PROBLEM SOLVER®

REGISTERED TRADEMARK

in

BUSINESS, MANAGEMENT, and FINANCE

Staff of Research and Education Association,

Dr. M. Fogiel, Director

Research and Education Association
505 Eighth Avenue
New York, N. Y. 10018

PROBLEM SOLVER®
IN
BUSINESS, MANAGEMENT, AND FINANCE

Printed in the United States of America

Library of Congress Catalog Card Number 78-64582

International Standard Book Number 0-87891-516-8

Revised Printing, 1985

WHAT THIS BOOK IS FOR

Students have found business, management, and finance generally a difficult subject to understand and learn. Despite the publication of hundreds of textbooks in this field, each one intended to provide an improvement over previous textbooks, students continue to remain perplexed as a result of the numerous conditions that must often be remembered and correlated in solving a problem. Various possible interpretations of terms used in the business field also have contributed to much of the difficulties experienced by students.

In a study of the problem, REA found the following basic reasons underlying students' difficulties with business, management, and finance taught in schools:

(a) No systematic rules of analysis have been developed which students may follow in a step-by-step manner to solve the usual problems encountered. This results from the fact that the numerous different conditions and principles which may be involved in a problem, lead to many possible different methods of solution. To prescribe a set of rules to be followed for each of the possible variations, would involve an enormous number of rules and steps to be searched through by students, and this task would perhaps be more burdensome than solving the problem directly with some accompanying trial and error to find the correct solution route.

(b) Textbooks currently available will usually explain a given principle in a few pages written by a professional who has an insight in the subject matter that is not shared by students. The explanations are often written in an abstract manner which leaves the students confused as to the application of the principle. The explanations given are not sufficiently detailed and extensive to make the student aware of the wide range of applications and different aspects of the principle being studied. The numerous possible variations of principles and their applications are usually not discussed, and it is left for the students to discover these for themselves while doing exercises.

Accordingly, the average student is expected to rediscover that which has been long known and practiced, but not published or explained extensively.

(c) The examples usually following the explanation of a topic are too few in number and too simple to enable the student to obtain a thorough grasp of the principles involved. The explanations do not provide sufficient basis to enable a student to solve problems that may be subsequently assigned for homework or given on examinations.

The examples are presented in abbreviated form which leaves out much material between steps, and requires that students derive the omitted material themselves. As a result, students find the examples difficult to understand--contrary to the purpose of the examples.

The examples are presented in abbreviated form which leaves out much material between steps, and requires that students derive the omitted material themselves. As a result, students find the examples difficult to understand--contrary to the purpose of the examples.

Examples are, furthermore, often worded in a confusing manner. They do not state the problem and then present the solution. Instead, they pass through a general discussion, never revealing what is to be solved for.

Examples, also, do not always include diagrams/graphs, wherever appropriate, and students do not obtain the training to draw diagrams or graphs to simplify and organize their thinking.

(d) Students can learn the subject only by doing the exercises themselves and reviewing them in class, to obtain experience in applying the principles with their different ramifications.

In doing the exercises by themselves, students find that they are required to devote considerably more time to business, management, and finance than to other subjects of comparable credits, because they are uncertain with regard to the selection and application of the theorems and principles involved. It is also often necessary for students to discover those "tricks" not revealed in their texts(or review books), that make it possible to solve problems easily. Students must usually resort to methods of trial-and-error to discover these "tricks", and as a result thay find that they may sometimes spend several hours to solve a single problem.

(e) When reviewing the exercises in classrooms, instructors usually request students to take turns in writing solutions on the boards and explaining them to the class. Students often find it difficult to explain in a manner that holds the interest of the class, and enables the remaining students to follow the material written on the boards. The remaining students seated in the class are, furthermore, too occupied with copying the material from the boards, to listen to the oral explanations and concentrate on the methods of solution.

This book is intended to aid students in business, management, and finance to overcome the difficulties described, by supplying detailed illustrations of the solution methods which are usually not apparent to students. The solution methods are illustrated by problems selected from those that are most often assigned for class work and given on examinations. The problems are arranged in order of complexity to enable students to learn and understand a particular topic by reviewing the problems in sequence. The problems are illustrated with detailed step-by-step explanations, to save the students the large amount of time that is often needed to fill in the gaps that are usually found between steps of illustrations in textbooks or review/outline books.

The staff of REA considers business, management, and finance a subject that is best learned by allowing students to view the methods of analysis and solution techniques themselves. This approach to learning the subject matter is similar to that practiced in various scientific laboratories, particularly in the medical fields.

In using this book, students may review and study the illustrated problems at their own pace; they are not limited to the time allowed for explaining problems on the board in class.

When students want to look up a particular type of problem and solution, they can readily locate it in the book by referring to the index which has been extensively prepared. It is also possible to locate a particular type of problem by glancing at just the material within the boxed portions. To facilitate rapid scanning of the problems, each problem has a heavy border around it. Furthermore, each problem is identified with a number immediately above the problem at the right-hand margin.

To obtain maximum benefit from the book, students should familiarize themselves with the section, "How To Use This Book," located in the front pages.

To meet the objectives of this book, staff members of REA have selected problems usually encountered in assignments and examinations, and have solved each problem meticulously to illustrate the steps which are usually difficult for students to comprehend. Gratitude for their patient work in this area is due to Jose Bittar, Steven Leitman, Richard Payne, Shira Rubinstein, Lewis Stern and the contributors who devoted short periods of time to this work.

Gratitude is also expressed to the many persons involved in the difficult task of typing the manuscript with its endless changes, and to the REA art staff who prepared the numerous detailed illustrations together with the layout and physical features of the book.

Finally, special thanks are due to Helen Kaufmann for her unique talents to render those difficult border-line decisions and constructive suggestions related to the design and organization of the book.

Max Fogiel, Ph.D.
Program Director

HOW TO USE THIS BOOK

This book can be an invaluable aid to students in business, management, and finance as a supplement to their textbooks. The book is subdivided into 34 chapters, each dealing with a separate topic. The subject matter is developed beginning with basic math skills and extends through cost accounting, banking, and statistics. Also included are sections on taxes, insurance, micro- and macro-economics, corporate operations, financial management, data processing, operations research, and computer science.

TO LEARN AND UNDERSTAND A TOPIC THOROUGHLY

1. Refer to your class text and read there the section pertaining to the topic. You should become acquainted with the principles dicussed there. These principles, however, may not be clear to you at that time.

2. Then locate the topic you are looking for by referring to the "Table of Contents" in the front of this book, "Problem Solver in Business, Management, and Finance."

3. Turn to the page where the topic begins and review the problems under each topic, in the order given. For each topic, the problems are arranged in order of complexity, from the simplest to the most difficult. Some problems may appear similar to others, but each problem has been selected to illustrate a different point or solution method.

To learn and understand a topic thoroughly and retain its contents, it will be generally necessary for students to review the problems several times. Repeated review is essential in order to gain experience in recognizing the principles that should be applied, and to select the best solution technique.

TO FIND A PARTICULAR PROBLEM

To locate one or more problems related to a particular subject matter, refer to the index. In using the index, be certain to note that the numbers given there refer to problem numbers, not to page numbers. This arrangement of the index is intended to facilitate finding a problem more rapidly, since two or more problems may appear on a page.

If a particular type of problem cannot be found readily, it is recommended that the student refer to the "Table of Contents" in the front pages, and then turn to the chapter which is applicable to the problem being sought. By scanning or glancing at the material that is boxed, it will generally be possible to find problems related to the one being sought, without consuming considerable time. After the problems have been located, the solutions can be reviewed and studied in detail. For this purpose of locating problems rapidly, students should acquaint themselves with the organization of the books as found in the "Table of Contents."

In preparing for an exam, it is useful to find the topics to be covered in the exam from the Table of Contents, and then review the problems under those topics several times. This should equip the student with what might be needed for the exam.

CONTENTS

Chapter No. **Page No.**

1 **BASIC MATH SKILLS** 1
- Addition and Subtraction 1
- Multiplication 16
- Division 25
- Averages 28
- Ratios and Percents 33
- Conversion of Units 48

2 **TAXES** 51
- Sales Tax 51
- Income Tax 54
- Property Tax 62

3 **INSURANCE** 77
- Life Insurance 77
- Social Security 84
- Health Insurance 88
- Automobile Insurance 89
- Fire Insurance 100

4 **INTERMEDIATE MATH SKILLS** 118
- Algebraic Equations 118
- Cost, Revenue, and Production Functions 126

5 **ECONOMIC THEORY** 141
- Microeconomics 141
  - Indifference and Demand Curve Analysis 141
  - Production and Cost Functions: Perfect and Imperfect Competition 158
- Macroeconomics 180
  - Production Possibilities Frontiers 180
  - Keynesian Macroeconomics 184
  - Monetary Problems 194

6 **ADVANCED MATH SKILLS** 198
- Rate of Change; Marginal Costs and Revenue 198
- Cost Minimization 206

Profit Maximization Through Production Adjustments 214
Profit Maximization Through Price Adjustments 222

MANAGEMENT THEORY AND SKILLS

7 **PAYROLL** 228
Wage Rates and Gross Earnings 228
Bonuses and Piece Rate Wage Basis 238
Payroll Tax Deductions 243

8 **COMMISSIONS** 251

9 **ADVERTISING** 261
Rate Per Advertisement 261
Milline Rate 264

10 **TRANSPORTATION** 266
Shipping and Mailing 266
Vehicle Rental 267

11 **WHOLESALE DISCOUNTS** 270
Discounts and Discount Rates 270
Series Discounts 274
Terms of Discount 285

12 **RETAILING** 293
Markdowns and Discounts 293
Markups 295

13 **PURCHASING DECISIONS** 305

14 **ANALYSIS OF COSTS AND PROFITS** 324
Fundamentals 324
Present Worth 327
Rate of Return 333

15 **CORPORATE OPERATIONS** 340
Costs and Price 340
Sales and Corporate Income 346
Accounting Systems 356

ACCOUNTING SKILLS

16 **BALANCE SHEETS** 362
Structure of the Balance Sheet 362
Journals, Ledgers, and Trial Balances 372
Rates and Ratios 395

17 FINANCIAL STATEMENTS 416
Ratios and Minor Documents 416
Income Statements and Net Profits 424

18 INVENTORY 434
Methods of Valuation 434
Open-to-Buy and Stockturn Rate 453

19 DEPRECIATION 458
Units of Production/Use Method and Straight Line Method 458
Declining Balance Method 465
Sum of the Years' Digits Method and Comprehensive Problem 470

20 OVERHEAD DISTRIBUTION 480
Floor Space Basis 480
Cost/Profit Basis 484

21 PARTNERSHIPS 488

22 COST ACCOUNTING 497
Standard Costs 497
Breakeven Ananlysis and Pricing 522

FINANCIAL MANAGEMENT

23 INTEREST 541
Simple Interest 541
Exact Interest 553
Compound Interest 555
Effective Interest 563

24 INSTALLMENT PLANS 567
Installment Cost and Finance Charges 567
Percent of Finance Charges 577

25 BANKING 583
Bank Statements and Deposit Accumulation 583
Bank Notes and Mortgages 587
Loans and Nominal Vs. True Interest Rate 590

26 STOCKS 598
Cost 598
Yield Rate and Income From Stocks 603

27 BONDS 612
Characteristics of Bonds 612
Cost and Face Value 614
Interest Rates 616

28 NOTES AND DRAFTS 625
Notes 625
Drafts 641

29 PERSONAL FINANCE 651
Expenditures and Choices 651
Savings and Funds 659

ADVANCED TECHNIQUES

30 LINEAR PROGRAMMING 669
Maximization and Minimization Problems 669
Games, Business Applications and Advanced Problems 688

31 DATA PROCESSING 700

32 STATISTICS 724

33 USING OPERATIONS RESEARCH FOR BUSINESS, MANAGEMENT, AND FINANCE 753

34 USING COMPUTERS FOR BUSINESS APPLICATIONS 785
Depreciation, Interest and Commission 785
Optimizing Production 791
Operations Research 801

TABLES FOR SELECTED PROBLEMS 817
(selected problems refer to the following tables which may be found on pages indicated)

Discount Tables 817
Automobile Insurance 819
Fire Insurance 823
Retirement Income 825
Ecomony Study 762
Interest Tables 827

INDEX 833

CHAPTER 1

BASIC MATH SKILLS

ADDITION AND SUBTRACTION

• PROBLEM 1-1

Add the following dollar amounts:

$85.75
$75.34
$84
$92.80
$ 8.05
$123

Solution: When adding dollars it is important to realize that whole dollars have a ".00" following the given digits. We then arrange the number so that the decimal points are one under the other. We then add up each column of numbers and keep the decimal point after the second digit from the right.

```
  $ 85.75
+ $ 75.34
+ $ 84.00
+ $ 92.80
+ $  8.05
+ $123.00
---------
  $468.94
```

• PROBLEM 1-2

Tom O'Brien is a checker at the Diamond Supermarket. Tell precisely how he would count out the change due the following costomers.

a. Costomer A's total purchases are $16.88. He gives Tom two $10 bills.

b. Customer B's total purchases are $6.16. She hands Tom a $20 bill.

c. Customer C's total purchases are $13.40. She wants to write a check for $40 and Tom receives approval to accept it.

d. Customer D's total purchases are $26.07. She presents coupons worth 80 cents and hands Tom three $10 bills.

e. Customer E's total purchases are $4.88. He returns soft drink bottles worth 90 cents and gives Tom a $5 bill.

Solution: The correct way to count out the change, for a customer, is to start with the loose change and build it up to the amount of change that you were given. If none, then you must build it up to the next dollar. After that, you build up the dollars to the amount which you were paid.

(a) Customer A purchased $16.88 worth of goods, and he gave Tom two $10 bills, which is equal to $20. Since he did not give Tom any change, Tom first takes the 88 ¢, then he says 88 ¢ and 12 ¢ make 1 dollar.(He finds this number by mentally subtracting the 88 ¢ from $1, and getting $.12 as an answer.) Therefore, he gives Customer A 12 ¢. Now Customer A has $16.88 worth of goods and $.12 of the supermarket's money. He now owns $17 worth of the supermarket's supplies (16.88 + .12 = 17.00). Now Tom figures out the difference of the $20 that Customer A paid and the $17 that he now owes. He subtracts 17 from 20 and gets 3, he would say, "$17 and $3 makes $20." Tom then pays the Customer $3.

(b) From Customer B, Tom receives $20 for a purchase of $6.16. Again, he first figures out the loose change. 1.00 - .16 = .84, so he gives Customer B 84 ¢. Now Customer B has $6.16 worth of goods and 84 ¢ of their cash, a total of $7. Tom now figures $20 - $7 = $13, therefore he gives Customer B $13. The way he counts it out should be to give Customer B 3 singles, and then a $10 bill. He would say as he was giving out the change, "16 ¢ and 84 ¢ makes 1 dollar, 7 dollars and 3 dollars make 10 dollars, 10 dollars and 10 dollars make $20."

(c) Customer C paid $40 for purchases of $13.40. Tom calculates that 1.00 - .40 = .60, and gives Customer C 60¢, leaving Customer C with $14 worth of goods and cash. Then Tom figures $40 -

$14 = $26, and gives her $1 and $5, saying that $14 and $1 is $15 and another $5 makes $20. Finally he gives her an additional $20, raising the total to $40.

(d) Customer D purchased $26.07 worth of goods and presented Tom with three $10 bills and 80¢ worth of coupons, totaling $30.80. Tom figures .80 - .07 = .73 and so gives Customer D 73¢. Tom still owes her $4 ($36.80 - $26.80) and so gives her four single dollars to terminate the exchange.

(e) Customer E purchased $4.88 worth of goods and gave the supermarket a $5 bill and 90¢ worth of bottles, a total of $5.90. Since he has given Tom change, Tom figures out that 90¢ paid minus 88¢ due equals 2¢ due. Thus he gives Customer E 2¢. Now Customer E has a total of $4.90 of goods and cash. Since he paid $5.90, all Tom has to do is subtract $5 - $4 = $1 and give that amount to the customer. He does not have to subtract the cents part because he has already established that they are equal, thus all he subtracts are the total dollar amounts.

• PROBLEM 1-3

Complete the following. Verify the accuracy of your work by adding the subtrahend and the difference to get the minuend.

a.	Amount	277.85	e.	Total charges	4,616.42
	Less	27.70		Less payments	1,916.43
	Net			Balance	
b.	Amount	1,384.47	f.	Total charges	949.99
	Less	138.45		Less payments	727.72
	Net			Balance	
c.	Gross earnings	275.75	g.	Gross earnings	788.80
	Deductions	64.40		Deductions	126.92
	Net pay			Net pay	
d.	Total purchases	1,287.87	h.	Total purchases	721.12
	Less Returns	16.90		Less returns	474.12
	Amount due			Amount due	

Solution: In order to solve all these problems one must only subtract the given subtrahend from the minuend in order to get their differences. In order to check, you add the difference to the number you subtracted (subtrahend) to get the original number (minuend).

(a)	277.85 - 27.70 250.15	check	250.15 + 27.70 277.85
(b)	1,384.47 - 138.45 1,246.02	check	1,246.02 + 138.45 1,384.47
(c)	275.75 - 64.40 211.35	check	211.35 + 64.40 275.75
(d)	1,287.87 - 16.90 1,270.97	check	1,270.97 + 16.90 1,287.87
(e)	4,616.42 -1,916.43 2,699.99	check	2,699.99 + 1,916.43 4,616.42
(f)	949.99 - 727.72 222.27	check	222.27 + 727.72 949.99
(g)	788.80 - 126.92 661.88	check	661.88 + 126.92 788.80
(h)	721.12 - 474.12 247.00	check	247.00 + 474.12 721.12

• PROBLEM 1-4

Bob Gardner, an accounting clerk at Cleverdon Novelties, prepares a deposit slip each day and takes it to the bank along with the cash and checks to be placed on deposit. Two deposit slips that Mr. Gardner prepared follow. Find the total amount to be deposited in the bank on each of the two days.

Currency	26.00	Currency	146.00
Coin	1.34	Coin	12.78
Checks	8.75	Checks	2385.00
	14.98		540.00
	125.00		76.82
	34.50		251.65

	8.29		87.98
	2.50		64.50
Total		Total	

CENTRAL NATIONAL BANK

Solution: In order to find the total for each day's deposits, we must add all the checks to the coin and currency that he deposited. Thus to find the total for each day, we simply add all the numbers.

	Currency	26.00		Currency	146.00
+	Coin	1.34	+	Coin	12.78
+	Checks	8.75	+	Checks	2,385.00
+		14.98	+		540.00
+		125.00	+		76.82
+		34.50	+		251.65
+		8.29	+		87.98
+		2.50	+		64.50
	Total	221.36		Total	3,564.73

• PROBLEM 1-5

The monthly totals of new subscribers to Golden West magazine are shown on the report below. The report covers a two-year period. Find (a) the monthly increases from year to year and (b) the total number of new subscribers over the two-year period. Verify your results.

Month	19 × 5	19 × 6	Increase
January	1409	2417	
February	1959	3005	
March	1322	2585	
April	2661	3924	
May	2132	3536	
June	2817	4102	
July	2946	4347	
August	1980	3368	
September	3141	3241	
October	2666	2998	

November	1784	1937
December	2102	2386
Totals	____	____

Solution: (a) To find the monthly increases from year 19×5 to 19×6, we take the monthly total of new subscribers in year 19×5 and subtract it from that of 19×6, for each month. We can check our results by finding the total number of new subscribers in 19×5 and subtracting that from the total number of new subscribers for year 19×6, giving the yearly increase. The result from that must equal the sum of the monthly increases, if they are correct.

Month	19×5	19×6	Increase	
January	1,409	2,417	1,008	(2,417-1,409=1,008)
February	1,959	3,005	1,046	(3,005-1,959=1,046)
March	1,322	2,585	1,263	(2,585-1,322=1,263)
April	2,661	3,924	1,263	(3,924-2,661=1,263)
May	2,132	3,536	1,404	(3,536-2,132=1,404)
June	2,817	4,102	1,285	(4,102-2,817=1,285)
July	2,946	4,347	1,401	(4,347-2,946=1,401)
August	1,980	3,368	1,388	(3,368-1,980=1,388)
September	3,141	3,241	100	(3,241-3,141=100)
October	2,666	2,998	332	(2,998-2,666=332)
November	1,784	1,937	153	(1,937-1,784=153)
December	2,102	2,386	284	(2,386-2,102=284)

Now to check our results we sum up the total of new subscribers for year 19×6, and get 37,846. We then sum up the total of new subscribers for year 19×5, and get 26,919. To find the yearly increase we subtract the yearly total of 19×5 from 19×6 and get 10,927. (37,846 - 26,919 = 10,927). Now if we sum up the 12 monthy increases, we also get 10,927, so our figures are correct.

(b) To find the total number of new subscribers over the two year period, we must first find the total number of new subscriptions in each year and then add those totals, for our answer. We already figured the totals for 19×5 and 19×6 in part (a). Our results were, in 19×5 there were 26,919 new subscriptions, and in 19×6 there were 37,846 new subscriptions. Thus, the total number of new subscriptions for the two year period is 64,765. (37,846 + 26,919 = 64,765).

The following tables show the prices a department store charges its customers for certain items of merchandise and the cost of each item to the store. The difference is the amount of profit the store makes on each item. Find the profit on each item and the total profit.

Musical Instruments

Article	Selling Price	Cost to Store	Profit
Banjo	45.50	27.30	
Cello	97.95	81.39	
Drums	110.00	76.40	
Flute	50.75	26.87	
Guitar	42.50	24.50	
Harp	350.00	223.00	
Oboe	196.25	140.25	
Violin	249.75	176.85	
Viola	320.65	208.60	
Totals	______	______	

Solution: The profit that a store makes on an item, is found by subtracting how much the item costs the store from the amount that the store charges for the item. Thus, in order to find the profit the store makes on the banjo, we take its selling price of $45.50 and subtract its cost, $27.30. Thus the profit is $45.50 - $27.30 = $18.20. Similarly, we find the profits of the other items.

	Cello	Drums	Flute	Guitar	Harp	Oboe
Selling price	97.95	110.00	50.75	42.50	350.00	196.25
- Cost to store	-81.39	- 76.40	-26.87	-24.50	-223.00	-140.25
Profit	16.56	33.60	23.88	18.00	127.00	56.00

	Violin	Viola
Selling price	294.75	320.65
- Cost to Store	-176.85	-208.60
Profit	117.90	112.05

To find the total profit, we must take the total cost to the store of all the items and subtract that amount from the total selling price. We find these by adding up the costs of each item to get the total cost, and adding up the selling price of each item to get the total selling price.

Selling Price	Cost to store
45.50	27.30
+ 97.95	+ 81.39
+ 110.00	+ 76.40
+ 50.75	+ 26.87
+ 42.50	+ 24.50
+ 350.00	+ 223.00
+ 196.25	+ 140.25
+ 294.75	+ 176.85
+ 320.65	+ 208.60
1,508.35	985.16

Therefore, the total profit is the total selling price of $1,508.35 less the total cost to the store of $985.16, which is $523.19 ($1,508.35 - $985.16 = $523.19). In order to check this result, we can see that the total profit is also equal to the sum of all the individual profits. Thus to check our work, we can take all of the profits which we found earlier and add them up.

18.20	(profit on Banjo)
+ 16.56	(profit on Cello)
+ 33.60	(profit on Drums)
+ 23.88	(profit on Flute)
+ 18.00	(profit on Guitar)
+ 127.00	(profit on Harp)
+ 56.00	(profit on Oboe)
+ 117.90	(profit on Violin)
+ 112.05	(profit on Viola)
523.19	Total profit

Note: We arrived at the same answer, so it is correct. The total profit is $523.19.

• PROBLEM 1-7

The Universal Book Company sets a quota of $4,000 as the amount of sales each sales representative should make per month. The following are weekly reports of sales made in February by its three representatives. By how much did each one exceed or fail to reach the quota?

Representative	Week 1	Week 2	Week 3	Week 4
Billup	$1,240.50	$970.20	$1,340.90	$1,295.70
Margolies	1,098.75	820.82	1,120.40	845.20
Storch	1,247.50	722.80	1,150.25	870.70

Solution: This problem requires that we take weekly sales reports and convert them into monthly sales reports, in order to check if the representatives exceeded or failed to reach their quota of $4,000 a month. To do this conversion one must sum up the weekly sales reports of the given four weeks, since a month is equal to four weeks in business transactions. Billup had $1,240.50 in week one, $970.20 in week 2, $1340.90 in week 3 and $1,295.70 in week 4. Therefore his total sales for the four week period was $1,240.50 + $970.20 + $1,340.90 + $1,295.70 = $4,847.30. Expressed in other terms, Billup made $4,847.30 of sales in the month. Now the quota was $4,000, therefore, Billup exceeded the quota (he sold more than he had to) Similarly, the monthly sales for Margolies and Storch can be obtained

	Margolies	Storch
Week 1	$1,098.75	$1,247.50
+ Week 2	820.82	722.80
+ Week 3	1,120.40	1,150.25
+ Week 4	845.20	870.70
Month	$3,885.17	$3,991.25

by comparing the month's sales of Margolies and of Storch to the set quota of $4,000. we can see that both of them failed to sell their quota of $4,000 for the month. Billup exceeded the quota by $4,847.30. Margolies and Storch failed to meet the quota by $114.83, ($4,000 - $3,885.17) and $8.75, ($4,000 - $3,911.25) respectively.

• PROBLEM 1-8

How many days would be included in a loan from September 2 until December 3?

Solution: To find out how many days there are between two dates, one must find out how many days there are in the months that he will have the loan. Thus to find out how many days he will have the loan we will consider how many days in September, in October, in November, and in December, then we will add up the number of days in each month to get the total number of days in the loan period.

The loan period in September is 28 days. This is calculated since September has 30 days, and the loan starts on the second, thus 30 - 2 = 28. The loan period in October is the full 31 days, the loan period in November is its full 30 days.

Finally, the loan period in December is 3 days, for it will have to be repaid on December 3.

28	days in September
+ 31	days in October
+ 30	days in November
+ 3	days in December
92	total number of days

• PROBLEM 1-9

What was the amount of an invoice for which $416.50 was payment in full after a cash discount of $8.50 was taken?

Solution: A cash discount is the amount the seller of the merchandise charges you less then the invoice asks for. Thus if the discount was $8.50, and the payment was $416.50, then the invoice was for $416.50 + $8.50 = $425.00.

• PROBLEM 1-10

A loan is made on December 17 for a time period of 120 days. When is it due (not a leap year)?

Solution: To find out what date a loan is due, we must first subtract the number or remaining days in that month from the time period of the loan. We then subtract the number of days in the months ahead until there are not enough days left for a total month. Our answer is then the number of days left in the next month. Thus since the 120 day loan is made on December 17 we must first subtract the remaining days in December.

31	number of days in December
- 17	the date in Dec. the loan was made
14	the loan period in December

Thus after December there are 120 - 14 = 106 days left to the loan. We now subtract the 31 days of January to leave us with 75 days.

Now, subtracting the 28 days in February (not a leap year) we are left with 47 days. We now subtract 31 days for March and are left with 16 days. Since there are not enough days for another month to be subtracted, the loan is due April (month after March, which was the last one we subtracted) 16.

• PROBLEM 1-11

While she was on a recent business trip, May C. Carlisle spent the following amounts: hotel, $63; meals, 42.90; laundry, $3.75; tips, $9.50; taxis, $7.85; telephone, $11.30; customer entertainment, $36.60; and supplies, $4.30. If Ms. Carlisle started out with $300 and paid cash while she was away, how much did she have left?

Solution: This problem reguires us to find out Ms. Carlisle's total expenditures on her trip. We do this by adding up all of the given amounts. We then take the total expenses and subtract it from the amount which she started with, in order to find out how much she had left.

In this problem Ms. Carlisle spent.

$63.00	hotel
+ $42.90	meals
+ $ 3.75	laundry
+ $ 9.50	tips
+ $ 7.85	taxis
+ $11.30	telephone
+ $36.60	entertainment
+ $ 4.30	supplies
$179.20	total expenses

She spent $179.20 of her $300.00, so she was left with $120.80. (300.00 - 179.20 = 120.80)

• PROBLEM 1-12

At the beginning of the year the Flynn Family estimated they would spend the following amounts during the year: rent, $2,700; food, $4,300; furniture and household needs, $700; clothing, $1,000; car expenses, $2,100; medical expenses, $700; vacation and entertainment, $500; insurance, $1,260; and miscellaneous expenses, $500. Actual expenses for the year amounted to $13,720. (a) Was their estimate of expenses too low or too high? (b) By how much were they "off"?

Solution: In order to find out if their estimate of their expenses was too high or too low, we need to find their estimate for their total expenses of the year. We do this by adding up their estimates for the individual expenses.

$2,700	rent
+ $4,300	food
+ $ 700	furniture and houshold needs
+ $1,000	clothing
+ $2,100	car expenses
+ $ 700	medical expenses
+ $ 500	vacation and entertainment
+ $1,260	insurance
+ $ 500	miscellaneous expenses
$13,760	total expenses

By comparing this figure to the actual expenses, we can see that they overestimated their expenses, for $13,760 is greater than the actual $13,720. In order to find out how much they were "off" we have to find the difference between the two numbers. What we do is subtract the smaller number (here the actual $13,720) from the larger number (here the estimated $13,760). Thus we find that they were off by $40. (13,760 - 13,720 = 40)

• PROBLEM 1-13

Henry Manners, a salesman for the Modern Dye Works, is paid a salary of $5,200 a year. Last year, in addition to his salary, he also earned the following monthly commissions: $518.25, $604.86, $833, $499.17, $617.84, $568.24, $751.09, $900.17, $824.35, $714.34, $628.28, and $928.58. Find his total earnings for the year.

Solution: In order to find out his total earnings, we must sum his yearly salary with all of his monthy commissions.

	$5,200.00	salary
+	$ 518.25	month 1
+	$ 604.86	month 2
+	$ 833.00	month 3
+	$ 499.17	month 4
+	$ 617.84	month 5
+	$ 568.24	month 6
+	$ 751.09	month 7
+	$ 900.17	month 8
+	$ 824.35	month 9
+	$ 714.34	month 10
+	$ 628.28	month 11
+	$ 928.58	month 12
	$ 13,588.17	total earnings for the year

• PROBLEM 1-14

Lois Frankel is office manager of the word prosessing department of Pilgrim Insurance Company. A summary of the pages typed by each employee for the past four months is shown below. For each employee, find (a) the total number of pages typed each month. (b) the total typed in four months, and (c) the grand total for the four month period.

Employee	Sept.	Oct.	Nov.	Dec.	Totals
Binns	157	196	143	158	____
Boch	216	193	184	159	____
Coffey	186	213	173	164	____
DuBois	167	184	179	152	____
Linkletter	169	168	196	182	____
Totals	___	___	___	___	

Solution: (a) In this problem we have to find the total number of pages that were typed each month. We do this by adding up the number of pages each employee had typed during that month.

Employee	Sept.	Oct.	Nov.	Dec.
Binns	157	196	143	158
+ Boch	+ 216	+ 193	+ 184	+ 159
+ Coffey	+ 186	+ 213	+ 173	+ 164
+ DuBois	+ 167	+ 184	+ 179	+ 152
+ Linkletter	+ 169	+ 168	+ 196	+ 182
Monthly sum	895	954	875	815

(b) To get the total number typed for each employee, in the 4 months, we need to sum up the number of pages that the employee typed in each month.

Employee	Sept.	+ Oct.	+ Nov.	+ Dec.	= Total
Binns	157	+ 196	+ 143	+ 158	= 654
Boch	216	+ 193	+ 184	+ 159	= 752
Coffey	186	+ 213	+ 173	+ 164	= 736
DuBois	167	+ 184	+ 179	+ 152	= 682
Linkletter	169	+ 168	+ 196	+ 182	= 715

(c) In order to get the grand total for the four months, we add up the total of pages each employee had typed during the four-month period. We can then check our answers by adding up the monthly total of pages typed, and if our numbers were correct we would get the same answers.

654	(total for Binns)
+ 752	(total for Boch)
+ 736	(total for Coffey)
+ 682	(total for DuBois)
+ 715	(total for Linkletter)
3,539	(grand total)

check

895	(sum for Sept.)
+ 954	(sum for Oct.)
+ 875	(sum for Nov.)
+ 815	(sum for Dec.)
3,539	(grand total)

• PROBLEM 1-15

Elaine Morris, assistant to the sales manager of Cox Distributors, prepares a weekly summary of sales representatives' expenses. The following figures are taken from the records for the first week in September: Danvers, $203,75; Halleck, $187.50; Isaac, $185; Meade, $176.85; Munez, $163.90; Wooten, $214.

Arrange the expenses in a column; then find the total of all representatives' expenses for the week.

Solution: Record of first week in September's sales representative's expenses

Employee	expense
Danvers	203.75
Halleck	+ 187.50
Isaac	+ 185.00
Meade	+ 176.85
Munez	+ 163.90
Wooten	+ 214.00
Total	$1,131.00

• PROBLEM 1-16

The Judith Franklyn Corporation offered on-the-job training to 1,240 employees. Their expenses for the training were as follows:

part-time instruction	$114,770
janitorial services	$ 6,080
books	$ 12,370
supplies	$ 4,160
miscellaneous	$ 6,150

Find the cost of the on-the-job training per employee.

Solution: The first thing we must do to solve this problem, is to find the total cost of the training. We find this by adding up all the expenses.

$114,770	(part-time instruction)
+ $ 6,080	(janitorial services)
+ $ 12,370	(books)
+ $ 4,160	(supplies)
+ $ 6,150	(miscellanoeus)
$143,530	(total)

We now take the total cost and divide it by the number of trainees in the program (1,240), to get a cost of on-the-job training per employee of $115.75 ($143,530.00 ÷ 1,240 = $115.75).

• PROBLEM 1-17

Compute the following:

(a) $37\frac{1}{8} - 12\frac{3}{4}$

(b) $49\frac{1}{16} - 31\frac{1}{8}$

Solution: In order to subract the mixed numbers, it is easiest to convert them to decimals and then subtract.

(a) $37\frac{1}{8} = 37.125$, and $12\frac{3}{4} = 12.750$. We now subtract the numbers in decimal form as such.

$$\begin{array}{r} 37.125 \\ -\ 12.750 \\ \hline 24.375 \end{array} = 24\frac{3}{8}$$

(b) $49\frac{1}{16} = 49.0625$, and $31\frac{1}{8} = 31.1250$. Thus, their difference is

$$\begin{array}{r} 49.0625 \\ -\ 31.1250 \\ \hline 17.9375 \end{array} = 17\frac{15}{16}$$

MULTIPLICATION

• PROBLEM 1-18

Prepare the following for multiplication. You do not have to do the final multiplication itself; just show what numbers you would multiply to arrive at an answer.

(a) 12,750 @ $2.95 per C
(b) 8,200 @ $1.50 per M
(c) 675 @ $3.00 per cwt
(d) 840 @ $2.00 per M
(e) 67 @ $1.95 per C
(f) 50 @ $5.99 per M.

Solution: "Per C" means per 100, "per M" means per 1,000, and "per cwt" means per hundred weight (a hundred weight is equal to 100 pounds). When working with a price per some amount, what we have to do is divide the quantity of the object by the given amount, and then multiply by the price. When dividing by 100, all one has to do is move the decimal point (if it does not exist, assume it exists at the extreme right side of the number) two places to the left. When dividing by 1,000 all one has to do is move the decimal point 3 places to the left.

(a) $\$2.95 \times 127.50 = \$2.95 \times (12,750 \div 100)$

(b) $\$1.50 \times 8.200 = \$1.50 \times (8,200 \div 1,000)$

(c) $\$3.00 \times 6.75 = \$3.00 \times (675 \div 100)$

(d) $\$2.00 \times .840 = \$2.00 \times (840 \div 1,000)$

(e) $\$1.95 \times .67 = \$1.95 \times (67 \div 100)$

(f) $\$5.99 \times .050 = \$5.99 \times (50 \div 1,000)$

• PROBLEM 1-19

Compute the selling price for the quantities of lumber in the table below.

Quantity in Board Feet	Kind	Price per M	Amount
8,640	Flooring, No. 1	$135	$______
6,860	Siding	$ 95	______
12,600	Floor timbers	$115	______
6,530	Flooring, No. 2	$ 93	______
3,750	Scantlings	$107	______
9,500	Sheathing boards	$ 89	______
		Total	$______

Solution: "Price per M" means the price of 1,000 units. Now to find out the amount for each object, we have to find out how many thousands there are of the object and then multiply that number by its price per thousand. To find out how many thousands there are, you take the quantity and divide it by 1,000. This is the same as taking the quantity and moving the decimal point (if none exists, assume it is at the extreme right of the number) three places towards the left. For example, for $8,640 \div 1,000 = 8.64$. We can now find out how many thousands there are of each.

Kind	Quantity in Board feet	Quantity in 1,000 board ft.
Flooring, No.1	8,640	8.64
Siding	6,860	6.86
Floor timbers	12,600	12.6
Flooring,No.2	6,530	6.53
Scantlings	3,750	3.75
Sheathing boards	9,500	9.5

We can now find out the amounts of each.

Kind	Quantity in 1,000 bd.ft.	Price Per M	Amount
Flooring,No.1	8.64	$135	$1,166.40(8.64 × $135)
Siding	6.86	$ 95	+$651.70 (6.86 × $95)
Floor timbers	12.6	$115	+$1,449.00(12.6 × $115)
Flooring,No.2	6.53	$ 93	+$607.29(6.53 × $93)
Scantlings	3.75	$107	+$401.25(3.75 × $107)
Sheathing boards	9.5	$ 89	+$845.50(9.5 × $89)
		total cost	$5,121.14

• PROBLEM 1-20

Find the cost of each order.

(a) 346 glasses @ 50 ¢ each

(b) 870 nails @ 3 $\frac{1}{2}$ ¢ each

(c) 125 chains @ $16.48 each.

Solution: The symbol @ means "at the cost of". Thus, to find the cost of each, we multiply the quantity by the price of each one.

(a) 346 @ 50 ¢ each costs 346 × $.50 = $173.00

(b) 870 @ 3 $\frac{1}{2}$ ¢ each costs 870 × $.035 = $30.45

(c) 125 @ $16.48 = $2,060.00.

• PROBLEM 1-21

Find the total sale in a gas station if a motorist purchases 13 6/10 gallons of gas at $.539 a gallon and 2 quarts of oil at $1.10 a quart.

Solution: Before we can find the total sale, we must find out how much he spent for the gasoline. We do this by multiplying the cost per gallon ($.539) by the number of gallons (13.6) and rounding the answer to the nearest penny.

$$\$.539 \times 13.6 = \$7.3304$$

He is therefore charged $7.33 for the gasoline. To find out how much he paid for the oil, we must multiply the cost per quart ($1.10) by the number of quarts (2), given a total of $2.20 ($1.10×2 = $2.20). Now to find the total sale, we must add the cost for the gasoline ($7.33) to the cost of the oil ($2.20), getting $9.53.

• PROBLEM 1-22

Find the total of the following purchase order.

To: Miner Candy Mfr.
Durham, N.C.

Order No. 472
Date 10/6/19--

Quantity in Pounds	Description	Amount	
400	Frozen milk caramels @ 59¢		
350	Red & black pectin berries @ 69¢		
475	Miniature fruit slices @ 73¢		
648	Toasted coconut @ 64¢		
1,100	Licorice berries @ 38¢		
176	Crystallized jelly frappe @ 91¢		
506	Chocolate-miniature cherries @ 85¢		
739	Chocolate-large cherries @ $1.07		
	Total		

Solution: The symbol @ means the cost per unit of each item. The units in this problem are pounds. In order to find the total, we must add all the individual amounts. The amounts are computed by multiplying the cost of a pound of the object by the quantity of pounds there are.

Quantity in Pounds	Object	Price per pound	Amount
400	milk caramels	59¢	$236 (400×$.59)
350	pectin berries	69¢	+ $241.50(350×$.69)
475	fruit slices	73¢	+ $346.75(575×$.73)
648	coconut	64¢	+ $414.72(648×$.64)
1,100	licorice berries	38¢	+ $418.00(1,100×$.38)
176	jelly frappe	91¢	+ $160.16(176×$.91)
506	chocolate cherries-min.	85¢	+ $430.10(506×$.85)
736	chocolate cherries-lg.	$1.07	+ $787.52(736×$1.07)
	Total		$3,034.75

• PROBLEM 1-23

The J & L Floor Covering Shop sold the following quantities of carpeting on a recent day. (a) What was the total received for each type of carpeting? (b) What was the total dollar-value of carpeting sales for the day?

Type of Carpeting	Square Yards Sold	Price per Square Yard	Total
Diamond tuft	320	$10.50	$________
Guild	436	$12.70	________
Kirk	280	$14.95	________
Krishna	170	$21.45	________
Heather	330	$ 8.85	________
		Total	$________

Solution: (a) In order to get the total for each type of carpeting, we must multiply the number of square yards sold by the price per square yard.

Type	Sq.yards sold	Price per sq.yd.	Total
Diamond tuft	320	$10.50	$3,360.00
Guild	436	$12.70	$5,537.20
Kirk	280	$14.95	$4,186.00
Krishna	170	$21.45	$3,646.50
Heather	330	$ 8.85	$2,920.50

(b) The total dollar-value of the carpeting sold that day is the sum of the totals for each type of carpeting

\$3,360.00	(Diamond tuft)
\$5,537.20	(Guild)
\$4,186.00	(Kirk)
\$3,646.50	(Krishna)
\$2,920.50	(Heather)
\$19,650.20	(total)

• PROBLEM 1-24

A furniture manufacturer wants to find out how many end tables he produced during a certain week. He knows that 8 employees produced 16 end tables each, 21 employees produced 23 each, 7 produced 27 each, and 4 produced 29 each. Find the total number of end tables produced during that week.

Solution: To solve this problem, we must multiply the number of tables by the number of employees that produced at the various rates. Then total these quantities from the different amounts of tables.

8 × 16 end tables = 128 end tables
21 × 23 end tables = 483 end tables
7 × 27 end tables = 189 end tables
4 × 29 end tables = 116 end tables

Thus 128 + 483 + 189 + 116 = 916 end tables were produced during the week.

• PROBLEM 1-25

How many 9-inch-by-9-inch tiles are needed to cover a floor which is 9 feet long and 6 feet wide? Find the cost if each tile costs 75 cents.

Solution: In order to find out how many tiles would be needed, we first must find the area of the floor that we want to cover. Since the floor's dimensions are given in feet, and the tile's dimensions are given in inches, we must convert the dimensions of the floor to inches so we can find out how many tiles would be required. There are 12 inches in a foot, thus the length of the floor is 108 inches (9 × 12 inches = 108 inches), and the width is 72 inches (6 × 12 inches = 72 inches). Now the area of the floor is found by multiplying the floor's length (108 inches) and width (72 inches), giving 7,776 sq. inches (108 inches × 72 inches = 7,776 sq. inches). Now we must find out how much area each tile covers. This is found by computing the area of a tile (length × width). Thus a tile covers an area of 9 inches × 9 inches, or 81 sq. inches.

Now, since we know that each tile covers an area of 81 sq. inches, and we need to cover 7,776 sq. inches of floor, we can see that the number of tiles we require would be the area to be covered (7,776 sq. in.) divided by the area each tile covers (81 sq. in.). Thus we would require 96 tiles (7,776 ÷ 81 = 96) to cover the floor. To find the cost, we must take the cost of each tile ($.75) and multiply it by the number of tiles that are required (96), giving a cost of $72.00 (96 × $.75 = $72.00).

• PROBLEM 1-26

The cost of lumber at one lumberyard is $140 per 1,000 board feet. Find the charge for 300 pieces of lumber that are 2 inches thick, 6 inches wide, and 12 feet long.

Solution: In order to solve this problem, we must find out how many board feet there are in the lumber we wish to purchase. A board foot is a unit of measure of lumber equal to a board one foot square and one inch thick. Each piece of lumber is 12 feet long, 1/2 foot wide and 2 inches thick. Thus it is 6 sq. ft. and 2 inches thick. Thus it is equal to 12 board feet (6 sq. ft. × 2 inches = 12 board feet). Therefore, since we are buying 300 pieces of lumber, we are buying 300 × 12 board feet, or 3,600 board feet.

Since the lumber is sold in units of thousands of board feet, we must find out how many thousands of board feet we require. This is accomplished by dividing the total board feet (3,600) by 1,000, giving 3.6. So the cost of the lumber is 3.6 thousand board feet X $140 per thousand board feet, giving $504.

• PROBLEM 1-27

Find the amount and cost of paint required to cover the walls of a room 20 feet long, 16 feet wide, and 10 feet high, given the following information.

Amount of paint	Area it covers	Cost
1 gallon	400 - 425 sq.ft.	$7.95
1 quart	100 - 110 sq.ft.	$2.20

Solution: Before we can find out how much paint will be needed, we must first find out how large an area we have to cover. We are given that the dimensions of the room are 20 feet by 10 feet by 16 feet. Thus we know that the four walls are 20 ft. by 10 ft.,20 ft. by 10 ft, 16 ft. by 10 ft., and 16 ft. by 10 ft. We can now find the areas of each wall. Area of a rectangle (a wall is a rectangle) is found by multiplying length by width.

20 ft. × 10 ft.= 200 square feet   20 ft. × 10 ft.=200 sq.ft.

16 ft. × 10 ft.= 160 square feet   16 ft. × 10 ft.=160 sq.ft.

Now since we must paint all four walls, the total area that we must paint is equal to the sum of the areas of the four walls. Thus the total area we must paint is 200 sq. ft. + 200 sq. ft. + 160 sq. ft. + 160 sq. ft. = 720 sq. ft.

Now we need to know how much paint we will need to cover this. When calculating this you must assume that the paint will only cover 100 sq. ft. per quart, and 400 sq. ft. per gallon, because the painter would not want to run out of paint before he is finished. Since we must cover 720 square feet we need 8 quarts of paint. (8 x 100 sq. ft.that a quart covers = 800 sq. ft. which is more paint than we need, however if we had ordered 7 quarts, it would only be sufficient for covering 700 sq. ft. (7 × 100 sq. ft. = 700 sq. ft.) which would be less than the required 720 sq. ft.) or we would need 2 gallons of paint. (2 × 400 sq. ft. that a gallon covers = 800 sq. ft.) 8 quarts would cost $2.20 × 8 = $17.60. 2 gallons would cost 2 × $7.95 = $15.90. So we would buy 2 gallons of paint and the cost would be $15.90.

• PROBLEM 1-28

Find the number of single rolls required to paper a room 18 feet long, 12 feet wide, and 10 feet high, allowing for a 10% waste of paper. A single roll consists of 36 square feet of paper. Make allowance for openings, which include one window 3 feet by 8 feet and one door 4 feet by 9 feet.

Solution: We must first find out how many sq. feet we must cover. In order to find that out, we must find the total area of the walls, then subtract the area of the openings from that. Then we make an allowance for the waste. The total area of the walls consists of the sum of the areas of the four walls. From the dimensions of the room, we see that the walls are 10 feet by 18 feet, 10 feet by 18 feet, 10 feet by 12 feet, and 10 feet by 12 feet. To find the areas of the walls we multiply the length by the width. Thus the areas of the walls are:

10 ft. × 18 ft. = 180 sq.ft.   10 ft. × 18 ft. = 180 sq.ft.

10 ft. × 12 ft. = 120 sq.ft.   10 ft. × 12 ft. = 120 sq.ft.

Thus the total area is 180 sq.ft. + 180 sq.ft. + 120 sq.ft. + 120 sq.ft. = 600 sq.ft. Now we must find the areas of the openings. The area of the door is 36 sq. ft. (4 ft. × 9 ft. = 36 sq.ft.), and the area of the window is 24 sq.ft. (3 ft. × 8 ft. = 24 sq.ft.). We can now find the area that we must cover by subtracting the area of the openings from the total area. Thus the area to be covered is equal to 600 sq.ft. - 24 sq.ft. (window) - 36 sq.ft. (door) = 540 sq.ft. We must now consider the waste allowance of 10%. To find out how much we must allow for, we must multiply the 10% by the area to be covered (540 sq.ft.), giving 54 sq.ft. Thus we require 594 sq.ft. of paper (540 sq.ft. (to cover walls) + 54 sq.ft. (waste allowance) = 594 sq.ft.). In order to find out how many single rolls are needed, we must divide the number of sq.ft. we need (594) by the number of sq.ft. in a roll (36), giving 16.5 (594 ÷ 36 = 16.5). Thus we need 17 rolls of paper in order to paper the room.

• PROBLEM 1-29

Frank Burger owns a paint and wallpaper store. A customer wishes to paper a room that is 24 feet long, 18 feet wide, and 9 feet high. There is a window 3 feet by 8 feet and a door 4 feet by 9 feet. Allowing for a 10% waste of paper, how many single rolls of paper (36 square feet of paper in a single roll) will be required?

Solution: In order to solve this problem, we must find out how many sq. feet we have to cover. In order to compute that, we must find the total area of the walls, and then subtract the area of the openings from that figure. Then we will make an allowance for the waste of paper. This waste of paper is caused by having to match the patterns, and is estimated as 10%.

The total area of the walls is found by finding the area of each of the four walls, and adding them together. The dimensions of the room are given as 24 × 18 × 9, and thus the walls are 24 ft. by 9 ft., 24 ft. by 9 ft., 18 ft. by 9 ft., and 18 ft. by 9 ft. The areas of the walls are

24 ft. × 9 ft. = 216 sq. ft.   24 ft. × 9 ft. = 216 sq.ft.

18 ft. × 9 ft. = 162 sq. ft.   18 ft. × 9 ft. = 162 sq.ft.

Thus the total area is 216 sq. ft. + 216 sq. ft. + 162 sq. ft. + 162 sq. ft. = 756 sq. ft. Now we need

to find the areas of the openings. The door's area is 36 sq. ft. (4 ft. × 9 ft. = 36 sq. ft.), and the window area is 24 sq. ft. (3 ft. × 8 ft. = 24 sq. ft.). So we now know the area to be covered is equal to 696 sq. ft. (756 sq. ft. (total area) -24 sq. ft. (window) -36 sq. ft. (door) = 696 sq. ft.).
Now we must add an allowance for the waste. The allowance is 10% of the area to be covered (696 sq. ft.), 69.6 sq. ft. (696 × .10 = 69.6). We therefore require 765.6 sq. ft. (696 + 69.6 = 765.6) of paper. In order to compute how many rolls will be required, we must divide the amount of sq. ft. we require (765.6 by the number of sq. ft. in a roll (36), giving $21\frac{4}{15}$ $\left(765.6 \div 36 = 21\frac{4}{15}\right)$. We therefore require 22 rolls to paper the room.

DIVISION

• PROBLEM 1-30

Good-day Tire Company wishes to find out its cost per tire. The managers know that during the past 6 months their expenses came to $820,600, and they produced 110,000 tires. Find their cost per tire.

Solution: To find out how much each tire costs, we take the total cost for all the tires ($820,600) and divide it by the number or tires (110,000), giving $7.46 for each tire ($820,600 ÷ 110,000 = $7.46).

• PROBLEM 1-31

Steven Moore purchased a new car for $3,462.20, including taxes and all other charges. He wishes to pay for it in 35 months. Find his monthly payments.

Solution: Since Mr. Moore wishes to pay for his car in 35 months, the amount he must pay each month is computed by dividing the cost of the car ($3,462.20) by the 35 months in which he wishes to pay, resulting in a monthly charge of $98.92 ($3,462.20 ÷ 35 = $98.92).

• PROBLEM 1-32

A super market has two cans of the same brand of tuna fish. The $7\frac{1}{2}$ ounce can sells for 57 cents, and the $8\frac{1}{4}$ ounce can sells for 64 cents. Which can is the better buy?

Solution: In order to find out which is the better buy, we must find out the cost of the goods for the same amounts of the goods. This is usually done best by finding, in this case, the cost of the tuna fish per ounce. To do this we need only divide the given cost of the can of tuna fish by the number of ounces in the can.

The can which sells for 57 ¢ for a $7\frac{1}{2}$ ounce can, sells for $.57 ÷ 7.5 per ounce, which is 7.6 ¢ an ounce. The other can sells for 64 ¢ an $8\frac{1}{4}$ ounce can, which per ounce is $.64 ÷ 8.25, which is 7.7 ¢ an ounce. Thus by comparison we can see that the first can was the better buy.

• PROBLEM 1-33

The Stadlow family, consisting of two adults and two children, went to the amusement park. The rides at the park are 75 cents for adults and 50 cents for children. Mr. Stadlow has $10, how many rides can the family go on?

Solution: In order to find out how many rides they could purchase, we must first find out how much one ride will cost them. Since the family consists of 2 adults and 2 children, then a ride will require two adult tickets, and two children's tickets. Thus the ride will cost 2 × $.75 (adult ticket) + 2 × $.50 (children's ticket) $1.50 + $1.00 = $2.50. Now in order to find out how many rides the family could go on for $10.00, we must divide the $10.00 by the cost per ride ($2.50), giving 4 rides ($10.00 ÷ $2.50 per ride = 4 rides).

• PROBLEM 1-34

James Milford spent $348.88 for tea this year. The tea sells for $.98 a kilogram (kilo), how many kilos did Milford purchase?

Solution: In order to find out how many kilos Milford purchased, we must divide the price he paid ($348.88) by the price per kilo. ($.98). Thus we see Mr. Milford purchased 356 kilos of tea (348.88 ÷ .98 = 356).

• PROBLEM 1-35

Fred Murphy is a New York City cab driver. He recorded the mileage and gas he used for five days. Find (a) his average mileage, and (b) how many miles-per-gallon his car averages.

Day	# of miles	# of gallons of gas
1	269	16
2	280	15.4
3	195	15.9
4	140	11.3
5	275	12.7

Solution: (a) In order to find his average mileage we must find out his total mileage, and divide it by the number of days.

```
   269 miles in day 1
+  280 miles in day 2
+  195 miles in day 3
+  140 miles in day 4
+  275 miles in day 5
 1,159 total number of miles
```

Thus his average mileage is 1,159 miles divided by 5 days, giving 231.8 miles per day.

(b) To find the miles per gallon, we must divide the total number of miles by the total number of gallons used.

```
16    gallons
15.4  gallons
15.9  gallons
11.3  gallons
12.7  gallons
71.3  total number of gallons used
```

We already have the total number of miles from part a. Thus the miles-per-gallon is 1,159 miles ÷ 71.3 gallons = 16.26 miles per gallon (rounded to 2 decimal places).

• **PROBLEM 1-36**

Solve the following problems.

(a) A plot of land containing 487 1/2 acres were broken up into smaller plots containg 3 1/4 acres apiece. Find the number of smaller plots that were formed.

(b) 450 freshmen entered a highschool. Of these only 2/3 will graduate four years later. Of those that graduate, 1/6 will receive an A average. Find how many graduating seniors will have an A average.

(c) The Goreman's Glue Factory wishes to package 4,000 pints of glue in container thst hold 2/3 pint each. How may containers are needed?

Solution: (a) To solve this problem we must realize that we will have to change the numbers into decimal form. Thus 487 1/2 acres becomes 487.5 acres, and 3 1/4 acre plots become 3.25 acre plots. Now to find out how many plots were formed, divide the total acreage (487.5) by the plot size (3.25); therefore, 150 plots were formed.

(b) To find out how many graduates will have an A average, we first must find out how many graduates there will be. To do this, we take the number of Freshman (450) and multiply it by 2/3 (the amount that will graduate). Thus there will be 300 graduates ($450 \times 2/3 = 900 \times 1/3 = 900 \div 3 = 300$).

Now of the 300 graduates since only 1/6 will receive an A average, we multiply $300 \times 1/6 = 300 \div 6 = 50$. Thus 50 graduating seniors will have an A average.

(c) Since they have 4,000 pints and are placing them in 2/3 pint containers, to find out how many containers are needed, we must divide the number of pints (4,000) by the size of the container (2/3 pint). To divide a number by a fraction is equivalent to multiplying by the fraction's inverse. A fraction's inverse is obtained by switching the top and bottom numbers. Thus the number of containers is equal to $4{,}000 \div 2/3 = 4{,}000 \times 3/2 = 6{,}000$ containers.

AVERAGES

• **PROBLEM 1-37**

A plane left Seattle at 1:00 p.m., traveled 540 miles and arrived at its destination at 2:30 p.m. Find the average speed of the plane in miles per hour.

Solution: The average speed of the plane is the fraction $\frac{\text{total number miles traveled}}{\text{total hours traveling time}}$.

The total traveling time is the difference between the original and final time.

$$\text{Therefore, average speed} = \frac{\text{total miles traveled}}{\text{total traveling time}}$$

$$= \frac{540 \text{ miles}}{1\ 1/2 \text{ hrs}}$$

$$= \frac{540}{3/2} \text{ mph} = 540 \times \frac{2}{3} \text{ mph}$$

$$= 360 \text{ mph}$$

• PROBLEM 1-38

Agatha Malm, supervisor of the word-processing department of Hallway Printing Company, wanted to find out how many pages of work the average typist in her department produces. She decided to keep a record for a two-week period. Here is the information she gathered.

Typist	First Week	Second Week
Gordon	206	208
Phipps	180	188
Porter	176	180
Stanislaus	190	178
Tomas	200	200
Zecchi	170	180

Solution: To solve this problem we will find out the total number of pages typed in the two weeks. We will then divide by 2 to find out the total number of pages typed in an average week. We will divide that number by the number of people in Agatha's department in order to get the number of pages typed by an average typist.

Typist	First Week		Second Week
Gordon	206		208
Phipps	+ 180		+ 188
Porter	+ 176		+ 180
Stanislaus	+ 190		+ 178
Tomas	+ 200		+ 200
Zecchi	+ 170		+ 180
Total for each wk.	1,122	+	1,134 = 2,256 (total number of pages)

Thus in two weeks 2,256 pages were typed, giving 1,128 pages typed in the average week (2,256 ÷ 2 = 1,128).

We now know that the number of pages typed by an average typist is 188 pages (1,128 pages ÷ 6 typists = 188). In order to check this we can find the number of pages an average typist typed in week 1, and in week 2, and then add them together and divide by two for their average.

Week 1		Week 2	
1,122	(pages typed in the week	1,134	(pages typed in the week)
÷ 6	(number of typists)	÷ 6	(number of typists)
187	(avg.typist in week 1)	189	(avg.typist in week 2)

Thus the sum of the pages typed by an average typist in the two weeks is 376 (187 + 189), and the number of pages an average typist types is 188 (376 ÷ 2 (weeks) = 188).

• PROBLEM 1-39

While on a trip to St. Louis, Howard Travers made the following purchases:

10 gal	@	33.9¢
14 gal	@	32.9¢
12 gal	@	31.9¢
8 gal	@	29.9¢

What was the average cost per gallon, to the nearest tenth of a cent?

Solution: This is a weighted average problem. When a quantity at any given price is more than one unit, first multiply each quantity by its unit price. Then, add all the products to obtain the total amount spent. Divide this by the total number of units to obtain the weighted average. Consequently, the weighted

$$\text{average} = \frac{\text{total amount spent}}{\text{total number of units}}\ .$$

Here, the total amount spent = (33.9¢ × 10 gal) + (32.9¢ × 14 gal) + (31.9¢ × 12 gal) + (29.9¢ × 8 gal) = \$14.216 = \$14.22

The total number of units is the sum of the individual quantities = 10 + 14 + 12 + 8 = 44.

Therefore, the weighted average = $\dfrac{\text{total amount spent}}{\text{total number of units}}$ =

$$\frac{\$14.22}{44} = 32.3¢$$

The weighted average problem is a generalization of the standard average problem. For the standard average problem, the quantity of each unit is always one.

• PROBLEM 1-40

Florence Lesson is a saleswoman. She uses her own car to call on customers. The company reimburses her 10 ¢ for every mile she drives, and pays for parking and tolls. During the past year Ms. Lesson drove 11,472 miles and her expenses for parking and tolls amounted to $787.44. Find (a) the cost to the company for Ms. Lesson's automobile expenses, and (b) the average cost to the company per month.

Solution: (a) In order to find out how much money Ms. Lesson's automobile expenses cost the company for the year, we must first find out how much money the company reinbursed her. Since she was reimbursed 10 ¢ for every mile she had driven (11,472), she was given $1,147.20 (11,472 × $.10). Thus the company spent $1,147.20 (for the reimbursement) + $787.44 (for parking and tolls). The company therefore spent $1,934.64 on Ms. Lesson's automobile expense for the year.

(b) In order to find out the company's avarege cost per month, we must take the cost per year ($1,934.64) and divide it by the number of months in a year (12). Thus the average cost per month was $161.22 ($1,934.64 ÷ 12 = $161.22)

• PROBLEM 1-41

Transportation expenses of various departments in the Raytown Sporting Goods Corporation for a three-month period were as follows:

Field sales	$655
Market research	$385
Direct-mail promotion	$474
Space advertising	$282
Market services	$394

a. What was the total cost of transportation for all departments for the three-month period?
b. What was the average cost of transportation for all departments for the period?
c. What was the average cost per month for transportation?
d. Verify the accuracy of each answer.

Solution: (a) To find the total cost of transportation, we must add up the transportation costs of the various departments.

\$655	(field sales)
+ \$385	(market research)
+ \$474	(direct-mail promotion)
+ \$282	(space advertising)
+ \$394	(market services)
\$2,190	(total cost of transportation)

(b) To get the average cost of transportation, we take the total cost of transportation (\$2,190) and divide it by the number of departments (5). Thus the average cost of transportation is \$438(\$2,190÷5= \$438).

(c) In order to find the average cost per month of transportation, we take the average cost of transportation, and we divide it by the number of months in the period (3), giving \$146 (\$438÷3= \$146).

(d) To verify our answers, we can find the average cost per month of transportation through another method. We can first find the average cost per month of each department's transportation, then sum them up to have a total cost for an average month, and finally find the average cost per month by dividing by the number of departments.

Department	Cost	Cost per average month	
Field sales	\$655	$\$218\frac{1}{3}$	$\left[655 \div 3 = 218\frac{1}{3}\right]$
Market research	\$385	$+\ \$128\frac{1}{3}$	$\left[385 \div 3 = 128\frac{1}{3}\right]$
Direct-mail promotion	\$474	+ \$158	$\left[474 \div 3 = 158\right]$
Space Advertising	\$282	+ \$94	$(282 \div 3 = 94)$
Market services	\$394	$+\ \$131\frac{1}{3}$	$\left[394 \div 3 = 131\frac{1}{3}\right]$
Total of average cost		\$730	

We can now check our answer to part (a), for 730 is the cost per average month, and thus the cost per average month times the number of months in the period (3) is the total cost (730 × 3 = 2190). We now take the cost per average month and divide it by the number of departments (5) to get the average cost per month. Thus the average cost per month is \$146 (730 ÷ 5 = 146) as before.

RATIOS AND PERCENTS

• PROBLEM 1-42

The Lyons family estimated that 20% of its net income is spent on food each week. If Mrs. Lyons spent \$36 on food shopping last week, what was the family's net income for that week?

Solution: Percent (%) refers to "parts per hundred". Thus 20% means "20 parts per hundred" or $\frac{20}{100}$ × the amount you are taking the percentage of. Note $\frac{20}{100} = .20$.

Since 20% of the family's net income is spent on food, then the amount spent on food = .20 × net income for the week.

Thus .20 × net income = \$36. If we divide both sides by .20 we get the solution to the problem:

net income = \$36 ÷ .20 = \$180.

• PROBLEM 1-43

Compute $\frac{1}{3}$ % of 1,109.

Solution: Convert $\frac{1}{3}$ % to its decimal form.

$\frac{1}{3}\% = .33\frac{1}{3}\% = .0033.$

$.0033 \times 1109 = 3.6597.$

Thus 3.6597 is $\frac{1}{3}$ % of 1,109.

• PROBLEM 1-44

A stock was sold at a gain of 13.5 percent on its original cost. Find the percent the selling price is of the original cost.

Solution: A gain of 13.5% means that the stock has sold for 13.5% of its original cost + its original cost. 100%

of something is itself, for multiplying by 100% is the same as multiplying by one. Thus the selling cost = 100% × original cost + 13.5% × original cost (the gain) = 113.5% × original cost (100% + 13.5% = 113.5%).

• PROBLEM 1-45

Change the following decimals to percents: .06, 2.00, .084, .0035, 3.6.

Solution: The symbol % means hundredths. For example, 40% means forty hundredths:

$$40\% = \frac{40}{100} = .40.$$

$$.06 = \frac{6}{100} = 6\%.$$

To eliminate the middle step, notice that we have moved the decimal point two places to the right and affixed the percent sign. Thus 2.00 = 200.%, .084 = 8.4%, .0035 = .35% and 3.6 = 360%.

• PROBLEM 1-46

Martha Michael spends $360 on her monthly telephone bills. This amounts to $6\frac{1}{4}$ % of her earnings for the year. Find her yearly earnings.

Solution: We know that her earnings × $6\frac{1}{4}$ % = $360, so to solve for her earnings we get $360 ÷ $6\frac{1}{4}$ %

$$= 360 \div .0625 = \$5{,}760.$$

• PROBLEM 1-47

Express $\frac{2}{5}$ and $\frac{1}{400}$ as a percentage.

Solution: The easiest way to express a fraction as a percentage, is to express it as a decimal. Then, move the decimal point two places to the right to make it a percentage.

$$\frac{2}{5} = .4 = 40\%$$

$$\frac{1}{400} = .0025 = .25\%$$

• PROBLEM 1-48

What percent of .065% is .42%?

Solution: Convert the two percents to decimals. $0.065\% = \frac{0.065}{100} = .00065$ and $.42\% = \frac{.42}{100} = .0042$. Since a percentage is a ratio based on 100, we can use the formula $\frac{a}{b} = \frac{x}{100}$, which gives the percent of b, that is a. In this problem a = .0042 and b = .00065. Now

$$\frac{.0042}{.00065} = \frac{100\ (.0042)}{100\ (.00065)} = \frac{.42}{.065} = \frac{100\ (.42)}{100\ (.065)} = \frac{42}{6.5} = 6.46$$

$$= \frac{646}{100} = 646\%.$$

Thus .42% is 646% of .065%.

• PROBLEM 1-49

Find 3% of 548. Compute $9\frac{1}{8}$% of \$6244 using two different methods.

Solution: 3% of 548 means $\frac{3}{100} \times 548$. $\frac{3}{100}$ can be written .03. Now we can multiply .03 × 548 = 16.44.

$9\frac{1}{8}$% of 6244 can be computed by two methods:

(1) $$9\frac{1}{8}\% = \left(9 + \frac{1}{8}\right)\% = \left(\frac{9\text{x}8}{8} + \frac{1}{8}\right)\% = \left(\frac{72}{8} + \frac{1}{8}\right)\% = \frac{73}{8}\%$$

$$= \frac{\frac{73}{8}}{100} = \frac{9.125}{100} = .09125.$$

Now multiply: .09125 × \$6244 = \$569.765.

(2) The second method is

$$
\begin{array}{llll}
9\ \% & \text{of}\ \$6244 & = .09 \times 6244 & = 561.96 \\
+\frac{1}{8}\ \% & \text{of}\ \$6244 & = \frac{1}{8} \times 62.44 & = +\ 7.805 \\
\hline
9\frac{1}{8}\ \% & \text{of}\ \$6244 & & = \$569.765.
\end{array}
$$

• PROBLEM 1-50

Find $4\frac{3}{4}$ % of \$24.85.

Solution: To find a fractional percent of a number, convert the fraction to decimal form.

$$4\frac{3}{4}\ \% = 4\% + \frac{3}{4}\ \% = \frac{16}{4}\ \% + \frac{3}{4}\ \% = \frac{16 + 3}{4}\ \%$$

$$= \frac{19}{4}\ \% = 4.75\% = \frac{4.75}{100} = .0475.$$

Now multiply this by \$24.85: .0475 × \$24.85 = \$1.18. Therefore, \$1.18 is $4\frac{3}{4}$ % of \$24.85.

• PROBLEM 1-51

What percent is 131 of 42?

Solution: In order to find what percent a number is of another number, the easiest procedure is to take the number that the word "is" refers to, and divide it by the number that "of" refers to. We then take our answer and multiply it by 100%. To do that, we need only move the decimal point (if it does not exist, we assume the decimal point is at the extreme right of the number) 2 places to the right, and follow the number by a "%" sign. If there are not enough places to the right of the number we add zeros to the right of the number.

Example: 15.2 × 100% = 1520%

Thus, the solution to our problem is,

131 ÷ 42 = 3.119, and 3.119 × 100% = 311.9%.

• PROBLEM 1-52

Bob, Carol, Ted and Alice win $20,000 in a television game show. They decide to divide it by the ratio 7 : 6 : 4 : 3. What is each one's share?

Solution: Add the digits of the ratio, then divide each digit by the total number. 7 + 6 + 4 + 3 = 20.

Bob receives $\frac{7}{20}$ of $20,000 = $7,000. Carol receives $\frac{6}{20}$ of $20,000 = $6,000. Ted receives $\frac{4}{20}$ of $20,000 = $4,000. Alice receives $\frac{3}{20}$ of $20,000 = $3,000.

Notice that $\frac{7+6+4+3}{20} = \frac{20}{20} = 1$ and $7,000 + 6,000 + 4,000 + 3,000 = $20,000.

• PROBLEM 1-53

The dividend return per annum on an investment was $900. Given this was an annual return of 6 percent, how much was invested?

Solution: The dividend return per annum, is the amount of money you get paid per year for investing your money in the stock. In our problem it is stated that this annual return is 6% of the investment.

Thus, annual return = 6% × investment = .06 × investment (since 6% = 6 ÷ 100 = .06).

If we now divide both sides by .06, we are able to solve for the investment,

investment = annual return ÷ .06.

The investment was $900.00 (annual return) ÷ .06 = $15,000.00.

• PROBLEM 1-54

The Alexander's monthly telephone bill averaged $17.05 last year, which was 10% more than the monthly charge for the previous year. What was the monthly charge the previous year?

Solution: To solve this problem one must first become familiar with the concept of "percentage increase". Quantity A is Y% more than quantity B, means that Quantity A can be obtained by increasing quantity B by Y%. Therefore, if Quantity A is Y% more than Quantity B we may write:

Quantity A = Quantity B + Y% of Quantity B (1)

This principle will be seen more clearly when specifically applied to the problem.

In this problem we are told that the monthly bill last year averaged 10% more than the monthly charge for the previous year. Last year's monthly bill is given as \$17.05. Letting P represent the monthly charge for the previous year, we substitute into equation (1) and obtain:

$$\$17.05 = P + 10\% \text{ of } P$$

The term "per cent" (symbolized by %) means "parts per hundred", and the word "of" means multiplication. Our equation can therefore be rewritten as:

$$\$17.05 = P + \left(\frac{10}{100} \times P\right)$$

so:

$$\$17.05 = P + .1\,P$$

$$\$17.05 = 1.1\,P$$

Solving for P we obtain:

$$P = \$15.50$$

The monthly charge for the previous year was \$15.50.

• PROBLEM 1-55

The selling price of a piano which cost \$18,000 is \$22,950. Find the percent the selling price is of the cost.

Solution: To find what percent the selling price is of the cost, we must take the number referred to by the verb "is" (the selling cost of \$22,950.00) and divide it by the number referred to by the word "of" (the cost of \$18,000.00). Then we multiply that number by 100% to get it into percent form.

Thus the answer to the problem is

$$\$22,950.00 \div \$18,000.00 = 1.275 = 127.5\%.$$

• PROBLEM 1-56

Mary Anne, a piece-worker, makes 370 units each day. A consultant advises that a change in her method would result in 30% more units. Assuming the change really has this result, how many units should Mary Anne produce?

Solution: Find 30% of 370 and add that number to 370 to find the new quantity. 30% of 370 is .30 × 370 = 111. 370 + 111 = 481 units.

• PROBLEM 1-57

A manufacturer sells his merchandise at 135 percent of the cost. Find his percent of gain.

Solution: The gain is the difference between the selling price and the cost of the merchandise, when the selling price is higher than the cost. Thus the gain = Selling price - cost. Since the selling price = 135% × cost and cost = 100% × cost, the gain = 135% × cost - 100% × cost = 35% x cost (135% - 100% = 35%)

• PROBLEM 1-58

A salesman sold 927 brushes one week and 1,059 brushes the next week. Find his percent of increase.

Solution: The percent of increase is found by dividing the amount of increase by the original number before the increase; and multiplying by 100%. The amount of increase is the difference between the two numbers.

Amount of increase = 1,059 - 927 = 132

Percent of increase = 132 ÷ 927 × 100%

= .14239 × 100% = 14.239%.

• PROBLEM 1-59

The population of Victoria is approximately 42,600. Ten years ago, the population was approximately 30,000. Find the percent of increase.

Solution: We are seeking the percent of increase of the population as it becomes larger over a 10 year time span. The percent or rate of increase is the fraction $\frac{\text{increase of population}}{\text{original population}}$. We first find the amount of change or increase between the original size and the final population size. This is found by subtracting 30,000 from 42,600 which equals 12,600. Substituting into the formula for percent of increase, we find

$$\text{rate or percent of increase} = \frac{\text{increase of population}}{\text{original population}}$$

$$= \frac{12,600}{30,000}$$

$$= \frac{126}{300}$$

$$= \frac{63}{150}$$

The answer is given in terms of a fraction. We can equally well put the answer in terms of a percentage or "parts per hundred".

Since $\frac{63}{150} = .42$, and .42 means 42 parts per hundred, $.42 = \frac{42}{100} = 42\%$. Therefore, the rate or percent increase is 42%. We can derive a general equation for the percent of increase from the above example.

$$\text{percent of increase of x} = \frac{\text{increase in x}}{\text{original x}} \cdot 100$$

where x is any given quantity.

• PROBLEM 1-60

George and Richard Martin, partners in a law firm, pay $6300 in annual rent. When their lease expires, their new rent will be $715 per month. What percent of increase will they be paying?

Solution: $715 per month × 12 months = $8580. The difference between the new and old annual rents is $8,580 - $6,300 = $2,280. To determine what percent of $6,300 is $2,280, divide as follows:

$$\frac{\$2,280}{\$6,300} = .3619 = 36\%.$$

This is the percent of increase.

• **PROBLEM 1-61**

Mike sold an automobile that cost him $12,640 for $11,628.80. What percent is the selling price of the cost?

Solution: In order to find out what percent the selling price is of the cost, we must divide the number referred to by the word "is" (the selling price of $11,628.80) by the number referred to by the word "of" (the cost of $12,640). We then multiply our result by 100%, which means moving the decimal point 2 places to the right and following the number by a "%" sign.

$11,628.80 (selling price) ÷ $12,640.00 (cost) = .92

and .92 × 100% = 92%.

Thus the selling price is 92% of the cost.

• **PROBLEM 1-62**

A pair of hiking boots costs $25 to produce. The Sure-grip Shoe Co. wishes to sell these booths for 15 percent more than they cost to produce. What is the manufacturer's increase over the cost?

Solution: What we must do in this problem is to find out how much money the manufacturer will charge for his goods. Since the problem states that he is selling them for an additional 15% of his cost, we must multiply his cost ($25) by 15%. To do this we must convert 15% into a decimal. What percent means is, the given number should be divided by 100, thus 15% = 15 ÷ 100 = .15.

The solution to our problem is

$25 × .15 = $3.75.

Thus the manufacturer is charging $3.75 over the cost.

• **PROBLEM 1-63**

A wholesaler was going out of business so he sold merchandise for $1,288 at a loss of 8 percent of his original cost. Find the original cost of the merchandise.

Solution: Since the wholesaler sold the merchandise for a loss of 8%, we know that the price he sold it for was 92% of the original cost (100% cost - 8% loss = 92%). Thus we see that the selling price = 92% × cost, or, since 92% = .92, selling price = .92 × cost. By dividing both sides by .92 we can find the cost = selling price ÷ .92. Thus the cost = $1,288.00 ÷ .92 = $1,400.00.

• PROBLEM 1-64

A department store had gross sales this month of $72,800, and returns and allowances were 12 percent of the net sales. If net sales + returns and allowances = gross sales, find the net sales in dollars.

Solution: The gross sales are comprised of the net sales and the returns and allowances. The returns and allowances are equal to 12% of the net sales. Thus, gross sales are equal to 100% net sales (all of the net sales) + 12% of the net sales (being the returns and allowances), or, gross sales = 112% (100% + 12%) of the net sales. Now, 112% = 112 ÷ 100 = 1.12, thus we see gross sales = 1.12 × net sales, or if we divide both sides of the equation by 1.12 we see net sales = gross sales ÷ 1.12. Thus the solution to our problem is

$72,800.00 (gross sales) ÷ 1.12 = $65,000.00 (net sales).

• PROBLEM 1-65

Joe, Barbara, and Susie purchased a $40 lottery ticket. Joe paid $19, Barbara paid $12, and Susie paid $9. The ticket won, and they decided to share the $20,000 prize by the ratio of the amount they had spent for the ticket. Find each person's share of the prize.

Solution: To find each person's share, we take the ratio of the amount he paid for the ticket to the cost of the ticket, and multiply that by the $20,000 prize. Joe paid $19 for the ticket, thus his share is 19/40 × $20,000 = .475 × $20,000 = $9,500. Barbara paid $12 for the ticket, thus her share is 12/40 × $20,000 = .3 × $20,000 = $6,000. Susie paid $9 for the ticket, thus her share is 9/40 × $20,000 = .225 × $20,000 = $4,500.
To check we add up each person's share and should get $20,000.

Joe	$9,500
Barbara	+ $6,000
Susie	+ $4,500
Total	20,000

• PROBLEM 1-66

Three partners - Alton, Birch, and Castor - invested \$4,000, \$5,000, and \$11,000, respectively, in a retail hardware store. The net profit for a recent year was \$15,000. If profits are to be shared in proportion to each man's investment, what amount of money should Birch receive?

Solution: One must first calculate the proportion of each partner's investment. The proportion of the profit that each partner will receive will be equal to the proportion of the total investment that he contributed.

(1) Proportion of investment contributed = Proportion of profits received. Using the proportion of profits received and the given net profit, the profit of each partner can then be calculated. To calculate the proportion of the investment contributed by each partner, we note that:

(2) Proportion of investment contributed

$$= \frac{\text{Individual's Investment}}{\text{Total Investment}} .$$

The three partners - Alton, Birch, and Castor - invest \$4,000, \$5,000, and \$11,000, respectively. The total investment is therefore:

$$\$4,000 + \$5,000 + \$11,000 = \$20,000.$$

Birch's individual investment is given as \$5,000. Using Equation (2) one obtains the

$$\text{Proportion of investment contributed by Birch} = \frac{\$5,000}{\$20,000} = \frac{1}{4} .$$

Birch's investment represents $\frac{1}{4}$ of the total investment. By equation (1), his proportion of the profits is also $\frac{1}{4}$. Therefore, if the total profits are \$15,000, Birch receives $\frac{1}{4}$ (\$15,000) = \$3,750.

• PROBLEM 1-67

Bob had debts totaling \$25,000. When he went into bankruptcy, it was found that he had only \$15,000 available to pay his creditors. How many cents on the dollar does Bob have to pay each creditor? How much money was paid to a creditor who had a claim for \$4,500?

Solution: If a business is continually operating at a loss, then the owner or owners may find that they can't pay all their debts. If a court agrees, the owners can be declared bankrupt. When this happens, someone is appointed to sell all the assets and distribute them among the creditors - those to whom money is owed. Bob can only pay out $15,000 even though he has debts of $25,000. This means that for every dollar owed, he can only pay out

$$\frac{\text{the cash available}}{\text{total debts}} = \frac{\$15,000}{\$25,000} = \frac{3}{5} \text{ of a dollar}$$

$$= 60 \text{ cents.}$$

Bob pays 60 cents on the dollar to each creditor. If a creditor has a claim, he will receive the dollar amount of the claim × 60 cents. For a claim of $4,500 a creditor will receive

$$\$4,500 \times 60 \text{ cents} = \$4,500 \times \$.6 = \$2,700.$$

• PROBLEM 1-68

The Jeffersons have a combined income of $12,600. They spent 28% for food; 20% for housing; 12% for clothing; $12\frac{1}{2}$% for entertainment; 8% for car expenses; 19% for miscellaneous expenses, and they saved the rest. Find (a) how much was spent in each category, and (b) how much was saved.

Solution: (a) In order to find out how much money was spent in each category, we take its corresponding percentage and multiply it by the income.

Category	Amount Spent
Food	$3,528 ($12,600 × .28)
housing	$2,520 ($12,600 × .20)
clothing	$1,512 ($12,600 × .12)
car expenses	$1,008 ($12,600 × .08)
entertainment	$1,575 ($12,600 × .125)
misc. expenses	$2,394 ($12,600 × .19)

(b) To find out how much they saved, we first must find out how much they spent, and subtract that from their income. To find out how much was spent over the year we must sum up the amounts spent for all the categories.

$ 3,528	food
$ 2,520	housing
$ 1,512	clothing
$ 1,008	car expenses
$ 1,575	entertainment
$ 2,394	misc. expenses
$12,537	total spent

We now take the total spent ($12,537) and subtract it from the income ($12,600), giving the amount saved.

$12,600	income
- $12,537	total spent
$ 63	amount saved

We can check this result by seeing what percentage of the money was saved. To do this we must find out the total percentage that was spent, and subtract that from 100%.

28%	(food)
+ 20%	(housing)
+ 12%	(clothing)
+ 8%	(car expenses)
+ $12\frac{1}{2}$ %	(entertainment)
+ 19%	(miscellaneous expenses)
$99\frac{1}{2}$ %	(total expense)

Thus they saved $\frac{1}{2}$ % $\left(100\% - 99\frac{1}{2}\%\right)$ of their income, which is $12,600 × .005 = $63.

• PROBLEM 1-69

What percent of sales does the selling cost represent for each of the three years of the Marison Milk Farm?

Marison Milk Farm			
Sales and Selling Costs 19X3 - 19X5			
	19X3	19X4	19X5
Sales	$700,000	$800,000	$900,000
Selling Costs	$154,000	$168,000	$184,500

Solution: In order to find the percent of sales that the selling costs represent, we must use the formula $\frac{\text{selling costs}}{\text{sales}} \times 100\%$.

In 19X3

$$\frac{\text{Selling Costs (\$154,000)}}{\text{Sales (\$700,000)}} \times 100\% = .22 \times 100\% = 22\%$$

In 19X4

$$\frac{\$168,000}{\$800,000} \times 100\% = .21 \times 100\% = 21\%$$

In 19X5

$$\frac{\$184,500}{\$900,000} \times 100\% = .205 \times 100\% = 20.5\% = 20\frac{1}{2}\%.$$

Notice in the last one we converted the decimal .5 to the fraction $\frac{1}{2}$. This is usually done for clarity.

• PROBLEM 1-70

Alan Jacobs has an income of \$9,260. He spent $26\frac{1}{3}\%$ for rent; 28% for food; 12% for clothing; $16\frac{2}{3}\%$ for other items, and he saved the rest. Find (a) the amount he spent in each category, and (b) the amount he saved.

Solution: (a) In order to find out how much money was spent in each category, we take its corresponding percentage and multiply it by the income. When you have to multiply by a fraction of a percent it is easiest to take 1% of the number, and then multiply your result by the fraction required.

Alan Jacobs spent $26\frac{1}{3}\%$ of his income on rent. To figure out how much he spent, we multiply his income (\$9,260) by $.26\frac{1}{3}$. To do this we break it up into two problems.

(1) $\$9,260 \times .26$

(2) $\$9,260 \times .01 \times \frac{1}{3}$ (one-third of one percent of his income)

and then sum the two problems for our answer.

$$\$9,260 \times .26\frac{1}{3} = (\$,9,260 \times .26) + \left(\$9,260 \times .1 \times \frac{1}{3}\right)$$

$$= \$2,407.60 + \$30.87 = \$2,438.47.$$

Similarly, we do this for food, clothing, and other items.

Food

$\$9,260 \times .28 = \$2,592.80$

Clothing

$\$9,260 \times .12 = \$1,111.20$

Other items

$$\$9,260 \times .16\frac{2}{3} = (\$9,260 \times .16) + \left(\$9,260 \times .01 \times \frac{2}{3}\right)$$

$$= \$1,481.60 + \$61.73 = \$1,543.33.$$

(b) To find our how much he saved, all one needs to do is add up all of the money he spent, and subtract the total from his income.

Money spent

\$2,438.47	(rent)
\$2,592.80	(food)
\$1,111.20	(clothing)
\$1,543.33	(other items)
\$7,685.80	(total spent)

Total saved is equal to income (\$9,260.00) less total spent (\$7,685.80), which is \$1,574.20.

We can check this answer by finding what percent of the money was not spent. To do this we must total the percents of money that was spent,and then subtract that total from 100%.

$26\frac{1}{3}$ %	rent
28%	food
12%	clothing
$16\frac{2}{3}$ %	other items
83%	total percent spent

This leaves 17% (100% - 83%) to be saved. To check if our answer was correct, just take 17% of his income which should come out to his total savings.

$$\$9,260 \times .17 = \$1,574.20.$$

• PROBLEM 1-71

The average salary of the Bedford Manufacturing Co. rose 60% during a 10-year period. This rise amounted to \$42.50 a week. (a) Find the average weekly salary at the beginning of the 10-year period, and (b) at the end of the 10-year period.

Solution: (a) To solve this problem, we must find out what the weekly salary was at the beginning of the 10-year period. We are given that over the 10 years the salary rose 60% which amounted to a rise of \$42.50.

From this we see that \$42.50 is equal to 60% of the starting salary. So we get an equation of the form \$42.50 = .60 × n, where n is the beginning salary.

To solve this equation we divide both sides of the equation by .60, in order to get rid of the unknown's multiplier.

$$\frac{\$42.50}{.60} = \frac{n \times .60}{.60} = n \times 1 = n$$

Thus by dividing \$42.50 by .60 we get n = \$70.83. Expressed in other terms, the beginning salary was \$70.83.

(b) To find out what the average weekly salary was after the 10-year period, we need only add the rise (\$42.50) to the beginning salary (\$70.83). Thus the weekly salary after the 10-year period was \$113.33 (\$70.83 + 42.50).

CONVERSION OF UNITS

• PROBLEM 1-72

Round .1476 to (a) 2 decimal places (b) 3 decimal places (c) 1 decimal place.

Solution: To round a decimal to a certain place, we look at the next place. If that digit is less than 5 we simply take the required digits, otherwise we add 1 to the last digit we are taking.

(a) .1476 becomes .15 to 2 decimal places

(b) .1476 becomes .148 to 3 decimal places

(c) .1476 becomes .1 to 1 decimal place.

• PROBLEM 1-73

Metric to Customary Units	Customary to Metric Units
1 liter = 1.057 quarts, .264 gallon	1 quart = .946 liter
	1 gallon = 3.785 liters
1 milliliter = .0338 ounce	1 ounce = 29.57 milliliters

(A) How many gallons are there in 12 liters?

(B) How many liters are there in 10 quarts?

Solution: (A) In order to find out how many gallons there are in 12 liters, we must find out how many gallons there are in 1 liter (a constant from the above table) and then multiply that number by the number of liters we wish to convert (12). Since 1 liter = .264 gallon, we know that 12 liters = 12 × .264 = 3.168 gallons.

(B) To do this conversion, we need to find out from the table how many liters there are in 1 quart, and then multiply that by the number of quarts (10). Since 1 quart = .946 liter, we know that 10 quarts = 10 × .946 = 9.46 liters.

• PROBLEM 1-74

(a) Convert 678 cm to feet.
(b) Convert 316 liters to dry pints.
(c) Convert 50 kg to pounds.

Solution: To convert from one scale to another,one must take the number that is in the first scale and multiply it by the constant for changing 1 unit in one scale to one unit in the other scale. Note, that the constants that will be used are all approximate.

(a) To change 678 cm to feet, we must multiply 678 by .0325 (1 cm = .0325 ft.), giving 22 ft. (approximately).

(b) To change 316 liters to dry pints, we must multiply 316 by 1.82 (1 liter = 1.82 pints), giving 575.12 pints.

(c) To change 50 kg. to pounds, we must multiply 50 by 2.2 (1 kg = 2.2 lbs.), giving 110 pounds.

• PROBLEM 1-75

A man shipped his car to Israel. In the United States his car averaged 10 miles to the gallon of gas. He now wishes to convert this figure in order to compare his car's efficiency to that of the Israeli cars. Convert the miles per gallon to kilometers per liter.

Solution: Converting from miles per gallon to kilometers per liter is a two step process. The first step is to convert the miles to kilometers. This is done by multiplying by $\frac{8}{5}$ (1 mile = $\frac{8}{5}$ kilometers). We then must convert the the gallons to liters. In this conversion we must multiply by .26 (1 gallon = $\frac{1}{.26}$ liters). The reason we are using .26 and not $\frac{1}{.26}$ is that since we are really dividing the number of kilometers by the number of gallons, we should have to divide by the constant $\left(\frac{1}{.26}\right)$ to convert to kilometers per liter. However, division by a fraction is the same as multiplying by its inverse, thus we multiply by .26.

$$10 \text{ mpg} = 16 \text{ kilometers per gallon } \left(10 \times \frac{8}{5} = 16\right)$$

16 kilometers per gallon = 4.16 kilometers per liter (16 × .26 = 4.16).

CHAPTER 2

TAXES

SALES TAX

• PROBLEM 2-1

Complete the table below.

Purchase	Selling Price	Tax Rate	Sales Tax	Actual Price
a	$2,000.00	5%	$______	$______
b	$ 65.00	4%	$______	$______
c	$ 4.98	4 1/2%	$______	$______
d	$ 79.95	6%	$______	$______

Solution: Multiply the tax rate by the selling price to find the sales tax. Then add the sales tax to the selling price to find the actual price.

Sales Tax	Actual Price
.05 x $2,000 = $100.00	$100 + $2,000 = $2,100
.04 x $65.00 = $2.60	$2.60 + $65.00 = $67.60
.045 x $4.98 = $0.22	$0.22 + $4.98 = $5.20
.06 x $79.95 = $4.80 (to the nearest cent)	$4.80 + $79.95 = $84.75

• PROBLEM 2-2

Steve King buys dress slacks on sale at $33.15 for two pairs, the sales tax is 5.5%. How much does he pay for four pairs of slacks?

Solution: Four pairs cost 2 x $33.15 = $66.30. The sales tax is 5.5% of $66.30 = .055 x 66.30 = $3.65. The total cost is $66.30 + $3.65 = $69.95.

• PROBLEM 2-3

John Cowan and his family were traveling through a state in which the sales tax was 3%. They spent $6.75, $5.50, $2.35 and $1.95 for their meals, all of which were put on one check. How much did they pay? If separate checks had been issued, how much would they have had to pay?

Solution: On one check, the cost of the individual meals is added before the sales tax is calculated. We have $6.75 + $5.50 + $2.35 + $1.95 = $16.55. The sales tax is 3% of $16.55 = $0.50. John's family paid $16.55 + $0.50 = $17.05. If separate checks were issued, the sales tax would be computed for each meal, as follows:

Cost of meal	Tax	Total	
$6.75	$0.20	$6.95	
5.50	0.17	5.67	
2.35	0.07	2.42	
1.95	0.06	2.01	
$16.55	$0.50	$17.05	total

The total cost would have been the same.

• PROBLEM 2-4

Pauline DiNardi has a choice between buying a stereo set in New Jersey for $698.50 and buying it in New York for $684.75 plus a 4% state tax and a 2% city tax. Which stereo should she buy?

Solution: Compute the total tax on the New York price ($684.75) and add it to the price. Then compare the sum to the New Jersey price.

4% + 2% = 6% of $684.75 = $41.09 (to the nearest cent.)

$684.75 + $41.09 = $725.84.

The New Jersey price is less.

• PROBLEM 2-5

Jack bought 3 auto tires at $17.95 per tire. The excise tax per tire was $2.86. A 4.2% sales tax was added. How much did Jack spend?

Solution: The sales tax is based on the cost of the three tires including excise tax. The tires cost 3 x $17.95 = $53.85. The excise tax is 3 X $2.86 = $8.58. Cost = $53.85 + $8.58 = $62.43. Now we compute the sales tax:

4.2% of $62.43 = .042 x $62.43 = $2.62. Add the sales tax to the cost to obtain $62.43 + $2.62 = $65.05.

• PROBLEM 2-6

Peter bought a typewriter for $125, less a 5% discount. The state sales tax was 4.5% and the city tax was 2.5%. How much did Peter pay?

Solution: To find the net price, compute the discount (5% of $125) and subtract it from the original price ($125).

5% of $125 = .05 X $125 = $6.25.

Net price = $125.00 - $6.25 = $118.75.

The total sales tax is 4.5% + 2.5% = 7% of the net price, or 7% of $118.75 = .07 X $118.75 = $8.31.
The total cost is the net price + sales tax = $118.75 + $8.31 = $127.06.

• PROBLEM 2-7

Jim Miller bought a vacuum cleaner priced at $69.75, with a 5% discount. The state sales tax was 3% and the city sales tax was 4%. How much did Jim pay for the cleaner?

Solution: There are four steps in computing the cost. The first is to find the discount, which is 5% of %69.75 = .05 x $69.75 = $3.49. Net price = (list price) - discount = $69.75 - $3.49 = $66.26. Now compute the total sales tax on the net price: 3% + 4% = 7% of $66.25 = .07 x $66.25 = $4.64 to the nearest cent.

Total cost = (net price) + (total sales tax) = $66.25 + $4.64 = $70.90.

• PROBLEM 2-8

Paul owed $56.30 plus a 3% sales tax to a sporting goods store. The terms were 2/10, n/30. If Paul paid one week after the agreement, how much did he pay?

Solution: The terms 2/10, n/30 mean that a 2% discount is allowed if payment is made within ten days of the invoice date, and that the net amount (the original price, with no discount allowed) is due from the 11th to 30th day. Since Paul paid one week after his purchase, he was entitled to the 2% discount on the net amount due (56.30). 2% of $56.30 = .02 X $56.30 = $1.13. The sales tax was 3% of $56.30 = .03 X $56.30 = $1.69. The total amount due was (net amount) + (sales tax) = $56.30 + $1.69 = $57.99. The amount that Paul paid was (total due) - (discount) = $57.99 - $1.13 = $56.86.

• **PROBLEM 2-9**

A dress with an original price of $47.50, was marked down 30% in a clearance sale. If a sales tax of 6% was paid on the dress, what was its total price?

Solution: Since the price of the dress was reduced by 30% (= .30), the discount on the dress was $47.50 x .30 = $14.25. This leaves a discounted price of $47.50 - $14.25 = $33.25. The sales tax was $33.25 X .06 = $2.00, resulting in a total price of $33.25 + $2.00 = $35.25.

INCOME TAX

• **PROBLEM 2-10**

ABC Corporation had a 1976 net income of $1,000,000. If ABC pays 50% taxes, what was its income before taxes?

Solution: Since ABC pays 50% (or 1/2) of its income in taxes, the corporation's net income of $1,000,000 represents only 1/2 of the income before taxes. The income before taxes was therefore twice the $1,000,000 or $2,000,000.

• **PROBLEM 2-11**

Mrs. Bracken is a widow who maintains a home for herself, her dependent father, and her two children.

(a) What filing status should she claim?

(b) How many exemptions is she allowed?

Solution: Since Mrs. Bracken maintains a home for herself, her father, and her two children, she should claim a filing status of head of household. Also, she would be allowed one exemption for herself, one for her father, and one for each of her children for a total of four exemptions.

• **PROBLEM 2-12**

Angela Rodriguez is single, not head of any household, and claims one exemption. She earned $9,357 during the year, of which $1,397 was withheld as federal tax. She has decided to take a standard deduction. Using the table for standard deductions, calculate how much additional tax Angela must pay.

Solution: Using the table for standard deductions, we see that the total tax due on an income of $9,357 (at least $9,350 but less than $9,400) for a single person, not head of household, is $1,403. Since Angela has already had $1,397 withheld for federal taxes, she must pay an additional

$1,403 - $1,397 = $6

in federal taxes.

• PROBLEM 2-13

Using the table below, find the federal income tax for Jerry Kohen, who has an annual income of $8,975. He is married, has two dependent children, and will be filing a joint tax return with his wife.

PARTIAL TAX TABLE STANDARD DEDUCTION, FOUR EXEMPTIONS			
If adjusted gross income is		And you are	
At least	But less than	Single, not head of household	Married, filing joint return
$4950	$ 5000	$ 96	$ 95
5950	6000	255	241
6950	7000	438	398
7950	8000	628	565
8950	9000	822	739
9950	10,000	1001	901

Solution: Since Mr. Kohen is filing a joint return with his wife, and they have 2 dependent children, they have a total of 4 dependents. Looking down the adjusted gross income column of the Standard Deduction, Four Exemptions table for an adjusted gross income of $8975 (which is in the "at least $8950 but less than $9000" row), and across to the Married, filing joint return column, we find that the tax due the federal government for the year is $739.

• PROBLEM 2-14

Tom Lewis is married, earns $153.75 a week and claims four exemptions. How much is deducted from his weekly paycheck for witholding tax? How much is withheld in a one-year period?

Solution: Consulting a partial table of Federal Withholding Tax, we see that the salary of $153.75 falls in the row listed as "at least $150 but less than $160". Reading across the row to the entry for four exemptions, the amount withheld is $13.30 per week. Since there are 52 weeks in a year, the total amount withheld in a 52 week period is

$$52 \times 13.30 = \$691.60 .$$

• PROBLEM 2-15

How much would an employer pay to the federal and state governments in unemployment insurance taxes on a total taxable payroll of $100,000 if 0.4% is sent to the federal government and 2.7% is sent to the state government?

Solution: Since the federal unemployment tax is

$$\frac{4}{10}\ \% \ (=.004)$$

of the total taxable payroll, the federal tax would be $100,000 × .004 = $400. The state tax, which is 2.7% (.027) of the total taxable payroll, would be

$$\$100,000 \times .027 = \$2,700.$$

• PROBLEM 2-16

Lester Lang, married and earning $7995 a year, claims four exemptions. If he has $1480 in itemized deductions, what tax should he pay for the year?

PARTIAL TAX RATE SCHEDULE WHEN TAX TABLES ARE NOT USED MARRIED TAXPAYERS FILING JOINT RETURN		
If taxable income is		Tax is
Over	But not over	
$3000	$4000	$450+17% of excess over $3000
$4000	$8000	$620+19% of excess over $4000
$8000	$12,000	$1380+22% of excess over $8000
$12,000	$16,000	$2260+25% of excess over $12,000
$16,000	$20,000	$3260+28% of excess over $16,000

Solution: Since Mr. Lang earns \$7995 a year, and has itemized deductions of \$1480, he has a net income of \$7995 - \$1480 = \$6515. His four exemptions, at \$750 per exemption, total \$750 × 4 = \$3000. Subtracting this from the net income, we get a taxable income of \$6515 - \$3000 = \$3515. Consulting the above table, we see that the tax on a taxable income of \$3515 is \$450 plus 17% (=.17) of the taxable income over \$3000. Since the taxable income over \$3000 is \$515, the tax is

$$\$450 + .17 \times \$515 = \$450 + \$87.55 = \$537.55.$$

• PROBLEM 2-17

Lucy Johnson earns \$26,300 a year and supports her disabled husband and three children. Her husband does some work at home for which he earns \$3,200 during the year. The Johnsons have itemized deductions amounting to \$3,100 for the year. What is their federal income tax?

Solution: Since Mrs. Johnson earned \$26,300 and her husband earned \$3,200, they have a combined income of \$26,300 + \$3,200 = \$29,500. Subtracting the itemized deductions of \$3,100, we get a net income of

$$\$29,500 - \$3,100 = \$26,400.$$

The Johnsons have 5 exemptions, at \$750 each, for a total exemption of \$3750. The Johnson's total taxable income, which is net income less exemptions, is

$$\$26,400 - \$3,750 = \$22,650.$$

Using the table for Married Taxpayers Filing Joint Returns, we see that the tax due on a total taxable income of \$22,650 is \$4,380 + 32% of the amount over \$20,000. The Johnson's total taxable income is \$22,650, so the excess amount over \$20,000 is \$22,650 - \$20,000 = \$2,650. The federal tax is then

$$\$4,380 + .32 \times \$2,650 = \$4,380 + \$848 = \$5,228 .$$

• PROBLEM 2-18

Mr. Wilson earns \$153.75 a week. His adjusted gross income is the same as his total income. A total of \$691.60 has been withheld from his paychecks for the year. If he claims four exemptions and takes the standard deduction, what is the amount of tax he pays for the year? Will he pay more or receive a refund?

PARTIAL TAX TABLE STANDARD DEDUCTION, FOUR EXEMPTIONS			
If adjusted gross income is		And you are	
At least	But less than	Single, not head of household	Married, filing joint return
$4950	$ 5000	$ 96	$ 95
5950	6000	255	241
6950	7000	438	398
7950	8000	628	565
8950	9000	822	739
9950	10,000	1001	901

Solution: Since Mr. Wilson earns $153.75 a week, his total earnings for the year are $153.75 × 52 = $7995. Consulting the Partial Tax Table for Standard Deduction, Four Deductions, we see that the tax due on an adjusted gross income of $7995 (which is at least $7950 but less than $8000) for the heading Married, Filing Joint Return is $565.

Since Mr. Wilson has already had $691.60 withheld, he is due for a refund of

$691.60 - $565 = $126.60.

• PROBLEM 2-19

Using the tax table (see figure below) find the income tax due the federal government from:

(A) A single person, head of household, one exemption, with an adjusted gross income of $9,187.80.

(B) A single person, not head of household, one exemption, with an adjusted gross income of $9,000.

(C) A married person, one exemption, claiming standard deduction with an adjusted gross income of $8,188.85.

Solution: The amount of income tax due the federal government from each of the individuals listed above is dependent on two things: (1) their adjusted gross salary, and (2) their classification, according to

If line 15 (adjusted gross income) is—		And you are—			
				Married filing separate return claiming—	
At least	But less than	Single, not head of household	Head of household	Low income allowance	%Standard deduction
		Your tax is—			
$6,250	$6,300	$737	$703	$883	$818
6,300	6,350	748	712	894	828
6,350	6,400	758	722	905	837
6,400	6,450	769	731	916	846
6,450	6,500	779	741	927	856
6,500	6,550	790	750	938	865
6,550	6,600	800	760	949	875
6,600	6,650	811	769	960	884
6,650	6,700	821	779	971	894
6,700	6,750	832	788	982	905
6,750	6,800	842	798	993	916
6,800	6,850	853	807	1,004	927
6,850	6,900	863	817	1,015	938
6,900	6,950	874	826	1,026	949
6,950	7,000	884	836	1,037	960
7,000	7,050	895	845	1,048	971
7,050	7,100	905	855	1,059	982
7,100	7,150	916	864	1,070	993
7,150	7,200	926	874	1,081	1,004
7,200	7,250	937	883	1,092	1,015
7,250	7,300	947	893	1,103	1,026
7,300	7,350	958	902	1,114	1,037
7,350	7,400	968	912	1,125	1,048
7,400	7,450	979	921	1,136	1,059
7,450	7,500	989	931	1,149	1,070
7,500	7,550	1,000	940	1,161	1,081
7,550	7,600	1,010	950	1,174	1,092
7,600	7,650	1,021	959	1,186	1,103
7,650	7,700	1,031	969	1,199	1,114
7,700	7,750	1,042	978	1,211	1,125
7,750	7,800	1,052	988	1,224	1,136
7,800	7,850	1,063	997	1,236	1,149
7,850	7,900	1,073	1,007	1,249	1,161
7,900	7,950	1,084	1,016	1,261	1,174
7,950	8,000	1,094	1,026	1,274	1,186
8,000	8,050	1,105	1,035	1,286	1,199
8,050	8,100	1,116	1,046	1,299	1,211
8,100	8,150	1,128	1,057	1,311	1,224
8,150	8,200	1,140	1,068	1,324	1,236
8,200	8,250	1,152	1,079	1,336	1,249
8,250	8,300	1,164	1,090	1,349	1,261
8,300	8,350	1,176	1,101	1,361	1,274
8,350	8,400	1,188	1,112	1,374	1,286
8,400	8,450	1,200	1,123	1,386	1,299
8,450	8,500	1,212	1,134	1,399	1,311
8,500	8,550	1,224	1,145	1,411	1,324
8,550	8,600	1,236	1,156	1,424	1,336
8,600	8,650	1,248	1,167	1,436	1,349
8,650	8,700	1,260	1,177	1,449	1,361
8,700	8,750	1,270	1,187	1,461	1,374
8,750	8,800	1,280	1,196	1,474	1,386
8,800	8,850	1,290	1,205	1,486	1,399
8,850	8,900	1,301	1,215	1,499	1,411
8,900	8,950	1,311	1,224	1,511	1,424
8,950	9,000	1,321	1,233	1,524	1,436
9,000	9,050	1,331	1,243	1,536	1,449
9,050	9,100	1,341	1,252	1,549	1,461
9,100	9,150	1,352	1,261	1,561	1,474
9,150	9,200	1,362	1,271	1,574	1,486
9,200	9,250	1,372	1,280	1,586	1,499
9,250	9,300	1,382	1,289	1,599	1,511
9,300	9,350	1,392	1,299	1,611	1,524
9,350	9,400	1,403	1,308	1,624	1,536
9,400	9,450	1,413	1,317	1,637	1,549
9,450	9,500	1,423	1,327	1,651	1,561

the table listed above. For example, to find the tax due from the individual in example (a), we would first find the adjusted gross salary of $9,187.80, which falls into the "at least $9,150 but less than $9,200" category.

Reading across this line to the tax due for a head of household, we find an amount due to the federal government of $1,271. Following the same procedure, the tax due from the individuals in examples (b) and (c) is $1,331 and $1,236, respectively.

• PROBLEM 2-20

Find the income tax due from each of the following single persons if they decide to itemize their deductions:

Name	Exemp.	Adjusted Gross Income	Itemized Deductions	Tax Due
Bruce Jacobus	1	$16,500	$2,710	$______
Marcia Jasko	2	$22,650	$3,640	$______
Rita Jurasch	3	$31,100	$2,753	$______
Paul E.Cordazzo	2	$17,820	$2,940	$______
David Schwann	1	$ 6,772	$1,500	$______

Solution: The income tax due in each of the above examples is based on the total taxable income, which is adjusted gross income less itemized deductions less exemptions at $750 each. For example, consider Bruce Jacobus. His total adjusted gross income is $16,500 and his itemized deductions amount to $2,710, so his net income is

$$\$16,500 - \$2,710 = \$13,790.$$

Deducting his one exemption of $750, we get a total taxable income of $13,790 - $750 = $13,040.

From the Schedule X table (Single Taxpayers Not Qualifying for Rates in Schedule Y or Z), we see that the tax due on a total taxable income of $13,040 is $2,630 + 29% of the amount over $12,000. Since the amount over $12,000 is $13,040 - $12,000 = $1,040, the total tax due is

$$\$2,630 + .29 \times \$1,040 = \$2,932$$

(rounded to the nearest dollar).
Following the same procedure,the remaining taxes due have been computed and are summarized in the following table:

Name	Net Income	Total Taxable Income	Total Tax Due (Rounded) (to nearest dollar)
Bruce Jacobus	$13,790	$13,040	$2,630+.29 × $1,040= $2932
Marcia Jasko	$19,010	$17,510	$3,830+.34 × $1,510= $4343
Rita Jurasch	$28,347	$26,097	$7,590+.45 × $97= $7634
Paul E. Cordazzo	$14,880	$13,380	$2630+.29 × $1,380= $3030
David Schwann	$5,272	$ 4,522	$690+.21 × $522= $800

• PROBLEM 2-21

Find the federal income tax due from each of the following. Assume that the figures represent married taxpayers filing joint returns.

	Adjusted Gross Income	Itemized Deductions	No of Exemptions
(A)	$26,380	$2,400	3
(B)	$19,650	$2,720	2
(C)	$41,290	$4,200	5
(D)	$21,850	$2,350	3
(E)	$36,400	$2,900	4

Solution: The income tax due from each of the above joint returns will be based on taxable income. In order to find the taxable income, we must first take the adjusted gross incomes, and subtract the itemized deductions to yield net income. From the net incomes, we subtract the exemptions (at $750 each), to obtain the total taxable income. We would then look up the tax due on the total taxable income, in the Married Taxpayers Filing Joint Returns table. For example, the couple in part (a) has an adjusted gross income of $26,380 and itemized deductions of $2,400. Their net income is therefore

$26,380 - $2,400 = $23,980.

They have three exemptions, at $750 each, for a total of $750 × 3 = $2,250 in exemptions. Their total taxable income is

$\$23,980 - \$2,250 = \$21,730.$

Consulting the Married Taxpayers Filing Joint Returns table, we see that the amount due on the $21,730 is $4,380 plus 32% of the excess over $20,000. Since the amount over $20,000 is $21,730 - $20,000 = $1,730, the total tax due is

$$\$4,380 + (.32 \times \$1,730) = \text{(to the nearest dollar)}$$

$$\$4,380 + \$554 = \$4,034.$$

The same method is followed for the remaining problems and the results have been summarized in the table below:

Example	Net Income	Total Taxable Income	Tax Due (Rounded)
A	$23,980	$21,730	$4,380+.32 × $1,730= $4,9334
B	$16,930	$15,430	$2,260+.25× $3,430= $3,118
C	$37,090	$33,340	$8,660+.42× $1,340= $9,223
D	$19,500	$17,250	$3,260+.28 × $1,250= $3,610
E	$33,500	$30,500	$7,100+.39 × $2,500= $8,075

PROPERTY TAX

• PROBLEM 2-22

A tax of $800 is paid on a property with an assessed value of $20,000. If the tax rate is increased 1%. what will the new tax cost be?

Solution: We can use the formula:

$$\text{Tax Rate} = \frac{\text{Tax}}{\text{Assessed Value}}$$ to find the old tax rate.

Substituting a tax of $800 and an assessed value of $20,000, we get

$$\text{Tax Rate} = \frac{\$800}{\$20,000} = .04.$$

The old tax rate was therefore .04. Increasing this by 1% (=.01) we get a new tax rate of

$$.04 + .01 = .05.$$

The new tax would then be

$$\$20,000 \times .05 = \$1,000$$

• PROBLEM 2-23

What is the tax on a store with an assessed valuation of \$6,640, if the tax rate is \$3.87 per \$100 and an additional charge of 2% of the tax is added as a collector's fee?

Solution: The tax rate of \$3.87 per \$100 as a decimal would be

$$\frac{\$3.87}{\$100} = .0387.$$

The tax on the store would then be assessed valuation × tax rate =

$$\$6,640 \times .0387 = \$256.97.$$

The collector's fee, which is 2% (=.02) of this would be \$256.97 × .02 = \$5.14.

The total payment, which is tax plus collector's fee, is then

$$\$256.97 + \$5.14 = \$262.11.$$

• PROBLEM 2-24

Mr. Okada owns a home worth \$28,750 in a town where homes are assessed at 38% of their market value. If Mr. Okada pays property taxes at the rate of \$8.42 per \$100, and 47% of his property taxes is spent on education, how much of his taxes goes toward education?

Solution: Since Mr. Okada's house is in a town where the assessment rate is 38% = .38, and the house is worth \$28,750, its assessed value is

$$\$28,750 \times .38 = \$10,925.$$

The tax rate, which is \$8.42 per \$100, as a decimal is

$$\frac{\$8.42}{\$100} = .0842.$$

The property tax that Mr. Okada pays is assessed value times tax rate = $10,025 × .0842 = $919.89.

Of this, only 47% goes towards education. The amount that goes toward education would then be

$919.89 × .47 = $432.35.

• PROBLEM 2-25

In Browningtown, water is sold to home owners by the cubic foot at the rate of $15.31 for up to and including 3,600 cubic feet, and $.15 for each 100 cubic feet over 3,600 cubic feet. Local taxes on water usage are 4%. If the Thomas family recently received a bill for 35,700 cubic feet of water, how much were they charged?

Solution: Since the Thomas family used 35,700 cubic feet of water, they would be charged $15.31 for the first 3,600 cubic feet, and $.15 for each cubic foot for the remaining 32,100 feet used. The charge for the additional 32,100 cubic feet would be

$$\frac{32{,}100 \times \$.15}{100} = \$48.15.$$

The charge for the total 35,700 feet would then be

$15.31 + $48.15 = $63.46.

Since a tax of 4% was also levied the tax would be $63.46 × .04 = $2.54. The total bill would then be

$63.46 + $2.54 = $66.

• PROBLEM 2-26

Mr. Golden owns property with a market value of $16,500. The property is located in a city where assessed valuation is 40% of actual value. If the tax rate in the city is 21.3 mills per dollar, how much does Mr. Golden pay in real estate taxes?

Solution: The city where Mr. Golden's property is located computes assessed valuation as 40% of actual value. The assessed valuation of his property is 40% of $16,500, which is

$.40 \times \$16,500 = \$6,600.$

Also, the tax rate, which is 21.3 mills per dollar (1000 mills = 1 dollar), as a decimal is

$$\frac{21.3}{1000} = .0213.$$

Mr. Golden's real estate tax, which is based on assessed value, is

$\$6,600 \times .0213 = \$140.58.$

• PROBLEM 2-27

Ms. Finer owns two houses in a town where the tax rate is \$43.72 per \$1000. Their market values are \$17,000 and \$25,000, respectively. If the houses are assessed at the rate of 75%, how much real estate tax does Ms. Finer pay?

Solution: Since Ms. Finer owns two houses, valued at \$17,000 and \$25,000 respectively, she has a total of

$\$17,000 + \$25,000 = \$42,000$

in property. The assessed value of the property, which is at a 75% rate, would be 75% of \$42,000, which is

$\$42,000 \times .75 = \$31,500.$

The tax rate, which is \$43.72 per \$1000, as a decimal is

$$\frac{\$43.72}{\$1000} = .04372.$$

Ms. Finer's tax, which is assessed value times tax rate, is

$\$31,500 \times .04372 = \$1,377.18.$

• PROBLEM 2-28

What is the property tax on a house worth \$17,500 if the rate of assessment is 28% and the tax rate is \$9.16667 per \$100.

Solution: Since the house has a value of \$17,500, and the rate of assessment is 28% = .28, the assessed value of the house is

$\$17,500 \times .28 = \$4,900.$

The tax rate, which is \$9.16667 per \$100, as a decimal would be

$$\frac{\$9.16667}{\$100} = .0916667.$$

The property tax, which is assessed value times tax rate, would be

$\$4,900 \times .0916667 = \$449.17$

• PROBLEM 2-29

What is the tax on a house with a market value of \$18,400, if the assessed value is at 65% and the tax rate is \$4.57 per \$100.

Solution: Since the house has a market value of \$18,400, and the assessed value is 65% of that, the assessed value is

$\$18,400 \times .65 = \$11,960.$

The tax rate, which is \$4.57 per \$100, as a decimal would be

$$\frac{\$4.57}{\$100} = .0457.$$

The tax, which is based on assessed value, would then be

$\$11,960 \times .0457 = \$546.57.$

• PROBLEM 2-30

What is the property tax on a house with an assessed value of \$3,250 if the tax rate charged is 2.351%.

Solution: Since the tax rate is 2.351% = .02351, the property tax on the house (which is tax rate times assessed value), is

$\$3,250 \times .02351 = \$76.41.$

• PROBLEM 2-31

> Mr. Williams owns a piece of property assessed at $7,800 in a city which has a tax rate of $2.80 per $100. How much in property taxes does he pay?

Solution: Since Mr. Williams pays a tax rate of $2.80 per $100, his tax rate, as a decimal, is

$$\frac{\$2.80}{\$100} = .028.$$

His taxes would then be

$$\$7,800 \times .028 = \$218.40$$

• PROBLEM 2-32

> What is the property tax on a building assessed at $125,000 if the tax rate is $7.24 per $100.

Solution: The tax rate, which is $7.24 per $100, as a decimal would be

$$\frac{\$7.24}{\$100} = .0724.$$

The property tax, which is tax rate times assessed value, would be

$$\$125,000 \times .0724 = \$9,050.$$

• PROBLEM 2-33

> Norman Stevens lives in a town where 28% of the property tax is passed along to the county government. Mr. Stevens owns a home which was assessed for $17,400. If the town's tax rate is $24.90 per $1,000, how much of his tax was passed along to the county government?

Solution: Since Mr. Stevens pays a tax rate of $24.90 per $1,000, his rate, as a decimal, is .0249. This means that on his house, which has an assessed value of $17,400, his total property tax would be

$$\$17,400 \times .0249 = \$433.26.$$

Of his total property tax of $433.26, 28% = .28 is

passed along to the county government. This amount would be

$$\$433.26 \times .28 = \$121.31.$$

• PROBLEM 2-34

A town needs $465,000 to meet its financial obligations for the year. If the assessed valuation of the property in the town is $10,000,000, what should the town's tax rate be?

Solution: We can calculate the tax rate for the town using the formula:

$$\text{Tax Rate} = \frac{\text{Income Required}}{\text{Assessed Valuation of Property}}$$

Substituting $465,000 for the income required and $10,000,000 for the assessed valuation, we get:

$$\text{Tax Rate} = \frac{\$465,000}{\$10,000,000} = .0465,$$

which is 4.65%.

• PROBLEM 2-35

Express the tax rates (A) 3.06% (B) 6.85% as mills per dollar of assessed valuation.

Solution: A tax rate of 3.06% is equivalent to .0306. On a per dollar basis, this is

$$.0306 \times \$1.00 = \$.0306 = 3.06 \text{ cents per dollar.}$$

Since 1 cent = 10 mills, 3.06 cents per dollar is equal to

$$3.06 \times 10 = 30.6 \text{ mills per dollar.}$$

Similarly a rate of 6.85% = .0685, is, on a per dollar basis, 6.85 cents per dollar. This is equivalent to

$$6.85 \times 10 = 68.5 \text{ mills per dollar.}$$

• PROBLEM 2-36

The tax rate in the town of Centerville is 11 1/2%. If a tax of \$1,794 was paid on a piece of property and the assessment rate in Centerville is 30%, what is the expected market value of the property?

Solution: Since a tax of \$1,794 was charged on a piece of property, and this amount represents 11 1/2% = .115 of the assessed valuation of the property, we know that \$1,794 = .115 × assessed valuation. Dividing both sides by .115, we get:

$$\text{assessed valuation} = \frac{\$1,794}{.115} = \$15,600.$$

We also know that the assessed valuation of \$15,600 represents 30% = .30 of the market price. We can express this relationship as \$15,600 = .30 × market price. Dividing both sides by .30 we get:

$$\text{market price} = \frac{\$15,600}{.30} = \$52,000.$$

The expected market price of the property is therefore \$52,000.

• PROBLEM 2-37

A city has a tax budget totaling \$2,455,335. The tax rate is comprised of 52¢ per \$100 for construction, 31¢ per \$100 for general health and welfare and \$1.42 per \$100 for education. What is the assessed valuation of the taxable property?

Solution: Since the tax rate contains 52¢ per \$100 for construction, 31¢ per \$100 for health and welfare and \$1.42 per \$100 for education, the total tax rate is 52¢ + 31¢ + \$1.42 = \$2.25 per \$100, which, as a decimal, is

$$\frac{\$2.25}{\$100} = .0225.$$

Using the formula $\text{Tax Rate} = \dfrac{\text{Income}}{\text{Assessed Valuation of Property}}$

we can calculate the assessed valuation of the taxable property. Substituting a tax rate of .0225 and an income of \$2,455,335 we get:

$$.0225 = \frac{\$2,455,335}{\text{Assessed Valuation}}, \text{ so}$$

$$\text{Assessed Valuation} = \frac{\$2,455,335}{.0225}, \text{ which is } \$109,126,000.$$

• **PROBLEM 2-38**

Mrs. Valdez pays a property tax of 2.432 percent on her home. In addition, a collection fee of 1% of the tax is charged. If the total charge on her home was $70.62, what is its assessed valuation?

Solution: The $70.62 Mrs. Valdez paid represents 101% of the tax due (100% of tax plus 1% collectors fee). We therefore know that 1.01 × tax = $70.62. Dividing both sides by 1.01 we get that the actual tax

(exclusive of collectors fee) is $\frac{\$70.62}{1.01} = \$69.92$.

We can now use the formula:

$\text{Tax Rate} = \frac{\text{Income}}{\text{Assessed Valuation}}$ to determine the assessed

valuation of Mrs. Valdez's home. Substituting a tax rate of 2.432% = .02432, and an income from tax of $69.92, we get:

$$.02432 = \frac{\$69.92}{\text{Assessed Valuation}}, \text{ so}$$

$$\text{Assessed Valuation} = \frac{\$69.92}{.02432}, \text{ which equals } \$2,875.$$

• **PROBLEM 2-39**

The assessed valuation of the taxable property in the town of Smithville is $52,384,600. The taxes to be raised are $123,475 for a new local project, $931,442.75 for educational purposes, and $319,878 for health and welfare needs. Find the town's tax rate (a) to thousandths of a percent, (b) in mills per $1 of assessed value (c) in cents per $100 of assessed value, and (d) in mills per $1,000 of assessed value.

Solution: Since Smithville requires $123,475 for a new project, $931,442.75 for education and $319,878 for health and welfare needs, the town requires a total of

$$\$123,475 + \$931,442.75 + \$319,878 = \$1,374,795.75.$$

We can calculate the tax rate necessary to generate this income via the formula:

$$\text{Tax Rate} = \frac{\text{Income Required}}{\text{Assessed Valuation of Property}}$$

Subtituting an income of $1,374,795.75 and an assessed valuation of $52,384,600, we get

$$\text{Tax Rate} = \frac{\$1,374,795.75}{\$52,384,600},$$

which to the nearest thousandth of a percent is

$$.02624 = 2.624\%.$$

Since there are 1000 mills in a dollar (10 mills = 1 cent) this rate in mills per $1 would be $.02624 \times 1000 = 26.24$ mills per $1 of assessed value. In cents per $100 of assessed value (since there are 10,000 cents in $100) this is

$$.02624 \times 10{,}000¢ = 262.4¢ \text{ per \$100 of assessed value.}$$

In mills per $1000 of assessed value (since $1000 = 1,000,000 mills) this is

$$.02624 \times 1{,}000{,}000 = 26{,}240 \text{ mills per \$1000 of}$$

assessed value.

• PROBLEM 2-40

> The village of Lynbrook has a capital budget of $125,626.79 for the current year. Through fines and issuing of licenses, the village expects to raise $4,256.30. If the total assessed valuation of the property in Lynbrook is $2,697,112, what is the town's tax rate in dollars per $1,000?

Solution: Since the town requires $125,626.79 and they expect to raise $4,256.30, an additional

$$\$125,626.79 - \$4,256.30 = \$121,370.49$$

must be generated by property taxes. We can calculate the tax rate necessary to do this via the formula:

$$\text{Tax Rate} = \frac{\text{Income Required}}{\text{Assessed Valuation of Property}}$$

Substituting an income of $121,370.49 and an assessed valuation of $2,697,112, we get:

$$\text{Tax Rate} = \frac{\$121,370.49}{\$2,697,112}, \text{ which is approximately } .045.$$

The tax rate in dollars per $1,000 would then be

$$.045 \times \$1,000 = \$45 \text{ per } \$1,000$$

of assessed valuation.

• PROBLEM 2-41

> New City has an annual budget of \$4,221,890.49. Its property has a total assessed valuation of \$150,781,803.21. What is the city's tax rate if other estimated receipts total \$385,000.

Solution: Since New City has other receipts of \$385,000, the amount that it must raise in property taxes is

$$\$4,221,890.49 - \$385,000 = \$3,836,890.49.$$

We can calculate the tax rate necessary to generate this income by using the formula:

$$\text{Tax Rate} = \frac{\text{Income Required}}{\text{Assessed Valuation of Property}}$$

Substituting an income of \$3,836,890.49 and an assessed valuation of \$150,781,803.21, we get

$$\text{Tax Rate} = \frac{\$3,836,890.49}{\$150,781,803.21}\text{, which is approximately}$$

$$.0254 = 2.54\%.$$

• PROBLEM 2-42

> The assessed valuation of the property of the city of Booksville is \$50,600,000. Booksville requires property taxes of \$4,500,000. What is its tax rate? Per \$100? Per \$1,000? (Carry division to 5 decimal places.)

Solution: We can calculate the tax rate in Booksville by using the formula:

$$\text{Tax Rate} = \frac{\text{Income Required}}{\text{Assessed Valuation of Property}}$$

Substituting \$4,500,000 for the income required and \$50,600,000 for the assessed valuation, we get:

$$\text{Tax Rate} = \frac{\$4,500,000}{\$50,600,000}\text{,}$$

which, to 5 decimal places is .08893 = 8.893%.

The rate per \$100 is .08893 × \$100 = \$8.893. The rate per \$1,000 is

$$.08893 \times \$1,000 = \$88.93.$$

• PROBLEM 2-43

Williamsville has a total assessed valuation of property of $6,250,000. The town requires $360,000 for educational purposes and $115,000 for health and welfare needs. What is the town's tax rate in dollars per $100.

Solution: Since the town requires $360,000 for educational purposes and $115,000 for health and welfare needs, it requires a total of

$$\$360,000 + \$115,000 = \$475,000.$$

We can calculate the tax rate necessary to generate this income by using the formula:

$$\text{Tax Rate} = \frac{\text{Income Required}}{\text{Assessed Valuation of Property.}}$$

Substituting an income of $475,000, and an assessed valuation of $6,250,000, we get

$$\text{Tax Rate} = \frac{\$475,000}{\$6,250,000} = .076.$$

The town's tax rate in dollars per $100 is then

$$.076 \times \$100 = \$7.60 \text{ per } \$100.$$

• PROBLEM 2-44

Find the tax on each of the following:

Property No.	Assessed Value	Tax Rate
1	$ 6,000	$4.27 per $100
2	$ 7,400	$5.36 per $100
3	$12,300	$4.98 per $100
4	$15,650	$2.27 per $100
5	$ 7,800	$54.20 per $1000
6	$10,500	$85.70 per $1000
7	$25,400	$17.60 per $1000
8	$ 8,700	$.057 per $1
9	$11,450	$.0628 per $1
10	$33,500	$.072 per $1

Solution: Since property number 1 has a tax rate of $4.27 per $100, the tax rate as a decimal is

$$\frac{\$4.27}{\$100} = .0427.$$

The property tax, which is based on assessed value, is then

$6,000 × .0427 = $256.20.

Following the same procedure for the remaining properties, and summarizing the results in table form, we get:

Property No.	Assessed Value	Tax Rate As A Decimal	Calculation For Tax
2	$ 7,400	.0536	$7,400 × .0536 = $396.64
3	$12,300	.0498	$12,300 × .0498 = $612.54
4	$15,650	.0227	$15,650 × .0227 = $355.25
5	$ 7,800	.0542	$7,800 × .0542 = $422.76
6	$10,500	.0857	$10,500 × .0857 = $899.85
7	$25,400	.0176	$25,400 × .0176 = $447.04
8	$ 8,700	.057	$8,700 × .057 = $495.90
9	$11,450	.0628	$11,450 × .0628 = $719.06
10	$33,500	.072	$33,500 × .072 = $2,412

• PROBLEM 2-45

Mr. Howard owns a house worth $16,500 which is assessed at the rate of 22%. His tax rates are as follows:

$.41 per $100 for a local college fund

$.02 per $100 for special education

$.001 per $100 for health and welfare

$.089 per $100 for community construction

How much tax does Mr. Howard pay for each of these needs? What was the total tax?

Solution: Since Mr. Howard's house has a value of $16,500, and is assessed at a rate of 22%, the house's assessed value is

$16,500 × .22 = $3,630.

His tax rate for the local college fund, which is $.41 per $100, as a decimal is

$$\frac{\$.41}{\$100} = .0041.$$

The tax that Mr. Howard paid for the local college fund was then

$$\$3,630 \times .0041 = \$14.88.$$

Following the same procedure, we can calculate the tax that Mr. Howard paid for special education, health and welfare, and community construction. The results have been summarized in the tabel below:

Tax For	Assessed Value	Tax Rate As A Decimal	Tax Computation
College Fund	\$3,630	$\frac{\$.41}{\$100}$ =.0041	\$3630 × .0041 = \$14.88
Special Education	\$3,630	$\frac{\$.02}{\$100}$ =.0002	\$3630 × .0002 = \$.73
Health & Welfare	\$3,630	$\frac{\$.001}{\$100}$ =.00001	\$3630 × .00001 = \$.04
Community Constr.	\$3,630	$\frac{\$.089}{\$100}$ =.00089	\$3630 × .00089 = \$3.23

The total tax Mr. Howard paid was then

$$\$14.88 + \$.73 + \$.04 + \$3.23 = \$18.88.$$

• PROBLEM 2-46

Mr. Wong owns a piece of property which is assessed at \$1,320, with improvements assessed at \$2,750. He pays taxes at the following rates:

\$2.95 per \$100 School tax

\$5.04 per \$100 Construction tax

\$.53 per \$100 Special Projects tax

Find the amount of tax he pays for each, as well as the total tax that Mr. Wong pays. Compute all taxes to 3 decimal places.

Solution: Since Mr. Wong owns property assessed at \$1,320, as well as improvements assessed at \$2,750, the total assessed value of his property is

$$\$1,320 + \$2,750 = \$4,070.$$

His School Tax rate is $2.95 per $100. As a decimal, this is

$$\frac{\$2.95}{\$100} = .0295.$$

The amount of School Tax that Mr. Wong pays is

$$\$4,070 \times .0295 = \$120.07.$$

Following a similar procedure, we can calculate the remaining taxes to be paid. This has been summarized in the table below:

Tax For	Assessed Value	Tax Rate As A Decimal	Tax Computation
School	$4,070	$\frac{\$2.95}{\$100} = .0295$	$4070 × .0295= $120.07
Construction	$4,070	$\frac{\$5.04}{\$100} = .0504$	$4070 × .0504= $205.13
Special Projects	$4,070	$\frac{\$.53}{\$100} = .0053$	$4070 × .0053= $21.57

The total tax that Mr. Wong pays is

$$\$120.07 + \$205.13 + \$21.57 = \$346.77$$

CHAPTER 3

INSURANCE

LIFE INSURANCE

• PROBLEM 3-1

Mr. Dalton, age 45, has been paying for a $15,000 ordinary life insurance since age 30. What is its cash surrender value?

Solution: Since Mr. Dalton is now 45, and he has been paying for the policy since age 30, the policy is in the end of its 45 - 30 = 15th year. From the Ordinary Life Policy table, we see that the cash surrender value of a policy in its 15th year, purchased at age 30 is $251.18. per $1,000. Mr. Dalton's policy is for $15,000, so its cash surrender value is $251.18 × 15 = $3,767.70.

• PROBLEM 3-2

Mr. Ozaku, age 20 recently took out a $5,000 ordinary life insurance policy. If he pays a semiannual premium until age 75, how much will he pay in premiums? If he dies, how much will his beneficiary receive?

Solution: Consulting the table of premiums for ordinary life policies, we see that the semiannual premium for a 20-year old is $8.73 per $1,000. Mr. Ozaku has a $5,000 policy, so his semiannual premium is $8.73 × 5 = $43.65. If he pays his semiannual premium until age 75, he will be paying twice a year for 75 - 20 = 55 years, for a total of 55 × 2 = 110 payments. The total amount he pays is therefore $43.65 × 110 = $4,801.50.

In the event of his death, Mr. Ozaku's beneficiary will receive the face of the policy, namely $5,000.

• **PROBLEM 3-3**

A father, age 50, takes out a 5-year term insurance policy to ensure his son's education.

(a) How much is his semiannual premium for $15,000 worth of insurance?

(b) How much will he pay in over the five years?

(c) How much will he receive at the end of the five years?

(d) If he died at age 51, what would his beneficiary receive?

Solution: Consulting the Five-Year Term Insurance Premium table, we see that the semiannual premium for a 50-year old is $9.53 per $1,000 of insurance. Since the father wants a $15,000 policy, his semiannual premium would be $9.53 × 15 = $142.95.

Over the 5-year period, he would make ten payments, for a total of $142.95 × 10 = $1429.50. If he were still alive after the five years he would receive nothing, since a policy of this type doesn't have a cash value. However, if he died at age 51 (with the policy in effect) his beneficiary would receive the face amount of the policy, namely $15,000.

• **PROBLEM 3-4**

Find the annual premiums for each policy.

Policy	Age at Issue	Face Value	Premium Per $1000	Annual Premium
a. 10-year term	30	$ 5,000	$____	$____
b. 20-payment life	45	$10,000	$____	$____
c. 30-yr. endowment	25	$20,000	$____	$____
d. Whole life	40	$ 2,000	$____	$____
e. 20-yr. endowment	20	$24,000	$____	$____
f. 15-year term	30	$ 5,000	$____	$____
g. 30-payment life	45	$ 7,000	$____	$____
h. Whole life	30	$12,000	$____	$____
i. 30-yr. endowment	20	$15,000	$____	$____
j. 10-year term	45	$25,000	$____	$____

Solution: The annual premium for each of the above policies can be found by consulting the Annual Premiums Per $1,000 of Insurance table. For example, consider problem (a). The annual premium for a 10-year term policy, issued at age 30, is $5.77 per $1 , 000, so the annual premium for a $5,000 policy is simply $5.77 × 5 = $28.85.

The remaining problems were completed in a similar fashion, and have been summarized in the table that follows:

Policy	Face Value	Premium per $1,000	Annual Premium
a	$ 5,000	$ 5.77	$5.77×5 = $28.85
b	$10,000	$36.49	$36.49×10 = $364.90
c	$20,000	$26.50	$26.50×20 = $530
d	$ 2,000	$22.55	$22.55×2 = $45.10
e	$24,000	$42.55	$42.55×24 = $1021.20
f	$ 5,000	$ 6.20	$6.20×5 = $31
g	$ 7,000	$29.79	$29.79×7 = $208.53
h	$12,000	$15.65	$15.65×12 = $187.80
i	$15,000	$26.15	$26.15×15 = $392.25
j	$25,000	$12.74	$12.74×25 = $318.50

• PROBLEM 3-5

Find the periodic payment on each policy.

Policy	Age at Issue	Face Value	Period	Premium
a. Whole life	25	$ 1,000	Semiannually	$______
b. 20-payment life	30	$20,000	Semiannually	$______
c. 30-year endowment	20	$ 4,000	Semiannually	$______
d. 15-year term	40	$ 8,000	Semiannually	$______
e. 30-payment life	45	$14,000	Semiannually	$______
f. 10-year term	25	$ 9,000	Quarterly	$______

g. 20-year endowment	30	$16,000	Quarterly	$_______
h. Whole life	15	$ 5,000	Quarterly	$_______
i. 20-year endowment	20	$15,000	Monthly	$_______
j. 30-payment life	25	$18,000	Monthly	$_______

Solution: In order to find the periodic payment on each of the above policies, we must first find the annual premiums for each. After that, we take a percentage of the annual premium, depending on the number of payments made per year, as listed in the Periodic Premium Table. To illustrate the procedure, consider the first problem. The Annual Premiums table lists an annual premium for whole life insurance, issued at age 25 of $13.35 per $1,000. Since the first policy is a $1,000 policy, the annual premium would be $13.35. Now consulting the Periodic Premium table, we see that a semiannual payment is .51 of the annual premium. The semiannual premium for the first policy would therefore be .51 x $13.35 = $6.81. Following the same procedure, the remaining premiums have been calculated and are summarized in the table below:

Policy	Annual Premium Per $1,000	Face Value	Annual Premium	Calc.for Periodic Premium
a	$13.35	$ 1,000	$ 13.35	$13.35×.51=$6.81
b	$24.73	$20,000	$494.60	$494.60×.51=$252.25
c	$26.15	$ 4,000	$104.60	$104.60×.51=$53.35
d	$ 9.67	$ 8,000	$ 77.36	$77.36×.51=$39.45
e	$29.79	$14,000	$417.06	$417.06×.51=$212.70
f	$ 5.19	$ 9,000	$ 46.71	$46.71×.26=$12.14
g	$43.01	$16,000	$688.16	$688.16×.26=$178.92
h	$10.11	$ 5,000	$ 50.55	$50.55×.26=$13.14
i	$42.55	$15,000	$638.25	$638.25×.087=$55.53
j	$17.03	$18,000	$306,54	$306.54×.087=$26.67

• PROBLEM 3-6

How much per year will a 25-year old save on a $5,000 20-year endowment policy by making annual instead of quarterly payments?

Solution: Consulting the Annual Premiums Per $1,000 of Insurance tables, we see that the premium for a 25-year old for a 20-year endowment policy is $42.69 per $1,000. For a $5,000 policy, the annual premium is therefore $42.69 × 5 = $213.45. The quarterly premium, which is .26 (from the Periodic Premium table) of the annual premium, is $213.45 × .26 = $55.50. This must be paid four times a year, so the yearly cost via quarterly payments is $55.50 × 4 = $222. The savings by making annual payments instead of quarterly payments is then $222 - $213.45 = $8.55.

• PROBLEM 3-7

What is the annual cost of a 20-payment life policy with a face of $4,000 for a 25-year old, if the payments are made (a) annually (b) semiannually (c) quarterly?

Solution: From the Annual Premium table, we see that the annual premium for a 20-payment life policy for a 25-year old is $22.07 per $1,000. The annual premium for a $4,000 policy would therefore be $88.28.

The semiannual premium, which is .51 (from the Periodic Premium table) of the annual premium, would be .51 × $88.28 = $45.02. Since two payments must be made each year, the annual cost of semiannual payments is $45.02 × 2 = $90.04.

Finally, the quarterly premium, which is .26 (from the Periodic Premium table) of the annual premium, would be .26 × $88.28 = $22.95. Since four payments must be made each year, the annual cost of quarterly payments is $22.95 × 4 = $91.80.

• PROBLEM 3-8

What is the difference in annual premiums of a $10,000 20-payment life policy purchased at age 30, as opposed to the same policy purchased at age 20?

Solution: The Annual Premiums per $1,000 of Insurance table lists an annual premium for a 20-payment life policy, issued at age 30, of $24.73 per $1,000. The same policy, issued at age 20 would cost $19.84 per $1,000. This represents a difference of $24.73 - $19.84 = $4.89 per $1,000 of insurance. Since the policy in the problem is a $10,000 policy, the difference in annual premiums would be 10 × $4.89 = $48.90.

• PROBLEM 3-9

Compare the costs of a $5,000 20-year endowment policy with a $5,000 20-year limited payment policy if each were to be purchased at age 45.

Solution: Consulting the table of Annual Premiums we see that the annual premium for a 20-year endowment policy, purchased at age 45 is $46.67 per $1,000. The cost for a $5,000 endowment policy would therefore be $46.67 × 5 = $233.35. Consulting the same table, the cost for a 20-year limited payment policy, also purchased at age 45, is $36.49 per $1,000. The cost for a $5,000 policy of this type is therefore $36.49 × 5 = $182.45. The difference in cost between the two policies is therefore $233.35 - $182.45 = $50.90.

• PROBLEM 3-10

Assuming that each lived for the term of the policy, compare the cost of a $5,000 20-payment life insurance policy for a young man 25 years of age with a man 45 years of age.

Solution: The Annual Premium Per $1,000 of Insurance table lists an annual premium for a 20-payment policy, issued at age 25, of $22.07 per $1,000. The annual premium for a $5,000 policy would therefore be $22.07 × 5 = $110.35, and., assuming all 20 payments were made, the total cost would be $110.35 × 20 = $2207.

The annual premium for the same policy issued to a 45-year old (from the Annual Premium table) is $36.49 per $1,000. The annual premium for a $5,000 policy is $36.49 × 5 = $182.45, and the cost of the total 20 payments would be $182.45 × 20 = $3649.

• PROBLEM 3-11

Mr. Norman Schwartz, age 30, wants to take out a $15,000 insurance policy. What will be his difference in annual premiums between a 20-payment life policy and an ordinary life paid-up-at 65 policy? If he dies at age 62, how much will he have paid in for each policy?

Solution: From the Annual Premiums table, we see that for a limited payment policy for 20 years the annual premium for a 30-year old is $24.73 per $1,000. Mr. Schwartz wants a $15,000 policy, so his annual premium would be $24.73 × 15 = 370.95

The table for ordinary life paid-up-at-65 lists an annual premium for a 30-year old of $26.70 per $1,000. The annual premium for a $15,000 policy would therefore be $26.70 × 15 = $400.50. The difference between the two policies annually is $400.50 - $370.05 = $29.55.

If Mr. Schwartz were to die at age 62, he would have made 62 - 30 = 32 payments on the ordinary life policy for a total payout of $400.50 × 32 = $12,816. However, by age 62 he would have made all 20 payments on the 20-payment life policy for a total of $370.95 × 20 = $7419.

• PROBLEM 3-12

A 40-year old man decides to buy some kind of endowment policy that will mature when he reaches age 60. What is his difference in premium semiannually between a $100 monthly retirement-income policy and a $15,000 20-year endowment policy? How much would this difference amount to over 20 years? If he lives to age 85, how much will he receive from the retirement-income policy?

Solution: From the table for Retirement-Income Policy Premiums, we see that the premium for a 40-year old man, making semiannual payments is $44.24 per $10 of monthly income desired. The man wishes a retirement income of $100 per month, so his semiannual premium for the retirement-income policy would be $44.24 × 10 = $442.40. The Annual Premiums table lists for a 20-year endowment policy an annual premium (for a 40-year old man) of $44.76 per $1,000. The semiannual premium, which is .51 of this amount would be $44.76 × .51 = $22.83 per $1,000. He wants a $15,000 policy, so the semiannual premium for the endowment policy would be $22.83 × 15 = $342.45.

The difference between the two semi-annual premiums is therefore $442.40 - $342.45 = $99.95. Since there are 40 premium payments to be made over the 20 year period, the difference in premiums over the 20 years would total $99.95 × 40 = $3,998. If the retirement-income policy went into effect at age 60, and the man lived to 85, he would receive 12 payments per year of $100 for a period of 85 - 60 = 25 years, for a total of $100 × 12 × 25 = $30,000.

SOCIAL SECURITY

• PROBLEM 3-13

John Wilson retired at age 62 with average yearly earnings of $5400. His wife was also 62 when he retired. How much do the Wilsons receive each month?

Solution: From the Examples of Monthly Cash Payments table we see that a retired worker, age 62, with average yearly earnings of $5400 is entitled to a monthly benefit of $200.50. In addition, his wife, at 62, is entitled to a monthly benefit of $94.00. Their total monthly benefit is therefore $200.50 + $94 = $294.50.

• PROBLEM 3-14

Mr. Thomas retired at age 65 with average yearly earnings of $6000. Estimate his monthly benefit.

Solution: Since Mr. Thomas had an average yearly earning of $6000, which is mid-way between the $5400 and $6600 columns on the Examples of Monthly Cash Payments table, the benefit paid to Mr. Thomas, retired worker 65 years old, will be approximately mid-way between the monthly benefits of $250.60 (for average earnings of $5400) and $288.40 (for average earnings of $6600). Mr. Thomas' monthly benefit will then be approximately

$$\frac{\$250.60 + \$288.40}{2} = \frac{\$539}{2} = \$269.50.$$

• PROBLEM 3-15

Mr. Johnson is a retired 62-year old with an "average yearly earnings" of $5400. His wife is also 62. If Mr. Johnson died, what lump-sum payment would Mrs. Johnson receive? What would her monthly benefit be?

Solution: As a retired worker at 62, with "average yearly earnings" of $5400, Mr. Johnson receives a monthly benefit of $200.50. Upon his death, Mrs. Johnson would receive a lump-sum payment of three times Mr. Johnson's monthly benefit, up to a maximum of $255. Since 3 × $200.50 = $601.50 exceeds the $255 limit, Mrs. Johnson's lump-sum payment would be $255. Also, after Mr. Johnson's death, as a widow, age 62, Mrs. Johnson would receive a monthly benefit of $206.80.

• PROBLEM 3-16

Paul Roberts earned $12,880 during 1976. How much did he contribute to the Social Security fund? How much did his employer contribute? What amount did he contribute to hospitalization? Use the Social Security Contribution Table given below.

Years	Employees $ Employers(each)			Self-employed People		
	A	B	Total	A	B	Total
1972	4.6%	.6%	5.2%	6.9%	.6%	7.5%
1973-1977	4.85%	1.0%	5.85%	7.0%	1.0%	8.0%
1978-1980	4.80%	1.25%	6.05%	7.0%	1.25%	8.25%
1981-1985	4.80%	1.35%	6.15%	7.0%	1.35%	8.35%
1986-2010	4.80%	1.45%	6.25%	7.0%	1.45%	8.45%

A denotes contributions for retirement, survivors, and disability insurance; B, for hospital insurance.

Solution: Since Mr. Robert's contribution in 1976 is 5.85% (= .0585) of his salary, and he earned $12,880 during the year, his total contribution will be $12,880 × .0585 = $753.48. His employer contributed the same amount, namely $753.48. Mr. Robert's contribution to hospitalization was 1% (= .01) of his annual salary, or $12,880 × .01 = $128.80.

In 1977, Ms. Jean Carter retired at age 62. Her annual covered earnings since 1953 are listed below:

Years	Earnings
1953-1955	$5000 per year
1956-1960	$5350 per year
1961	$2700 per year
1962-1964	$5500 per year
1965-1967	$5825 per year
1968	$3000 per year
1969-1971	$6000 per year
1972-1976	$10,000 per year

In calculating "average yearly earnings" Social Security lists the following maximum earnings per year that can be applied:

Years	Amount
1951-1954	$3600
1955-1958	$4200
1959-1965	$4800
1966-1967	$6600
1968-1971	$7800
1972	$9000
1973	$10800
1974-1976	$12000

Social Security also requires that the number of years to be counted in the calculation of average yearly earnings is the number of years from 1956 to the year that you become 62 years old. Keeping all these contraints in mind, calculate Ms. Carter's "average yearly earnings."

Solution: Since Ms. Carter reached 62 in 1977, the number of years from 1956 to the year that she reached 62 is 1977-1956 = 21 years. This means that she must use 21 years of earnings to calculate her "average yearly earnings." Since she wants her "average yearly earnings" to be as high as possible, she will choose the 21 years in which she made the most income. They are:

Year	Amount
1954	$5000
1955	$5000
1956	$5350
1957	$5350
1958	$5350
1959	$5350
1960	$5350
1962	$5500
1963	$5500
1964	$5500
1965	$5825
1966	$5825
1967	$5825

Year	Amount
1969	$6000
1970	$6000
1971	$6000
1972	$10000
1973	$10000
1974	$10000
1975	$10000
1976	$10000

Ms. Carter, however, is limited by the maximum earnings per year allowed by Social Security that were listed in the problem. Listing her maximum earnings allowed in each of those years we get:

Year	Maximum Earnings Allowed To Be Counted
1954	$3600
1955	$4200
1956	$4200
1957	$4200
1958	$4200
1959	$4800
1960	$4800
1962	$4800
1963	$4800
1964	$4800
1965	$4800
1966	$5825
1967	$5825
1969	$6000
1970	$6000
1971	$6000
1972	$9000
1973	$10000
1974	$10000
1975	$10000
1976	$10000
Total =	$127850

Her total earnings allowed during the 21 year period, which is simply the sum of the maximum earnings column listed above,is $127,850. Since she is credited with this amount over a period of 21 years, her "average yearly earnings" are

$$\frac{\$127,850}{21} = \$6088.10$$

HEALTH INSURANCE

• **PROBLEM** 3-18

Shown below are the yearly rates for a health insurance policy, with benefits, with $750 deductible, to a maximum of $45,000 for each person:

Age	Individual (Male or Female)	Husband and Wife
20	$102.45	$178.35
30	111.00	195.45
40	143.70	261.00
50	200.40	374.25

For one child, add $25.80

For two or more children, add $51.60

Using the rates, calculate the premium for a husband, age 40, his wife, and three children.

Solution: Consulting the table given, we see that the premium for a husband, age 40, and wife, is $261.00. We then add to this the additional $51.60 (for two or more children), yielding a total premium of $261 + $51.60 = $312.60

• **PROBLEM** 3-19

Ted Logan, as a result of a recent illness, spent 72 days in a hospital at $52 a day and 30 days in a convalescent home at $13 a day. After returning home, he had a visiting nurse calling on him three times a week for ten weeks at $12 a call. In addition, he had doctor's bills totaling $1335. Mr. Logan is covered by Medicare hospitalization and medical insurance. The coverage he is entitled to is listed below:

Medicare Coverage Schedule

Type of Expense	Coverage
1. Hospitalization	$0 for first $72 of expense. Up to $75 per day for up to 60 days thereafter, and up to $34 per day thereafter.
2. Convalescent home	Up to $15 per day for days 1-20 and up to $4.50 per day thereafter

3. Visiting nurse service Up to $20 per visit

4. Doctor's service 80% of the first $1275.

What are Mr. Logan's total medical expenses? How much of them will Medicare pay? How much must Mr. Logan pay?

Solution: Mr. Logan's total medical expense will be the sum of his hospital, convalescent home, visiting nurse, and doctor's bills. The hospital bill, at $52 a day for 75 days is $52 × 75 = $3900. The bill for the convalescent home at $13 per day for 30 days is $13 × 30 = $390. The visiting nurse, calling three times a week for ten weeks made a total of 30 visits. At $12 per visit, the bill for the visiting nurse was $12 × 30 = $360. Adding on $1335 in doctor's bills, we get total expenses of $3900 + $390 + $360 + $1335 = $5985.

Since Medicare will pay up to $75 per day for up to 60 days of hospitalization over the first $72 of expense, and $34 per day thereafter, for the first 60 days of hospitalization Mr. Logan would be convered for $52 × 60 - $72 = $3120 - $72 = $3048 by Medicare. He would be covered for the remaining 15 days at the rate of $34 per day for a total of 15 × $34 = $510. Mr. Logan's total hospitalization coverage is therefore $3048 + $510 = $3558.

Since the convalescent home is covered at a rate of up to $15 per day for the first 20 days, the $13 per day total of $13 × 20 = $260 would be completely covered by Medicare. The remaining 10 days would be covered at the rate of $4.50 per day for 10 × $4.50 = $45. The Medicare coverage for the convalescent home totals $260 + $45 = $305.

The visiting nurse allotment is up to $20 per visit, so the total visiting nurse bill of $360 is covered. The $1335 doctor's bill, covered at an 80% (= .80) rate of the first $1275, is covered for $1275 × .80 = $1020. The total amount covered by Medicare is then $3558 + $305 + $360 + $1020 = $5243. Mr. Logan is responsible for the balance of the $5985 bill, namely $5985 - $5243 = $742.

AUTOMOBILE INSURANCE

• PROBLEM 3-20

Find the cost of each of the following. (Bodily injury is abbreviated b.i.; property damage, p.d.; and medical payments, m.p.)

Operator	Driver Training	Use of Car	Territory	Accidents	Coverage	Cost
a. Male, 42	No	Business	02	1	50-and-100 b.i.	$____
b. Female, 17 unmarried	Yes	Work, 6 miles	06	0	$10,000 p.d.	$____
c. Male, 17, unmarried, owner	Yes	Pleasure	06	0	$10,000 p.d.	$____
d. Female, 46, only operator	No	Business	05	0	$5,000 m.p.	$____
e. Male, 24, married	No	Work, 8 miles	03	3	25-and-50 b.i.	$____
f. Male, 67	No	Farm	04	2	$25,000 p.d.	$____

Solution: The cost of bodily injury, property damage, and medical payments insurance coverage is dependent on two factors: (1) the type of coverage desired and (2) the history of the driver of the car. Depending on the type of coverage desired, a base premium is established. The driver's history is then evaluated, and factors are assigned according to age, number of accidents during the past three years, and the purpose for which the car is used.

For example, consider example (a). From table A of Base Premium Schedule, we see that the base premium for 50-and-100 bodily injury (abbreviated as b.i.) coverage for a car kept in 02 territory is \$72. Also, the factor for a male operator, age 42 (from the Factors For No Youthful Operator table in table B-3), using the car for business is 1.45. The factor for 1 accident during the past three years (from Table C, Accident Factors) is 0.40. The total factor is therefore

$$1.45 + .40 = 1.85.$$

Now applying the formula:

Total Premium = Base Premium × Total Factor,

and substituting a base premium of \$72 and a total factor of 1.85, we get a total premium of

$$\$72 \times 1.85 = \$133.20,$$

which, rounded to the nearest dollar is \$133. Following the same procedure, the total premiums for the remaining examples have been computed and summarized in the table below:

Example	Base Premium	Total Factor	Total Premium(Rounded)
a	$72	1.85	$72 × 1.85 = $133
b	$37	1.75	$37 × 1.75 = $ 65
c	$37	3.10	$37 × 3.10 = $115
d	$13	1.35	$13 × 1.35 = $ 18
e	$38	2.85	$38 × 2.85 = $108
f	$42	1.70	$42 × 1.70 = $ 71

• PROBLEM 3-21

Find the cost of each.

Operator	Use of Car	Accidents	Age Group	Car Symbol	Territory	Policy	Cost
a. Male, 45	Business	0	New	3	04	$50 ded.	$___
b. Female, 36, only operator	Pleasure	1	2 yrs.	5	05	Comp.	$___
c. Male, 24, married	Work, under 10 mi	2	6 yrs.	2	01	Comp.	$___
d. Male, 68	Pleasure	0	4 yrs.	4	06	$100 ded.	$___
e. Female, 22	Business	3	3 yrs.	1	02	Comp.	$___
f. Male, 19, unmarried, owner*	Farm	1	5 yrs.	3	03	$50 ded.	$___
g. Female, 17*	Work, under 10 mi	0	New	5	04	Comp.	$___

*Has had driver education

Solution: The cost of collision and comprehensive insurance is dependent on three factors: (1) type of coverage desired, (2) type of car to be insured, and (3) record of the person or persons driving the car. Depending on the type of coverage desired, and the type of car to be insured, the base premium is established. Then, depending on the record of the driver, a multiplication factor (known as the Total Factor) is determined, and the total premium, which is base premium times total factor, is determined. For instance, in example (a), Table B of the Base Premium Schedule lists for a new car, kept in 04 territory, classified as symbol 3, a base premium of $136 for $50-deductible collision coverage. The factor for a 45-year-old male operator using the auto for business (from the Factors For No Youthful Operator, table B-3) is 1.45. The total premium is therefore

$$\$136 \times 1.45 = \$197.20,$$

which is rounded to $197.

Following the same procedure, the remaining premiums have been calculated and summarized in the below table:

Consult Table C for the accident factors.			
Example	Base Premium	Total Factor	Total Premium (Rounded)
a	$136	1.45	$136 × 1.45 = $197
b	$ 45	.90+.40 = 1.30	$ 45 × 1.30 = $ 59
c	$ 17	1.35+.90 = 2.25	$ 17 × 2.25 = $ 38
d	$ 76	.95	$ 76 × .95 = $ 72
e	$ 33	1.25+1.50= 2.75	$ 33 × 2.75 = $ 91
f	$ 70	2.70+ .40= 3.10	$ 70 × 3.10 = $217
g	$ 54	1.75	$ 54 × 1.75 = $ 95

• PROBLEM 3-22

Phil LeFranc purchased 25/50 bodily injury insurance and $10,000 property damage insurance. The base premium for the bodily injury insurance was $101, while the base premium for the property damage coverage was $48. If Phil had a total factor of 1.37 for bodily injury and a total factor of 1.10 for property damage, what was his premium for each type of coverage?

Solution: We can calculate the premiums for each type of the coverage by using the formula:

Total Premium = Base Premium × Total Factor.

Substituting a base premium of $101 and a Total Factor of 1.37 for bodily injury coverage, we get a total premium of

$$\$101 \times 1.37 = \$138.37$$

for bodily injury coverage.

Substituting a base premium of $48 and a total factor of

1.10 for property damage coverage, we get a total premium of

$$\$48 \times 1.10 = \$52.80$$

for property damage coverage.

• PROBLEM 3-23

Mr. Green, who is 35 years old, has just purchased a new car. The car is classified as symbol 5, and is kept in 06 territory. He has had one accident in the last three years. If he uses the new car for business, what is the difference in cost between $50-deductible and $100-deductible collision insurance?

Solution: From the Factors for No Youthful Operators table (Table B-3) we see that the factor for a 35 year old male, using the car for business is 1.45. Also, according to table C, the factor for one accident in the last three years is .40. Mr. Green's total factor is therefore

$$1.45 + .40 = 1.85.$$

From table B of the Base Premium Schedule, the base premium for a new car kept in 06 territory, and classified as symbol 5 is $161 for $50-deductible coverage and $137 for $100-deductible coverage.

Using the formula,

Total Premium = Base Premium × Total Factor,

we get a total premium of

$$\$161 \times 1.85 = \$297.85$$

(which rounds to $298) for $50-deductible coverage and a premium of

$$\$137 \times 1.85 = \$253.45$$

(which rounds to $253) for $100-deductible coverage. The difference in cost between the two is therefore

$$\$298 - \$253 = \$45.$$

• PROBLEM 3-24

Mr. Richard Denton, a resident of Richmond, Virginia, has just purchased a new car. He has decided to get the following insurance on it: comprehensive, property damage and bodily injury, medical payments, and uninsured motorist. Using the table of Automobile Insurance Rates below, find his premium for six months.

Automobile Insurance rates					
	Six Month Rates in Selected Locations				
Types of Insurance	Los Angeles, California	Richmond, Virginia	Manhattan, New York	Valdosta, Georgia	Springfield, Missouri
Comprehensive	$22.60	$41.90	$91.00	$11.80	$11.40
Collision: 50$ deductable	40.20	16.20	118.00	32.10	28.80
Property-damage: $10,000 and Bodily injury: $25,000 per person, $50,000 per accident	43.70	30.10	106.80	21.20	26.10
Medical payments: 2,000 per person	7.00	5.30	7.40	4.00	3.90
Uninsured motorist	8.00	2.00	1.80	3.50	3.00

Solution: Mr. Denton's total premium for six months is the sum of the premiums for each of the types of coverage he wants. Consulting the Automobile Insurance Rates table above under the column for Richmond, Virginia, we see that the insurance premiums for each of the types of coverage is as follows:

Comprehensive	$41.90
property damage and bodily injury	$39.10
medical payments	$ 5.30
uninsured motorist	$ 2.00

Mr. Denton's total premium is then

$$\$41.90 + \$39.10 + \$5.30 + \$2.00 = \$88.30.$$

• PROBLEM 3-25

Mr. Griffin, age 22 and single, uses his car strictly for pleasure. His insurance coverage includes 25-and-50 bodily injury liability and $10,000 property damage insurance. If Mr. Griffin lives in 04 territory and has had no accidents, what is the cost of his coverage?

Solution: Consulting table A of the Base Premium Schedule, we see that the base premium for a 25-and-50 bodily injury liability in 04 territory is $37. The base premium for $10,000 property damage in 04 territory is $41. Mr. Griffin's total base premium is therefore

$$\$37 + \$41 = \$78.$$

The youthful operator factor for a 22-year-old unmarried male, who owns the car and uses it for pleasure (from the Factors for Youthful Operators, table B-1) is 2.35. We use the with or Without Driver Training Listing because we don't know whether or not Mr. Griffin has had driver training. Since Mr. Griffin has had no accidents, his accident factor is 0. Mr. Griffin's total factor is therefore 2.35.

Using the formula,

Total Premium = Base Premium × Total Factor,

with a base premium of $78 and a total factor of 2.35, we get

Total Premium = $78 × 2.35 = $183.30.

The cost of Mr. Griffin's coverage is therefore $183.30.

• PROBLEM 3-26

John Harwick, 24 years-old and single, owns a two-year-old car which he drives to work (a distance of 7½ miles, round trip). He keeps the car in 03 territory, and has had one car accident during the past three years. How much would John save on a combination of $100-deductible collision and comprehensive coverage if he drove a car classified as symbol 1 rather than as symbol 5? We do not know whether John has had driver training.

Solution: From table B-2, the Factors for Youthful Operators table, we see that the factor for an unmarried 24-year-old male owner, using the car to drive to work 10 miles or less, is 2.20. We use the With or Without Driver Training classification as we don't know whether John has received any training. Also the factor for one accident during the past three years (from the table of Accident Factors) is .40. Mr. Harwick's total factor is then

$$2.20 + .40 = 2.60.$$

Assuming a symbol 5 classification, table B of the Base Premium Schedule lists for a 2-year-old car kept in 03 territory base premiums of $33 and $97 for comprehensive, and \$100-deductible collision coverage respectively. The total base premium under symbol 5 classification is therefore

$$\$33 + \$97 = \$130.$$

Using the formula

Total Premium = Base Premium × Total Factor,

and substituting (for the symbol 5 classification) a base premium of \$130 and a total factor of 2.60, we get a total premium of

$$\$130 \times 2.60 = \$338.$$

Under the symbol 1 classification, the Base Premium Schedule B lists base premiums of \$11 and \$52 respectively for the comprehensive and \$100-deductible collision coverage, for a total base premium of \$11 + \$52 = \$63. Under a symbol 1 classification, the total premium would be

$$\$63 \times 2.60 = \$163.80,$$

which we would round off to \$164.

The savings to John Harwick in driving a car classified as symbol 1 rather than as symbol 5 would be

$$\$338 - \$164 = \$174.$$

• PROBLEM 3-27

> Mr. and Mrs. Tobin carry 50-and-100 bodily injury, \$10,000 property damage, and \$2,000 medical payments coverage on their car. They have had three accidents in the last three years, and keep their car in 02 territory. How much would the couple have saved on their car insurance premium this year if they had had no accidents?

Solution: Consulting Table A of the Base Premium Schedule, we see that the base premium for a car kept in 02 territory for 50-and-100 bodily injury is \$72, the base premium for \$10,000 property damage is \$47, and the base premium for \$2,000 medical payments is \$11. The total base premium for the Tobin's car is therefore

$$\$72 + \$47 + \$11 = \$130.$$

The Accident Factor table (table C) lists a factor of 1.50 for 3 accidents during the last three-years. Using the formula,

Premium = Base Premium × Additional Factor,

we can calculate the difference in the Tobin's premium between the three accident charge and zero accident charge. Since the three accidents caused their total factor to increase by 1.50, the increase in their premium was

$$1.50 \times \$130 = \$195.$$

The Tobins would therefore would have saved $195 on their premium for the year if they had had no accidents.

• PROBLEM 3-28

How much would a $100-deductible collision insurance policy pay on an accident causing a repair bill of $89.90. How much would be paid against a $50-deductible policy on a repair bill of $76.40 resulting from a collision?

Solution: With a $100-deductible insurance policy, the first $100 of repair expenses are paid by the owner of the automobile, with the remaining expenses being paid by the insurance company. A repair bill of $89.90 would therefore be paid entirely by the owner of the car, since it falls within the first $100 of expenses. The insurance company would not pay anything at all for the repair.

With the $50-deductible policy, the first $50 of expenses would be paid by the owner of the automobile, and the remainder paid by the insurance company. On a repair bill of $76.40, the insurance company would pay

$$\$76.40 - \$50 = \$26.40.$$

• PROBLEM 3-29

During a riot, Mr. Winter's car was overturned causing $346.50 in damage. Mr. Winter had $50-deductible collision insurance, but no comprehensive coverage. How much will the insurance company pay Mr. Winter?

Solution: In order to receive payment under a collision policy, a car must be damaged because it hit an object or was struck by another vehicle. Turning a car over during a riot, which is an example of vandalism, is covered under comprehensive coverage, but not under collision insurance . Since Mr. Winter does not have comprehensive coverage, his insurance company will not pay him anything.

• PROBLEM 3-30

Thomas Siden carries property-damage insurance on his car with a limit of $5,000. He damages Frank Hartman's car in an accident to the extent of $2,350. How much will his insurance company pay?

Solution: Since Mr. Siden carries property-damage insurance on his car with a limit of $5,000, his company will pay any amount up to $5,000 for any damage he causes. He caused only $2,350 worth of damage to Mr. Hartman's car (which is less than the $5,000 limit), so his insurance company will pay the full amount of $2,350.

• PROBLEM 3-31

After crossing through a red light, Tom Patrick's car struck another car, injuring five persons. Through a court action, he was required to pay them $27,000, $14,000, $6,000, $5,000 and $2,700, respectively. If Mr. Patrick has 50-and-100 bodily injury insurance, how much did his insurance company pay?

Solution: Under a 50-and-100 bodily injury insurance policy, an insurance company will pay, when their client is found liable, up to a maximum of $50,000 to each injured person, with a maximum total of $100,000 in payments for any one accident. Since each of the amounts awarded to the people whom Mr. Patrick injured was less than $50,000, and the total amount awarded was

$27,000 + $14,000 $6,000 +$5,000 + $2,700 = $54,700

which is less than the $100,000 maximum total per accident, the insurance company was liable for the entire $54,700.

• PROBLEM 3-32

As a result of a blow-out, Frank Lincoln's car swerved and hit John Martin's car. Leon Taylor, a passenger in Mr. Martin's car, had medical expenses of $6,251. Mr. Martin's medical bills came to $75. If Lincoln had 5/10 bodily injury insurance, how much will his insurance company pay?

Solution: Under a 5/10 bodily injury policy, an insurance company will pay, when their client is liable, up to a maximum of $5,000 per person to each injured claimant, with a maximum payment on any one accident of $10,000. Since Leon Taylor's medical expenses exceeded $5,000, the company will only pay up to the $5,000 limit on his claim, with Mr. Lincoln being liable for the remainder. The insurance company will also pay the $75 for Mr. Martin's claim, bringing the total amount they will pay to

$$\$5,000 + \$75 = \$5,075.$$

• PROBLEM 3-33

An automobile insurance policy purchased on March 10, with a $155 premium, was cancelled on September 6 by the owner of the car.
How much was the refund on the policy?

Solution: Since the insurance policy was purchased on March 10 and cancelled September 6, it was in effect for the remaining 21 days of March, the 30 days of April, the 31 days of May, the 30 days of June, the 31 days of July, the 31 days of August, and 6 days in September for a total of

$$21 + 30 + 31 + 30 + 31 + 31 + 6 = 180 \text{ days.}$$

From the table for Premium Charges for Cancelled Policies, we see that the charge for 180 days is 60%. This means that the insurance company charge is 60% of $155 = .60 × $155 = $93.

The refund is therefore

$$\$155 - \$93 = \$62.$$

• PROBLEM 3-34

Mr. Wingate's automobile insurance cost $173.50 per year. His policy was cancelled 115 days after it went into effect. How much was his refund if (a) he cancelled the policy or (b) the insurance company cancelled the policy?

Solution: (a) From the Premium Charges for Cancelled Policies, we see that the insurance company charge for a policy cancelled after 115 days is 42%. The insurance company would therefore have charged Mr. Wingate 42% (= .42) of his annual premium of $173.50 if he cancelled the policy. The charge can be calculated as follows:

$$42\% \text{ of } \$173.50 = .42 \times \$173.50 = \$72.87.$$

The refund to Mr. Wingate would then have been

$$\$173.50 - \$72.87 = \$100.63.$$

(b) If the insurance company had cancelled the policy, they would charged him a daily rate of 1/365 of his premium for each of the days that the policy was in effect. Since the policy had been in effect for 115 days, Mr. Wingate would have been charged

$$\frac{115}{365} \times \$173.50, \text{ or } \$54.66$$

rounded to the nearest cent. His refund would therefore have been

$$\$173.50 - \$54.66 = \$118.84.$$

FIRE INSURANCE

• PROBLEM 3-35

Mr. and Mrs. Miller paid $32,700 for their house and land. They estimate that the land is worth $5,500. If they want to insure the house at 80% of its estimated value, how much insurance should they purchase?

Solution: Since the house and the land together are worth $32,700, and the land alone is worth approximately $5,500, the estimated value of the house is $32,700 - $5,500 = $27,200. The Millers want to insure the house for 80% (=.80) of this, so they should insure the house for $27,200 × .80 = $21,760.

• PROBLEM 3-36

Harrison's Bookstore has an inventory with an estimated value of $500,000. They wish to insure it with a policy covering 70% of its value. If the insurance company charges $.50 per $100, what annual premium will Harrison's pay for its coverage?

Solution: Since Harrison's wishes to insure its $500,000 inventory at 70% (=.70) of its value, the store will need a policy for

$$\$500{,}000 \times .70 = \$350{,}000$$

worth of coverage.

The premium rate of \$.50 per \$100 is equivalent to the decimal of

$$\frac{\$.50}{\$100} = .0050.$$

The premium for \$350,000 worth of coverage would therefore be

$$\$350{,}000 \times .0050 = \$1{,}750.$$

• PROBLEM 3-37

> What is the premium for a 15-day policy on a piece of furniture valued at \$1,500 if the annual premium is \$1.25 per \$100?

Solution: The annual premium of \$1.25 per \$100 is equivalent to a rate of

$$\frac{\$1.25}{\$100} = .0125.$$

The annual premium for the \$1,500 worth of furniture is therefore

$$\$1{,}500 \times .0125 = \$18.75.$$

From the table for Rates of Charge for Premium Cancellation, we see that the charge for a 15-day policy is 13% (=.13) of the annual premium. Since the annual premium is \$18.75, the charge for the 15-day policy is

$$\$18.75 \times .13 = \$2.44.$$

• PROBLEM 3-38

> Mr. Charles owns a brick building, worth \$35,000, and stock, valued at \$9,500. He wishes to insure each at 4/5 of their value. If the insurance rates are \$.23 per \$100 and \$.21 per \$100, respectively, what is the cost of his coverage?

Solution: Since Mr. Charles wishes to insure the building for

$\frac{4}{5}$ of its \$35,000 value, he will need

$$\frac{4}{5} \times \$35,000 = \$28,000$$

worth of coverage.

The premium rate of \$.23 per \$100, which is equivalent to

$$\frac{\$.23}{\$100} = .0023,$$

when applied to a \$28,000 policy requires a premium of

$$\$28,000 \times .0023 = \$64.40,$$

which would be rounded to \$64.

The stock, insured for $\frac{4}{5}$ of its \$9,500 value, requires

$$\frac{4}{5} \times \$9,500 = \$7,600$$

worth of coverage. The premium rate of \$.21 per \$100, which is equivalent to

$$\frac{\$.21}{\$100} = .0021,$$

when applied to a \$7,600 policy, yields a premium of \$7,600 × .0021 = \$15.96, which would be rounded to \$16.

The total premium that Mr. Charles pays for his coverage is therefore \$64 + \$16 = \$80 per year.

• PROBLEM 3-39

Which requires a greater annual insurance premium: a frame house, located in a Class A town, insured for \$24,000, or the same frame house, located in a Class B town, insured for the same \$24,000? How much of a difference is there?

Solution: From the Annual Premium Rates for Fire Insurance table, we see that the annual premium for \$24,000 of insurance for a frame house, located in a Class A town, is \$40.10 plus \$.14 per \$100 of insurance above \$20,000.

Since we are computing the premium for \$24,000 worth of insurance, the premium would be \$40.10 plus

$.14 per $100 for the additional $4,000 amount. The rate of $.14 per $100 is equivalent to a rate of

$$\frac{\$.14}{\$100} = .0014,$$

so the charge for the additional $4,000 worth of coverage is

$$\$4,000 \times .0014 = \$5.60.$$

The total charge for the $24,000 worth of coverage for the house located in the Class A town is therefore

$$\$40.10 + \$5.60 = \$45.70.$$

For the same house located in a Class B town, the Annual Premium Rates table lists a premium of $46.10 plus $.17 per $100 for the amount over $20,000. The rate of $.17 per $100, which is equivalent to

$$\frac{\$.17}{\$100} = .0017,$$

when applied to the additional $4,000 (over the $20,000), would result in a charge of

$$\$4,000 \times .0017 = \$6.80.$$

The total premium for the house located in the Class B town would therefore be

$$\$46.10 + \$6.80 = \$52.90.$$

The house in the Class B town therefore requires the higher premium. The difference in premiums is

$$\$52.90 - \$45.70 = \$7.20.$$

• PROBLEM 3-40

Find the premium for each of the following:

Policy	Face Value of Policy	Premium Rate	Term of Policy	Premium
1	$ 9,000	$.28 per$100	1 year	
2	$52,000	$.35 per$100	3 years	
3	$28,000	$.42 per$100	1 year	

Solution: The premium rate for policy number 1 of $.28 per $100 is equivalent to

$$\frac{\$.28}{\$100} = .0028.$$

This means that the premium for a one-year policy with \$9,000 worth of coverage is

$$\$9,000 \times .0028 = \$25.20.$$

The premium rate for policy number 2 of \$.25 per \$100 is equivalent to

$$\frac{\$.35}{\$100} = .0035.$$

This means that the premium for a one-year policy with \$52,000 worth of coverage is

$$\$52,000 \times .0035 = \$182.$$

Since the premium for a 3-year policy is 2.7 times the annual premium, the premium for policy number 2 is

$$\$182 \times 2.7 = \$491.40.$$

The premium rate for policy number 3, which is

$$\frac{\$.42}{\$100} = .0042,$$

when applied to \$28,000 worth of coverage, yields a premium for policy number 3 of

$$\$28,000 \times .0042 = \$117.60.$$

• PROBLEM 3-41

> The premium rate on homeowners insurance for the ABC Insurance Company is \$.96 per \$100. In addition, ABC allows a discount of 20% of the premium if the homeowner accepts a policy containing a \$250 deductible clause. Calculate the premium for a homeowners policy for \$27,000 containing a \$250 deductible clause.

<u>Solution</u>: The premium rate of \$.96 per \$100 is equivalent to a rate of $\frac{\$.96}{\$100}$ = .0096. The premium for a \$27,000 policy would therefore be \$27,000 × .0096 = \$259.20. However, since the policy described in the problem is \$250 deductible, a discount of 20% (= .20) would be deducted from the premium. The discount would therefore be \$259.20 × .20 = \$51.84. The premium to be paid would then be \$259.20 - \$51.84 = \$207.36, which would be rounded to \$207.

Since the policy is \$250 deductible, on a loss of \$352, the insurance company would pay the amount over \$250, namely \$352 - \$250 = \$102.

• PROBLEM 3-42

What is the difference in cost between three consecutive one-year policies and a 3-year policy for \$28,000 worth of coverage if the rate is \$.23 per \$100?

Solution: The premium rate of \$.23 per \$100 is equivalent to a rate of

$$\frac{\$.23}{\$100} = .0023.$$

The annual premium for \$28,000 worth of coverage is therefore

$$\$28,000 \times .0023 = \$64.40.$$

The cost for three consecutive one-year policies would then be

$$\$64.40 \times 3 = \$193.20.$$

The cost for a 3-year policy (from the table for multi-year policies) is 2.7 times the annual premium, namely

$$2.7 \times \$64.40 = \$173.88.$$

The difference in cost is therefore

$$\$193.20 - \$173.88 = \$19.32.$$

• PROBLEM 3-43

Montgomery's Department Store insured one of its buildings for \$30,000 at the rate of \$2.50 per \$1,000. What would the cost be for three consecutive one-year policies? What would the cost be for a 3-year policy? What is the difference between the two?

Solution: The premium rate of \$2.50 per \$1,000 is equivalent to a rate of

$$\frac{\$2.50}{\$1,000} = .00250$$

The annual premium for a $30,000 policy is therefore

$30,000 × .00250 = $75.

The premium for three consecutive one-year policies is

3 × $75 = $225.

The cost for a 3-year policy (from the table for multi-year policies) is 2.7 times the annual premium, namely

2.7 × $75 = $202.50.

The difference in cost is then

$225 - $202.50 = $22.50.

• PROBLEM 3-44

What is the difference in cost between a 3-year policy and 3 one-year policies for $22,000 worth of coverage, if the rate is $1.19 per $1,000?

Solution: The premium rate of $1.19 per $1,000 is equivalent to

$$\frac{\$1.19}{\$1,000} = .00119.$$

The annual premium for $22,000 worth of coverage is therefore

$22,000 × .00119 = $26.18.

The cost for three consecutive one-year policies would be

$26.18 × 3 = $78.54.

The cost for a 3-year policy (from the table for multi-year policies) is 2.7 times the annual premium, namely

2.7 × $26.18 = $70.69.

The difference in cost is therefore

$78.54 - $70.69 = $7.85.

• PROBLEM 3-45

Of the following types of insurance, which is the least costly for a depreciable asset?

1) term insurance
2) decreasing term insurance
3) increasing principal coverage
4) permanent insurance
5) fixed total loss coverage

Solution: The premium of an insurance policy is based, among other factors, upon the amount which the insurer may be required to pay on the policy. The amount which the insurer may be required to pay is known as the principal of the policy.

With decreasing term insurance, the principal and related premium decreases with the age of the assets being insured. As a result, it is usually the least costly type of insurance for a depreciable capital asset.

• PROBLEM 3-46

Adams Manufacturing Company recently suffered a fire loss of $45,000. Their insurance was distributed between two insurance companies as follows:

Company Name	Amount of Policy
Acme Insurance	$50,000
Safe Way Insurance	$30,000

How much of the loss did each of the insurance companies pay to Adams?

Solution: Adams carries a total of

$$\$50,000 + \$30,000 = \$80,000$$

worth of insurance, $50,000 of which is with the Acme Insurance Company. Acme is therefore responsible for

$$\frac{\$50,000}{\$80,000} = \frac{5}{8}$$

of the $45,000 loss, which is

$$\frac{5}{8} \times \$45,000 = \$28,125.$$

Similarly, Safe Way is responsible for

$$\frac{\$30,000}{\$80,000} = \frac{3}{8} \text{ of the loss, which is}$$

$$\frac{3}{8} \times \$45,000 = \$16,875.$$

• PROBLEM 3-47

What is the premium on a \$60,000 policy if the rate is \$.2065 per \$100? How much would the insurance company pay on a loss of \$61,000?

Solution: The insurance rate of \$.2065 per \$100 is equivalent to

$$\frac{\$.2065}{\$100} = .002065.$$

The premium for a \$60,000 policy would therefore be

$$\$60,000 \times .002065 = \$123.90,$$

which would be rounded to \$124.

On a \$61,000 loss, the company would pay \$60,000, since that was the limit of the policy.

• PROBLEM 3-48

A building damaged by fire to the extent of \$52,000, was insured with a number of insurance companies as follows:

Insurance Company	Face Value of Policy
A	\$15,000
B	\$10,000
C	\$12,500
D	\$37,500

How much did each company pay on the loss?

Solution: The building carries a total of

$$\$15,000 + \$10,000 + \$12,500 + \$37,500 = \$75,000$$

worth of insurance, \$15,000 of which is with Company A. This means that Company A is responsible for

$$\frac{\$15,000}{\$75,000} = \frac{1}{5} \text{ of the damage.}$$

Company A therefore pays

$$\frac{1}{5} \times \$52,000 = \$10,400.$$

Company B is responsible for

$$\frac{\$10,000}{\$75,000} = \frac{2}{15} \text{ of the damage, so it pays}$$

$$\frac{2}{15} \times \$52,000 = \$6,933.33.$$

Company C pays

$$\frac{\$12,500}{\$75,000} = \frac{1}{6} \text{ of the damage, so it pays}$$

$$\frac{1}{6} \times \$52,000 = \$8,666.67.$$

Company D pays

$$\frac{\$37,500}{\$75,000} = \frac{1}{2} \text{ of the damage, so it pays}$$

$$\frac{1}{2} \times \$52,000 = \$26,000.$$

• PROBLEM 3-49

Mr. Smith carries a $10,000 homeowners insurance policy with Company A and a $3,000 policy with Company B. If a fire causes $2,900 worth of damage to his house, how much would he collect from each company?

Solution: Mr. Smith carries a total of

$$\$10,000 + \$3,000 = \$13,000$$

worth of insurance on his house. Since $10,000 of this is carried with Company A, Company A is responsible for

$$\frac{\$10,000}{\$13,000} = \frac{10}{13}$$

of the damage to Mr. Smith's house.

Company A is therefore liable for $\frac{10}{13}$ of $2,900, which is

$$\frac{10}{13} \times \$2,900 = \$2,230.77 .$$

Similarly, Company B is responsible for

$$\frac{\$3,000}{\$13,000} = \frac{3}{13} \text{ of } \$2,900,$$

which is

$$\frac{3}{13} \times \$2,900 = \$669.23.$$

• PROBLEM 3-50

A building, damaged by fire to the extent of $78,000, carries insurance as follows:

Insurance Company	Face Value of Policy
A	$15,000
B	$10,000
C	$12,500
D	$37,500

How much would each of the companies pay on the loss?

Solution: When property is covered by more than one insurance company, the claims must be shared by the insurance companies according to the percentage of the total coverage which is theirs. The building carried a total of

$$\$15,000 + \$10,000 + \$12,500 + \$37,500 = \$75,000$$

worth of insurance. However, the loss (which was $78,000) exceeded the insurance coverage. Since the insurance companies are only liable up to the face values of the policies, each company would pay just the amount it carries, i.e.

Company A pays $15,000
Company B pays $10,000
Company C pays $12,500
Company D pays $37,500

with the owner suffering the remaining $3,000 loss.

• PROBLEM 3-51

A house, valued at $10,000 and insured for $7,000 with an 80% coinsurance clause, is damaged by fire to the extent of $8,500. How much will the insurance company pay on the loss? How much of the loss must the owner assume?

Solution: We can calculate the amount that the insurance company will pay on the loss by using the formula:

$$\text{Payment on Loss} = \frac{\text{Amount of Insurance Coverage}}{(\text{Coinsurance \%})(\text{Value of Property})} \times \text{Amount of Loss}$$

Substituting $7,000 for the amount of insurance coverage, 80% (=.80) for the coinsurance percentage, $10,000 for the value of the house, and $8,500 for the amount of the loss, we get:

$$\text{Payment on Loss} = \frac{\$7,000}{(.80)(\$10,000)} \times \$8,500 = \frac{\$7,000}{\$8,000} \times \$8,500 = \$7,437.50.$$

However, since the face value of the insurance policy is only $7,000, the insurance company is required to pay only $7,000. The owner would then be responsible for the remaining

$$\$8,500 - \$7,000 = \$1,500$$

of the loss.

• PROBLEM 3-52

Mr. Fields owns a house worth $30,000. He insures it with a $20,000 fire insurance policy that contains an 80% coinsurance clause. As a result of fire, the house is damaged to the extent of $10,800. How much will the insurance company pay on the loss?

Solution: We can calculate the amount that the insurance company will pay on the loss by using the formula:

$$\text{Payment on Loss} = \frac{\text{Amount of Insurance Coverage}}{(\text{Coinsurance \%}) \times (\text{Value of Property})} \times \text{Amount of Loss}$$

Substituting $20,000 for the amount of insurance coverage, 80% (=.80) for the coinsurance percentage, $30,000 for the value of the property, and $10,800 for the amount of loss, we get a payment of

$$\frac{\$20,000}{(.80)(\$30,000)} \times \$10,800 = \frac{\$20,000}{\$24,000} \times \$10,800 =$$

$9,000.

The insurance company would therefore pay $9,000.

• PROBLEM 3-53

> The Ace Furniture Company owns a warehouse valued at $90,000, stocked with furniture worth an additional $200,000. The company insures the warehouse for $50,000 and the contents for $150,000, with an insurance policy containing an 80% coinsurance clause. If a fire destroyed 2/3 of the building and 1/2 of its contents, how much did the insurance company pay on the loss? What was the total loss to the Furniture company?

Solution: Since the fire destroyed 2/3 of the building, the loss due to the building was

$$\frac{2}{3} \times \$90,000 = \$60,000.$$

Similarly, the loss due to the contents was

$$\frac{1}{2} \times \$200,000 = \$100,000.$$

We can now use the formula:

$$\text{Payment on Loss} = \frac{\text{Amount of Insurance Coverage}}{(\text{Coinsurance }\%)(\text{Value of Property})} \times \text{Amount of Loss}$$

to calculate the amount of payment on each of the losses. Substituting $50,000 for the amount of insurance coverage, 80% (=.80) for the coinsurance percentage, $90,000 for the value, and $60,000 for the amount of loss for the building, we get:

$$\text{Payment on Warehouse} = \frac{\$50,000}{(.80)(\$90,000)} \times \$60,000 =$$

$$\frac{\$50,000}{\$72,000} \times \$60,000 = \$41,666.66.$$

Substituting $150,000 for the amount of insurance coverage, 80% (=.80) for the coinsurance percentage, $200,000 for the value, and $100,000 for the amount of damage to the furniture, we get:

$$\text{Payment on Furniture} = \frac{\$150,000}{(.80)(\$200,000)} \times \$100.000$$

$$\frac{\$150,000}{\$160,000} \times \$100,000 = \$93,750.$$

The total payment was then

$$\$41,666.66 + \$93,750 = \$135,416.66.$$

Since the damages amounted to

$$\$60,000 + \$100,000 = \$160,000,$$

and the insurance company paid only \$135,416.67, the total loss to the furniture company was

$$\$160,000 - \$135,416.66 = \$24,583.34.$$

• PROBLEM 3-54

Mr. Singer insured his house for \$36,000 with a policy containing an 80% coinsurance clause. If the house has a value of \$45,000 and he suffers a fire loss of \$10,500, how much will the insurance company pay?

Solution: We can calculate the amount that the insurance company will pay by using the formula:

$$\text{Payment on Loss} = \frac{\text{Amount of Insurance Coverage}}{(\text{Coinsurance \%})(\text{Value of Property})} \times \text{Amount of Loss.}$$

Substituting \$36,000 for the amount of insurance coverage, 80% (=.80) for the coinsurance percentage, \$45,000 for the value of the house, and \$10,500 for the amount of loss, we get:

$$\text{Payment on Loss} = \frac{\$36,000}{(.80)(\$45,000)} \times \$10,500 = \frac{\$36,000}{\$36,000} \times \$10,500 = \$10,500.$$

The insurance company would therefore pay the entire \$10,500.

• PROBLEM 3-55

A building valued at \$10,000 and insured for \$6,000 with an 80% coinsurance clause suffers damage in a fire to the extent of \$5,000. How much will the insurance company pay on the loss? What part of the loss does the owner bear?

Solution: We can calculate the amount that the insurance company will pay on the loss by using the formula:

$$\text{Payment on Loss} = \frac{\text{Amount of Insurance Coverage}}{(\text{Coinsurance \%})(\text{Value of Property})} \times \text{Amount of Loss}$$

Subtituting \$6,000 for the amount of coverage, 80% (=.80) for the coinsurance percentage, \$10,000 for the value of the building, and \$5,000 for the amount of loss, we get:

$$\text{Payment on Loss} = \frac{\$6,000}{(.80)(\$10,000)} \times \$5,000 = \frac{\$6,000}{\$8,000} \times \$5,000 = \$3,750.$$

The insurance company would therefore pay \$3,750 on the %5,000 loss, with the owner responsible for the remaining

$$\$5,000 - \$3,750 = \$1,250 \text{ of the loss.}$$

• PROBLEM 3-56

What is the refund on an insurance policy with an annual premium of \$37 that is canceled 33 days after it was purchased?

Solution: Consulting the table for Rates of Charge for Premium Cancellation, we see that the charge to a policy holder for cancelling the policy after 33 days is 20% (=.20) of the annual premium. Since the premium is \$37, the charge is

$$\$37 \times .20 = \$7.40.$$

The refund would therefore be

$$\$37 - \$7.40 = \$29.60.$$

• PROBLEM 3-57

Mr. I.F. Sarbo purchased a fire insurance policy for his home with an annual premium of \$32 on July 17. On September 22 he canceled his policy. What was his refund?

Solution: Since Mr. Sarbo purchased the policy on July 17 and canceled it on September 22, the policy was in effect for the remaining 14 days of July, the 31 days in August, and 22 days in September for a total of

$$14 + 31 + 22 = 67 \text{ days.}$$

Consulting the table for Rates of Charge for Premium Cancellation, we see that the charge to a policy holder for canceling his policy after 67 days is 29% (=.29) of the annual premium. Since the premium is $32, the charge is

$$\$32 \times .29 = \$9.28.$$

The refund is therefore

$$\$32 - \$9.28 = \$22.72.$$

• PROBLEM 3-58

On January 3, Mr. Totten insured his store against fire loss for $350,000 at $.95 per $100, as well as the contents of the store for $500,000 at $.86 per $100. On July 6 he canceled the policy. What was his refund?

Solution: The insurance rate for Mr. Totten's store was $.95 per $100, which is equivalent to

$$\frac{\$.95}{\$100} = .0095.$$

Since the store was insured for $350,000, his premium for that coverage was

$$\$350,000 \times .0095 = \$3,325.$$

The insurance rate for the contents of the store was

$$\frac{\$.86}{\$100} = .0086.$$

The contents were insured for $500,000, so the premium for the contents was

$$\$500,000 \times .0086 = \$4,300.$$

The total annual premium to cover both the store and its contents was

$$\$3,325 + \$4,300 = \$7,625.$$

Since the policy went into effect on January 3 and was canceled on July 6, it was in effect for the remaining 28 days of January, the 28 days of February, the 31 days of March, the 30 days of April, the 31 days of May, the 30 days of June and 6 days in July of a total of

$$28+28+31+30+31+30+6 = 184 \text{ days.}$$

Consulting the table for Rates of Charge for Premium Cancellation, we see that the charge to the charge to the policy holder for cancelling his policy after 184 days is 39% (=.39) of the annual premium. Since the annual premium for his coverage was $7,625, the charge to Mr. Totten was

$$\$7,625 \times .39 = \$2,973.75.$$

His refund was therefore

$$\$7,625 - \$2,973.75 = \$4,651.25$$

• PROBLEM 3-59

Barnes and Sons, Co. insured its offices at an annual premium of $130 on March 3. On October 15, the carrier canceled the policy. What was the refund due Barnes and Sons?

Solution: When the carrier cancels an insurance policy, the charge for the time that the policy is in effect is 1/365 of the annual premium for each day that the policy is in effect. Since the policy was issued March 3 and canceled October 15, it was in effect for the remaining 28 days of March, the 30 days of April, the 31 days of May, the 30 days of June, the 31 days of July, the 31 days of August, the 30 days of September, and 15 days of October for a total of

$$28+30+31+30+31+31+30+15 = 226 \text{ days.}$$

The charge for the policy was therefore

$$\$130 \times \frac{226}{365} = \$80.49.$$

The refund to Barnes and Trust was then

$$\$130 - \$80.49 = \$49.51.$$

• **PROBLEM 3-60**

> Mr. Laker purchased a one-year insurance policy with a premium of $42 on August 15. He canceled it on October 12. How much was his refund?

<u>Solution:</u> Since Mr. Laker purchased the policy on August 15 and canceled it on October 12, it was in effect for the remaining 16 days of August, the 30 days of September, and 12 days of October, for a total of

16 + 30 + 12 = 58 days.

Consulting the table for Rates of Charge for Premium Cancellation, we see that the charge to a policy holder for terminating his policy after 58 days is 26% (=.26) of the annual premium. Since the premium is $42, the charge is

$42 × .26 = $10.92.

The refund is therefore

$42 - $10.92 = $31.08.

• **PROBLEM 3-61**

> A fire insurance policy with an annual premium of $40 was canceled 90 days after it took effect. What was the refund to the insured if:
>
> (a) the insurance was canceled by the policy holder?
> (b) the insurance was canceled by the carrier?

<u>Solution:</u> (a) Consulting the table for Rates of Charge for Premium Cancellation, we see that the charge to the policy holder for cancelling the policy after 90 days is 35% (=.35) of the annual premium. Since the premium is $40, the charge was

$40 × .35 = $14.
The refund was then
$40 - $14 = $26.

(b) When the carrier cancels the policy, they charge 1/365 of the annual premium for each day that the policy was is effect. Since the policy was in effect for 90 days, the charge was 90/365 of the premium, which is

$$\frac{90}{365} \times \$40 = \$9.86.$$

The refund would then be
$40 - $9.86 = $30.14

CHAPTER 4

INTERMEDIATE MATH SKILLS

ALGEBRAIC EQUATIONS

• PROBLEM 4-1

A programmer earns \$6.50 an hour. His take-home pay amounts to 81% of his gross pay. Find a function for determining his take-home pay. How many hours must he work to take home \$200?

Solution: The function for his take-home pay will have to vary with the number of hours he works. Let X stand for the number of hours he works. Since he is paid \$6.50 an hour, his gross pay is \$6.50 · X. Of this he takes home 81%. Thus his take-home pay

$$= 81\% \text{ of } \$6.50X = (.81) \times (\$6.50X) =$$

$$\$5.265\ X.$$

The function is therefore

Take-home pay = \$5.265 X .

If he wishes to take home \$200, we substitute \$200 for his take-home pay getting:

$$\$200 = \$5.265\ X\ .$$

We now solve for X by dividing both sides of the equation by \$5.265 getting

$$\$200 \div \$5.265 = X$$

or

$$X = 38 \text{ (rounding to nearest hour)}.$$

Thus he must work 38 hours to take home \$200.

• PROBLEM 4-2

Determine the number of men needed to build a boat in 77 days if it takes 36 men 132 days to build one.

Solution: As the number of days required to build a boat decreases, the number of men needed increases. We say that these two numbers are inversely proportional. If the number of men and number of days were directly proportional, we would write $\frac{36}{x} = \frac{132}{77}$ and solve for x. But because they are inversely proportional, we write $\frac{x}{36} = \frac{132}{77}$.

Now we solve for x : $77\,x = 36 \times 132$.

$x = \frac{36\times 132}{77} = \frac{4752}{77} = 61\,\frac{5}{7}$. Thus, 62 men would be needed.

• PROBLEM 4-3

A shoe factory has fixed costs of \$1200 per day, and variable costs of \$1.50 per shoe. Find a linear cost function to represent their daily costs.

Solution: A linear cost function is a function which will be in terms of the number of shoes produced. It will give the daily cost for each number of shoes produced. Let X stand for the number of shoes. Then the variable cost is \$1.50 X . Adding to that the daily fixed cost, we get \$1200 + \$1.50 X.

This can be expressed without the dollar signs as the cost function.

$$\text{Cost} = 1200 + 1.5\,X\ .$$

To find the cost for a certain day, merely substitute the number of shoes made that day, and solve the equation.

• PROBLEM 4-4

Tom can buy shirts wholesale, at \$60 per dozen. A minimum of 5 dozen shirts must be bought before further purchases may be made at \$30 per dozen. There is a customer limit of 12 dozen.

(i) What is the cost of 10 dozen?

(ii) Express the cost of purchases as a function of the number of dozen bought.

Solution: (i) We are told that the first five dozen shirts must be bought at \$60.

$$\therefore \text{Cost of shirts} = 5 \text{ dz.} \times \$60/\text{dz} + 5 \text{ dz.} \times \$30/\text{dz}$$
$$= \$300 + \$150$$
$$= \$450 .$$

(ii) Let z = number of dozen

s = cost of shirts.

Then

$$s = F(z) = \begin{cases} 60z & \text{when } 0 \le z \le 5 \\ \$30(z - 5) + \$300 & \text{when } 5 < z \le 12 \end{cases}$$

• PROBLEM 4-5

Industry "V" contributes \$400,000,000. to the Gross National Product. However, industry "V" also creates pollution which costs the public \$300 for every \$80,000. contributed to the G.N.P., plus a contant cost of \$6,000.

(i) Express the cost of industrial pollution algebraically.

(ii) What is the pollution cost in monetary terms at \$400,000,000 ?

Solution:

(i) Let $p = \dfrac{\$ \text{ Product of Industry'V'}}{\$80,000}$,

and pollution cost is C_I (in dollars)
Then

$$C_I = \$300\, p + \$6,000.$$

(ii) $$p = \frac{\$400,000,000}{\$80,000} = 5000$$

$$\therefore C_I = (\$3000)(5000) + \$6000$$
$$= \$1,506,000.$$

• PROBLEM 4-6

Four highschool and college friends started a business of remodeling and selling old automobiles during the summer. For this purpose they paid \$600 to rent an empty barn for the summer. They obtained the cars from a dealer for \$250 each, and it takes an average of \$410 in materials to remodel each car. How many automobiles must the students sell at \$1,440. each to obtain a gross profit of \$7,000?

Solution: Total Revenues - Total Cost = Gross profit

$$\text{Revenue} - \left[\text{Variable Cost} + \text{Fixed Cost}\right] = \text{Gross profit}$$

Let a = number of cars

Revenue = $1,440a

$$\text{Total Cost}\begin{cases}\text{Variable Cost} = (\$250 + 410)a \\ \text{Fixed Cost} = \$600\end{cases}$$

The desired gross profit is $7,000.

Using the equation for the gross profit,

$$\begin{aligned} 1{,}440a - \left[660a + 600\right] &= 7{,}000 \\ 1440a - 600 &= 7000 \\ 780a &= 7000 + 600 \\ 780a &= 7600 \\ a &= 9.74 \end{aligned}$$

or to the nearest car, a = 10 .

• PROBLEM 4-7

A record shop operates with a monthly overhead cost of $800.

(i) If they buy records at $21.00 per dozen, and sell them at $3.60 each, how many must they sell per month to break even?

(ii) What effect on the break-even point will a $20. per month reduction in overhead have?

Solution: (i) To break even,
Total Revenue = Total Cost

Let r = no. of records sold

T.R. = Total Revenue = $3.60r

$$\text{T.C.} = \text{Total cost} = \left(\frac{\$21}{12}\right) r + \$800$$

$$\begin{aligned} \$3.60r &= \$1.75r + \$800 \\ \$1.85r &= \$800 \\ r &= 432.43 \approx 433 \text{ records.} \end{aligned}$$

The break-even point will be approximated when 433 records are sold monthly.

(ii) With a $20. reduction in overhead,

$$\begin{aligned} T.R. &= T.C \\ \$3.60r &= \$1.75r + \$780 \\ \$1.85r &= \$780 \\ r &= 421.62 \approx 422 \text{ records} \end{aligned}$$

have to be sold monthly to break even.

• PROBLEM 4-8

A resort computes its guest fees on the basis of the duration of the visit (D), plus the amount of time spent in the steam-massage room. Tom spends 4 days at the resort and 10 hours in the steam-massage. In a 7 day stay, Jane spends 30 hours with masseurs. Their bills are \$500, and \$1,125, respectively. The cost of a visit (C) is given by the following linear equation:

$$C = xD + yH.$$

Find the values of the constants x and y.

Solution: We are given data for two equations (the stay of Tom and of Jane). We can set up the following system of equations.

$$Dx + Hy = C$$

(Tom) $4x + 10y = \$500.$ Eq.i

(Jane) $7x + 30y = \$1,125.$ Eq.ii

Eliminate one unknown:

$$3\,(4x + 10y) = \$\ 500. \times 3$$

$$-1\,(7x + 30y) = 1,125. \times -1$$

$$\begin{aligned} 12x + 30y &= \$1,500. \\ -7x - 30y &= -1,125. \\ \hline 5x + 0 &= \$\ 375. \end{aligned}$$

$$x = \frac{375}{5}$$

$$x = \$75.$$

Now, to find y, simply write the value of x into one of the original equations:

(Jane) $7x + 30y = \$1,125.$

$$7(\$75.) + 30y = 1,125.$$

$$\$525. + 30y = 1,125.$$

Subtract \$525. from both sides.

$$\begin{array}{r} \$525. + 30\,y = \$1,125. \\ -\ 525. \qquad\qquad -\ 525. \\ \hline \end{array}$$

$$30\,y = \$600.$$

$$y = \frac{600.}{30}$$

$$y = \$20.$$

The cost function is

$$C = 75\,D + 20\,H.$$

• PROBLEM 4-9

> In one year Juan earned \$30,000. and Don earned \$20,000 as free-lance commercial artists. Juan paid \$10,000. in taxes. Don paid \$6,000. They know that
>
> $Ib + a = T$ is the linear equation used in
>
> computing their tax payments, where I stands for 'income' and T, the amount of tax to be paid. What are the values of the constants a and b ?

Solution: We are supplied with enough information to get a system of simultaneous equations.

$$Ib + a = T$$

Note: I and T values $\times 10^3$

(J) $(\$30.)b + a = \$10.$ Eq.i

(D) $(\$20.)b + a = \$\ 6.$ Eq.ii

$$\$30b + a = \$10.$$
$$-1\ (20b + a) = \$\ 6. \times (-1)$$

$$\begin{array}{ll} \$30b + a & = \$10. \\ -20b - a & = -\ 6. \\ \hline \$10b & = \$\ 4. \end{array}$$

$$b = \frac{\$\ 4.}{\$10.} = .4$$

Substitute this value for b in any one of the equations above to get a.

Take $30b + a = 10$

$(30)(.4) + a = 10$

$12 + a = 10$ or $a = -2$.

Remembering the proper units we have

$T = 0.4b - \$2,000$ is the required equation.

• PROBLEM 4-10

In an effort to gain a larger share of the energy market, Experimental Company is shipping L.N.G. (a grade of gas) by supertanker.

It costs $5 per ton to ship the gas from the source to the depot and $12 per nautical mile for each ton that is shipped from the depot to the distribution point.

(i) Derive an algebraic expression showing all transportation costs.

(Hint: Let C = total cost ; let n = no.of miles from depot to distribution point;
let t = no. of metric tons of cargo.)

(ii) Express the total cost per ton algebraically.

(iii) What is the cost of shipping 200,000 tons of L.N.G. fifty miles to a distribution point (15 miles of the journey is from the source to the depot)?

Solution:

(i)

Total cost = $5.per ton × number of tons shipped
+ $12.per (mile • ton) × no.miles × no.tons

$$C = 5t + 12nt .$$

(ii)

$$\text{Cost per ton: } \frac{C}{t} = \frac{5t + 12nt}{t}$$

$$\frac{C}{t} = \frac{t(5 + 12n)}{t}$$

$$\frac{C}{t} = 12n + 5 .$$

(iii)

Distribution point is (50 - 15) miles from the depot.

$$C = 5t + 12nt$$
$$C = \$5 \times (200{,}000) + \$12. \times 35 \times 200{,}000$$
$$C = \$1{,}000{,}000. + \$84{,}000{,}000.$$
$$C = \$85{,}000{,}000.$$

• PROBLEM 4-11

It has been found that hours of recreation (r) and wages (W) have a direct effect on productivity (P),

so that : $P = ar + bW.$

In two surveys it was found that

Survey 1 $P = 170 : r = 51 : W = 136$
Survey 2 $P = 425 : r = 68 : W = 204$

What are the values of a and b?

Solution: Again we have a linear simultaneous equation:

$$P = ar + bW$$

$$170 = 51a + 136b$$
$$425 = 68a + 204b$$

$$-680 = (51a + 136b)(-4)$$
$$1,275 = (68a + 204b)3$$

$$-680 = -204a - 544b$$
$$1,275 = 204a + 612b$$

$$595 = +68b$$

$$b = \frac{595}{68} = 8\frac{3}{4}$$

Substituting into the original equation:

$$170 = 51a + 136\,b$$
$$170 = 51a + 136\,(8.75)$$
$$170 = 51a + 1190$$
$$-1020 = 51a$$
$$-20 = a\ .$$

• PROBLEM 4-12

Charles has $22.50 to spend on a canoe rental at a resort. If the rental rate is $15 plus $.60 per hour, (a) how long can he keep the boat out and (b) how would he express the rental cost as a function of hours spent?

Solution: It might be easier to answer part (b) first.

Total funds = \$.60 (no. of hours) + \$15.

$$F(h) = .60\,(h) + 15\ .$$

(a) $$\$22.50 = \$.60h + \$15.$$

$$22.50 - 15 = .60h$$
$$7.5 = .60h$$
$$\frac{7.5}{.60} = h = 12.5\ .$$

COST, REVENUE, AND PRODUCTION FUNCTIONS

• PROBLEM 4-13

J. S. Bacq & Co. runs a "penny arcade" with the following fixed costs:

Wages and electricity: \$500 per week
Upkeep and miscellaneous: \$100 per week.

As a sales incentive, the Arcade distributes a surprise gift to each customer. Each gift costs the Arcade \$2.00.

The sole charge in the Arcade is \$6.00 for admission. Management wants to make \$1,000 profit each week. How many people must visit the Arcade weekly to realize this much profit?

Solution:

Fixed cost = \$500 + 100 = \$600

Variable cost = \$2 × no. of customers

Revenues (Y) = \$6 × no. of customers

Desired profit (¶) = \$1,000.

When n = no. of customers

$$\text{Total Cost } (C) = FC + VC = 600 + 2n$$
$$Y = 6n$$

and setting ¶ = Y - C

$$1{,}000 = 6n - (600 + 2n)$$
$$1{,}000 = 6n - 600 - 2n$$
$$1{,}000 = 4n - 600$$
$$1{,}000 + 600 = 4n$$
$$1{,}600 = 4n$$
$$\frac{1{,}600}{4} = n$$
$$400 = n$$

Four hundred customers must visit each week to yield \$1,000 in profits.

• PROBLEM 4-14

A factory can produce 699 units of type I automobile suspension struts in an hour (using a new machine) at an average cost of \$1.20 per unit. It also can produce type Y struts from the machine (30 per hr.) at a cost of \$1.30 per unit. Each 24 hour production day has a budget of \$4,005.

The factory wants to produce as many type Y struts as possible, but has a quota of 2,700 type I struts per day.

(i) How many type Y struts are produced daily?

(ii) Is the factory's budget sufficient?

Solution:

i) No. of type I per day = 2,700

no produced/hr. = 600

Time req'd. to produce quota $= \dfrac{2,700}{600} = 4.5$ hr

Daily # of hrs. of production = 24.

No of hrs to produce type Y = 24 - 4.5 = 19.5

Hourly rate of type Y production = 30.

$\therefore$ no of type Y made per day = 30/hr × 19.5 hr
= 585 .

ii) Daily budget = \$4,005.

Cost of type I = 2,700 × \$1.20
= \$3,240.

Cost of type Y = 585 × \$1.30
= 760.50

Cost of I + Y types = \$4,000.50

$\therefore$ the budget is sufficient.

• **PROBLEM 4-15**

William Accra has found that his company's output is increasing radically each week. When t is the number of weeks of production, output is a direct function F(t) such that

$$F(t) = -10,000 + 50t^4 .$$

How many weeks of work will it require them to reach an output of 190,000 ?

Solution:

$$F(t) = -10,000 + 50t^4$$

$$190,000 = -10,000 + 50t^4$$

$$200,000 = 50t^4$$

$$\frac{200,000}{50} = t^4$$

$$4{,}000 = t^4$$

and $\quad t - (4000)^{\frac{1}{4}} = 7.95 \text{ weeks} \;\; = 8 \text{ weeks.}$

• PROBLEM 4-16

The distributors of oil from the Molo Republic are willing to buy 60-p barrels per day, when p = dollars per barrel. The Republic's officials are willing to supply $\frac{p^2}{10}$ barrels per day.

(i) What is the equilibrium price of oil?

(ii) How many barrels will be sold at the equilibrium price?

Solution: (i) At equilibrium price,

$$\text{Demand} = \text{Supply}$$

i.e.
$$60 - p = \frac{p^2}{10}$$
$$600 = p^2 + 10p$$
$$0 = p^2 + 10p - 600 .$$

The right side can be factored into

$$(p - 20)(p + 20) = 0 .$$

The roots are p = 20 and p = -30.

The negative root is meaningless in this example so that p = 20 dollars is the equlibrium price of oil.

(ii) Number of barrels sold $= 60 - p$
$$= 60 - 20$$
$$= 40 \text{ per day} .$$

• PROBLEM 4-17

The exclusive designer of custom suits has found that at a certain point of output, the price that customers are willing to pay for a suit begins to decline. His variable weekly cost is $255 for the first suit produced, and $107 for each suit thereafter. Other data is as follows:

Output	Price per Suit	Total Revenue	Total Cost
1	$785	$ 785	$2,255
2	800	1,600	2,362
3	842	2,526	2,469
4	818	3,272	2,576
5	705	3,525	2,683
6	627	3,762	2,790
7	606	4,242	2,897
8	593	4,744	3,004
9	539	4,851	3,111
10	473	4,730	3,218
11	430	4,730	3,325
12	403	4,836	3,432

(i) What is the designer's weekly fixed cost?

(ii) At what point is profit maximized?

(iii) What are the values of Marginal Revenue and Marginal Cost at the point of maximum profit?

Solution: (i) Total Cost = Fixed Cost + Variable Cost From line 1 of the table.

TC = $2,255
2,255 = FC + 255
$2,000 = FC.

(ii) Profit = Total Revenue - Total Cost By examining the table one can see that maximum profit occurs at 9 units ($1,740 profit).

(iii) Marginal Cost = the change (Δ) in total cost (TC) for each unit change in output.

MC = $107 (everywhere except for the first unit produced in this case).

Marginal Revenue = the change (Δ) in total revenue (TR) for each additional unit produced (After the production of the second unit, MR is less than price: MR < P.)

The designer's maximum profit occurs when MR = MC. The point of maximum profit is thus,

MR = MC = $107.

Since we already knew that the maximum profit was obtained at an output of 9 suits, where MC = $107, we can similarly see that the marginal cost of the ninth suit is also $107.

• **PROBLEM 4-18**

It costs $5.00 to transport one pound of merchandise 100 miles and $28.50 to transport one pound of merchandise 700 miles. Assuming the relationship between the cost of transportation and mileage is linear, find the function describing the relationship. How much does it cost per pound to transport merchandise 200 miles? 400 miles?

Solution: To find the function, we must first determine the added cost per mile for the increase in miles. To do this, we divide the difference of the costs by the diffence of the mileage.

$$\frac{\$28.50 - \$5.00}{700 - 100} = \frac{\$23.50}{600} = \$.039 \text{ per mile.}$$

Thus, it costs $.039 per mile for every mile over 100 miles, and $5 for the first 100 miles. Hence the cost = $5.00 + $.039 (X - 100) where X is the number of miles [it is shipped]. For shipping the merchandise 200 miles, the cost can be found by substituting 200 for X.

$$\text{Cost} = \$5.00 + \$.039\ (200 - 100) =$$

$$\$5.00 + \$.039\ (100) =$$

$$\$5.00 + \$3.90 = \$8.90\ .$$

For shipping the merchandise 400 miles, the cost will be

$$\text{Cost} = \$5.00 + \$.039\ (400 - 100) =$$

$$\$5.00 + \$.039\ (300) =$$

$$\$5.00 + \$11.70 = \$16.70\ .$$

• **PROBLEM 4-19**

The owner of a local department store gives presents to his regular costomers at Christmas time. The gifts bought are: (i) bottles of perfume, at a manufacturer's price of $48. per dozen, (ii) men's wallets, at $3.00 each (iii) wooden salad bowls, at $.50 each. He spends $157.50, and wants to purchase three times as many bottles of perfume as wallets. Also, the number of salad bowls is one-half the number of bottles of perfume.

i) How many of each kind of gift has he bought?

ii) What is the total cost of each kind of gift?

Solution: The basic concept in the solution of this type of problem is, the algebraic relationship between the proportions of items purchased, and the total payment. Choose the quantity of an item as a constant, and express the other items in terms of this.

i) In this problem,

let p = the number of bottles of perfume

then $\frac{1}{3}p$ = the number of wallets

and $\frac{1}{2}p$ = the number of salad bowls .

Now all items are expressed in terms of p instead of using a different symbol for each item

$$\text{perfume cost/per bottle} = \frac{\$48./\text{dzn.}}{12}$$

$$= \$4.00$$

men's wallet = \$3.00 each

salad bowl = \$ .50 each

total to be spent on all items = \$157.50 .

The sum of the separate costs equals the total amount to be spent.

$$(\$4)p + (\$3)\frac{1}{3}p + (\$.50)\frac{1}{2}p = \$157.50$$

$$\$(4p + 1p + \frac{1}{4}p) = 157.50$$

$$\$5\frac{1}{4}p = 157.50$$

$$\$5.25p = 157.50$$

$$p = \frac{\$157.50}{\$\ \ 5.25}$$

$$p = 30 .$$

Now that we know that the number of bottles of perfume $p = 30$, it is an easy matter to find the amount of the other items.

no. of wallets = $\frac{1}{3}p = 10$,

no. of salad bowls = $\frac{1}{2}p = 15$.

ii) The answers to this question will serve as a check to part (i).

Cost of wallets	= \$3 × 10	=	\$ 30.00
Cost of bowls	= \$.50 × 15	=	7.50
Cost of perfume	= \$4 × 30	=	120.00
Total cost		=	157.50 .

• PROBLEM 4-20

A publisher has fixed daily costs of \$300. His books sell for \$1.00 a piece, and they cost him 75¢ a piece. Find the breakeven point.

Solution: The breakeven point is the number of books he must publish in order that the costs of publishing them equals the revenue [earned] from them. To do this, we first must find the linear cost and revenue functions.

Let X stand for the number of books. The revenue is equal to the amount of revenue per book times the number of books. In function form this becomes:

$$R = \$1\ X \quad (R = \text{revenue})\ .$$

The daily cost is equal to the variable cost times the number of books plus the daily fixed cost. Hence the linear cost function is:

$$C = \$.75\ X + \$300\ .$$

We can now find the breakeven point. To do this we set the cost and revenue functions equal to each other, and solve for X (the number of books).

$$\$1 \cdot X = \$.75\ X + \$300\ ,$$

subtract \$.75 X from each side of the equation and we get:

$$\$.25\ X = \$300\ .$$

Finally, dividing both sides by \$.25 we find:

$$X = \$300 \div \$.25 = 1{,}200 \text{ books.}$$

• PROBLEM 4-21

A company manager found that the company's revenue function is $R = 90\sqrt{2X}$ where X is the number of units made, and their cost function is $C = 3X + 1200$. Find the breakeven point, and how many units to produce (in terms of an in inequality) to make a profit.

Solution: The break even point, is the number of units reguired to be made in order that cost is equal to the revenue. To find this, we set the two equations, profit and cost, equal to each other and solve for X .

$$90\sqrt{2X} = 3X + 1200$$

or dividing each term by 3

$$30\sqrt{2X} = X + 400\ .$$

We now must get rid of the square root term. To do this, we square each side, that is, multiply each side by itself.

$$(30\sqrt{2X})(30\sqrt{2X}) = (X + 400)(X + 400)$$

or

$$900 \cdot 2X = X^2 + 800X + 160000$$

or

$$1800x = X^2 + 800X + 160000$$

now subtract 1800X from both sides

$$0 = X^2 - 1000X + 160000.$$

To solve for X we now factor the right hand side into $(X - 800)(X - 200)$ so the equation now reads

$$(X - 800)(X - 200) = 0.$$

If $X = 800$ then the equation is true, and it is also true for $X = 200$.

Hence there are two breakeven points. We can now see where the company makes its profits. If they produce less than 200 units they lose money for it is less then the first breakeven point. If they make between 200 and 800 units the company makes a profit, but if they make more then 800 units, they lose money again. Hence profits occur for

$$200 < X < 800.$$

• PROBLEM 4-22

A plastics company has determined that the cost of waste is fixed at \$12 for up to 20 modules. After this, the waste cost increases according to the function $\$4\ (p - 20)^2$ where p is the modules in excess of 20 produced.

(i) What is the total waste cost in producing 45 modules?

(ii) What number minimizes waste cost?

Solution: (i) Fixed waste = \$12

when $0 < p \leq 20$.

To this we add the varying rate of waste cost: $p > 20$,

$$\text{Varying waste} = \$4\ (p - 20)^2,$$

$$\therefore \text{Total waste cost} = \$4\ (p - 20)^2 + 12$$

when $p = 45$.

$$\text{Total waste cost} = 4\ (45 - 20)^2 + 12$$

$$= 4\ (625) + 12$$
$$= \$2{,}512.$$

(ii) Total waste $= F(p) = 4(p - 20)^2 + 12$

$$F(p) = 4(p^2 - 40p + 400) + 12$$
$$F(p) = 4p^2 - 160p + 1{,}612\ .$$

To find the minimum waste, take the first derivative:

$$F^1(p) = 8p - 160.$$

Let $8p - 160 = 0$

then $p = \frac{160}{8} = 20$ modules as we should expect.

• PROBLEM 4-23

> The Tiller Company is considering manufacturing rings. Through a market survey it has found that when the number of rings bought (r) is expressed in terms of its price p (in dollars), the demand function is
>
> $$r = 1{,}125 - 375\ p\ .$$
>
> The company has fixed costs of $3,000 and each ring cost $9 to produce. How many rings can the company produce at the price which gives maximum profit?

Solution: Since Profit = Revenue - Cost,

we must (a) derive the Revenue function at price in terms of p.

(b) Derive the Cost function. likewise

$$\text{Revenue } (R) = \text{no. of rings} \times \text{price/ring}$$
$$= (r)(p)$$
$$= (-375\ p + 1{,}125)\ p$$
$$= -375\ p^2 + 1{,}125\ p\ .$$

Total Cost (C_T) = fixed cost + variable cost

$C_T = \$3{,}000 + \$9r$ (no. of rings)

$C_T = \$3{,}000 + \$9r = \$3000 + \$9\ (-375\ p + 1{,}125)$

$C_T = -\ 3{,}375\ p + 13{,}125$

Profit = Revenues - Cost

$$= (-375p^2 + 1{,}125p) - (-3{,}375p + 13{,}125)$$

$$f(p) = -375p^2 + 4,500p - 13,125 .$$

Finding the maximum at the first derivative of f(p), we have

$$f^1(p) = -750p + 4,500 .$$

Letting $f^1(p) = 0$, we find the critical point:

$$-750p + 4,500 = 0 .$$

$$750p = 4,500$$

$$p = \frac{4,500}{750} = \$6.$$

So that maximum profit is obtained when the price of each ring is 6 dollars per ring, but if it costs the Tiller Company $9 to make a ring then it should not bother entering the ring market.

• PROBLEM 4-24

The unit demand function of a jeweler is p = 52 - 2x, where p is the price and x = number of units. The average unit cost of production is $4.00.

(i) What is the cost of producing x units?

(ii) What is the revenue function?

(iii) What is the profit function?

(iv) What is the jeweler's maximum profit?

Solution: (i) Total Cost = unit cost × no. of units

$$C_T = 4x .$$

(ii) Revenue = unit price × no. of units

$$= (52 - 2x)\, x$$

$$= -2x^2 + 52x .$$

(iii) Profit = Total Revenue - Total Cost

$$= -2x^2 + 52x - (4x)$$

$$\text{Profit} = F(x) = -2x^2 + 48x .$$

(iv) Taking the first derivative of F(x)

$$F^1(x) = -4x + 48.$$

Setting $F^1(x) = 0$, we have

$$-4x + 48 = 0$$
$$4x = 48$$
$$x = \frac{48}{4} = 12 .$$

This, then is the critical value of x.

Since, when $x < 12$, $F^1(x) > 0$

and when $x > 12$, $F^1(x) < 0$

for values near $x = 12$, there is a relative maximum at $x = 12$.

The jeweler's maximum profit therefore occurs when $x = 12$.

As before,

$$\text{Profit} = F(x) = -2x^2 + 48x$$
$$= -2(144) + 48(12)$$
$$= -288 + 576$$
$$= \$288.$$

• PROBLEM 4-25

Find the break-even point for the cost of production C and the revenue R received for each of the following:

(a) $C = \$10x + \$600$, $R = \$30x$
(b) $C = \$5x + \$200$, $R = \$8x$
(c) $C = \$0.2x + \$50$, $R = \$0.3x$
(d) $C = \$1800x + \$3000$, $R = \$2500x$

Solution: The break-even point is the number of items produced so that the cost of producing them is equal to the revenue (earned by) received from selling them. To find this point, we set the cost function equal to the revenue function, and solve for the unknown.

(a) $C = \$10x + \$600$ $R = \$30x$

By setting them equal we get:

$\$10x + \$600 = \$30x$.

We now subtract \$10x from each side and get:

$\$600 = 20x$.

We now divide both sides by 20 and get:

$30 = x$ or the break even point is when we produce 30 units.

(b) $C = \$5x + \$200$ $\qquad R = \$8x$

Following the same procedure:

$\$5x + \$200 = \$8x$

$\$200 = \$3x$

$\$200 \div \$3 = x$ or $x = 66\ 2/3$ units.

(c) $C = \$0.2x + \$50$ $\qquad R = \$0.3x$

$\$.2x + \$50 = \$.3x$

$\$50 = \$.1x$

$500 = x$

(d) $C = \$1800x + \$3000$ $\qquad R = \$2500x$

$\$1800x + \$3000 = \$2500x$

$\$3,000 = \$700x$

$\frac{3000}{700} = x$ or $x = 4\frac{2}{7}$ units.

• PROBLEM 4-26

Assume that some function, $K = F(i)$ is the cost of the production and marketing of a product, and the total cost (K) is solely dependant upon the number of items produced, where i stands for the number of items produced. Then, the average rate of change in cost

$$= \frac{\text{change in total cost}}{\text{change in number of items}} ; \frac{\Delta K}{\Delta i} = \frac{F(i_2) - F(i_1)}{i_2 - i_1} .$$

Suppose the production and marketing cost of a pair of compasses is

$$K = F(i) = 3\sqrt{i} .$$

When $0 \leq i \leq 250$.

What then, is the average rate of change in cost,

(a) from $i = 25$ to $i = 100$?

(b) from $i = 25$ to $i = 225$?

Solution: $\frac{\Delta K}{\Delta i} = \frac{F(i_2) - F(i_1)}{i_2 - i,}$.

(a) $\Delta K = 3\sqrt{100} - 3\sqrt{25} = 30 - 15 = 15$

$\Delta i = 100 - 25 = 75$

$\frac{\Delta K}{\Delta i} = \frac{15}{75} = \frac{1}{5} = .2$.

(b) $\Delta K = 3\sqrt{225} - 3\sqrt{25} = 45 - 15 = 30$

$\Delta i = 225 - 25 = 200$

$\frac{\Delta K}{\Delta i} = \frac{30}{200} = .15$.

This states that it costs an average of \$.20 per unit for each extra item produced from 25 to 100, but only \$.15 per unit for up to 200 extra items, beginning at item number 25.

In other words, the average cost rate diminishes as more items are produced. These returns to scale are observed as a major advantage of large industry.

• PROBLEM 4-27

Mrs. Accra owns a bakery which has an average cost per unit function C = 4u when u = number of large cakes. The price is given by p = 20 - 2u. Her revenue function then, is

R = unit demand × number of cakes

$R = (20 - 2u)\ u = -2u^2 + 20u$.

(i) Derive Mrs. Accra's profit function in terms of u.

How many cakes maximize the profit?

Solution: (i) Profit = Revenue - Cost

i.e. $P(u) = -2u^2 + 20u - (4u)$

$= -2u^2 + 16u$.

(ii) Taking the first derivative of P (u) we have;

$P^1(u) = -4u + 16$.

Since, at the maximum (vertex) of the curve $P(u) = -2u^2 + 16u$, $P'(u) = 0$, let us solve for u.

$0 = -4u + 16$

$-16 = -4u$

$u = 4$ cakes .

The maximum profit

occurs when u = 4

$$P(4) = -2(4)^2 + 16(4)$$
$$= -32 + 64$$
$$= 32 .$$

• PROBLEM 4-28

At the Harris foundry, the total daily cost of manufacturing m pieces of metal is represented by the following equation:

$$C \text{ (in dollars)} = 3m^2 + m + 9 .$$

If the cost of the work produced by 9:00 am is $4,849 and the rate of manufacture after 9:00 am is 10 pieces per hr.,

(i) how many pieces of metal will have been produced by lunch hour (12 noon)? Hint: use the quadratic formula:

$$m = \frac{-b \pm \sqrt{b^2 - 4ac}}{2a} ,$$

and other calculations.

(ii) When t represents the number of hours past 9:00 am., express the total cost as a function of t.

Solution: (i) 10 pcs./hr. × 3 hrs. = 30 pieces

To this we must add the number produced before 9 a.m. which we find using

$$C = 3m^2 + m + 9 .$$

$$\$4,849 = 3m^2 + m + 9 .$$

To use the quadratic formula, set the equation = 0.

$$0 = 3m^2 + m - 4840 .$$

In to above equation:

$a = 3 \qquad b = 1 \qquad C = 4840$

$$m = \frac{-b \pm \sqrt{b^2 - 4ac}}{2a}$$

$$m = \frac{-1 \pm \sqrt{1^2 - 4(3 \times -4840)}}{2 \times 3}$$

$$m = \frac{-1 \pm \sqrt{58,081}}{6}$$

$$m = \frac{-1}{6} \pm \frac{241}{6}$$

$$m = \frac{240}{6} = 40 \ .$$

The root $m = 40\frac{1}{3}$ is meaningless in this example, and may be ignored.

$\therefore$ m = 40 is the proper amount.

Amount of metal up to 9: a.m.	= 40 pieces
" " " from 9: a.m. to 12: noon	= 30 pieces
Total	70 pieces .

(ii) First of all, we have

$$m = 10t + 40 ;$$

i.e. the total number pieces equals the number of hours past 9 a.m. times 10 , plus the 40 pieces completed before 9 a.m.

Now let us express the cost C .

$$C = 3m^2 + m + 9$$

$$C = 3(10t + 40)^2 + (10t + 40) + 9$$

$$C = 300t^2 + 2,410t + 4849.$$

CHAPTER 5

ECONOMIC THEORY

MICROECONOMICS

INDIFFERENCE AND DEMAND CURVE ANALYSIS

• PROBLEM 5-1

Describe, using indifference curves, the preferences of the following consumers, that is, for each consumer draw a few representative indifference curves. Both consumers consume only two commodities which are measured in ounces: ginger ale (G) and whiskey (W). Place whiskey on the vertical axis and ginger ale on the horizontal axis. Assume the drinks are not premixed.

1. Betty likes her G and W mixed in exactly a 3 to 1 ratio, respectively. If she is given any other proportion, she just won't use the excess commodity. If she has to choose between two drinks, both of which are mixed in a 3 to 1 ratio, she chooses the one with more liquid. (i.e., she chooses 6 to 2 = 8 ounces over 3 to 1 = 4 ounces).
2. Bob always prefers to drink ginger ale without any whiskey. If he has any W he just doesn't use it.

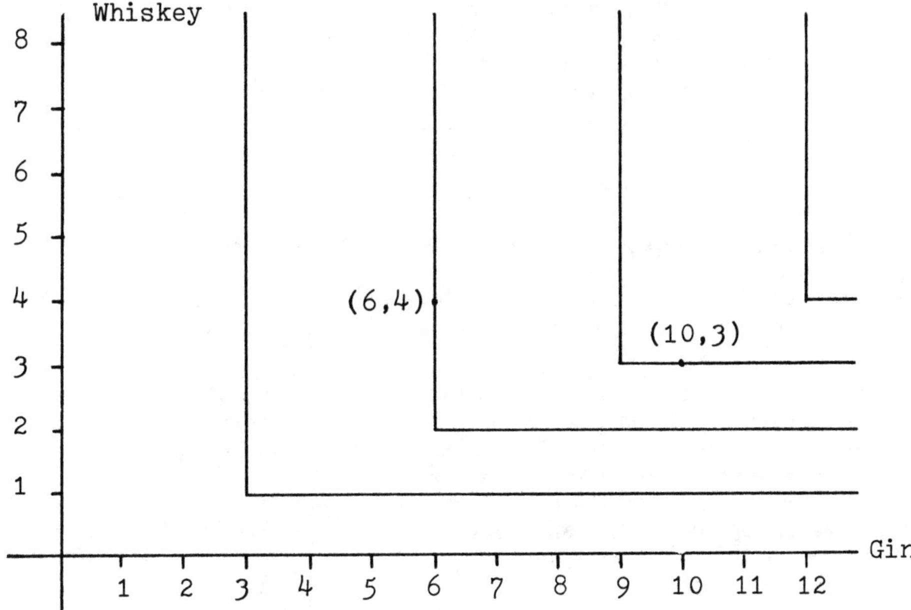

Solution: An indifference curve is the locus of all points giving the consumer the same level of satisfaction. As the curves shift away from the origin, the consumer reaches higher and higher levels of satisfaction. Let us consider points (6,4) and (10,3) on the graph. Although neither is in a 3 to 1 ratio, the question said Betty wouldn't use the excess commodity; thus we must find the 3 to 1 ratio having the largest volume. She would prefer the point (10,3), since it gives her a 9 to 3 mixture with one ounce of ginger ale in excess, whereas the point (6,4) gives her at most a 6 to 2 mixture with two ounces of whiskey in excess. She therefore would choose the point (10,3) because there is more liquid (9+3 > 6+2).

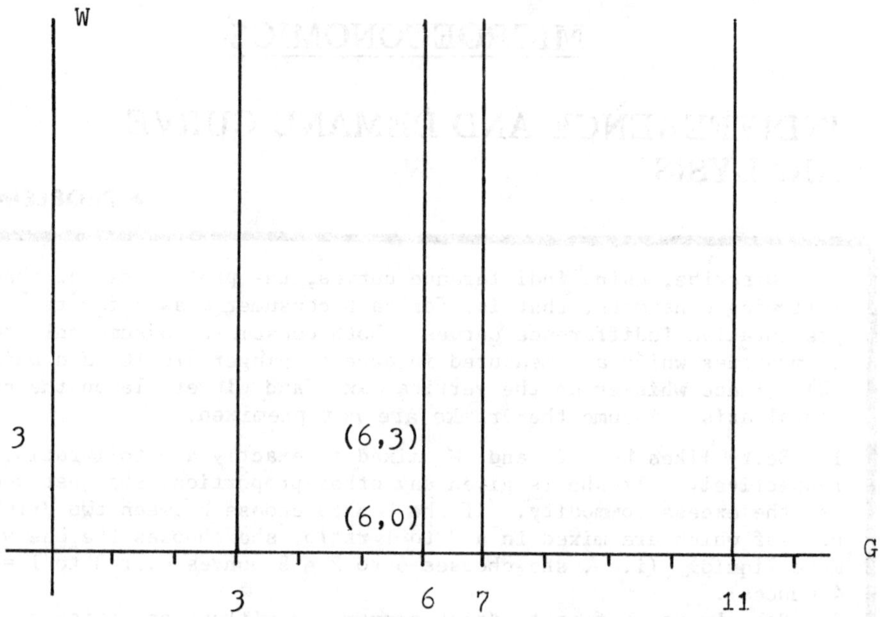

Any vertical line would satisfy Bob's needs. He only drinks ginger ale, so for example, he will choose the combinations 6 ginger ale and 0 whiskey with the same desire as 6 ginger ale and 3 whiskey. As the question stated "if he has any W he just doesn't use it." Again we would choose an indifference curve as far to the right as possible, since the more ginger ale, the better.

• PROBLEM 5-2

Suppose an individual's preference ordering over the two goods food and warmth can be represented numerically by the equation

$$SV(F,W) = fw^2 ,$$

where SV is the subjective valuation of any bundle containing food and warmth, f is the amount of food in the bundle (measured in pounds per week), w is the amount of warmth in the bundle (measured in equivalent hundred weight of coal per week).

(a) If f = 10 and w = 27, and the amount of f more than doubles to 22.5, by how much can w decline without leaving the individual worse off?

(b) If the individual's satisfaction is obtained when he spends his entire income on 10f and 27w, what happens as income doubles while prices remain unchanged? Will he increase his consumption of food by more than his consumption of warmth, or visa versa?

(c) Now suppose the same conditions hold as in (b) but $SV(F,W) = Kf^{\frac{1}{2}}w^{\frac{1}{2}}$. Which increases in larger proportion now when income doubles?

(d) Same exercise except $SV(F,W) = f^{\frac{1}{3}}w^{\frac{2}{3}}$.

Solution: In discussing an individual's preference for two goods we are able to plot the information on an indifference curve. This curve illustrates all accepted combinations of two goods so that if the consumer had to pick a point on the curve he would not care which one he chose (i.e., he would be indifferent).

By substituting $f = 10$ and $w = 27$ into the function $SV(F,W) = afw^2$ we get $SV(F,W) = 729 \times 10 = 7290$. If f is being more then doubled to 22.5 and we are on the same indifference curve,(so we don't become worse off), $[SV(F,W) = 7290]$, w will have to decrease correspondingly. By dividing 7290 by 22.5 we get $324 = w^2$ and $w = 18$. w will decrease from 27 to 18.

(b) We use the budget constraint line, because we are discussing an indifference curve with a fixed income and fixed prices. When income increases in this case, the budget line will shift outward, still having the same slope, see figure below.

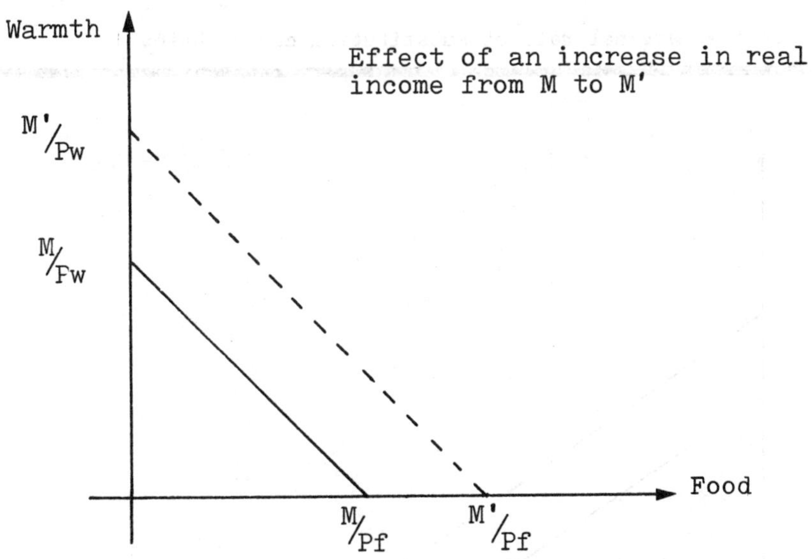

$SV(F,W) = fw^2$ tells us that f is valued more than w since w must be squared to be on the same level as f. We will then increase consumption of food more than the consumption of warmth.

(c) If food and warmth are each raised to the same power, that means that each grow in the same proportion. A doubling of income will result in the same proportion increase in f and w.

(d) We apply the same thought here as in "b" and "c". $SV(F,W) = f^{\frac{1}{3}} w^{\frac{2}{3}}$ shows that food is valued more than warmth. If you were to cube each variable you would get fw^2, where w still must be squared to be on the same level as f.

• PROBLEM 5-3

Suppose there are two consumers, Fred and Robert. W represents the number of units of wine consumed, while C represents the number of units of cheese consumed. Thus, W_R represents the number of units of wine consumed by Robert. Fred and Robert live in an economy that has produced 1400 units of wine and 900 units of cheese. These supplies have been divided evenly between Robert and Fred. Assume that the price of wine is P_W = \$1.50/unit and the price of cheese is P_C = \$.33/unit. At these prices each consumer's allocation of wine and cheese can be sold to him at $\$1\frac{1}{2}(700) + \$\frac{1}{3}(450) = \$1200$. This income (which goes to the producer) can then be used to buy any desired wine-cheese (WC) bundle which satisfies the budget constraint of $\$1\frac{1}{2}W + \$1/3C = \$1200$.

1) Which (WC) bundle will Fred choose?

2) Which (WC) bundle will Robert choose?

3) Is the total demand for wine and cheese equal to the supply of wine and cheese when $P_W = \$1\frac{1}{2}$/unit and $P_C = \$\frac{1}{3}$/unit?

Use the marginal rate of substitution curves below.

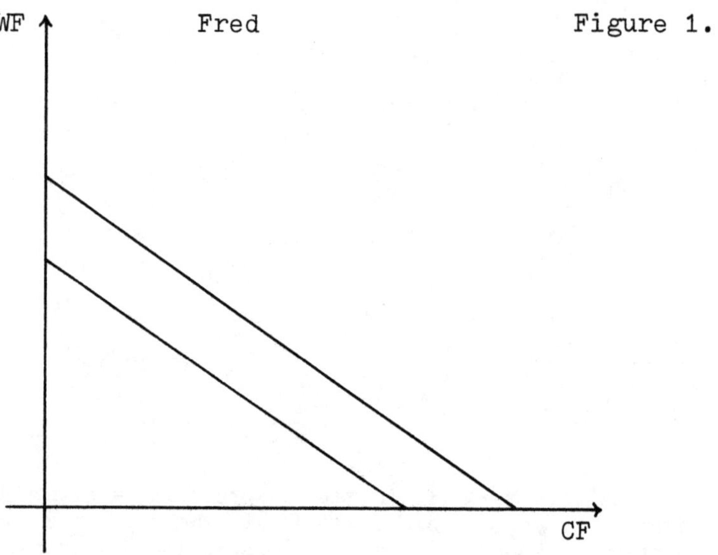

Figure 1.

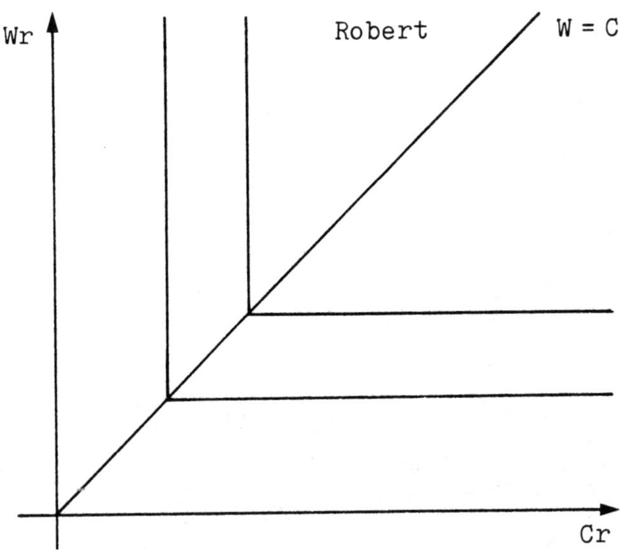

Solution: Consumer satisfaction will not be maximized unless the marginal rate of product transformation (MRPT) between two goods is equal to the marginal rate of substitution (MRS). The MRS which we are given on the above graph, tells the rate at which the consumer is willing to substitute one good for the other while maintaining the same level of satisfaction. $MRS_{X \text{ for } Y}$ is the change in Y divided by the change in X, and is the negative of the slope of the indifference curve. The isocost line • MRPT, which we must superimpose over the existing graph, tells the rate at which the producer is able to substitute one good for the other while maintaining the same production costs. The intersection of the two curves will give us the optimal amounts of both cheese and wine that Fred and Robert can buy, given product prices and a limited supply of products. To graph the MRPT lines we use the equation $\$1\frac{1}{2}W + \frac{1}{3}C = 1200$ or $1.50W + .33C = 1200$. To find the axial intercepts of the isocost line, put the cost equation into the standard linear form $W = MC + b$, where W is the coordinate of the vertical axis, M is the slope of the line, C is the coordinate of the horizontal axis, b is the value of W where the line crosses the vertical axis; i.e., b is the one of the two intercepts.

$$1.5W + 0.33C = 1200$$
$$1.5W = 1200 - .33C$$
$$W = 800 - .222C = -2/9\ C + 800$$

The slope of the budget constraint line is $-2/9$ and the intercept of the vertical axis is 800. The intercept of the horizontal axis is found by setting W equal to zero.

$$W = -2/9\ C + 800$$

$$0 = -\ 2/9\ C + 800$$

$$9/2 \times 2/9\ C = 800 \times 9/2$$

$$C = 3600\ ,$$

the intercept of the horizontal axis. The intersecting points will be 3600 on the "C" axis and 800 on the "W" axis as seen below.

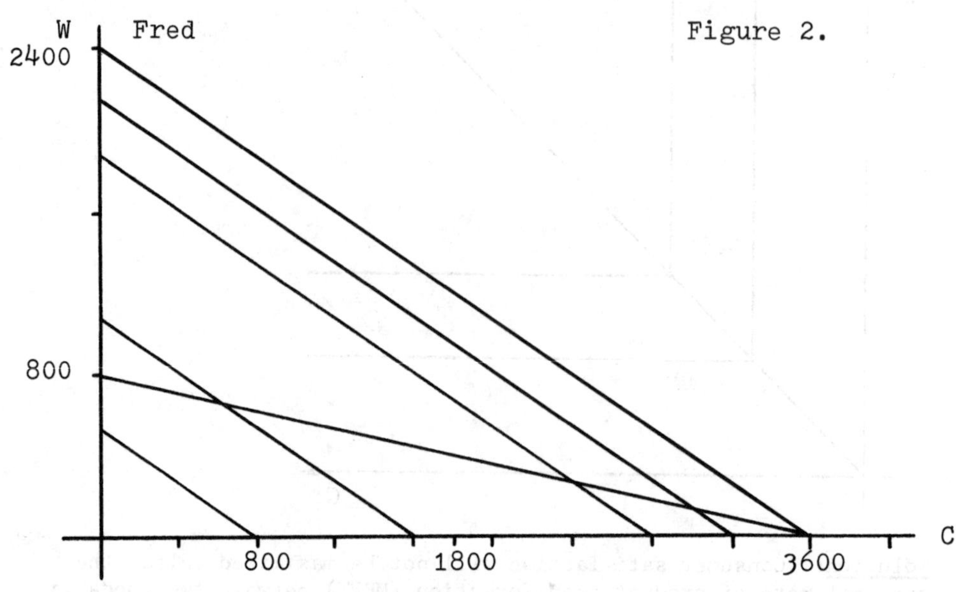

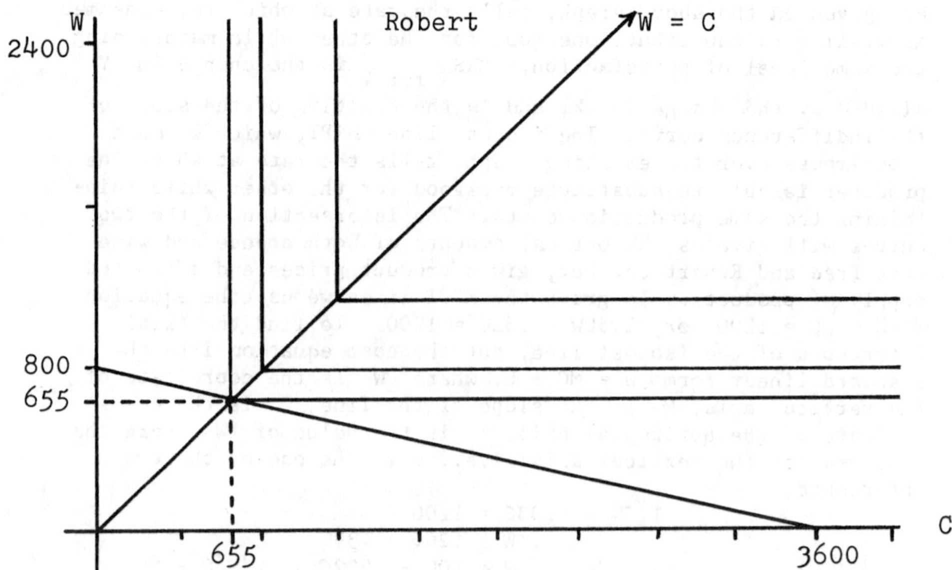

Interpreting these results: 1) Fred will choose to take 3600 units of cheese and no units of wine. 2) Robert will demand 655 units each of wine and cheese. On the graph of Robert's marginal rate of substitution curve, it is stated that $W = C$, that the amount of wine demanded equals the amount of cheese desired. Robert's point of maximum satisfaction, where his marginal rate of substitution $W = C$, is equal to MRPT, is $W = -2/9C + 800$. Because $W = C$, we can write MRPT as

$$C = -2/9C + 800$$

$$\frac{9}{11} \times \frac{11}{9} C = 800 \times \frac{9}{11}$$

$$C \approx 655$$

$$W = C \approx 655 .$$

3) The total demand of wine is 0(Robert) + 655(Fred) = 655.

The market supply of wine is 1400, therefore, there is a surplus of wine (1400 > 655). The total demand of cheese is 3600 (Robert) + 655 (Fred) = 4255. The total supply of cheese is 900 so there is a large excess demand (900 < 4255).

• PROBLEM 5-4

The Heino fan club sponsored a film on Finnish art. The demand curve is given by

$$x = \frac{a}{p} - b \tag{1}$$

where x is the number of viewers, p is the uniform price and a and b are constants. The theatre has 3000 seats. The following figures were previously observed; when

$$p_1 = \$3.00 \ , \ x_1 = 1500 \tag{2}$$

$$p_2 = \$2.00 \ , \ x_2 = 2000 \tag{3}$$

Find the constants a and b. Then find the price at which the theatre is filled.

Solution: Substituting (2) and (3) successively into (1) we obtain the pair of simultaneous equations

$$1500 = \frac{a}{3} - b \tag{4}$$

$$2000 = \frac{a}{2} - b \ . \tag{5}$$

From (4), $-b = 1500 - a/3$. Substituting this result into (5) we obtain:

$$2000 = \frac{a}{2} + 1500 - \frac{a}{3}$$

$$500 = \frac{3a - 2a}{6} = \frac{a}{6}$$

and $a = 3000$.

Then, from (4)

$$-b = 1500 - \frac{3000}{3} = 500 \ .$$

Thus, (1) becomes

$$x = \frac{3000}{p} - 500 \ . \tag{6}$$

We are given that $x_{maximum} = 3000$. Substituting this into (6),

$$3000 = \frac{3000}{p} - 500$$

$$3500p = 3000; \quad p = \frac{3000}{3500} \approx \$0.86 \ .$$

The theatre will be filled when p is \$0.86.

• PROBLEM 5-5

The Grover Cleveland Motel has 25 rooms. The demand curve is $p = \sqrt{225 - 9x}$ which means that x number of rooms will be occupied at price p. Graph this demand schedule and comment on its appropriateness.

Solution: Let us first find the intercepts of the curve on the p and x axes. The given curve is

$$p = \sqrt{225 - 9x}\ , \qquad (1)$$

where only the positive square root of 225 - 9x is under consideration, since the price, p, cannot be zero. Letting x = 0 in (1), we find $p = \sqrt{225} = 15$. Similarly, letting p = 0 in (1),

$$\sqrt{225 - 9x} = 0\ ,$$

$$225 - 9x = 0^2 = 0\ ,$$

$$x = 25\ .$$

Next we must tabulate some other points on the graph.

x	0	1	2	3	6	9	12	15	18	21	24	25
P	15	14.8	14.4	14.1	13.1	12	10.8	9.5	7.9	6	3	0

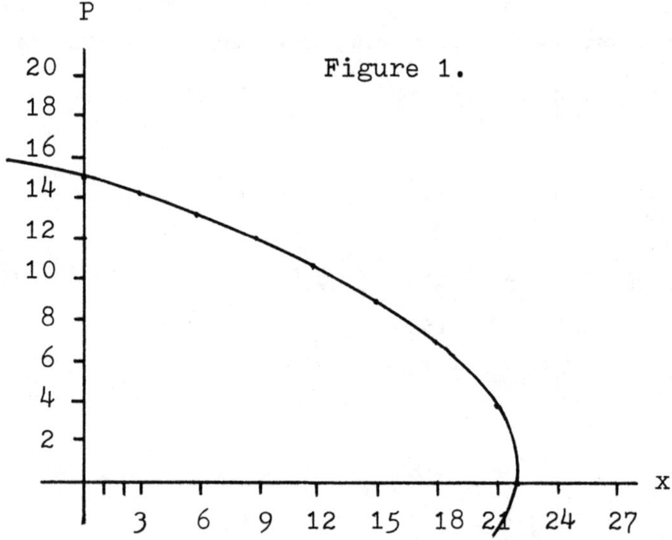

Figure 1.

Examining the graph, we see that the demand curve is a parabola with vertex at (25,0). The curve is not shaped as the demand curve for a commodity is usually shaped. Consider the following analogy with figure 1.

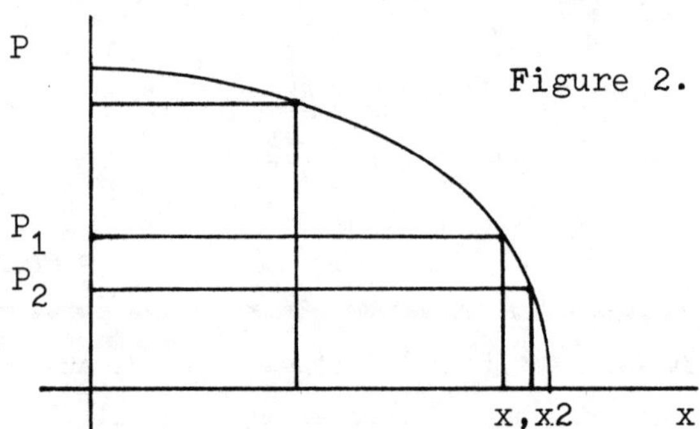

Figure 2.

As price falls beyond a certain point, further reductions in price call forth very small changes in quantity demanded. This suggests that there is a fairly fixed demand for rooms at the motel.

• PROBLEM 5-6

If the price of an item increases 50% what will happen to the quantity demanded if demand is elastic; inelastic; unitary elastic? In each case will the change in quantity demanded be greater, less, or equal to 50% ?

Solution: First, in an ordinary demand schedule, an increase in price causes a decrease in the quantity demanded and viee versa.

Where demand is elastic, the percentage change in quantity demanded will be greater than the percentage change in price. Elastic demand shows a greater responsiveness to changes in price. In the problem, quantity demanded will decrease by more than 50% when price increases 50%, if the demand is elastic. Inelastic demand means that the quantity demanded is not affected very much by changes in price. The percentage change in quantity is less than the percentage change in price. If price increases by 50%, quantity demanded will decrease by less than 50%.

With unitary elasticity, the percentage change in quantity demanded is equal to the percentage change in price. Quantity demanded will decrease 50% when price increases 50%.

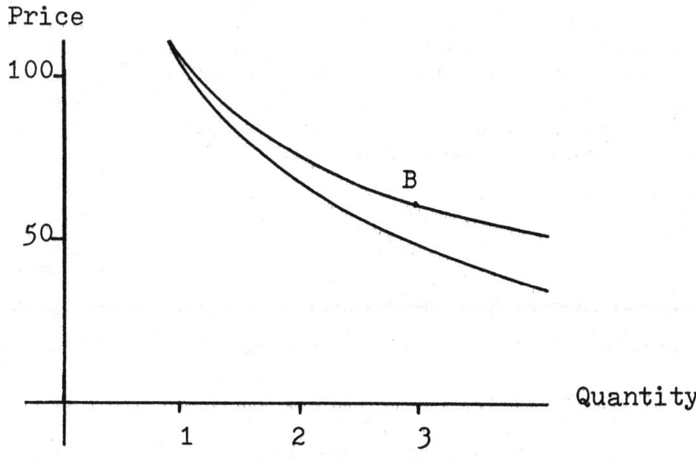

• PROBLEM 5-7

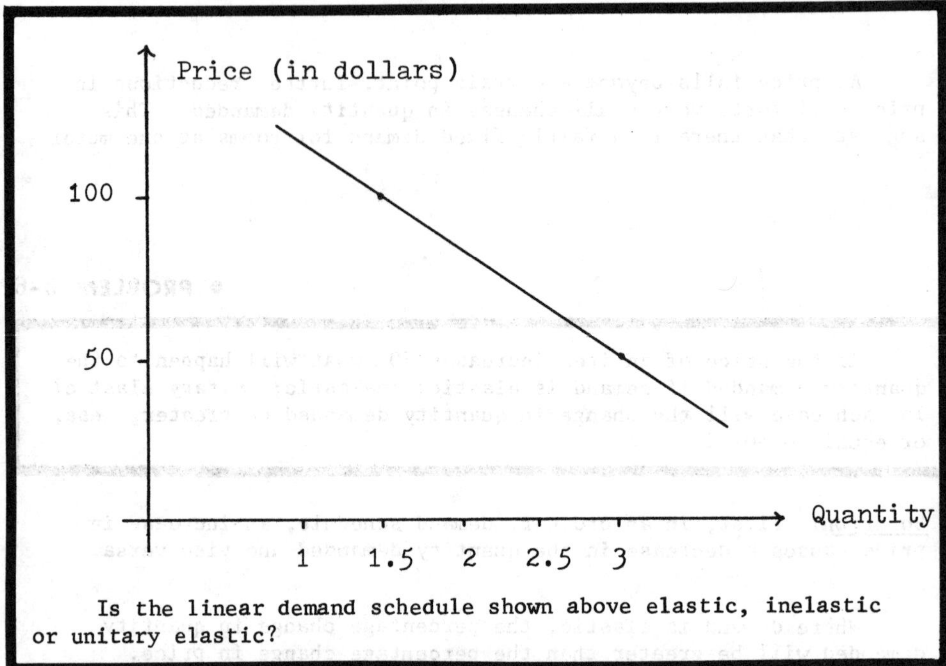

Is the linear demand schedule shown above elastic, inelastic or unitary elastic?

Solution: How demand for a product will respond to a change in the product's price is measured by elasticity of demand. One way to judge the elasticity of a demand schedule is to see the effect of a decrease in price on total revenue. Total revenue is equal to the price of an item multiplied by the quantity demanded at that price. A decrease in price will, for most products, cause an increse in quantity demanded.

Where demand is elastic, the increase in quantity demanded will be greater than the decrease in price. This will cause total revenue to increase. Where demand is inelastic, the increase in quantity demanded will not be enough to offset the price decrease. Revenue will drop when the price drops.

When elasticity is unitary, the decrease in price will be exactly offset by the increase in quantity demanded. Total revenue will not change at all.

In this example, when price drops from \$100 per unit to \$50, total revenue does not change. When the price is \$100, demand is 1.5 units. Total revenue is \$150. When the price drops to \$50, demand goes up to 3 units. Total revenue is still \$150. Elasticity of demand is therefore unitary.

• PROBLEM 5-8

Consider the demand curve given by the following equation

$$p = \frac{a}{q+b} + c \ , \quad a > 0 \ , \ b > 0 \ , \ c > 0 \ . \qquad (1)$$

Assuming that a/b is small, show that a change in price causes a more than proportionate change in demand.

Solution: Recall that in microeconomic theory, p is considered the independent variable that causes changes in the dependent variable, quantity demanded. But (1) has price dependent on quantity. Let us first find the quantity as a function of the price. Thus, from (1),

$$p - c = \frac{a}{q+b}$$

$$(q+b)(p-c) = a$$

$$q = \frac{a}{p-c} - b \;. \tag{2}$$

When q equals zero, $p = a/b + c$. Examining (1) we see that when q becomes very large $a/q+b$ approaches zero and hence the limiting price is $p_0 = c$.

Using the above analysis we construct the graph below:

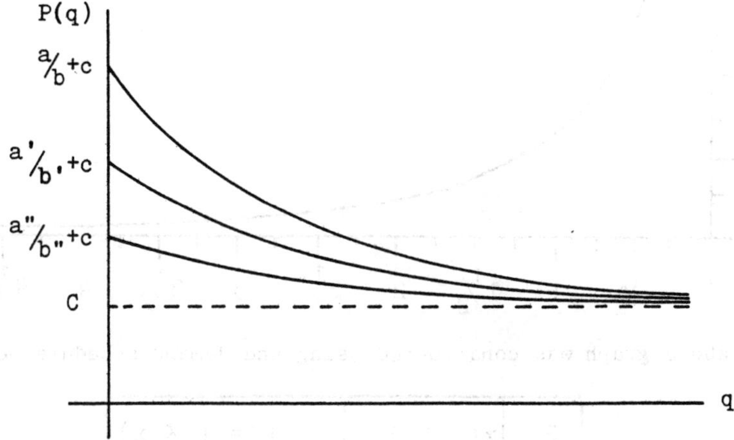

Consider the point $(0, \frac{a}{b} + c)$. Directly below it is the point $(0, \frac{a'}{b'} + c)$ where $a'/b' < a/b$. We note that as a/b becomes smaller, the demand curve becomes flatter, i.e., more elastic. A curve $p = f(q)$ is said to be elastic if a change in price causes a more than proportionate change in quantity demanded. This is what you were asked to show.

• PROBLEM 5-9

Let the demand for a product be given by the following demand law

$$p = \frac{a}{x} - c \;, \quad a > 0 \;, \; c \geq 0 \;. \tag{1}$$

Graph the relation (1) and show that total revenue falls or at least remains constant as output rises.

Solution: For simplicity, assume that $a = 1$ and $c = 0$. Then,

(1) reduces to

$$p = \frac{1}{x} . \tag{2}$$

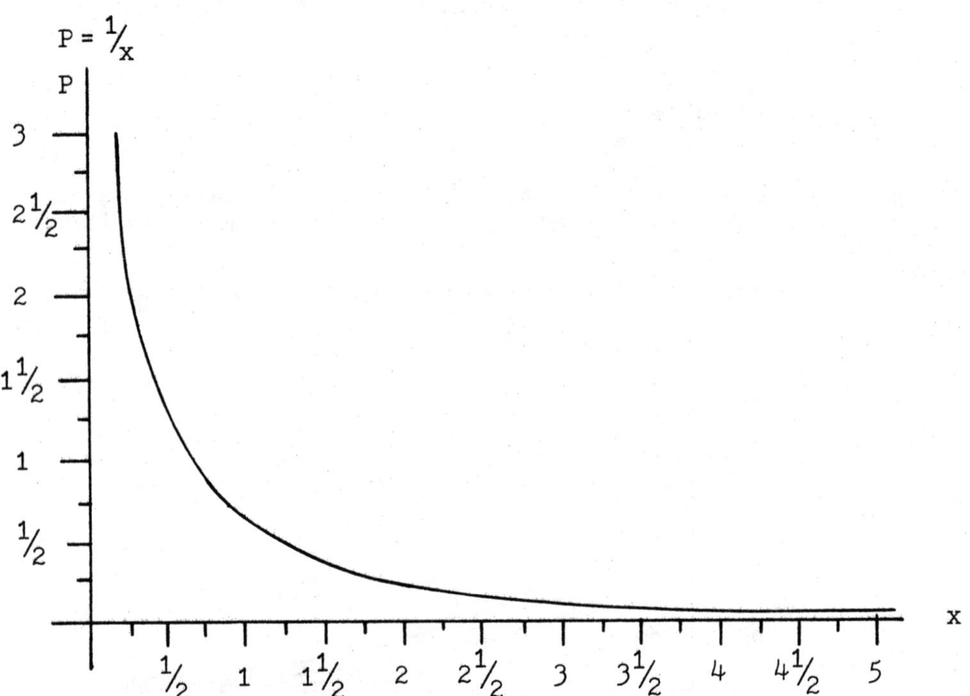

The above graph was constructed using the demand schedule below.

P	x(= 1/p)	TR(= P × x)
1/4	4	1
1/2	2	1
3/4	1.33	1
1	1	1
5/4	4/5	1
6/4	4/6	1
7/4	4/7	1
2	1/2	1
3	1/3	1

Note that although p = f(q), it is actually price that is the independent, (i.e., determining), variable while quantity is the dependent, (i.e., determined), variable. The convention in economics, however, is to graph demand and supply relations with price on the vertical, (i.e., dependent), axis and quantity on the horizontal, (i.e., independent), axis.

• PROBLEM 5-10

The Metropolitan Bus Company offers service to the airport. The demand for the service follows a curve

$$p = (3 - \frac{1}{40} x)^2 . \qquad (1)$$

Graph the demand curve and the total revenue curve. Then consider the demand function

$$p = (a - bx)^2 \qquad (2)$$

in the light of your analysis.

Solution: We first find the intercepts, i.e., the values of (1) when $p = 0$ and $x = 0$. We find

i) $x = 0$ implies $p = 9$

ii) $p = 0$ implies $x = 120$.

Next we tabulate a few points to get a good idea of the shape of the graph.

x	0	40	80	120	160	200	240	280
P	9	4	1	0	1	4	9	16

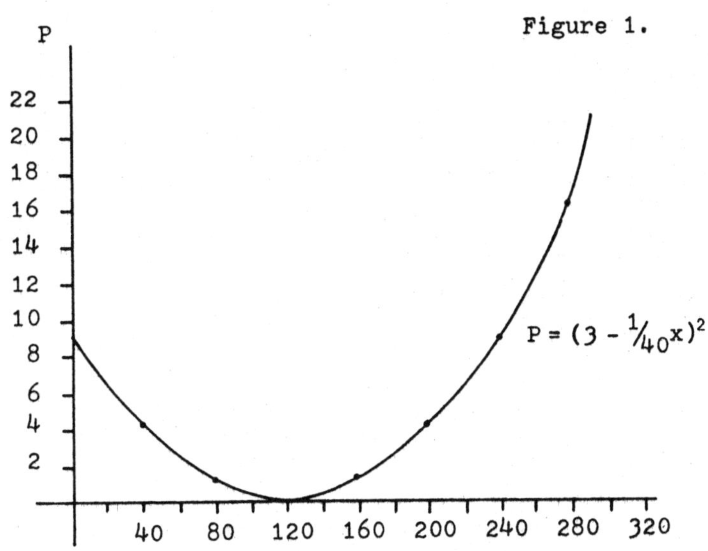

Figure 1.

Next, we must construct the revenue curve. Total revenue is defined as

$$TR = p \cdot X. \qquad (3)$$

Substituting (1) into (3),

$$TR = (3 - \frac{1}{40} x)^2 x$$

$$= (9 - \frac{3}{20} x + \frac{1}{1600} x^2) x$$

$$= \frac{1}{1600}x^3 - \frac{3}{20}x^2 + 9x . \qquad (4)$$

We must have recourse to the techniques of calculus to construct the graph of (4). Differentiating (4) and setting the result equal to zero,

$$\frac{3}{1600}x^2 - \frac{6}{20}x + 9 = 0 . \qquad (5)$$

The roots of (5) are, using the quadratic formula,

$$x_1 = 120 ; \quad x_2 = 40 .$$

Using the above table, we find that

$$TR_{x=40} = p_x = 4(40) = 160$$

$$TR_{x=120} = p_x = 0(120) = 0 .$$

We know also that total revenue equals zero when $x = 0$. Hence, we realize that the total revenue function reaches a maximum quickly (at $x = 40$) and then slowly declines afterwards until $x = 120$, at which point total revenue reaches another minimum. Then it rises again without stopping.

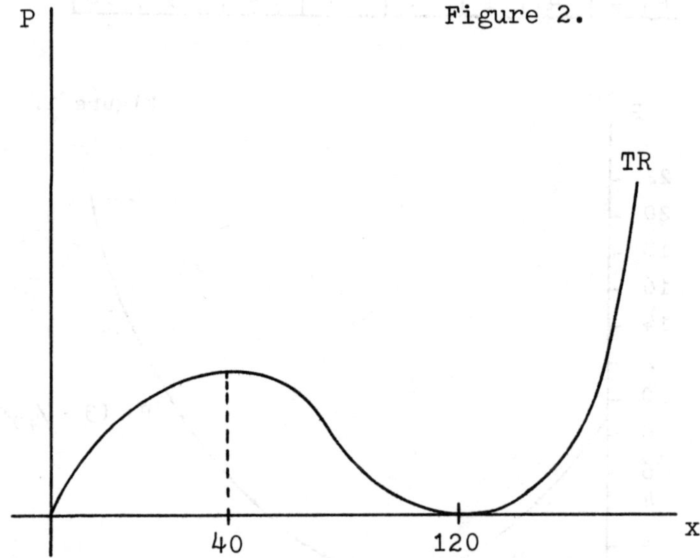

Figure 2.

From the information ascertained above, let us analyze the general demand function

$$p = (a - bx)^2 . \qquad (6)$$

We note first that $p > 0$ and $x > 0$ by the economic conditions. To find the p-intercept we set (6) equal to zero and solve for x.

$$(a - bx)^2 = 0 ,$$

$$a - bx = 0 ,$$

$$x = a/b$$

when $x = 0$, $p = a^2$.

Thus the vertex of the parabola generated by (6) passes through (a/b, 0) and the p-intercept is given by $p = a^2$.

Finally, let us find the inflection points of the total revenue curve.

$$TR = p_x$$
$$= (a - bx)^2 x$$
$$= b^2x^3 - 2abx^2 + a^2x , \qquad (7)$$

$$\frac{dTR}{dx} = 3b^2x^2 - 4abx + a^2 . \qquad (8)$$

Setting (8) equal to zero, and solving for x

$$x = \frac{4ab \pm \sqrt{16a^2b^2 - 12a^2b^2}}{6b^2} . \qquad (9)$$

Since $b > 0$, (9) reduces to

$$x = \frac{4ab \pm 2ab}{6b^2}$$

or

$$x_1 = \frac{a}{b} \; ; \; x_2 = \frac{1}{3}\frac{a}{b} .$$

This makes sense in terms of the inflection points we found earlier; a/b = 120 = x_1 and 1/3(a/b) = 40 = x_2 .

• PROBLEM 5-11

Suppose that the demand curve for a firm's product is as follows:

Output	Price of Good
23	$ 5.00
32	4.00
40	3.50
47	3.00
53	2.00

Also, suppose that the marginal product and total product of labor is:

Amount of Labor	Marginal Product of Labor	Total Output
2	10	23
3	9	32
4	8	40
5	7	47
6	6	53

(Note that the figures regarding marginal product pertain to the interval between the indicated amount of labor and one unit less than the indicated amount of labor.) Given this data, how much labor should the firm employ if labor costs $12 a unit?

Solution: In this case we are assuming that the only variable input is labor. The demand curve for such a firm will show the quantity of labor that the firm will employ at various possible prices of labor. We also assume that the firm wishes to maximize its profit so it will choose the quantity of labor where the value of extra output produced by an extra unit of labor is equal to the price of labor. In other words we need to find the Marginal Revenue Product of Labor, which is the increase in total revenue due to the use of an additional unit of input.

Quantity of labor	Marginal Product of labor	Total Output	Price of Good	Total Revenue	Marginal Revenue Product of Labor
2	10	23	$5.00	115.	---
3	9	32	4.00	128.	13.
4	8	40	3.50	140.	12.
5	7	47	3.00	141.	1.
6	6	53	2.00	106.	-35.

By setting the marginal revenue product of input equal to the price of input x a firm maximizes its profit. This can be explained as follows: The marginal revenue product of input x is equal to the marginal product of input x times the firm's marginal revenue. We can compare this to the equation $MP_x \cdot MR = P_x$ where MP_x is the marginal product of input x, MR is the marginal revenue and P_x is the price of x. This is the condition for maximization of profit by a firm.

Thus, by setting $MRP_x = P_x$ (marginal revenue product of x) a firm maximizes profit, and we can then determine the necessary quantity desired at a particular price. Plotting the MRP_{Labor} on a graph we see that at the cost of $12. per unit of labor we would hire 4 workers.

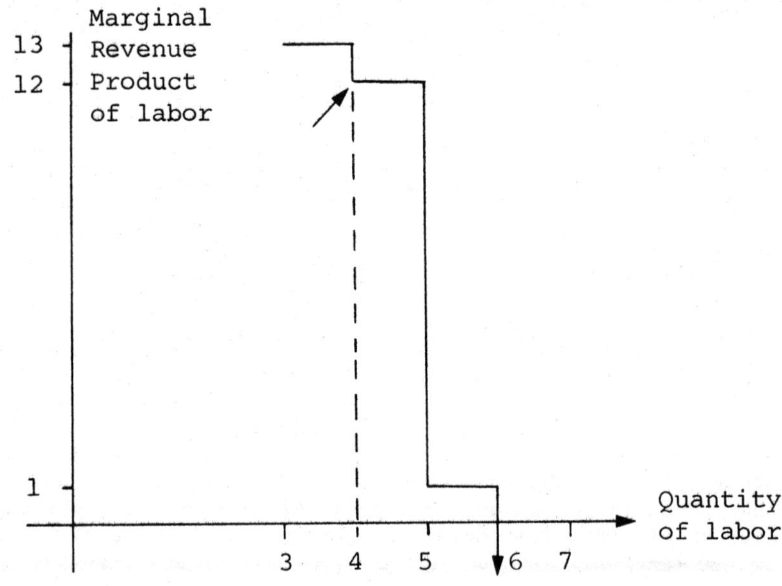

• **PROBLEM** 5-12

A ceramics craftsman has found that $Qd = 48 - 6p$ and $Qs = 2p + 16$ apply respectively to the market demand and supply for his products.

(i) Find the equilibrium price (\$p).

(ii) Assume that the government sets a floor price of \$8.00 to help bolster the ceramics industry. What will the excess supply be?

(iii) Graph the functions, indicating the excess demand for a ceiling price of \$3.00.

Solution: (i) Equilibrium price occurs where supply = demand, $Qd = Qs$, or $48 - 6p = 2p + 16$,

$$48 - 16 = 2p + 6p$$
$$32 = 8p$$
$$\$4. = p,$$

equilibrium price.

Equilibrium quantity = $2p + 16$ (or $= 48 - 6p$) . When $p = 4$, $2p + 16 = 24$ units .

(ii) Excess supply is

$$Qs - Qd, = (2p + 16) - (48 - 6p) .$$

Since the floor price (pf) = \$8,

$$Qs - Qd = [2(8) + 16] - [48 - 6(8)]$$
$$= [16 + 16] - [48 - 48]$$
$$= 32 - 0$$
$$= 32 \text{ units.}$$

(iii) When the price of an item increases from the equilibrium price, the demand for it will decrease; i.e., an excess supply will exist.

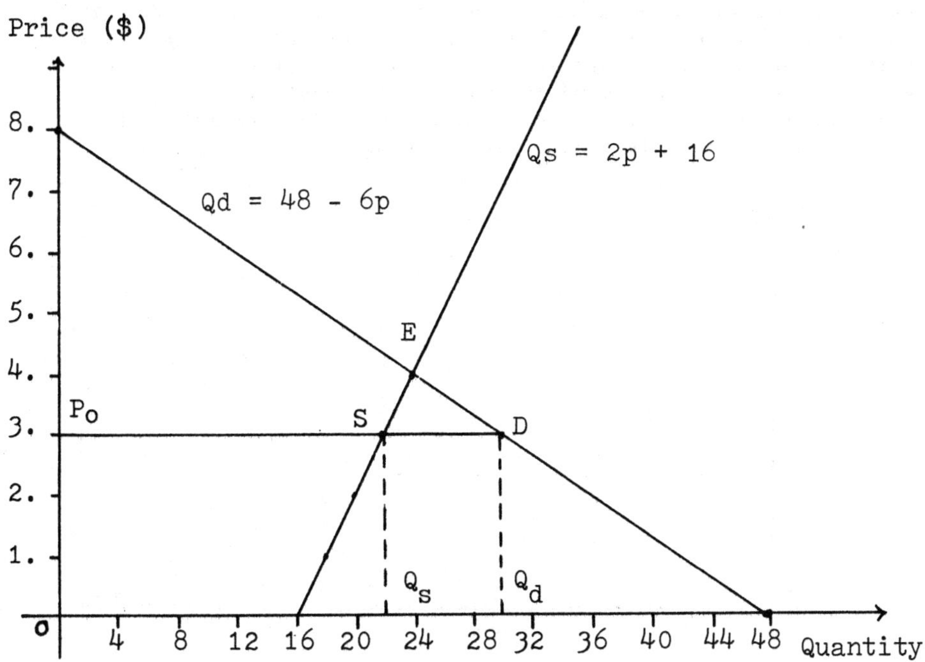

The supply and demand functions intersect at equilibrium point E. When a ceiling price of \$3. is instituted, rectangle OP_0DQ_d represents the potential revenue from the resulting demand of quantity OQ_d (30 units)

Only 0 Qs (22 units) is supplied at a price of \$3. per unit, however. The revenue at this level of supply is shown by rectangle OP_0SQ_s, and is equal to 22 units × \$3/unit = \$66.

The excess demand, then, is (0 Qd) - (0 Qs) = (48 - 6p) - (2p + 16) = [48 - 6(3)] - [2(3) + 16] = 30 - 22 = 8 . The loss of potential revenue is the rectangle Q_sSDQ_d.

PRODUCTION AND COST FUNCTIONS: PERFECT AND IMPERFECT COMPETITION

• PROBLEM 5-13

Give an example of a real market operating approximately under pure and perfect competition.

Solution: The wheat market is a good example of perfect competition. In a market operating under pure and perfect competition, no seller is in a position to alter the price which is taken as constant by buyers and sellers alike. It is assumed that sellers can sell all they are capable of producing without affecting the market price of the product. Also no buyer can change the price individually.

The product being sold on this sort of market is usually undifferentiable or homogeneous, meaning that units of the product made by different producers have the same quality. In the wheat market, this is true. Differences in nutritional value of wheat grown in different parts of the country are negligible. The price of a bushel of wheat is fixed for a certain period of time. The demand schedule is a line with zero slope for a specific

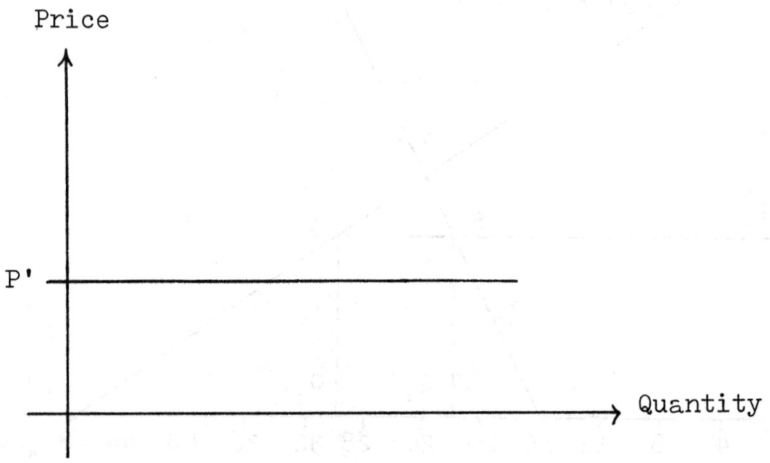

period. Given that the supply schedule is a straight line with positive slope as shown below, the quantity sold will be set at Q'.

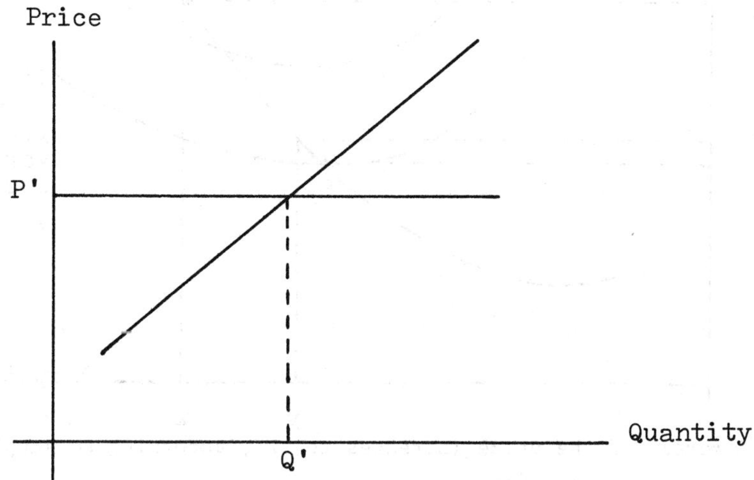

In reality, due to weather and extraordinary changes in demand, the price may fluctuate from period to period, yet we are to understand that it maintains a set value within one period. The limitation of classical market theory lies in its static nature, i.e., time is not considered. When dealing with microeconomic models we should keep this fact in mind.

• PROBLEM 5-14

Describe the actions of a firm operating in the short run, and how it would alter its strategies when faced with a long run situation.

Solution: In the short run, a firm is in a rather inflexible position, not being able to change its plant size, while in the long run it has this option. In the short run, if the price of a product is given, the firm will choose the output level where price equals marginal cost. If the price is less than the firm's average variable cost at any level of output, the firm will discontinue production. Assume the graph below describes the firm's short run cost curves.

The marginal cost (MC) curve intersects the average variable cost (VC") curve at point B, its minimum. Curve AC' is the average fixed and variable cost curve. As long as the price is above P_3 the firm will keep operating. However, once the price drops below this minimum the firm will produce nothing because the price will no longer cover its variable costs. If the firm sets its price at P_2 it will produce at output Y . Similarly, if it sets price at P_1 it will produce at output level X; at price P_2 , the firm will wish to sell

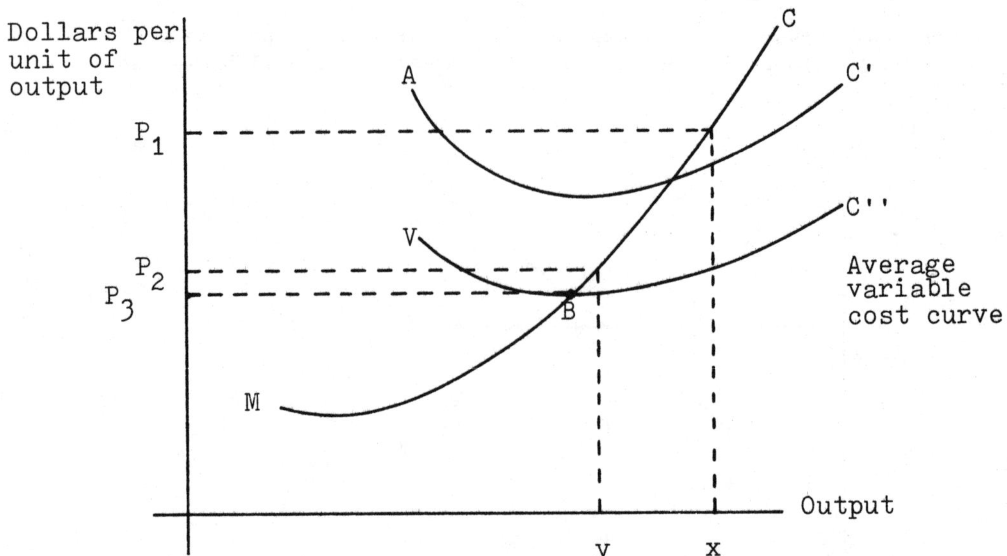

y units. However, if the price increases to P_1, according to supply and demand theory the firm will wish to produce and sell more units and will increase output to X.

In the long run since the firm can change its plant size, those firms that are not doing well and that cannot expand plant size can withdraw from the industry. New firms may also be able to enter the industry, if it has above average profits. Suppose the firm has average and marginal cost curves A_0A_0' and M_0M_0' as shown in the diagram below, and has a price of OP. This means the firm is operating at a profit.

In the long run the firm could operate a plant corresponding to any of the short-run cost curves. It could build one at A_1A_1' and M_1M_1' but will chose to build one at A_2A_2' and M_2M_2'. This will

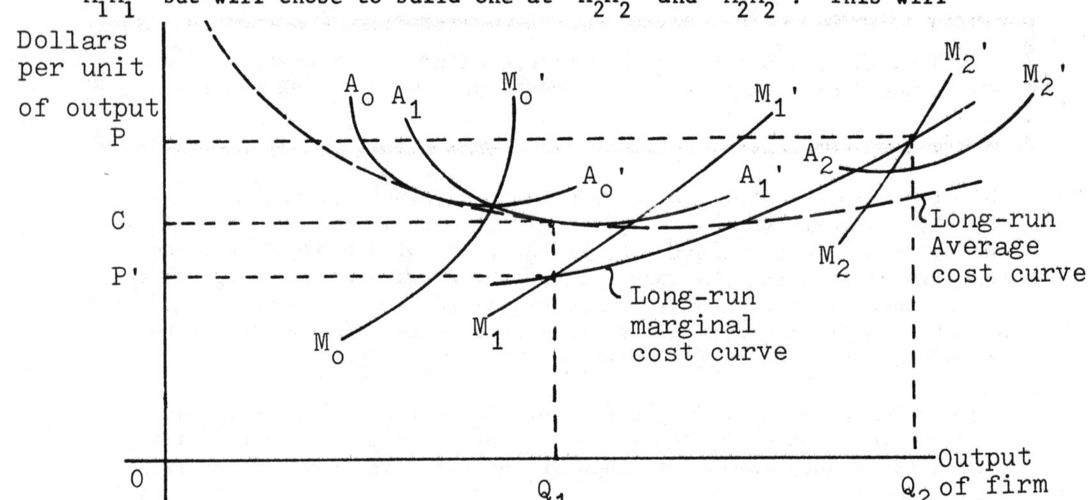

give the plant the maximum attainable profit. The maximum profit will be obtained by producing at an output rate and with a plant such that the long-run marginal cost is equal to price at the point where the short run marginal cost of the plant is equal to price. This occurs at price OP and quantity OQ_2.

An automobile manufacturer produces identical cars (A) using two inputs, capital (K) and labor (L). The production function which characterizes this process is:

$$A = \begin{cases} 20K & \text{if } K \le \tfrac{1}{2}L \\ 6K + 7L & \text{if } \tfrac{1}{2}L < K \le 3L \\ 25L & \text{if } 3L < K \end{cases}$$

(The isoquants representing automobile production should be drawn with K on the vertical axis and L on the horizontal axis.)

Assume the price of capital P_K = \$15 /unit and the price of labor P_L = \$20./unit.

a. Derive the graph of the automobile plant's total cost curve.
b. Does the plant face constant marginal cost, increasing marginal cost or decreasing marginal cost?

Solution: An isoquant is a curve which represents all possible efficient combinations of inputs capable of producing a certain output level. An isoquant line is similar to an indifference curve in that all the points on the same line are equally feasible, however, we can assign various levels of output to the isoquant, while we can't assign specific numbers to the indifference curves. Given the production function, one can derive the isoquant pertaining to any level of output.

First, draw the shape of the isoquants by looking at the production function. From the first constraint, A = 20K, if $K \le \tfrac{1}{2}L$, we plot points on the line $K = \tfrac{1}{2}L$ or $L = 2K$. We do the same for $A = 25L$, i.e. if $3L < K$, plotting points satisfying $3L = K$. If K lies somewhere between these points, we use the constraint $6K + 7L$, if $\tfrac{1}{2}L \le K \le 3L$. Next we pick values for "A" (output) and substitute them into each of the constraints. The calculations will result in the following figure.

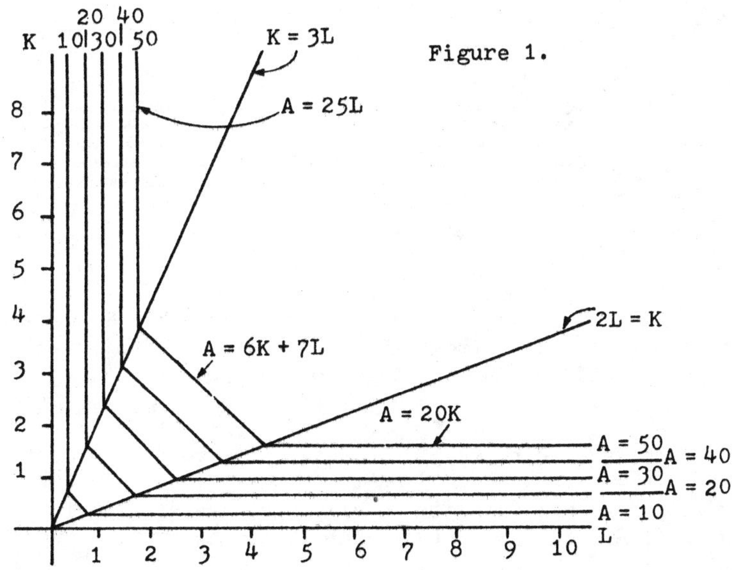

Figure 1.

To derive total cost curve, first find the points of intersection between the isoquants and isocost curves. The isocost lines show the locus of different input combinations that can be purchased for specific cost levels. If we superimpose the isocost curves on the isoquant map we can graphically determine which combination of inputs will maximize the output for a given expenditure. These points are the equilibrium points. Equilibrium occurs in an economic model when supply equals demand so that both suppliers and demanders are willing and able to sell or buy the same quantity of goods. In this particular case of isoquants and isocosts, it is the same analogy. Equilibrium occurs when the isoquant combinations of inputs (supply) capable of producing a given output (supply) intersects with the isocost curve which shows input combinations that can be purchased (demanded) for specific cost levels. The firm should pick that point on the isocost curve which is on the highest isoquant, where the isocost curve is tangent to the isoquant. From our previous graph and the new isocost curves we see on the graph below where our lines intersect.

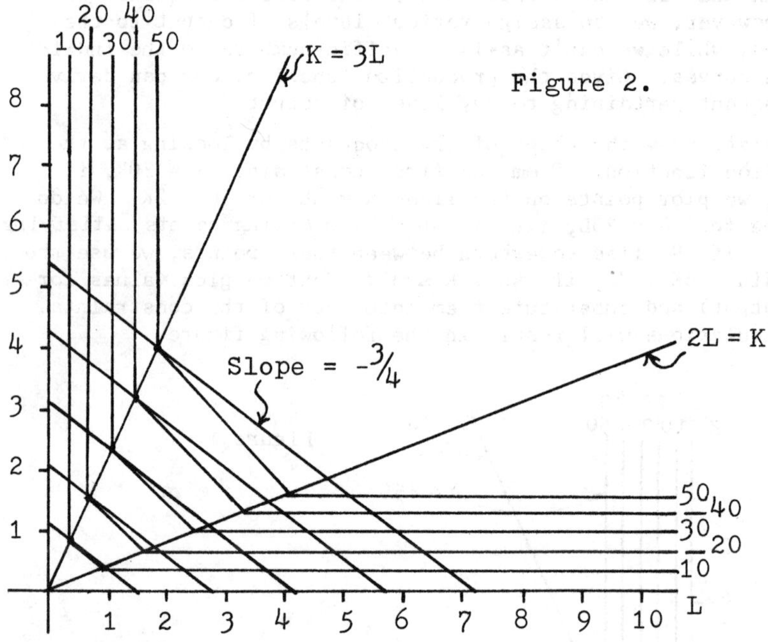

The isocost lines have a slope of -3/4 which is determined by multiplying \$15/unit times labor and adding \$20/unit times capital, which equals 15K + 20L = A, then solving for L:

$$L = \frac{A}{20} - \frac{15K}{20} = \frac{A}{20} - \frac{3}{4}K.$$

Since we wish to graph the total cost curve, we must plot on one axis the total cost and on the other output. To obtain total cost we substitute each of the values of the equilibrium points into the 15K + 20L equation. The following graph shows the results.

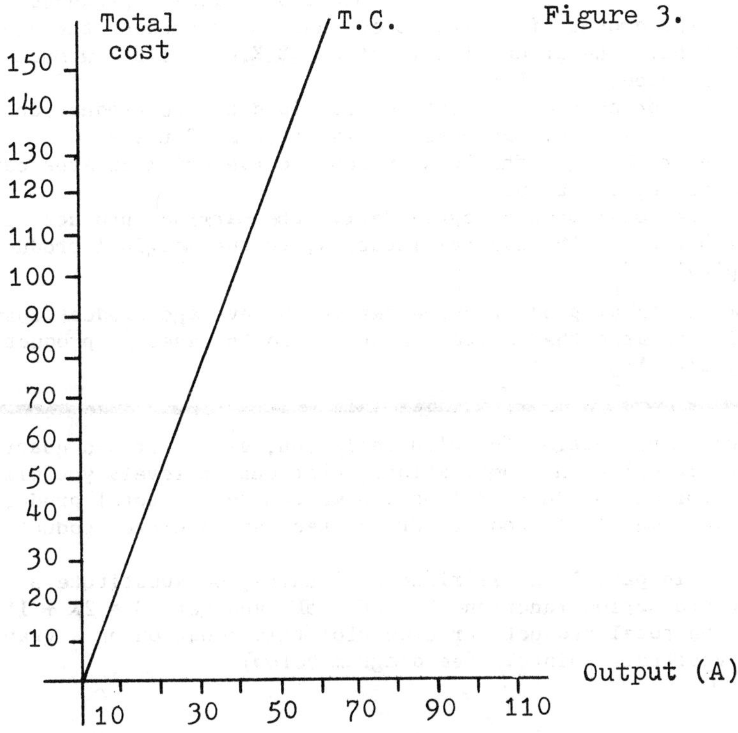

The equilibrium values are found by combining the equations whose lines intersected, A = 25L and K = 3L. Since L = A/25 and K = 3L, K = 3A/25 . Thus (3A/25, A/25) are the points we are looking for. Substituting then into 15K + 20L = total cost, we get

$$\frac{45A}{25} + \frac{20A}{25} = \frac{65A}{25} .$$

Now we tabulate the equation

$$\frac{65A}{25} = \text{T.C.}$$

for different values of output A (See table below).

B. The plant faces constant marginal costs since the total cost curve is a straight line with a constant slope of 2.6. Marginal Cost (MC) =

A =	10	20	30	40	50
T.C.	26	52	78	104	130
M.C.	-	26/10	26/10	26/10	26/10

Note that when output increases by 10, total costs always go up by the same amount, 26. This shows that the slope is constant and that average cost per unit (Total Costs/Total Units) = Marginal Costs.

• **PROBLEM 5-16**

Suppose that a building is produced using two inputs, capital and labor. Let B represent the amount of building produced, K represent the amount of capital used, and L represent the amount of labor used. The production function, B(K,L) tells how much B will be produced, [B = B(K,L)].

Let the production process be described by the production function B = 2K + 5L. Suppose L is fixed at 3 units

a) Derive graphically the total product curve which relates capital inputs, K, to output B.

b) From the total product curve derive the marginal product curve which relates the capital input, K, to the marginal product of capital, MP_K .

c) From the total product curve derive the average product curve which relates the capital input, K, to the average product of capital, AP_K .

Solution: A production function tells you, given certain quantities of inputs in different combinations, what output levels you will obtain. For any production function we can derive total product (TP) curves, marginal product (MP) curves, and average product (AP) curves.

Since in part A, L is fixed at 3 units, we substitute 3 for L into the production function B = 2K + 5L and get B = 2K + 15. To draw the total product curve we plot this equation on a graph by picking arbitrary points. (See diagram below)

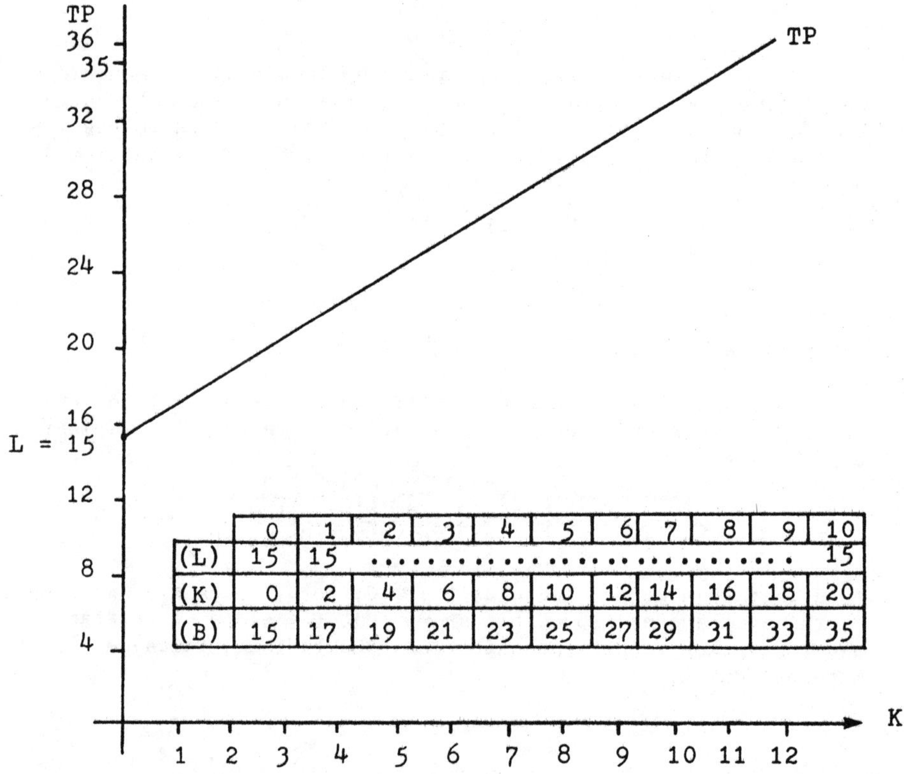

The marginal product curve is derived by dividing the change in total product by the change in quantity and plotting the results. Since labor is fixed at 3 units and K increases at a constant rate, total product increases at a constant rate and marginal product remains constant, thus appearing horizontal. The average product curve is derived by dividing total product (B) by capital (K).

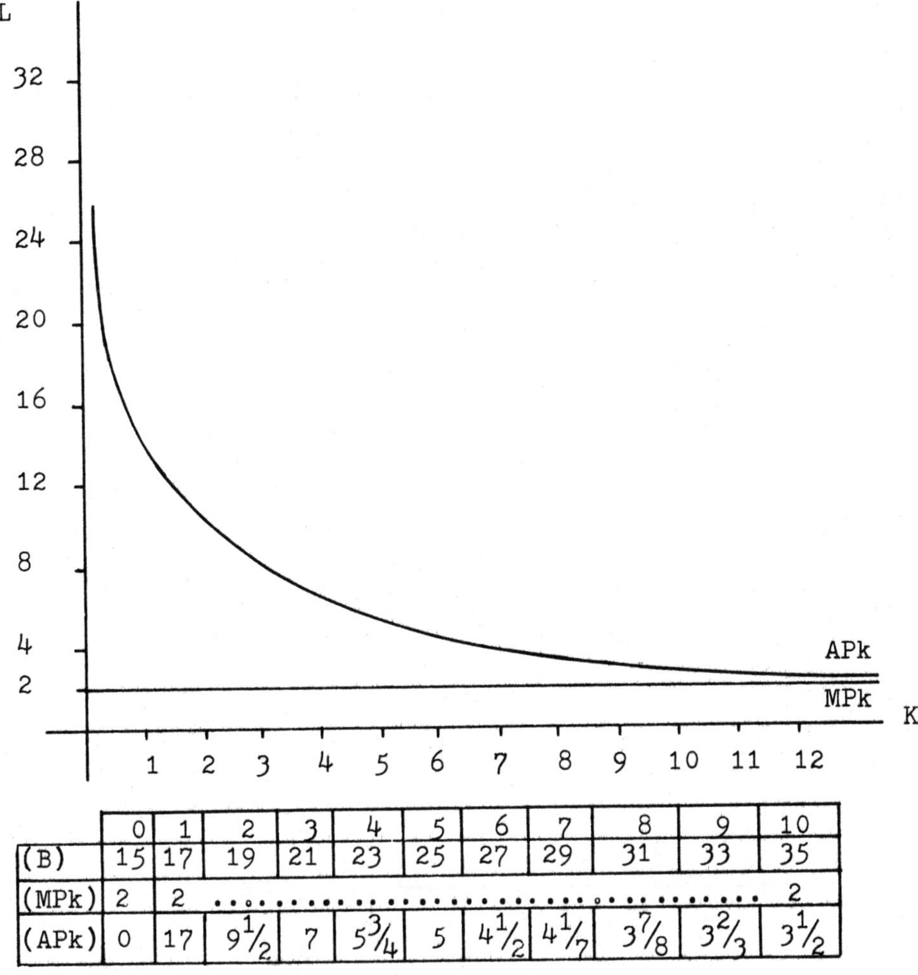

	0	1	2	3	4	5	6	7	8	9	10
(B)	15	17	19	21	23	25	27	29	31	33	35
(MPk)	2	2	....								2
(APk)	0	17	$9\frac{1}{2}$	7	$5\frac{3}{4}$	5	$4\frac{1}{2}$	$4\frac{1}{7}$	$3\frac{7}{8}$	$3\frac{2}{3}$	$3\frac{1}{2}$

See the above graph and computations.

Note: The Average Product line approaches but never intersects the marginal product line.

• PROBLEM 5-17

Given production function $x = f(a)$ where x is the number of units produced and a is the factor input, prove the firm obtains the largest physical output when the marginal product curve cuts the average product curve at its maximum.

Solution: The marginal product is the derivative of the production function, i.e., MP (marginal product) = dx/da . The average product is the number of units of x produced divided by the number of units it took to make them, i.e., AP (average product = x/a . The problem asks us to prove that MP = $df/da = x/a$ = AP when AP is a maximum.

To find the maximum of the function $g(a) \equiv x/a$, take the derivative of $g(a)$ with respect to a and set equal to zero.

$$\frac{dg}{da} = \frac{a\frac{dx}{da} - x\frac{da}{da}}{a^2} = 0 \ .$$

Multiplying both sides by a^2 we get $a\frac{dx}{da} - x = 0$. Add x to both sides then divide by a to get $dx/da = x/a$. This is what we wanted to prove. We know this point is a maximum because the average product curve is concave downward as shown below.

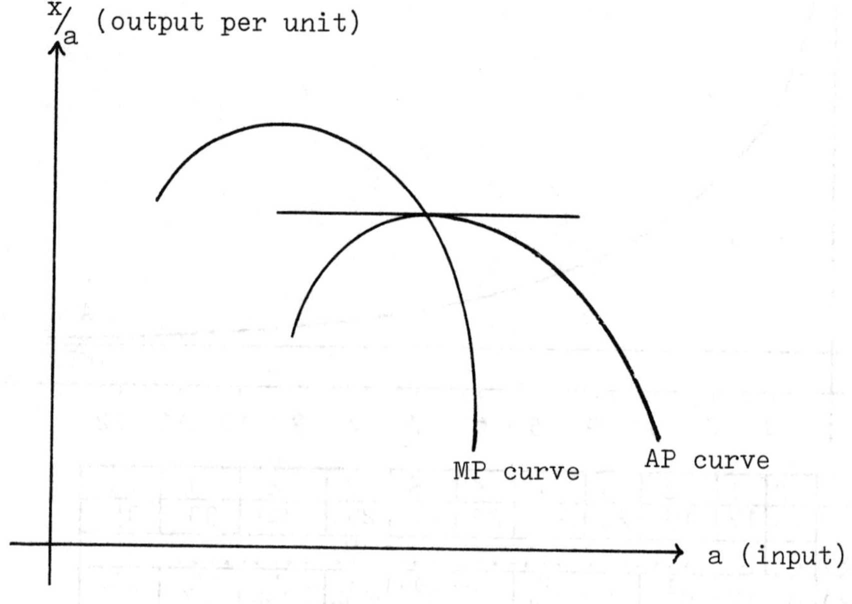

• **PROBLEM** 5-18

There are three regions of production in the theory of perfect competition:
a) decreasing costs, b) constant costs and c) increasing costs. Show that, in the case of b), the average cost curve is a rectangular hyperbola. Then consider the following problem. Miss Eija Heino, an up-and-coming artist has fixed overheads at $2,000 per year (studio, agency, etc.) and variable costs are always $120 per picture. Graph the curve showing average cost per painting when a variable number x are done per year.

Solution: When costs are constant, the cost function assumes the form

$$C = ax + b \ , \qquad (1)$$

where "b" are fixed costs and variable costs are "ax". If we graph this function we obtain a straight line with slope "a" passing through the points

$$(0,b) \ (\frac{-b}{a} \ , \ 0) \ .$$

Figure 1.

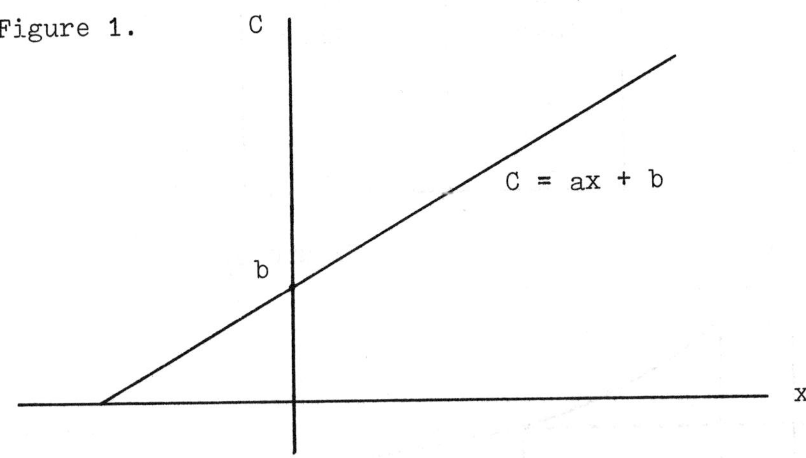

Next, we find the average cost

$$AC = \frac{C}{x} = \frac{ax + b}{x} = a + \frac{b}{x} \ . \qquad (2)$$

As x increases to infinity $b/x \to 0$ and average cost falls continuously towards a. The function (2) is a hyperbola with asymptote a.

Figure 2.

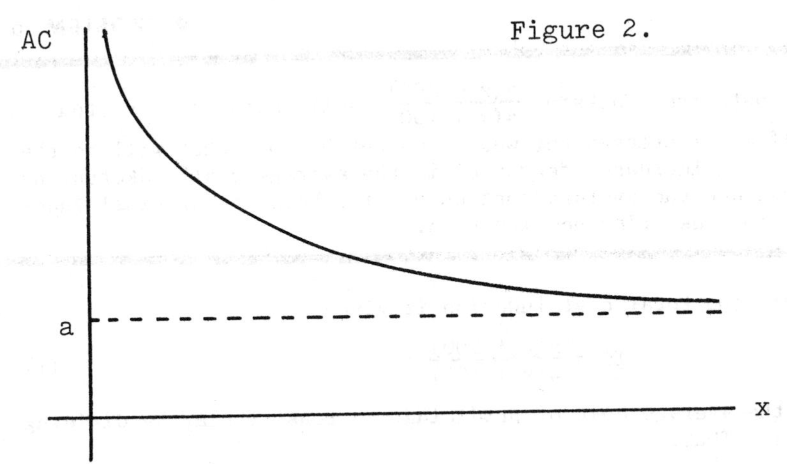

Finally, we graph the average cost curve of Miss Eija Heino. The fixed cost is $b = 2000$ and the average cost is $a = \$120$.

Tabulating a few points,

X	$120 + \frac{2,000}{X}$
10	320
100	140
1,000	122
2,000	121
10,000	120.2
.	.
.	.
.	.
.	120

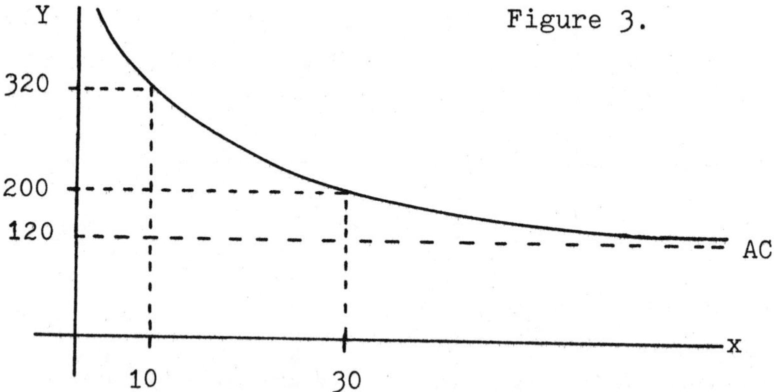

Figure 3.

• PROBLEM 5-19

> It costs Mrs. Jackson $\frac{x(x + 200)}{4(x + 100)}$ dollars to make x tons of clay. If she increases her weekly output by 15%, what will be the corresponding increase (decrease) in the average cost? Sketch the total cost and the average cost curves for both the original function and the resulting new function.

Solution: The total cost function is given by

$$TC = \frac{x(x + 200)}{4(x + 100)} . \qquad (1)$$

We find the average cost of producing x tons of clay by dividing (1) by x. Thus,

$$AC = \frac{x + 200}{4(x + 100)} . \qquad (2)$$

Assume now that Mrs. Jackson increases her output by 15%. Then her total cost curve becomes

$$TC_1 = \frac{1.15x(1.15x + 200)}{4(x + 100)} \quad (3)$$

and her average cost curve becomes

$$AC_1 = \frac{1.15x + 200}{4(1.15x + 100)} \quad . \quad (4)$$

We now graph (1) and (2) and superimpose our adjusted totals (3) and (4) in:

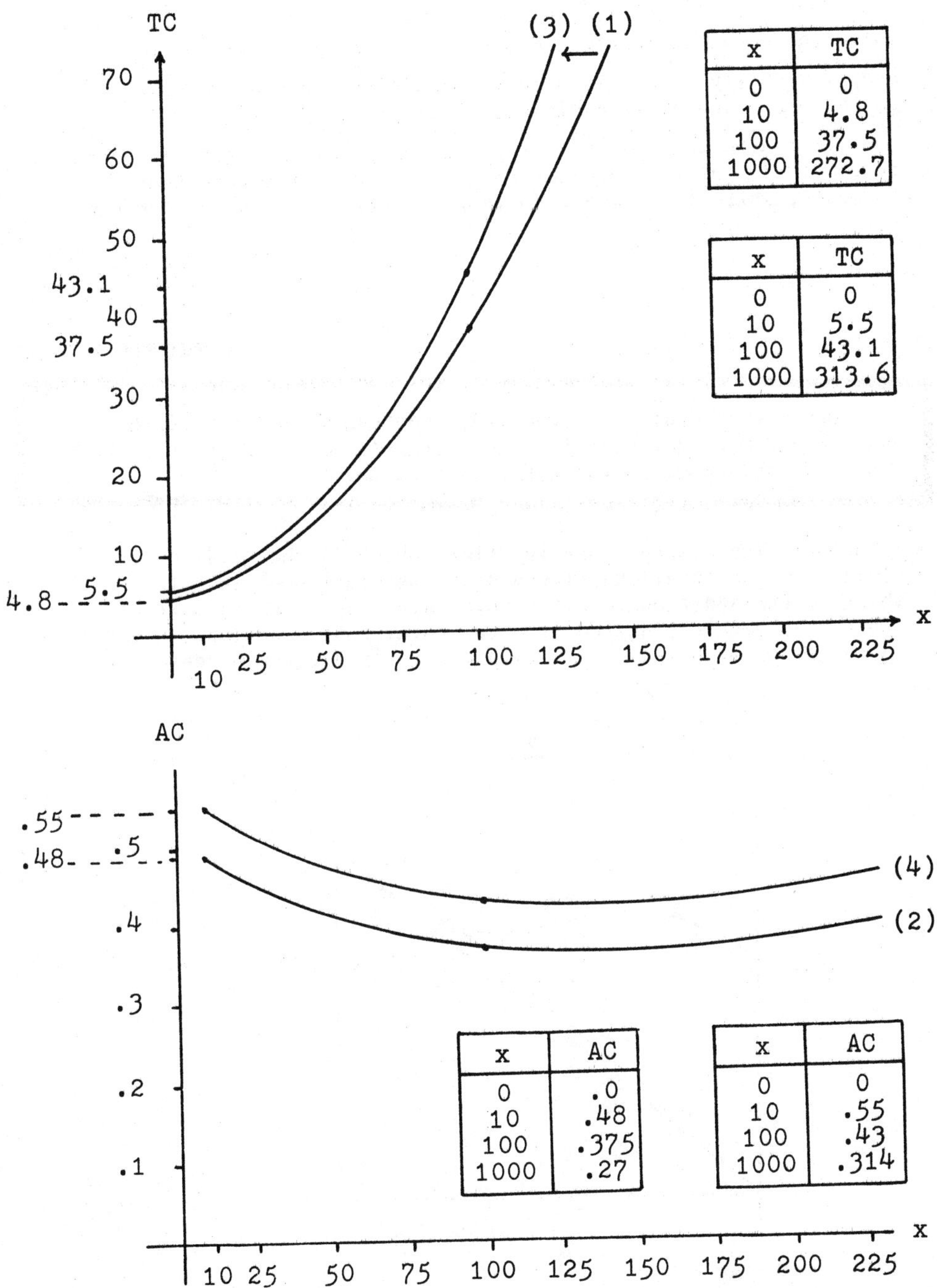

x	TC
0	0
10	4.8
100	37.5
1000	272.7

x	TC
0	0
10	5.5
100	43.1
1000	313.6

x	AC
0	.0
10	.48
100	.375
1000	.27

x	AC
0	0
10	.55
100	.43
1000	.314

We see from this comparison that the new total cost curve is growing increasingly farther away from the original one as the quantity of tons of clay increase. This shows that the slope of curve (3) is growing faster than that of (1), thus the cost is increasing at a faster rate.

In comparing the two average cost curves, we notice that they are almost parallel. The curve (2), in $y = Mx + b$ form, where

$$X = \frac{x + 200}{4(x + 100)} \quad \text{is} \quad Y = x,$$

while the curve (4) has the equation $y = 1.15x_0$. Although the slopes visually appear identical, we see that since M is equal to the slope, there is a difference of .15.

In conclusion the total costs corresponding to the increased input of 15%, will be greater and rise at a faster rate than formerly, while the average costs will increase at about the same rate.

• PROBLEM 5-20

Given the total cost function, show how we can derive the average and marginal cost functions graphically. (Hint: use the slope of tangencies to the total cost curve).

Solution: The average cost function, which is the total cost divided by the total quantity and the marginal cost function, which is the additional cost brought about by an extra unit of input, can both be derived from the total cost function. Refer to the diagrams below. The average cost is derived by calcula-

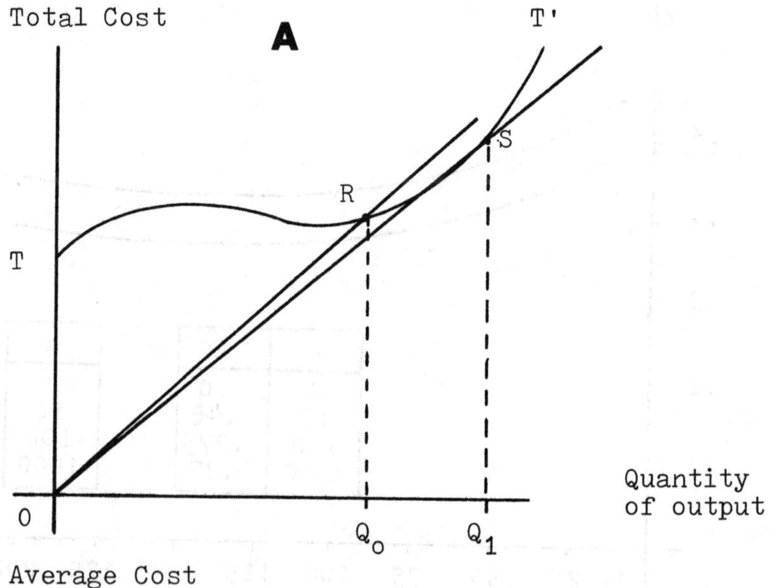

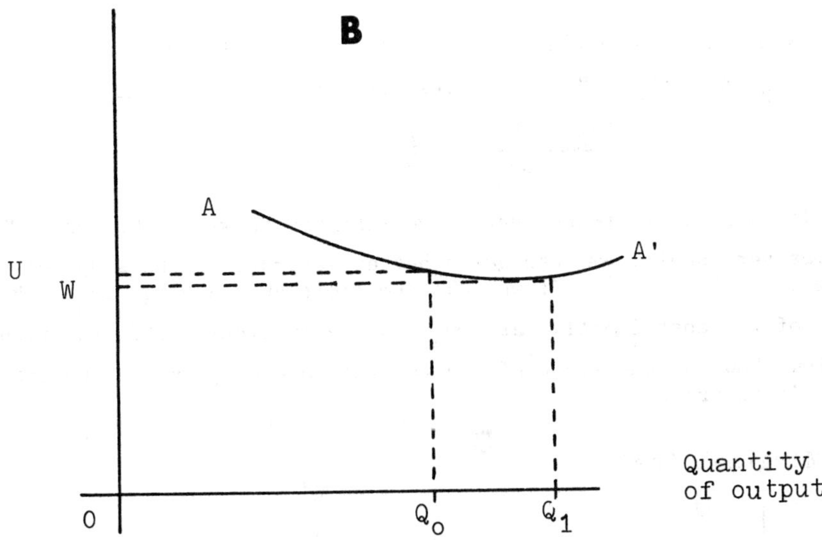

ting the value of the slope of a ray drawn from the origin to a particular output level on the total cost curve (TT'). In diagram "A," the average cost at output OQ_0 is the slope of line segment. We plot this slope on the vertical axis of panel "B" and get the segment OU for the same level of output OQ_0. If we follow this same procedure for each quantity desired on the total cost curve we will construct an Average Cost Curve as was done in panel "B". We see that increases in output result in decreases in average cost, until we reach a minimum at OQ. To the right of this point, as can be seen from panel "A," the slope begins to increase; therefore, average cost will begin to increase past this point. The figures below illustrates the derivation of the marginal cost function.

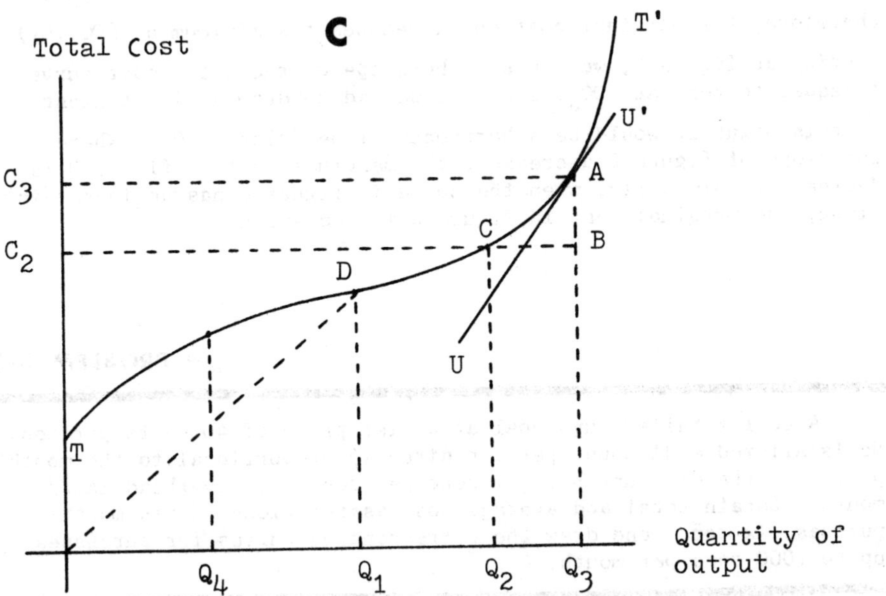

As we increase output from OQ_2 to OQ_3, total cost increases from OC_2 to OC_3. The extra cost per unit of output is

$$\frac{OC_3 - OC_2}{OQ_3 - OQ_2} = \frac{BA}{CB}$$

If OQ_2 is increased until the distance between OQ_2 and OQ_3 becomes very small, we can get a better estimate of the slope of tangent UU′ at A. If we take the limit approaching OQ_3, the slope of the cost function at OQ_3 is the marginal cost. The figure D below shows us the slope of the tangent to each point on the cost curve in figure C.

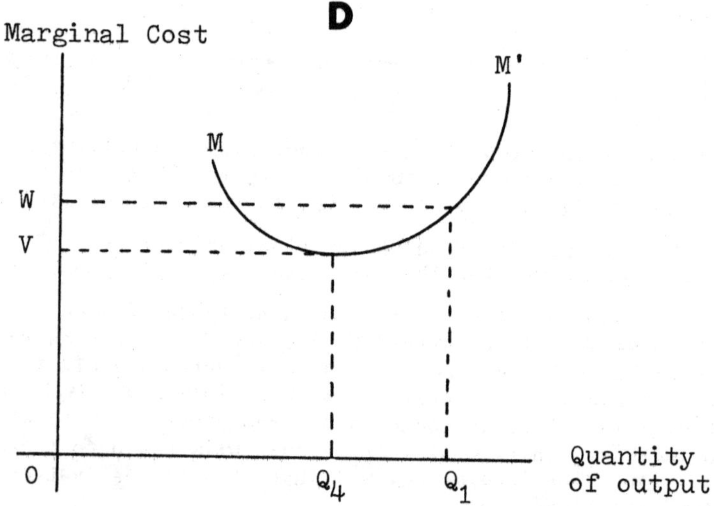

The slope of the tangent in figure C at OQ_4 is a minimum; therefore, the marginal cost curve reaches its minimum at (OQ_4, OV). Looking at figure C, we can see the slope of the total cost curve is equal to zero at OQ_4, since if we had to draw a line tangent to this point it would be a horizontal line (slope = 0). Where the slope of figure C decreases, the marginal cost in figure D is decreased. Similarly, when the curve in figure C has an increasing slope, the marginal cost in figure D is increasing.

• PROBLEM 5-21

A coal retailer buys coal at a list price of 40 cents per ton. He is allowed a discount per ton directly proportional to the monthly purchase, the discount being 1 cent per ton. His overhead is $50 per month. Obtain total and average cost as functions of his monthly purchase (x tons) and draw the corresponding curves for purchases up to 1000 tons per month.

Solution: Conceptually the retailer's total cost is

variable cost + fixed cost - discount,

where fixed cost is synonymous with overhead. Let x be the variable representing the amount of tons the retailer purchases during one particular month. The variable cost is therefore 0.40x dollars. The overhead is given as $50. For every ton purchased, there will be a 1 cent discount, i.e., if x tons are purchased the discount is (0.01)x dollars. The total cost function is (TC is total cost)

$$TC = 50. + 0.40x - 0.01x$$
$$= 50. + 0.39x \quad \text{(in dollars)} .$$

This is a straight line with slope 0.39 and y-intercept of 50. It is sketched below:

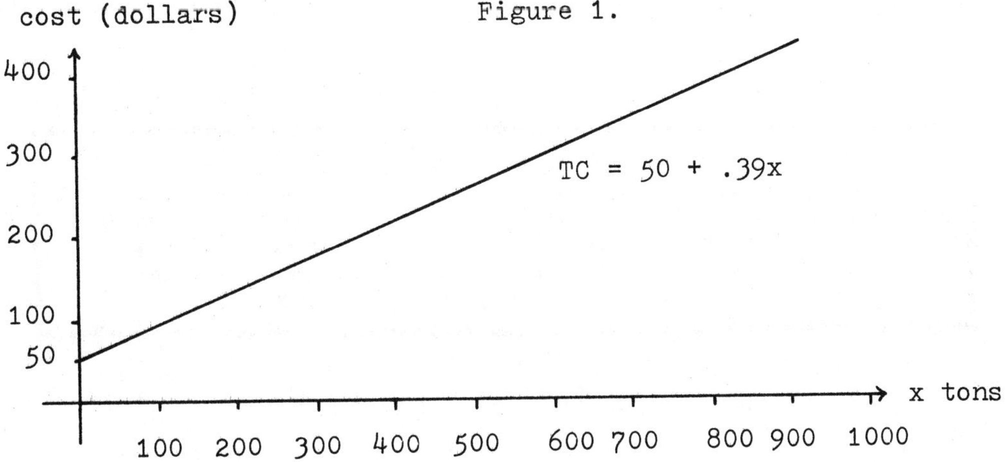

The average cost of purchasing x tons is the total cost of purchasing x tons, 50 + .39x divided by the amount x tons

$$AC = \frac{TC}{x} = \frac{50}{x} + .39 \quad \text{(dollars/ton)} .$$

Note that x cannot be zero since division by zero is not allowed. As x increases the average cost in dollars per ton decreases, never becoming less than or equal to 39 cents. For each value of x given in the graph below 100, 200, ... get the corresponding value for the average cost and construct a table.

x	100	200	300	400	500	600	700	800	900	1000	tons
AC	0.89	0.64	0.56	0.52	0.49	0.47	0.46	0.45	0.445	0.44	dollars

This curve approaches the y = $0.39 line, but will never cross it. The y = $0.39 line is called an asymptote. For large values of x, the average cost will be a little bit above 39 cents.

(Graph on the following page.)

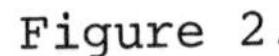

Figure 2.

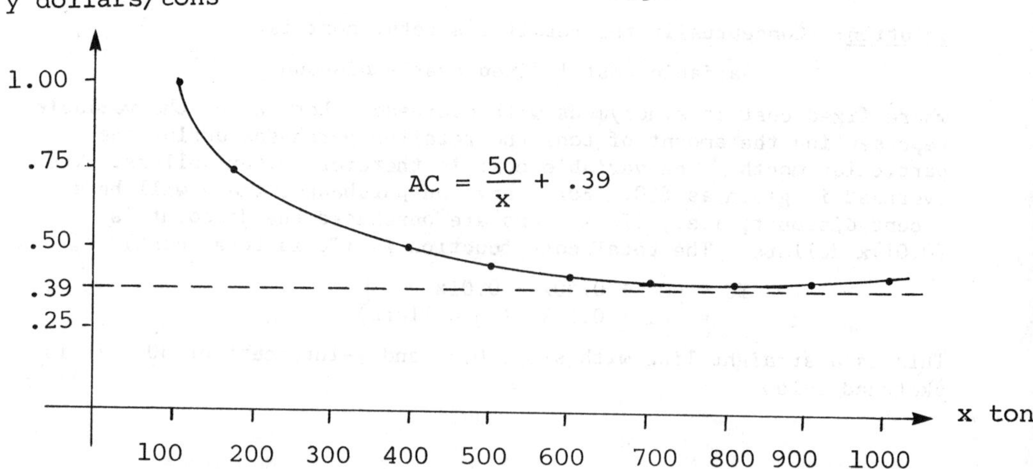

• **PROBLEM 5-22**

> **Draw a diagram showing how price could drop below the lowest point on the average total unit cost curve, and indicate the loss the firm would suffer. Explain by means of a diagram why a manufacturer may remain in business even though he cannot sell his output for the full cost of producing it. What will determine whether or not it is worth his while to quit entirely?**

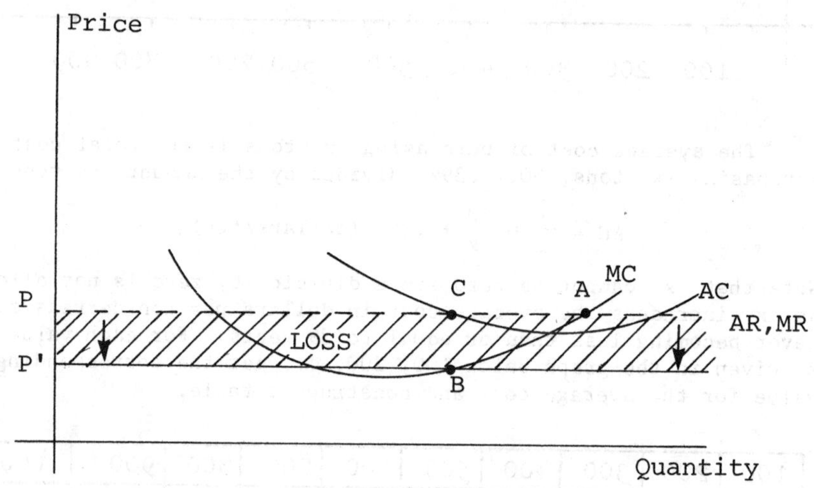

Solution: With reference to the above diagram the optimal level of output is determined by the intersection of the marginal cost and marginal revenus curves. With the price set at P, the point A satisfies this condition since in a competitive firm such as this one, price equals marginal revenue and average revenue MC = MR at point A. If price drops to P' then the new optimum level will be point B. At this point we see that the average cost curve is above the average revenue curve which results in a loss to the firm. Since we are now producing at point B, and at the same quantity level at the old price the output would have been producing point C (Quantity × AC = output) the loss incurred by the firm is the difference between the two points. The firm will not quit here since this decision would bring about larger losses. Fixed costs, (depreciation, interest, etc.) must be paid if production ceases, therefore, as long as price is at least as high as marginal cost, a firm will continue to produce. Each additional unit of output contributes something over and above variable cost to fixed cost. The length of time this can continue depends either on (1) how quickly it can terminate its fixed costs or (2) how long it can maintain a loss without going bankrupt.

In the diagram below we see that at price P'' we would close down our firm since we no longer pay off any of our fixed costs.

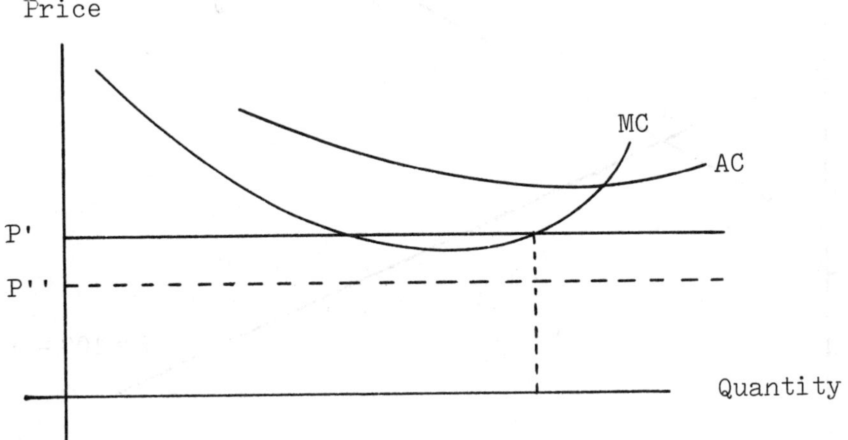

• PROBLEM 5-23

> Suppose that you are the owner of a metals producing firm that has an unregulated monopoly. After considerable experimentation and research, you find that your marginal cost can be approximated by a straight line, MC = 60 + 2Q, where MC is marginal cost (in dollars) and Q is output. Moreover, suppose that the demand curve for your product is p = 100 - Q, where p is the product price and Q is the output. If you want to maximize profit, what output should you choose?

Solution: Under perfect competition the profit maximizing output is the one at which price equals marginal cost. In a monopoly position, the firm will maximize profit if it sets its output rate at the point at which marginal cost equals marginal revenue. Since the monopolist is the only firm producing a product in a given market, anyone demanding that product will have to buy it from him. He controls the consumer demand in the market and will want to obtain the maximum profit that can be obtained. He will not produce at an output level where marginal revenue exceeds marginal cost because by increasing output he can still increase profit.

The extra revenue obtained will be greater than the extra cost. Similarly, he will not produce at an output where marginal cost exceeds marginal revenue, since profit can be increased by reducing output; the decrease in cost will exceed the decrease in revenue. In this problem the marginal cost curve is the linear function MC = 60 + 2A, where Q is output.

In the demand curve, p = 100 - Q, p is price and Q is output. Plotting the two curves you get:

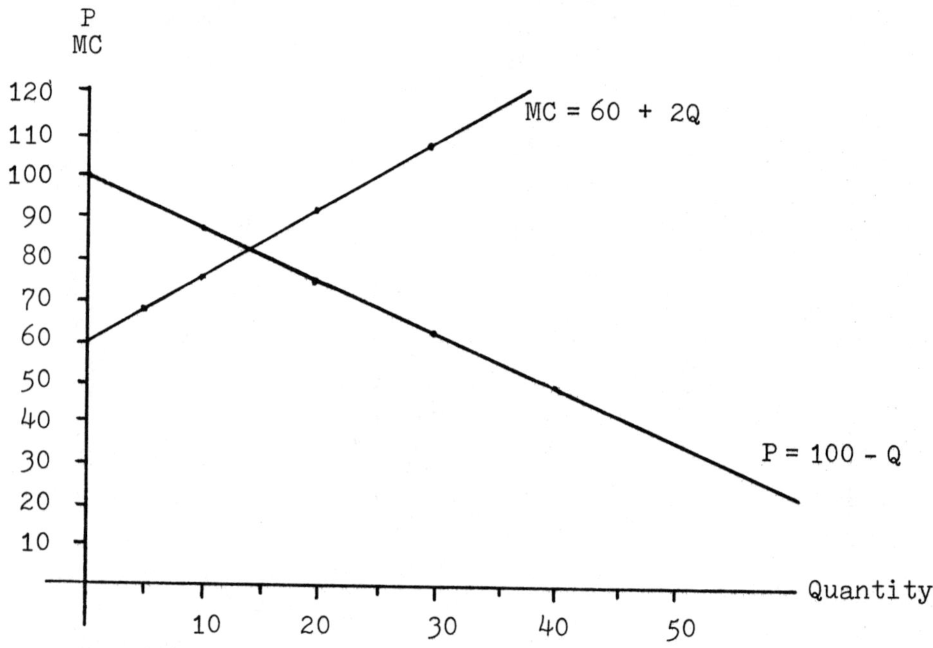

From the demand curve derive the total revenue and then the marginal revenue curves needed for solving this equilibium.

Quantity	Price	Total revenue		Marginal revenue
0	100	0		0
9	91	819	819-0/9	= 91
10	90	900	900-819/1	= 81
20	80	1600	1600-900/10	= 70
30	70	2100	2100-1600/10	= 50
40	60	2400	2400-2100/10	= 30
50	50	2500	2500-2400/10	= 10

We can now plot the marginal revenue curve, and see the intersection of that and the marginal revenue curve to get the output which the monopolistic firm will want to produce. The approximate answer, as shown by the graph is Q = 10. We just showed that the marginal revenue at Q = 10 is 81. The marginal cost (MC) at Q = 10, is consequently 80, from the equa-

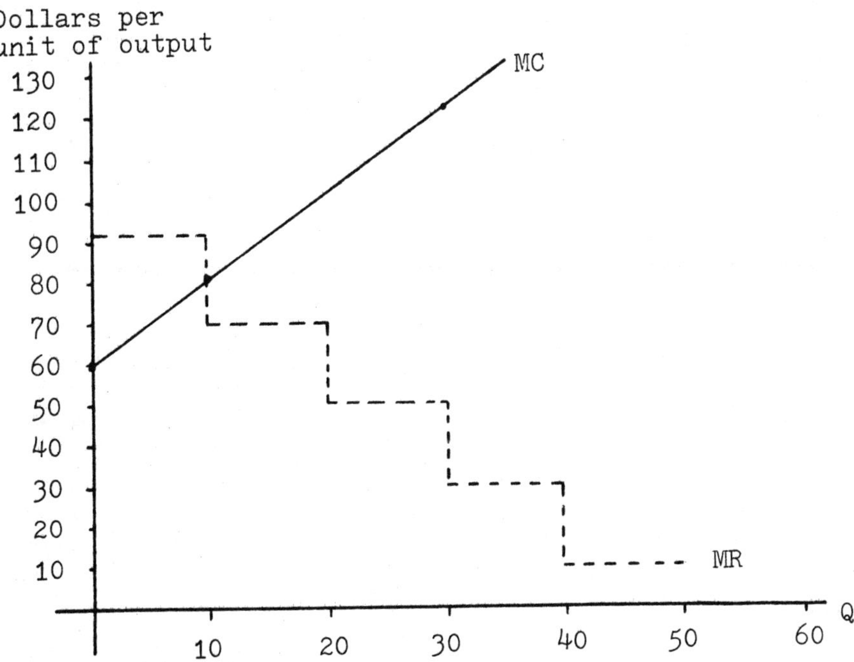

tion MC = 60 + 2Q . This satisfies our requirement

Q	MC
9	60 + 18 = 78
10	60 + 20 = 80
11	60 + 22 = 82
20	60 + 40 = 100
30	60 + 60 = 120
.	.
.	.
.	.

of MR = MC at equilibrium ($80 \approx 81$).

• PROBLEM 5-24

Marlowe Department Store is experiencing declining sales in many of its departments. It is located in a section of town that was previously quite prosperous but is presently deteriorating. Two miles down Main Street, the Elysium Department Store provides stiff competition, not because it offers many bargains but precisely because it does not. The Elysium is a "prestige" store.

Marlowe's management intends to raise the store to the prestige category.

Many departments are being upgraded and some, like the hardware army surplus department, will be eliminated.

More recently, the stereo department has had a poor sales record being left with $350,000 worth of high-priced, very advanced equipment in inventory by the middle of January and selling only $40,000 all of last year. Management is considering two options (1) markdown the price of the systems by as much as 50% for a Washington's Birthday sale, (2) have gradual sales with less drastic markdowns. The first option will mean a loss. The second option may be equally disastrous since the "latest" in stereos will reach the market in September, perhaps making many of the present units obsolete.

Keeping in mind that Marlow Department Store must also contend with local stereo shops, what decision should the store make on its stereo department?

Solution: MARKET THEORY APPROACH.

Classic market theory may be useless in deciding what to do here. Very expensive, well-equipped stereos are, like diamonds and fur coats, "status" items; the average, middle-class economical buyers are not running to the store in droves requesting these items.

This example illustrates the distinction between a mathematical model and the reality it claims to describe. The demand curve in the perfect market is downward sloping. A drop in price will result in increased demand.

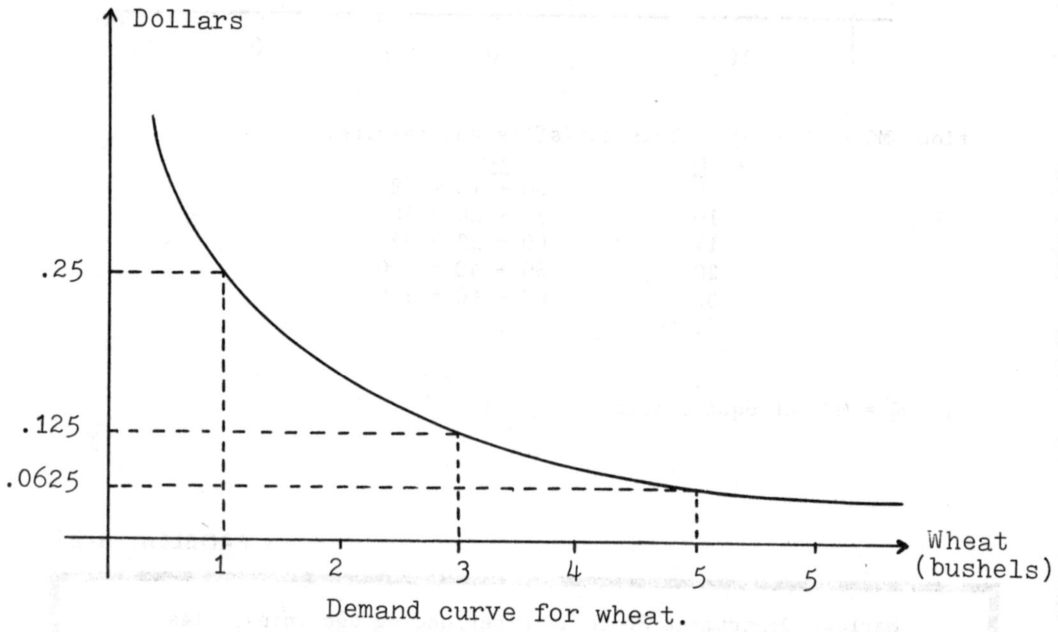

Demand curve for wheat.

In a perfect market where wheat is sold, the demand curve may look like the one shown above. At a price of 25¢ per bushel, buyers are willing to purchase 1 bushel. If the price were to drop to 12½¢, 3 bushels would be demanded at that price. The lower price, the more quantity demanded.

This is not necessarily true in status commodities. The price of a fur coat may be associated with its quality, the higher the price, the higher its quality. This is a matter of product differentiation. One bushel of wheat, as far as most people are concerned, is just the same as another. A farmer may sell his bushels at a higher price than the equilibrium price and get away with it by convincing his buyers that the wheat was grown on holy land; this farmer has found a way to differentiate his product.

Beyond a certain point, stereos, like cars or furs, become status items. A buyer may purchase an expensive unit, say one priced at $3,500, simply because he or she believes that it must sound better than a unit priced at $850. He may stay away from lower-priced units because he associates price with quality. The demand curve may not be downward sloping at all. The decision of Marlowe's management to lower prices to liquidate a large portion of its inventory is founded on the assumption of a downward sloping demand curve -- lower prices and the quantity demanded will be increased. This may be true for wheat. It may not be true for high-priced stereos.

Should the store liquidate its inventory via the Washington Birthday Sale and incur a frightening loss, what will be the fate of the stereo department? The "upgrading" of the store requires that it have a prosperous stereo department. A hasty sale may retard its growth and should not be undertaken. The market environment is not such that we may use the classic market model.

SYSTEMS APPROACH

The miserable performance of the stereo department may be more of a symptom than part of the disease. The store may be in a bad location, and no amount of "upgrading" may help. A decision to move the store to a new location and presently ignore the performance of each department would be based on the decision criterion: upgrade the store to the level of Elysium Department Store. This is a long-term goal whereas the liquidation of inventory is a short-term goal. Given that management consider upgrading very important, it should not get tangled in departmental changes until a decision is made on the environment in which the store will operate. The stereo department problem has now been placed in a new perspective. If management decided not to move, then a gradual sales, with modest discounts is preferable because a buyer may purchase a unit originally priced at $3,500 if it is discounted by $150 to $3,350; if the department offers a 50% discount, the unit will sell at $1,750; the buyer might think there is something wrong with the units.

This problem illustrates the concept of the demand for a luxury good is an exception to the downward sloping demand curve in the perfect market. For a certain price range, the demand for the product may increase with price.

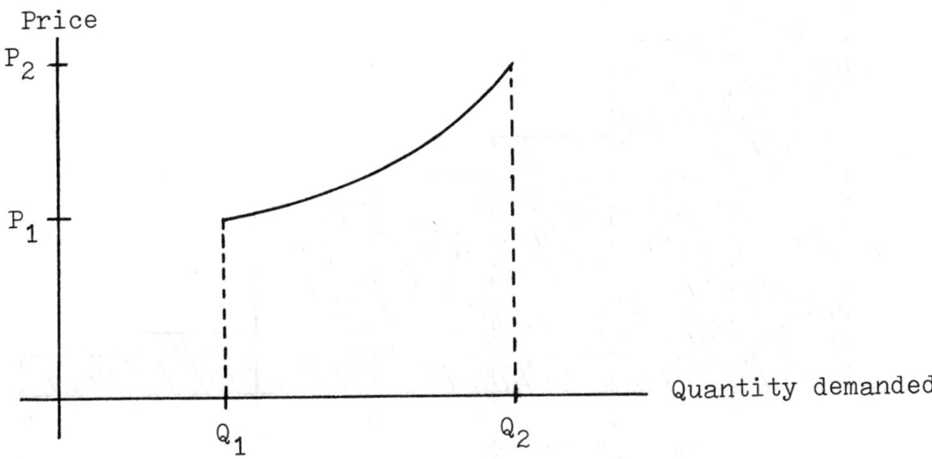

MACROECONOMICS

PRODUCTION POSSIBILITIES FRONTIERS

• PROBLEM 5-25

The table below shows the number of units produced at the given employment level.

Workers employed	Units produced
0	0
1	900
2	1450
3	1850
4	2200
5	2500
6	2600
7	2675

Construct a bar graph that shows the marginal physical product on the vertical axis and the employment level on the horizontal axis.

Solution: The marginal physical product is defined as the number of units added per worker, per input, to the total output on the addition of one extra worker.

The first worker adds 900 units to total output; the second worker adds 1450 - 900 = 550 units; the third worker adds 1850 - 1450 = 400 units; the fourth adds 2200 - 1850 = 350; and so on.

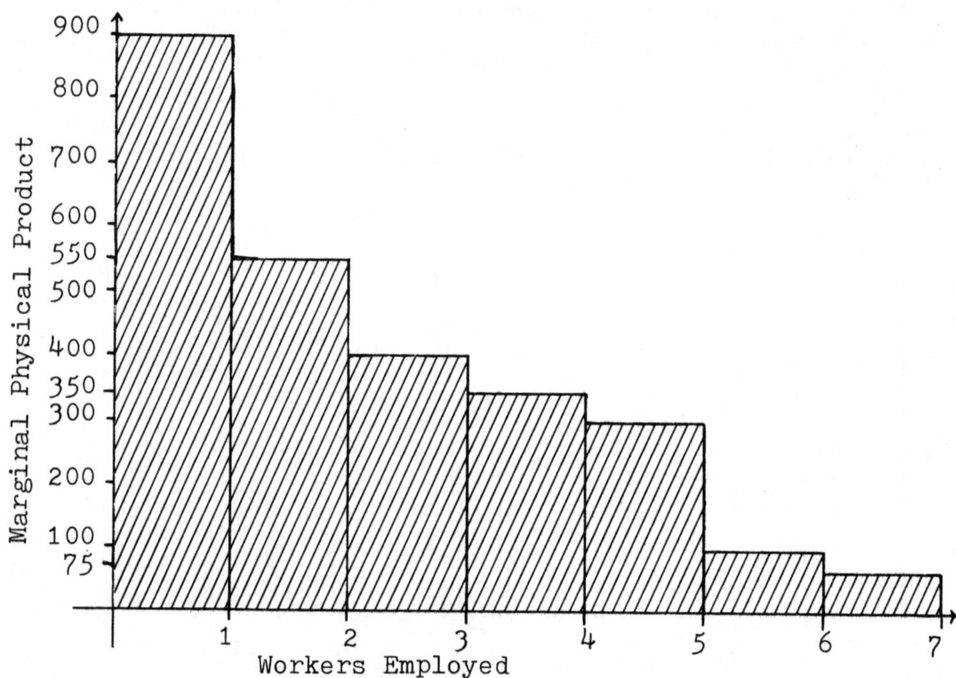

The last worker adds 2675 - 2600 = 75 units to the total output. Associated with every level of employment we have a number called the marginal physical product as shown below.

Workers employed	Marginal-physical product
1	900 units
2	550 units
3	400 units
4	350 units
5	300 units
6	100 units
7	75 units

The bar graph is shown.

• PROBLEM 5-26

A country produces only two goods, food and clothing, using two factors of production, land and labor. The country has 1 million workers and 2 million acres. If all workers were employed in the clothing sector 1 million units of clothes would be produced and if they were employed in the food sector 1 million units of food would be produced. The production-possibility curve (P-P), is a straight line connecting these production choices. Four acres of land employed solely for food production bring ½ million units of food. Four acres of land used only for clothing production yields 2 million units of clothes. The production possibility curve is a straight line connecting these extreme production cases. Assuming that we may have some of the land and labor unemployed, what is the maximum number of goods (food + clothing) that can be produced, subject to the land and labor constraints?

Solution: What we are trying to do in this problem is known as optimization and the mathematical procedure used is called linear programming.

Graphically the labor constraint is shown below.

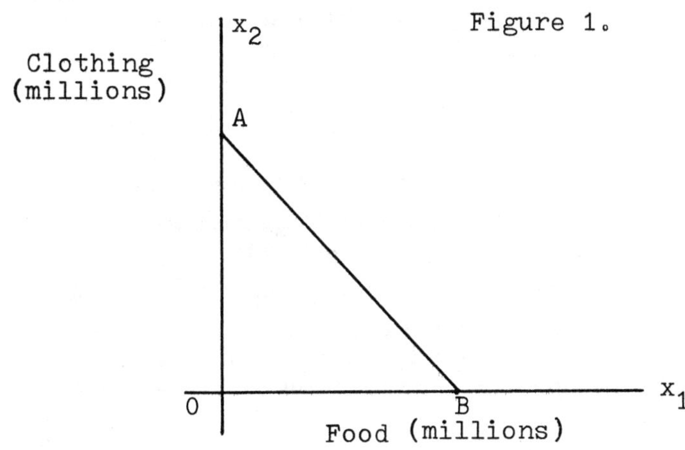

Figure 1.

The p-p frontier is the line AB as given in the problem. With 1 million workers we could produce these combinations of food and clothing. The line above has a slope of -1 and its equation is $X_2 = 1 - X_1$, or $X_1 + X_2 = 1$. Producing at any point inside triangle OAB means that we are not using all the labor that is available.

The land constraint is similarly sketched and its equation is given by $4X_1 + X_2 = 2$. Both constraints are sketched on the same set of axes below.

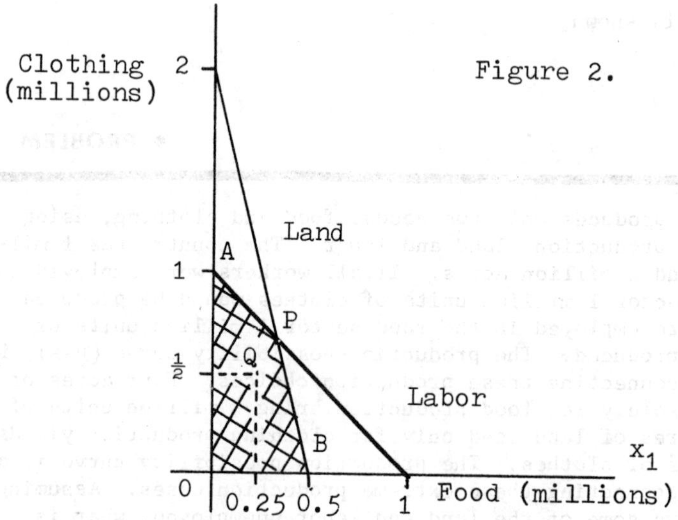

The shaded region represents the possible combinations of food and clothing that can be produced with the available land and labor. For example, Q above is the point (0.25,.5), i.e., 250,000 units of food and 500,000 units of clothing; these production levels can be reached with the available inputs. Any production combination inside this region or on the boundary can be made. Specifically, we want to maximize the sum of the outputs.

Mathematically our problem can be stated as follows:

maximize $X_1 + X_2$

subject to

$X_1 + X_2 \leq 1$ (labor constraint)

$4X_1 + X_2 \leq 2$ (land constraint)

and $X_1 \geq 0$, $X_2 \geq 0$ (no negative values are allowed).

This set of constraints is the shaded region shown before.

The procedure for solving this problem is called the simplex method and basically it ignores all the combinations inside the feasible region and just tests the corner-point solutions on the boundary.

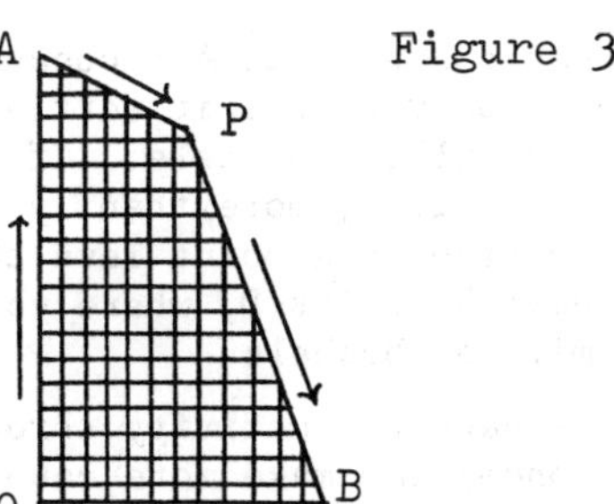

Figure 3.

From test point 0, go on to point A, then to point P and last to point B. Stop when the value of the objective function, $X_1 + X_2$ decreases. Point 0 is (0,0) no units of cloths or food are produced, the value of the objective function is 0 + 0 = 0. Point A is (0,1), here we produce 1 million units of clothes. Point P is the intersection of the lines $X_1 + X_2 = 1$ and $4X_1 + X_2 = 2$. Omitting the algebra involved (or the graphical manipulations) P is $(\frac{1}{3},\frac{2}{3})$, i.e., $X_1 = \frac{1}{3}$, $X_2 = \frac{2}{3}$. The total production is $\frac{1}{3} + \frac{2}{3} = 1$; this is not less than the previous value so we try point B. Point B is (0.5,0) and total production would then be 500,000 units of food. This is less than the previous value and so point P or point A can be chosen as the combination that gives the largest mixed output. For the sake of variation and not just numerical output the workers are capable of producint 333,333 units of food and 666,666 units of clothing.

• PROBLEM 5-27

A society produces only two goods, television sets and cabbages. Recent advances in agricultural technology have greatly increased the productivity of cabbages. What has happened to the production-possibility frontier?

Solution: The production-possibility frontier is a curve showing the combinations of products that can be produced by the economy. The production-possibility curve (p-p curve) shows we have finite resources to employ. If we want more TV sets we have to reduce cabbage production and vice versa. This situation is shown below.

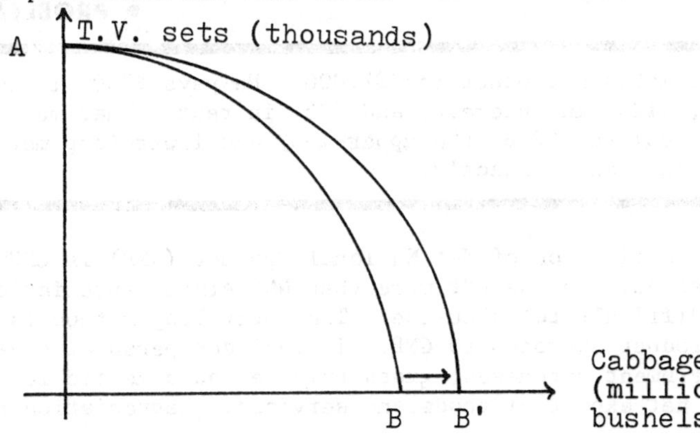

At most the economy can produce A thousand TV sets or B million bushels of cabbage, however at C it settles for producing y thousand TV sets and x million bushels. If the economy decides to produce more TV sets, i.e., more than y thousand, it must reduce cabbage production to a point less than x. The new combination would be shown by point D, where you produce y' thousand TV sets and x' million bushels.

Increasing cabbage productivity through improved technology means that the economy can make more cabbages than before using the same amount of resources. For example, if it were initially producing x million bushels with Q number of workers, after the improvements in technology we would be producing some amount x" greater than x still using the same number of workers.

The revised p-p curve has been shifted to the right as shown below. The economy is, now on the A-B' curve.

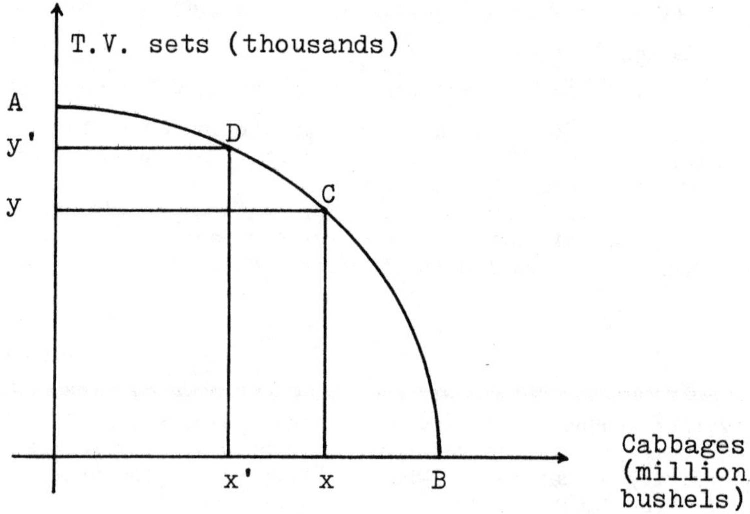

KEYNESIAN MACROECONOMICS

• PROBLEM 5-28

R. Crusoe makes a product for $1,000. He pays $750 in wages and materials, $125 in interest, and $75 in rent. What must his profit be? Calculate NNP by the upper-loop and lower-loop methods and show they must agree exactly.

Solution: The definition of Net National Product (NNP) is GNP minus depreciation. We use GNP more than NNP since depreciation is extremely difficult to calculate. The upper-loop method is the flow-of-product approach to GNP. It includes personal consumption, government purchases, gross private and domestic investment, and net export of goods and services. Depreciation has not yet been deducted from this sum. The lower loop, earning cost approach, includes wages and materials, interest, rent, and depreciation, income of unincorporated enterprises and corporate profits (before taxes). The basic difference between the two categories is that the upper-loop gross private investment makes no allowance for depreciation of capital. The lower-loop flow-of-product approach is also known as GNI (Gross National Income) = W (Wage and material costs) + T(Taxes) + D (Depreciation) + R (Rent).

Since we know that all costs of the product are $1,000, of which rent income and wages account for $750 + 125 + 75 = $950, depreciation must be $1,000 - 950 = $50. Since the total of the upper-loop equals GNP, by subtracting depreciation we can obtain the NNP. $1,000 (GNP) - 50 (depreciation) = $950 (NNP).

The price of products can be analyzed as cost (GNI) components or as income (GNP) components. The cost components are wages and materials, rent, interest and depreciation. The income components are sales to consumers, investors, government and foreign consumers. Since both the cost and sales components add up to the price, they are equal. GNP (the upper-loop method) = GNI (the lower-loop method), with a GNP of $1,000 and an NNP of $950 .

Flow of Product Approach		Earnings and Cost Approach	
1. Consumption		Wages and other employee supplements	$750
2. Investment		Net Interest	$125
3. Government purchases		Rent Income of persons	$75
4. Export of goods		Depreciation	$50
GNP	$1,000	GNI	$1,000
Less Depreciation	-$50	Less Depreciation	-$50
Net National Product	$950	Net National Product	$950

• PROBLEM 5-29

Ms. Edwards' disposable income (that is, her income after taxes have been paid) has risen from $19,000 to $20,000. Her expenditures have risen from $15,200 to $15,950.
1) What is her marginal propensity to consume?
2) What is her marginal propensity to save?

Solution: Marginal propensity to consume is the fraction of each additional unit of disposable income that will be spent or consumed. It is calculated by dividing the increase in consumption by the increase in income. The increase in consumption is $15,950 - $15,200 = $750. The increase in income is $1,000. Marginal propensity to consume is then 750/1000 or .75. This means that for each unit of increase in income .75 of it will be used for consumption. Note that we are not concerned with total income and consumption. We deal only with the actual increases or decreases in income and consumption when we work with marginal propensity to consume.

2. Marginal propensity to save is the fraction of a unit of increase in income that is saved rather than spent. Since an increase in income can be either spent or saved ,marginal propensity to save can be considered the difference between one unit of income increase and the fraction of it that will be spent (marginal propensity to consume). Therefore if 750/1000 or .75 of the unit of increase in income will be spent, 250/100 or .25 will be saved.

• PROBLEM 5-30

The equation for a particular consumption curve is C (consumption) = 200 + 2/3 D.I. (disposable income). Calculate the marginal propensity to consume (MPC). Find the equation for the savings (S) schedule and the marginal propensity to save.

Solution: The consumption schedule demonstrates the relationship between income and consumption. MPC = dC/d(DI), the derivative of C (consumption) with respect to D.I. (disposable income). This derivative represents the change in C for every 1-unit change in DI. The derivative of the equation for C, 200 + 2/3 DI, is 2/3. Therefore, MPC = 2/3 and every 1-unit (1 dollar) increase in disposable income causes an increase in consumption of 2/3 of a unit (67¢). Since income is either saved or spent,

Disposable Income = Savings + Consumption

$$DI = S + C$$

$$DI = S + 200 + 2/3\ DI .$$

Solving for S,

$$S = 1/3\ DI - 200 .$$

If disposable income is 600, savings is 1/3(600) - 200 = 200 - 200 = 0 . If DI is less than 600,people will not be able to save; they will have to use up what they have already saved.

The derivative of the savings equation, dS/d(DI), is MPS = 1/3. This checks with the principle that income is either spent or saved; each additional dollar of disposable income is either spent or saved. Therefore MPC + MPS = 1 dollar, since each represents the fraction of the dollar that is either spent or saved.

$$1 - MPC = MPS = 1 - 2/3 = 1/3 .$$

• PROBLEM 5-31

Let Y be GNP in billions of dollars. If $C = a + bY = 300 + 2/3Y$ and $I = \bar{I} = 200$, solve $Y = C + I = (300 + 2/3Y) + 200$ to get $Y^* = 500 + (1 - 2/3) = 1500$. Increase $\bar{I}$ by 1 and verify that Y^* goes up by 3. What is the multiplier?

Solution: The multiplier is defined as the number by which the change in investment must be multiplied in order to give the resulting change in income. The marginal propensity to consume tells out of a given dollar of income how much one is willing to spend on consumption. For example, in this problem the MPC = 2/3. This means a person will spend 2/3 and save 1/3 of every dollar. The change in income, using the multiplier, is equal to 1/1-MPC x change in investment. Substituting the numbers we get 1/1-2/3(1) = 3. This shows that a $1 increase in investment will stimulate the economy enough to generate three times the original input, or $3 in additional income.

$Y = C + I = 300 + 2/3\ Y + 200; \quad Y - 2/3\ Y = 500; \quad Y = \frac{500}{1-2/3}$ =1,500. This can be shown graphically.

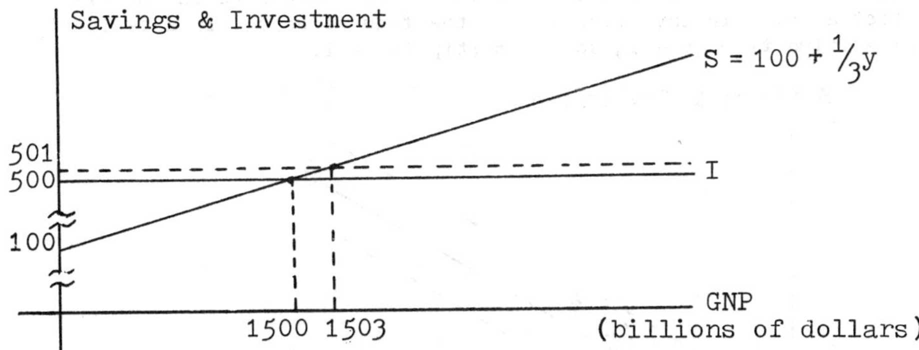

Since we know the consumption line to be C = 300 + 2/3 Y the savings line can be determined by S = C - I therefore 300 - 200 = 100 , S = 100 + 1/3 Y. A 1-unit increase in savings gives us a 3-unit increase in GNP.

• PROBLEM 5-32

If investment rises with income, instead of being horizontal, we must amplify the multiplier formula, 1/MPS = 1/(1-MPC), to the form 1/(MPS-MPI). Assume, MPI = 2/15. Show that the old multiplier of $3 = 1/(\frac{1}{3})$ now becomes $5 = 1/(\frac{1}{3} - 2/15) = 1/(3/15) = 1/(1/5)$; show

$$[Y = C + I = (A + \tfrac{2}{3}Y) + (B + \tfrac{2}{15}Y)] = [Y^* = 5(A+B)],$$

where a shift in the CC schedule is a shift in A, and a shift in investment is a shift in B.

Solution: The relationship between the marginal propensity to consume (MPC) and the marginal propensity to save (MPS) is MPC + MPS = 1. The MPS is the fraction of a dollar left after consumption, assuming that investment is constant. However, when investment varies, we must make the corresponding adjustment. The new formula is MPS + MPC - MPI = 1 or MPI = MPS + MPC - 1. MPI is the marginal propensity to invest. If MPI is 2/15 this says that a person will invest 2/15 of each additional dollar. Through the old multiplier, 3, we know the MPS is its inverse, 1/3. The new multiplier 1/MPS-MPI is then

$$\frac{1}{1/3 - 2/15} = 1/1/5 = S \ .$$

To arrive at the new value of Y^*, solve the equation $Y = C + I = A + 2/3Y + B + 2/15Y$.

$$Y = 4/5Y + A + B \Rightarrow 1/5Y = A + B \Rightarrow Y = S(A + B).$$

The equation for the consumption line is $A + 2/3Y$ where A is the intercept on the savings + investment axis. If A changes, since the slope remains the same; what will occur will be a shift upward or downward in the consumption curve. A change in B will affect a shift in investment. See the figures below. In a perfectly competitive firm $S = I$, so the multiplier = 1.

Savings & Investment

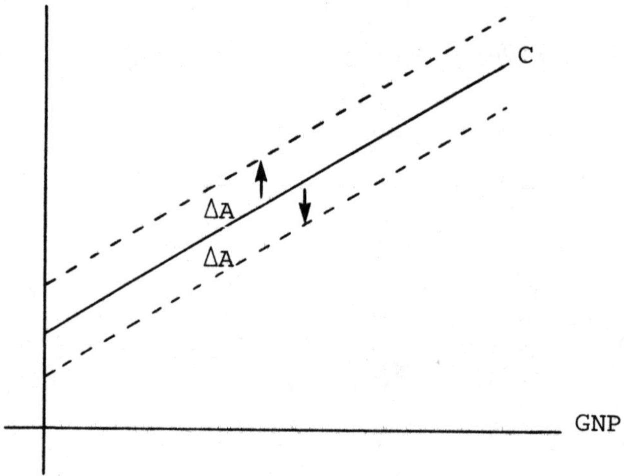

Shift in consumption

Savings & Investment

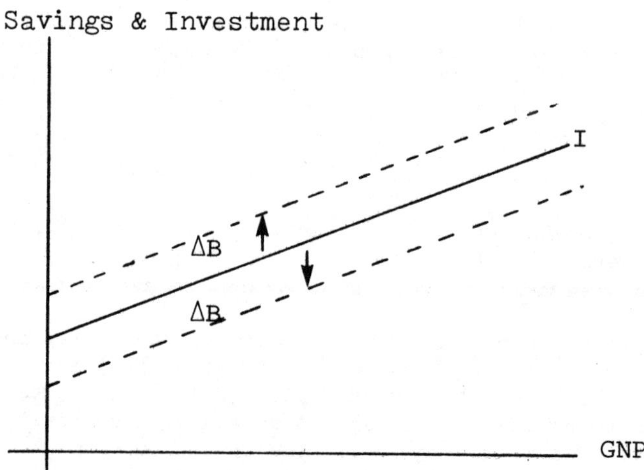

Shift in investment

Consider a simple macro-economic model which takes into account conditions in the money market. Assume the following relationships:

$$Y = C + I + G$$
$$C = 100 + 0.6Y$$
$$I = 0.2Y - 50i$$
$$M_D = 0.25Y - 30i$$
$$M_s = 65$$
$$G = 100$$

where Y is the gross national product, C is consumption, G is government expenditures, I is investment, M_D is money demanded, M_s is money supplied and i is the interest rate. Find (a) the equilibrium level of income, (b) the interest rate at that level.

Solution: To find the equilibrium level we must look for the intersection of the I.S. and L.M. curves. The I.S. curve demonstrates the relationship between the rate of interest and the equilibrium level of national income. The National Income equilibrium occurs when savings is equal to investment. By plotting national income on the "X" axis and the interest rate on the "Y" axis, we see, the lower the rate of interest, the greater the level of investment, and hence, the higher is the level of national income equilibrium consistent with that interest rate. See diagram "A" below:

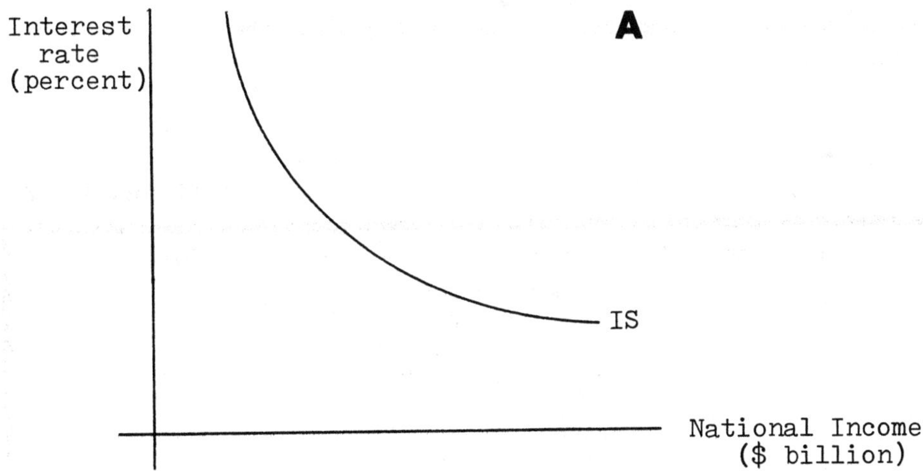

The L.M. curve, on the other hand, shows the relationship between the level of income and the rate of interest required to clear the money market given a fixed money supply. Since the rate of interest is determined by the equilibrium between money demand and money supply, assuming a fixed-money supply, the L.M. curve will be positively sloped.

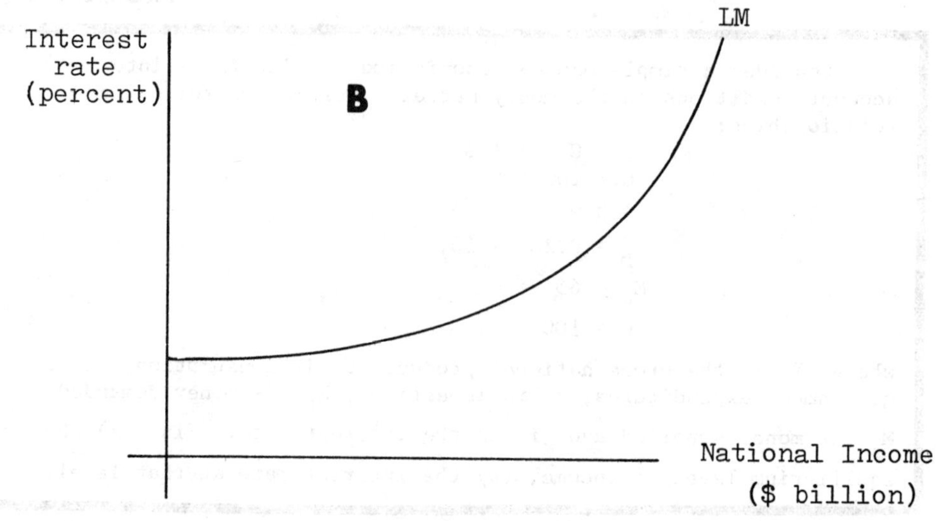

The intersection of the I.S. and L.M. curves, the general equilibrium level, involves the simultaneous determination of the interest rate and the level of income. Substituting the consumption and investment functions into the national income identity (Y = C + I + G) we derive the I.S. curve. Y = 200 + 0.8Y - 50i ; 0.2Y = 200 - 50i ; Y = 1000 - 250i. To get the L.M. curve, we set money demand (M_D) equal to the money supply (M_s). $M_D = M_s$; 0.25Y - 30i = 65; Y = 260 + 120i . Using simultaneous equations, we have

$$Y = 100 - 250i$$
$$Y = 260 + 120i\,.$$

Hence the equilibrium level of income is 500 and the interest rate is 2.

• PROBLEM 5-34

Assume the following model (from the preceding problem).

$$Y = C + I + G$$
$$C = 100 + 0.6Y$$
$$I = 0.2Y - 50i$$
$$M_D = 0.25Y - 30i$$
$$M_s = 65$$
$$G = 100$$

whose equilibrium level was found to be 500. Suppose that full employment level of income is 600, so that the desired change is 100. If the money supply is held constant, what change in government spending will be required to close the deflationary gap?

Solution: We first look at the income identity which states Y = consumption + investment + government expenditures. Since, in our model, G is held constant, we now must allow for a change in G to absorb the gap of 100. The new I.S. curve becomes $600 = C + I + G$, $600 = 200 + 0.8(600) - 50i + \Delta G$, $50i - 80 = \Delta G$. The new L.M. curve, $M_0 = M_s$, is $0.25Y - 30i = 65$, $Y = 260 + 120i$, $600 = 260 + 120i$, $120i = 340$, $i = 2.83$. Since the equilibrium rate of interest can be found from the L.M. curve when the equilibrium level of income is known, we can now determine the required change in G from I.S. Substituting $i = 2.83$ into $\Delta G = 50i - 80$ we get $50(2.83) - 80 = \Delta G = 141.5 - 80 = 61.5$.

A second way of deriving the required change in G is through the multiplier analysis. This analysis tells us that an increase in government expenditures by a given amount will result in an even larger generation of income. When M_s is assumed constant

$$\frac{\Delta Y}{\Delta G} = \frac{1}{1-b-d-}$$

where μ is the "monetary effect" reflecting the impact of the increase in demand on the interest rate, b is the coefficient relating consumption to income, $C = a + bY$ and d is the coefficient relating investment to income $I = h + dY$. From our model we see that $b = 0.6$ (from $c = 100 + 0.6Y$) and $d = 0.2$ (from $I = 0.2Y - 50i$). We solve for μ from the equation

$$\mu = \frac{(t-w)\ell}{j} .$$

We get the values of w, t, ℓ and j as following. "w" comes from the equation which generates the I.S. curve. $S = -a + sY + wi$, saving can be a function of both income and the interest rate. Since we assume no relationship between savings and interest rates, w equals zero. "t" comes from the investment function $I = dY + ti$, which shows how investment is also a function of income and the rate of interest. In this problem we are given $I = 0.2Y - 50i$ so $t = 50$. "ℓ" and "j" comes from the equation of money demanded. $M_D = \ell Y - ji$, the demand for transactions and speculative money balances is a function of both income and interest rate. We are given $M_D = 0.25Y - 30i$. Therefore, $\ell = 0.25$ and $j = 30$.

Substituting the values $t = -50$, $w = 0$, $\ell = 0.25$ and $j = 30$ we get

$$\mu = \frac{(-50-0)(0.25)}{30} = -0.415.$$

$$\frac{\Delta Y}{\Delta G} = \frac{1}{1-0.6-0.2+0.415} = \frac{1}{0.615} .$$

To induce a change in Y of 100 $\Delta G = 61.5$. We know that

$\frac{\Delta Y}{\Delta G} = \frac{1}{0.615}$; since $\Delta Y = 100$ and $\Delta G = 61.5$, $\frac{\Delta Y}{\Delta G} = \frac{100}{61.5} = \frac{1}{0.615}$.

• **PROBLEM 5-35**

Suppose the economy has a deflationary gap of \$200 million. With a multiplier of 5, this implies the required change in income is \$1 billion. Several alternative monetary and fiscal policies will be appropriate to bring income to its full employment level. Assume the marginal propensity to consume, b, is 0.7, the marginal propensity to import, m_i, is 0.1, and the investment function is $I = 0.2Y - 100i$. What are some of the ways of closing this deflationary gap that would bring the economy to a full-employment level of income?

Solution: A deflationary gap is the difference between equilibrium and full employment income, multiplied by the reciprocal of the multiplier. The deflationary gap is obviously smaller than the required change in income. There are many alternative measures to close this deflationary gap of \$200 million. The first way is through a change in government expenditures. An increase in demand is equal to the same increase in government expenditures. Therefore, government expenditures will have to increase by \$200 million. The second way is through a reduction in taxes. A change in demand is equal to a change in consumption, C, plus a change in net exports, X_n. In general, as taxes increase, demand decreases and vice-versa. Hence, $\Delta D = C\Delta T$, where $c < 0$, is a parameter to be estimated. This can also be written as $-(b - m)\Delta T$, where b is taken from the consumption equation $C = a + bY$ and m is taken from the export equation $X_n = E_C - mY$. Thus, ΔD, (a change in demand) $= -(b - m)\Delta T = -(0.7 - 0.1) = -0.6\Delta T$. A change in taxes will equal $1.66\Delta D$, so if ΔD is \$200 million, taxes will increase by \$332 million. A third way to reduce the gap is by decreasing interest rates; the effect of a change in demand will be equal to a change in i (investment), or as seen in notation form from the investment equation $I = dY - h_i$, a change in the coefficient $-h\Delta i$. We are given $I = 0.2Y - 100i$, therefore a change in demand equals $-100\Delta i$ or $-\Delta i = \frac{1}{100}\Delta D$. The fourth and last way of changing demand is by equal increases in G (government expenditures) and T (taxes). A change in demand is equal to a change in G + a change in C + a change in X_n. We already showed how $\Delta C + \Delta X_n$ was equal to $-(b-m)\Delta T$ so in this case $\Delta D = \Delta G - (b-m)\Delta G$ or $\Delta D = \Delta G - 0.6\Delta G = 0.4\Delta G$. A change in government expenditures will be equal to $2.5\Delta D$. Therefore, the actual change will be 200×2.5 or 500 million.

• **PROBLEM 5-36**

Demonstrate graphically the wage-price spiral and show the effects of a change in interest rates.

Solution: Money wages may rise due to increases in aggregate demand because of several factors. If demand increases, prices will rise and workers will request higher earnings to compensate for their loss in real income. In addition the level of employment will increase with this influx of demand so that the labor markets tighten. Companies will want to hire more workers during times of increased demand in order to match this demand with a large enough supply. Labor will then have greater bargaining power. This in turn will force the aggregate supply schedule upward and stimulate a rise in the general price level. The wage-price spiral thus shows how wages affect prices and prices consequently affect wages.

If there is a threat of war that causes the government to increase spending, demand will increase. This will lead to a price increase whose magnitude will be determined by the steepness of the price-employment relationship curve. If there is a very small excess of workers, prices would rise sharply, since resources would have to be transferred to the public sector from consumption and investment or other public uses. We see in the diagram below, how prices will rise from P_0 to P_1, as

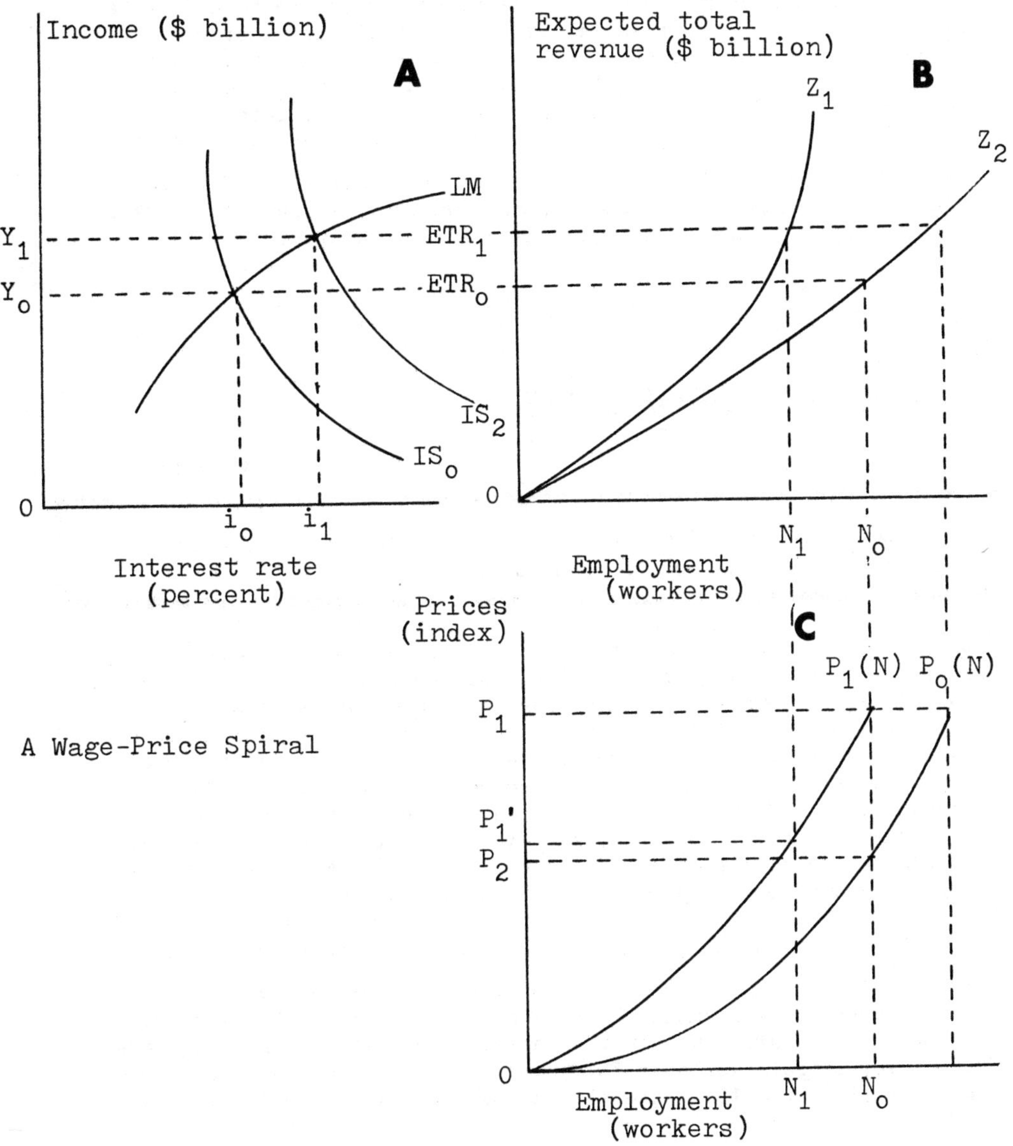

A Wage-Price Spiral

I.S. shifts from IS_0 to IS_1; if the initial price increase activates demand for higher wages, the aggregate supply curve and the price-employment relationship will shift from Z_0 to Z_1 and $P_0(N)$ to $P_1(N)$. In panel B, if Z_0 shifts to Z_1, this means that we will now employ fewer workers to reach the same level of expected total revenue. In panel C, if $P_0(N)$ shifts to $P_1(N)$, to reach the same price index level we now don't have to employ as many workers. In other words, as the I.S. curve shifts upward, instead of employing N_0 workers at a price level of P_0 and a level of income of Y_0, we now use only N_1 (fewer) employees and are at a higher price and income level.

The inflation will stop at this point, unless there is further impact on demand. One possibility is if fiscal and monetary authorities act against the increasing unemployment rates. Another possibility is if the Federal Reserve Board (the Fed) increases money supply to counteract the increase in interest rates which shifted from i_0 to i_1. If the Fed tries to prevent interest rates from rising, the L.M. curve will shift leftward. This would also lead increasing demand and prices which would in turn trigger wage increases. Thus, the wage-price spiral is created.

MONETARY PROBLEMS

• PROBLEM 5-37

Name the types of moneys in the U.S. economy, their uses and the factors which affect them the most.

Solution: M_1 is the amount of money demanded for transaction purposes. It consists of coin and paper currency (outside of banks), as well as bank money which includes demand deposits of all banks. Firms and households do not get their incomes and pay for goods and services at the same time; therefore they need to set aside money in their wallets and in checking accounts to take care of daily transactions. When income in an economy increases, there is a corresponding increase in the number of transactions in the economy. A rise in the number of transactions means that M_1 will increase. Figure 1 shows M_1 is related to the level of income.

M_2 is the amount of money demanded for speculative purposes. This includes time and savings deposits. Speculators buy assets when prices are low and sell them when prices are high. The prices of bond assets are low when the interest rate is high and high when the interest rate is low. For example, consider a government bond which yields 10 dollars annually no matter what its price is. If

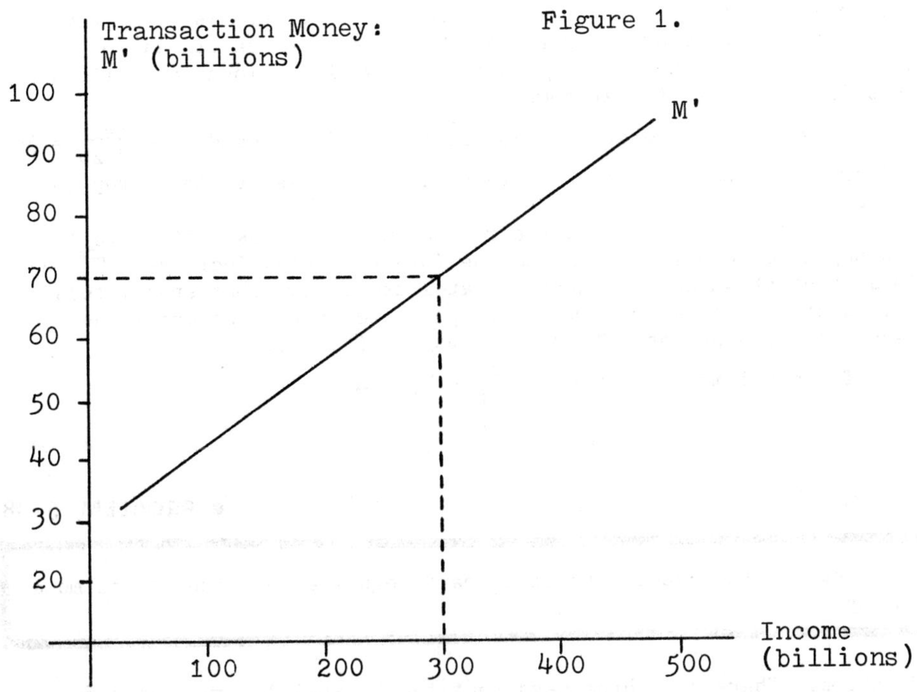
Transaction Money:
M' (billions)
Figure 1.
100
90
80
70
60
50
40
30
20
M'
Income
(billions)
100
200
300
400
500

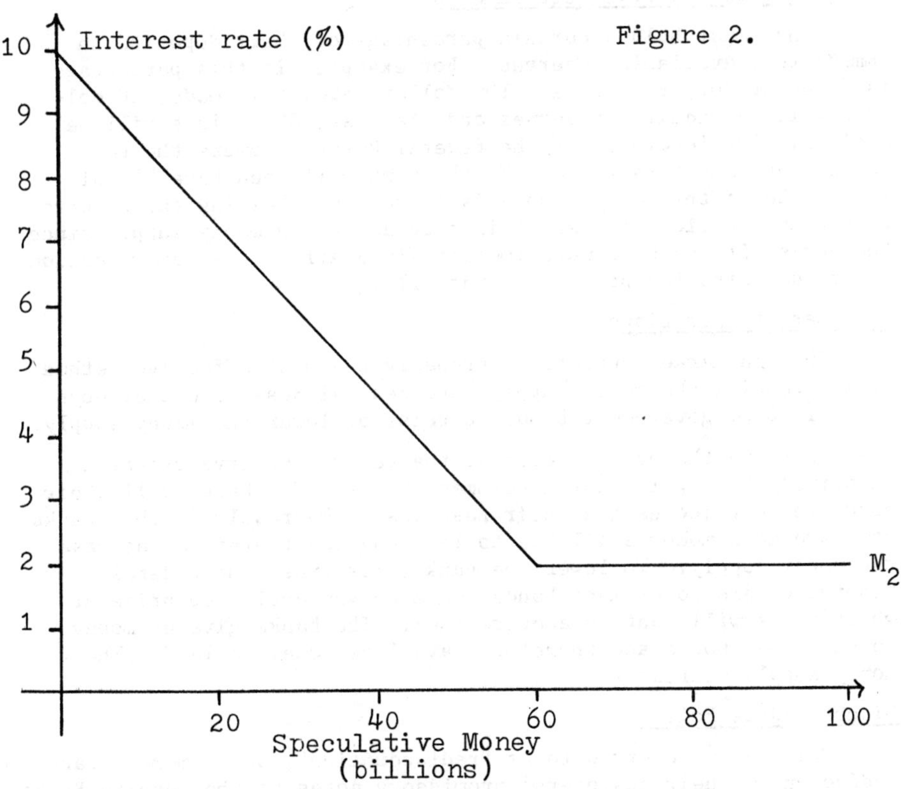
Interest rate (%)
Figure 2.
10
9
8
7
6
5
4
3
2
1
M_2
20
40
60
80
100
Speculative Money
(billions)

the bond is sold for 100 dollars, the rate of return is 10%. However, if the price of the bond is 50 dollars, the return is 20%. If this bond returned 25% then its price would be found as follows: 10 dollars is 25% of what number?

$10 = 0.25 \times p$ where p is the price of the bond $p = \frac{10}{0.25} = 40$ dollars. An increase in the rate of interest results in a drop in price.

Speculators hold on to their money when interest rates are low and begin to hold less money as the interest rates increase. There is a point at which the interest rates are so low that speculators will want to hold as much money as possible instead of acquiring assets at high prices. This is shown in figure 2.

The total money supply is $M_S = M_1 + M_2$.

• PROBLEM 5-38

How can the Federal Reserve Board regulate the size of the money supply?

Solution: There are three ways that the Federal Reserve can affect the supply of money in the American economy.

Changes in the Reserve Requirements

Banks must hold a certain percentage of their deposits in immediately available reserves. For example, if this percentage is fixed at 20%, then once a 100 dollar deposit is made, 20 dollars will be required reserves and the rest, 80 dollars will be available for lending. If the Federal Reserve lowers the reserve requirement ratio to 15%, the bank will then have 85 dollars to lend; the money supply is increased. Raising the reserve requirement ratio will result in decreasing the money supply since the banks will have to make immediately available a higher portion of the deposits for possible withdrawls.

Open Market Operations

In open market operations probably the most effective method of influencing the money supply, the Federal Reserve either buys or sells U.S. government bonds to raise or lower the money supply.

To raise the bank's reserves the Federal Reserve offers a relatively high price for government bonds. The banks sell their bonds thereby increasing their reserves. The result is that banks now have more money available to lend and can therefore increase the money supply. To lower the bank's reserves, the Federal Reserve offers government bonds for a conveniently low price at which banks will want to acquire them. The banks give up money to buy these bonds and therefore have less money to lend. The money supply decreases.

Discount-Rate Policy

Originally referred to as "rediscounting", where member banks rediscounted their customers' promissory notes at the Reserve Banks in return for cash, this system has since taken on a new direction. "Discounts" are loans that the Federal Reserve Banks make to member banks. By increasing or decreasing the amount of discounts, the money reserves grow or diminish correspondingly. The Federal Reserve Board (the Fed) is empowered to raise and lower the discount or interest rate on loans; to lower the rate increases loans which expands the money supply.

• PROBLEM 5-39

The public always holds the fraction $C = \frac{1}{21}$ of its M (money supply) in cash and $d = \frac{20}{21}$ of M in demand deposits, D. The bank is required by law to always have available a reserve ratio, r, of 1/5 of its deposits for withdrawal by bank customers. Verify that if D increases a) the change in the money supply, ΔM, will be

$$\frac{1}{\frac{1}{21} + (\frac{1}{5} \times \frac{20}{21})} = \frac{21}{5}\Delta D ,$$

b) the change in demand deposits will be $= 4\Delta D$, and
c) the change in cash will be $.195\ \Delta D$.

<u>Solution</u>: Reserve laws require member banks to hold a certain portion of its assets in non-earning cash. A fraction of demand deposits must be held on deposit with its regional Federal Reserve Bank or in its own vaults. In an economy where money is held either as currency or as demand deposits, the expansion in M caused by an increase in bank deposits is computed by the formula

$$\Delta M = \frac{1}{C + (r \times d)} \Delta D \quad \text{(deposits)} .$$

In this problem,

$$\Delta M = \frac{1}{\frac{1}{21} + (\frac{1}{5} \times \frac{20}{21})} \Delta D = \frac{21}{5} \Delta D .$$

The money in demand deposits will therefore be multiplied by 21/5, and result in a rise in the money supply.

$$\frac{20}{21} \times \frac{21}{5} \Delta D = 4\Delta D = \text{the increase in deposits.}$$

The change in cash is $\frac{1}{21}(\frac{21}{5}\Delta D) = .2\Delta D$.

CHAPTER 6

ADVANCED MATH SKILLS

RATE OF CHANGE; MARGINAL COSTS AND REVENUE

• PROBLEM 6-1

Tencer Inc. has estimated its revenue function to be $r(x) = 3x^2$, where x is the number of years the company has been in business and r(x) is the total revenue earned up to year x in millions. The profit function is $f(x) = 2x^2 - 5x + 1$, f(x) is the total profit earned up to year x. What is the cost accrued over a three year period? What is the rate of change of cost of production by the end of the third year?

Solution: The revenue minus cost gives you the profit. Therefore, to get the cost subtract the profit from the revenue.

$$c(x) = r(x) - f(x) = 3x^2 - (2x^2 - 5x + 1)$$
$$= x^2 + 5x - 1 \quad \text{for} \quad x \geq 1 .$$

The cost accrued by the end of 3 years is $(3)^2 + 5(3) - 1 = \$23$ million.

The marginal cost is the first derivative of the cost function.

$$\text{Rate of change of cost} = \frac{dc(x)}{dx} = 2x + 5.$$

The cost rate of change at the end of the third year is

$$\left.\frac{dc}{dx}\right|_{x=3} = 2(3) + 5 = \$11 \text{ million.}$$

• PROBLEM 6-2

The marginal cost of producing an item is $y' = 3 + x + \frac{e^{-x}}{4}$. What does it cost to produce one item if the fixed cost is $4?

Solution: If $y = f(x)$ is the total cost of producing and selling x items, then the marginal cost of producing an item is defined as the derivative $y' = dy/dx$. In this problem we are given the derivative and asked to find the total cost. $y = f(x)$ can be obtained by integrating y':

$$y = \int y'dx = \int (3 + x + \frac{e^{-x}}{4})\,dx$$

$$y = 3x + \frac{x^2}{2} - \frac{e^{-x}}{4} + c\ .$$

We are told that the fixed cost is \$4. This means that there is a \$4 cost ($y = 4$) when no items are being produced ($x = 0$). Substituting in our equation for y, we have

$$y = 4 = 0 + \frac{0^2}{2} - \tfrac{1}{4} + c$$

$$4 + \tfrac{1}{4} = \frac{17}{4} = c\ .$$

It follows that $y = 3x + \frac{x^2}{2} - \frac{e^{-x}}{4} + \frac{17}{4}$. The cost of producing one item is

$$y = 3(1) + \frac{1^2}{2} - \frac{e^{-1}}{4} + \frac{17}{4} = 3 + \tfrac{1}{2} - \frac{1}{4e} + \frac{17}{4}$$

$$= \frac{12 + 2 + 17}{4} - \frac{1}{4e} = \frac{31}{4} - \frac{1}{4e} = \frac{31e - 1}{4e} = \$7.66.$$

• PROBLEM 6-3

The daily cost of producing n Caped Ghouls at the Star Toys Factory is $C(n) = 0.2n^2 + n + 900$ where $C(n)$ is in dollars. It has been found that $t^2 + 100t$ Caped Ghouls can be produced in t hours. What is the formula for the rate of change of the total cost with respect to time?

Solution: The rate of change of the cost with respect to the number of Ghouls made is

$$\frac{dC(n)}{dn} = \frac{d}{dn}(0.2n^2 + n + 900) = 0.4n + 1\ .$$

The rate of change of the number of Ghouls made with respect to time is

$$\frac{d}{dt}(t^2 + 100t) = 2t + 100\ .$$

But we actually want $\frac{dC(n)}{dt}$. By the chain rule we have $\frac{dC(n)}{dt} = \frac{dC(n)}{dn}\frac{dn}{dt}$

or

$$\frac{dC(n)}{dt} = (0.4n + 1)(2t + 100)$$

$$= 0.8nt + 40n + 2t + 100$$

but we know that $n = t^2 + 100t$ so that we can substitute this value for n in the expression above to get $dC(n)/dt$ as a function of t alone. And $dC(n)/dt$ is the rate of change of the cost with respect to time.

$$0.8(t^2 + 100t)t + 40(t^2 + 100t) + 2t + 100$$

$$= 0.8t^3 + 80t^2 + 40t^2 + 4000t + 2t + 100$$

$$= 0.8t^3 + 120t^2 + 4002t + 100 \ .$$

This is the rate of change of the total cost with respect to time. Note that for $t = 0$, there is a fixed cost of 100.

• PROBLEM 6-4

> The total cost of producing x cameras is $C(x) = 2 + x^3$. What is the average cost if 10 cameras are made? What is the marginal cost of producing 10 cameras?

Solution: The average cost is the change in total cost divided by the number of units produced which brought about that cost. For example, if it costs \$100 to produce 10 units of a product, then the average cost is \$100/10 = 10/unit. Thus the average cost is also interpreted as the cost per unit made.

In this example, if no cameras are made there is still an operating cost of \$2; i.e., $C(0) = 2$. If ten units are made then the total cost is $c(10) = 2 + (10)^3 = \$1002$. The total change in the cost of going from 0 units to 10 units produced is $\Delta c = 1002 - 2 = \$1000$. The number of units produced is $\Delta x = 10$, where Δx is the change in units produced, i.e., $\Delta x = 10 - 0 = 10$. The average cost is

$$\frac{\Delta c}{\Delta x} = \frac{\$1000}{10} = \$100/\text{unit.}$$

The marginal cost is defined to be the instantaneous rate of change of the average cost as Δx approaches zero. It is the derivative of the cost function. The marginal cost of producing 10 units is then the value of the derivative at $x = 10$.

The derivative of $c(x)$ is $c'(x) = 3x^2$. At $x = 10$, $c'(10) = 3(10)^2 = \$300$.

• PROBLEM 6-5

> Quinones Bros. has been in business for four years. Management has estimated the gross annual earnings after t years to be
>
> $\sqrt{10t^2 + t + 236}$ in thousands of dollars. What was the annual rate of growth of earnings after four years? As a percentage, what was the rate of growth of the earnings after four years?

Solution: The annual gross income is given as a function of t. When we ask for the rate, we mean the derivative of this income function. More specifically, the rate of income growth after four years is the derivative of the income function at $t = 4$ years.

$$f(t) = \sqrt{10t^2 + t + 236}$$

$$\frac{df(t)}{dt} = \frac{d}{dt}\left(\sqrt{10t^2 + t + 236}\right)$$

$$= \tfrac{1}{2}(10t^2 + t + 236)^{-\frac{1}{2}} \cdot (20t + 1)$$

$$= \frac{20t + 1}{2\sqrt{10t^2 + t + 236}} \quad .$$

At $t = 4$ we have,

$$\frac{20(4) + 1}{2\sqrt{1,840}} = .944 \text{ thousands} \quad ,$$

so that gross earnings are increasing \$944 annually after four years in business. The gross amount earned by this time is

$$\sqrt{10(4)^2 + (4) + 236} = \sqrt{1840} = 42.9 \text{ thousands.}$$

The annual percentage rate of growth is therefore

$$\frac{.944}{42.9} \times 100\% = 2.20\%$$

• PROBLEM 6-6

Retail City sold 1,000 Morris the Cat T-shirts at \$5 each last week. This week they sold 1,200 T-shirts at \$4 each. Derive the demand and the revenue functions.

Solution: The demand function relates quantity demanded to the price of the product. It is usually a decreasing function, meaning that an increase in price will reduce demand and vice versa. This is true in this example where a one dollar decrease in the price of a T-shirt resulted in a rise in demand of 200. Assuming the function to be a straight line, we can find such a line because we know two points on it. The slope of a line is

$$\frac{\Delta Y}{\Delta X} = \frac{\text{the change in } Y}{\text{the change in } X} \, ,$$

from the points (1,000,5), (1,200,4) the slope is

$$\frac{\Delta Y}{\Delta X} = \frac{4 - 5}{1200 - 1000} = \frac{-1}{200} \; .$$

Given a point $(X_1 Y_1)$ on a line and the slope of the line m, the equation of the line is $Y - Y_1 = m(X - X_1)$. Use $(q,p) = (1200,4)$ and $m = \frac{-1}{200}$ to get

$$p - 4 = \frac{-1}{200}(q - 1200)$$

where q is the quantity on the horizontal axis and p is the price on the vertical axis. Expressing p explicitly as a function of the quantity q we have

$$p - 4 = -\frac{q}{200} + 6$$

$$p = \frac{-q}{200} + 10 \; .$$

A sketch of the function appears below.

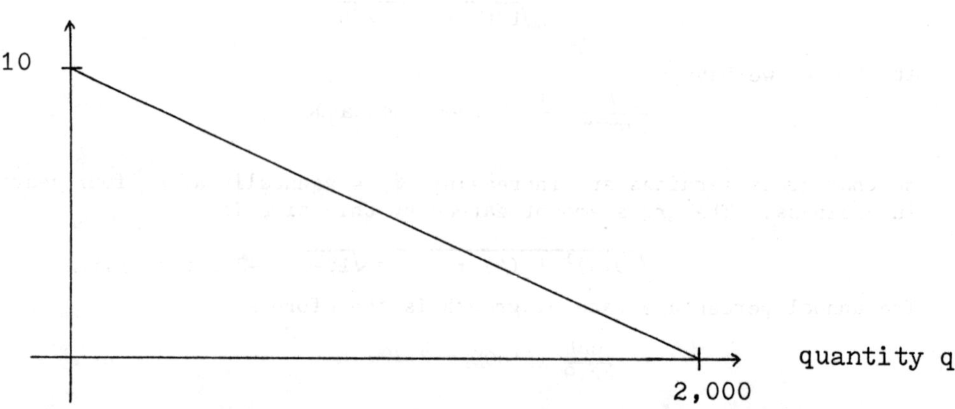

Note that at $p = 0$ 2,000 T-shirts would be "given away". At $p = \$10$ no T-shirts would be sold.

Revenue is the price of the product times the number of units sold. We can express the revenue function in terms of p or in terms of q. As a function of the quantity:

$$R(q) = pq = q\left(\frac{-q}{200} + 10\right) = \frac{-q^2}{200} + 10q$$

and as a function of price: Solve for q in terms of p.

$$p = \frac{-q}{200} + 10$$

$$p - 10 = \frac{-q}{200}$$

$$-200(p - 10) = -200p + 2000 = q\ .$$

So that $R(p) = pq = p(-200p + 2000) = -200p^2 + 2000p$. The functions are sketched below.

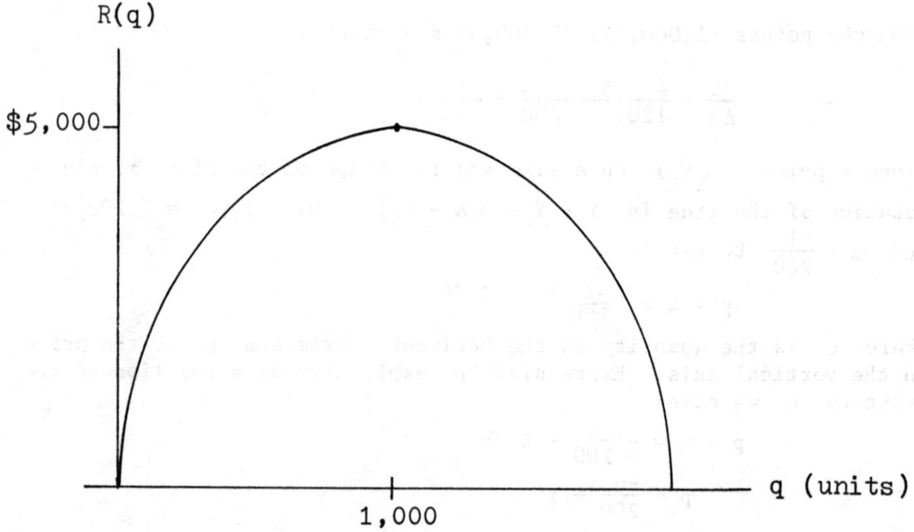

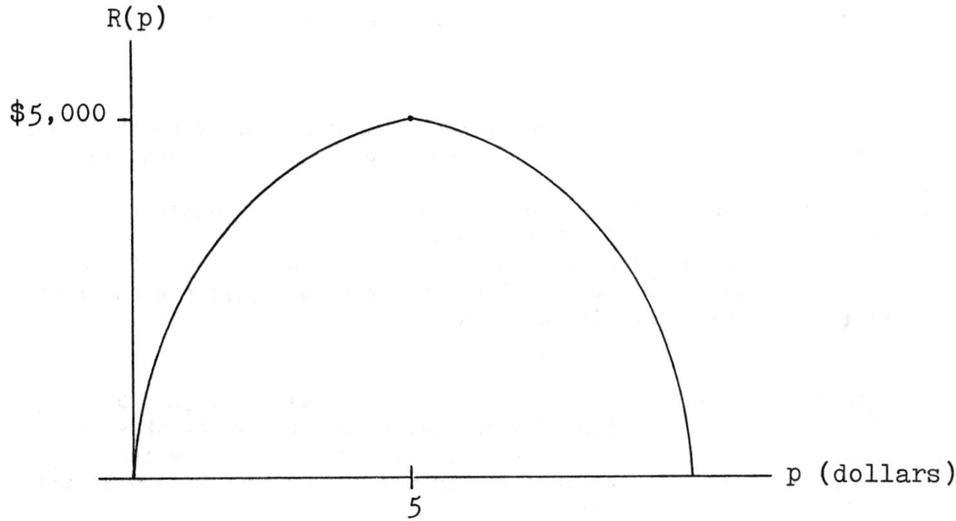

• PROBLEM 6-7

The Blue Eagle Rum factory has estimated that its cost function and its revenue function for next year will be $C(x) = 2x + 5$ and $R(x) = 8x - x^2$ respectively, where x is in thousands and the corresponding revenue is in millions.

(a) What are the marginal revenue, marginal cost and profit functions?

(b) What are the values of the functions in (a) at the break-even point(s)?

(c) Find the most profitable level of output and the values of the functions in (a) and the revenue and cost functions at this level.

Solution: (a) Profit equals revenue minus cost whether the revenue and the cost are functions or specific numerical values. Here the profit will be a function. Let the profit function be called $P(x)$.

$$P(x) = R(x) - C(x) = 8x - x^2 - 2x - 5 = -x^2 + 6x - 5 .$$

At different levels of production there are different profits (or losses) made.

Marginal revenue is the revenue earned for each additional unit of output. This can be expressed as the ratio $\Delta R/\Delta x$ which is the change in revenue divided by the change in production. The ratio $\Delta R/\Delta x$ approaches the derivative of the revenue function. To find this derivative means to find the expression for the ratio $\Delta R/\Delta x$ as the change in x, Δx, becomes very small. Marginal revenue:

$$\frac{\Delta R}{\Delta x} = \frac{dR(x)}{dx} = 8 - 2x .$$

Marginal cost is the expense incurred for each additional unit of output. Therefore the same reasoning is used in finding the marginal cost function except that now the ratio is $\Delta C/\Delta x$, or the change in the cost divided by the change in production level. Marginal cost:

$$\frac{\Delta C}{\Delta x} = \frac{dC(x)}{dx} = 2 .$$

In this case, the rate of change of the cost with respect to the level of production is constant. This is the slope of the cost function C(x).

(b) The break-even point is the point where the cost equals the revenue, or in this example $R(x) = C(x)$.

We solve the equation $8x - x^2 = 2x + 5$. Adding $-2x - 5$ to both sides, to get $-x^2 + 6x - 5 = 0$ and then multiplying both sides by -1 we get the quadratic equation

$$x^2 - 6x + 5 = 0 .$$

By factoring this equation, we get $(x - 5)(x - 1) = 0$. $x = 5, x = 1$ are the roots of the equation. Note that there are two break-even points which means the cost function intersects the revenue function: $P(x) = -x^2 + 6x - 5$. At the break-even points we have $P(1) = 0$ and $P(5) = 0$. Revenue function:

$$R(x) = 8x - x^2$$
$$R(1) = 7 \quad R(5) = 15 .$$

Marginal Cost function:

$$C(x) = 2x + 5$$
$$C(1) = 7 \quad C(5) = 15$$

(c) To find at what level of production profit is maximized, find the derivative of profit function and set it equal to zero

$$P(x) = -x^2 + 6x - 5, \quad \frac{dP(x)}{dx} = -2x + 6 .$$

$$\frac{dP(x)}{dx} = -2x + 6 = 0 \quad \text{and} \quad x = 3 \quad \text{or } 3000$$

is the most profitable level of production. Profit made at this level:

$$P(3) = -(3)^2 + 6(3) - 5 = 18 - 14 = 4 \text{ million.}$$

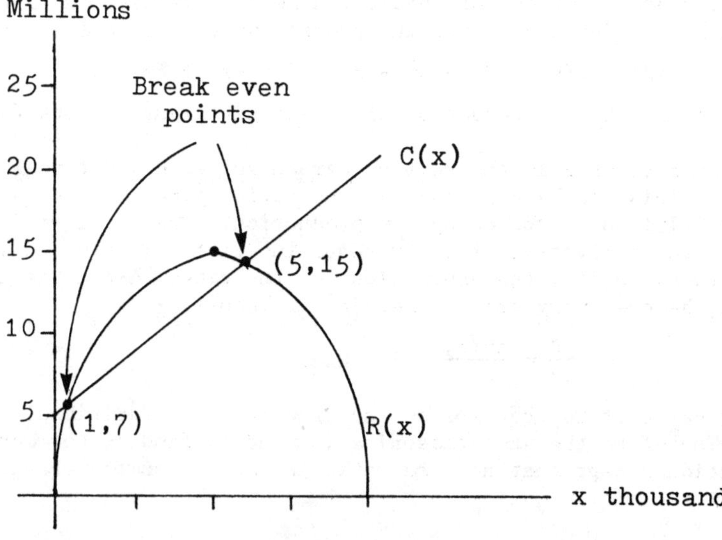

Costs at this level: $C(3) = 2(3) + 5 = 11$ million.

Marginal revenue: $R'(3) = 8 - 2(3) = 2$ million.

Margin cost: $C'(x) = 2$ million (constantly) .

As we can see from the marginal cost and marginal revenue figures, profit is maximized when $R'(x) = C'(x)$. A sketch of $R(x)$ and $C(x)$ is shown.

• PROBLEM 6-8

Home Video Products has just put on the market a new game set. Management has estimated the demand will increase every year. Let x be the number of years the product has been on the market and $f(x)$ the demand in year x, then the demand as a function of the year is estimated to be $f(x) = 2000 - 1000e^{-x}$.

Assuming that the price of a set, \$35, will remain constant over a 10 year period:

(a) At what annual rate is the gross revenue increasing after 2 years assuming that Home Video Products will be able to satisfy the demand fully?

(b) What is the actual change in gross revenue between years 2 and 3; between years 1.5 and 2.5?

Solution: (a) If p is the price of a product and d is the number of units sold then pd is the gross revenue obtained. Similarly, when either the price or the demand vary as a function of some independent variable, the revenue will also be a function of the variable. In this case the revenue function is

$$R(x) = \$35 \cdot f(x) = 70{,}000 - 35{,}000e^{-x} .$$

When we ask, "What is the annual 'rate'?" in this problem, we mean specifically the derivative of the revenue function. 'After two years' means at $x = 2$ years where $x = 0$ referes to the year when the product was put on the market.

$$\frac{dR(x)}{dx} = 35{,}000e^{-x} , \quad \text{at } x = 2 \text{ this is } 4{,}736$$

but this is not the rate of increase.

In year x the annual rate of increase will simply be e^{-x} since the rate of increase does not depend on the constant 35,000 but only on e^{-x}. Therefore e^{-2} is the rate of increase for the gross revenues in year 2, or approximately 13.5% will be $(e^{-5}) \times 100\% = 0.67\%$, and in year 10 the rate of increase will be

$$(e^{-10}) \times 100\% = 0.0045\% .$$

Note that at first the rate of increase is rapid but then it slows down considerably. The annual gross revenues finally settle down to about

$$R(10) = 70{,}000 - 35{,}000e^{-10} \cong \$70{,}000 .$$

The graph illustrates this:

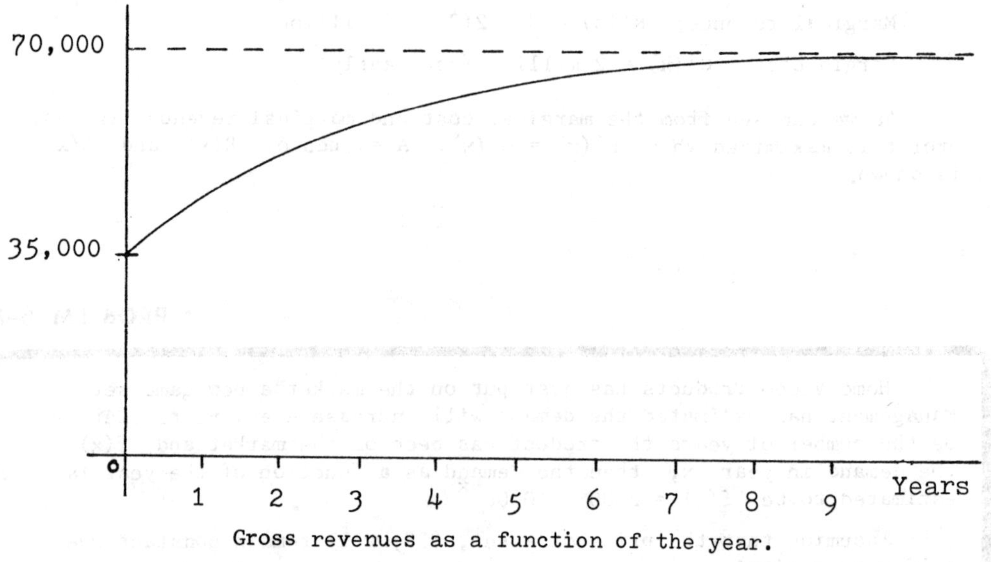

Gross revenues as a function of the year.

(b) The change in gross revenue between years 2 and 3 is R(3) -R(2).

$$R(3) = 70,000 - 35,000e^{-3} = 68,257$$

$$R(2) = 70,000 - 35,000e^{-2} = 65,263$$

and so R(3) - R(2) = $2,994.

Between years 1.5 and 2.5 the change in gross revenue is R(2.5) - R(1.5).

$$R(2.5) = 70,000 - 35,000e^{-2.5} = \$67,127$$

$$R(1.5) = 70,000 - 35,000e^{-1.5} = \$62,190$$

$$R(2.5) - R(1.5) = \$4,937 .$$

As we expected, the increase in gross revenue between the second and the third year is less than the increase between x = 1.5 and x = 2.5. The rate of increase is decreasing.

COST MINIMIZATION

• PROBLEM 6-9

Given that the cost of mimeographing x number of copies is

$$C(x) = 0.005x + \frac{4500}{x},$$

what is the number of copies that will minimize the cost?

Solution: We take the first derivative of the cost function, C(x), set it equal to zero and solve for x. The derivative of C(x) is

$$\frac{dC(x)}{dx} = \frac{d}{dx}\left(0.005x + \frac{4500}{x}\right) = 0.005 - \frac{4500}{x^2}$$

$$= \frac{0.005x^2 - 4500}{x^2} .$$

Set this to zero:

$$\frac{0.005x^2 - 4500}{x^2} = 0$$

to get

$$0.005x^2 - 4500 = 0 \quad \text{or} \quad 0.005x^2 = 4500$$

$$x^2 = \frac{4500}{0.005} \quad \text{and} \quad x = \sqrt{\frac{4500}{0.005}} \cong 949 \quad \text{copies.}$$

The cost of making this many copies is

$$C(949) = (0.005)(949) + \frac{4500}{949} = \$9.49.$$

We know this cost is a minimum because the second derivative of C(x) is a positive number. This means that the curve for C(x) is concave upward.

• PROBLEM 6-10

A cylindrical container is to be produced whose capacity is 10 cubic feet. The top and bottom of the container are to be made of a material that costs \$2 per square foot, while the side of the container is made of material costing \$1.50 per square foot. Find the dimensions that will minimize the total cost of the container.

Solution: We need to get an expression for the cost as a function of the dimensions of the cylinder, which are its radius r and its height h. The total cost is composed of two separate costs, the cost of the top and bottom of the container and the cost of the sides of the container.

The total area of the circular sections of the cylinder is $\pi r^2 + \pi r^2 = 2\pi r^2$ square feet so that the cost of these sections is $\$2(2\pi r^2) = \$4\pi r^2$. The units are correct since we have (dollars/sq.ft.) x (sq.ft.) = dollars.The total area of the side section is $2\pi rh$(the circumference of the cylinder times the height h of the cylinder). The cost of this section is $\$1.5(2\pi rh) = \$3\pi rh$. The total cost as a function of two variables is $C(r,h) = 4\pi r^2 + 3\pi rh$. If the volume of the container is to be 10 cubic feet, then the following relation must be true. Volume $= \pi r^2 h = 10$ since the left side of the equation is the volume of the cylinder with radius r and height h. We can get the cost as a function of one variable, say r by solving for h in the equation above and substituting into C(r,h).

$$h = \frac{10}{\pi r^2}$$

$$C(r,h) = 4\pi r^2 + 3\pi rh$$
$$C(r) = 4\pi r^2 + 3\pi r\left(\frac{10}{\pi r^2}\right)$$

$$= 4\pi r^2 + \frac{30}{r} .$$

We can now proceed to minimize the cost. The first derivative of $C(r)$ is

$$C'(r) = 8\pi r - \frac{30}{r^2} .$$

Set this equal to zero and solve for r.

$$8\pi r - \frac{30}{r^2} = 0 , \quad \frac{8\pi r^3}{r^2} - \frac{30}{r^2} = 0 ,$$

$$\frac{8\pi r^3 - 30}{r^2} = 0 ,$$

$$8\pi r^3 - 30 = 0 \quad \text{(multiply both sides by } r^2\text{)}$$

$$8\pi r^3 = 30 , \quad r^3 = \frac{30}{8\pi}$$

or

$$r = \sqrt[3]{\frac{15}{4\pi}} \approx 1.061 \quad \text{feet}$$

and

$$h = \frac{10}{\pi r^2} \approx \frac{10}{\pi(1.061)^2} \approx 2.828 \text{ feet.}$$

The radius of the cylinder is $r = 1.061$ feet and the height is 2.828 feet.

• PROBLEM 6-11

Finch Analysts installed a new computer terminal in their main offices. It has been estimated that the average cost of repair will be \$50 per repair and should the terminal be in service for t years, the number of breakdowns will be about $t^{4/3}$.

If the replacement cost of the terminal is \$250, when should Finch Analysts get a new terminal?

Solution: A repair follows every breakdown. The cost accrued over t years because of breakdowns is $\$50t^{4/3}$ and the total lifetime cost of getting rid of the terminal is

$$\$50t^{4/3} + \$250$$

which is the accrued cost plus the \$250 replacement cost. The annual cost is therefore

$$\frac{\$50t^{4/3} + \$250}{t} \text{ (dollars/year)} .$$

This is the cost function that is to be minimized and not simply $50t^{4/3} + 250$, since it is clear that the minimum of this latter function occurs only at $t = 0$, where no purchase is made. The repair cost is one of the things we shall always have with the terminal and the accrued costs will never decrease, so we know costs can't be zero. The problem now becomes:

Given the annual cost function

$$C(t) = \frac{50t^{4/3} + 250}{t} = 50t^{\frac{1}{3}} + \frac{250}{t} ,$$

what is the value of t for which $C(t)$ is a minimum? In other words, we want to find out what number of years of owning the machine will minimize the cost of maintaining it.

Differentiating C(t) we get,

$$C'(t) = \frac{50}{3} t^{-\frac{2}{3}} - \frac{250}{t^2} .$$

We can simplify the equation,

$$= \frac{50}{3} \frac{t^{-\frac{2}{3}} \cdot t^2}{t^2} - \frac{250}{t^2} = \frac{\frac{50}{3} t^{4/3} - 250}{t^2}$$

Setting this equal to 0 we have,

$$\frac{50}{3} t^{4/3} = 250$$

$$t^{4/3} = \frac{3}{50} \cdot 250 = 15$$

and $t = (15)^{3/4}$ years. This is approximately 7.6 years. The accrued cost will be

$$\$50(7.6)^{4/3} + \$250 = \$997.12$$

and the annual cost is

$$\frac{\$997}{7.6} = \$131.18 .$$

Finch Analysts should replace the terminal after 7.6 years, since from that point on the annual costs begin to increase indefinitely.

• PROBLEM 6-12

> An inventory manager knows that he has an ordering cost of \$40 per order, an inventory cost of \$2 per item per year, and an annual demand of 4000 per year. However, his warehouse allows a maximum order size of 100. How many should he order to minimize cost?

Solution: If x is the number of orders to be placed, then $\frac{4000}{x}$ is the number of units per order, since a total of 4000 units will be ordered during the year. The cost of ordering is $40x$, that is, forty dollars per order. The storage cost is $\$2(4000)/x$, two dollars for every unit stored. The total cost is

$$c(x) = 40x + \frac{8000}{x} .$$

This is the function to minimize. To find the x that minimizes $c(x)$, take the derivative of $c(x)$, set it equal to zero and solve for x.

$$\frac{dc(x)}{dx} = \frac{d}{dx}(40x + \frac{8000}{x}) = 40 - \frac{8000}{x^2} = 0$$

or

$$40 = \frac{8000}{x^2}, \quad x^2 = 200, \quad x \approx 14.14 \text{ orders.}$$

This minimizes $c(x)$ because $\frac{d^2 c(x)}{dx^2}$, the second derivative of $c(x)$ is positive.

There is a problem. If 14.14 orders are placed then the order size is $4000/14.14 \approx 283$ units, but the warehouse holds at most 100 units so that the manager cannot minimize his cost as much as is possible.

Sketch the cost function to get a feel of what is happening.

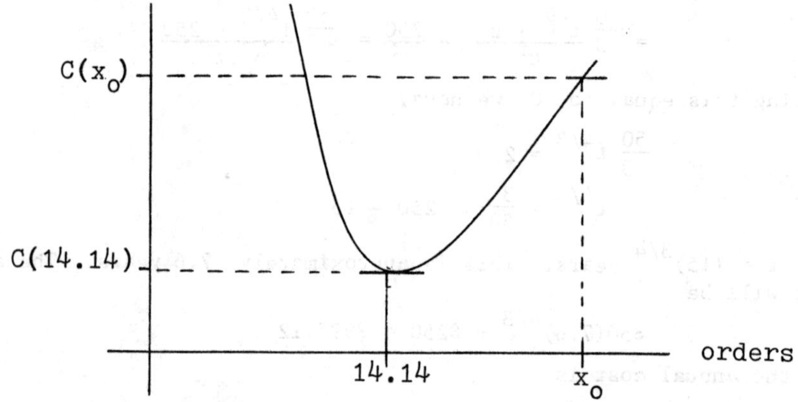

At 14.14 orders, the total cost is a minimum. The manager is forced to order more often since every order contains less units. Let the amount of these orders be x_0 and the corresponding cost $c(x_0)$. The constraint is that the order size not exceed 100:

$$\left(\frac{4000}{x}\right) \le 100 \quad \text{or} \quad x \ge \left(\frac{4000}{100} = 40\right)$$

x, the number of orders has to be greater than or equal to 40, i.e. x_0 has to be either 40 or greater than 40. If x_0 is greater than forty, the cost is higher. Sketch a portion of the curve for $40 \le x$. The total cost increases for $x > 40$. In fact, our problem

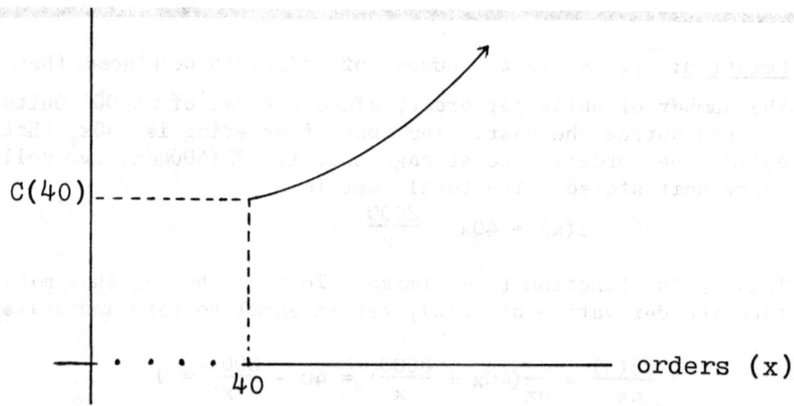

is now to minimize $c(x)$ in the interval $40 \le x < 4000$. The minimum is clearly at $x = 40$. The manager should place 40 orders which is the same as $4000/40 = 100$ units per order. The cost is

$$c(40) = 40(40) + \frac{8000}{40} = \$1,800,$$

and the loss from not minimizing with an order size of 14.14 is

$$c(40) - c(14.14) = \$1800 - \$1130 = \$670.$$

• PROBLEM 6-13

Leo's Summer Camp for Dogs is preparing for the June canine arrivals. The owners of these dogs have been promised that their animals will receive the best of treatment which includes meat every day.

The meat, although low grade and improper for human consumption, has no additives or artificial ingredients. The meat conveniently comes in boxes of 10 hamburger patties. Last summer the camp required a total of 45,000 patties. On an average day, 475 patties were avidly consumed by the voracious canines and 25 were simply wasted because of more refined tastes. The storage cost per box is 2 cents and it costs the camp 45¢ every time an order is placed. Assuming the demand for this summer is the same as for the last one, how many orders should be placed by Leo's Camp over the course of the summer and how many boxes are contained in each order to minimize costs?

Solution: The total cost is a function of the storage cost and the purchase order cost. Clearly, we must add these costs to obtain a preliminary relationship:

$$(\text{total costs}) = (\text{storage cost}) + (\text{order cost}).$$

Let x denote the number of boxes to be ordered. Then $\$0.02x$ is the term corresponding to the storage cost. Forty-five thousand patties are needed, at 10 patties per box this is actually

$$\frac{45,000}{10} = 4,500 \text{ boxes.}$$

Suppose that you have decided to order 500 boxes every time, how many orders will you have to place to satisfy demand? It is clearly $4,500/500 = 9$ orders. More generally, if x is the number of boxes in each order then $4,500/x$ is the number of orders placed. At 45¢ per order, the order cost is therefore

$$\$.045\left(\frac{4,500}{x}\right) .$$

The cost function with x as the independent variable is, (x boxes)

$$c(x) = \$0.02x + \$0.45\left(\frac{4,500}{x}\right) .$$

This is the function we have to minimize. Taking the first derivative of the above we get

$$\frac{dc(x)}{dx} = 0.02 - \frac{2025}{x^2} .$$

Set this equal to zero and solve for x to find the number of orders and the cost $c(x)$.

$$0.02 - \frac{2025}{x^2} = 0$$

$$0.02x^2 = 2025$$

$$x^2 = \frac{2025}{0.02} = 101250$$

and

$$x = \sqrt{101250} \cong 318.2 \quad \text{boxes.}$$

This is an approximate value. The number of orders placed is therefore 4,500/318.2 = 14.14 orders. The total cost is

$$c(318.2) = (0.02)(318.2) + .45(14.14) = \$12.73.$$

A sketch of the cost function is shown below:

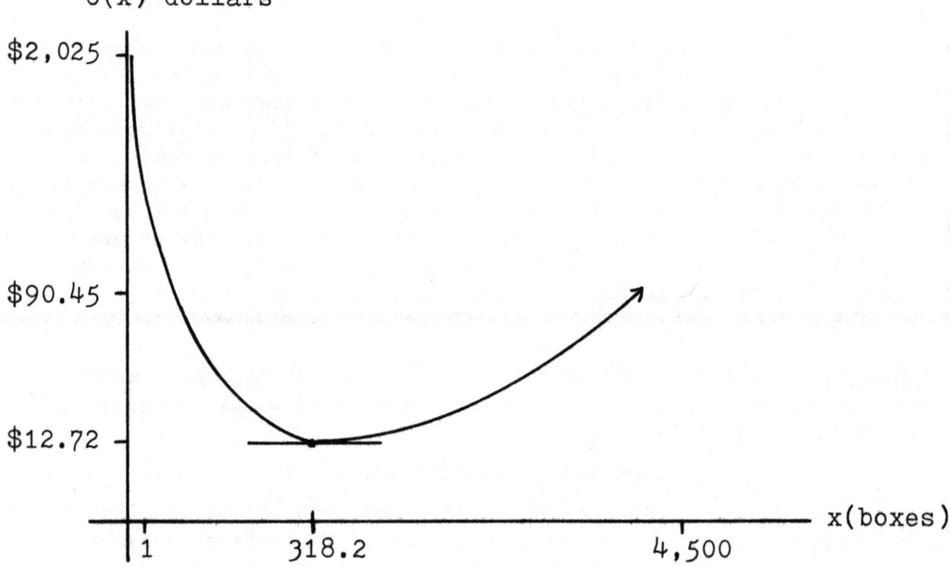

Note: We know that the critical point (318.2, 12.72) is a minimum because the second derivative of $c(x)$,

$$\frac{d^2(x)}{dx^2} = \frac{4050}{x^3}$$

is positive for all positive values of x meaning that $c(x)$ is concave upward and thus (318.2, 12.73) is a minimum.

• PROBLEM 6-14

An enterprising student at Rapid River State College has contracted to produce 150 candles in the shape of the college mascot, the otter. He plans to buy a quantity of reusable candle molds from a local metal works at \$3 apiece, and then hire a freshman at \$1.50 an hour to fill the molds with wax. It takes 3 hours to produce a single candle from a mold.

(a) How many molds should the student buy to keep his costs as small as possible?
(b) How much money will the freshman earn if the optimal number of molds is used?

Solution: (a) In a problem like this one, it is best to denote the principal quantity you are looking for as x and then derive all other intermediate quantities like labor costs and material costs in terms of x. The problem is how the student should distribute his resources between the two factors of production; materials and labor.

Increasing the use of one decreases the need for the other. The student can purchase 150 molds and have his freshman employee do the entire procedure in 3 hours, or he could choose the other extreme and purchase one mold and have the freshman work 150.3 = 450 hours. The basic relation is this:

total costs = labor costs + materials cost.

Let x be the number of molds the student is to purchase. The material cost is $3x$ where we assume that the student incurs no cost in acquiring wax.

To get the labor costs in terms of x is not so obvious. There are three distinct steps.

(i) The number of candles to a mold is $\frac{150}{x}$. To see this, note that if there are 30 molds available, the number of candles per mold is $\frac{150}{30} = 5$.

(ii) The number of hours the freshman works is $3\left(\frac{150}{x}\right) = \frac{450}{x}$ since each candle takes 3 hours in each mold, $\left(\frac{150}{x}\right)$ candles will take $3\left(\frac{150}{x}\right)$ hours in the respective molds they have been assigned to.

(iii) The total cost of labor is $\$1.50\left(\frac{450}{x}\right) = \frac{675}{x}$ dollars, i.e., the number of hours times the wage rate.

The cost function can now be stated as

$$C(x) = 3x + \frac{675}{x}$$

$$\uparrow \qquad \uparrow$$

material cost labor cost

The problem is to find x which minimizes this cost. Take the first derivative of $C(x)$, set equal to zero and solve for x.

$$\frac{dC(x)}{dx} = \frac{d}{dx}\left(3x + \frac{675}{x}\right) = 3 - \frac{675}{x^2} = 0$$

or

$$3 = \frac{675}{x^2}, \quad x^2 = \frac{675}{3} = 225$$

$$x = \sqrt{225} = 15 \text{ molds}.$$

The cost is minimized when 15 molds are purchased. The cost is

$$C(15) = 3 \cdot 15 + \frac{675}{15} = \$90.$$

The point (15,90) is a minimum because the second derivative of $C(x)$, $C''(x) = \frac{1350}{x^3}$ is positive when $x = 15$.

(b) The freshman will earn $\frac{675}{15} = \$45$.

PROFIT MAXIMIZATION THROUGH PRODUCTION ADJUSTMENTS

• PROBLEM 6-15

Circle Electronics can produce and sell x number of calculators a month. If it costs x^2 dollars to produce x number of calculators and each calculator is sold wholesale at $100, how many calculators should Circle Electronics produce monthly to maximize its profit?

Solution: First, obtain an expression for the profit in terms of the number of units produced. The gross profit is the total revenue minus the total cost. If x units are produced the total cost is x^2 and the total revenue is 100x. So, the gross profit will be $p(x) = 100x - x^2$. To find the production level which maximizes the profit function, take the derivative of p(x) and set it equal to zero and solve for x.

$$\frac{dp(x)}{dx} = \frac{d}{dx}(100x - x^2) = 100 - 2x .$$

Set to zero, $100 - 2x = 0$ to get $x = 50$ as the number of calculators that will maximize the profit. The gross profit will be

$$(100)(50) - (50)^2 = 5\,000 - 2500 = \$2,500.$$

We can verify that p(50) is a maximum rather than a minimum by seeing that the second derivative $p''(x) = -2$ is negative.

• PROBLEM 6-16

Margaret's Toyland can sell x bags of marbles at a price of p cents per bag where $p = 20 - 0.03x$. If the cost of x bags is $C = 3 + 0.02x$, then how many bags will the store have to sell to maximize the profit?

Solution: If p is the price of a product and x the number of units sold, then the revenue is xp. For this case, the revenue is

$$xp = x(20 - 0.03x) = 20x - 0.03x^2 .$$

Profit is revenue minus cost,

$$\begin{aligned} p(x) &= r(x) - c(x) \\ &= 20x - 0.03x^2 - 3 - 0.02x \\ &= -0.03x^2 + 19.98x - 3 . \end{aligned}$$

To find the maximum of this function, take the first derivative, set equal to zero and solve for x.

$$\frac{dp(x)}{dx} = -.06x + 19.98$$

$$19.98 = 0.06x, \quad x = \frac{19.98}{0.06} = 333.$$

The store will have to sell 333 bags of marbles to obtain the maximum profit.

We know that p(333) represents a maximum point since the second derivative of the profit function $p''(x) = -0.06$ is negative.

• PROBLEM 6-17

Heavenly Flights charter club charges its members $200 annually. The club's director is considering reducing the annual fee by $2 for all members whenever applicants in excess of 60 members join. For example, if club membership stands at 60 and two new members are added, this will decrease everyone's fee by $4 and the new annual fee would be $196 per member. How many extra members maximize revenue?

Solution: The first thing to do is to find an algebraic expression for the total revenue as a function of the number of new members added. Let x be the number of new members added. Then (60 + x) is the total number of club members. The annual fee is 200 - 2x since we reduce the present $200 fee by $2 for every new member. The revenue is then the fee multiplied by the number of club members

$$R(x) = (200 - 2x)(60 + x) \quad \text{(in dollars)}$$

$$= 12{,}000 + 80x - 2x^2 .$$

To find the value of x that maximizes this function, take the first derivative of R(x), set this to zero and solve for x.

$$\frac{dR(x)}{dx} = \frac{d}{dx}(12{,}000 + 80x - 2x^2)$$

$$= 80 - 4x.$$

Set equal to zero: $80 - 4x = 0$, $80 = 4x$ and $x = 20$

is the value which maximizes R(x) because $R''(x)$ is negative. The club size which maximizes revenue is 60 + 20 = 80.

• PROBLEM 6-18

The price of a product p is $50. The cost per unit is $C(x) = 1000 + 0.01x^2$, where x is the number of units produced and C(x) is in dollars. (a) What is the profit function? (b) At what value of x is profit maximized?

Solution: (a) We have the basic relationship gross profit = total revenue - total costs. The total revenue from x units sold is price times quantity, or $50x. The costs are given as a function of x, $C(x) = 1000 + 0.01x^2$. The gross profit will also be given as a function of x.

$$P(x) = R(x) - C(x)$$

$$= 50x - 1000 - 0.01x^2 .$$

So the profit function is

$$P(x) = -0.01x^2 + 50x - 1000 .$$

(b) To find x where P(x) is a maximum, take the derivative of P(x) with respect to x, set equal to zero and solve for x.

$$\frac{dP(x)}{dx} = \frac{d}{dx}(-0.01x^2 + 50x - 1000)$$

$$= -0.02x + 50 = 0$$

$$50 = 0.02x \quad \text{and} \quad x = \frac{50}{0.02} = 2{,}500 \text{ units.}$$

P(x) is a maximum at $x = 2500$ because $P''(x)$ is negative.

• PROBLEM 6-19

Mcguill Photo estimates the receipts from selling x telescopic lenses will be

$$R(x) = 140x\left(1 - \frac{x}{10{,}000}\right) .$$

How many lenses must be sold to maximize the receipts?

Solution: To maximize, R(x), the receipt function, take the first derivative, set equal to zero and solve for x.

$$R(x) = 140x - \frac{140x^2}{10{,}000}$$

$$\frac{dR(x)}{dx} = 140 - \frac{2\cdot 140x}{10{,}000} .$$

Setting this equal to zero we get the equation,

$$140 = \frac{140x}{5{,}000} \quad \text{and}$$

$$x = \frac{140 \times 5000}{140} = 5{,}000 \text{ lenses} .$$

The receipts for this number of lenses are

$$140(5{,}000)\left(1 - \frac{5000}{10{,}000}\right) = \$350{,}000 .$$

We know this is a maximum because the second derivative $\frac{d^2R(x)}{dx^2}$ is $-\frac{280}{1000}$, a negative number. Therefore R(x) is concave downward and so this critical point must be a maximum.

• PROBLEM 6-20

Company A has found that if it offers a guarantee on its transistor radios, more will be sold than without the guarantee. In a year, the company expects to sell 100 radios if no guarantee is offered, but if the length of the guarantee is t years then the number sold will be $Q = 100 + 5t$. It is known that 10% of radios sold will fail each year. The cost of fixing a radio is $1 and a profit of $2.80 is made on every radio sold. What is the length of the guarantee period t that maximizes profit?

Solution: The object is to obtain the profit as a function of t. Since 10% of the radios sold will fail, then this is $0.10Q$ where Q is the number of radios sold. The cost is $1 per repair or $\$1(0.10Q) = 0.10Q$ dollars. Furthermore, if the guarantee period is t years, then the cost of repairs over t years is $0.10Qt$. Total profit for one year is $2.80Q. We are looking to maximize the annual profit. The profit function is

$$P(t) = \$2.80Q - 0.10Qt.$$

Substituting $Q = (100 + 5t)$, we get

$$P(t) = \$2.80(100 + 5t) - 0.10(100 + 5t)t$$

$$= 280 + 14t - .10(100t + 5t^2)$$

$$= 280 + 14t - 10t - .5t^2 = 280 + 4t - .5t^2 .$$

To find the value of t which maximizes $P(t)$, get $P'(t)$, the derivative of $P(t)$, set equal to zero, and solve for t.

$P'(t) = 4 - t = 0$ and $t = 4$ is the maximum $P(t)$ because $P''(t)$ is negative.

Annual profits will be at a maximum if

$$P(4) = 280 + 4(4) - .5(16) = \$288.$$

A warranty period of 4 years should be offered in order to maximize profits.

• PROBLEM 6-21

A wholesaler is willing to reduce the price of his $60 calculators by 50 cents for each purchase in excess of 35. For example, if the retailer buys 36 calculators, the price of each will be $59.50. What is the number of calculators that maximizes revenues under this scheme?

Solution: The basic relation is, (revenue) = (number of units sold) × (price per unit.) The price changes in response to the number of units sold. What is important is the number of units over 35. Let x represent this quantity.

The number of units sold is clearly $35 + x$. The price per unit is $60 less 50 cents for every unit over 35 or $(60 - 0.50x)$, therefore, our revenue function is

$$R(x) = (35 + x)(60 - 0.5x) = 2100 + 42.5x - 0.5x^2 ,$$

To find the value of x that maximizes R, take the derivative of R with respect to x, set equal to zero and solve for x.

$$\frac{dR}{dx} = 42.5 - x = 0 \quad \text{and} \quad x = 42.5.$$

The only problem is that the seller cannot sell one-half of a calculator. There is nothing in the mathematical model that guarantees us an integral solution. We adopt a continuous model for the revenue to be able to use calculus, but the real situation is shown below.

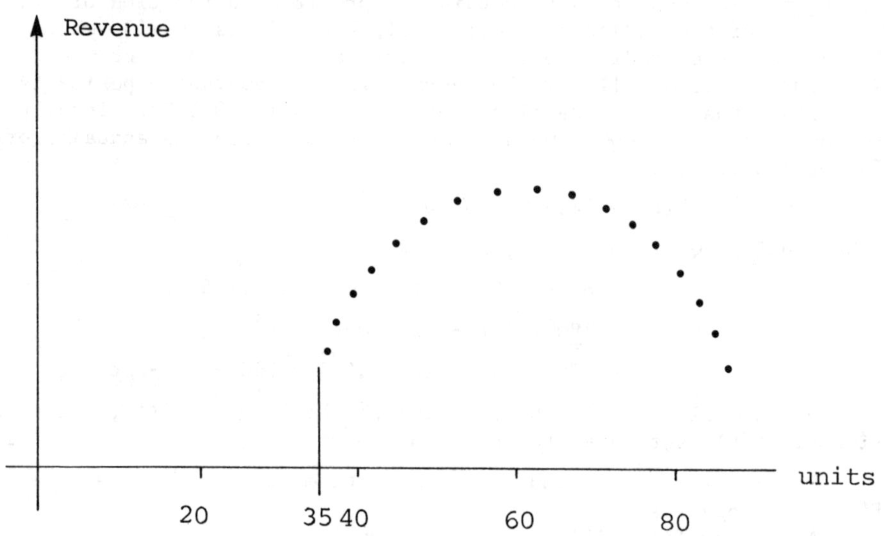

There is a series of isolated points corresponding to integral units of 35, 36, 37,... etc. The continuous model nevertheless tells us in what region $(35 + x)$ should maximize R. Try $x = 42$ which for $(35 + x)$ gives a total of 77 units.

$$R(42) = 2100 + 42.5(42) - 0.5(42)^2 = 3003.$$

For $x = 43$,

$$R(43) = 2100 + 42.5(43) - 0.5(43)^2 = 3003.$$

The nearest integers to 42.5 give the same value for the revenue and thus either one can be used to maximize $R(x)$. The number of calculators that maximizes revenue is $35 + 42 = 77$ or $35 + 43 = 78$, and the revenue in either case is 3003.

• PROBLEM 6-22

Harker Air Conditioners is selling their new car air conditioner to car manufacturers at a price of $200 each for orders of 150 or less. For each unit purchased in excess of 150 the price of all units in the purchase order will be reduced by one dollar, For example, if a customer buys 155 air conditioners, or 5 units over 150, the price per unit will now be reduced $5 to $195. What is the size of the purchase lot that maximizes the revenue?

Solution: The first step is to find the algebraic expression for the revenue. We are using the definition of revenue as

(Price per unit sold) × (number of units sold).

Let X represent the number of units sold. Given that this amount was sold, what was the price per unit? If x is less than or equal to 150, the price is \$200. If x is greater than 150 sets, the price per set is then[\$200 - \$(x - 150)] where (x - 150) is the number of sets in excess of \$150.

The revenue is given by different expressions depending on whether $0 \le x \le 150$ or $x > 150$. This revenue function has two parts corresponding to each domain of x. For $0 \le x \le 150$ the revenue is $R(x) = \$(200x)$.

For $x > 150$, the revenue is

$$R(x) = \underbrace{x}_{\text{number of units}}\underbrace{[(200 - (x - 150)]}_{\text{price per unit.}} = 350x - x^2$$

A sketch of this revenue function is shown below.

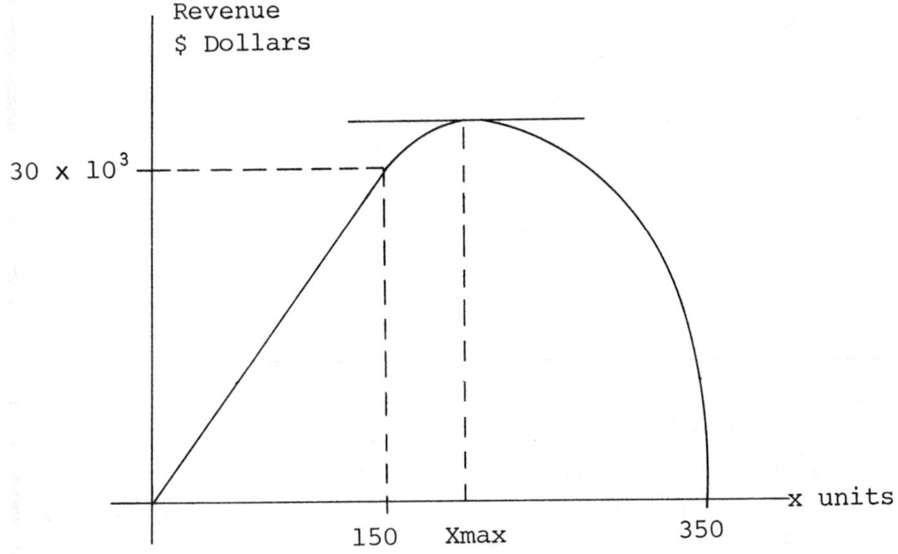

$$R(x) = \begin{cases} 200x, & \text{for } 0 \le x \le 150 \\ 350x - x^2, & \text{for } x > 150 . \end{cases}$$

Our problem is to find x_{max}. Ignore the expression for $0 \le x \le 150$ in maximizing the revenue function. The manufacturer will not offer the price reduction plan if $x_{max} = 150$ units. Then we maximize $R(x) = 350x - x^2$ for $x > 150$, by taking the first derivative of R(x) and setting it equal to zero.

$$\frac{dR(x)}{dx} = 350 - 2x_{max} = 0 \quad \text{and} \quad x_{max} = 175 \text{ units.}$$

The revenue for this amount is

$$350(175) - (175)^2 = \$30,625.$$

If we had not sketched the function we would nevertheless know this is a maximum since the second derivative of $R(x)$,

$$\frac{d^2R(x)}{dx^2} = -2$$

is negative, $R(x)$ is concave downward and therefore $(x_{max}, R(x_{max}))$ is the maximum.

• PROBLEM 6-23

The demand function of a product is shown below, and is $P(x) = 1000 - 0.005x$. The lower the price, the more quantity is demanded.

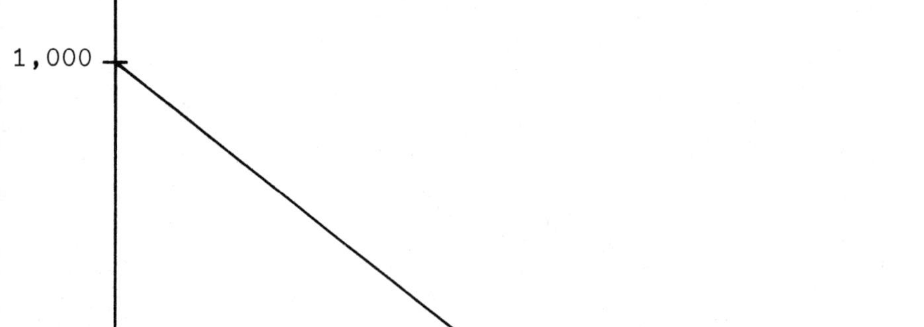

(a) What is the revenue function?

(b) What is the marginal revenue when $x = 20$?

(c) If the cost of producing x units is $C(x) = 0.5x^2 + 3.13x + 500$, how many units must be produced to maximize profit?

<u>Solution</u>: (a) If the price of a product is p and x units of the products are sold, the revenue obtained is px. The price p is a function of x, therefore the revenue is a function of x.

$$R(x) = xp(x) = x(1000 - 0.005x) = 1000x - 0.005x^2 .$$

(b) The marginal revenue function is the derivative of the revenue function.

Marginal revenue $= \frac{dR(x)}{dx} = 1000 - 0.010x$ or abbreviating,

$MR(x) = 1000 - (0.01)x$. When $x = 20$, $MR(20) = 1000 - .2 = 999.8$.

(c) Derive the profit function using $R(x)$, the revenue function, and $C(x)$, the cost function. The basic relationship is gross profit = total revenue - total costs. The profit will be a function of x.

$$P(x) = R(x) - C(x) = (1000x - 0.005x^2) - (0.5x^2 + 3.13x + 500)$$

$$= -0.505x^2 + 996.97x - 500 .$$

To find the number of units of x which maximizes $P(x)$, obtain the derivative $P'(x)$, set equal to zero and solve for x.

$$P'(x) = -1.01x + 996.97 = 0$$

or

$$996.97 = 1.01x \quad \text{and}$$

$$x = \frac{996.97}{1.01} = 987 \text{ units} .$$

A proof that the point $(987, P(987))$ is a maximum is that $P''(x) = -1.01$ is negative for all values of x.

• PROBLEM 6-24

The price of a barrel of crude oil stands at \$2 per barrel for a whole month. North Sea Wells is trying to decide how many barrels of oil a day it should extract to maximize profits. The cost of extracting x barrels of oil a day is

$$C(x) = \frac{x^2}{10,000} + 500 ,$$

where $C(x)$ is in dollars. How many barrels of oil a day will maximize profits?

Solution: The first step is to find the profit function from the information given. Keep in mind that gross profit equals total revenue minus total cost.

(a) Total revenue.

If the price per barrel is \$2, then the revenue from selling x barrels is $2x$. The revenue function is therefore $R(x) = 2x$

(b) Profit function.

Gross Profit = Total Revenue - Total Cost.

We already know the total cost of producing x units is

$$C(x) = \frac{x^2}{10,000} + 500.$$

$$P(x) = 2x - \frac{x^2}{10,000} + 500 .$$

This is the function we want to maximize.

To maximize $P(x)$, take its derivative, then set the derivative equal to zero and solve for x

$$P'(x) = 2 - \frac{x}{5000} = 0$$

or

$$2 = \frac{x}{5000} \quad \text{and} \quad x = 10,000$$

barrels a day. At $P(10,000)$ there is a maximum because $P''(x)$ is negative. From the above equation $2 = x/5000$ we note the maximum profit is obtained when marginal revenue (the derivative of the revenue function) equals the marginal cost (the derivative of the cost function). This can be proven for all cases. Given that the profit is $P(x) = R(x) - C(x)$, taking derivatives with respect to x we get,

$$\frac{dP(x)}{dx} = \frac{dR(x)}{dx} - \frac{dC(x)}{dx} .$$

Since profit is maximized when $\frac{dP(x)}{dx}$ is set equal to zero the above becomes $\frac{dR(x)}{dx} = \frac{dC(x)}{dx}$.

PROFIT MAXIMIZATION THROUGH PRICE ADJUSTMENTS

• PROBLEM 6-25

Van Helsing's Photo Shop bought a number of exposure meters for \$10 each from a manufacturer. Van Helsing estimates he will sell $(50 - x)$ meters, where x is the selling price of each meter in dollars. What selling price should Van Helsing set to maximize his profit and what is the profit made at this price?

Solution: Find an expression for the profit earned as a function of the selling price. If the selling price is x, then the profit made per meter is $(x - 10)$ dollars. The total profit is then the number of meters sold times the profit per meter:

$$P(x) = (x - 10)(50 - x) = -x^2 + 60x - 500 .$$

To maximize this take the first derivative of $P(x)$ and set it equal to zero.

$$\frac{dP(x)}{dx} = -2x + 60 = 0$$

or

$$2x = 60 \quad \text{and} \quad x = 30 \quad \text{dollars.}$$

The profit made at this price is

$$P(30) = -(30)^2 + 60(30) - 500 = \$400.$$

The profit as a function of price is sketched below.

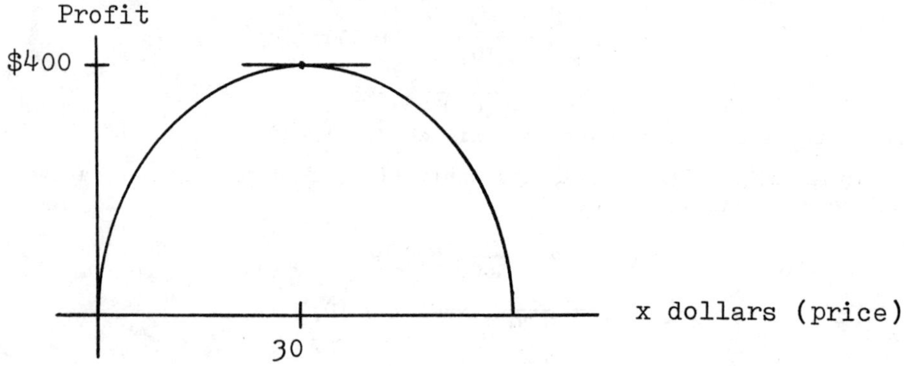

Profit

\$400

x dollars (price)

30

• PROBLEM 6-26

A single train set costs \$10 to produce no matter how many such sets are made. The demand function is $p = 90 - 0.02x$, where x is the number of sets sold and p the price paid by retailers.

(a) What is the profit function and the amount of units that should be made to maximize the profit?

(b) What price do retailers pay for the train set?

Solution: (a) If each unit will be sold at a price p, then x units will bring xp dollars in revenues. The revenue function is

$$R(x) = xp = 90x - 0.02x^2 .$$

The profit function is then the revenue function minus the cost function,

$$R(x) - C(x) = 90x - 0.02x^2 - 10x$$

$$P(x) = 80x - 0.02x^2 .$$

To maximize this profit function, differentiate and set to zero.

$$\frac{dP(x)}{dx} = 80 - 0.04x = 0$$

or $$x = \frac{80}{0.04} = 2{,}000 \text{ sets should be sold to maximize profit.}$$

The profit made is

$$P(2000) = 80(2000) - 0.02(2000)^2$$

$$= \$80{,}000 .$$

(b) The price of the train set to retailers is

$$p = 90 - 0.02x = 90 - 0.02(2000) = \$50 .$$

• PROBLEM 6-27

The managers of Disney World are considering changing the amount charged on their Humpty Dumpty ride. Presently they charge 25 cents a mile and this results in about 6,000 passengers each day. The managers believe the number of daily passengers will rise by 400 for each 1 cent decrease in the admission charge and drop by 400 for each 1 cent increase. What is the admission charge which maximizes the daily revenue?

Solution: The daily revenue is the daily volume times the rate. If the rate was 24 cents, the volume would increase by 400 and the total volume would be 6,400. Similarly, if the ride were free, $(r = 0)$ then according to this rule 6,400 + (400)(24) = 16,000 persons would ride through Humpty Dumpty Land. Given admission price r, the volume of passengers will then be $V(r) = 16{,}000 - 400r$. See that this checks with the value for $r = 25¢$. Since the daily revenue is the volume times the rate, the revenue function is in cents

$$S(r) = r\,V(r) = r(16{,}000 - 400r)$$

$$= 16{,}000r - 400r^2 .$$

To maximize, take the first derivative of $S(r)$, set it equal to zero and solve for r.

$$\frac{dS(r)}{dr} = 16,000 - 800r$$

$$16,000 = 800r, \; r = \frac{16,000}{800} = 20¢ .$$

The fare should be reduced to 20¢ to get the greatest revenue. We know that $(r = 20, V(r) = 8000)$ is a maximum because the second derivative of $S(r)$ is negative, i.e.

$$\frac{d^2S(r)}{dr^2} = -800 .$$

• PROBLEM 6-28

Ms. Hamilton knows the demand function for her sea shell ash trays is $d(p) = 20 - p$, where p is the selling price of each ash tray and $d(p)$ is the number of ash trays she can sell at price p. What price should Ms. Hamilton set on each tray to maximize revenues? Assuming that each ash tray costs \$3 to make, what price should she set on each tray to maximize profits?

Solution: We first find the revenue function. The number of units sold of a product times the price of a product is the revenue. So if the price of an ash tray is p and the number of units that are demanded is $(20 - p)$, then the revenue function is $R(p) = p(20 - p)$. We have assumed that Ms. Hamilton will be able to meet the demand fully. Given this revenue function, maximize by taking its first derivative, setting it equal to zero and solving for p.

$$\frac{dR(p)}{dp} = 20 - 2p \; ; \; 20 - 2p = 0$$

and $p = 10$ is the price at which the revenue is maximized because the second derivative of $R(p)$, $d^2R(p)/dp^2$ is negative. The maximum point is $(10,R(10))$ or $(10,100)$.

To answer the second question, we must get the profit function. Profit is defined as the revenue minus the cost of obtaining the revenue. In this case, if the cost is \$3 a unit and $(20 - p)$ units are sold then the total cost will be $3(20 - p)$. The profit function is therefore

$$f(p) = R(p) - C(p) = 20p - p^2 - 3(20 - p) = -p^2 + 23p - 60.$$

To maximize this, do the same thing we did before when maximizing revenue

$$\frac{df(p)}{dp} = -2p + 23 \; ; \; 23 = 2p \text{ and } p = \$11.50.$$

The price that maximizes profit is not necessarily the same as the price that maximizes revenue.

• PROBLEM 6-29

Grey's Truck Rental Service currently charges \$180 per week for the use of one of their moving trucks. Presently, Ms. Grey is renting out an average of 200 trucks per week. She estimates there will be a drop in demand of 1 truck per week if she raises the rental price by \$1 a truck. What is the price that will maximize revenues?

Solution: The number of trucks rented per week depends on the price increase and so does the rental charge per week. Let x be the proposed price increase and also be the resulting decrease in demand for trucks, since the amount of price increase will be equal to the number of trucks by which demand is decreased. Then $(200 - x)$ is the number of trucks rented per week. The rental price per truck is now $\$(180 + x)$.

Since revenue is price times the number of units sold (rented in our case), the revenue as a function of the price increase is

$$R(x) = (200 - x)(180 + x)$$

$$= 3600 + 20x - x^2 .$$

To find the x which maximizes this function, take the first derivative of $R(x)$, set it equal to zero and solve for x.

$$\frac{dR(x)}{dx} = \frac{d}{dx}(3600 + 20x - x^2)$$

$$= 20 - 2x .$$

Setting this equal to zero:

$$20 = 2x \quad \text{and} \quad x = 10.$$

The rental service should raise the price per truck to \$190 to maximize revenues. We know the revenue function reaches a maximum at $x = 10$ because the second derivative of $R(x)$ is negative. Thus $R(x)$ is concave downward and $(x = 10, R(10))$ is a maximum.

• PROBLEM 6-30

A bookstore can obtain from a publisher 200 anthropology textbooks for \$3 each. The store believes it can sell these books at \$15 each, but will be able to sell 10 more for every 50 cent reduction in the price. What is the price that maximizes its profit per book?

Solution: We must find an expression for the profit as a function of the price decrease. To do this we must find the revenue function and the cost function. The profit function is just the revenue function minus the cost function.

(i) Revenue function.

Let x be the number of 50 cent deductions. Then the selling price of the textbook is $(15 - 0.5x)$. For example, when $x = 4$ there have been four 50 cent deductions or a \$2 reduction, setting the selling price at \$13.

For every deduction, there will be an increase of 10 books sold so that the total number of books sold at price $(15 - 0.5x)$ is $(200 + 10x)$. From the basic relation,

$$\text{revenue} = (\text{price/unit}) \times (\text{number of units})$$

we get the revenue function

$$R(x) = (15 - 0.5x)(200 + 10x) .$$

Multiplying this out and simplifying, we get

$$R(x) = 3000 + 50x - 5x^2 .$$

(ii) Cost function

The cost function is easier to derive. The number of books is $(200 + 10x)$. At \$3 each, the total cost is

$$c(x) = 3(200 + 10x) = 600 + 30x.$$

(iii) Profit function

The profit function is $R(x) - c(x)$, revenue minus the cost.

$$p(x) = 3000 + 50x - 5x^2 - 600 - 30x$$

$$= 2400 + 20x - 5x^2 .$$

To find the value of x that maximizes $p(x)$, take the derivative of x, set it equal to zero and solve for x.

$$p'(x) = 20 - 10x = 0, \quad 20 = 10x$$

and $x = 2$ is the number of 50 cent deductions that maximize $p(x)$. The selling price of the book is

$$15 - 2(0.5) = \$14.$$

Note: $p(x)$ is a maximum at $x = 14$ because $p''(x)$ is negative.

• PROBLEM 6-31

A manufacturer is currently selling 2000 units each month of a product at \$2 per unit. The manufacturer estimates that for every 1-cent increase there will be a drop in sales by 10 units. If the fixed costs are \$500 and the material and labor costs total 40 cents a unit, at what price will the manufacturer maximize the profit?

Solution: Obtain expressions for the total revenue and total cost as a function of x. Then find the profit function, which equals the revenue function minus the cost function.

(1) Revenue function.

If x is the increase in cents of the price then the price after the increase is $200 + x$, where 200 cents = 2 dollars. We must be careful to keep track of the units. The number of units sold at $(200 + x)$ cents is $(2000 - 10x)$, i.e., for every 1 cent increase there is a drop in sales of 10 units. The revenue, $(\text{units}) \times (\text{price/unit})$ is

$$R(x) = (2000 - 10x)(200 + x) = (400{,}000 - 10x^2) .$$

(ii) Cost function.

The labor and material costs are 40 cents per unit. Since $(2000 - 10x)$ units are sold, the variable costs amount to

$$40(2000 - 10x)$$

and

$$C(x) = 50{,}000 + 40(2000 - 10x) \qquad (\$500 = 50{,}000 \text{ cents})$$
$$= 130{,}000 - 400x$$

where \$500 is the fixed cost.

(iii) Profit function.

$$P(x) = R(x) - C(x)$$

or

$$400{,}000 - 10x^2 - 130{,}000 + 400x$$
$$= 270{,}000 + 400x - 10x^2 \ .$$

To find the value of x which maximizes $P(x)$, take the derivative $P'(x)$, set this equal to zero and solve for x.

$$P'(x) = 400 - 20x = 0$$

and

$$20x = 400$$
$$x = 20 \text{ cents.}$$

The price increase should be 20 cents to maximize profits. This sets the selling price of each unit at \$2.20. The profit made is

$$\frac{P(20)}{100} = \frac{270{,}000 + 400(20) - 10(20)^2}{100} = \$2{,}740 \ .$$

We divide by 100 to convert from cents to dollars.

CHAPTER 7

PAYROLL

WAGE RATES AND GROSS EARNINGS

• PROBLEM 7-1

Harry Hyppe is paid a straight wage of $\$2.89\frac{1}{2}$ per hour. If he works 9 hours a day in a six-day week, how much will he be paid?

Solution: Wages = days/week × hours/day × wages/hour

= 6 × 9 × \$2.895

= \$156.33

• PROBLEM 7-2

L. Thea Greene is a policewoman whose standard work week is 40 hours. She is paid \$7.80 per hour. She gets time-and-a-half for working over 40 hours in a week. She worked 44 hours during the week of a power failure. How much was she paid?

In this problem, bear in mind that base pay (regular pay) is calculated on a set number of hours weekly (or daily). Hours in excess of 'regular time' are called 'overtime' and are (usually) computed at 1.5 times regular pay rate.

Solution: Regular time = 40 hrs.
Regular rate = \$7.80/hr.

Overtime = Time worked - Regular time
= 44 hrs. - 40 hrs.
= 4 hours .

Overtime rate = Regular rate × 1 ½
= \$7.80/hr × 1.5
= \$11.70/hr.

I. Regular (base) pay = Regular time × Regular rate
= 40 hrs × 7.80/hr.
= $312.00

II. Overtime pay = Overtime hours × Overtime rate
= 4 hrs × $11.70/hr
= $46.80

Total pay (I + II) = $312.00
+ 46.80
$358.80

• PROBLEM 7-3

In Neartown, there are three factories. The income data for the employees of these factories is as follows:

	Number of Employees	Average Income	Total Income
Factory A	100	$ 8,000	$800,000.
Factory B	80	$ 5,000	$400,000.
Factory C	20	$20,000	$400,000.

What is the average income of the factory workers of Neartown?

Solution: To obtain the average income of the workers for all three factories, one must add the total incomes for all three factories:

$800,000. + $400,000. + $400,000. = $1,600,000.

and divide the result by the total number of employees for all three factories.

Total of employees for 3 factories = 100 + 80 + 20 = 200

$$\text{Total Average} = \frac{\$1{,}600{,}000.}{200} = \$8{,}000. \text{ per employee.}$$

• PROBLEM 7-4

John Steiner owns a restaurant and wants to determine his average earnings over a seven year period. After all costs were paid, his annual income was as follows:

Year		Amount
1970	=	$ 7,150
1971	=	7,335

1972	=	6,520
1973	=	6,600
1974	=	6,600
1975	=	7,025
1976	=	7,810
Total for 7 years	=	$49,040.

Solution: To determine the average yearly income, add each year's income to get the total for the seven year period (see above) and then divide by the number of years (7):

$$\$49,040 \div 7 = \$7,005.7142.$$

We may round this off to the nearest dollar to get $7,006.00.

• PROBLEM 7-5

Corporation Q has the following pay scale for a laborer.

Base pay rate = $2.50/hour
Over 8 hours a day, or Saturday = Time-and-a-half
Sunday = Double time

The weekly pay period is from Saturday to Friday, and a laborer's hours of work are as follows:

Saturday,	5 hours
Sunday,	5 hours
Monday,	6 hours
Tuesday,	8 hours
Wednesday,	10 hours
Thursday,	7 hours
Friday,	9 hours.

What are his earnings for the week?

Solution: There are three rates of payment in this problem, and one must find the total number of hours at each rate, and the hourly rates.

Regular time: (2.50/hr.)

6 hr. (Mn) + 8 hr. (Tu) + 8 hr. (W) + 7 hr. (Th) + 8 hr. (F)

= 37 hours .

Time-and-a-half: $(1\frac{1}{2} \times 2.50 = 3.75/\text{hr.})$

2 hr. (W) + 1hr. (F) + 5 hr. (Sat.) = 8 hrs.

Double time: (2 × 2.50 = 5.00/hr.)

5 hr. (Sun).

Now multiply the three hourly rates by the number of hours worked at each rate:

$2.50/hr. × 37 hrs. = $ 92.50
$3.75/hr. × 8 hrs. = $ 30.00
$5.00/hr. × 5 hrs. = $ 25.00 and add the three

results for the salary = $147.50.

• **PROBLEM 7-6**

ACEPLUS SALES COMPANY wants to pay its employees a bonus as an incentive. It is decided that 70% of the labor-cost savings for the quarter will be distributed to the employees. The employer will retain 30%. The quarterly sales information is:

Total Sales	Total Labor cost
$100,000.	$32,000.

The standard total cost of labor is 40% of the adjusted sales price.

(i) What is the total amount to be paid to the employees as an incentive?

(ii) What percentage of wages earned in the quarter will the workers receive as bonus? (The bonus will be paid as a set percentage of the employee's earnings).

Solution:

(i) Total sales = $100,000.
Standard cost of labor = 40% = 0.40
Total labor cost at standard = $100,000. × .40
= $40,000.

Actual total labor cost = $32,000.

Labor cost savings to be shared (ie., Standard labor - Actual labor cost) = $8,000.

Share of labor cost savings for workers = 70% = 0.70

Amount allocated to workers = .70 × $8,000.
= $5,600.

(ii) Workers' share of labor-cost savings = $5,600.

Actual labor cost = $32,000.

Percent of share to labor cost $= \$ \frac{5,600.}{32,000} \cdot 100$

= 17.5%

• PROBLEM 7-7

Four working students have different pay periods:

Y is paid \$380 semi-monthly.

W receives \$55 per day, and works four days each week.

U is paid \$480.00 per month

S makes a bi-weekly salary of \$515.

All are paid for a 52-week year

a) What is the yearly salary of each?

b) How much does each student make, per week?

<u>Solution:</u> Income of Y :

a) \$380 semi-monthly = ? yearly
No. of monthly periods per yr. = 12
∴ no. of semi-monthly periods per yr. = 12 × 2 = 24.

Hence, annual income of Y = \$380 × 24
= \$9, 120.

b) No. of weeks per year = 52

∴ salary per week $= \frac{\$9,120}{52}$

= \$175.38

Income of W :

a) \$220 per week × 52 weeks/yr = \$11,440 per year

b) \$55 per day (4 day week) = \$220. per week

Income of U :

a) \$480 per month = ? yearly
Months per year = 12

∴ income per yr. = \$480 × 12 = \$5,760.

b) \$5,760 per yr ÷ 52 weeks/yr = \$110.77

Income of S :

a) \$515 bi-weekly = ? yearly
No. of weekly periods per yr = 52

∴ no. of bi-weekly periods per yr. $= \frac{52}{2} = 26.$

\$515 × 26 = \$13,390 per year

b_1) \$515 ÷ 2 = \$257.50 per week
(Note: \$515 bi-weekly is <u>not</u> the same as
\$515 semi-monthly.)
or
b_2) \$13,390 per year ÷ 52 weeks/yr = \$257.50 per week

• PROBLEM 7-8

> If a plumber is paid $4.50 per hour for all time worked up to 40 hours, and $1\frac{3}{4}$ time for work in excess of 40 hours. What is his pay for a 50-hour work week?

Solution:

Overtime	= total hours - regular hours
	= 50 hours - 40 hours
	= 10 hours
Regular pay	= regular hrs. × regular rate
	= 40 hrs. × $4.50/hour
	= $180.00
Overtime pay	= overtime × overtime rate
	= 10 hr × $4.50 × $1\frac{3}{4}$ = 10 × $7.88
	= $78.80
Total pay	= $180.00 + $78.80
	= $258.80

• PROBLEM 7-9

> George Henderson worked 46 hours last week. His salary provides for a base rate of $3.00 per hour and time and a half for overtime. What were George's gross earnings last week? The standard work week is 40 hours.

Solution: Gross earnings are the total amount earned before taxes and social security are deducted. To find George's total earnings, we add his pay for 40 regular hours to his pay for 6 hours (overtime). His regular salary is 40 hours × $3/hour = $120. "Time-and-a-half" means George is paid 1 1/2 times the regular rate per hour, or 1 1/2 × 3.00/hr. = 4.50/hr. His overtime wages were, therefore, 6 hours × $4.50/hr. = $27.00. His gross earnings last week were $120.00 + $27.00 = $147.00.

• PROBLEM 7-10

> Pauline Kay earns $3.50 per hour. She is paid time and a half for all hours worked over 40 per week and double the regular rate for Sunday work. Last week she worked 48 hours during the regular week and $4\frac{1}{2}$ hours on Sunday. What were her gross earnings for the week?

Solution: Pauline worked 8 hours over 40 during the week. Her time and a half rate is $\$3.50 + \frac{\$3.50}{2} =$ $\$3.50 + \$1.75 = \$5.25$. She was paid $\$3.50 \times 40$ hours + $\$5.25 \times 8$ hours + Sunday pay, which is $\$7 \times 4\frac{1}{2}$ hours = $28 + $3.50 = $31.50. Thus her gross earnings were

$$\$140 + \$42 + \$31.50 = \$182 + \$31.50 = \$213.50.$$

• PROBLEM 7-11

A machinist spent 23 1/2 hours working on a part. If he is paid at the rate of $3.90 per hour , what was the cost of his labor for the part.

Solution: The cost of the machinist's labor for the part equals his rate of pay per hour multiplied by the number of hours he worked on the part. Therefore, the cost of his labor equals

$3.90 per hour × 23 1/2 hours = $91.65.

• PROBLEM 7-12

Mary O'Grady recently worked 44 hours during a regular (Monday-Friday) week. In addition, she worked $4\frac{1}{2}$ hours on Saturday and 3 hours on Sunday. Time and a half is paid for all hours worked over 40 during the regular week and for all Saturday work. Double time is paid for all hours worked on Sunday. What were her gross earnings for the week if her regular rate is $3.10 an hour?

Solution: To do this problem, we break up her hours into regular hours, overtime and Saturday hours, and Sunday hours.

	Regular hours	Overtime and Saturday	Sunday
	40	4 (44 - 40)	3
		$4\frac{1}{2}$ (Saturday)	
Total	40	$8\frac{1}{2}$	3

We can now find her wages by multiplying her regular

hours by \$3.10, her overtime and Saturday hours by 1.5 (time and a half) times \$3.10, and her Sunday hours by 2 (double time) times \$3.10.

We then sum all the figures to get her weekly pay.

Regular hours	:	$40 \times \$3.10 = \$124.00$
Overtime & Sat.	:	$8\frac{1}{2} \times 1\frac{1}{2} \times \$3.10 = \$39.53$
Sunday	:	$3 \times 2 \times \$3.10 = \$18.60$
Total		\$182.13

• PROBLEM 7-13

Find the total earnings of an employee who worked 43 hours and earns \$3.00 per hour with time and a half for more than 40 hours per week.

Solution: To do this problem, one must first understand the terms, regular time, overtime, and time-and-a-half. Regular time is the standard number of hours worked per pay period. Regular time can be specified in terms of hours per week or hours per day. Overtime is the number of hours worked in excess of regular time. During overtime, the employee is paid more than his hourly wage. Usually he is paid time and a half. Time and a half is the sum of the hourly wage plus half the hourly wage. Here, time and half is $\$3.00 + \frac{\$3.00}{2} = \$4.50$. Total earnings equals the regular time multiplied by the hourly wage plus the overtime multiplied by time and a half. In this problem, the standard number of hours is 40, therefore since the employee worked 43 hours, he worked 3 hours overtime and 40 hours regular time.

Consequently,

$$\begin{aligned}\text{Total earnings} &= \text{regular time} \times \text{hourly wage plus overtime} \times \text{time-and-a half} \\ &= 40 \text{ hours} \times \$3 \text{ per hour} + 3 \text{ hours} \times 4.50 \text{ per hr.} \\ &= \$120 + \$13.50 \\ &= \$133.50 .\end{aligned}$$

• PROBLEM 7-14

Find the total earnings of an employee who earns \$2.40 per hour with time and a half for more than 8 hours per day if he worked 8 hours on Monday, 7 hours on Tuesday, 9 hours on Wednesday, 9 hours on Thursday, and 10 hours on Friday.

Solution: First, we must separate each day into regular time hours and overtime hours. On Monday, the employee worked 8 hours, therefore he worked 8 hours of regular time and 0 hours of overtime. We can continue like this for Tuesday through Friday, and thus obtain a chart for the number of hours of overtime and regular time each day:

	M	T	W	Th	F	Total
total hours	8	7	9	9	10	43
regular time	8	7	8	8	8	39
overtime	0	0	1	1	2	4

We see the employee worked 8+7+8+8+8= 39 regular time hours and 4 overtime hours. The overtime wage rate is $1\frac{1}{2}$ times the regular time rate or $1\frac{1}{2} \times 2.40/\text{hr} =$ \$3.60/hr. Total wages for the week were, therefore:

Regular time: 39 hours ×\$2.40/hr ...	\$93.60
Plus Overtime 4 hours ×\$3.60/hr ...	14.40
Total wages	\$108.00

• PROBLEM 7-15

John Bindels earns \$300 a month. He worked 4 hours overtime last month, for which he was paid time and a half. What were his total earnings for the month?

Solution: We need to compute John's hourly and overtime rates. When we know them, we can calculate his overtime pay, which we will add to his regular monthly pay to obtain his total earnings. The hourly rate is found by dividing the regular salary for a year(\$300/month ×12 months) by the number of regular hours in a year (40 hrs/week 52 weeks):

$$\frac{\$300 \times 12}{40 \times 52} = \frac{30 \times 12}{4 \times 52} = \frac{30}{52} \times \frac{12}{4} = \frac{30}{52} \times 3 = \frac{90}{52} = \$1.7308 .$$

The overtime rate is $1\frac{1}{2} \times$ hourly rate $= 1\frac{1}{2} \times 1.7308 = 1.5 \times 1.7308 = \$2.596$.

John's overtime pay were 4 hrs × \$2.596 = \$10.38. Therefore, his total earnings were \$300.00 + \$10.38 = \$310.38

• PROBLEM 7-16

Tim is a salesman who earns a guaranteed salary of \$4,800/year plus 4% of all sales up to \$12,000; 5% of sales from \$12,000 to \$20,000; 6% of sales over \$20,000 in any month. Last month Tim's sales were \$21,750. Compute his gross earnings for last month.

Solution: Tim receives \$4,800 + (4% × \$12,000) + 5% × (\$20,000 - \$12,000) + 6% × (\$21,750 - \$20,000) = \$4,800 + \$480 + \$400 + \$105 = \$5785. We have found the individual amounts for each percentage, and added them.

• PROBLEM 7-17

Paul Hilton receives time and a half for all work over 8 hours in a day, time and a half for all Saturday work, and double time for holidays and Sundays. During a recent week, Paul worked the following hours.

Monday	10	Friday	$9\frac{1}{2}$
Tuesday	7	Saturday	6
Wednesday	8	Sunday	4
Thursday	9		

If his regular hourly rate is \$4, what were Paul's gross earnings for the week?

Solution: If the regular hourly rate is \$4, the time and a half hourly rate is $\$4 \times 1\frac{1}{2} = \$6$ and the double time hourly rate is $\$4 \times 2 = \$8$.
Monday's wages are computed as follows: for the first 8 hours, Hilton is paid the regular \$4/hr. or 8 × \$4 = \$32 and for the rest, 10 hours - 8 hours = 2 hours he is paid the time and a half rate, 2 × \$6 = \$12. Hilton's wages for monday are \$32 + \$12 = \$44. The wages for the rest of the week are computed similarly as follows:

	Regular Time	Time and a half	Double Time	Total
Monday	8hrs x \$4 = \$32	2hrs x \$6 = \$12		\$44
Teusday	7hrs x \$4 = \$28			\$28
Wednesday	8hrs x \$4 = \$32			\$32
Thursday	8hrs x \$4 = \$32	1 hr x \$6 = \$6		\$38
Friday	8hrs x \$4 = \$32	$1\frac{1}{2}$hrs x \$6 = \$9		\$41
Saturday		6hrs x \$6 = \$36		\$36
Sunday			4hrs x \$8 = \$32	\$32
Total	39hrs x \$4 = \$156	10.5hrs x 6 = \$63	4hrs x \$8 = \$32	\$251

• PROBLEM 7-18

Buzz Reinhaus worked 63 hours last week. He was paid time and a half for 15 hours and double time for 9 hours. His regular rate was \$2.60 per hour. Calculate Buzz's total earnings for the week.

Solution: We will determine the overtime and double time rates, then compute the overtime pay and double time pay. We will then add these to Buzz's regular pay to obtain his total earnings.

Buzz is paid time and a half for overtime. As we saw in a previous problem, this is equivalent to $1\frac{1}{2}$ times the hourly rate of pay. Thus, Buzz's overtime rate is

$$1\tfrac{1}{2} \times \$2.60 = \$3.90.$$

His double time rate is $2 \times \$2.60 = \$5.20$.

Overtime pay = (number of hours overtime) × (overtime hourly rate) = $15 \times \$3.90 = \$58.50$.

Double time pay = (hours at double time) × (double time hourly rate) = $9 \times \$5.20 = \$46.80$.

Regular pay = 39 hours × \$2.60/hour = \$101.40.

Total earnings are the sum of the regular, overtime and double time pay, which is

$$\$101.40 + \$58.50 + \$46.80 = \$206.70 .$$

BONUSES AND PIECE-RATE WAGE BASIS

• PROBLEM 7-19

Leroi Wilson has a business supplying hand-made belts to boutique chains. He receives \$2.80 per belt. During a six day work week, he finishes the following number of belts: 56 on Monday, 126 on Tuesday, 130 on Wednesday, 110 on Thursday, 118 on Friday, and 56 on Saturday. What is his gross revenue for the week?

Solution: Since payment is made per piece (i.e., per belt), one must determine how many belts are produced, and multiply the total times the rate per piece (\$2.80 per belt).

(Mn)	56
(Tu)	+ 126

(We)	+ 130
(Th)	+ 110
(Fr)	+ 118
(Sat)	+ 56
	596 pcs. × \$2.80 per pc. = \$1,668.80 .

• PROBLEM 7-20

Sam's factory has four workers: Arnold, Betty, Charles and Doreen. They are paid 40 cents for each pair of pants they sew. How much must Sam pay in wages if, in one week:

Arnold sews 22 pairs of pants
Betty sews 40 pairs
Charles sews 35 pairs
and Doreen sews 114 pairs?

Solution: To find the answer, one must:

(i) multiply the number of pairs each worker sews times the rate,

(ii) and add the four wages, to obtain the total.

Arnold	=	22 pr. × \$.40	=	\$ 8.80
Betty	=	40 pr. × \$.40	=	+ \$16.00
Charles	=	35 pr. × \$.40	=	+ \$14.00
Doreen	=	114 pr. × \$.40	=	+ \$45.60
Total			=	\$84.40

Alternate Solution: Since all four workers receive the same amount per pair, we may total the number of pairs of pants completed, and multiply by \$.40:

Total number of pairs of pants = 22 + 40 + 35 + 114 = 211
Wages paid = 211 pr. × \$.40 per pr.
= \$84.40.

• PROBLEM 7-21

The Colonial Cookie Company pays on a piece-rate basis at the rate of 80 cents a piece. Mrs. Batter completed the following number of acceptable pieces last week: Monday 45, Tuesday 41, Wednesday 49, Thursday 47, and Friday 43. What were her total earnings for the week?

Solution: Some businesses pay on a piece-rate basis. This is when an employee is paid a given amount for each piece completed. The amount of money received per piece completed is known as the piece-rate. Therefore, the total earnings equal the total number of pieces completed × the amount of money received per piece, i.e., the piecerate. The number of pieces completed during the week = 45+41+49+47+43= 225 . Therefore, total earnings = 225 × 80¢ = 225 ×$.8 = $180.

• PROBLEM 7-22

Assume that you are managing a department of a store which pays its salesmen by the quota-bonus method. Each salesman receives a weekly wage for each quarterly period (13 weeks), which is 6% of his sales for the previous quarter and each new quarterly amount is the quota for the following quarter.

Question 1: Salesman 'A' sells $22,100. during the first quarter. (a) What is his quota for the second quarter? (b) What is his new guaranteed wage?

Question 2: Salesman 'A' sells $26,500. in the second 13 week period. (a) What is his bonus at 6% of sales in excess of the quota? Bonuses are 6% of the excess of actual sales over the sales quota for a period. (b) What is his quota for the third quarter? (c) What will be his weekly wage in the third quarter?

Question 3: If the sales of salesman 'O' are $23,040 in the second quarter, and $21,550. in the third quarter; (a) What is his third quarter quota? (b) What is his bonus in the third quarter? (c) What will be his weekly wage for the fourth quarter?

Solution: Part 1. (a) The salesman sells $22,100., so that becomes his new quota in the second quarter.

(b) The new guaranteed wage is 6% of the previous quarter's sales. But this has to be divided into 13 weekly payments (for the quarter-year). Therefore, we have:

$$\text{guaranteed weekly wage} = (\text{Previous sales}) \times .06 \div 13$$

$$= \frac{\$22,100. \times .06}{13}$$

$$= \frac{\$1,326.}{13} = \$102.00.$$

Part 2: (a) Amount in excess of the quota for the second quarter = $26,500. - $22,100. = $4,400.
(sales 2nd quarter) - (quota, 2nd quarter) = excess.

The salesman's bonus is 6% of this excess:

$\$4,400 \times .06 = \$264.00.$

(b) The sales amount of quarter two, $26,500, becomes the quota for the quarter three.

(c) The weekly wage for quarter three, is 6% of the sales of quarter two divided by 13 weeks

$$\frac{\$26,500. \times .06}{13 \text{ weeks}} = \frac{\$1,590.}{13 \text{ weeks}} = \$122.31 \text{ per week.}$$

Part 3: (a) $23,040 (the amount of second quarter sales).

(b) He gets no bonus. (There is no quota excess.)

(c) $\text{His wage} = \frac{.06 \times \$21,550.}{13}$

$= \$99.46\ .$

• PROBLEM 7-23

The workers of "K. Industry" are paid a bonus if they produce more than 180 micro circuits in a 40-hour workweek. The premium paid is 50% of the hours saved. They are paid $2.40 an hour. If worker 'A' completes 150 circuits in a week, and worker 'B' completes 198 circuits, how much more than worker 'A' must worker 'B' be paid?

Solution: Worker 'A' completed fewer than 180 circuits in the work week. Consequently, he does not receive a bonus.

$$\text{Worker 'A' wages} = \$2.40/\text{hr.} \times 40 \text{ hrs.}$$
$$= \$96.00 .$$

Worker 'B' gets a bonus. We must determine what value this extra productivity has with respect to future time saved.

$$\text{Work completed} = \frac{198 \text{ circ.}}{180 \text{ circ.}} \times 40 \text{ hrs.}$$
$$= 44 \text{ hr. standard.}$$

$$\therefore \text{Worker 'B' wages} = (\$2.40/\text{hr} \times 40 \text{ hrs}) + .50 \times (44-40)\text{hours} \times \$2.40/\text{hour} .$$

$$= \$96.00 + (4 \times \$1.20)$$

$$= \$96.00 + 4.80$$

$$= \$100.80$$

Note: (a) In the above computation the ".50" refers to the 50% premium paid on hours saved.

(b) The (44-40) represents the hours saved.

• PROBLEM 7-24

Barry Presco has set a task rate of 32 pieces per day at his garment shop. Workers, who complete that amount or more are paid 120% of the minimum wage rate of $2.50 per hour. The work day is 10 hours. If (i) five employees complete 26 pieces each, (ii) ten others complete 32 pieces each, and (iii) five more complete 40 pieces each, how much must Presco pay in wages for that day?

Solution:

i) Wages of first five employees = (hourly rate × no.of hrs × no. workers)

= $2.50/hr. × 10 hrs × 5

= $125.00 for the day.

Note:

These employees each completed fewer than the task number. They are paid the regular daily rate.

ii) Ten employees completed 32 pieces each. They completed the task amount, but since they did not do over the task amount, we do not have to establish a standard for hours of work saved.

Note:

Work completed = 10 hrs × $\frac{32}{32}$ = 10 hrs × 1

= 10 hr.standard (Regular day).

Therefore, the wage paid these workers will be as follows:

W = (120% × hourly rate × no.of hours × no.of workers)

= 1.20 × $2.50/hr × 10 hr. × 10

= $300.00 for the day.

iii) Five workers completed 40 pieces each. This means that we must determine an hour standard for their work. To establish a standard for hours worked means to make an equivalent in hours for a number of units produced. In part (iii), to have produced more than the standard 32 units means to have worked more than the standard 10-hour day. If a worker produced 40 units, he worked the equivalent of $\frac{40}{32}$ of a day. Although the workers who produced 26 units can be said to have worked only $\frac{26}{32}$ of a day, Presco has evidently decided to pay such workers for a ten-hour day.

$$\text{Work completed} = 10 \times \frac{40}{32} = 12.5 \text{ hour standard}$$

$$\text{Wage} = 1.20 \times \$2.50/\text{hr.} \times 12.5 \text{ hr.} \times 5$$

$$= 187.50 \quad \text{for the day}.$$

The employer, then, must pay:

$$\begin{array}{r} \$\ 125.00 \\ +\ 300.00 \\ +\ 187.50 \\ \hline \$\ 612.50 \end{array}$$

in total wages for the day.

PAYROLL TAX DEDUCTIONS

• PROBLEM 7-25

Mr. Baxter, age 68, earns $750.48 a month. Mrs. Baxter, who is three years her husband's senior, does not work. How much income tax will be withheld from Mr. Baxter's paycheck? See table on following page.
(Note: If a worker and his wife are both over 65, he can claim two exemptions for himself, and two for his wife).

Solution:

Mr. Baxter earns ($750.48/mo. ÷ 4 wk/mo)
= $187.62 per week.

He and his wife are over 65, and therefore may claim (2+2) = 4 withholding exemptions. On the table shown, follow the line which reads that wages are "at least $180, but less than $190" to the 4 exemption column. The answer is $18.30 withheld.

At least	But less than	4
180	190	18.30

MARRIED Persons — WEEKLY Payroll Period

And the wages are		And the number of withholding exemptions claimed is -										
At least	But less than	0	1	2	3	4	5	6	7	8	9	10 or more
		The amount of income tax to be withheld shall be -										
$100	$105	$13.10	$11.10	$9.10	$7.00	$4.80	$2.80	$1.00	$0	$0	$0	$0
105	110	13.90	11.90	9.90	7.80	5.70	3.60	1.70	0	0	0	0
110	115	14.70	12.70	10.70	8.70	6.50	4.40	2.40	.70	0	0	0
115	120	15.50	13.50	11.50	9.50	7.40	5.30	3.10	1.40	0	0	0
120	125	16.30	14.30	12.30	10.30	8.20	6.10	4.00	2.10	.30	0	0
125	130	17.10	15.10	13.10	11.10	9.10	7.00	4.80	2.80	1.00	0	0
130	135	17.90	15.90	13.90	11.90	9.90	7.80	5.70	3.60	1.70	0	0
135	140	18.70	16.70	14.70	12.70	10.70	8.70	6.50	4.40	2.40	.70	0
140	145	19.50	17.50	15.50	13.50	11.50	9.50	7.40	5.30	3.10	1.40	0
145	150	20.30	18.30	16.30	14.30	12.30	10.30	8.20	6.10	4.00	2.10	.30
150	160	21.50	19.50	17.50	15.50	13.50	11.50	9.50	7.40	5.30	3.10	1.40
160	170	23.10	21.10	19.10	17.10	15.10	13.10	11.10	9.10	7.00	4.80	2.80
170	180	25.00	22.70	20.70	18.70	16.70	14.70	12.70	10.70	8.70	6.50	4.40
180	190	26.90	24.50	22.30	20.30	18.30	16.30	14.30	12.30	10.30	8.20	6.10
190	200	28.80	26.40	24.10	21.90	19.90	17.90	15.90	13.90	11.90	9.90	7.80
200	210	30.70	28.30	26.00	23.60	21.50	19.50	17.50	15.50	13.50	11.50	9.50
210	220	32.60	30.20	27.90	25.50	23.10	21.10	19.10	17.10	15.10	13.10	11.10
220	230	34.50	32.10	29.80	27.40	25.00	22.70	20.70	18.70	16.70	14.70	12.70
230	240	36.40	34.00	31.70	29.30	26.90	24.50	22.30	20.30	18.30	16.30	14.30
240	250	38.30	35.90	33.60	31.20	28.80	26.40	24.10	21.90	19.90	17.90	15.90
250	260	40.20	37.80	35.50	33.10	30.70	28.30	26.00	23.60	21.50	19.50	17.50
260	270	42.10	39.70	37.40	35.00	32.60	30.20	27.90	25.50	23.10	21.10	19.10
270	280	44.10	41.60	39.30	36.90	34.50	32.10	29.80	27.40	25.00	22.70	20.70
280	290	46.20	43.60	41.20	38.80	36.40	34.00	31.70	29.30	26.90	24.50	22.30
290	300	48.30	45.70	43.10	40.70	38.30	35.90	33.60	31.20	28.80	26.40	24.10
300	310	50.40	47.80	45.20	42.60	40.20	37.80	35.50	33.10	30.70	28.30	26.00
310	320	52.50	49.90	47.30	44.70	42.10	39.70	37.40	35.00	32.60	30.20	27.90
320	330	54.60	52.00	49.40	46.80	44.10	41.60	39.30	36.90	34.50	32.10	29.80
330	340	56.70	54.10	51.50	48.90	46.20	43.60	41.20	38.80	36.40	34.00	31.70
340	350	58.80	56.20	53.60	51.00	48.30	45.70	43.10	40.70	38.30	35.90	33.60
350	360	60.90	58.30	55.70	53.10	50.40	47.80	45.20	42.60	40.20	37.80	35.50
360	370	63.00	60.40	57.80	55.20	52.50	49.90	47.30	44.70	42.10	39.70	37.40
370	380	65.10	62.50	59.90	57.30	54.60	52.00	49.40	46.80	44.10	41.60	39.30
380	390	67.30	64.60	62.00	59.40	56.70	54.10	51.50	48.90	46.20	43.60	41.20
390	400	69.80	66.70	64.10	61.50	58.80	56.20	53.60	51.00	48.30	45.70	43.10
400	410	72.30	69.10	66.20	63.60	60.90	58.30	55.70	53.10	50.40	47.80	45.20
410	420	74.80	71.60	68.50	65.70	63.00	60.40	57.80	55.20	52.50	49.90	47.30
420	430	77.30	74.10	71.00	67.90	65.10	62.50	59.90	57.30	54.60	52.00	49.40
430	440	79.80	76.60	73.50	70.40	67.30	64.60	62.00	59.40	56.70	54.10	51.50
440	450	82.30	79.10	76.00	72.90	69.80	66.70	64.10	61.50	58.80	56.20	53.60
450	460	84.80	81.60	78.50	75.40	72.30	69.10	66.20	63.60	60.90	58.30	55.70
460	470	87.30	84.10	81.00	77.90	74.80	71.60	68.50	65.70	63.00	60.40	57.80
470	480	89.80	86.60	83.50	80.40	77.30	74.10	71.00	67.90	65.10	62.50	59.90
480	490	92.30	89.10	86.00	82.90	79.80	76.60	73.50	70.40	67.30	64.60	62.00
490	500	94.80	91.60	88.50	85.40	82.30	79.10	76.00	72.90	69.80	66.70	64.10
500	510	97.30	94.10	91.00	87.90	84.80	81.60	78.50	75.40	72.30	69.10	66.20
510	520	99.80	96.60	93.50	90.40	87.30	84.10	81.00	77.90	74.80	71.60	68.50
520	530	102.30	99.10	96.00	92.90	89.80	86.60	83.50	80.40	77.30	74.10	71.00
		25 percent of the excess over $530 plus -										
$530 and over		103.50	100.40	97.30	94.10	91.00	87.90	84.80	81.60	78.50	75.40	72.30

• PROBLEM 7-26

Ms. Riggs works in the payroll department of her company, and is furnished with the following information for this week:

	Harrie O.	Jim B.	Mathew H.
Gross Earnings	$180.00	$123.16	$94.80
F.I.C.A.	8.64	0.	4.55
F.W.T.	33.70	12.50	5.40
S.W.T.	2.20	1.40	0.

(a) What should her payroll journal look like?
(b) How should her crossfoot check be done?

Solution: (a) Put the Gross Wages, F.I.C.A., F.W.T. and S.W.T. in columns so that they may be totaled. Also, there must be a Total Deductions column and a Net Wages column.

Name	1 Gross Wages	2 FICA	3 FWT	4 SWT	5 Total Deductions	6 Net Wages
Harrie O.	180.00	8.64	33.70	2.20	44.54	135.46
Jim B.	123.16	0	12.50	1.40	13.90	109.26
Mathew H.	94.80	4.55	5.40	0	9.95	84.85
Totals	397.96	13.19	51.60	3.60	68.39	329.57

To obtain the Total Deductions: One must, of course, add the deductions of each employee (i.e. F.I.C.A. + F.W.T. + S.W.T.). In Jim B.'s case, for example, there are 0 + 12.50 + 1.40 = 13.90.

When the Total Deductions are subtracted from the Gross Earnings, the result is Net Earnings. In Mathew H.'s case, this = 94.80 - 9.95 = 84.85.

(b) The procedure for a crossfoot check is as follows:

Col. 2	13.19
Col. 3	51.60
Col. 4	3.60
Sum	68.39
Col. 5	68.39

(i) Add the "Totals" of columns 2, 3 and 4 (deductions columns). This gives the sum column 5 (Total Deductions column). The two figures must be equal.

Col. 5	68.39
Col. 6	329.57
Sum	397.96
Col. 1	397.96

(ii) Next, add the Totals of columns 5 and 6 (Total Deductions column + Net Wages column). This sum must equal the Total of the Gross Wages column (column 1).

• PROBLEM 7-27

Make up a payroll, in alphabetical order from the information given below. What is the total of net incomes? Note: (i) The overtime rate (for time in excess of

40 hours a week) is 1 1/2 times the regular rate per hour. (ii) The F.I.C.A. tax rate is 5.85%. (iii) Make all deductions (F.I.C.A., F.W.T. etc.) when computing the net incomes.

Employee	Marital Status	Exemptions	Total Hours	Hourly Rate	Other Deductions
M. Snyder	M	4	42	$3.30	$4.75
G. Carver	S	6	48	$3.55	$6.25
A. Bell	S	1	45	$2.95	$4.00
J. Bose	M	2	44	$4.10	$6.10
L. Randolph	S	2	40	$4.35	$ .15

Solution:

Gross Earnings

M. Snyder : (40 × $3.30) + (2 × $4.95) = $(132. + 9.90)
= $141.90

G. Carver : (40 × $3.55) + (8 × $5.33) = $(142. + 42.64)
= $184.64

A. Bell : (40 × $2.95) + (5 × $4.43) = $(118. + 22.15)
= $140.15

J. Bose : (40 × $4.10) + (4 × $6.15) = $(164. + 24.60)
= $188.60

L. Randolph : (40 × $4.35) = $(174.) = $174.00

To be able to calculate the F.I.C.A. and other deductions, we must first know the gross earnings of each employee. This is calculated in the following manner:

Subtract 40 from the Total Hours of an employee, (provided that he/she has worked 40 hrs. or over). You now have the number of hours of overtime worked. Multiply the number of regular hours by the Hourly Rate, and then multiply the number of overtime hours by 1.5 times the hourly rate. Add the two. This is the Gross Earnings. Note M. Snyder's income:

Reg. Hrs. × Reg. Rate + Overtime × Overtime Rate = Gross
40 × $3.30 + 2 × $4.95 = $141.90

Next we must enter all information on the payroll and make all necessary calculations.

Employee	Exemp-tions	Gross Wages	Deductions				Net Wages
			FICA	FWT	Other	Total Deduc.	
Bell, A.	S-1	$140.15	$ 8.20	$20.20	$ 4.00	$ 32.40	$107.75
Bose, J.	M-2	$188.60	$11.03	$22.30	$ 6.10	$ 39.43	$149.17
Carver, G.	S-6	$184.64	$10.80	$16.60	$ 6.25	$ 33.65	$150.99
Randolph, L.	S-2	$174.00	$10.18	$24.20	$ .15	$ 34.53	$139.47
Snyder, M.	M-4	$141.90	$ 8.30	$11.50	$ 4.75	$ 24.55	$117.35
Totals		$829.29	$48.51	$94.80	$21.25	$164.56	$664.73

It is stated that the F.I.C.A. rate is 5.85% (of the Gross Wage). Therefore the F.I.C.A. tax for J. Bose

$$= \frac{\$188.60}{1} \times \frac{5.85}{100} = \$11.03.$$

The Federal Income Tax Withholding varies in amount, depending upon the worker's earnings, marital status, and the number of exemptions claimed. The amounts are found in the Federal Income Tax Withholding Table (SEE TABLE). To find the income tax of L. Randolph, for example, find the line "At least (170); But less than (180)", on the "Single Persons - WEEKLY Payroll Period" table, and follow the lines to the Two Exemption column. The amount to be deducted (in this case) is $24.20.

The Total Deductions is the sum of the F.I.C.A. + F.W.T. + Other.

Gross Wages - Total Deductions = Net Wages,

and the sum of Net Wages is found at the bottom of the Net Wages column ($664.73).

• **PROBLEM** 7-28

G. Kahn receives a wage of $3.50 an hour, and always works an 8 hour day. This week, he worked in his factory for five days. If he is married and has four exemptions (see table) for federal income tax withholdings, and pays F.I.C.A. tax (at.0585) and $5.70 in other deductions, what will Mr. Kahn's net wages be?

Solution: G. Kahn's gross wages = hourly rate × no. hours × no.days

= $3.50/hr. × 8 hrs/day × 5 days.

= $140.00

G. Kahn's deductions:

F.W.T. (wages at least $140, 4 exemptions)	= $11.50
F.I.C.A. = (.0585 × $140.)	= $ 8.19
Other deductions	= $ 5.70
Total deductions	$25.39

Gross wages	= $140.00	
- Total deductions	= - 25.39	
Net wages	= $114.61	answer.

MARRIED Persons — WEEKLY Payroll Period

And the wages are		And the number of withholding exemptions claimed is -										
At least	But less than	0	1	2	3	4	5	6	7	8	9	10 or more
		The amount of income tax to be withheld shall be -										
$100	$105	$13 10	$11 10	$9 10	$7.00	$4 80	$2 80	$1 00	$0	$0	$0	$0
105	110	13 90	11 90	9 90	7 80	5 70	3 60	1 70	0	0	0	0
110	115	14 70	12 70	10 70	8 70	6 50	4 40	2 40	70	0	0	0
115	120	15 50	13 50	11 50	9 50	7 40	5 30	3 10	1 40	0	0	0
120	125	16 30	14 30	12 30	10 30	8 20	6 10	4 00	2 10	30	0	0
125	130	17 10	15 10	13 10	11 10	9 10	7 00	4 80	2 80	1 00	0	0
130	135	17 90	15 90	13 90	11 90	9 90	7 80	5 70	3 60	1 70	0	0
135	140	18 70	16 70	14 70	12 70	10 70	8 70	6.50	4 40	2 40	70	0
140	145	19 50	17 50	15 50	13 50	11 50	9 50	7 40	5 30	3 10	1 40	0
145	150	20 30	18 30	16 30	14 30	12 30	10 30	8.20	6.10	4.00	2 10	.30
150	160	21 50	19 50	17 50	15 50	13 50	11 50	9 50	7 40	5 30	3 10	1 40
160	170	23 10	21 10	19 10	17 10	15 10	13 10	11 10	9 10	7 00	4 80	2 80
170	180	25 00	22 70	20 70	18 70	16 70	14 70	12 70	10 70	8 70	6 50	4 40
180	190	26 90	24 50	22 30	20.30	18.30	16 30	14 30	12 30	10 30	8 20	6 10
190	200	28 80	26 40	24 10	21 90	19.90	17.90	15 90	13 90	11 90	9 90	7 80
200	210	30.70	28 30	26 00	23 60	21.50	19 50	17 50	15 50	13 50	11 50	9 50
210	220	32 60	30.20	27 90	25.50	23 10	21 10	19 10	17 10	15 10	13 10	11 10
220	230	34 50	32 10	29 80	27 40	25 00	22 70	20 70	18 70	16 70	14 70	12 70
230	240	36 40	34 00	31 70	29 30	26 90	24 50	22 30	20 30	18 30	16 30	14 30
240	250	38 30	35.90	33 60	31 20	28 80	26 40	24 10	21 90	19 90	17 90	15 90
250	260	40 20	37 80	35 50	33 10	30 70	28 30	26 00	23 60	21 50	19 50	17 50
260	270	42 10	39 70	37 40	35 00	32 60	30 20	27 90	25 50	23 10	21 10	19 10
270	280	44 10	41 60	39 30	36 90	34 50	32 10	29 80	27 40	25 00	22 70	20 70
280	290	46.20	43 60	41 20	38 80	36 40	34 00	31 70	29 30	26 90	24 50	22 30
290	300	48 30	45 70	43 10	40 70	38 30	35 90	33 60	31 20	28 80	26 40	24 10
300	310	50 40	47.80	45 20	42 60	40.20	37 80	35 50	33 10	30 70	28 30	26 00
310	320	52 50	49 90	47.30	44 70	42.10	39 70	37 40	35 00	32 60	30 20	27 90
320	330	54 60	52 00	49 40	46 80	44 10	41.60	39 30	36 90	34 50	32 10	29 80
330	340	56.70	54 10	51.50	48 90	46.20	43.60	41.20	38 80	36 40	34 00	31 70
340	350	58.80	56.20	53 60	51 00	48 30	45 70	43 10	40 70	38 30	35 90	33 60
350	360	60.90	58.30	55 70	53.10	50 40	47 80	45 20	42 60	40 20	37 80	35 50
360	370	63 00	60 40	57 80	55.20	52 50	49 90	47.30	44 70	42 10	39 70	37 40
370	380	65 10	62 50	59.90	57.30	54.60	52 00	49 40	46 80	44 10	41 60	39 30
380	390	67 30	64 60	62 00	59 40	56 70	54 10	51.50	48 90	46.20	43 60	41 20
390	400	69 80	66 70	64 10	61 50	58 80	56 20	53 60	51 00	48.30	45 70	43 10
400	410	72.30	69 10	66 20	63 60	60 90	58 30	55 70	53 10	50 40	47.80	45 20
410	420	74 80	71 60	68 50	65 70	63 00	60 40	57 80	55 20	52 50	49 90	47 30
420	430	77 30	74 10	71 00	67 90	65 10	62 50	59 90	57 30	54 60	52 00	49 40
430	440	79 80	76 60	73 50	70 40	67 30	64 60	62 00	59 40	56 70	54 10	51 50
440	450	82.30	79 10	76 00	72 90	69 80	66 70	64 10	61 50	58.80	56 20	53 60
450	460	84.80	81 60	78 50	75 40	72 30	69 10	66 20	63 60	60 90	58 30	55 70
460	470	87.30	84 10	81.00	77 90	74 80	71.60	68 50	65 70	63.00	60 40	57.80
470	480	89 80	86 60	83 50	80 40	77 30	74 10	71 00	67 90	65 10	62 50	59 90
480	490	92.30	89 10	86 00	82.90	79 80	76.80	73.50	70 40	67 30	64 60	62 00
490	500	94.80	91.60	88 50	85 40	82 30	79 10	76.00	72 90	69.80	66 70	64 10
500	510	97 30	94 10	91 00	87.90	84 80	81.60	78.50	75 40	72 30	69 10	66 20
510	520	99 80	96.60	93 50	90.40	87 30	84.10	81 00	77.90	74.80	71 60	68 50
520	530	102.30	99 10	96 00	92 90	99 80	86 60	83.50	80 40	77 30	74 10	71 00
		25 percent of the excess over $530 plus -										
$530 and over		103 50	100 40	97 30	94 10	91 00	87 90	84 80	81 60	78 50	75 40	72 30

• PROBLEM 7-29

Joseph Kafka worked 7, 10, 8 1/2, 6 1/4 and 15 hours last week. He is paid $6.25 per hour for up to 40 hours/week and time and a half for over 40 hours. He is married and claims 4 exemptions. Compute his regular earnings, overtime earnings, and gross earnings. Find the FICA (Social Security) taxes, income tax withheld, total deductions, and net earnings.

Solution: Regular earnings are found by multiplying 40 hours by the regular hourly rate of pay, \$6.25. Joseph's regular earnings are:

$$40 \times \$6.25 = \$250.00 .$$

Overtime earnings are computed in the same way. Joseph worked a total of 46 3/4 hours, of which 46 3/4 - 40 = 6 3/4 were overtime. The time-and-a-half rate is

$$1.5 \times \$6.25 = \$9.375.$$

So Joseph's overtime pay was

$$6\ 3/4 \times \$9.375 = \$63.28 .$$

Gross earnings are the sum of regular earnings and overtime earnings:

$$\begin{array}{r} \$250.00 \\ +\quad 63.28 \\ \hline \$313.28 \end{array} .$$

The official FICA rate for 1976 - 1979 is 5.7% of gross earnings. 5.7% of \$313.28 is

$$.057 \times \$313.28 = \$17.86 .$$

Reading the table for weekly income tax withheld (ITW) we find that for 4 exemptions and salary between \$310 and \$320, the ITW is \$42.10. Total deductions are

$$\$17.86 + 42.10 = \$59.96.$$

Now we subtract total deductions from gross earnings to yield Joseph's net earnings.

Gross earnings	=	\$313.28
Total deductions	=	59.96
Net earnings		\$253.32 .

• PROBLEM 7-30

Louise Layne earns 692.50 bi-weekly. She supports her parents, and her son, her husband and an elderly aunt. How much will be withheld from her paycheck for taxes? See table in problem 7-28.

Solution: Louise's weekly salary = (\$692.50 ÷ 2)

= \$346.25.

She can claim six exemptions: herself, her parents (2), son, husband and aunt.

Follow the line that indicates: "At least \$340, but less than \$350" to the six exemption column in the table below. Note that all salaries are based on a weekly payroll period. From the table, one may see that the " ... Amount of income tax to be withheld" = \$43.10.

CHAPTER 8

COMMISSIONS

• **PROBLEM** 8-1

George sells vacuum cleaners for \$75 each. He receives a 30% commission on each cleaner. Last week he sold 13 machines. What were his total earnings?

Solution: George's total earnings for last week were

= number machines sold × price per machine × commission per machine as percent

= 13 × \$75 × 30%

= \$975 × .3 = \$292.50.

• **PROBLEM** 8-2

Jack receives a 5% commission on all sales. If his sales for the week are \$1,200, how much commission does he earn?

Solution: Jack's commission is a percentage of his net or total sales. Percent (%) or percentage means parts per hundred. Therefore, Jack's commission is 5/100 x (his total sales). Since his total sales are \$1,200, Jack's commission is

$$\frac{5}{100} \times (1{,}200) = \$60.$$

We can also write a formula for commission:

commission = (rate of commission) x (total sales).

• **PROBLEM** 8-3

Harry is paid a 4% commission on all sales. If he sold \$2,100 worth of goods last week, what was his commission?

Solution: Harry's commission is paid as a percentage of his sales. To determine his commission, one can use the following general formula:

$$\text{Amount of Commission} = \frac{\text{\% of sales received as a commission}}{100} \times \text{Amount Sold.}$$

% means "per 100" . Therefore, Harry receives 4% or 4/100 of his total sales as a commission. His sales last week were \$2,100. Substituting the proper values into the equation, we obtain:

$$\text{Amount of commission} = \frac{4}{100} \times \$2,100 = \$84.$$

• PROBLEM 8-4

A plot of land 100 feet by 40 feet is sold for \$75 a front foot. Compute the gross selling price. The broker receives a 7½ % commission. Find the net selling price.

Solution: The front of a plot is normally its shorter side. Thus the plot in this problem has 40 front feet. The gross selling price is the product of the rate per front foot and the number of front feet. We have

(\$75 per front foot) × (40 front feet) =

\$3,000 gross price.

The broker is paid 7½ % of the gross price, which is .075 × \$3,000 = \$225 commission. The gross price has been decreased by \$225. Therefore the net selling price is

\$3,000 - 225 = \$2,775.00

• PROBLEM 8-5

Albert Morgan sells C.B. radios. He works on a straight 5% commission basis. His sales this week were \$3,500. How much did he earn?

Solution: Mr. Morgan is paid on a straight commission basis. That means he receives a certain percentage (5%) of what he sells. This provides an incentive to increase his sales. To compute his earnings for the week, we multiply his sales for the week by his 5% commission. Note: multiplying by 5% is the same as multiplying by .05. Thus, his earnings for the week were .05 X \$3,500 = \$175.00.

• **PROBLEM 8-6**

The salesman for the Fabulous Footwear Co., receive a 1.5% commission on all sales. What would a salesman's income be for the month in which he sold $54,600 worth of shoes?

Solution: The salesman's income is computed by multiplying the percent of his commission by his sales (in dollars) for the month. Thus, the salesman's income for the month is $54,600 (sales) X .015 (commission of 1.5%) = $819.

• **PROBLEM 8-7**

Jack sells magazine subscriptions door to door after school. He is paid 85 cents commission on every subscription he sells. Last week, he sold 17 subscriptions. What was the amount of his commission?

Solution: Instead of a fixed salary, some salesmen are paid a commission. The commission could be a certain amount per article sold or a given percent of the value of the goods sold. Jack's rate of commission is $.85 for each subscription sold. Therefore his total commission for all subscriptions sold is the number of subscriptions sold multiplied by his rate of commission. Hence,

total commission = number of subscriptions X rate of commission

= 17 X $.85

= $14.45

• **PROBLEM 8-8**

Fred Lowes is a typewriter salesman. He receives $15 for each typewriter sold. If he sells 12 typewriters,what is his commission?

Solution: To compute Fred's commission, we simply multiply the number of sales by the amount he gets for each sale.

$ 15	for each sale
X 12	sales
$180	commission

• **PROBLEM 8-9**

Steven Fox is a salesman for the Maxi-Power Vacuum Cleaner Co. He receives $32.50 for each cleaner he sells,plus a 25% commission on all the accessories and supplies he sells. Find his total income for the month during which he sells 14 cleaners and $237.40 worth of accessories and supplies.

Solution: Mr. Fox's income from selling vacuum cleaners equals the commission per vacuum cleaner sold x the number of cleaners sold. His income from selling accessories and supplies equals the dollar amount of his sales x the rate of commission, i.e., 25% . Mr. Fox's total income is therefore:

14 vacuum cleaners x \$32.50 per cleaner +
\$237.40 x 25% (or .25)
= \$455.00 + 59.35
= \$514.35 .

• PROBLEM 8-10

If Susan received a \$250 commission on \$10, 000 in sales, what rate of commission did she receive?

Solution: S rate of commission is a percentage of sales, received as salary. To find what percentage Susan received, use the following formula:

$$\text{rate of commission} = \frac{\text{commission (in dollars)}}{\text{sales (in dollars)}} \times 100\%$$

$$= \frac{\$250}{\$10,000} \times 100\%$$

$$= 2.5\% .$$

• PROBLEM 8-11

Daniel receives at 6.5% commission on all sales. If he received a \$275.08 commission, what were his sales?

Solution: A commission is a certain percentage of sales paid as salary to a salesperson. Daniel's \$275.08 commission is 6.5% of his sales. If his sales equal S, then

$$\$275.08 = 6.5\% \cdot S .$$

Dividing both sides of the equation by 6.5%, or rather by .065, we get

$$\frac{\$275.08}{.065} = S$$

$$\$4243. = S = \text{sales}.$$

In general:

$$\text{total sales} = \frac{\text{commission (in dollars)}}{\text{percent of commission}} .$$

• PROBLEM 8-12

Jim Dagney is a salesman for the Beeswax Co. His weekly sales average $2,000, and his average weekly earnings (salary plus commission) are $120. Find his selling cost percentage.

Solution: The selling cost percentage is one way of determining the efficiency of a salesman. It is found by dividing his earnings by his sales. Thus Jim Dagney has a selling cost percentage of $120 (earnings) ÷ $2000 (average sales) = .06 = 6%.

• PROBLEM 8-13

Edith Calder receives a weekly salary of $80, plus a 5% commission on her sales over $1,000. Last week her sales were $1,354.20. What were her earnings for the week?

Solution: Edith Calder is working on a salary-plus-commission basis. This means that besides her salary, she receives a percentage (5%) of what she sells over a certain amount. To compute her earnings for the week, we first compute her commission, and then add her salary. To find her commission we subtract $1,000 from her sales, $1,354.20, and take 5% of the result, $354.20.

To take 5% of $354.20 is the same as multiplying $354.20 by .05. Her commission for the week was:

$354.20	(sales over $1,000)
X .05	(commission rate)
$ 17.71	(commission)

Her total earnings for the week were:

$ 17.71	(commission)
80.00	(salary)
$ 97.71	(total earnings)

• PROBLEM 8-14

Mary Rogers is a saleswoman at a department store. She has a sales quota of $900. She receives a weekly salary of $80, plus a commission of 5% on all sales and an additional 2½% on sales over her quota. What are her earnings for a week in which her sales totaled $1,200?

Solution: Ms. Roger's earnings are composed of her salary ($80) and her commission. Her commission has two parts. First, she gets a 5% commission on all of her sales ($1,200) and also a 2½% commission on all sales above her quota. Since her quota is $900, and she sold

$1,200 worth of goods, her $2\frac{1}{2}\%$ commission is paid on $300($1,200 - $900 = $300). Her commission on the $1,200 is:

$$5\% \text{ of } \$1,200 = .05 \times \$1,200 = \$60.00 \quad (5\% \text{ commission})$$
$$2\tfrac{1}{2}\% \text{ of } \$300 = .025 \times \$300 = \$7.50 \quad (2\tfrac{1}{2}\% \text{ commission})$$

Thus, her total commission is $60.00 + $7.50 = $67.50. Therefore her earnings are $80 (salary) + $67.50(commissions) = $147.50.

• PROBLEM 8-15

Salesmen for the Yearly Almanac Co. receive a 10% commission on all sales above $2,500, and a salary of $300 per month. What would a salesman's income be if his total sales in one month were $5,070.20?

Solution: The salesman's total income is comprised of his salary and commissions for the month. The salesman's commissions are paid on all sales above $2,500. Thus if he sells $5,070.20, his commission would be 10% of $5,070.20 - $2,500, or $2,570.20. Therefore, his commission would be $2,570.20 X .10 = $257.02.

His total income would be $300.00(salary) + $257.02 = $557.02.

• PROBLEM 8-16

Miss Florence Parrish earns a semi-monthly salary of $160, plus a commission of 1% of her monthly sales. During January she sold $3,680 worth of goods. What were her total earnings for the month?

Solution: Miss Parrish's total earnings for the month are the sum of her salary for the month, and her commission for the month. Her semi-monthly salary is $160.00 which means she is paid $160 twice a month. Therefore, her salary for the month was 2 x $160 = $320.00. Miss Parrish also received a 1% commission on her sales for the month ($3,680). Thus, her commission was .01 x $3,680 = $36.80. Her total earnings were $36.80 (in commissions) + $320.00 (in salary) = $356.80.

• PROBLEM 8-17

Freddy Prince is a bicycle salesman. He receives an 8% commission on all sales, plus an additional 2% commission on all sales over $5,000 a month. If he sold $7,500 worth of bicycles in May, what was his commission?

Solution: Freddy Prince's earnings are composed of a straight commission on his total sales, plus an additional commission on all sales over \$5,000 per month, which in May were (\$7,500 - \$5,000) = \$2,500. Thus, his commission was:

8% of \$7,500 = .08 x \$7,500 =	\$600
+ 2% of \$2,500 = .02 x \$2,500 =	50
Total commission =	\$650

• PROBLEM 8-18

Jack Conlon is employed on a salary-plus-commission basis. He receives a salary,of \$200 a week, plus a commission of 3% of his sales. He had sales of \$3,550 over a two week period. What were his earnings for the two weeks?

Solution: Mr. Conlon is employed on a salary-plus-commission basis. This is done frequently by companies in order to encourage salesmen to sell more goods. To compute his earnings for the two weeks, we first compute his salary. Since he is paid \$200 a week, and he worked two weeks, he was paid 2 x \$200 = \$400.00. To compute Mr. Conlon's commission, we take 3% of his sales. Taking 3% of a number is the same as multiplying the number by .03. Since he got a 3% commission on \$3,550, his commission was .03 x \$3,550 = \$106.50. Since his total earnings were the sum of his salary and commission, they equaled:

	\$106.50	(commission)
+	\$400.00	(salary)
	\$506.50	(total earnings)

• PROBLEM 8-19

Mr. Brown receives a 1% commission on all his sales. He receives an additional 1½% on all of his sales above \$1,000,000. How much will he earn if he sells \$1,200,000 worth of goods?

Solution: If Mr. Brown receives a 1% commission on all of his sales he will make a commission of .01 x \$1,200,000 = \$12,000. Since he has sold \$1,200,000 he will also receive a 1½% commission for all sales over \$1,000,000. Thus he will receive a 1½% commission on \$200,000 (\$1,200,00 - \$1,000,000 = \$200,000), of .015 x \$200,000 = \$3,000.

Mr. Brown will therefore receive a total of \$12,000 + \$3,000 = \$15,000 in commissions.

• PROBLEM 8-20

> Frank Bryant is a salesman for the Fast Cool Refrigerator Co. He is compensated for all travel expenses, and is allowed a drawing account of $600 per month. He receives a monthly commission of 2% of his first $30,000 of sales, 2.5% of the next $10,000 of sales, and 3% of all sales in excess of $40,000. Find the amount due him for a month in which his travel expenses paid out of pocket are $332.75, his drawings are $600, and his sales total $41,180.

Solution: A drawing account allows a worker to use the company's money for personal reasons; it is similar to the company giving the worker an advance of his wages. Thus, if the salesman uses the drawing account, we must subtract the amount he withdrew from what the company owes him.

Mr. Bryant's commission must be figured out in steps. He receives a 2% commission on the first $30,000 in sales, which is $600.00 (.02 × $30,000 = $600.00). Bryant had $41,180 worth of sales, so he receives another 2.5% on the next $10,000,giving an additional $250.00 (.025 × $10,000 = $250.00). He then receives a 3% commission on all sales over $40,000. This commission is .03 × $1,180 ($41,180 - $40,000) = $35.40. Thus his total commissions on the $41,180 are:

$ 600.00	on	$30,000
250.00	on	10,000
35.40	on	1,180
$ 886.40	on	$41,180

Therefore, the total amount that the company owes him is the total commission ($885.40), plus $332.75 for travel expenses. So the total amount is $1,218.15 ($332.75 + $885.40).

The actual amount due him is the total ($1,218.15) less the amount he received from his drawing account ($600.00) which is

$618.15 ($1,218.15 - $600.00).

• PROBLEM 8-21

> Loretta Gould has been offered a position as salesperson for the Houston Oil Company. Her manager estimates that her sales will amount to approximately $80,000 the first year. She may accept one of two pay schedules: (1) a salary of $8,000 plus commission of 1% of sales or (2) a salary of $5,800 plus a commission of 5% of sales over $30,000. Which pay schedule is better? By how much is it better?

Solution: Houston Oil's manager has estimated that she will sell about $80,000 worth of oil, so she computes how much she would earn under each schedule. Under (1), she finds 1% of $80,000 = 1/100 × $80,000 = 80,000/100 = $800. She adds this to her salary to obtain

$8,800($8,800 = $800 + $8,000).

She then calculates that under schedule (2) her commission will be

$$\frac{5}{100} \times (\$80,000 - \$30,000)$$

(she is not paid for the first $30,000) =

$$\frac{5}{100} \times \$50,000 = 5 \times \frac{\$50,000}{100} = 5 \times \$500 = \$2,500.$$

She adds to this her salary, which is $5,800, to obtain $8,300. Schedule (1) will pay Loretta $500 more. ($8,800 - $8,300 = $500).

If Loretta does not think she can make sales over $30,000, she might take schedule (1) where she would earn more if she didn't sell $30,000 worth of oil.

• PROBLEM 8-22

Find the gross monthly earnings of the following straight-commission sales supervisors. All of them receive 3% on the sales they make plus a 1% override on the sales made by their sales representatives.

Supervisor	Own Sales	Commission	Representatives Sales	Commission	Total Commissions
McVeigh	$25,400	$____	$31,200	$____	$____
Myerson	$16,000	$____	$ 8,800	$____	$____
Nabors	$18,250	$____	$57,745	$____	$____
Nyland	$ 8,680	$____	$121,400	$____	$____
Ormond	$20,100	$____	$45,500	$____	$____

Solution: To find the total commission of each supervisor, we multiply his own sales by his 3% (or .03) commission and his representative's sales by a 1% (or .01) commission. Then we add the two results for the total commission.

Supervisor	Commission on own sales	+	Commission on representatives' sales	=	total commission
McVeigh	($25,400x.03) = $762.00	+	(31,200x.01) = $312.00	=	$1,074.00
Meyerson	($16,000x.03) = $480.00	+	($8,800x.01) = $88.00	=	$568.00
Nabors	($18,250x.03) = $547.50	+	($57,745x.01) = $577.45	=	$1,124.95
Nyland	($8,680x.03) = $260.40	+	($121,400x.01) = $1,214.00	=	$1,474.40
Ormond	($20,100x.03) = $603.00	+	($45,500x.01) = $455.00	=	$1,058.00

Robert Rogers is a real estate salesman whose commission is 3.5% of his sales. He is married and claims three exemptions. Last month his sales were $256,225. What were Robert's gross earnings, standard deductions, and net earnings?

Solution: Robert's gross earnings are his commissions, which are 3.5% of $256,225= .035 × $256,225 = $8967.875 = $8967.88 rounded to the nearest cent. The official FICA rate for 1976-1979 is 5.7% of gross earnings, so Robert's FICA (Social Security) tax is .057 × $8967.88 = $511.17. Consulting the table for Income Tax Withheld (ITW), we find that for 3 exemptions Robert's ITW is 403.70 + 25% of excess over $2,280, which is .25 × (8967.88 - 2280.00) = .25 × 6687.88 = 1,671.97. The ITW is $403.70 + 1671.97 = $2075.67. Robert's total deductions are the sum of his ITW and FICA taxes: $2075.67 + $511.17 = $2586.84. We subtract total deductions from gross earnings to find the net earnings: $8967.88 - $2586.84 = $6381.04.

CHAPTER 9

ADVERTISING

RATE PER ADVERTISEMENT

• PROBLEM 9-1

An advertisement for a black-and-white full-page ad in Camera Magazine costs \$20,000. If the circulation of the magazine is 2,000,000, what is the cost per thousand for a single ad?

Solution: Cost per Thousand Circulation =

$$\frac{1{,}000}{\text{Circulation}} \times \text{Cost per page}$$

$$\frac{1{,}000}{2{,}000{,}000} \times \$20{,}000 = \$10.00$$

The term cost per thousand refers to the cost of reaching 1,000 readers. This is used to gauge the effectiveness of alternate magazines.

• PROBLEM 9-2

Rates for 1 Color Ad

Page	1 time basis	6 time basis
1	\$1000	\$900
2/3	\$690	\$665
1/2	\$520	\$500
1/3	\$350	\$335
1/6	\$175	\$170

\$150 charge per additional color

What is the price of one page and 5 one-sixth page advertisements within one year?

Solution: Since there are a total of 6 advertisements, we use the rates listed in the 6 time basis column.

1 page at \$900	= \$900
5 1/6 page at \$170	= \$850
Total	\$1,750

• PROBLEM 9-3

Using the schedule of rates from the previous problem, find the cost of 6 one half page advertisements.

Solution: We look up the charge for one-half page under the 6 time basis and we find a charge of \$500. Thus, since there are 6 ads, the total charge is

$$6 \times \$500 = \$3,000.$$

• PROBLEM 9-4

Using the schedule of rates from the previous problem, find the cost of a 2/3 page advertisement in 2 colors.

Solution: By looking in the schedule of rates for 1 time basis, a 2/3 page ad. costs \$690. We must add to that the extra charge of \$150 for the second color. Thus, the total charge is

$$\$690 + \$150 = \$840.$$

• PROBLEM 9-5

Popsi Soda Company had over the period of 1 year placed 12,000 lines of advertisement in the Jamestown Daily. Given the schedule of volume discounts for the Jamestown Daily, determine the cost of the advertising.

Linage Within One Year	Rate per Line or Discount per Line
Open	.50 per line
5,000 lines	10% discount
10,000 lines	12% discount
20,000 lines	14% discount

Solution: The newpaper gives a discount on its rate per line depending on the number of lines that were used by the customer. To find the applicable line rate, we take the percent of the discount, multiply it by the open rate, and subtract that result from the open rate. Then the total cost is found by multiplying the applicable line rate by the total number of lines. By consulting the table, we see that the open rate is \$.50 per line. The discount for

10,000 lines (the next discount rate is only if 20,000 lines) is 12%. Thus, the applicable line rate is:

Applicable Line Rate = Open Rate - (% of Discount × Open Rate)

$= \$.50 - (12\% \times \$.50) = \$.50 - (.12 \times \$.50)$

$= \$.50 - (\$.06) = \$.44$

Thus the total cost is equal to $\$.44 \times 12{,}000$ (lines) $= \$5{,}280$.

• PROBLEM 9-6

The Quick-Slick Hamburger Chain is extensive in the Eastern and Central regions of the U.S. They are expanding to the other regions of the U.S. They found that Good Food magazine is their best advertising medium. Below are the rates for a full page ad in the magazine. What is the difference in cost, if they advertise 6 times a year, between advertising in the Eastern & Central editions only, or advertising in the entire edition? What would it be if they advertised 12 times a year?

	1 Time	6 Times	12 Times
Entire edition	\$765	\$715	\$640
Eastern edition	340	320	290
Central edition	405	380	350
Southern edition	245	225	205
Western edition	195	180	165

Solution: On a six-time basis, a full page ad for the entire edition would cost \$715. A full page ad for the Eastern and Central editions would cost

\$320 (Eastern) + \$380 (Central) = \$700.

Thus, the difference is \$715 - \$700 = \$15 per ad. Hence the difference in the cost is

\$15 per ad × 6 ads = \$90.

If it is on the 12-time basis, a full page ad for the entire edition would cost \$640. A full page ad for the Eastern and Central editions would cost

\$290 (Eastern) + \$350 (Central) = \$640.

So there is no difference in cost on a 12-time basis.

MILLINE RATE

• PROBLEM 9-7

The milline rate is the cost of placing one agate line of space for one million readers. What is the milline rate for newspaper Y whose circulation is 878,000 and whose cost is \$1.70 per line.

Solution:

$$\text{Milline rate} = \frac{1,000,000}{\text{circulation}} \times \text{Cost per Agate Line}$$

$$\frac{1,000,000}{878,000} \times \$1.70 = 1.138 \times \$1.70 = \$1.94$$

• PROBLEM 9-8

The Daily Beetle has a circulation of 400,000. If the newspaper's rate is \$1.20 per agate line, find the milline rate.

Solution: The milline rate is the cost of reaching 1,000,000 people with one agate line. An agate line is a line of small print. To find out the milline rate we divide 1,000,000 by the circulation and multiply that result by the cost per agate line.

$$\text{Milline rate} = \frac{1,000,000}{400,000} \times \$1.20 = 2.5 \times \$1.20 = \$3.00$$

• PROBLEM 9-9

The Weekly Globe has a circulation of 352,579. Its rate is \$1.18 per agate line. What is the milline rate?

Solution: The milline rate is the cost of reaching 1,000,000 people with one agate line. An agate line is a line of small print. To find out the milline rate we divide 1,000,000 by the circulation and multiply that result by the cost per agate line.

$$\text{Milline rate} = \frac{1{,}000{,}000}{\text{circulation}} \times \text{cost per line}$$

$$= \frac{1{,}000{,}000}{352{,}579} \times \$1.18 = 2.836 \times \$1.18$$

$$= \$3.35.$$

• PROBLEM 9-10

The Daily Planet's rate for one agate line of print is \$4. It has a circulation of 2 million. What is the milline rate?

Solution: The milline rate is the cost of reaching 1,000,000 people with one agate line of print. It is used by customers in order to compare the rates of advertising of competing newspapers.

To find out the milline rate, we divide 1,000,000 by the newspaper's circulation, and multiply the result by the cost per agate line.

$$\text{Milline rate} = \frac{1{,}000{,}000}{\text{Circulation}} \times \text{Cost per line}$$

$$= \frac{1{,}000{,}000}{2{,}000{,}000} \times \$4 = \frac{1}{2} \times \$4 = \$2.00.$$

CHAPTER 10

TRANSPORTATION

SHIPPING AND MAILING

• PROBLEM 10-1

ABC Trucking Company charges a rate of $.084 per pound to transport equipment from New York City to Albany. What would they charge to ship a 275-pound washing machine?

Solution: Since ABC Trucking charges a flat rate of $.084 per pound from New York City to Albany, and the washing machine weighs 275 pounds, the shipping charge would be 275 x $.084 = $23.10.

• PROBLEM 10-2

What is the estimated REA charge for shipping a 34-pound item 295 miles?

ESTIMATED REA EXPRESS RATES
(Minimum charge will never be less than $6.75)

Weight	Up to 100 Miles	101 to 200	201 to 300	301 to 400	401 to 500	501 to 700
1 to 25 pounds	$7.30	$7.80	$8.05	$8.60	$8.90	$9.60
26 to 50 pounds	8.05	8.85	9.20	10.00	10.45	11.55
51 to 75 pounds	8.85	9.85	10.40	11.45	12.00	13.40
76 to 100 pounds	9.60	10.85	11.50	12.75	13.50	15.25

Solution: Consulting the above REA Express Rates table we see that the weight of 34 pounds falls into the 26 to 50 pounds category. Reading across the 26 to 50 pounds line to the 201 to 300 miles column, we see that the estimated REA charge is $9.20.

• PROBLEM 10-3

What is the total cost of mailing to an overseas country a $3\frac{1}{2}$ ounce letter that contains documents valued at $225 by registered mail? The overseas postal rates are 31¢ for each $\frac{1}{2}$ ounce up to 2 ounces, and 26¢ for each additional $\frac{1}{2}$ ounce. The registry fee for a letter worth $225 is $2.60.

Solution: Of the $3\frac{1}{2}$ ounces, 2 ounces will be charged 31¢ per $\frac{1}{2}$ ounce, leaving $3\frac{1}{2} - 2 = 1\frac{1}{2}$ ounces to be charged at 26¢ per $\frac{1}{2}$ ounce. The total mailing cost is:

4 × 31¢ =	$1.24
3 × 26¢ =	.78
Registry fee =	2.60
	$4.62

We multiply 31¢ by 4, because there are 4 one-half ounces in the first 2 ounces; $4 \times \frac{1}{2} = 2$. We multiply 26¢ by 3 because there are 3 one-half ounces in the additional $1\frac{1}{2}$ ounces; $3 \times \frac{1}{2} = 1\frac{1}{2}$.

VEHICLE RENTAL

• PROBLEM 10-4

Margaret Denault recently rented a truck to drive 516 miles in 3 days and 17 hours, using 54 gallons of gasoline. The rental company charged her $32 per day, $.22 per mile, and $.445 per gallon of gas. Extra hours were charged $2.75 per hour. Find the total cost of the rental.

Solution: The total cost of the rental was the sum of the time rental, mileage, and gasoline charges. The three full days, at the rate of $32 per day, cost $32 × 3 = $96. The 17 extra hours, at the rate of $2.75 per hour, cost 17 × $2.75 = $46.75. The total charge for time rental was then $96 + $46.75 = $142.75. The mileage charge at the rate of $.22 per mile for 516 miles was 516 × $.22 = $113.52. The gasoline charge, at the rate of $.445 per gallon for 54 gallons was 54 × $.445 = $24.03.

The total rental charge was then $142.75 + $113.52 + $24.03 = $280.30.

• PROBLEM 10-5

Armco Truck Rental Co. charges $32 per day, $.22 per mile, and $.55 per gallon of gasoline for renting its trucks. Additional hours a day are charged at $2.75 per hour. Mr. Williams rented a truck for 2 days and 3 hours. He drove it 320 miles, and used 30 gallons of gasoline. What was the total cost?

Solution: The total cost to Mr. Williams was the sum of the daily rental, mileage, and gasoline charges. The two full days, at the rate of $32 per day, cost $32 x 2 = $64. The additional 3 hours, at the rate of $2.75 per hour, cost 3 x $2.75 = $8.25. The total daily rental charge was then $64 + $8.25 = $72.25. The mileage charge, at the rate of $.22 per mile was 320 x $.22 = $70.40. The gasoline cost, at the rate of $.55 per gallon, 30 x $.55 = $16.50.

The total cost to Mr. Williams was $72.25 + $70.40 + $16.50 = $159.15.

• PROBLEM 10-6

CAR RENTAL SCHEDULE
Local and One-Way

Car	Rate per Day	Rate per Week	Rate for Extra Hours
Compact	$12.00 per day $.14 per mile gas included	$60.00 per week $.14 per mile gas included	$2.75 per hour over 24 $.14 per mile gas included
Standard	$16.00 per day $.16 per mile gas included	$80.00 per week $.16 per mile gas included	$2.75 per hour over 24 $.16 per mile gas included
Luxury	$20.00 per day $.18 per mile gas included	$100.00 per week $.18 per mile gas included	$2.75 per hour over 24 $.18 per mile gas included

MINIMUM CHARGE: 24-hour rate
INSURANCE (per day or any part thereof): Collision, $1.20; Liability, $1.20

What is the cost of renting a compact car for 2 days and 4 hours, and driving it 364 miles?

Solution: The total cost of the car rental is the sum of the daily rental charge and the mileage charge. The rental charge for the two days at $12 per day is $12 x 2 = $24. The rental charge for the additional 4 hours at $2.75 per hour is $2.75 x 4 = $11. The daily rental charge is then $24 + $11 = $35. The mileage charge, at $.14 per mile for 364 miles, is 364 x $.14 = $50.96.

The cost of insurance is computed on the basis of $2.40 per day for a total of 3 days equals $7.20.

The total cost of renting the compact car is therefore $35 + $50.96 + $7.20 = $93.16.

• PROBLEM 10-7

Paul Kelley used a rented compact car on a 520-mile trip that took two weeks and ten hours. Compute the charge for the extra 10 hours, the charge for mileage, and the total charge. Use the table below.

CAR RENTAL SCHEDULE Local and One-Way			
Car	Rate per day	Rate per week	Rate for extra hours
Compact	$12.00 per day $.14 per mile gas included	$60.00 per week $.14 per mile gas included	$2.75 per hour over 24 $.14 per mile gas included
Standard	$16.00 per day $.16 per mile gas included	$80.00 per week $.16 per mile gas included	$2.75 per hour over 24 $.16 per mile gas included
Luxury	$20.00 per day $.18 per mile gas included	$100.00 per week $.18 per mile gas included	$2.75 per hour over 24 $.18 per mile gas included

Minimum charge: 24-hour rate
Insurance (per day or any part thereof): Collision $1.20; Liability $1.20

Solution: The Car Rental Schedule gives the $60 per week for a compact car. The charge for 2 weeks is then 2 × $60 = $120. The charge for the 10 extra hours is 10 × $2.75 = $27.50. Thus the rental charge is

$120 + $27.50 = $147.50.

The mileage charge is $.14 per mile × 520 miles = $72.80. The total charge is the sum of the rental charge and the mileage charge,

$147.50 + 72.80 = $220.30.

CHAPTER 11

WHOLESALE DISCOUNTS

DISCOUNTS AND DISCOUNT RATES

• **PROBLEM 11-1**

What is the net cost of a tape recorder whose list price is \$32 and on which the discount rate is 30%?

Solution: Find the discount and subtract it from the list price to get the net price.

Discount: 30% of \$32 = .30 × \$32 = 9.60

Net cost = List price - Discount

\$22.40 = \$32.00 - \$9.60.

The net cost of the recorder is \$22.40.

• **PROBLEM 11-2**

Family Games Wholesalers is offering the Captain Marvel Pinball Machine at a list price of \$900 with a 25% discount. What is the net price of the pinball machine?

Solution: The net price = list price - discount

= list price - (discount rate × list price)

= \$900 - (.25 × 900)

= \$900 - \$225

= \$675.

• PROBLEM 11-3

A reclining chair has a list price of \$635 with a trade discount of 16%. What is the net price, i.e., the market price?

Solution: Discount:

16% of \$635 = 0.16 × \$635 = \$101.60

List Price - Discount = Net Price

= \$635 - \$101.60 = \$533.40

• PROBLEM 11-4

Handy Dandy Speakers is selling each unit to Tech High-Fi for \$299.50 with a trade discount of 36%. What is Tech High-Fi paying for each set, i.e., what is the net price?

Solution: The net price is the list price, in this case, \$299.50 minus the discount.

The amount of the discount is

(0.36) × (\$299.50) = \$107.82

The net price =

\$299.50 - \$107.82 = \$191.68.

• PROBLEM 11-5

Weiser Inc. is offering a discount of \$21.90 on dinette tables. The discount rate is 12½ %. What is the list price and the net price of the tables?

Solution: Ask yourself, "Twelve and a half percent of what number gives \$21.90?" In equation form, let p be this number; the question becomes,

(.125) × (p) = \$21.90.

Divide both sides of the equation by .125 to get p = \$175.20. This is the list price.

Since the net price is equal to the list price minus the discount, it is

\$175.20 - \$21.90 = \$153.30.

List price: \$175.20 Net price: \$153.30 .

• PROBLEM 11-6

You can buy a sewing machine selling for \$275 net price, or one listed at \$320 less a $12\frac{1}{2}$ % discount. Which is the best buy and how much will you save by buying it instead of the other one?

Solution: A $12\frac{1}{2}$ % discount on the \$320 sewing machine is

$$.125 \times \$320 = \$40.$$

The net price of the \$320 machine is therefore

$$\$320 - \$40 = \$280.00.$$

But this is \$280 - \$275 = \$5 dollars more than you pay if you purchase the \$275 machine.

• PROBLEM 11-7

With the invoice amount of \$190.55, and a discount rate of 2 % on a partial payment of \$90.00, what is the balance due and the discount?

Solution: To be given a discount on this invoice price is the same as having your cash payment worth more than the actual amount paid. If the actual cash payment is \$90, more than \$90 will be credited to your account, as if you had paid more than \$90. The account rate is 2% so that the amount credited to the account is

$$\$90 \div (1 - 0.02) = 90 \div .98 = \$91.84$$

to the nearest cent. The discount = amount credited - actual payment

$$= \$91.84 - \$90.00$$

$$= \$1.84$$

Balance due = invoice amount - amount credited

$$= \$190.55 - \$91.84$$

$$= \$98.71$$

In general, if the discount rate is r% and the payment made is q, then the amount credited, s, will be

$$s = q \div (1 - \frac{r}{100}).$$

The amount of the discount is $s - q$.

Given that the amount of the invoice is p, the balance due is then $p - s$.

• PROBLEM 11-8

A portable color television, listed at \$280, is being sold at a discount, net price \$196. What is the discount rate?

Solution: The discount is the list price minus the net price, in this case

$$\$280 - \$196 = \$84.$$

$$\text{The discount rate} = \frac{\text{discount (in dollars)}}{\text{list price}} \times 100\%$$

$$= \frac{\$84}{\$280} \times 100\% = 30\%$$

• PROBLEM 11-9

A calculator has a list price of \$10.00 and the seller is offering a \$4.00 trade discount. What is the percentage of the discount?

Solution: The percentage of a trade discount is calculated as

$$\%\text{ of discount} = \frac{\text{Amount of discount (in dollars)}}{\text{List price}} \times 100\%$$

$$= \frac{\$4.00}{\$10.00} \times 100\%$$

$$= 40\%$$

• PROBLEM 11-10

If the list price of a watch is \$300 and the net price is \$174, what is the percentage discount offered?

Solution: Since the list price minus the discount is the net price, to compute the discount, subtract the net price from the list price:

Amount of discount: $\$300 - \$174 = \$126.$

The percentage of the discount is then

$$\frac{\text{discount}}{\text{list price}} \times 100\% \quad \text{or} \quad \frac{\$126}{\$300} \times 100\% = 42\%.$$

SERIES DISCOUNTS

• PROBLEM 11-11

Find the NDE for the following series discounts

	Series	Net Decimal Equivalent (NDE)
	15-10-7½ %	.70763
(a)	$16\frac{2}{3}$-10-10%	______
(b)	25-10%	______
(c)	60-7½-5%	______
(d)	35-10-10-5%	______
(e)	35-10%	______

Solution: Consult the Discount Table. This gives the net value of $1 after the discount series is subtracted.

(a) Find the vertical column headed by $16\frac{2}{3}$. Move down the column to the row pair 10-10%. Read 0.675 as the NDE.

(b) Find the 25% column. Move down the column to row 10% where the required NDE is again 0.675

(c) Find the 60% column in the NDE Table. Move down the column to the row 7½, 5 and read 0.3515 as the NDE.

(d) Find the 35% column in the NDE Table. Move down to row 10, 10, 5 to find 0.50018 as the NDE.

(e) Along the same column, move up to row 10 and read 0.585 as the NDE.

In general, if the series is, say, a-b-c-d-e%, locate the a column, then move up or down the column to locate row b, c, d, e. The interesction of the row and column is the required NDE.

• PROBLEM 11-12

How can you express the discount series 20-10% as one single discount?

Solution: Multiply the complements of 20% and 10% to get the percentage of the original price that will be left after the discounts are deducted. The complement of 20% is (100% - 20%) = 80% and that of 10% is (100% - 10%) = 90%. Change 80% and 90% to decimals and multiply: (.80) (.90) = 0.72 or 72%.

Since 72% of the original price will be left, this means that 100% - 72% = 28% will be discounted.

This is equivalent to discounting 20 - 10% from the original price.

• PROBLEM 11-13

What is the net price of a bed that is list-priced at $300 and discounted first at 30%, and then at 20%?

Solution: First, discount 30% from the list price of $300:

30% of $300 = 0.3 × $300 = $90

The first discount is $90. The amount left after the first discount is $300 - $90 = $210.

Now discount 20% from this intermediate price of $210:

20% of $210 = 0.2 × $210 = $42.

This is the second and last discount.

The net price is $210 - $42 = $168.

Another method to calculate the net price of a multiple discount is to multiply the complements of the two discount rates and then to multiply this result times the list price.

The complement of the 20% discount is (100% - 20%) = 80%. The complement of the 30% discount is (100% - 30%) = 70%

80% × 70% = 0.8 × 0.7 = 0.56 = 56%.

This means that after both discounts are deducted from the original list price, 56% of the list price will be left.

Net price = $300 × 56% = 300 × 0.56 = $168.

• PROBLEM 11-14

If 10% and 20% discounts are both given on the"Speedway Racing Set", list-priced at $32, what is the net price?

Solution: It does not matter whether you discount first 10% and then 20% or vice versa. You will get the same answer.

First discount: (10%) of ($32) = $3.20

Amount left after first discount: $32 - $3.20 = $28.80

Second discount: (20%) of ($28.80) = (0.2)×($28.80) = $5.76

Net price: $28.80 - $5.76 = $23.04

• PROBLEM 11-15

Ringlet Wholesalers discounted its old line of dining-room sets at a chain discount of 30% and 10%. If the discount offered was $248.40, what was the list price and the net price of each set?

Solution: Step 1.

Find a single discount rate for the chain discount series 30% and 10%. If 30% is taken from a whole, (100%), 70% is left. If we then take 10% of this 70% we are left with 70% - 7% = 63% of the amount we started with. This means that we took out 100% - 63% = 37% of the whole. This is the single discount rate we want.

Step 2.

Ask "Thirty-seven percent of what number will equal $248.40?" This will be the list price; that is, 37% of list price = $248.40.

Therefore the list price will be $248.40 divided by the decimal equivalent of 37% or

$248.40 ÷ .37 = $671.35.

The net price equals the list price, $671.35, minus the discount, $248.40, which is $422.95. This will be the price paid by anyone buying the dining-room set.

• PROBLEM 11-16

Baskow Toys Wholesalers is offering Albee Stores the new Captain Kirk doll at 25-20% offthe retail price. If Albee Stores is buying each doll for $2.10, for what will it sell the dolls, i.e., what is the retail price?

Solution: First, find a single equivalent discount for the chain discount 25-20%. Do this by subtracting from 100% the product of the complements of 25% and 20%.

Complement of 25%: (100% - 25%) = 75%

Complement of 20%: (100% - 20%) = 80%

$$(80\%) \times (75\%) = (.80) \times (.75) = 0.6 \text{ or } 60\%$$

Single discount equivalent: 100% - 60% = 40%

The wholesale price is equal to the retail price minus the discount (40% of the retail price.)

$$\$2.10 = (\text{retail price}) - .40\ (\text{retail price}) \text{ or}$$

$$\$2.10 = .60\ (\text{retail price})$$

$$\text{and retail price} = \frac{\$2.10}{.60} = \$3.50$$

Albee Stores will sell the Captain Kirk doll for $3.50.

• PROBLEM 11-17

Alfors Motors is purchasing some new European cars which are list-priced at $6,238.42. What will it pay for each car if a chain discount of 11%, 4% and 21% is being offered?

Solution: Step 1.

Find one equivalent discount for the chain discount 11-4-21%. Taking 11% from 100% of any amount leaves you with 89% of the amount. Then subtract 4% from the 89% that is left:

$$4\% \text{ of } 89\% = 0.04 \times .89 = 0.0356 \text{ or } 3.56\%$$

This leaves you with 89% - 3.56% = 85.44% of the original amount.

Now subtract 21% of 85.44% from 85.44% to get the final percentage.

$$21\% \text{ of } 85.44\% = 0.21 \times .8544 = 0.179424 \text{ or } 17.9424\%$$

Final percentage: 85.44% - 17.94% = 67.4976% ≈ 67.5%

This means that 100% - 67.5% = 32.5 was taken out and this is the single discount equivalent of 11-4-21%.

Step 2.

The single discount applied to the list price of

$6,238.42 is 0.325024 × $6,238.42 = $2,027.64,

to the nearest cent.

Alfors Motors will then pay

$6,238.42 - $2,027.64 = $4,210.78

for each car.

• PROBLEM 11-18

Is the discount series 10-5% the same as 15%? Is a 10-10-5% discount the same as a 25% discount?

Solution: Applying the discount rate of 15% on the given amount $24.00, subtract (24 × .15) = $3.60 from $24.00. $20.40 is the amount to be paid.

The discount series 10-5% means that you will discount 10% from the given base and then 5% from the new base.

(a) Base: $24.00 First discount rate: 10%

Amount discounted: (24 × .10) = $2.40
Net amount (New base) : $24.00 - $2.40 = $21.60
(b) Base: $21.60 Second discount rate: 5%

Amount discounted: (21.60 × .05) = $1.08

Net amount: $21.60 - $1.08 = $20.52

To see that the series 10-10-5% is not the same as 25%, discount from the gross amount $24.00 as follows:

(a) Amount discounted at a 25% discount rate is

24 × .25 = $6

The net amount is

$24 - $6 = $18

(b) First amount discounted from $24 with a 10-10-5% discount series is

24 × .10 = 2.40

Net amount is $24 - $2.40 = $21.60.

Using this net amount as a new base gives the discount

$$21.60 \times .10 = 2.16. \quad \text{Net amount is}$$

$$\$21.60 - 2.16 = \$19.44.$$

Last of all, use $19.44 as the new base. A 5% discount on this yields a final price of 19.44 -(.05 × 19.44) = $18.47

So, we see that a 10-10-5% discount is not the same as a 25% discount.

• PROBLEM 11-19

What is the net cost of a $120 television set discounted at 30% and 20%?

Solution: The discounts refer to successive discounts. It does not matter if we take a 30% discount and then 20% from what remains or take the 20% discount first, and then take 30% of what remains.

First discount: (.30)×($120) = $36

Amount left after the first discount: $120 - $36 = $84

Second discount: (.20)×($84) = $16.80

Net cost is = $84.00 - $16.80 = $67.20.

• PROBLEM 11-20

A Speedway Racing Set is list-priced at $84. It is later discounted at 20% and 10%. What is the net price?

Solution: The net price is the list price minus the discount(s). First, the 20% discount is taken:

Amount of 20% discount: (0.20) × ($84) = $16.80

Amount left after discount: $84 - $16.80 = $67.20

Amount of 10% discount: (0.10) × ($67.20) = $6.72

Net price: $67.20 - $6.72 = $60.48.

• **PROBLEM 11-21**

What is the net price of a calculator list-priced at $100.00 and discounted at 40% and 25%?

Solution: First discount 40% from $100, then discount 25% from the amount you found from the first discount.

The first discount is $0.4 \times \$100 = \$40.$

The amount left after the first discount is

$$\$100 - \$40 = \$60.$$

Now take the 25% discount from $60.

The second discount is $0.25 \times \$60 = \$15$

The net price of the calculator is

$$\$60 - \$15 = \$45.$$

• **PROBLEM 11-22**

A typewriter is priced at $80, less series discounts of 20%, 10%, 5%. What is the net price?

Solution: Take the 20% discount from the list price $80.

1st discount: $0.20 \times \$80 = \$16$

The amount left after 1st discount is

$$\$80 - \$16 = \$64$$

As a second step, discount 10% from this amount, $64.

2nd discount: $0.10 \times \$64 = \$6.40$

The amount left after 2nd discount is

$$\$64 - \$6.40 = \$57.60$$

Finally, discount 5% from this last amount, $57.60.

3rd discount: $0.05 \times \$57.60 = \$2.88$

The net cost of the typewriter is

$$\$57.60 - \$2.88 = \$54.72.$$

• PROBLEM 11-23

What is the net decimal equivalent for the series 12½ - 7½ - 10%?

Solution: First method: To find the net decimal equivalent is to discount the series from an initial amount of $1.

First discount: $1.00 × 0.125 = .125

net amount : 100 - 12.50 = .875

Second discount: 0.875 is the new amount to be discounted, so

$$0.875 \times 0.075 = .065625$$

net amount: 0.8750 - 0.065625 = .809375

Third discount: 0.809375 is the last amount to be discounted; the discount is

$$80.9375 \times 0.10 = .0809375.$$

The final net amount is

$$80.9375 - 0.0809375 = 0.7284375.$$

Second method: The percent complement of any number is the difference between it and 100 percent. The complement of 12½ % is 87½ % because

$$12\tfrac{1}{2}\ \% + 87\tfrac{1}{2}\ \% = 100\%.$$

The complement of 7½ % is 92½ % since 7½ % + 92½ % = 100%,

and 90% is the complement of 10% since 90% + 10% = 100%.

To get the NDE just multiply the decimal equivalents of the complements of the discount series:

$$\text{NDE} = 0.875 \times 0.925 \times 0.90 = 0.7284375.$$

• PROBLEM 11-24

What is the net amount obtained from $4,500.00 successively discounted at 20%, 15% and 2½ %?

Solution: First method:
Use 'complements', i.e., the complement of 20% is 100% - 20% = 80%, of 15% is 100% - 15% = 85%, and of the 2½ % is 100% - 2½ % = 97½ %.

First, take 80% of \$4,500, then of this new amount, take 85%, and finally from this last figure, take $97\frac{1}{2}\%$.

$$(\$4,500 \times .80) = \$3,600 \quad \text{first amount}$$

$$(\$3,600 \times .85) = \$3,060 \quad \text{second amount}$$

$$(\$3,060 \times 0.975) = \$2,983.50 \text{ net amount}$$

But we can just as well multiply \$4,500 by

$$(0.80 \times 0.85 \times 0.975) = .663,$$

$$\$4,500 \times 0.663 = \$2,983.50$$

The order of multiplication does not matter.

Second method

The amount discounted from 4,500 at 20% is \$4,500 × 0.20 = \$900. The net amount is \$4,500 - \$900 = \$3,600. This net amount becomes our new base amount i.e., the amount from which to discount. A 15% discount on \$3,600 is \$3,600 × .15 = \$540. The net amount is \$3,600 - \$540 = \$3,060. This net amount becomes our last base amount. A $2\frac{1}{2}$ % discount on \$3,060 is

$$\$3,060 \times 0.025 = \$76.50.$$

The final net amount is

$$\$3,060 - \$76.50 = \$2,983.50.$$

• PROBLEM 11-25

(a) Given the two discount series of 30-10-$2\frac{1}{2}$ % and 25-15-2%, which is better?

(b) Given the discount series 15-15% and the single rate of 30%, which is better?

Solution: We will find what fraction of the total amount we eventually pay after the discounts.

(a) Let y be the original list price.

Series: 30-10-$2\frac{1}{2}$ %

First discount: $0.30y$; $y - 0.30y = 0.7y$. The base is $0.70y$

Second discount: $(0.70y) \times (0.10) = 0.07y$

The base is $0.70y - 0.07y = 0.63y$

Third discount: $(0.63y) \times (0.025) = 0.01575y$

The final base is $0.63y - 0.01575y = 0.61425y$

So, we end up by paying 0.61425 of the base amount y.

Series: 25-15-2%

First discount: $0.25y$, $y - 0.25y = 0.75y$. The base is $0.75y$

Second discount: $(0.75y)\times(.15) = 0.1125y$;

$(0.75y)-(0.1125y) = 0.6375y$; base $0.6375y$

Third discount: $(0.6375y)\times(0.02) = 0.01275y$

$(0.6375y)-(0.01275y) = 0.62475y$

Final base is $0.62475y$, i.e., we pay 0.62475 of the base amount y.

Since $0.62475 > 0.61425$, the series 30-10-2½ % is better, i.e., we eventually pay a smaller portion of the original price y.

(b) Let y be the base amount

Series: 15-15%

First discount: $0.15y$; $y-0.15y = 0.85y$; base $.85y$

Second discount: $(0.85y)\times(0.15) = 0.1275y$

$(0.85y) - (0.1275y) = 0.7225y$

So we finally pay 0.7225 of the base amount y.

Discount rate: 30%

Discount: $0.30y$; $y - 0.30y = 0.70y$

We pay only 0.7 of the original price, y, so the discount rate 30% is better than the series 15-15%.

• PROBLEM 11-26

Sometimes, when the percentages in a discount series are familiar fractions, such as

33 1/2% = 1/3 , 12 1/2% = 1/8 or 6 1/4% = 1/16

you can solve the problem more easily if you change the order of the discounting. What is the net amount you get from (a) \$63.60 less 16 2/3% and 10% (b) \$126.00 less 2% and 66 2/3%?

Solution: (a) We know that 16 2/3% = 1/6 and 1/6 of $63.60 is $10.60. This is the first discount. The net amount is $63.60 - 10.60 = $53.00. And 10% of $53.00 is $5.30, the second discount. The final net amount is

$53.00 - $5.30 = $47.70.

(b) The percentage 66 2/3% = 2/3.

Two thirds of $126.00 is $84.00, the first discount. The net amount is

$126.00 - $84.00 = $42.00.

This becomes the new base amount. Two percent of

42.00 = 0.02 × $42.00 = $0.84.

This is the second discount.

$42.00 - $0.84 = $41.16

The final net amount is $41.16.

• PROBLEM 11-27

Parks Wholesalers are offering a chain discount of 25-10-5% on sofas. What is an equivalent single discount for this series?

Solution: Multiply the complements of 25%, 10% and 5% to find what percentage of any given list price will be left after the discounts are deducted

Complement of 25%: (100% - 25%) = 75%

Complement of 10%: (100% - 10%) = 90%

Complement of 5%: (100% - 5%) = 95%

Product of the complements in decimal form:

(.75)×(.90)×(.95) = (.64125) or 64.125%

Since 64.125% of the original amount will be left then

(100% - 64.125%) = 35.875%

will have been taken out. This is equal to the series discount 25-10-5%.

• **PROBLEM 11-28**

ABC Publications bought 50 reams of paper at \$2.76 a ream, with a 50-10% discount . A further discount of 1% is given if payment is received within 10 days from the date of purchase. What was the amount paid if the cash discount was taken?

Solution: The gross amount to be paid is

$$50 \times \$2.76 = \$138.00.$$

We now apply the 50-10% discount. First, discount 50% from \$138.00, or

$$0.50 \times \$138 = \$69.$$

The new amount to be discounted is \$138.00 - \$69 = \$69. Now, discount 10% from this new base amount

$$\$69 - (0.10 \times \$69) = \$69 - \$6.90 = \$62.10.$$

The 1% cash discount is taken from the net amount \$62.10 and not from the gross amount.

The amount discounted is

$$62.10 \times 0.01 = 0.62, \text{ to the nearest cent}$$

The amount paid is therefore the net amount less the cash discount, or

$$\$62.10 - 0.62 = \$61.48.$$

TERMS OF DISCOUNT

• **PROBLEM 11-29**

2/10, E.O.M. E.O.M. means that the time is computed from the end of the month. In this case, a 2% discount is available if the invoice is paid within 10 days from the end of the month.

3/10, 1/30, n/60 Either of two different discounts is available depending upon when the invoice is paid: a 3% discount is paid within 10 days; a 1% discount if paid within 11 to 30 days.

2/10, R.O.G. R.O.G. stands for receipt of goods. A 2% discount is available if the invoice is paid within 10 days from the receipt of the goods (merchandise).

2/10, 30 extra Extra refers to the extra number of days allotted for the discount. In this case, a 2% discount would be available if the invoice is paid within 40 days. Extra is abbreviated as "x".

$1.55/10 Deduct $1.55 if the invoice is paid within 10 days.

2/10 as of Jan. 1 Deduct 2% if the invoice is paid within 10 days following January 1.

Menlo Wholesalers has sold one lot of electric fans to Star Hardware for $247.32 on May 17. If the terms of the discount are 3/10, 1/30, n/60, what are the net amounts due during the different time periods at the different rates?

Solution: 3/10 means that Star Hardware will get a 3% cash discount if it pays within ten days of the date of purchase. This will be on or before May 27 since the lot of fans was purchased on May 17.

Amount discounted: $247,32 × .03 = $7.42

The net amount due before or on May 27:

$247.32 - $7.42 = $239.90

Star Hardware may instead choose the terms 1/30 which mean that it will get a 1% discount if it pays within 30 days, in this case, on or before June 16. With these discount terms paying the invoice between May 27 and June 16 will give Star Hardware a discount of

$247.32 × 0.01 = $2.47.

If Star Hardware pays before May 27, it will get the 3% discount. Due between May 27 and June 16 is

$247.32 - $2.47 = $244.85.

The term n/60 means that Star Hardware must pay the full $247.32 60 days after May 17, or in other words, any time between June 16 and July 16.

• PROBLEM 11-30

The term "2/10 net 60" is an example of

(A) a quantity discount
(B) a cash discount
(C) a trade discount
(D) fair trade laws
(E) basing point pricing

Solution: When most companies sell their products, they usually have to wait some period of time before they receive payment from the customer purchasing the goods. It is almost always beneficial for the company selling the product to keep the time they have to wait for payment to a minimum. One way of doing this is to offer a "cash discount" to customers that pay their bills promptly. A cash discount is an agreement under which the customer is permitted to deduct a certain percentage from the bill if the bill is paid within a specified period of time. For example, the term 2/10 net 60 refers to an agreement under which the customer is allowed to deduct 2% of the bill if the bill is paid within 10 days; otherwise, the full amount of the bill is to be paid within 60 days. The correct answer to the problem is therefore (B).

• PROBLEM 11-31

Explain what the term 7/10 EOM means.

Solution: It is very important to many companies to receive payment for merchandise delivered to their clients as quickly as possible. In an effort to motivate quick payment, these companies will offer various bonuses for prompt payment. The term 7/10 EOM is an example of such a bonus. This term means that a customer may deduct 7% of the amount of the invoice if payment is made no later than the tenth day after the end of the month.

• PROBLEM 11-32

An invoice dated March 2 in the amount of $416.50, less 15% and 2½ % with terms of 2% 10-EOM, was paid on April 10. What was the amount remitted in payment?

Solution: Since the first discount of 15% (=.15) was allowed on the $416.50 invoice, the amount of the first discount was $416.50 × .15 = $62.48, leaving a balance of $416.50 - $62.48 = $354.02. The second discount for 2½ % (=.025) is to be taken on the $354.02, so the amount of the second discount is

$354.02 × .025 = $8.85.

This leaves a net balance due of $354.02 - $8.85 = $345.17. The term 2% 10-EOM means that if payment is made not later than the tenth day after the end of the month, an additional 2% discount may be taken. Since payment was made within the time required (before April 11) the additional discount allowed is

$$\$345.17 \times .02 = \$6.90,$$

leaving an amount to be remitted of

$$\$345.17 - \$6.90 = \$338.27.$$

• PROBLEM 11-33

On June 8, Danny's Furniture bought a set of living room furniture from Swift Wholesalers for $1,426 with discount terms of 3/15, n/30. What was the amount due if payment was made on June 22?

Solution: The term 3/15 means that a 3% discount can be taken if payment is made within 15 days from the date of purchase, on or before June 8 + 15 days, or June 23. The payment was made on June 22, in time to take the discount.

Discount given: ($1,426)×(0.03) = $42.78

Amount due: $1,426 - $42.78 = $1,383.22

So, Danny's Furniture paid $1,383.22 on June 22.

• PROBLEM 11-34

On September 17, Morley Construction purchased two hydraulic lifts for a total of $837.50 with discount terms of 5/10, 3/30, n/45. If payment was made on October 16, what was the amount due?

Solution:

The meanings of the discount terms are as follows.

5/10 - If payment is made within ten days of the date of purchase, a 5% discount can be taken. For Morley Construction this can be any time before September 27 (September 17 + 10).

3/30 - If payment is made within 30 days of the invoice date (date of purchase), a 3% discount will be given. October 17 (September 17 + 30) is the last day to take the 3% discount. This 3% discount holds for the period September 28 to October 17, since a 5% discount can be taken up until September 27.

n/45 - Full payment must be made within forty-five days of the date of purchase. November 1 (September 17 + 45 days) is the last payment day. Between October 18 and November 1 no discount is given and the entire $837.50 must be paid.

Morley Construction paid on October 16, in time to take advantage of the 3% discount.

Discount: 3% of $837.50 = 0.03 × $837.50 = $25.12

Net price: list price - discount = $837.50 - $25.12 =

$812.38

Morley Construction paid $812.38 on October 16.

• PROBLEM 11-35

The Jones House Furnishings Store purchased the articles shown on the invoice below from the Howard Hardware Company on August 3. The list price of the entire purchase is $165.06. This was discounted at 8% and 5% to get the net price of $144.27.

Payment of this amount has the discount terms of 3/10 and n/60.

(a) How much will Jones Furnishings pay if it pays on August 12?

(b) What will the payment be if it is made on August 14?

INVOICE

Frank Jones — **Buffalo, N.Y., August 3, 19__**
Jones House Furnishings Store
St. Louis, Missouri

Bought of: THE HOWARD HARDWARE COMPANY

Terms: BUFFALO, NEW YORK 14202
3/10, n/60

3¼ doz.	Strap Hinges No. S. H. 92	@ $8.28	$ 26.91
18 doz.	Carriage Bolts No. C. B. 1337	@ 5.65	101.70
9 doz.	Pkg. ¼ Rivers No. W. B. 30	@ 1.45	13.05
15 doz.	Pkg. Steel Rivers No. F. S. 17	@ 1.56	23.40
			$165.06
		Less 8% and 5%	20.79
			$144.27

Solution: (a) The term 3/10 means that if payment is made within ten days of the date of purchase, a three per cent discount will be given on the net price. Ten days after August 3 is August 13; If Jones Furnishings pays the entire bill on or before August 13, the 3% discount can be taken.

Discount: $(0.03)\times(\$144.27) = \$4.33$

Subtract the $4.33 from the net price $144.27 to get the amount paid by Jones Furnishings on August 12.

$\$144.27 - \$4.33 = \$139.94$. (Amount due.)

(b) The term n/60 means that payment may be made 60 days after the date of purchase at the latest. The 3% discount will not be given after August 13, but full payment must be made within the period August 14 to October 2. (August 3 + 60 days)

Jones Furnishings will pay $144.27 if payment is made on August 14.

• PROBLEM 11-36

On December 10, Shepp's Store bought a set of camping hotplates from Wilderness Wholesalers for $56.65 minus a trade discount of 10%. The terms offered were 2/10, n/30. If Shepp's Store paid the bill on December 20, what was the amount paid?

Solution: First, find the amount left to pay after the 10% trade discount is taken. Multiply $56.65 by .10, the decimal equivalent of 10%, to get $5.66 as the amount of the trade discount. Now, subtract $5.66 from the gross amount, $56.65, to get $50.99 as the amount left after the discount.

Any subsequent discounts will be deducted from this amount.

The terms 2/10 mean that a 2% discount will be given if payment is made within ten days. Ten days from December 10, the date of purchase, is December 20. Since payment was made on December 20, the discount could be taken.

Discount: 2% of $\$50.99 = 0.2 \times \$50.99 = \$1.02$

This discount is deducted from $50.99 to get the amount of the payment:

$\$50.99 - \$1.02 = \$49.97$

Shepp's Store paid Wilderness Wholesalers $49.97 on December 20. Had Shepp's Store waited one more day to pay, the discount would not have been in effect. The term n/30 tells us that $50.99, the price without the 3% discount, was due by January 9 (December 10 + 30 days).

• PROBLEM 11-37

Leo's Restaurant purchased a neon sign on July 1 for $202, discount terms 3/10, n/30 R.O.G. If the sign was delivered on July 12 and payment was made on July 20, what was the amount paid?

Solution: The term 3/10 R.O.G. means that a 3% discount will be given if payment is made within 10 days of the receipt of goods (R.O.G.). The sign was delivered on July 12 so July 12 + 10 days, or July 22, is the final day the discount may be taken or anytime prior to this. The term n/30 means that payment must be made by July 12 + 30 days, or August 11. Paying during the period from July 23 to August 11 will not give any discount, so the full amount, $202, must be payed.

Leo's Restaurant paid before July 22 and could therefore take the 3% discount.

Discount: 3% of $202 = 0.03 × $202 = $6.06

To find the amount paid, subtract the $6.06 discount from the list price, $202, to get $195.94.

• PROBLEM 11-38

Shipley and Star ordered one lot of portable cassette machines from Stereo Electonics, list-priced at $987.70, on June 3. The invoice was dated June 10 and the terms were n/30 ROG.

(a) On what date would the payment be due if the machines were received July 30?

(b) If the terms 2/10, n/30 were offered, payment was made on August 4 and the invoice was date July 30, what was the amount paid?

Solution: (a) n/30 ROG means that full payment must be made within 30 days after receipt of goods (ROG), without any discount.

Thirty days after July 30 is August 29. \$987.70 was supposed to be paid by this day.

(b) 2/10 means that if payment is made within 10 days after the date of purchase, a 2% discount will be given. Payment must be made on or before August 9 (July 30 + 10 days) for the discount to be given. The payment was made on August 4 so the 2% discount was given.

Discount: (2%) of (list price)

$$(0.02)\times(\$987.70) = \$19.75$$

(rounded to the nearest cent)

(list price) - (discount) = (net price)

$$\$987.70 - \$19.75 = \$967.95.$$

Shipley and Star paid Stereo Electronics \$967.95 on August 4.

• PROBLEM 11-39

An invoice of \$10,000 is marked 6/10, n/30. Find the annual percentage rate.

Solution: The marking 6/10, n/30 means if the invoice is paid within 10 days you can apply a 6% discount, and the invoice must be paid in 30 days. Since if the bill is paid promptly we have a 6% discount, we can consider it as saying the amount due is the invoice less the discount, and you are charged at a certain rate for holding the payments for 30 days. To get the rate we divide the amount of the discount by the amount due, and then multiply by 12 because the charge was for one month and there are 12 months in a year.

$$\text{Discount} = 6\% \times \$1{,}000 = .06 \times \$1{,}000 = \$60$$

$$\text{Amount due} = \$1{,}000 - \$60 = \$940$$

$$\text{Monthly rate} = \frac{60}{940} = .0638 = 6.38\%$$

$$\text{Annual percentage rate} = 6.38\% \times 12 = 76.56\%.$$

CHAPTER 12

RETAILING

RETAILING MARKDOWNS AND DISCOUNTS

• PROBLEM 12-1

The list price of a book is \$4.95. It sells in a bookstore at a net price of \$2.95. What is the amount of trade discount?

Solution: The trade discount is the amount of money that the book is discounted from the list price. To find it we subtract the net price from the list price, giving \$4.95 - \$2.95 = \$2.00.

• PROBLEM 12-2

What is the percent markdown on an item that was reduced from \$10.00 to \$8.00 ?

Solution: We find the difference between the original and the reduced prices and divide it by the reduced price.

$$\text{Markdown percent} = \frac{\text{Original Price - Reduced Price}}{\text{Reduced Price}}$$

$$= \frac{\$10 - \$8}{\$8} = \frac{\$2}{\$8} = .25 = 25\%$$

• PROBLEM 12-3

Bob's Camera Shop reduced the price of their worst selling camera by $8\frac{1}{3}$ %.
The camera originally sold for \$65. How much is the camera selling for now?

Solution: We subtract the $8\frac{1}{3}$ % discount from

the original selling price. The discount is equal to $8\frac{1}{3}\%$ of $\$65 = (0.08333) \times \$65 = \$5.42$ to the nearest cent. The selling price is therefore

$$\$65 - \$5.42 = \$59.58.$$

• PROBLEM 12-4

Herbie's Service Station bought a water pump from his supplier that has a list price of $40. His trade discount is $16. Find the net price.

Solution: The net price is the list price minus the trade discount. This is the amount of money (not including taxes) that the service station must pay. It is $\$40 - \$16 = \$24$.

• PROBLEM 12-5

A toy was originally priced at $2.25 and was later marked down to sell at $2.00. Find the percent of markdown.

Solution: Find the difference between the original and the reduced prices and divide it by the reduced price.

$$\text{Markdown percent} = \frac{\text{Original Price} - \text{Reduced Price}}{\text{Reduced Price}}$$

$$= \frac{\$2.25 - \$2.00}{\$2.00} = \frac{\$.25}{\$2.00} = .125 = 12.5\%$$

• PROBLEM 12-6

A store put an item on sale discounting it by 10%. The next day they decided to discount it another 10%. What was the total discount over the two days?

Solution: The total discount of the item can be found by noticing that after the first discount of 10% the new selling price was 90% (100% - 10%) of the original selling price. The next 10% discount is applied to the current selling price. Thus, the discount is 10% of 90% of the original selling price. In other terms it is .10 × .90 = .09 or 9% of the original selling price. Subtracting the discount from the price we find the price to be 81% of the original selling price (90% - 9% = 81%). Thus, the total discount was 100% (original price) - 81% (new price) = 19%.

• PROBLEM 12-7

A shirt in Fabers Clothing Store originally sold for $6.75. During a storewide sale it was reduced to $4.50. After the sale the price was changed to $5.50. Find the gross and net markdown in dollars, and the net markdown as a percent of the current price.

Solution: The gross markdown is found by subtracting the new selling price from the original, in this case $6.75 - $4.50 = $2.25. The net markdown is the gross markdown less the markdown cancellation. The markdown cancellation is the new price less the sale price, giving $5.50 - 4.50=$1. Hence the net markdown is $2.25 - $1.00 = $1.25. The net markdown in percent is found by dividing the net markdown by the current price. It is

$$\frac{\$1.25}{\$5.50} \times 100\% = 22.7\%$$

MARKUPS

• PROBLEM 12-8

A stereo system sells for $200. The cost to the store is $120. Find the dollar markup.

Solution: The selling price of the stereo is equal to the cost plus the markup. Thus the markup can be found by subtracting the cost from the selling price.

$$\begin{aligned} \text{Markup} &= \text{Selling Price} - \text{Cost} \\ &= \$200.00 - \$120.00 \\ &= \$80.00 \end{aligned}$$

• PROBLEM 12-9

A dress sells for $50.00. It has a percent markup of 40% based on the selling price. Find the markup in dollars.

Solution: The percent markup based on the selling price means that the markup is 40% of the selling price. To find the markup in dollars, we multiply the selling price (\$50.00) by the percent markup (40%), giving 40% of \$50.00 = .40 × \$50.00 = \$20.00. Hence the markup in dollars is \$20.00.

• PROBLEM 12-10

A tapedeck sells for \$200. The dollar markup is \$80. Find the percent markup based on the selling price.

Solution: The percent markup based on the selling price is the markup divided by the selling price times 100%.

$$\text{percent markup} = \frac{\text{markup in \$}}{\text{selling price}} = \frac{\$80}{\$200} = .4 = 40\ \%$$

• PROBLEM 12-11

The markup on a camera is 20% based on the cost. Find the percent markup based on the selling price.

Solution: The selling price is equal to the cost plus the markup. Since the markup is 20% of the cost, the selling price is equal to cost + 20% × cost = 100% × cost + 20% × cost = 120% × cost. The markup based on the selling price is equal to the markup divided by the selling price.

$$\frac{\text{markup}}{\text{selling price}} = \frac{20\% \times \text{cost}}{120\% \times \text{cost}} = \frac{.2}{1.2} = .1667 \text{ or } 16\ \frac{2}{3}\ \%.$$

• PROBLEM 12-12

A C.B. radio sells for \$89.95. The store pays \$65.05 for each. Find the percent markup based on the cost and also based on the selling price.

Solution: The selling price is made up of the cost plus the markup. To find the markup, we subtract the cost from the selling price, giving \$89.95 - \$65.05 =

$24.90. To find the percent markup based on the cost, we divide the markup by the cost, giving $24.90 ÷ $65.05 = .3828 = 38.28%. The percent markup based on the selling price is the markup divided by the selling price, giving $24.90 ÷ $89.95 = .2768 = 27.68%.

• PROBLEM 12-13

Joe's Department Store wishes to sell a coat with a 20% margin on the selling price. The cost of the coat is $40. Find their selling price.

Solution: They wish to sell the coat for a 20% margin; that means that the amount by which the selling price exceeds the cost is 20% of the selling price. The cost is 80% (100% - 20%) of the selling price. Thus, we can find the selling price.

Cost = 80% of selling price

$40 = .80 × selling price

$$\$\frac{40}{.80} = \text{selling price}$$

$50 = selling price

• PROBLEM 12-14

Jane's Bargain store buys children's shirts for $3.00 and sells them for $4.00. Find the percent markup based on the cost.

Solution: The markup in dollars is the selling price minus the cost, being $4.00 - $3.00 = $1.00. The percent markup based on the cost is found by dividing the markup by the cost and converting the resulting decimal to a percentage.

$$\text{percent markup} = \frac{\text{markup}}{\text{cost}} = \frac{\$1.00}{\$3.00} = .3333 = 33\tfrac{1}{3}\%$$

• PROBLEM 12-15

A television sells for $180. It costs the retailer $136.50. Find the percent markup based on the selling price.

Solution: The markup is equal to the selling price minus the cost, giving $180.00 - $136.50 = $43.50. The percent markup based on the selling price is found by dividing the markup by the selling price and then converting the resulting decimal to a percentage

$$\text{percent markup} = \$43.50 \div \$180.00 = .2417 \text{ or } 24.17\%$$

• PROBLEM 12-16

A radio was originally priced at $2.25. This week it was marked up and sold at $2.50. Find the percent of the markup.

Solution: The markup percentage is found by dividing the difference between the new and the original prices by the new price.

$$\text{Markup percent} = \frac{\text{New Price - Original Price}}{\text{New Price}}$$

$$= \frac{\$2.50 - \$2.25}{\$2.50} = \frac{\$.25}{\$2.50} = .10 = 10\%$$

• PROBLEM 12-17

Jackson and Co. are buying electric blankets for $18.75 each. They wish to have a markup of 40% on the cost. Find their selling price.

Solution: The selling price is equal to the sum of the cost and the markup. Since the markup is 40% of the cost, we know selling price = cost + 40% of cost or

$$\text{selling price} = \$18.75 + (0.4) \times \$18.75$$

$$= \$18.75 + \$7.50 = \$26.25$$

• PROBLEM 12-18

A record sells for $3.24. There is a 35% markup based on the selling price. Find the cost of the record.

Solution: The selling price is the cost plus the markup. Since the markup is 35% of the selling price, we see that the cost is 65% (100% - 35%) of the selling price. Hence the cost is equal to 65% of \$3.24 (selling price) = .65 × \$3.24 = \$2.11, rounding off to the nearest cent.

• PROBLEM 12-19

A sofa has a markup of 20% based on its selling price. Find the percent markup based on the cost.

Solution: The selling price is equal to the cost plus the markup. Since the markup is 20% of the selling price, we see that the cost is 80% (100% - 20%) of the selling price. The percent markup based on cost can be found by dividing the markup by the cost.

$$\text{percent markup} = \frac{\text{markup}}{\text{cost}} = \frac{20\% \times \text{selling price}}{80\% \times \text{selling price}}$$

$$= \frac{.2}{.8} = .25 \text{ or } 25\%.$$

• PROBLEM 12-20

A television sells for \$226.50. The markup is 30% based on the cost. Find the cost.

Solution: The selling price is equal to the cost plus the markup. Since the markup is equal to 30% of the cost, the selling price is equal to the cost plus 30% of the cost.

$$\text{Selling Price} = \text{Cost} + (30\% \text{ of the cost})$$

$$= \text{cost} + .30 \text{ cost} = 1.3 \text{ cost}$$

or

$$\$226.50 = 1.3 \text{ cost}$$

and the cost is $\frac{\$226.50}{1.3} = \$174.23.$

• PROBLEM 12-21

Find the cost in dollars of \$200,000 worth of stock at retail if the markup is 30% of selling price.

Solution: The worth of the stock is equal to the cost plus the markup. Hence, the cost is 100% - 30%= 70% of the worth. The cost in dollars can be found by multiplying the worth of the stock by 70%, obtaining 70% of \$200,000 = .70 × \$200,000 = \$140,000.

• PROBLEM 12-22

Vinnie wishes to sell an item that cost him \$18.20 at a 40% markup based on the selling price. What is his selling price?

Solution: The selling price is the sum of the cost and markup. Being that the markup is 40% of the selling price we see that the cost must be 60% (100% - 40%) of the selling price.

Cost = 60% of selling price

or cost = (0.6) × (selling price)

We know the cost is 18.20, so the equation becomes \$18.20 = (0.6) × (selling price)
Therefore the selling price is

$$\text{selling price} = \frac{\$18.20}{0.6} = \$30.33.$$

• PROBLEM 12-23

Find the markup in dollars on \$230,000 worth of stock at retail if the cost is 70% of this selling price.

Solution: The selling price is equal to the cost plus the markup. Since the cost is 70% of the selling price, the markup is 100% - 70% = 30% of the selling price. We have,

$$\begin{aligned}\text{markup} &= 30\% \text{ of } 230{,}000\\ &= (0.30) \times 230{,}000 = \$69{,}000\ .\end{aligned}$$

As a check, 70% of 230,000 = 161,000
and \$69,000 + \$161,000 = \$230,000
(markup) + (cost) = (selling price).

• PROBLEM 12-24

A glass vase sells for \$25.00. The net profit is 7%, and the operating expenses are 39%. Find the gross profit on the vase.

Solution: The gross profit is equal to the net profit plus the operating expenses. The net profit is 7% of the selling cost; thus it is equal to 7% × \$25.00 = .07 × \$25 = \$1.75
The operating expenses are 39% of the selling price, thus equal to 39% × \$25 = .30 × \$25 = \$9.75

\$1.75	net profit
+ \$9.75	operating expenses
\$11.50	gross profit

• PROBLEM 12-25

Two competing department stores have a radio whose cost is \$10.82. Both stores advertise that they sell the radio on a 70% markup. However, store A bases the markup on the selling price, while store B bases it on the cost price. What is the selling price of the radio in the two stores?

Solution: The markup is the amount of money that is charged over the cost. Store A sells the radio on a 70% markup based on the selling price. This means the markup is 70% of the selling price, and the other 30% of the selling price is the cost. Thus, Cost = 30% of selling price, or

$$\frac{\text{cost}}{.30} = \text{selling price.}$$

Hence the selling price in store A is
\$10.82 ÷ .30 = \$36.07 (rounding to the nearest cent). Store B bases the markup on the cost. That means the markup is 70% of the cost, or markup = 70% × cost = 70% × \$10.82 = .70 × \$10.82 = \$7.57 (rounding to the nearest penny). The selling price is equal to the cost plus the markup, thus it is equal to \$10.82 + \$7.57 = \$18.39.

• PROBLEM 12-26

Field and Co. purchased 100 dolls at \$3.25 each. They sold 25 of them for \$6 each. What is the minimum retail price that Field and Co. may charge for the rest of the dolls in order that the average retail markup is 35%?

Solution: The total cost of the dolls is 100 × \$3.25 = \$325. The retail price is equal to the cost plus the markup. Since the markup is to be 35%, we see that the cost is 65% (100% - 35%) of the retail price. Hence, the retail price is equal to the cost divided by 65%, giving \$325 ÷ .65 = \$500. Thus, to make a 35% markup they must sell all their dolls for \$500. Now they already sold 25 dolls at \$6 each, for 25 × \$6 = \$150. The remaining 75 (100 - 25) dolls must sell for \$500 - \$150 = \$350 in order to have a 35% markup. Thus, each doll must sell for \$350 ÷ 75 = \$4.67.

• PROBLEM 12-27

The markup in the radio department of the R.L. Electronics store is 30%. Its sales for this past month were \$15,000. The markup in the tube department is 25% and its sales for the month were \$40,000. Find the average markup on sales for the two departments.

Solution: To find the average markup, we cannot simply average the two markups because they are based on different amounts of sales. Rather, we find the total markup and divide it by the total sales. The markup on the radios is 30% of \$15,000 = .30 × \$15,000 = \$4,500. The markup on the tubes is 25% of \$40,000 = .25 × \$40,000 = \$10,000. Thus the total markup is \$ 4,500 + \$10,000 = \$ 14,500. The total sales is \$15,000 (radios) + \$40,000 (tubes) = \$55,000. Thus the average markup on sales is \$14,500 ÷ \$55,000 = .263636 = 26.36% (rounding to two decimal places).

• PROBLEM 12-28

A store sells two items for \$10 each. One item costs \$5.25, while the other costs \$6.50. What ratio of items at each price must be purchased in order to have an average markup based on the selling price of 40%?

Solution: To find out the required ratio, we first find out the average markup,and from that the average cost. From this, we can see how much each cost deviates from the average; thus we can find the ratio needed. The average markup is 40%. Since selling price = cost + markup, Cost = selling price - markup = selling price -

40% of selling price = 60% of selling price. Since the selling price is $10 apiece, the average cost is 60% of $10 = $10 × .60 = $6.00. We can now find out by how much each one deviates from the average cost.

	Average cost	$6.00	$6.00
Less:	Actual cost	-5.25	-6.50
	Gain or loss	$ .75	-$.50

From here we see that every $6.50 item loses $.50 of profit, while every $5.25 item gains $.75 of profit. Therefore we can purchase 75 $6.50 items to every 50 $5.25 items in order to have the desired profit. The required ratio is 75 to 50 or 3 to 2.

• PROBLEM 12-29

A store wishes to make $12,000 profit on sales of $200,000. Find the markup percent on the selling price needed if expenses will be $56,000, markdowns $15,000, shortages $5,000, alteration costs $2,500, and cash discounts earned from vendors $ 4,500.

Solution: The markup percent on sales is found by dividing the markup by the selling price and multiplying it by 100%. The selling price is equal to sales plus the markdown plus the shortages, or $200,000 + $15,000 + $5,000 = $220,000. The markup must be equal to the profit and it must cover all the expenses. However we must subtract the cash discount. Thus, the amount of markup can be computed as follows:

$56,000	expenses
+ $12,000	profit
+ $15,000	markdowns
+ $ 5,000	shortages
+ $ 2,500	alteration costs
- $ 4,500	discounts
$86,000	markup

Thus, the markup percent is

$86,000 ÷ 220,000 × 100% = .3909 × 100% = 39.09%.

• PROBLEM 12-30

The owner of a small store plans on purchasing $1,500 worth of goods to be marked up 40% based on the selling price. Of this he will have purchased $200 worth of "floor goods", which will sell for $250. If he is to maintain the desired 40% markup on the total purchase, what markup % is needed on the balance of the purchases?

Solution: We must find out what the selling price of the entire amount purchased is. We can then find out the balance needed to have a markup of 40%. Recall that selling price = cost + markup, or for this problem selling price = cost + 0.4 (Selling Price), since the markup is 40% of the selling price. The cost is given to us as $1,500 so that we can solve the given equation for the selling price:

$$\text{Selling Price} = \$1,500 + 0.4\times(\text{Selling Price})$$

$$0.6\ (\text{Selling Price}) = \$1,500$$

$$\text{or Selling Price} = \frac{\$1,500}{0.6} = \$2,500$$

	Cost	Selling Price
Total planned purchase	$1,500	$2,500
Less floor purchase made	$200	$250
Balance needed	$1,300	$2,250

Thus, the remaining $1,300 worth of goods must sell for $2,250. Recalling that Markup = Selling price - Cost, we find that the markup is equal to $2,250 - $1,300 = $950.

To find the markup percentage we divide the markup by the selling price, and multiply by 100%, obtaining ($950 ÷ $2,250) × 100% = .4222 × 100% = 42.22%.

CHAPTER 13

PURCHASING DECISIONS

• **PROBLEM** 13-1

Mr. Lai owns a rental property close to what will become a country club. He receives $10,000 annually from a single tenant who is willing to renew the lease for 25 years for the same rent. Mr. Lai is being offered $120,000 by the club owners for his property.

The total annual cost of maintenance, insurance and taxes is $4,070. Assuming that annual disbursements and receipts will remain constant over 25 years, and Mr. Lai can sell the property at the end of the twenty-five years for $40,000, should Mr. Lai sell his property now to the club, or in 25 years? He considers $5\frac{1}{2}\%$ interest the minimum adequate rate of return. Round all calculations to the nearest dollar.

Solution: If the present value of the total receipts expected over twenty-five years is greater than the amount offered by the club investors, then Mr. Lai should not sell his property. The net annual receipts are $10,000 - $4,070 = $5,930. A series of $5,930 receipts over 25 years at $5\frac{1}{2}\%$ interest has a present value of ($5,930)(13.414) = $79,545. The factor 13.414 is obtained from the $5\frac{1}{2}\%$ compound interest table under the annual series section, present worth column, for n = 25 years. The single receipt of $40,000 to be received from selling the property has a present value, for n = 25, $5\frac{1}{2}\%$, of

$$(\$40{,}000)(0.2622) = \$10{,}488.$$

The factor 0.2622 is found under the single payment column of the $5\frac{1}{2}\%$ table. The total present worth is

$$(\$79{,}545 + \$10{,}488) = \$90{,}033.$$

Clearly, this is less than the $120,000 offered by the club owners; Mr. Lai should accept their offer.

• **PROBLEM** 13-2

Mr. Louis is presently considering buying a new boat to give rides to tourists. He has two alternatives: Boat A costs $10,000 and consumes $2,000 in fuel per year. Boat B costs $7,000 and consumes $2,500. Both boats have a zero salvage value at the end of 10 years. If Mr. Louis considers a rate of return of 6% acceptable,

(a) which boat should he purchase?

(b) how much will he charge each tourist if there are 3 tourists to a ride and Mr. Louis plans to have 125 rides each year?

Solution: (a) In order to decide which boat to purchase, find the total annual cost of each one. This cost consists of (1) the cost of the fuel, and (2) Mr. Louis' annual capital recovery cost at 6% over 10 years of operation.

Find the annual capital recovery amount for each boat. Look at the table, "Capital Recovery Factors for Interest Rates from 0% to 25%". Move down the 6% column to n = 10 years; 0.13587 is the capital recovery factor. Multiply the amounts Mr. Louis plans to invest by this factor to get the capital recovery amount.

Capital recovery of a $10,000 investment over a 10 year period at a 6% rate of return is

$$(0.13587)(\$10{,}000) = \$1{,}358.70.$$

Capital recovery of a $7,000 investment over a 10 year period at a 6% rate of return is

$$(0.13587)(\$7{,}000) = \$951.09\ .$$

The total annual cost of boat A is

$$\$1{,}358.70 + \$2{,}000 = \$3{,}358.70.$$

The total annual cost of boat B is

$$\$951.09 + \$2{,}500 = \$3{,}451.09\ .$$

Mr. Louis should buy boat A because total annual cost of boat A is less than boat B.

(b) The cost per passenger

$$= \frac{\text{cost per tour}}{\text{passengers per tour}}$$

$$= \frac{\text{cost per year} \div \text{tours per year}}{\text{passengers per tour}}$$

$$= \frac{\$3{,}358.70 \div 125}{3}$$

$$= \$8.96, \text{ to the nearest cent.}$$

To cover costs, Mr. Louis should charge at least $8.96 per passenger.

If there should be no available capital recovery factors table, use the formula,

$$\frac{i(1+i)^n}{(1+i)^n - 1}\ ,$$

for an investment period of n years and an i rate of interest.

• PROBLEM 13-3

Derman and Klein are the sole stockholders of the Leather Products Corporation. It is estimated that Leather Products will have a taxable income of $30,000 this year. The stock is evenly divided between Mr. Derman and Mr. Klein, so that resulting dividends will also be equally shared. Both Mr. Derman and Mr. Klein expect to receive from other sources a net taxable income of $12,000. All profit after taxes Leather Products makes this year will be paid out as dividends. Mr. Derman wants to introduce a new product. Should this venture succeed, the annual income before taxes will increase by $10,000. What will be the increase in stockholders' income after taxes? Use the tables "Federal Taxes Rates on 1949 Net Incomes of Corporations in the United States", and "Federal Tax Rates on 1949 Incomes of Individuals in the United States."

Solution: Step 1. Find the increase in stockholders' income after taxes if Mr. Derman's suggestion is followed.

(a) Net Corporate Income.

The Leather Products Corporation's $30,000 income is taxed, according to the 1949 corporate income tax table, $5,750 plus 53% of the excess income over $25,000.

Taxes = $5,750 + 53% of ($30,000 - 25,000)

= $5,750 + (.53)(5,000)
= $8,400 .

Net income to be paid as dividends

= $30,000 - $8,400 = $21,600

(b) Net Income per Stockholder.

$$\text{Dividends per stockholder: } \frac{\text{net income}}{\text{number of stockholders}} = \frac{21,600}{2}$$
$$= \$10,800 .$$

Other income per stockholder:	12,000
Taxable Income:	22,800
less: Income taxes of individuals in $22,000 - 25,999 bracket -[$7,354.70 + 51.92% of (22,800 - 20,000)]:	- (7,769.76)
Net Income of each stockholder:	15,030.24

Step 2. with new product

(a) Corporate Net Income.

If the new product is introduced and successful, taxable income will be $30,000 + $10,000 = $40,000, which will still be in the $25,000 - $49,999 bracket, with the same tax rate as before.

Corporate Taxable Income:	$40,000
less taxes: $5,750 + 53% of ($40,000 - 25,000)	13,700
Net Income to be paid in dividends	26,300

(b) Net Income per Stockholder

Dividends per stockholder: $\frac{26,300}{2}$	$13,150
Other Income per Stockholder:	12,000
Taxable Income per Stockholder:	$25,150
less: Income taxes of individuals in $22,000 - 25,999 bracket - $7,354.40 + 51.92% of ($25,150 - 22,000)	8,989.88
Income per Stockholder	$16,160.12

If the new product is successfully introduced, each stockholder's income will increase by

$16,160.12 - $15,030.24 = $1,129.88.

• PROBLEM 13-4

A small airline is considering installing computerized fuel allocation systems in all its planes to reduce fuel costs.

The $8,000 investment will reduce fuel costs annually by $1,000 over a ten year period. If the minimum acceptable rate of return is 7%,

(a) is the investment worthwhile?

(b) if fuel costs increase 5% each year, is the investment worthwhile?

Solution: (a) Find the capital recovery cost of the $8,000 investment at 7% over 10 years.

The capital recovery factor for i(interest) = 7% and n = 10 years, 0.14238, is in the "7% Compound Interest Factors" table.

An $8,000 investment over a 10 year period at 7% interest should then yield annually

$$(\$8,000)(0.14238) = \$1,139.04$$

as a return to satisfy the investor. In the airline's case, its costs are reduced only by $1,000; the return on the investment is inadequate, the investment should not be made.

(b) If the fuel cost for the first year is $1,000, and if it increases 5% each year, the fuel cost for the second year will be

$$\$1,000 + (.05)(\$1,000) = \$1,050.$$

A simpler way to get the cost of $1,000 worth of fuel n years from now, knowing that there is a price increase of 5% annually, is to use the compound formula $P_{n-1} = P(1+i)^{n-1}$, where i is the rate of increase, n is the year (calling the second year 1), and P is the principle, $1,000. For the 2nd year, n = 1, we have

$$P_1 = (\$1,000)(1.05)^1 = \$1,050.$$

For the remaining years:

$$P_2 = (\$1,000)(1.05)^2 = (\$1,000)(1.103) = \$1,103 \text{ third}$$

$$P_3 = (\$1,000)(1.05)^3 = (\$1,000)(1.158) = 1,158 \text{ fourth}$$

$$P_4 = (\$1,000)(1.05)^4 = (\$1,000)(1.216) = 1,216 \text{ fifth}$$

$$P_5 = (\$1,000)(1.05)^5 = (\$1,000)(1.276) = 1.276 \text{ sixth}$$

$$P_6 = (\$1,000)(1.05)^6 = (\$1,000)(1.340) = 1,340 \text{ seventh}$$

$$P_7 = (\$1,000)(1.05)^7 = (\$1,000)(1.407) = 1,407 \text{ eighth}$$

$$P_8 = (\$1,000)(1.05)^8 = (\$1,000)(1.477) = 1,477 \text{ ninth}$$

$$P_9 = (\$1,000)(1.05)^9 = (\$1,000)(1.551) = 1,551 \text{ tenth}$$

You can find all the factors $(1.05)^n$ in the 5% compound interest table, so you do not need a calculator. The factors are rounded off. The costs calculated above must now be changed to present worth amounts calculated at the minimum rate of return of 7%. Look at the table for "7% Compound Interest Factors" and read the factors under the "Single Payment"present worth factors column from n = 1 to n = 10. Multiply the cost corresponding to each year by the appropriate factors and add to get the total present worth.

($1,000)(0.9346) = $935 (nearest dollar)
($1,050)(0.8734) = $917
($1,103)(0.8163) = $900
($1,158)(0.7629) = $883
($1,216)(0.7130) = $867
($1,276)(0.6663) = $850
($1,340)(0.6227) = $834
($1,407)(0.5820) = $819
($1,477)(0.5439) = $803
($1,551)(0.5083) = $788
$8,596.

The total fuel cost over the ten years is greater than the amount invested to reduce fuel consumption; the investment should be undertaken.

• PROBLEM 13-5

Two pumping systems are being considered for use on a project. The gasoline pump will cost $3,500, has a 6 year life year, and a $500 salvage value. Annual operating and repair costs would be $2,000 the first year, and would rise $300 each succeeding year. The electric pumping system costs $12,000, has a life of 6 years and a salvage value of $1,000. Annual operating and maintenance costs would be $1,000 the first year, and would rise $150 each year. If the current interest rate is 10%, compare the equivalent annual costs of the two pumping systems. Assume all maintenance and repair costs are paid at the end of each year.

Solution: Gasoline pump

First, find the amount actually paid for the pump, considering there is a salvage value of $500 at the end of six years. At 10%, the present value of $500 obtained six years from now is

(0.5645)($500) = $282,

to the nearest dollar. The number 0.5645 is the present worth factor for a single payment given i = 10%, n = 6 periods (years). This factor is found in the table "Single Payment Present Worth Factors for Interest Rates from 0% to 25%." The actual amount paid, and to be recovered during the six years, is $3,500 - $282 = $3,218. The annual capital recovery amount for this investment at 10% interest over 6 years is, to the nearest dollar, ($3,218)(0.22961) = $739 annually. Find this factor in the table "Capital Recovery Factors for Interest Rates from 0% to 25%." This is added to the other costs to find the total annual costs. Costs rise by $300 each year.

TOTAL ANNUAL COSTS:

Year 1: $739 + $2,000 = $2,739
Year 2: $739 + $2,300 = $3,039
Year 3: $739 + $2,600 = $3,339
Year 4: $739 + $2,900 = $3,639
Year 5: $739 + $3,200 = $3,939
Year 6: $739 + $3,500 = $4,239

Total Costs $20,934

Electric Pumping System

The same procedure is applied in this case.

Net capital investment

(i) A salvage value of $1,000 six years from now is ($1,000)(0.5645) = $565 at 10% interest.

(ii) The amount of capital to be recovered during six years is $12,000 - $565 = $11,435.

(iii) To recover this amount at 10%, the annual addition to costs is ($11,435)(0.22961) = $2,626, to the nearest dollar.

The total annual costs are shown below.

Year 1: $2,626 + $1,000 = $3,626
Year 2: $2,626 + $1,150 = $3,776
Year 3: $2,626 + $1,300 = $3,926
Year 4: $2,626 + $1,450 = $4,076
Year 5: $2,626 + $1,600 = $4,226
Year 6: $2,626 + $1,750 = $4,376

Total Costs $24,006

The gasoline pump is more economical.

• PROBLEM 13-6

The Dickenson Company has purchased a hand-operated machine of the following description; after a year, it can purchase an automatic machine of equal capacity and sell the first machine for $1,600. The following data is available:

	Hand-Operated Machine	Automatic Machine
Purchase price	$4,400	$6,200
Expected Useful life	5 years	4 years
Expected salvage value	$0	$0
Annual operating costs	$2,600	$800

The current interest rate is 8%. Which of the following options should the company chose?

Option A - Keep the hand-operated machine 5 years.

Option B - Keep the hand-operated machine 1 year, sell it, and purchase the automatic to use for 4 years.

Round all calculations to the nearest dollar.

Solution: Option A

To find the annual capital recovery cost of the machine, multiply its price, $4,400, by the capital recovery factor for n = 5 years, i = 8%. Look in the table named "Capital Recovery Factors for Interest Rates from 0% to 25%". The factor in the 8% column, five rows down is 0.25046. To recover $4,400 in 5 years, the company must recover

($4,400)(0.25046) = $1,102 per year for five years.

Therefore, total annual expenses are Capital Recovery Cost + Operating Costs = $1,102 + $2,600 = $3,702 .

Option B

At the end of one year, the company will receive $1,600 for this hand-operated machine, of which the present worth (what would be received today) is (0.9259)($1,600) = $1,481. The multiplier, 0.9259, is the single-payment present worth factor obtained from the compound interest table for 8%, n = 1 year (period). The net capital disbursement is therefore $4,400 (price of the machine) - $1,481 (resale value) = $2,919.

If we recover this amount in one year (n = 1), when 8% = i (interest), the capital recovery cost of the machine is (1.08)($2,919) = $3,153. Operating costs are $2,600, so that under Option B, the cost of the manual machine is $2,600 + $3,153 = $5,753 the first year.

For the new machine, the annual capital recovery cost of $6,200 at 8% over 4 years is ($6,200)(0.30192) = $1,872. The factor 0.30192 is from the capital recovery factors table for i = 8%, n = 4 periods (years). Adding annual operating costs, we get annual costs for each of years two through five of $1,872 + $800 = $2,672.

If the Dickenson Company chooses Option A, it will save $5,753 - $3,702 = $2,051 the first year. If the company chooses Option B, it will save $3,702 - $2,672 = $1,030 per year for years two through five, or $1,030 x 4 = $4,120. The company should choose Option B, because, over the five years, it would save more money.

• PROBLEM 13-7

Mr. Fields is considering selling a property acquired 15 years ago for $65,000; $10,000 was for the land, and $55,000 was for the building. Mr. Fields can now sell the property for $120,000. He can also keep it and continue to collect the annual rent from the building. If Mr. Fields decides to keep the property, he will keep it for another 25 years and will, at that time, sell it for $40,000. The annual rent receipts will be $5,930 for the next twenty-five years. Should Mr. Fields sell the property now or in twenty-five years? Assume that the building, but not the land, has been depreciated using the straight line method at 2%, long term gains are taxable at a rate of 25%, Mr. Fields' income tax rate is 56%, the minimum attractive rate of return after taxes is $2\frac{1}{2}$%, and taxes will hold for the next 25 years. Make all calculations to the nearest dollar.

Solution: The decision criterion in this problem is the present worth of both investment options after taxes.

Decision A - Sell now for $120,000.

The long-term gain will be $120,000 less the net book value of the property. The book value is the original price of $65,000 less accumulated depreciation on the building. Straight line depreciation at 2% means that the annual depreciation on the building is (0.02)($55,000) = $1,100. Mr. Fields has held this property for 15 years and thus the accumulated depreciation is (15)($1,100) = $16,500. The book value of the property is therefore $65,000 - $16,500 = $48,500. The long term gain is $120,000 - $48,500 = $71,500. This long term gain is taxable at 25% so that the tax paid on the transaction is (0.25)($71,500) = $17,875. After paying this tax, Mr. Fields will have $120,000 - $17,875 = $102,125 left. This is the present worth of the receipts from selling now.

Decision B - Keep another 25 years.

The total revenue generated from the property will be the annual rent receipts plus the receipts from selling the property after 25 years.

Present worth of rent receipts:

the annual tax on the rent income, $5,930, is (0.56)($5,930) = $3,321. The net annual receipts are $5,930 - $3,321 = $2,609. The minimum attractive rate of return after taxes is 2½%, so that the present worth of a series of $2,609 receipts over 25 years is

($2,609)(18.424) = $48,068.

The factor 18.424 is obtained from the "2½% Compound Interest Factors" in the "Uniform Annual Series" section's "Present Worth Factor" column, for n = 25.

Present worth of resale value:

In 25 years the building will have been used for 15 + 25 = 40 years and the accumulated depreciation will be (40)($1,100) = $44,000. The book value will be $65,000 - $44,000 = $21,000.

The long term gain will be $40,000 - $21,000 = $19,000. The tax paid on the $40,000 transaction will be (0.25)($19,000) = $4,750 and so the net long term gain will be $40,000 - $4,750 = $35,250.

The present worth of $35,250 obtained in 25 years at a 2½% rate is:

($35,250)(0.5394) = $19,014.

The factor 0.5394 is obtained from the same 2½% table as before under the "Single Payment" section's present worth factor column and n = 25 years.

The total present worth of decision B is

$48,068 + $19,014 = $67,082

which is far less than the $102,125, obtained from selling the property today. Mr. Fields should sell the property now for $120,000.

• PROBLEM 13-8

A drama guild is renovating an old theater, hoping to use it for 15 years. The guild can follow one of two plans to finance the work:

Plan A is to use $5,000 collected from guild members to pay for a renovation job which would be done immediately and would last 15 years.

Plan B is to borrow $2,000 the year before the theater opens, and then in the 5th and 10th years of the theater's life to renovate it; each job will last five years. Interest is 6% for both plans.

(a) Which plan should the guild follow?

(b) If, in Plan B, the 2nd and 3rd renovation jobs will cost $3,000 each and the guild will not be able to borrow the money for any of the three jobs (i.e., the members will have to contribute), which plan should the guild follow?

Solution: (a) Plan A -

$5,000 paid immediately (i.e., in the 'present') as is the money for the 15 year renovation, has a present value of $5,000.

Plan B -

Find the annual payments on a 6%, 5 year loan of $2,000.

$$\text{Annual Payments} = \frac{\text{Amount of loan}}{\text{Uniform Annual Series Present Worth Factor,}}$$

$i = 6\%$, $n = 5$ years.

The present worth factor, 4.212, is in the uniform annual series section of the "6% Compound Interest Factor" table

$$\text{Annual Payments} = \frac{\$2,000}{4.212} = \$475\text{, to the nearest dollar.}$$

If the theater is to be renovated 3 times, there will be 3 five-year loans taken and 3(loans) × 5(payments per loan) = 15, $475 annual payments on the loans. The present worth (P.W.) of a series of 15 $475 payments where money is increasing nominally, through interest earned from savings accounts and other investments, by 6% a year (and the intrinsic worth of money is decreasing by 6% a year, so today's dollar is worth more than tomorrow's dollar) is = Uniform Annual Series P.W. factor, for $i = 6\%$, $n = 15$ × $475 = 9.712 × $475 = $4,613, to the nearest dollar.

Plan B is better because the present worth of its cost, $4,613, is less than the $5,000 paid in Plan A.

(b) The present worth of the $5,000 payment is still $5,000.

Since, if Plan B is followed, the first ($2,000) disbursement would be made immediately, the present worth of the $2,000 payment would be $2,000.

Since the 2nd and 3rd $3000 payments would be made in lump sums, their present worths are computed using their single payment present worth factors for $n = 5$ and $n = 10$, respectively (in the 6% Compound Interest Factor" table). The present worth of the Plan B payments is therefore:

$$\begin{aligned} &\$2,000 &&= \$2,000 \\ &\$3,000 \times 0.7473 &&= 2,241.9 \\ &\$3,000 \times 0.5584 &&= \underline{1,675.2} \\ & && \$5,917.1 \end{aligned}$$

The present worth of Plan A's costs is less than this sum; the guild should follow Plan A.

• PROBLEM 13-9

Two power line construction routes are being considered. Route A is 15 miles long and goes around a lake. Each mile will cost $6,000 to build and $2,000 a year to maintain. At the end of fifteen years, each mile will have a salvage value of $3,000.

Route B is an underwater line that cuts 5 miles across the lake. Construction costs will be $31,000 per mile and annual maintenance costs, $400 per mile. The salvage value at the end of fifteen years will be $6,000 per mile. Assuming interest is 8% and taxes are 3% of the construction costs of each power line, compare the annual costs of Route A and Route B for the first year.

Solution: Route A:

Construction costs of Route A are 15 miles x $6,000/mile = $90,000. At the end of fifteen years, the total salvage value will be $3,000/mile x 15 miles = $45,000. To receive $45,000 in 15 years is the same as receiving $45,000 x 0.3152 = $14,184 today. The number 0.3152 is the single-payment present worth factor from the 8% compound interest table for n = 15. The actual capital that must be recovered is therefore $90,000 - $14,184 = $75,816. To find how much must be recovered(earned back) annually, multiply $75,816 by the capital recovery factor in the 8% compound interest table for n = 15. This factor is 0.11683. Annual capital recovery cost for Route A is $75,816 x 0.11683 = $8,858 to the nearest dollar. The annual maintainence expense will be $2,000/mile x 15 miles = $30,000. Taxes are 3% of $90,000, or $2,700.

The total annual costs of Route A are $8,858 (capital recovery) + $2,700 (taxes) + $30,000 (maintenance) = $41,558.

Route B:

Construction costs: 5 miles x $31,000/mile = $155,000.

Total annual maintenance costs: 5 miles x $400/mile = $2,000.

Taxes: 0.03 x $155,000 = $4,650.

Total salvage value: 5 miles x $6,000/mile = $30,000.

Present worth of salvage value (i.e., what it would be worth if received today instead of in 15 years): $30,000 x 0.3152 (single payment present worth factor, n = 15 years, i = 8%) = $9,456.

Amount to be recovered: construction costs - Present Worth of Salvage Value = $155,000 - $9,456 = $145,544.

Amount to be recovered each year = $145,544 x 0.11683 (capital recovery factor, n = 15, i = 8%) = $17,004, to the nearest dollar.

Total annual costs of Route B are

= Recovery Cost + Taxes + Maintenance
= $17,004 + $4,650 + $2,000
= $23,654.

• PROBLEM 13-10

A water line will be constructed to reach a reservoir 2,000 ft. away. The three pipe sizes being considered, the pumping cost per hour for each size and the estimated cost of construction modifications in buildings and ground fixtures are shown below.

Pipe size, inches	Pumping cost/hr.	Construction modifications
8	$2.00	$19,000
10	1.50	37,000
12	0.75	62,000

The line will only have one pipe size, last 16 years and have no salvage value. Using an interest rate of 15%, answer the following questions:

(a) How many hours of pumping per year would be required to make the 8-inch and 10-inch pipes equally economical?

(b) How many hours of pumping per year would be required to make the 10-inch and 12-inch pipes equally economical?

(c) For what ranges of required pumping hours per year is each size of pipe most economical?

Solution: (a) Let x be the number of hours each line operates annually. Then if the line is constructed from 8-inch pipe, the annual pumping costs is (x hrs.)($2/hr) = $2x. The pumping cost of the 10-inch pipe is $1.5x.

The construction modifications represent a capital investment that is to be recovered in 16 years at a rate of 15%. To find how much to recover annually at this rate for the 8-inch pipe-line, multiply the initial investment $19,000 by the capital recovery factor in the 15% compound interest table for n = 16 periods (years). This factor is 0.16795. Find it in the table "Capital Recovery Factors for Interest Rates from 0% to 25%" for i(interest) = 15% and n(number of years) = 16. The amount that should be recovered annually is $19,000 x 0.16795 = $3,191, to the nearest dollar.

For the 10-inch pipe-line, the annual capital recovery cost is $37,000 x 0.16795 = $6,214, to the nearest dollar.

The total annual cost of the 8-inch pipe-line is $2x + $3,191. The total annual cost of the 10-inch pipe-line is $1.5x + $6,214. Setting these total costs equal to each other, we can solve for x.

$$2x + 3191 = 1.5x + 6{,}214$$
$$0.5x = 3023$$
$$x = \frac{3023}{0.5} = 6046 \text{ hours annually.}$$

(b) The annual capital recovery cost for the 12-inch pipe-line is $62,000 X 0.16795 = $10,413. The total annual cost of this line is

$$0.75x + 10{,}413.$$

Set this cost equation equal to the cost equation of the 10-inch pipe-line and solve for x.

$$0.75x + 10{,}413 = 1.5x + 6{,}214$$

$$0.75x = 4{,}199, \ x = \frac{4199}{0.75} = 5{,}598 \ 2/3 \text{ hours .}$$

(c) Plot the three cost relations on the same graph with the hours of operation on the horozontal axis and with the cost in dollars on the vertical axis.

Point A is the intersection of the 12-inch pipe-line and the 10-inch line

Point B is the intersection of the 8-inch pipe-line and the 10-inch pipe-line.

Point C is the intersection of the 8-inch pipe-line and the 12-inch pipe-line. The number of hours can be determined, in the manner shown before, to be 5777.6.

For any number of hours less than or equal to 5777.6, the 8-inch cost line is below the two other lines; therefore, it is the most economical size in this range. Beyond 5777.6 hours, the 12-inch line is the most economical size because it lies below the two other lines.

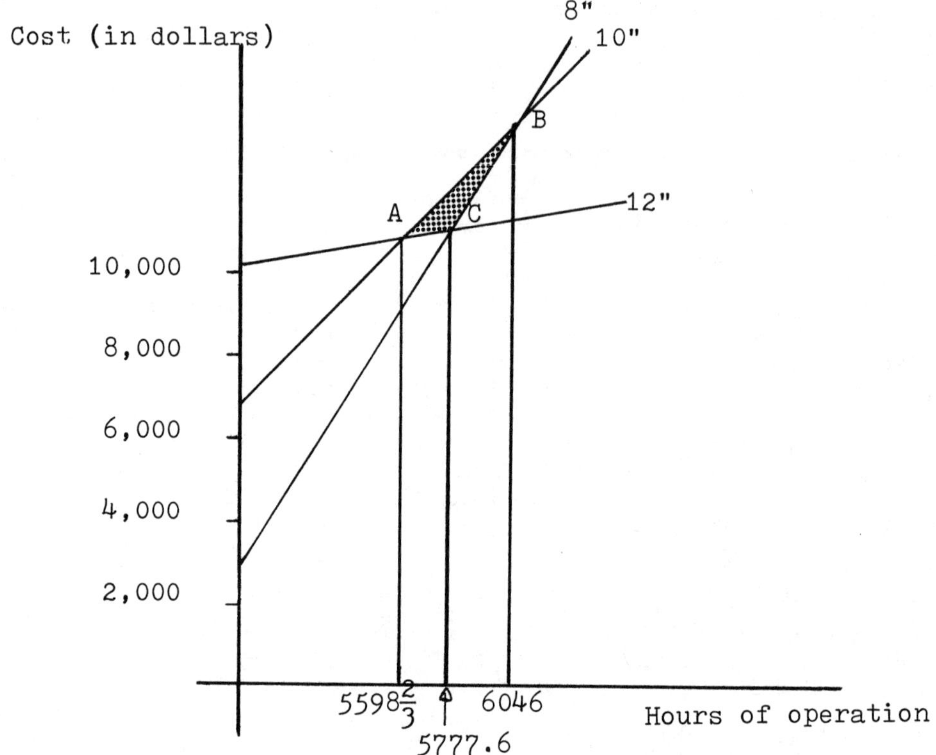

• **PROBLEM 13-11**

A factory is considering the purchase of a machine, for \$600,000, that is expected to reduce production costs by \$200,000 each year. The desired rate of return on this investment is 20%. What is the minimum life the machine must have to assure this rate of return?

Solution: The initial investment of \$600,000 is expected to be recovered at 20% interest over a number of years. The amount recovered each year is the \$200,000 in production costs saved by the machine. Given this information, we can set up the equation

$$\$600{,}000 \times Q = \$200{,}000,$$

where Q is the capital recovery factor from the capital recovery factors table for i(interest) = 20% and n = the minimum number of years the machine must last to make the investment worthwhile. Solve for Q directly

$$Q = \frac{\$200{,}000}{\$600{,}000} = \frac{1}{3} \approx 0.33333 \;.$$

In the 20% of the capital recovery factors table, find the factor closest to 0.33333, which, for n = 5, is 0.33438. Since 0.33438 is 0.33438 - 0.33333 = .00105 greater than 0.33333, and as the factors decrease, n decreases, 0.33333 corresponds to n slightly greater than 5 years.

• PROBLEM 13-12

Mr. Castle will buy one of two 10-HP motors offered to him. Motor A sells for $169 and has a full-load efficiency of 85.2%. Motor B costs $149 and has a full-load efficiency of 82.1%. The annual inspection and maintenance fee on both motors is 14.5% of the price. If electric energy costs 2.35 cents per kilowatt hour (1 HP = 0.746 kw.) find the number of hours per year at which the cost of both motors will be the same.

Solution: For each motor there will be two factors of the total operating cost: the inspection and maintenance fee and the cost of energy consumption.
Motor A - The inspection and maintenance charge is ($169)(0.145) = $24.51. The cost of energy for Motor A for x hours a year is found as follows: The motor will consume 10(0.746) or 7.46 kilowatts of energy at full load capacity. The 7.46 kilowatts will be multiplied by an "inefficiency factor" equal to

$$\frac{1}{\text{full load efficiency}} = \frac{1}{85.2\%} = \frac{1}{0.852} .$$

The higher the efficiency, the lower the inefficiency factor and vice versa. Therefore, the 7.46 kilowatts consumed are actually equivalent to (7.46)(1/.852) = 8.76 kilowatts. The cost of x hours of operation at 2.35 cents per kilowatt hour is

$$(8.76)(0.0235)x = 0.20586x .$$

The total cost of Motor A is therefore

$$24.51 + 0.20576x.$$

Motor B - The inspection and maintenance charge is, to the nearest cent, ($149)(0.145) = $21.61. The cost of energy is, with an inefficiency factor of

$$\frac{1}{82.1\%} = \frac{1}{0.821} ,$$

$$\frac{(10\text{ HP})(0.746\text{kw/HP})}{0.821}(\$0.0235)x = (9.09)(0.0235)x$$
$$= 0.2136x .$$

The total cost is 21.61 + 0.2136x.

To find the number of hours at which the costs are equal, set the two expressions equal to each other and solve for x:

$$24.51 + 0.20586x = 21.61 + 0.2136x$$
$$2.9 = 0.00774x$$
$$x = \frac{2.9}{0.00774} = 374.677\text{ hrs.} = 374\,\frac{2}{3}\text{ hrs.}$$

When both motors operate 374 2/3 hours, their operating costs are the same.

• PROBLEM 13-13

A company has a permit to mine for gold in a region of New Mexico for 3 years. Management is trying to decide how to finance the machinery. One option is to rent it for $130 per month over the three years. The deal includes the fuel needed to operate the equipment. The other option is to buy the equipment now and resell it after three years. The machinery costs $11,500. There is a down payment of $2,500, so that the balance due will be $11,500 - $2,500 = $9,000. This balance will be covered by a $5\frac{1}{2}$% loan to be paid in equal annual installments over 15 years. The annual fuel costs for the equipment would be $375. If the minimum attractive rate of return is 5%, at what resale value (end of third year) will both options be equally economical? Make all calculations to the nearest dollar.

Solution:

Rent option. (A)

The total annual disbursement is 12 × $130 = $1,560. The total present value of a series of annual payments of $1,560, at a rate of return of 5% over 3 years, is ($1,560)(2.723) = $4,248. The factor 2.723 is obtained from the **5%** table of compound interest factors in the "Present Worth Factor" column of the "Uniform Annual Series" section in the row n = 3 years.

Purchase option. (B)

The loan agreement requires a series of uniform annual payments over a period of 15 years. To find the annual payment, multiply the amount of the loan, $9,000, by the capital recovery factor present worth for n = 15 years and i = $5\frac{1}{2}$, 0.09963. This factor is also found in the $5\frac{1}{2}$% compound interest factors table. The annual repayment of the loan is ($9,000)(0.09963) = $897. The total annual disbursements including fuel costs, are $897 + $375 = $1,272. The present worth of a series of $1,272 disbursements over n = 3 years at 5% is ($1,272)(2.723) = $3,464. There is a $2,500 down payment. Total disbursements including this down payment are $3,464 + $2,500 = $5,964.

At the end of the third year, the equipment will be sold for a certain amount. Let x be the amount of dollars to be received from the sale over and above costs so that Option B is as economical as Option A. Then x(0.8638) is the present value of this amount, where the factor 0.8516 is obtained from the 5% interest table under the single payment column for n = 3. The expression for the total costs, so that this amount will be recovered, is $5,964 - x(0.8638). Setting this equal to the cost of option A, $5,964 - x(0.8638)= $4,248, and solving for x, we find x = 1,987. The amount owed on the loan at the end of three years is $897(8.863) = $7,950, where 8.863 is the present worth factor for n = 12 years (years remaining) at i = 5% for a series of annual payments. The sale price of the equipment must be $7,950 + $1,987 = $9,937 for the purchase option to cost the same as the rent option.

In this problem, the $5\frac{1}{2}$% table has only been used to compute the payments on the loan, because $5\frac{1}{2}$% is the rate on the loan. Present worth computations have been based on 5%.

• PROBLEM 13-14

A gas main carrying natural gas and laid in a corrosive soil ultimately reaches the point where it develops small leaks that increase as time goes on. Assume the cost per mile of main is $8,000, that no gas is lost for the first 15 years of life, and that a main has zero net salvage value whenever retired. Assume also that the mile of main loses $60 worth of gas in the 16th year of life and that the cost of lost gas increases $60 every year thereafter. Interest or minimum attractive return is at 7%. Compare the equivalent uniform annual cost over the life of a main retired after 20 years with the equivalent uniform annual cost over the life of the main retired after 25 years.

Solution: To lose $60 sixteen years from today is not the same as losing $60 today; the different disbursements must be converted to their present worth. Multiply each year's disbursement by the corresponding single payment present worth factor. The factors are found in the table "7% Compound Interest Factors", in the present worth factor column of the single payment section, in rows n = 16 through n = 25.

Year	Expected Loss	X	Present worth factor	=	Present worth
16	$60		0.3387		$20.32
17	120		0.3166		37.99
18	180		0.2959		53.26
19	240		0.2765		66.36
20	300		0.2584		77.52
21	360		0.2415		86.94
22	420		0.2257		94.79
23	480		0.2109		101.23
24	540		0.1971		106.43
25	600		0.1842		110.52

If we maintain the pipe for 20 years, the total present worth of the loss is

$$\$20.32 + \$37.99 + \$53.26 + \$66.36 + \$77.52 = \$255.45.$$

If the loss of $255.45 is considered to come in 20 equal annual installments of x dollars, the equation to find x is:

$255.45 = (x) (Present worth factor for n = 20 for the uniform annual series case).

The present worth factor is 10.594 and is found in the last column of the 7% table.

$$x = \frac{\$255.45}{10.594} = \$24.11 \text{ to the nearest cent.}$$

In other words, a series of twenty $24.11 losses at 7% equals $255.45. With the twenty-five year option, the total present value of the loss is:

$$\$255 + \$86.94 + \$94.79 + \$101.23 + \$106.43 + \$110.52 = \$755.36.$$

As before, use the following equation to find the uniform series payment.

755.36 = (x) (Present worth factor for n = 25 under uniform annual series section).

$$755 = (x)(11.654) \text{ and } x = \frac{755.36}{11.654} = 64.82.$$

At 7% interest, the capital recovery cost of the line for a 20 year life is found by multiplying 8,000 by the capital recovery factor in the 7% table for n = 20.

<u>20-year line</u>

Capital Recovery at 7% = ($8,000)(0.09439)	=	755.12.
Annual cost of lost gas	=	24.11
Total annual cost	=	779.23

The capital recovery factor for n = 25 years is 0.08581.

<u>25-year line</u>

Capital Recovery cost at 7% = ($8,000)(0.08581)	=	686.48
Annual cost of lost gas	=	64.82
Total annual cost	=	751.30

The total annual cost of the 25-year line is lower than that of the 20-year line.

• PROBLEM 13-15

Ten years ago a carnival purchased a candy-making machine for $3,000, which has been depreciated at $120 a year. The salvage value of the machine is $1,500. In five years, its value will be $700. The new machine being considered costs $4,500, and if acquired, will be depreciated by the straight line method over 5 years, with no salvage value. Some of the annual costs of the old machine are:

Sugar	$28,000
Maintenance and repair	50
Supplies other than sugar	45
Power	80

<u>New Machine</u> - annual costs

Sugar	$28,000
Maintenance and repair	30
Supplies other than sugar	25
Power	56

Labor costs are $1.80/hour for either machine. The manager estimates they will use either machine for 2,080 hours. However, it is estimated that 29½% less workers are needed to run the new machine.

Three percent of the candy made by the old machine and one percent of that made by the new one will be unsalable. The cost of spoilage is the percent of spoilage multiplied by the direct operating cost (i.e., cost of sugar and labor). Taxes are 3% of the present book value for the old machine and 3% of the first cost of the new machine Assume that rate of interest is 6%. Should the carnival keep the old machine, or sell it and buy the new one?

<u>Solution:</u> Find and compare the total annual operating costs of the two machines.

Annual cost of old machine

(a) Annual decrease of net value

The net realizable value of the machine will be $700 in five years so that it will have decreased by $1,500 - $700 = $800 over the five years or $800/5 = $160 each year.

(b) The labor cost is (2,080 hrs)($1.80/hr) = $3,744.

(c) Average interest cost

If the carnival keeps the old machine it may lose the opportunity to earn 6% interest. To compute an approximate value of this loss, use the average interest formula; if Q is the present salvage value of the asset, P is the salvage value of the asset in n years, and i is the rate of interest, then the average interest is

$$(Q - P)\left(\frac{i}{2}\right)\left(\frac{n+1}{n}\right) + Pi$$

$$= (\$1,500 - \$700)\left(\frac{0.06}{2}\right)\left(\frac{6}{5}\right) + (\$700)(0.06) = \$70.80.$$

(d) Spoilage cost

This is the cost incurred whenever unacceptable candy is made. The direct operating cost is $28,000 (materials) + $3,744 (labor) = $31,744. Of this amount, 3% is wasted every year. The spoilage cost is therefore

$$(0.03)(\$31,744) = \$952.32.$$

(e) Taxes

Total accumulated depreciation is 10 years x $120 per year = $1,200. The book value of the machine is therefore $3,000 - $1,200 = $1,800, and the tax paid on this asset is (0.03)($1,800) = $54. Add all the costs from (a) to (e) and the given costs for maintenance, supplies, and power previously given to get the total annual cost of keeping the old machine. Do not include the cost of sugar because it is the same for both machines and therefore will make no difference in the comparison of costs.

decrease of net value	160
labor costs	3,744
average interest cost	70.80
spoilage	952.32
taxes	54
supplies	45
maintenance	50
power	80
total annual cost	$5,156.12

Annual costs of new machine

(a) Annual decrease of net value

The salvage value is $0, so in five years, the value of the new machine will have decreased by $4,500/5 = $900 annually.

(b) Labor costs

Since the new machine uses 29½% less labor than the old one, labor cost is (100% - 29½%) = 70½% of that of the old machine. (0.705)($3,744) = $2,639.52 is the labor cost of the new machine.

(c) Average interest costs

There is no salvage value so that the average interest formula becomes

$$Q(\frac{i}{2})(\frac{n+1}{n}) = \$4,500(\frac{0.06}{2})(\frac{5}{6}) = \$162 .$$

(d) Spoilage cost
The total direct operating cost is

$$(\$28,000 + \$2,639.52) = \$30,639.52.$$

The new machine spoils 1% of the candy, so that the spoilage cost is (0.01)($30,639.52) = $306.40.

(e) Taxes
The tax paid is (0.03)($4,500) = $135.

Add up all the costs to get the total cost, again excluding the cost of sugar.

decrease of net value	900
labor costs	2,639.52
average interest cost	162
spoilage	306.40
taxes	135
supplies	25
maintenance	30
power	56
total annual cost	$4,253.92

The carnival should buy the new machine since it has a lower annual cost than the old machine.

• PROBLEM 13-16

Machine A costs $15,000 and has an expected life of 6 years with zero salvage value. Machine B, costing $25,000, is also expected to last 6 years with a salvage value of $2,993. The expected annual operating and maintenance costs are below.

Year	Machine A	Machine B
1	$2,000	$1,000
2	3,000	1,500
3	5,000	2,500
4	8,000	4,000
5	9,500	5,000
6	10,000	6,000

Using 8% interest, find and compare the total annual costs of the machines.

Solution: The total annual costs can be separated into two costs: the operating and maintenance costs given in the table and the capital recovery costs.

To find how much to recover each year for six years at 8% interest, given an initial capital investment of $15,000, multiply $15,000 by the capital recovery factor in the 8% compound interest table for n = 6 periods, (years). The annual capital recovery cost is:

$$\$15,000 \times 0.21632 = \$3,245, \text{ to the nearest dollar.}$$

This is added to each annual maintenance cost from the table to give the total annual costs for machine A.

Year	Machine A: Total annual costs
1	$2,000 + $3,245 = $5,245
2	3,000 + 3,245 = 6,245
3	5,000 + 3,245 = 8,245
4	8,000 + 3,245 = 11,245
5	9,500 + 3,245 = 12,745
6	10,000 + 3,245 = 13,245

Machine B has a salvage value of $2,993, that is, the company will receive $2,993 for it in six years. At 8% interest, the present value of this single payment is $2,993 x 0.6302 = $1,886.20. The number 0.6302 is the single payment present worth factor in the 8% table for n = 6. The $2,993 to be received six years from now is $1,886.20 today at 8% interest. The net value of Machine B is $25,000 - $1,886.20 = $23,113.80, which we have to recover over six years.

Use the same capital recovery factor to find the annual capital recovery cost:

$23,113.8 x 0.21632 = $5,000.

The total costs of B can now be found.

Year	Machine B: Total annual costs
1	$1,000 + 5,000 = $6,000
2	1,500 + 5,000 = 6,500
3	2,500 + 5,000 = 7,500
4	4,000 + 5,000 = 9,000
5	5,000 + 5,000 = 10,000
6	6,000 + 5,000 = 11,000

Machine A saves the company $755 the first year. The present value is $755 x 0.9259 = $699. Second year savings are $255, of which the present value is $255 x 0.8573 = $219. The total savings obtained from using Machine A instead of Machine B is $699 + $219 = $918 for the first 2 years.

The savings obtained from using Machine B, in terms of present value, are shown below.

Year		Net savings
3	$745 x 0.7938 =	$591
4	2,245 x 0.7350 =	1,650
5	2,745 x 0.6806 =	1,868
6	2,245 x 0.6302 =	1,415
	Total savings	5,524

Using B would save $5,524 - $918 = $4,606 more than using A.

CHAPTER 14

ANALYSIS OF COSTS AND PROFITS

FUNDAMENTALS

• PROBLEM 14-1

You invest $1,000 at 4 percent interest, compounded annually. Determine your balance at the end of 10 years (a) if you make no further deposits or withdrawals; (b) if you deposit $30 at the beginning of each year, including the tenth; (c) if you withdraw $30 at the end of each year, including the tenth.

Solution: (a) The single payment compound amount factor (SPCA) for i = 4%, n = 10years is 1.480. The balance at the end of 10 years is

$$(\$1,000)(1.480) = \$1,480.$$

(b) The amount at the beginning of the first year is $1,030. The interest is ($1,030)(0.04) = $41.20. The amount at the end of the first year is therefore $1,030 + $41.20 = $1,071.20. The amount in the beginning of the second year is $1,071.20 + $30 deposit = $1,101.20. The interest for the second year is ($1,101.20)(0.04) = 44.05 , to the nearest cent. The account at the end of the second year shows $1,101.20 + $44.05 = $1,145.25. Continue likewise for the remaining years, remembering to add 30 at the beginning of each year, to get the following table

Year	Beginning Amount (including yearly deposit of $30)	Interest	Ending Amount
1	1,030	41.20	1,071.20
2	1,101.20	44.05	1,145.25
3	1,175.25	47.01	1,222.26
4	1,252.26	50.09	1,302.35
5	1,332.35	53.29	1,385.64
6	1,415.64	56.62	1,472.26
7	1,502.26	60.09	1,562.35
8	1,592.35	63.69	1,656.04
9	1,686.04	67.44	1,763.48
10	1,783.48	71.33	1,854.81

(c) At the beginning of year one, the amount in the account is $1,000. Four percent interest on this is $40.00. But since $30 dollars are withdrawn at the end of each year, the amount at the beginning of the second year is \$1,000 + (\$40 - \$30) = \$1,010. The interest for the second year is (1,010)(0.04) = \$40.40. Again, deducting the amount withdrawn at the end of year 2 gives us a net increase of \$10.40. The beginning amount for the third year is \$1,010 + \$10.40 = \$1,020.40 and the interest for that year is (\$1,020.40)(0.04) = \$40.82 to the nearest cent. Continue this procedure to get the following table.

Year	Beginning Amount	Interest	Ending Amount (including withdrawal of \$30)
1	1,000.00	40.00	1,010.00
2	1,010.00	40.40	1,020.40
3	1,020.40	40.82	1,031.22
4	1,031.22	41.25	1,042.47
5	1,042.47	41.70	1,054.17
6	1,054.17	42.17	1,066.34
7	1,066.34	42.65	1,078.99
8	1,078.99	43.16	1,092.15
9	1,092.15	43.69	1,105.84
10	1,105.84	44.23	1,120.07

At the end of the ten years you have \$1,120.07 in your account.

• PROBLEM 14-2

The single-payment compound-amount factor, for interest rate i = 6.146% and number of periods n = 5, is $(1+i)^n = 1.3475$. For this i and n, find the
(a) single-payment present-worth factor (SPPW),
(b) uniform-series compound-amount factor (USCA),
(c) sinking-fund-payment factor (SFP),
(d) capital-recovery factor (CR)
(e) uniform-series present-worth factor (USPW).

Solution: (a) The single-payment present worth factor is the reciprocal of the single-payment compound-amount factor.

$$(SPPW)_{i,n} = \frac{1}{(1+i)^n}$$

$$(SPPW)_{6.146,5} = \frac{1}{1.3475} \approx 0.7421 .$$

(b) The formula for the uniform-series compound factor is

$$(USCA)_{i,n} = \frac{(1+i)^n - 1}{i}$$

therefore to get $(USCA)_{6.146,5}$, subtract 1 from 1.3475 (which equals $(1+i)^n$) and divide by 0.06146, the rate i in decimals.

$$(USCA)_{6.146,5} = \frac{1.3475 - 1}{0.06146} \approx 5.6541 .$$

(c) The sinking-fund factor is the reciprocal of the uniform-series compound-amount factor.

$$SFP = \frac{1}{USCA}$$

$$(SFP)_{6.146,5} = \frac{1}{5.6541} \approx 0.1769 \ .$$

(d) The capital-recovery factor (CR) is the product of the single-payment compound-amount factor and the sinking-fund factor, i.e.

$$CR = SPCA \times SFP$$

$$(CR)_{6.146,5} = 1.3475 \times 0.1769 \approx 0.2384 \ .$$

(e) The uniform-series present-worth factor (USPW) is the reciprocal of the capital recovery factor (CR)

$$(USPW)_{6.146,5} = \frac{1}{(CR)_{6.146,5}} = \frac{1}{0.2384} \approx 4.2 \ .$$

• PROBLEM 14-3

The sinking-fund-payment factor for $i = 5\frac{1}{2}\%$, $n = 4$ is 0.2303. For the same i and n, find the (a) uniform-series compound-amount factor, (b) capital-recovery factor, (c) uniform-series present-worth factor.

Solution: (a) The sinking-fund-payment factor is the reciprocal of the uniform-series compound amount factor so that

$$\text{USCA (Uniform Series Compound Amount)} = \frac{1}{0.2303} \approx 4.3422$$

for $i = 5\frac{1}{2}\%$, $n = 0.2303$.

(b) The capital recovery factor (CR) is given by

$$\frac{i(1+i)^n}{(1+i)^n - 1} = \left(\frac{i}{(1+i)^n - 1}\right)(1+i)^n$$

which is the sinking-fund-payment (SFP) factor multiplied by the simple payment component amount factor (SPCA) $(1+i)^n$. To obtain $(1+i)^n$ for $i = 5\frac{1}{2}$, $n = 4$, substitute directly, $(SPCA)_{5\frac{1}{2},4} = (1.055)^4 = 1.2388$ and the capital recovery factor is $(0.2303)(1.2388) \approx 0.2853$.

(c) The uniform-series present worth factor (USPW) is the reciprocal of the capital recovery factor: $(USPW)_{5\frac{1}{2},4} \approx 1/0.2853 \approx 3.5051$.

Summarizing the relationships:

$$USPW = \frac{1}{SFP}$$

$$CR = (SFP)(SPCA)$$

$$USPW = \frac{1}{CR} = \frac{1}{(SFP)(SPCA)}$$

• PROBLEM 14-4

A man arranges to repay a $1,000 loan in 15 equal annual installments. Interest is 4 percent. After his tenth payment, he wishes to pay the balance in a lump sum. Assuming he can do this without an additional penalty premium, how much does he owe?

Solution: This annual payment is found by multiplying the capital recovery factor in the 4% interest table, n = 15, by the $1,000 loan annual payment = ($1,000)(0.08994) = $89.94 .

The man has made 10 of these payments by the end of the 10th year. The amount paid is not ($89.94)(10) = $899.40, but less since the present value of a series of payments is less than the nominal value. To find the present value of this series of annual payments at 4%, n = 10 years, multiply $89.94 by the uniform-series present worth factor in the 4% interest table for n = 10 years. The present worth of the series is

($89.94)(8.111) = $729.50 ,

to the nearest cent. The man owes $1,000 - $729.50 = $270.50 after 10 payments.

• PROBLEM 14-5

You are considering the purchase of a machine which will give you an annual return of $1,000 a year for 20 years. The return will be received uniformly and continuously over the years. How much can you pay for the machine and still obtain at least a 10 percent effective annual return on your investment in the machine?

Solution: This problem asks the question, "What is the present worth of a uniform series of $1,000 receipts for 20 years at an annual rate of 10% ?" From the 10% compound interest table, the uniform series present worth factor for n = 20 periods is 8.514. To obtain a rate of return of 10% on the investment, pay

(8.514)($1,000) = $8,514 .

• PROBLEM 14-6

A man has the following debts outstanding: (a) 10 annual mortgage payments of $1,000, (b) 12 monthly payments of $100 on his automobile, (c) a bill for $2,000 due in two years, (d) a bill for $1,000 due today. Using an annual interest rate of 12 percent (nominal rate on the automobile loan and effective rate on all other debts), determine the annual amount necessary to retire the entire debt in 15 years.

Solution: Convert all the payments to their equivalent present worth and add these results to get the total amount to be paid in equal annual disbursements at a rate of 12% in 15 years.

(a) To get the present worth of a uniform series of annual payments, multiply one payment by the uniform series present worth factor for n = 10, i = 12%. There is no table from which to directly obtain this uniform series present worth factor. However, this factor is the reciprocal of the uniform series capital recovery (C.R.) factor, n = 10, i = 12%, which is found in the table named "Capital Recovery Factors for Interest Rates from 0% to 25%." The C.R. factor is 0.17698; therefore the present worth factor is

$$\frac{1}{0.17698} = 5.650,$$

to the nearest thousandth, and

$$\text{Present Worth} = 1,000 \times 5.650 = \$5650.$$

The series of ten equal payments, each $1,000, is equivalent to a lump sum of $5,650 today.

(b) Twelve monthly payments at a rate of 12% annually is the same as twelve month payments at a monthly rate of 1%. This uniform series of payments can be converted to an equivalent lump sum by using the 1% interest table for n = 12 periods.

$$\text{Present Worth} = 100 \times \text{Present Worth Factor for Uniform Series, } n = 12$$

$$= 100 \times 11.255 = \$1,125.50.$$

(c) We want to know the present worth of 2,000 paid 2 years from now if the interest rate is 12%. Consult the table for Present Worth Factors for Interest Rates from 0% to 25%.

$$\text{Present Worth} = 2,000 \times \text{Present Worth Factor of Single Payments, } n = 2$$

$$= 2,000 \times 0.7972 = \$1,594.40.$$

(d) The present worth of $1,000 today is $1,000. The total amount to be paid is:

$$\$5,650 + \$1,125.50 + \$1,594.40 + \$1,000 = \$9,369.90$$

To compute the annual payment for 15 years at a rate of 12% per year to retire the debt, use the capital recovery factor found in the Capital Recovery Table for Interest Rates from 0% to 25% for i = 12% and, n = 15 periods (years).

This factor is 0.14682.

$$\text{Annual Payment} = \$9,369.90 \times 0.14682 = \$1,375.69,$$

to the nearest cent.

• PROBLEM 14-7

Mr. Johnson, who already has a $20,000 annual salary, has purchased land for $8,000 and a house on the land for $50,000. He expects to sell the property in ten years. For the first 3 years, Johnson expects rent income from the property to be $7,000 and expenses to be $2,700. For the next 7 years, revenue will be $10,000 and expenses, $3,500.

Johnson will deduct a 2% depreciation allowance on the building from his taxable incomes.

If Johnson sells this property after 10 years for $61,500, what percent of his $58,000 investment will he have gained or lost from the rental and sales incomes? The current interest rate is 7%. The tax rates applied to rental and sales income, above and beyond the $20,000 salary, are:

Income	Rate
On the first $4,000	33.44% = 0.3344
On the second $4,000	37.84% = 0.3784
On the third $4,000	41.36% = 0.4136
On the fourth $4,000	44% = 0.44
On the fifth $4,000	46.64% = 0.4664

Solution: Find the present worth of all income from the property. The percentage ratio of the profit (or loss) to investment is

$$\frac{\text{Present worth of income-investment}}{\text{investment}} \times 100\% .$$

For each of the first 3 years, net annual receipts will be:

Gross Annual receipts - expenses
= $7,000 - $2,700 = $4,300.

Since the depreciation allowance on the building is tax deductible, i.e., it is not included in taxable income,

Taxable Income = Net Annual Receipts - Depreciation Allowance

= $4,300 - (2% x $50,000)

= $4,300 - $1,000 = $3,300.

Since $3,300 falls within the first $4,000 limit,

Income Taxes = 0.3344 x $3,300
= $1,104, to the nearest dollar,

and

Net Income
Net Annual Receipts - Income Taxes
= $4,300 - $1,104 = $3,196.

The depreciation allowance, since it is not an actual cash disbursement, is only deducted to find taxable income, but has no effect on actual net income.

Present worth is how much an expected future receipt is worth today. Money invested today earns interest in the future, $100 invested today at 6%, will be worth $106 a year from today, the present worth of the $106 is $100.

Consult the "7% Compound Interest Factors" table. Use the "Uniform Annual Series " section, since we are discussing 3 annual $3,196 payment, to find in the "Present Worth Factor" column, for n(number of years) = 3, the factor 2.624. The present worth factor for i(interest rate) = 7%, n = 3 can also be computed from the "Capital Recovery Factors for Interest Rates from 0% to 25%" table. The capital recovery factor is the reciprocal of the present worth factor in a uniform annual series. In this table there is no 7% column, but there is a 6% and an 8% column. Since 7% is halfway between 6% and 8%, its capital recovery is halfway between those of 6% and 8% for n = 3. The capital recovery (C.R.) factor of 7% is

$$\frac{\text{C.R. factor of 6\%} + \text{C.R. factor of 8\%}}{2}$$

$$= \frac{0.37411 + 0.38803}{2} = 0.38107.$$

The present worth factor, the reciprocal, is $\frac{1}{.38107} = 2.624$, (to the nearest thousandth). This is the same result obtained from the 7% table.

The present worth of 3 annual $3,196 payments is $3,169 x 2.624 = $8,386, to the nearest dollar. Over the next 7 years:

Net Annual Receipts = Gross Annual Receipts - Expenses

= $10,000 - $3,500 = $6,500 .

Taxable Income = Net Annual Receipts - Depreciation Allowance

= $6,500 - $1,000 = $5,500.

The first $4,000 of taxable income will be taxed at 33.44% and the remaining $5,000 - 4,000 = $1,500 will be taxed at 37.84%

Income Taxes = ($4,000 x .3344) + ($1,500 x .3784)

= 1337.6 + 567.6

= 1905.2, or $1,905 to the nearest dollar.

Net Income = Net Annual Receipts - Income Taxes

= $6,500 - $1,905 = $4,595 .

Since Johnson will not start receiving the annual $4,595 income until 3 years have passed, adjust the figure to what it would be if he were to begin receiving this income today; calculate its present value for n = 3, i = 7%. In the present worth column of the single payment section (since only the amount of one payment is being adjusted) of the "7% Compound Interest Factors" table, for n = 3, find the factor 0.8163. By interpolating from the capital recovery factor table, find that the present worth factor of 7 annual receipts of $3,751 at 7% interest is approximately 5.3879. It is equal to

$$\frac{1}{\frac{1}{2}(\text{C.R. factor } i = 6\%,\ n = 7 + \text{C.R. factor } i = 8\%,\ n = 7)}$$

$$= \frac{1}{\frac{1}{2}(.1794 + .19207)} = \frac{1}{.1856} = 5.3879.$$

The present worth factor in the 7% compound interest table, for 7 annual payments, is 5.389. Use this latter factor.

The present worth of 7 annual $3,751 payments, where the current interest rate is 7%, is $3,751 X 5.389 = $20,214, to the nearest dollar.

In ten years, when the property is sold, there will be a long-term taxable gain of :

Sales price	$61,500
less: purchase price	(58,000)
plus: depreciation allowance (10 years x $1,000/year)	10,000
	$13,500

According to the tax rates given in the problem, the taxes on this gain will be ($2,500 x .3784) + ($4,000 x .4136) + ($4,000 x .44) + ($3,000 x .4664) = $946 + $1,654.4 + $1,760 + $1,399.2 = $5,760, to the nearest dollar. Multiply the second tax rate, 37.84% by $2,500 because it is part of the tenth year income which also includes $4,000 to be taxed at the 33.44% rate and $1,500 to be taxed at 37.84%. There is another $4,000 - $1,500 = $2,500 that can be taxed at 37.84%.

The net receipts on the sale of the property
= sales price - taxes on taxable gain
= $61,500 - $5,760
= $55,740.

The present worth factor for this single receipt of $55,740, found in the 7% Compound Interest Factors" table in the present worth factors column of the single payment section, for n = 10, is 0.5803. The present worth of $55,740 received in 10 years, for

i(interest rate) = 7% is $55,740 x 0.5083 = $28,333,

to the nearest dollar.

The present worth of the property for 10 years = present worth of rent + present worth of net receipts from sale = $8,386 (3 years rent) + $20,214 (7 years rent) + $28,333 (net receipts) = $56,933.

Johnson has incurred a 58,000 - 56,933 = $1,067 loss, which is

$$\frac{\$1,060}{\$58,000} \times 100 = \text{(to the nearest 1/100\%) } 1.84\%$$

of his investment.

• PROBLEM 14-8

A bridge is expected to have maintenance and repair expenses of $2,000 in the first year. It is anticipated that these expenses will increase $500 each year over the bridge's expected lifetime of 20 years.

(i) Find a formula that will give the present worth of each annual disbursement, given the year in which the disbursement occurs.

(ii) Give the present worth of each annual disbursement for each year the bridge is in service.

(iii) What is the total, present worth of these maintenance and repair costs?

The current interest rate is 4%.

Solution: (i) The maintenance and repair costs of the bridge will be different each year. The first year, year 0, the disbursement will be $2,000 as stated before. In year 1, (second year) the disbursement will be $2,500; year 2, $2,500 + $500 or $3,000; year 3, $3,000 + $500 or $3,500; in general, if k is the year, $0 \leq k \leq 19$, the disbursement in year k is $2,000 + 500k.

To get the present value of any amount, be it a receipt or disbursement, in year n at a rate i, multiply the receipt or disbursement, by the "single payment present worth" factor, abbreviated SPPW. This factor is

$$\frac{1}{(1+i)^n}$$

and can be found in the compound interest table for the rate i. For this problem, the rate is 4% so that algebraically the factor is stated as

$$\frac{1}{1.04^n} .$$

The disbursement in year k, $0 \le k \le 19$, we previously found, is $2,000 + 500k$. Therefore the formula which gives the present worth of this disbursement in year k is

$$\underset{\text{DISBURSEMENT}}{\underset{\uparrow}{(2,000 + 500k)}} \cdot \underset{\text{PRESENT WORTH FACTOR for year } k \text{, at } 4\%}{\underset{\uparrow}{\left(\frac{1}{1.04^k}\right)}} = \frac{2,000 + 500k}{1.04^k}$$

(ii) Construct a table with three columns. Column one shows the year number from 0 to 19, year zero being the first year. Column two shows the disbursement in that year. Column three gives the present worth of the disbursement. Use the 4% compound interest factor table to get the present worth factors from period 1 to period 20 instead of using the formula derived in (i). For example, the SPPW factor for the 2nd year, (called year 1), is .9615. The disbursement for year 1, is \$2,500. Multiply the disbursement by its $n = i$, $i = 4\%$ present worth factor to compute present worth.

$$(\$2,500)(.9615) = \$2,404.$$

The present worth figures are rounded off to the nearest dollar. Continue this way to get the complete table shown below.

Year	Disbursement	Present Worth
n=0	\$2,000	\$2,000
n=1	2,500	2,404
n=2	3,000	2,774
n=3	3,500	3,112
n=4	4,000	3,419
n=5	4,500	3,699
n=6	5,000	3,952
n=7	5,500	4,180
n=8	6,000	4,384
n=9	6,500	4,567
n=10	7,000	4,729
n=11	7,500	4,872
n=12	8,000	4,997
n=13	8,500	5,105
n=14	9,000	5,197
n=15	9,500	5,275
n=16	10,000	5,339
n=17	10,500	5,390
n=18	11,000	5,430
n=19	11,500	5,458

(iii) To get the total cost of the bridge, add the numbers in the present worth column, \$86,283 are the maintenance and repair expenses of the bridge over 20 years.

RATE OF RETURN

• PROBLEM 14-9

Charles will pay Bernice \$800 five years from now if she lends him \$500 now. What is the rate of return on the \$500 loan?

Solution: \$500 is the present value of \$800 received 5 years from now, given interest rate i. (Assume compound interest). In general, given interest rate i, and a future receipt S to be received n periods from now, the present worth of the receipt, P, is given by the formula

$$P = S \frac{1}{(1+i)^n}$$

Multiply both sides of the equation by $(1+i)^n$ to obtain the more familiar compound interest formula:

$$P(1+i)^n = S .$$

P = 500, S = 800, n = 5 years, solve for i.

(i) $500(1+i)^5 = 800$ (initial equation).

(ii) Divide both sides by 500,

$$(1+i)^5 = 1.6 .$$

(iii) Take the fifth roots of both sides, using a calculator,

$$(1+i) = \sqrt[5]{1.6} = (1.6)^{0.2} \approx 1.0986$$

(iv) $i \approx 1.0986 - 1 = 0.0986$.

The rate of return of the \$500. loan is approximately

$$0.0986 \times 100\% = 9.86\% .$$

• PROBLEM 14-10

Ms. Derman expects \$500 annually for the next 10 years from her \$3,000 investment. What is the rate of return of this investment?

Solution: The Capital Recovery (C.R.) factor

$$= \frac{\text{expected annual return}}{\text{investment}}$$

$$= \frac{\$500}{\$3{,}000} = 0.16667 .$$

Look in the table "Capital Recovery Factors for Interest Rates from 0% to 25%". For n (number of periods) = 10 years and i (interest rate) = 10%, the capital recovery factor is 0.16275, which is less than 0.16667. For n = 10 and i = 12%, the capital recovery factor is 0.17698, which is greater than 0.16667. Thus the rate of return of the \$3,000 investment is between 10 and 12 percent. Use linear interpolation to get the approximate rate.

Linear Interpolation:

On a set of perpendicular axes, let the horizontal axis be the capital recovery factors and the vertical axis be the interest rates. Assume a line connects the two given points, (0.16275,10) and (0.17698,12), as shown below

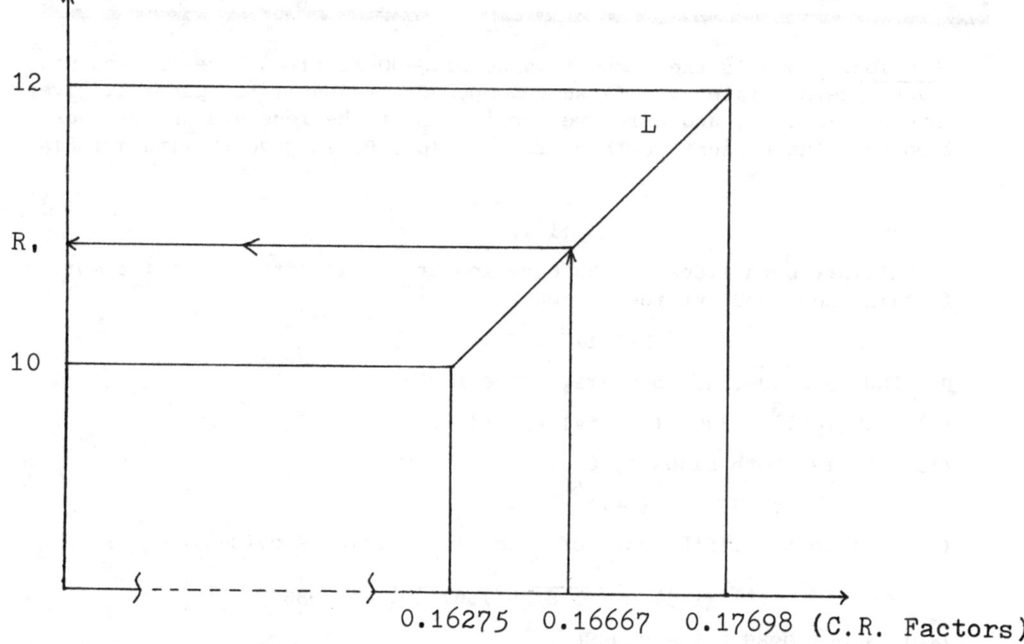

Given the capital recovery factor 0.16667, we want to find the corresponding R, assuming a linear relationship between interest rates and capital recovery factors. The slope of the line segment is

$$\frac{\text{change in interest rates}}{\text{change in C.R. factor}} = \frac{\Delta i}{\Delta \text{ C.R. factor}} = \frac{12 - 10}{.17698 - .16275}$$

$$= \frac{2}{0.01423} \approx 140.548 \text{ (to the nearest thousandth).}$$

$$R \approx 10 + (\text{increment in C.R. factor from 10\% to R\%} \times \text{slope})$$

$$\approx 10 + [(0.16667 - 0.16275) \times (140.548)]$$

$$\approx 10 + (.00392 \times 140.548)$$

$$\approx 10.55 .$$

The rate of return on the $3,000 investment is approximately 10.55%.

• PROBLEM 14-11

> You are willing to buy a new machine for $1,000 because it will save you $150 annually for the next 10 years. What is the rate of return on this investment?

Solution: Given the rate i, and n = 10 years the uniform-series present worth factor is given by

$$\text{USPWF(uniform series present worth factor)} = \frac{(1+i)^{10} - 1}{i(1+i)^{10}} .$$

This means that given ten annual receipts of $150, the present value of these receipts is 1,000 and we have the formula

$$1,000 = 150 \frac{(1+i)^{10} - 1}{i(1+i)^{10}} .$$

To get an approximation for i, (i) divide both sides by 150 to get the USPW factor for n = 10 and the unknown i,

$$\frac{(1+i)^{10} - 1}{i(1+i)^{10}} = (\text{SPPW})_{i,10} = 6.6667 ,$$

(ii) Look in the table of interests factors to a rate which has approximately 6.6667 in n = 10 periods under the uniform series present worth factor column. For example, i = 10%, n = 10 has 6.144 as the USPW factor. The 8% table has, for n = 10, a USPW factor of 6.710 which is closer to 6.6667 than is 6.144 in the 10% table.

The higher the percentage, the lower the uniform series present worth factor. Since 6.6667 is

$$\frac{6.710 - 6.6667}{6.710} \times 100\% = .645\%$$

lower than 6.710, the 8% factor, the unknown rate of interest must be .645% higher than 8%; the unknown rate must be 8% + (0.645% × 8%) = 8.0516% .

• PROBLEM 14-12

Mr. Haskell has decided to buy a rental property. The building costs $50,000 and the land costs $30,000. The annual rent income is estimated to be $10,450 and the annual expense, $3,200. Mr. Haskell plans to depreciate the building by the straight line method over 40 years. Mr. Haskell wants to choose the best of three investment plans.

Plan A

Pay the full $80,000 from personal account.

Plan B

Borrow $30,000 and pay $50,000 from personal account. Rate of interest is 4½%.

Plan C

Borrow $60,000 and pay $20,000 from personal account. Rate of interest is 5 1/4%. If the tax rate is 40%, which investment plan has the highest rate of return?

Solution: Find Rate of Return: Plan A.

The total annual expense will be the sum of (1) the interest payments (2) maintenance and insurance disbursements and (3) depreciation.

(1) No money is borrowed so the interest payments = $0.00
(2) We are told this is $3,200.
(3) The annual depreciation charge on the property is

$$\frac{\$50,000}{40} = \$1,250.$$

The annual expense is therefore, $3,200 + $1,250 = $4,450. Since the annual receipts are $10,450, the estimated annual profit is $10,450 - $4,450 = $6,000. The tax paid on this amount is (0.40)($6,000) = $2,400. Net income is $6,000 - $2,400 = $3,600.

$$\text{Rate of Return: } \frac{\text{Net Income}}{\text{investment}} \times 100\% = \left(\frac{3,600}{80,000}\right) \times 100\% = 4.5\%.$$

The rate of Return: Plan B.

Use same procedure. Expenses:

(1) The interest paid on $30,000 at an annual rate of $4\frac{1}{2}\%$ is (0.045)($30,000) = $1,350.
(2) Annual disbursements are $3,200.
(3) Depreciation remains at $1,250.

The total annual expense is therefore, $1,350 + $3,200 + $1,250 = $5,800. The total annual receipts is $10,450 so the income before taxes is $10,450 - $5,800 = $4,650. Forty percent of this is paid as taxes or (0.40)($4,650) = $1,860. The after tax income is $4,650 - $1,860 = $2,790. The rate of return on a personal investment of $50,000 is

$$\left(\frac{2,790}{50,000}\right) \times 100\% = 5.58\%.$$

Find Rate of Return: Plan C.

(1) The interest paid on $60,000 at an annual rate of $5\frac{1}{2}\%$ is (0.055)($60,000) = $3,300. Since the annual maintenance disbursements and the depreciation charge remain the same, the total annual expense is $3,300 + $3,200 + $1,250 = $7,750.

Income before taxes is $10,450 - $7,750 = $2,700 the tax rate is 40% so the tax paid on this amount is (0.4)($2,700) = $1,080 and the net income is $2,700 - $1,080 = $1,620. The rate of return on a $20,000 personal investment is

$$\left(\frac{\$1,620}{\$20,000}\right) \times 100\% = 8.1\%$$

Therefore, Mr. Haskell should choose Plan C; he should borrow $60,000 and use $20,000 of his money to get the greatest rate of return.

• PROBLEM 14-13

Mr. Stein wants to buy a new sawing unit worth $10,000 that will substantially speed up work. He estimates the total extra receipts from improved operations to be $7,000 per year during the first five years. Disbursements, excluding income taxes, will be $4,000. After 5 years the machine will be retired, although it will be retained in case of extraordinary demand. The machine will be depreciated on a straight line basis. If the tax rate is 60% and the minimum desirable rate of return is 4%, (a) during the first five years, what is the rate of return before taxes?

(b) what is the rate of return after taxes?
(c) and if Mr. Stein uses straight line depreciation over 25 years instead of 5, is the rate of return after taxes above or below 4% ?

Solution: (a) The net receipts are \$7,000 - \$4,000 = \$3,000. The capital recovery factor corresponding to this amount and the \$10,000 investment is

$$\frac{3,000}{10,000} = 0.3 .$$

Look in the table named "Capital Recovery Factors for Interest Rates from 0% to 25%. For n = 5 years, the factor 0.3 is close to 0.29832, the factor for 15% .

Interpolating: $15\% + \left(\frac{0.3}{0.29832}\right) \times (15\%) = 15.08\%$ is the rate of return before taxes for the five years.

(b) Straight line depreciation on \$10,000 over 5 years yields a

$$\frac{10,000}{5} = \$2,000$$

annual charge. There is a tax deduction for this amount on net income, so the taxable income resulting from this investment is \$3,000 - \$2,000 = \$1,000. The tax rate is 60%, therefore the tax paid on this amount is (\$1,000)(0.60) = \$600. The net receipts after taxes and other disbursements are

$$\$7,000 - (\$4,000 + \$600) = \$2,400.$$

The capital recovery factor is

$$\frac{\$2,400}{\$10,000} = 0.24 .$$

For n = 5, and table entry 0.24, (using the same table as before) we interpolate to find a rate of return of 6.06%:

$$\left(\frac{0.24}{0.23740}\right) \times 6\% = 6.06\% ,$$

where 0.23740 is the capital recovery factor of 6%.

(c) The annual straight line depreciation on \$10,000 over 25 years is

$$\frac{\$10,000}{25} = \$400 .$$

Excess receipts over disbursements:	\$3,000
Less: Annual depreciation:	400
Net taxable income:	\$2,600

The amount of tax is then 60% of \$2,600 = 0.60 × \$2,600 = \$1,560. During the first five years, the excess of receipts over disbursements will be

$$\$7,000 - (\$4,000 + \$1,560) = \$1,440.$$

For the next 20 years, the machine will be idle, but still depreciated \$400 per year. This depreciation is tax exempt; if it weren't, \$400 × 60% = \$240 would have to be paid in taxes. The \$240 saved is the receipt from owning the machine from years 6 through 25.

To calculate the percentage return on investment, find the present worth (P.W.) factors that make the annual receipts equal to the original \$10,000 investment. The interest rate corresponding to these factors is the percentage rate of return. The present worth will be:

Annual Receipts for 1st - 5th years: (\$1,440)(Uniform Annual Series Present Worth Factor for n = 5 years)

+ Annual Receipts for 6th - 25th years: (\$240)(Uniform Annual Series P.W. factor for n= 20 years)(Single Payment P.W. factor for n = 5)

The receipts of \$240 for years 6 - 25 are multiplied by the single payment, n = 5 factor because these 20 receipts will not be earned until year 6; to only multiply them by the uniform series n = 20 will convert them to their present worth in year 6. It is necessary to use the single payment n = 5 factor to convert the 20 \$240 receipts to today's present worth. This second conversion uses the single payment factor because the first conversion to present worth in year six gives the equivalent single payment of the 20 \$240 payments.

Since we know the return on investment net of taxes with a 5-year life is approximately 6%, and the returns with a 25-year life (net of taxes),it makes sense to use the 6% factors as a first trial. The present worth of all receipts for i(interest) = 6% is \$8,122.45, which is too low. For i = 1%, the present worth is \$11,109.30. This is too high, but closer to \$10,000. Try $1\frac{1}{2}$%, 2% then $2\frac{1}{2}$%, which is closest to the answer.

\$1,440 (4.646)	\$6,690.24
\$240(15.589)(0.8839)	3,306.99
	\$9,997.33

The approximate rate of return, $2\frac{1}{2}$%, is below the 4% minimum desirable rate.

• PROBLEM 14-14

Mr. Golden purchased 3 bonds, each with a maturity value of \$1,000, from the Suttonsmith Corporation. For each bond, he will receive \$15 semiannually for 20 years, after which time he will also receive the full face value of \$1,000. The \$15 payments will be made regardless of the interest rate. If the interest rate on one bond was 3%; on another, 4%; and on the third, 3.6%, what did Mr. Golden pay for each bond?

Solution: Although the maturity value of each of the bonds was \$1,000, Mr. Golden did not necessarily pay \$1,000 for each bond. Mr. Golden paid the sum of present worth of the future interest payments and the present worth of the maturity value. The present worth calculations are based on the semiannual interest rates. The semiannual rates of the annual rates 3%, 3.6% and 4% are 1.5%, 1.8%, and 2% respectively.

For the 1.5% semiannual bond

In twenty years, 40 $15-payments will have been made. Look at the table named "1½% Compound Interest Factors". For n = 40 periods, the present worth factor is 29.916. The present worth of the series of payments is ($15) x (29.916) = $448.74. The present worth factor for one single payment of $1,000 at the maturity date is found along the same row under the "single payment" section. The factor is 0.5513, and the present worth is

$$(\$1,000) \times (0.5513) = \$551.30.$$

The price of the bond was $448.74 + $551.30 = 1000.04, or $1,000 to the nearest dollar.

For the 2% semiannual bond

Use table named "2% Compound Interest Factors" to get the proper factors. For n = 40, under the present worth column for series payments, the factor is 27.355. The present worth of forty $15 payments is:

$$\$15 \times 27.355 = \$410.33 \text{ to be nearest cent.}$$

The present worth of a single $1,000 payment at the end of 40 periods is 0.4529 (the present worth factor for single payments, n = 40) x $1,000 = $452.90. The price of the 2% semiannual bond is

$$\$410.33 + \$452.90 = \$863.23.$$

The 1.8% semiannual bond

There is no table for 1.8%, but there is one for $1\frac{3}{4}$% table to estimate the present worth factors for the 1.8% interest rate.

The factor for the series of 40 payments is 28.594. The present worth of forty $15 payments is

$$\$15 \times 28.594 = \$428.91.$$

For a single payment of $1,000, the present worth, for n = 40, is $1,000 x .4996 (the present worth factor) = $499.60. The price of a 1.75% semiannual bond is therefore $428.91 + $499.60 = $928.51. To better estimate the price of a 1.8% bond, interpolate.

Interpolation

For any given number of periods, as the interest rates increase, the present worth factors for series payments decrease. The present worth factor for 1.8% is less than 28.594, the 1.75% factor, and greater than 27.355, the 2% factor. It is also closer to 28.594 than to 27.355, since 1.8% is closer to 1.75% than to 2.0%

$$1.8\% - 1.75\% = 0.05\%; \quad \frac{0.05\%}{1.75\%} = 0.0286 = 2.86\% .$$

1.75% and 1.8% differ by approximately 2.86% of 1.75%. The unknown present worth factor and 28.594 should differ by 2.86% of 28.594, which equals 0.0286 x 28.594 = 0.818. Therefore, the estimate for n = 40, i = 1.8% is 28.594 - 0.818 = 27.776.

The present worth of forty $15 payments is

$$\$15 \times 27.776 = \$416.64.$$

The present worth factor for a single payment is obtained the same way, keeping in mind that the factors decrease as the rates increase. The present worth factor for n = 40, i = 1.8% must be greater than 0.4529 (the factor for n = 40, i = 2%) and less than 0.4996 (the factor for n = 40, i = 1.75%). Interpolating as before, we find that the factor is 0.4853.

The present worth of the $1,000 payment is then

$$(\$1,000)(0.4853) = \$485.30.$$

The new estimate of the price of the bond is

$$\$416.70 + \$485.30 = \$902.00.$$

This is less than our previous figure, $928.51. Take the average of the two to get the final estimate of the price of the 1.8% bond:

$$\frac{\$928.51 + 902.00}{2} = \$915.26 \text{ to the nearest cent.}$$

CHAPTER 15

CORPORATE OPERATIONS

COSTS AND PRICE

• PROBLEM 15-1

A television manufacturing firm lowered the price of its deluxe portable television set from $350 to $320 per unit, in order to increase their revenues and profits. This price change resulted in an increase in sales from 1,000 units per month to 1,080 units per month. Assuming the unit production costs did not change, was their decision to lower prices a good one?

Solution: To find out if their decision was a good one, we must compare the revenue before the price reduction with the revenue after the price reduction. The revenue before the reduction in price was $350 times 1,000 units, or a total revenue of $350,000. The revenue after the reduction was $320 times 1,080 units or $345.600. Thus the revenue decreased, and the decision was a poor one.

• PROBLEM 15-2

Punk Magazine has a circulation of 2,000,000. They charge $20,000 for a full page ad in their magazine. What is the cost per thousand for a single ad?

Solution: The term "cost per thousand" refers to the cost of reaching 1,000 readers. This is used as a standard by which we can compare the costs of an ad in two different magazines. To find the cost per thousand, we must find the fraction obtained by dividing 1,000 by the circulation of the paper. We then multiply that fraction by the cost of the ad, to get our answer.

Thus, the cost per thousand for an ad in Punk Magazine is:

$$1,000 \div 2,000,000 \text{ (circulation)} \times \$20,000 = \frac{1}{2,000} \times \$20,000 = \$10.$$

• PROBLEM 15-3

> A manufacturer can produce a saw for $13 in direct costs and $10 in overhead or indirect costs. He needs to sell his saw for a minimum price. At what price must he sell his saw so that he will not incur a short term loss?

Solution: The manufacturer is not worried about a long term loss, thus he must only cover his direct costs. The indirect costs will not affect any short term losses, only long term. Thus, he need only charge $13.

• PROBLEM 15-4

> Costs for producing one widget:
>
> Materials: 2 parts (a) $25.00 per part
>
> Expenses : $10.00
>
> Labor : 20 operations (a) $5.00 per operation
>
> Based on the above information, which is the only valid conclusion?
>
> A) The selling price should be $160 per widget.
>
> B) labor rates are excessive
>
> C) output is labor intensive
>
> D) material costs are low

Solution: The costs for the production of one widget are:

Materials	2 × $25 =	$50
Expenses		$10
Labor	20 × $5 =	$100
Total		$160

The total cost is $160, thus the selling price should be greater than $160, otherwise they will earn no profit. We can say that the output is labor intensive, for most of the cost of the widget is due to labor. We cannot say from this information that the labor cost is excessive, for a widget may be very intricate and require a lot of labor. We also cannot say that the material costs are low, because there may be very little material in a widget. Thus the only conclusion we can arrive at is (C).

• PROBLEM 15-5

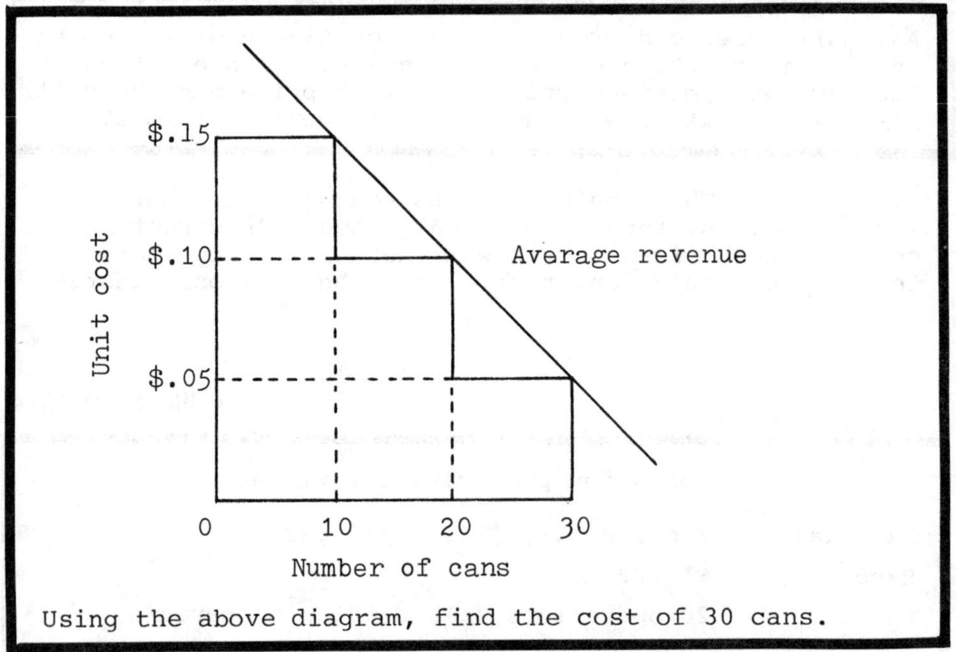

Using the above diagram, find the cost of 30 cans.

Solution: This is a typical case of differential pricing. Differential pricing is a method used to give a discount to customers who buy large lots of some items.

In this case, the first 10 cans of goods sell for 15¢ a can, for a total of $\$.15 \times 10 = \$1.50$. If the purchaser buys more than 10 cans, then for the number of cans above the previously paid for 10, and up to 20, he pays 10¢ a can. The number of cans purchased in excess of 20, up to 30 cans cost 5¢ a can. Thus, if he buys 30 cans, he pays

$$10 \times \$.15 = \$1.50 \quad \text{the first 10 cans}$$
$$(20 - 10) \times \$.10 = 10 \times \$.10 = \$1.00 \text{ the cans up to 20}$$
$$(30 - 20) \times \$.05 = 10 \times \$.05 = \$.50 \text{ the cans in excess of 20}$$

$$\$1.50 + \$1.00 + \$.50 = \$3.00 .$$

This is the total amount paid for all 30 cans. An example of differential pricing occurs in an insurance company. They charge a flat rate for the first $5,000 of coverage, then charge a rate for the next $5,000 of coverage, and a lower rate for any additional coverage. The customer must compute the fee using the above procedure.

• PROBLEM 15-6

A salesman for the Filler Brush Company is compensated for his auto costs at a rate of 8¢ a mile. His fixed costs are $500 and he has a variable cost of 5¢ a mile. How many miles would he have to travel in order to break even (cover expenses), yet still earn no profit over fixed costs?

Solution: The break-even point in miles is equal to the fixed costs divided by the difference between income and Variable Costs per mile. For each mile the salesman drives, he gets $.08 - $.05 (variable costs) = $.03 towards the $500 fixed costs. Thus he needs to drive

$500 ÷ $.03 (per mile) = 16,667 miles to break even.

• PROBLEM 15-7

Joe's Motorcycle Co. wishes to find the break-even point given the following data.

Labor Costs	$ 800	per motorcycle
Material Costs	$ 800	per motorcycle
Fixed Overhead	$100,000	
Variable Overhead	$ 400	per motorcycle
Selling Price	$ 2,500	per motorcycle

Solution: The break-even point is the number of motorcycles at which the total costs are equal to the total revenue. Another way of looking at it is that the break-even point is the number of motorcycles at which the sales revenue, less the Variable Costs, is equal to the Fixed Overhead. The Variable Costs in this example are the labor costs, material costs, variable overhead.

$800	Labor Costs per motorcycle
$800	Material Costs per motorcycle
$400	Variable Overhead per motorcycle
$2,000	Variable Costs per motorcycle

Thus, the selling Price less the Variable Costs is $2,500 - $2,000 = $500 per motorcycle.

We can now find the break-even point by the following equation:

$500 × X = $100,000 (Fixed Overhead)

where X is the number of motorcycles. If we divide both sides by $500, we get

X = $100,000 ÷ $500 = 200 motorcycles.

Thus, the break-even point is 200 motorcycles.

• **PROBLEM 15-8**

Find the cost of goods sold for each retail store .

Store No.	Beginning Inventory	Purchases	Ending Inventory	Cost of Goods Sold
1	\$ 6,000	\$ 1,000	\$ 3,800	\$ ______
2	\$17,200	\$13,700	\$16,400	\$ ______
3	\$33,750	\$ 9,780	\$31,420	\$ ______
4	\$ 1,245	\$ 4,650	\$ 2,445	\$ ______
5	\$162,000	\$47,500	\$129,980	\$ ______

Solution: The cost of goods sold is found by adding the beginning inventory and the purchases, and then subtracting the ending inventory.

Store No.	Beginning Inventory	+Purchases	-Ending Inventory	=	Cost of Goods Sold
1	\$ 6,000	+ \$ 1,000	- \$ 3,800	=	\$ 3,200
2	\$17,200	+ \$13,700	- \$16,400	=	\$14,500
3	\$33,750	+ \$ 9,780	- \$31,420	=	\$12,110
4	\$ 1,245	+ \$ 4,650	- \$ 2,445	=	\$ 3,450
5	\$162,000	+ \$47,500	-\$129,980	=	\$79,520

• **PROBLEM 15-9**

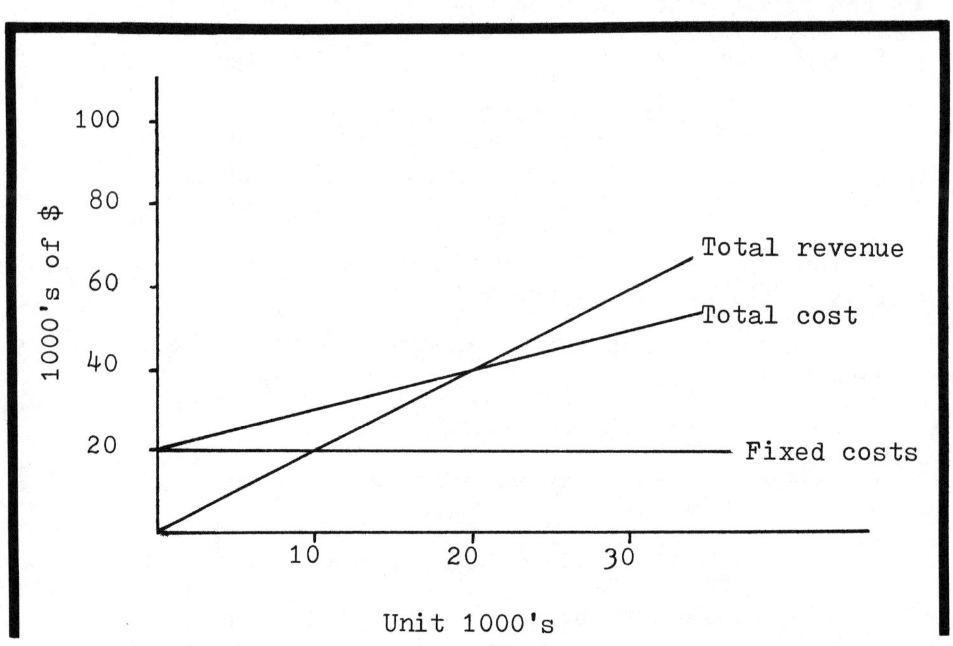

Using the above breakeven chart for the Hamilton Radio Co., how much is their total variable cost at the breakeven point?

Solution: The break-even point is the point on the chart where the total revenue equals the total cost (their lines intersect). The breakeven point for the Hamilton Radio Co. is 20,000 units or $40,000 -total costs. The variable costs are equal to the total costs less the fixed costs. The fixed costs are $20,000 (found by looking at the graph). Thus, the variable costs are equalto the total costs of $40,000 minus the fixed costs of $20,000,giving $20,000.

• PROBLEM 15-10

The Smart Calculator Corp. has total costs of $15,700 for producing 700 calculators, and total costs of $16,000 for producing 1,000 calculators. Find their variable and fixed costs.

Solution: The total costs are equal to the volume times the variable cost plus the fixed costs. To find the variable costs, we divide the difference of the two costs by the difference of the two volumes. This gives us the cost per calculator.

$16,000	for producing 1000 calculators
- $15,700	for producing 700 calculators
$ 300	for producing 300 (1000 - 700) calculators

Hence the variable cost is $300/300 calculators = $1 per calculator. We can now find the fixed costs by using the following formula:

Total Costs = Volume × Variable Costs + Fixed Costs

We can solve the equation for fixed costs by rewriting it:

Fixed Costs = Total Costs - Volume × Variable Costs

By substituting the values for 700 calculators we find:

Fixed Costs = $15,700 - 700 calculators × $1 =
$15,700 - $700 = $15,000.

We can check this by finding the total costs for producing 1000 calculators.

Total Cost = Volume × Variable Costs + Fixed Cost =

$$1{,}000 \times \$1 + \$15{,}000 = \$1{,}000 + \$15{,}000 = \$16{,}000.$$

SALES AND CORPORATE INCOME

• PROBLEM 15-11

A man sells novelty items for $1.25 each. His cost is $.75 apiece plus a fixed cost of $140,000. How many items must he sell to break even? What is his sales revenue at that point?

Solution: To find the break-even point, we divide the fixed costs by the selling price less the variable cost.

$$\text{Break-even point} = \frac{\$140{,}000}{\$1.25-\$.75} = \frac{\$140{,}000}{\$.50} = 280{,}000$$

units.

The sales revenue is found by multiplying the number of items sold by the price per item.

Thus, the sales revenue is

$\$1.25 \times 280{,}000 = \$350{,}000.$

• PROBLEM 15-12

Trinket Co.

Year	Number of Units Sold
1950	1000
1955	1100
1960	1210
1965	1331

Given the table above, Find the number of units sold in 1968.

Solution: To solve this problem, we must find out how much the number of units sold increased per year. By inspection, we can see that sales have increased 10% every five years for the past fifteen years. That suggests that in 1970 sales would have been 100% of sales in 1965 + 10% of sales in 1965 = 110% of sales in 1965 = 110% × 1331 = 1464.1 = 1464 units. Now we have to see how much was increased per year. In the five years the increase was 10% of 1331 or 133.1 units = 133 units. Thus, each year it was 133 ÷ 5 unit increase = 26.6, or approximately 27 units per year. So in 1968 the number of units sold was

$$1331 + 3 \times 26.6 = 1331 + 79.8 = 1411 \text{ (approximately)}.$$

What we did was add three times the yearly increase (for the three years from 1965 to 1968) to the number of units sold in 1965.

• PROBLEM 15-13

YEAR	NO. UNITS SOLD
1950	1000
1955	1100
1960	1210
1965	1331

If the past trend will continue, find the estimated sales in units for 1970.

Solution: The way we can estimate the sales for 1970, is to find the percentage increase in sales over each 5 year period. To find the percentage, we take the difference of the sales, and divide it by the sales in the earlier year. Thus, the percentage increase in 1955 is (Sales in 1955 - Sales in 1950) ÷ Sales in

$$1950 \times 100\% = (1100 - 1000) \div 1000 \times 100\% = 100 \div 1000 \times 100\% = .10 \times 100\% = 10\%.$$

The percentage increase in 1960 is (sales in 1960 - Sales in 1955) ÷ Sales in

$$1955 \times 100\% = (1210 - 1100) \div 1100 \times 100\% = 110 \div 1100$$
$$100\% = 10\%.$$

Similarly, the percent increase of 1965 is also 10%. Hence if we assume the trend to continue the percentage increase of 1970 will also be 10%.

To find the number of sales in units in 1970, we add to the sales of 1965 another 10% of the sales of 1965.

Sales in 1965 × 10% = 1331 × 10% = 133.1 = 133

(We round off because we are dealing with whole units.) Therefore, the number of sales in 1970 is

1331 (sales in 1965) + 133 (10% increase) = 1464.

• PROBLEM 15-14

M.K. Electronics wants to know what their approximate average sales value is. Given the following data, find the approximate average sales value.

Value of Sales	Number of sales
$0,000 - 2,000	6
$2,000 - 4,000	12
$4,000 - 6,000	2

Solution: The answer will be approximate because we do not know the exact value of each sale. What we will do is find the mid-point of each class of sales, and use that as the value of all the sales in that class. We then multiply the number of sales by their values. We find the average sales value by adding up the sales in each class and dividing by the total number of sales.

Class	Value of Sales	Class mid-point	×	Number of sales	=	Sales in the class
1	$0,000-2,000	$1,000	×	6	=	$ 6,000
2	$2,000-4,000	$3,000	×	12	=	$36,000
3	$4,000-6,000	$5,000	×	2	=	$10,000
Total				20		$52,000

Thus the average sales value is equal to

$52,000 ÷ 20 = $2,600 (approximately).

• PROBLEM 15-15

A.B.C. CORPORATION

Year Ending Dec. 31, 1965

	1966	1965
Sales	10,000,000	8,000,000
Net Income	1,000,000	800,000

Per Share Earnings	$2.00	$2.00

Find the percentage that sales have gone up in 1966 for the A.B.C. Corp.

Solution: To find the percentage increase in sales for 1966, we take the increase and divide it by the sales in 1965, then multiply by 100%.

(Sales in 1966 - Sales in 1965 [increase in sales]) ÷ Sales in 1965 × 100%

= ($10,000,000 - $8,000,000) ÷ $8,000,000 × 100% =

($2,000,000 ÷ $8,000,000)× 100% = .25 × 100% = 25%

• PROBLEM 15-16

McLevin's Sporting Goods Shop started the month of December with an inventory worth $27,300. During the month, it made additional purchases of skating goods for $3,940 and ski equipment costing $6,340. Some of the ski equipment was damaged, and $210 worth was returned by McLevin's for credit. At the end of the month the shop had made sales totaling $26,800 and had a merchandise inventory valued at $22,300.

a. Find the cost of goods sold.

b. Find the gross profit.

Solution: (a) To find the cost of goods sold, we add the purchases to the starting inventory, and subtract the returns, to get the cost of goods available for sale. We then subtract the ending inventory to get the cost of goods sold.

$27,300	starting inventory
+ $ 3,940	purchased skating goods
+ $ 6,340	purchased ski equipment
- $ 210	returns
$37,370	cost of goods available for sale

$37,370	cost of goods available for sale
- $22,300	ending inventory
$15,070	cost of goods sold

(b) The gross profit is found by subtracting the cost of goods sold from the sales.

$26,800	sales
- $15,070	cost of goods sold
$11,730	gross profit

• PROBLEM 15-17

Given the following information for the Fresh Fruit Store, calculate the store's gross profit.

Gross Sales	$30,000
Beginning Inventory	$ 7,000
Ending Inventory	$ 9,000
Sales Returns and Allowances	$ 1,500
Sales Discount	$ 300
Purchases	$20,000

Solution: To find the gross profit, we must find the net sales and cost of goods sold. We then subtract the cost of goods sold from the net sales, giving the gross profit.

The net sales are found by subtracting the discounts, and returns from the gross sales. The cost of goods sold is found by subtracting the ending inventory from the sum of the beginning inventory and purchases. This is all summarized by the following:

Gross Sales			$30,000
Less: Sales Discounts	$300		
Sales Returns & Allowances	1500		
Reductions from Sales		1,800	
Net Sales			$28,200
Purchases	$20,000		
Beginning Inventory	7,000		
Available for Sale	$27,000		
Less: Ending Inventory	9,000		
Cost of Goods Sold			$18,000
Gross Profit			$10,200

• PROBLEM 15-18

The Davidson Manufacturing Company sold $607,500 worth of steel products last year. However, customer returns and allowances amounted to $7,500. The cost of materials and labor for these products amounted to $320,000. Operating expenses included the following:

Salary Expense	$110,000
Delivery Expense	$ 12,000
Sales and Advertising Expense	$ 20,000
Rent Expense	$ 15,000
Insurance Expense	$ 4,000
Miscellaneous Expenses	$ 1,000

a. What was the gross profit?

b. What was the net income?

Solution: (a) The gross profit is found by subtracting the cost of goods sold from the net sales. The net sales is the total sales less the returns and allowances.

$607,500	Sales
- $ 7,500	Returns and Allowances
$600,000	Net Sales

$600,000	Net Sales
- $320,000	Cost of Goods Sold (Material and Labor)
$280,000	Gross profit

(b) The net income is equal to the gross profit less the total expenses:

$110,000	Salary Expense
+ $ 12,000	Delivery Expense
+ $ 20,000	Sales and Ad. Expense
+ $ 15,000	Rent Expense
+ $ 4,000	Insurance Expense
+ $ 1,000	Miscellaneous Expense
$162,000	Total Expense

$280,000	Gross profit
- $162,000	Total Expenses
$118,000	Net Income

• PROBLEM 15-19

Wiley's Gum Co. wishes to find their net income (or loss) for the last week. Their revenue from sales was $16,150. Their sales returns and allowances were $150. The cost of goods sold was $9,600. They also had the following expenses:

Rent	$ 800
Salaries	$3,200
Ultilities	$ 160
Miscellaneous	$ 575

Find their gross profit and net income for the week.

Solution: To find the gross profit, we must subtract the cost of goods sold from the net sales. The net sales is the revenue from sales less the sales returns and allowances. The net income (or loss) is found by subtracting the expenses from the gross profit.

Sales	\$16,150
Sales Returns	-\$ 150
Net Sales	\$16,000

Net Sales	\$16,000
Cost of Goods Sold	-\$ 9,600
Gross Profit	\$ 6,400

Rent	\$ 800
Salaries	+ \$ 3,200
Utilities	+ \$ 160
Miscellaneous	+\$ 575
Total Expenses	\$ 4,735

Gross profit	\$ 6,400
Total Expenses	-\$ 4,735
Net Income	\$ 1,665

• PROBLEM 15-20

The Danbury Hat Company has total fixed costs of \$10,500. They make summer hats at a cost of \$1.50 a hat. They sell the hats for \$5. How much profit will they make if they create and sell 46,500 summer hats?

Solution: To find out their profits, we must subtract their total costs from their total income. The total income is found by multiplying the selling price per hat by the amount of hats sold. Thus, the total income is \$5 (a hat) × 46,500 (sold) = \$232,500.

The total costs are the sum of the fixed costs and the variable costs. The variable costs are found by multiplying the cost per hat by the number of hats. Thus the variable costs equal

\$1.50 (per hat) × 46,500 (number of hats) = \$69,750.

The total costs are then:

\$10,500	(fixed costs)
+ \$69,750	(variable costs)
\$80,250	(total costs)

Now we can find the total profits.

$232,500 (total income)
- 80,250 (total costs)
$152,250 (total profits)

• PROBLEM 15-21

Joe's Five and Dime Store had sales and net profit on sales as shown below. Find the year with the highest absolute dollar profit.

Year	Sales	Net profit on sales
1963	$50,000	7%
1964	$55,000	10%
1965	$57,000	8%
1966	$60,000	6%
1967	$64,000	7%

Solution: To find out which year has the highest absolute dollar profit, we find the year which had the highest amount of net profit. To do this, we multiply the net profit on sales by the total sales, and get the net profit. The net profit on sales is the percentage of sales which are net profit. Note we will change the net profit on sales to a decimal for ease of computations.

Year	Sales	×	Net Profit on Sales	=	Net Profit
1963	$50,000	×	.07	=	$3,500
1964	$55,000	×	.10	=	$5,500
1965	$57,000	×	.08	=	$4,560
1966	$60,000	×	.06	=	$3,600
1967	$64,000	×	.07	=	$4,480

We can now see that 1964 was the year with the highest net profit.

• PROBLEM 15-22

Given the following statement of the Martin Paint Store, find their net profit for the week.

Cost of Goods Sold	$650
Sales	$800
Expenses (Fixed)	$ 25

Expenses (Variable)	$	5 per unit
Sales Volume		5 units

Solution: The Net Profit is found by subtracting the cost of Good Sold and Total Expenses from the Sales. The Total Expenses are found by adding the Fixed Expenses and the Variable Expenses.

The Variable Expenses is equal to the expense per unit times the number of units produced. We can now find the Net Profit

$5	per unit
× 5	units produced
$25	Variable Expenses
$25	Variable Expenses
+ $25	Fixed Expenses
$50	Total Expenses
$800	Sales
- $650	Cost of Goods Sold
- $ 50	Total Expenses
$100	Net Profit

• **PROBLEM** 15-23

The Bodie Candy Store paid $709.50 for merchandise during the month of May. Expenses were: rent, $130: advertising, $20.75; and store expenses, $12.70. On May 1 the inventory (cost of merchandise on hand) was $120.50; on May 31 it was $203.40. Receipts during May were $913.50. Was there a net profit or a net loss for the month? How much? At that rate, what would be Mrs. Bodie's total yearly income from the store?

Solution: The net profit (or loss) is found by subtracting the expenses from the gross profit (or loss). The gross profit (or loss) is found by subtracting the cost of goods sold from the receipts of the month. The cost of goods sold is found by subtracting the ending inventory from the sum of the purchases and the beginning inventory.

Beginning Inventory	$120.50
Purchases	+ $709.50
Ending Inventory	- $203.40
Cost of Goods Sold	$626.60
Receipts	$913.50
Cost of Goods Sold	-$626.60
Gross profit	$286.90

Gross profit	$286.90
Rent Expense	- $130.00
Advertising Expense	- $ 20.75
Other Expenses	- $ 12.70
Net profit	$123.45

If the net profit remains the same for the entire year, we multiply the net profit by the 12 months in the year, giving

$$\$123.45 \times 12 = \$1481.40 .$$

• PROBLEM 15-24

Investment $12,000

Year	Net Cash Benefits After Taxes
1	$4,000
2	$4,000
3	$4,000
4	$1,000

Find the percentage of the initial investment that the company will get after two years.

Solution: The percentage of the initial investment that the company gets is found by dividing the Net Cash Benefits After Taxes by the initial investment. The Net Cash Benefit After Taxes is equal to $4,000 (first year) + $4,000 (second year) = $8,000.

Thus the percentage is

$$\$8,000 \div \$12,000 = .667 = 66.7\%.$$

• PROBLEM 15-25

Net investments (December 31, 1966)	$250,000
Net investments (December 31, 1967)	$350,000
Net sales year ended December 31, 1967	$600,000
Net income year ended December 31, 1967	$ 25,000

Given the above information, what is the return on invested capital (to the nearest tenth of 1%)?

Solution: The return on invested capital is the percent of invested capital that is income. To find this, we divide the net income by the net invested capital. Since the capital changed within the year, we must divide it by the average net investment.

The average net investment is found by adding the beginning and ending net investments, and dividing their sum by 2.

$250,000	Net investment 12/31/66
+ $350,000	Net investment 12/31/67
$600,000	Total

$600,000 ÷ 2 = $300,000 (average net investment)

We can now find the return on invested capital.

$$\frac{\$25,000 \text{ (net income)}}{\$300,000 \text{ (average net investment)}} = .08333 = 8.3\%$$

ACCOUNTING SYSTEMS

• PROBLEM 15-26

A multi-product manufacturer, making only a nominal profit, decides to evaluate the profitability of each of his products. What systems change should be effected to do this?

(A) Cost accounting should be used
(B) Management control should be decentralized
(C) Time and motion studies should be instituted
(D) Cash accounting should be used
(E) PERT cost systems should be used

Solution: A process is a step in manufacturing a product, and a process cost accounting system is one in which costs are assembled in terms of the processes or manufacturing steps in producing a product. Under a process cost accounting system, a separate goods in process account is used for the costs of each department, allowing management to obtain an index of the profitability of each of the product lines.

PERT Cost systems are used in commercial, industrial, and other economic planning and control activities, and are generally applied to project type work rather than the process type work that a multiproduct manufacturer would be involved in performing. Time and motion studies are generally applied to examine the time required to complete each of the steps in the performance of a task, and while they would be useful in establishing work standards, they do not facilitate the gathering of accurate cost data. Cash accounting has to do with recording revenues at the time they are received in cash and expenses at the time cash is disbursed. It is not the type of system that would facilitate the type of cost analysis required. The correct answer is (A).

• PROBLEM 15-27

When a firm's accounting system is on an accrual basis, which of the following adjustments must be made at the end of each accounting period?

(A) accrued income receivable
(B) prepaid expenses
(C) unearned income
(D) depreciation
(E) all of the above

Solution: For income tax purposes, a business in which inventories are not a factor may report income on either a cash or accrual basis. Under the cash basis, revenues are considered earned at the time they are received in cash, and expenses are considered to be incurred at the time cash is disbursed in their payment. On the other hand, under the accrual basis of accounting, revenues are credited to the period in which they are earned, regardless of when payment is received. Also, expenses are charged to the period in which they are incurred, regardless of when cash is disbursed. As a result, a number of adjustments must be made at the end of each accounting period. Accrued income receivable (income that has been earned but not yet collected because payment is not due), prepaid expenses (expenses that have been paid for in advance of use), and unearned income (payment received for goods or services in advance of their delivery) must all be adjusted at the end of each accounting period.

In addition, depreciation is always adjusted at the end of each accounting period, regardless of the accounting system used. The correct answer is therefore (E).

• PROBLEM 15-28

A company wants to find the best estimate of their cost of capital. They have the following information available

	Current Market Value	Rate
Debt Capital	$100,000	5%
Equity Capital	$300,000	15%

Find their average cost of capital (in percent).

Solution: To find the best estimate of the cost of capital for a company using both debt and equity capital, is to find their weighted averages; we do this by finding the total cost of each type of capital, adding them up and dividing by the total capital.

Type	Value	Rate	Total
Debt	$100,000	5%	100,000 × .05 = $ 5,000
Equity	$300,000	15%	300,000 × .15 = $45,000
Total	$400,000	-	$50,000

Thus, the average cost of capital is

$50,000 ÷ $400,000 = .125 = 12.5%

• PROBLEM 15-29

Jefferson's Clothing has current assets of $150,000, current liabilities of $50,000, and capital of $200,000. What is their current ratio?

Solution: The current ratio is the ratio of current assets to current liabilities. This is also known as the working capital ratio, and is used as one measure of the ability of a business to pay promptly what it owes. To find it we divide the current assets by the current liabilities giving

$150,000 ÷ 50,000 = 3 .

• PROBLEM 15-30

What is the difference between assets and liabilities called?

Solution: In accounting, they have the equation

Assets = Liabilities + Capital (or Owner's Equity)

This means that the assets (or worth) of a company comes about from liabilities such as short term or long term loans, or stock etc., plus the amount of capital that was invested into the company. That includes putting in the profits of the year before. Thus, the difference between assets and liabilities is the capital (or sometimes in a one-owner business, called owner's equity).

• PROBLEM 15-31

Retained Earnings:

Reserved for contingencies	\$25,000
Reserved for plant expansion	\$20,000
Total reserves	\$45,000
Free retained earnings	\$50,000
Total retained earnings	\$95,000

Given the above statement, find what would happen to the free amount if the reserve for contingencies were to increase by \$10,000.

Solution: Retained earnings are the amount of profit that is not distributed, but is held by the company. These retained earnings may be reserved for a special use, such as plant expansion, or reserved for an error in judgment, such as a reserve for contingencies. The retained earnings which are not "earmarked" for any purpose are called "free retained earnings." Thus if you increase the reserve for contingencies, you would be deducting the \$10,000 from the free retained earnings, for you would be "earmarking" it for contingencies. Thus, the free retained earnings would be reduced to

$$\$50,000 - \$10,000 = \$40,000.$$

• PROBLEM 15-32

ABC CORPORATION

Income Statement for Year Ended December 31, 1967

Net Sales		\$ 5,000.00
Cost Of Goods Sold		
Merchandise Inventory		
Jan. 1, 1965	\$2,000.00	
Purchases	1,000.00	
Freight-In	50.00	

Cost of Goods Available for Sale	$ 3,050.00	
Merchandise Inventory Dec. 31, 1967	50.00	
Cost of Goods Sold		3,000.00
Gross Profit on Sales		2,000.00
Total Expenses		1,500.00
Net Income		$ 500.00

Given the above Income Statement for the ABC Corporation, find the Cost of Goods Sold if we included the following:

Purchase Returns and Allowances	$500
Discount on Purchases	$ 50

Solution: The Purchase Returns and Allowances and the Discount on Purchases are both subtracted from the Cost of Goods Sold. They are the amount of money that was given back to a customer if he did not keep his purchase, and the amount of money which the seller discounts the price of the goods for varying reasons. Thus the Cost of Good sold is:

	$3,000	(old Cost of Goods Sold)
-	$ 500	(Purchase Returns and Allowances)
-	$ 50	(Discount on Purchases)
	$2,450	(Cost of Goods Sold)

• PROBLEM 15-33

A firm produces three different products. They have determined the total cost function of each to be as follows:

Product A: Total Cost = $\$56 + 2X$

Product B: Total Cost = $\$56 + 2X + 4X^2$

Product C: Total Cost = $\$56 + 2X - 4X^2$

where X is the number of units produced. Determine from each products cost function whether its productivity is contant, increasing, or decreasing.

Solution: If the cost per unit increases with the number of units, the productivity decreases, and if the cost per unit decreases, the productivity increases.

Product A's cost function is a straight line, thus the cost per unit remains constant, and thus productivity remains constant.

Product B's cost function increases more rapidly for the more units produced, due to the X^2 term. Thus the cost per unit increases or the productivity decreases.

Finally, product C's cost function starts to decrease as the number of units increases. Hence, the productivity increases.

CHAPTER 16

BALANCE SHEETS

STRUCTURE OF THE BALANCE SHEET

• PROBLEM 16-1

What is the capital of a firm that has total assets of \$240,000, total liabilities of \$100,000, and an income of \$40,000 for one year?

Solution: Capital is synonymous with owner's equity, the amount invested in the company by its proprietors.

Liabilities: Are financial obligations which appear in the normal operation of the business. It could be short term (up to a year or less) or long term (over a year).

Assets: Are anything of value that is owned by the firm.

Income is the excess of sales over all expenses. From the elementary accounting equation,

C = Capital

L = Liabilities

A = Assets

$$C = A - L .$$

Assets	\$240,000
Less Liabilities	\$100,000
Capital	\$140,000

• PROBLEM 16-2

Where in the balance sheet does each of the following belong?

(A) Taxes payable

(B) Capital stock

(C) Retained earnings

(D) Administrative expense

(E) Prepaid expenses

Solution: (A) Taxes payable is a liability and is therefore placed in the liability section.

(B) Capital stock is entered in the Owner's Equity section.

(C) Retained earnings, also being a capital item like capital stock belongs in the owner's equity section.

(D) Administrative Expense does not belong anywhere on the balance sheet. It is an item we would place in the Income Statement.

(E) Prepaid expense is an asset and belongs on the asset side of the balance sheet.

It represents money paid for the future use of a good or service, as opposed to money paid for past use of a good or service. The latter would be recorded on the Income Statement, as an expense of the period accounting.

• PROBLEM 16-3

Prepare a balance sheet for Silvertown Office Supplies, C. H. Walters, owner, as of April 30 of the current year, based on the following information: Cash, $3,390; Notes Receivable, $2,905; Accounts Receivable, $8,215; Merchandise Inventory, $23,600; Store Supplies, $720; Store Fixtures, $2,895; Furniture and Equipment, $5,600; Notes Payable, $5,250; Accounts Payable, $4,800.

Solution: Silvertown Office Supplies

Balance Sheet as of April 30, 19X7

Assets		Liabilities	
Current Assets:			
Cash	3,390	Notes payable	5,250
Notes receivable	2,905	Accounts payable	4,800
Accounts receivable	8,215	Total	10,050
Store supplies	720		

Inventories	23,600	Owner's Equity	
Total current	38,830	C.H.Walter, capital	37,275
Fixed Assets		Total	37,275
Store fixtures	2,895	Total Liabilities + Owner's Equity	47,325
Furniture + equipment	5,600		
Total fixed	8,495		
Total assets	47,325		

Note that the owner's equity had to be found by subtracting total liabilities from the total assets to be able to satisfy the accounting equation,

Assets = Liabilities + Owners Equity.

• PROBLEM 16-4

Prepare a balance sheet for Cobbler Stationary as of Oct. 13, 19X7 from the following information.

Accounts Payable	2,720	Merchandise	10,670
Prepaid Rent	500	Taxes Payable	350
Inventory	2,500	Notes Payable	850
Salaries Payable	400	Cash	1,500
Store Equipment	7,910	Accounts Receivable	2,340

Comment on the liquidity of the business.

Solution: The first step is to decide in what section of the balance sheet each item belongs. The items considered as assets are cash, accounts receivable, prepaid rent, inventory, store equipment and merchandise. Items considered as liabilities are notes payable, taxes payable, accounts payable, and salaries payable. The owner's equity section in this case includes only one category - "Capital". The owner's equity will be calculated last.

Cobbler Stationary Balance Sheet as of 10/13/X7	
Assets	Liabilities

Cash	1,500	Notes payable	850
Accounts receivable	2,340	Accounts payable	2,720
Prepaid rent	500	Salaries payable	400
Merchandise	10,670	Taxes payable	455
Inventory	2,500	Total liabilities	4,425
Store equipment	3,940	Owner's equity	
Total Assets	21,450	Capital	17,025
Total Liabilites + Owner's Equity			21,450

The Capital figure was obtained by subtracting the total Liabilities from the Total Assets, since

Assets = Liabilities + Owners Equity

The total working capital, the current ratio, and the acid test ratio tell us about the liquidity of the business, i.e., its ability to convert a portion of its assets to cash relatively rapidly. The total working capital is total current assets minus total current liabilities. The total current assets are

$1,500 (cash) + $2,340 (accounts receivable) +

$10,670 (merchandise) + $2,500 (inventory) = $17,010.

The total Current Liabilities in this case is just the total Liabilities or $4,425. The working capital is $17,010 - $4,425 = $12,585.

The working capital sometimes is a deceptive figure because it doesn't say anything about the size of a business. The current ratio, being the total current assets divided by total current liabilities, is a more appropriate measure of liquidity, current ratio

$$= \frac{17,010}{4,425} = 3.84 .$$

For every dollar of liabilities there are $3.84 in assets. The acid-ratio test is similar to the current ratio except that only cash plus accounts receivable are divided by the total current liabilities.

$$\text{acid-ratio test} = \frac{1500 + 2340}{4425} = 0.86 .$$

This tells us that 1 dollar of liabilities is set against 86 cents of the most liquid assets. This is acceptable and does not signal any financial difficulties. Comparing the acid test ratio with the current ratio, we note that Cobbler Sta. may be wise to adopt a policy where it would not have to carry the present level of merchandise. The manager should devise ways of redistributing the asset composition so there are more of the most liquid assets. This will yield a higher acid test ratio.

• PROBLEM 16-5

From the following data, prepare a schedule of the cost of goods sold for the period ended December 31, 1976:

Balances in inventory accounts:	1/1/76	12/31/76
Raw materials	$17,420	$16,960
Work-in-process	34,750	26,220
Finished goods	74,700	91,400
Cost of resources acquired during 1976:		
Raw materials purchased		$88,310
Direct labor		144,700
Production overhead		51,910

Solution: Keep in mind that we are concerned with three inventories: (1) the raw materials inventory, (2) the work-in-process inventory, and (3) the finished goods inventory.

The solution involves finding how much was put into each inventory and how much came out of that inventory. We can solve the problem in three steps

I Find the total amount of raw material inventory handled during the year. This is beginning inventory plus any inventory acquired during the year. Subtract from this total amount the ending inventory. This difference is the amount that went into the work-in-process inventory.

II Find the total amount of work-in-process inventory handled during the year. This is the sum of the beginning work-in-process inventory and the amount obtained in I. Also, add to this labor and overhead costs. Now, subtract the ending work-in-process inventory to obtain the amount carried into the finished goods inventory.

III Find the total amount of finished goods inventory handled during the year. This equals the finished goods obtained from the work-in-process inventory plus the beginning finished goods inventory. Subtract from this amount the ending finished goods inventory to get the cost of goods sold.

Raw-material inventory

Beginning inventory	$17,420
plus acquired inventory	88,310
Total raw materials inventory 1976	105,730
less ending inventory	16,960
Amount taken to work-in-process	$88,770

Work-in-process inventory

Beginning inventory	$34,750
plus amount obtained from raw-materials . .	88,770
plus direct labor	144,700
plus production overhead	51,910
Total work-in-process inventory, 1976 . . .	320,130
less ending work-in-process inventory . . .	26,220
Amount taken to finished goods inventory . .	293,910

Finished goods inventory

Beginning inventory	74,700
plus amount obtained from work-in-process	293,910
less ending finished goods inventory . . .	91,400
Cost of goods sold	$277,210

• PROBLEM 16-6

Which of the following are sources of funds? Which are uses of funds?

I. Increase in inventories

II. Decrease in factory equipment

III. Increase in retained earnings

IV. Increase in Accounts Payable (within one year)

V. Increase in 5-year notes payable.

Solution: I. an increase in inventories results in neither a source nor use of funds. If inventory items have been purchased for cash, then one form of current asset has been given in exchange for another. If inventory items have been purchased on account, current assets,(inventory) and liabilities, (accounts payable), have been increased by the same amount causing no change in the excess of assets over liabilities, which is a company's fund.

II. Factory equipment is a long-lived asset. Decreases in long lived assets are sources of funds

III. Retained earnings is an owner's equity account. An increase in owner's equity is a source of funds.

IV. Accounts Payable is a current liability account. An increase in a current liability is a use of funds, since it causes a decrease in working capital

V. Five-year notes payable are, of course long term liabilities. An increase in long term liabilities is a source of funds.

• PROBLEM 16-7

Decide which of the following items are sources or uses of working capital.

1. Net income was $72,000.
2. Inventory sold was $14,000 on account.
3. Received $65,000 from a successful law suit.
4. Paid $1,500 of a short-term note.
5. Sold $68,000 in common stock.
6. Paid $42,000 in dividends to stockholders.
7. Purchased inventory of $19,000.
8. Invested in marketable securities.
9. Sold $50,000 of fixed assets.
10. Assumed a $150,000 mortgage for a new building.

Solution: By definition total working capital is the difference of current assets and current liabilities. Working capital includes current assets items like cash, accounts receivable, short-term notes payable, inventory. The sources of working capital are (1) sales of fixed assets, (2) increases in long-term debt, or (3) increases in owner's equity. Uses of working capital are (1) the purchase of fixed assets, (2) decreases in long-term debt, (3) decreases in owner's equity. It is important to remember that working capital does not refer exclusively to cash.

1. Net income is an increase to owner's equity. It is therefore a source of working capital.

2. This is neither a source or a use of total working capital because an exchange in current asset items is being made. For example, suppose we have the following situation,

Current assets		Current liabilities	
Cash	$10,000	Total current: . .	$21,000
Accounts receivable . .	5,000		

Inventory	18,000
Total current assets:	$33,000

Working capital = $33,000 - 21,000 = $12,000

Selling $14,000 of inventory results in the following,

Current Assets

Cash	$10,000
Accounts receivable	19,000
Inventory	4,000
Total current assets:	$33,000

The working capital remains $12,000 after the transaction since total current assets have not changed.

3. This is a source of working capital although it is more realistic to ask what the lawyer's fee was and consider the difference as increase (or decrease) in working capital, thereby determining if this is a source or use of working capital.

4. No change has taken place in the total working capital since the decrease in cash (a current asset) results in a corresponding decrease in the short-term notes account (a current liability account). There is neither a use or a source of working capital shown here.

5. This is a source of capital, an increase in cash brought about by an increase in owner's equity.

6. This is a use of capital. A decrease in cash produces a decrease in owner's equity.

7. This, like item 2., is neither a use nor a source of capital.

8. This is not a use of capital because marketable securities are current assets.

9. This is a source of working capital.

10. No change in working capital since there is no inflow or outflow of current assets. Working capital in the form of current assets could have been <u>used</u> to obtain the fixed asset. However, instead a mortgage liability was used. Also, this is no source of working capital, for even though long-term debt was increased, its increase was used to obtain a fixed asset, not working capital.

A condensed form of Morgan and Leed Inc. balance sheet as of January 1 is shown below. During the current year, sales totaled $1,200,000. The cost of goods sold was $750,000 and there was a $100,000 depreciation expense. The selling and administrative expenses were $350,000.

(a) What was the net profit or net loss made for the year?

(b) Suppose a capital recovery plan was to be made with the following percentages of the net proceeds going to different assets:

new plant and machinery - 50%

replacement of retired assets - 30%

inventory - 15%

cash - 5%

If the net revenues in excess of expenses is zero, this means that the capital recovery was financed through the depreciation charge.

What is the balance sheet at the end of the year?

Solution: (a) The materials cost is the cost of goods sold plus the $100,000 depreciation expense, this is $850,000. Total sales were $1,200,000 so that the gross profit on sales is

$1,200,000 - $850,000 = $350,000.

But there are also administrative and selling expenses to take care of, which amount to $350,000. The gross profit made, less this expense, leaves no net profit for the year.

(b) The important thing to note here is that the $100,000 depreciation charge resulted arbitrarily from the accountant's particular method of depreciation and in no way reflects a measure of the actual physical deterioration or obsolescence that actually took place during the year. For example, it could be that Morgan and Leed Inc. were operating far below capacity this year, say 45%, and still the depreciation charge was the same as when operating capacity was moderately high, say 70%.

The $100,000 amount taken from the total sales is therefore used to recover some of the capital 'lost' due to depreciation. Using the percentages given:

amount for new plant and machinery -

(0.5)($100,000) = $50,000

amount for replacement of retired assets -

(0.3)($100,000) = $30,000

amount for inventory -

(.15)($100,000) = $15,000

amount for cash -

(0.05)($100,000) = $5,000

This is how the $100,000 is distributed between the different assets. It is now a simple matter to draw up the balance sheet for the end of the year.

Balance Sheet for Morgan and Lood Inc.
Dec. 31, 19--

Assets			
Current assets:			
Cash		$305,000	
Accounts receivable		500,000	
Inventories		600,000	$1,400,000
Fixed assets:			
Land		150,000	
Plant and Machinery	$2,000,000		
less reserve for depreciation	800,000	1,200,000	1,350,000
			$2,750,000
Liabilities and Owner's Equity			
Current liabilities:			
Accounts payable		300,000	
Notes payable		200,000	$500,000
Fixed liabilities			
Mortgage bonds outstanding			500,000
Owners' Equity			
Capital Stock		1,500,000	
Surplus		250,000	1,750,000
			$2,750,000

The liabilities and owner's equity remains the same since we have not financed the capital recovery either by borrowing or taking from the surplus account.

The "reserve for depreciation" figure $870,000 was found in a roundabout way. The total assets had to remain at $2,750,000, and given that the total current assets was already $1,420,000, the value of the fixed assets must be

$2,750,000 - $1,420,000 = $1,330,000

Subtracting the value of the land from this amount gives

$1,330,000 - $150,000 = $1,180,000

as the amount left after the plant and machinery have been depreciated. Since the plant and machinery is worth 2,050,000, the amount for the depreciation reserve is 2,050,000 - $1,180,000 = $870,000.

Note that it would have been possible all along to have claimed the depreciation as being $90,000 which leaves the company with a net profit of $10,000. But again, the accountants decide how much to depreciate each year.

JOURNALS, LEDGERS, AND TRIAL BALANCES

• PROBLEM 16-9

Ambrose Stationery has the following accounts,

Inventory	Accounts receivable
Office supplies	
Salaries expense	Withdrawals
Utility expense	Accounts payable

In what accounts should the following transactions be placed? Credit and debit appropriately

(a) Gas and electricity expenses came to $75

(b) Received $420 from an account customer.

(c) Paid $2,150 to employees.

(d) Typewriter purchased for $160.

(e) Sold $1,200 on account.

(f) Bought inventory on account, $2,000.

(g) Owner withdrew $775. for personal use.

(h) Paid creditors $642 for inventory bought on account.

Solution: (a) Gas and electricity costs are expenses and thus belong under an owner's equity account. In this case the account is the "utility expense" account. Expenses are considered debits to their respective accounts. Something of value has been acquired and part of the Owner's Equity has been decreased by that amount. Since income increases owner's Equity, anything that decreases income, such as an expense, also decreases the Equity Account and therefore would be debited. Also, there will have to be a corresponding credit entry. If the expense is paid, the credit will be to cash. If not, the credit will go to Accounts Payable in order to record the debt of $75.

Owner's equity:

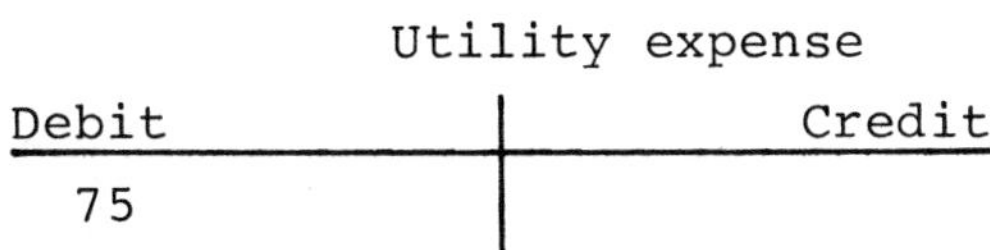

(b) This has decreased "Accounts Receivable" and is therefore a credit.

Assets: Accounts Receivable

Debit	Credit
	420

This decrease in Accounts Receivable was caused by a customer paying money that he/she owed to the company. Therefore cash has been increased, and should be debited for $420.

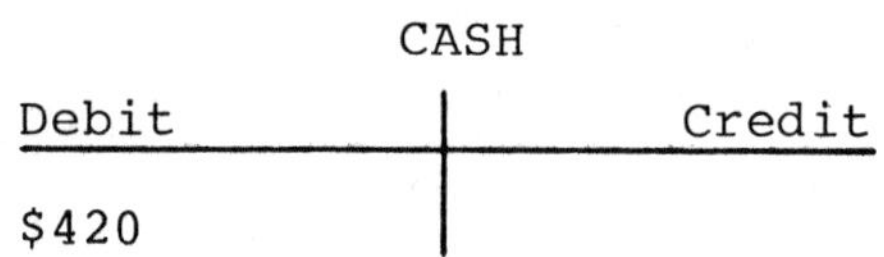

(c) Owner's equity:

Salaries expense

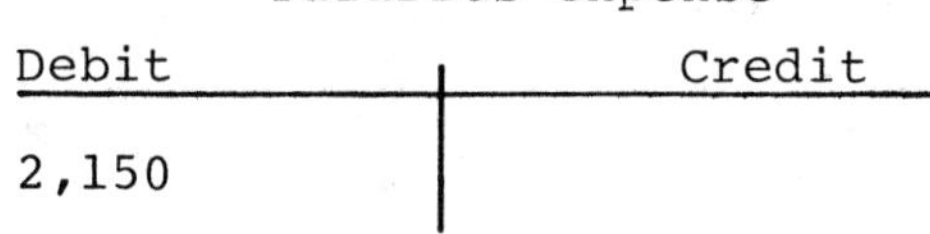

Just like any other expense, salaries expense is an owner's equity account and is debited when the service has been obtained. A credit entry must be made, either to cash, if the salaries have been paid, or to the liability Salaries Payable, if the money has not yet been paid.

(d) A typrewriter is an asset and thus belongs in the "Office supplies" account under the assets section. Since there has been an increase in an asset we debit.

Assets:

Office supplies

Debit	Credit
160	

Note that if the typewriter was paid for in cash, there would be an equivalent decrease (credit) to the asset "cash".

Cash

Debit	Credit
	160

(e) This is an increase to Accounts Receivable and a corresponding decrease to Inventory.

Assets:

Accounts receivable

Debit	Credit
1200	

Inventory

Debit	Credit
	1,200

(f) This is an increase to Inventory (debit) and an increase to Accounts Payable (credit).

Inventory

Debit	Credit
2,000	

Owner's equity:

Accounts payable

Debit	Credit
	2,000

(g) The withdrawals account belongs under Owner's Equity. An increase in this account means that the owner has drawn a certain amount. It is therefore considered a debit. Corresponding to this debit, there is a credit (decrease) on the cash account.

Owner's equity:

Withdrawals

Debit	Credit
775	

(h) This is a decrease (debit) to "Accounts payable".

Liabilities:

Accounts payable

Debit	Credit
642	

It is also a credit to Cash.

• PROBLEM 16-10

Given the following transactions make the appropriate credit-debit journal entries.

(a) Salaries paid, $4,298. cash
(b) Paid account creditors $2,500 in cash.
(c) Paid rent, $900 in cash
(d) Utilities bill paid, cash $150.
(e) Owner withdrew $100 for her personal use.
(f) Bought equipment for $17,500, paid $6,000 cash, leaving the rest as an Account Payable
(g) Bought $4,300 of inventory on account.

The accounts to refer to are,

cash	inventory	furniture + equipment
accounts receivable	prepaid insurance	accum. depreciation
office supplies	prepaid rent	withdrawals

Accounts payable	salaries expense
notes payable	office supplies expense
rent expense	depreciation expense
insurance expense	utilities expense.

Solution:

	Debit	Credit
(a) Salaries expense	$4,298	
Cash		4,298
To record payment of salaries		
(b) Accounts Payable	2,500	
Cash		2,500
To record payment of creditors		

	Debit	Credit
(c) Rent expense	900	
Cash		900
Payment of rent.		
(d) Utility expense	150	
Cash		150
To record payment of utilities.		
(e) Withdrawals	100	
Cash		100
To record withdrawal of cash by owner for personal use.		
(f) Furniture and Equipment	17,500	
Cash		6,000
Accounts payable		11,500
To record purchase of equipment and partial cash payment		
(g) Inventory	4,300	
Accounts payable		4,300
To record purchase of inventory on account.		

Remember, in each entry, the amount credited must equal the amount debited.

• PROBLEM 16-11

Morley Hardware balance sheet as of July 31 is shown below.

Morley Hardware
Balance Sheet as of July 31, 1974

Assets		Liabilities	
Current assets:		Current liabilities:	
Cash	5,500	Acc. payable	7,910
Accs.receivable ...	10,000	Long term liabilities:	
Inventory	14,750	Loan	4,500
Fixed assets:		Total liabilities ..	12,410
Store fixtures	1,640	Owner's equity	
Total assets	31,890	Mr.Morley, capital	19,480
			31,890

The following transactions were made during the month of August.

1. Purchased $7,300 of inventory on credit.
2. Sold $6,950 on account

3. Received $10,000 cash from account customers.

4. Paid $50 cash, advertising.

5. Paid $475 cash, rent.

6. Paid $1,700 cash, salaries

7. Purchased neon sign $980 cash.

8. Paid for installation of sink $75; $90 utilities.

9. Paid $7,910 to creditors.

10. Purchased a dog for Mr. Morley, cash $150.

Refer to the following accounts.

sales rent expense maintenance expense,
uitility expense withdrawals.

(a) Summarize transactions as a series of journal entries.

(b) Post the journal items to the Ledger t accounts indicating the changes in each account if any.

(c) Prepare a preliminary trial balance for August 31.

Solution: We must always have debits = credits

1. Increase (debit) to inventory account; increase (credit) to accounts payable.

Debit: Inventory 7,300
Credit: Accounts payable 7,300

2. Increase (debit) to accounts receivable; decrease (credit) for inventory.

Debit: Accounts receivable 6,950
Credit: Sales 6,950

3. Debit: Cash 10,000
Credit: Accounts receivable 10,000

4. Debit: Advertising expense 50
Credit: Cash 50

5. Debit: Rent expense 475
Credit: Cash 475

6. Debit: Salaries expense ...... $ 1,700
Credit: Cash $1,700

7. Debit: Store fixtures 980
Credit: Cash 980

8. Debit: Maintenance expense 75
Utility expense 90
Credit: Cash 165

9. Debit: Accounts payable 7,910
Credit: Cash 7,910

10. Debit: Withdrawals............. 150
Credit: Cash 150

Expenses are increased, (credited) the same way that assets are because a service has been obtained.

(b) Balance Sheet Accounts

Cash

Debit		Credit	
Bal. 7/31	5,500	50	(4)
(3)	10,000	475	(5)
Total	15,500	1,700	(6)
		980	(7)
		165	(8)
		7,910	(9)
		150	(10)
		total 11,430	
Bal. 8/31	4,070		

Accounts receivable

Debit		Credit	
Bal. 7/31	10,000	10,000	(3)
(2)	6,950		
Total	16,950		
Bal.8/31	6,950		

Inventory

Debit		Credit
Bal. 7/31	14,750	
(1)	7,300	
Total	22,050	

Store fixtures

Debit		Credit
Bal.7/31	1,640	
(7)	980	
Total	2,620	

Accounts payable

Debit		Credit	
(9)	7,910	7,910	Bal.7/31
		7,300	(1)
		15,210	Total
		7,300	Bal.8/31

Loan

Debit	Credit	
	4,500	Bal.7/31
	4,500	Bal.8/31

Morley - Capital

Debit	Credit	
	19,480	Bal.6/31

Morley - Withdrawal

Debit		Credit
(10)	150	

Income Statement Accounts

Sales

Debit	Credit	
	6,950	(2)

Rent expense

Debit		Credit
(5)	475	

Utilities expense

Debit		Credit
(8)	90	

Advertising expense

Debit		Credit
(4)	50	

Maintenance Expense

Debit		Credit
(8)	75	

Salaries expense

Debit		Credit
(5)	1,700	

(c) Morley Hardware
Trial Balance as of 8/31/74

Account	Debit	Credit
Cash	4,070	
Accounts receivable	6,950	
Inventory	22,050	

Store fixtures	2,620	
Accounts payable		7,300
Loan		4,500
Morley-capital account ...		19,480
Morley-withdrawalaccount .	150	
Sales		6,950
Rent expense	475	
Utilities expense	90	
Advertising expense	50	
Maintenance expense	75	
Salary expense	1,700	
	38,230	38,230

This is only a preliminary balance. We have yet to calculate cost of goods sold, depreciation expenses and other miscellaneous expenses.

• PROBLEM 16-12

The unadjusted trial balance for Jones Hardware Store at the end of the current fiscal year is:

Jones Company
Trial Balance
Dec 31, 19XX

	Debit	Credit
Cash	$1,080	
Accounts receivable	4,300	
Inventory	22,100	
Furniture and equipment	34,000	
Accum.deprec.-Furniture; equip.		$15,600
Office supplies	850	
Accounts payable		6,020
Jones-capital account		15,970
Jones-withdrawalaccount	2,000	
Sales		37,000
Rent expense	1,000	
Utilities expense	480	
Insurance expense	600	
Salaries expense	7,800	
Advertising expense	200	

Interest expense	180	
	$74,590	$74,590

The following accounts are also found in the ledger:

office supplies, prepaid insurance, depreciation expense, accrued salaries payable, cost of goods sold.

The following adjustments must be considered.

(a) Office supplies on hand total $320.

(b) An inventory was taken and $600 is left at the end of the fiscal year.

(c) Two month's rent, $800 has been prepaid in cash

(d) $60 of electricity and gas was consumed; the bill is due to be paid by the middle of next month.

(e) $300 is owed to employees for work done the present period. It will also be paid in the middle of next month.

(f) At the beginning of the fiscal year, a $600 premium was paid for a 3-year insurance policy. Two years of the policy are left at the end of the fiscal year.

(g) Furniture and equipment depreciation was $800 for the year.

Using a ten-column worksheet format,

(i) Record the trial balance and the adjustments.

(ii) Record the adjusted trial balance and the income statement.

(iii) On the same worksheet prepare the balance sheet

(iv) Prepare a formal income statement, and the formal balance sheet.

<u>Solution:</u> (i) Using the debit-credit format of the worksheet, simplifies our task. The thing to remember is that for every debit, there must be a corresponding credit of the same amount. It remains for us to enter the adjustments in the proper accounts. The trial balance and adjustments are as follows:

	TRIAL BALANCE		ADJUSTMENTS	
Accounts	Debit	Credit	Debit	Credit
Cash	1,080			(c) 800
Accounts receivable	4,300			

Inventory	22,100			(b) 21,500
Furniture and equipment	34,000			
Accum.deprec.-Furniture;equipment		15,600		(g) 800
Prepaid insurance	600			(f) 200
Prepaid rent			(c) 800	
Accounts payable		6,020		(d) 60
Jones-capital account		15,970		
Jones-withdrawal account	2,000			
Sales		37,000		
Rent expense	1,000			
Utilities expense	480		(d) 60	
Insurance expense			(f) 200	
Salaries expense	7,800		(e) 300	
Advertising expense	200			
Supplies expense			(a) 530	
Interest expense	180			
Depreciation expense			(g) 800	
Office supplies	850			(a) 530
Accrued salaries Payable				(e) 300
Cost of goods Sold			(b) 21,500	
	74,590	74,590	24,190	24,190

Note that on the worksheet we add any additional accounts needed in making adjustments to the list of those already on the list.

(a) Office Supplies are an asset. At first we are told that we have $850 left in the account. But then we find that at the end of the year we only have $320 left in the account, the account has been decreased by $530. Therefore we credit the asset $530 to show this decrease.

The purpose of expense accounts is to match any expenditure or decrease to the period in which it occurred, in order to determine, as precisely as possible, now much was spent in a period to generate that period's income. A decrease of $530 in Supplies for a period means that $530 was "spent" on supplies to help earn that period's income. Therefore, we have a $530 Supplies Expense which is debited, as it represents a decrease to the Capital account . (The Capital account can be increased or credited by a net profit. Therefore anything, such as an expense which decreases the net profit, also decreases the Capital Account).

(b) If $600 of inventory are left, then $22,100 - $600 = $21,500 was deducted (credited) from the 'Inventory' account. This also means that the cost of goods sold was $21,500 and this is debited to the Cost of Goods Sold account.

(c) Prepaid rent is an asset and is debited to the Prepaid Rent account. We can credit Cash for $800 to note the decrease, in cash resulting from payment.

(d) Utilities expense is $60 and is debited to the Utilities Expense account. Since this is to be paid next month, $60 is credited to Accounts Payable.

(e) $300 is debited to the Salaries Expense account since services have been realized, and therefore should be matched to the period just ending. The same amount is credited to the liabilities account, Accrued Salaries Payable, since the salaries have not been paid yet.

(f) The $600 premium giving 3 year's protection is the same as 3 premiums, each worth $200 and each giving 1 year of protection. After 1 year, there is $400 left in the Prepaid Insurance since there was a decrease, of $200. Since Prepaid Insurance is an asset, it is decreased by a credit. As has been already mentioned, expenses attributable to a particular period are debited to the expense accounts. Since $200 was "spent" on insurance during the period, there should be a debit to Insurance Expense. Next year when another $200 of the prepaid insurance is used up,an identical adjustment will have to be made on the balance sheet.

(g) Depreciation of an asset represents the asset's decline in value through time and is demonstrated by deducting a certain part of its original dollar cost each accounting period. In this example, the office furniture and equipment are considered to have declined in value by $800 in this period. The account Accumulated Depreciation is a contra-asset account; it shows how much value has been deducted from an asset's value so far. Since it represents a decrease in an asset, it is credited when additional depreciation is assigned to an asset.

Depreciation also represents which portion of the original cost of an asset was used during the period to add to a firm's productivity. It is therefore an expense and should be debited to the Depreciation Expense account.

(ii) Adjusted trial balance - To get the adjusted trial balance, in each account either subtract or add the amount found in the adjustments debit-credit columns. For example, Accounts Receivable remains the same since no adjustments were made. The entry for Accounts

Receivable would be unchanged in adjusted trial balance, namely, a debit of $4,300. For Inventory this is not the case. The adjustments require a credit (decrease) to the Inventory account. Subtract $21,500 from $22,100 to get a debit in the adjusted trial balance of $600.

For Utilities Expense, the corresponding adjustment is a debit and thus we would add $480 and $60 to obtain a utilities expense of $540 (debit) in the adjusted trial balance. Other entries are found in the same way, remembering that entries in debits have the opposite sign of credit entries. For example, if, before adjustment, there is some money in the Cash account, it is of course recorded as a debit and considered a positive amount. So, if there is an adjusting entry to this account in the credit column it represents an amount to be subtracted and is therefore a negative number.

The income statement column is prepared by just copying the sales,expense and cost of goods sold figures of the adjusted trial balance to a corresponding, worksheet format to find net income earned.

	ADJUSTED TRIAL		INCOME STATEMENT	
Accounts	Debit	Credit	Debit	Credit
Cash	280			
Accounts receivable	4,300			
Inventory	600			
Furniture and equipment	34,000			
Accum. deprec.-Furniture,equip.		16,400		
Accounts payable		6,080		
Jones-capital account	2,000			
Sales		37,000		37,000
Rent expense	1,000		1,000	
Utilities expense	540		540	
Insurance expense	200		200	
Salaries expense	8,100		8,100	
Advertising expense	200		200	
Supplies expense	530		530	
Interest expense	180		180	
Depreciation expense	800		800	

Office supplies	320			
Prepaid insurance	400			
Prepaid rent	800			
Accrued salaries payable		300		
Cost of Goods sold	21,500		21,500	
	75,750	75,750	33,050	37,000
Net income			3,950	
			37,000	37,000

	BALANCE SHEET.	
Accounts	Debit	Credit
Cash	280	
Accounts receivable	4,300	
Inventory	600	
Furniture and equipment	34,000	
Accum.deprec.-Furniture, equip.		16,400
Accounts payable		6,080
Jones-capital account		15,970
Jones-drawing account	2,000	
Sales		
Rent expense		
Utilities expense		
Insurance expense		
Salaries expense		
Advertising expense		
Supplies expense		
Interest expense		
Office supplies	320	
Prepaid insurance	400	
Prepaid rent	800	
Accrued salaries payable		300
Cost of Goods sold		

Net Income		3,950
	42,700	42,700

(iii) The balance sheet, like the income statement, is just a matter of taking the proper entries of the adjusted trial balance and putting these in credit-debit format in the worksheet. We take only "balance sheet accounts" in this case, the assets, liabilities and the owner's capital accounts. Under assets we have cash, accounts receivable, inventory, furniture and equipment, accumulated depreciation, office supplies, prepaid insurance and prepaid rent. The liability accounts are, Accounts Payable, and Salaries Payable. As for the owner's equity account on the balance sheet, the drawing account and the net income determine the change in the equity account. So we add the net income to and subract the amount of withdrawal from the "Jones-Capital" account. This is what will appear as the owner's capital on the balance sheet. The drawing and net income accounts do not appear separately on the balance sheet; we merely calculate their effect on the capital account and then just show what is left in the capital account.

(iv) Formal income statement and balance sheet are prepared directly from the worksheet figures.

Jones Hardware Store INCOME STATEMENT		
For Last Month of Current Fiscal Year.		
Sales		$37,000
less cost of goods sold		21,500
gross profit		15,500
Administrative expenses		
rent expense	$1,000	
utilities expense	540	
salaries expense	8,100	
insurance expense	200	
advertising expense	200	
supplies expense	530	
interest expense	180	
depreciation expense	800	11,550
Net income		3,950

Jones Hardware Store BALANCE SHEET AS OF THE END OF CURRENT FISCAL YEAR			
Assets		**Liabilities**	
Current:			
Cash	280	Acc.payable	6,080
Accounts receivable	4,300	Salaries payable	300
Inventory	600	Total	6.380
Office supplies	320	**Owner's equity**	
Prepaid rent	800	Jones capital -	17,920
Prepaid insurance	400	Liab.+ Equity	24,300
Total current assets	7,500		
Fixed:			
Furniture,equipment	34,000		
less accum.deprec.	16,400		
	17,600		
Total Assets	24,300		

• PROBLEM 16-13

The balance sheet for the Beckett Company as of January 1, 19X3 is shown below.

Beckett Company Balance Sheet as of January 1, 19X3			
Assets		**Liabilities**	
Current:		Current:	
Cash	$3,000	Acc.payable	$6,000
Accounts receivable ..	5,000	Current notes payable	1,000
Inventory	17,000	Long term:	
Total current assets .	25,000	Notes payable ...	4,000
Long lived:		Total liabilities	11,000
		Owner's equity	
Furniture and equipment	8,000	Ms.Beckett-capital	22,000
Total assets	33,000	Total claims	33,000

The following transactions took place in 19X3.

1. Total sales were $210,000; $10,000 was paid in cash, the remaining $200,000 were on account.

2. Inventory purchased on credit: $96,000

3. Accounts receivable collected was $202,000

4. Paid $99,000 on account.

5. The following expenses were incurred

Salaries:	$102,600	
Rent:	2,400	
Utilities:	800	(11 months)
Supplies:	200	

6. A new cash register was purchased in January for $1,500 with 1/3 down payment and the balance due January 31, 19X4.

7. Received $500 cash settlement from a law suit.

8. Ms. Beckett purchased a car for $5,000 with company money and registered car in her name.

9. Total current notes payable was paid.

Given this information,

(a) Journalize the transactions for 19X3.

(b) Post the transactions to ledger accounts.

(c) Prepare the preliminary trial balance.

For December of 19X3, the following adjustments have to be made.

10. Physical inventory at the end of December was $6,000.

11. $60 worth of supplies were acquired in December, to be paid for in January.

12. Depreciation charges for furniture and equipment is $950;

13. The rent for January and February of 19X4 was prepaid, $680 cash.

14. The utility expense for December was $75, will be paid next month.

(d) Journalize the adjusting entries.

(e) Post adjustments to ledger accounts.

(f) Prepare the adjusted trial balance.

(g) Prepare formal financial statements: income statements, balance sheet.

Solution: (a) Remember that for every credit, there must be a corresponding debit of the same amount. We must create the necessary accounts as we go along.

		Debit	Credit
1.	Cash	$10,000	
	Accounts receivable	200,000	
	Sales		$210,000
2.	Inventory	96,000	
	Accounts payable		96,000
3.	Cash	202,000	
	Accounts receivable		202,000
4.	Accounts payable	99,000	
	Cash		99,000
5.	Salaries expense	102,000	
	Cash		102,000
	Rent expense	2,400	
	Cash		2,400
	Utilities expense	800	
	Cash		800
	Supplies expense	200	
	Cash		200
6.	Furniture, equipment	1,500	
	Accounts payable		1,000
	Cash		500
7.	Cash	500	
	Beckett-capital		500
8.	Beckett withdrawals	$5,000	
	Cash		5,000
9.	Current notes payable	1,000	
	Cash		1,000

Comments:

1. The sales account is a temporary Owner's Equity account. That is, the sales account will be closed to the Owner's Equity account at the end of each period. However, during each period the Sales account is used to record increases to Owner's Equity through sales made in the period. Since increases to Owner's Equity are recorded by crediting the account, increases

through sales are recorded by crediting the sales account.

2. There was an increase (credit) in Accounts Payable (a liability account) and a corresponding increase (debit) on the asset side in Inventories.

3. When Accounts Receivable are collected, the account for the receivables is decreased and the cash account increases, there is a debit to cash and a credit to Accounts receivable. We have changed the assets from one form to another.

4. Accounts payable, a liability account, is debited (decreased). There is a corresponding decrease or credit in the Cash account.

5. Expense accounts are also temporary Owner's Equity accounts which record a decrease to Owner's Equity account. When ever an expense is incurred, these accounts are debited.

6. A new asset, a cash register, was acquired. Debit equipment \$1,500, credit 1/3 down-payment; \$1,500 x .333 = \$500 cash and credit the remainder, \$1,000, to accounts payable.

7. The proceeds from the lawsuit is addition to the cash of the firm and therefore represents an increase in Owner's Equity.

8. The withdrawal account is also a temporary Owner's Equity account which records decreases in Owner's Equity when an owner takes money from the business for his/her own use. The withdrawal account is debited when a withdrawal of cash is made from the firm by an owner. When Ms. Bennett used company money to buy a car to be registered in her name, she was in effect, using the money for herself and therefore withdrawing it from the company.

(b) Posting to ledger accounts:

Cash

Debit		Credit	
Bal 1/X3	\$3,000	\$99,000	(4)
(1)	10,000	102,000	(5)
(3)	202,000	2,400	(5)
(7)	500	800	(5)
	215,500		
		200	(5)
		500	(6)

Accounts receivable

Debit		Credit	
Bal 1/X3	\$5,000	\$202,000	(3)
(1)	200,000		
	205,000		
Bal	\$3,000		

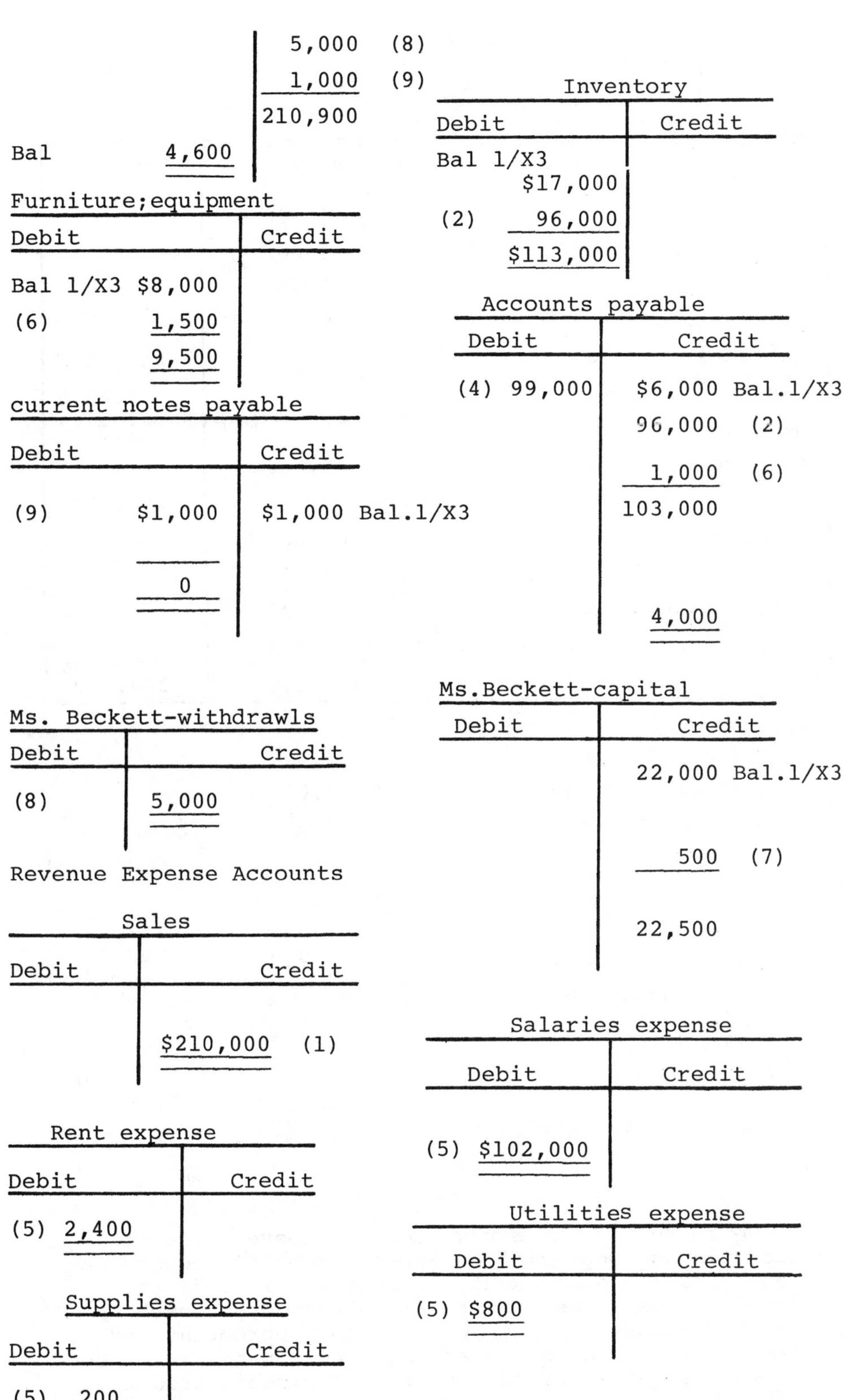

Debit		Credit	
		5,000	(8)
		1,000	(9)
		210,900	
Bal	4,600		

Inventory

Debit		Credit
Bal 1/X3	$17,000	
(2)	96,000	
	$113,000	

Furniture;equipment

Debit		Credit
Bal 1/X3	$8,000	
(6)	1,500	
	9,500	

Accounts payable

Debit		Credit	
(4)	99,000	$6,000	Bal.1/X3
		96,000	(2)
		1,000	(6)
		103,000	
		4,000	

current notes payable

Debit		Credit	
(9)	$1,000	$1,000	Bal.1/X3
	0		

Ms.Beckett-capital

Debit	Credit	
	22,000	Bal.1/X3
	500	(7)
	22,500	

Ms. Beckett-withdrawls

Debit		Credit
(8)	5,000	

Revenue Expense Accounts

Sales

Debit	Credit	
	$210,000	(1)

Salaries expense

Debit		Credit
(5)	$102,000	

Rent expense

Debit		Credit
(5)	2,400	

Utilities expense

Debit		Credit
(5)	$800	

Supplies expense

Debit		Credit
(5)	200	

(c)

The Beckett Company
Preliminary Trial Balance
December 31, 19X3

Account	Debit	Credit
Cash	$ 4,600	
Accounts receivable	3,000	
Inventory	113,000	
Furniture and equipment	9,500	
Accounts payable		$ 4,000
Long term notes payable		4,000
Beckett-capital		22,500
Beckett-withdrawls	5,000	
Sales		210,000
Salaries expense	102,000	
Rent expense	2,400	
Utilities expense	800	
Supplies expense	200	
	240,500	240,500

(d)

		Debit	Credit
10.	Cost of goods sold	$107,000	
	Inventory		$107,000
11.	Supplies	60	
	Accounts Payable		60
12.	Depreciation Expense	950	
	Accumulated Depreciation		950
13.	Prepaid rent	680	
	Cash		680
14.	Utilities Expense	75	
	Accounts Payable		75

We introduce three new accounts above, cost of goods sold and Depreciation Expense (owner's equity accounts) and Prepaid Rent (an asset). To make the ledger entries we use the totals obtained for each account previously. Once we make the appropriate adjustments in the accounts affected we can get the income statement and the balance sheet in the debit-credit worksheet format.

(e)

Inventory

Debit	Credit
$113,000	$107,000
(10)	
$ 6,000	

Cost of Goods Sold

Debit	Credit
$107,000	

Supplies

Debit	Credit
(11) $60	

Accounts payable

Debit	Credit
	$4,000
	60 (11)
	75 (14)
	4,135

Depreciation expense

Debit	Credit
(12) $950	

Accumulated depreciation

Debit	Credit
	$950 (12)

Cash

Debit	Credit
$4,600	$680 (13)
$3,920	

Prepaid rent

Debit	Credit
(13) $680	

Utility expense

Debit	Credit
$800	
(14) 75	
$875	

(f)

The Beckett Company
Adjusted Trial Balance
December 31, 19X3

Accounts	Debit	Credit
Cash	$ 3,920	

Accounts receivable	3,000	
Inventory	6,000	
Prepaid rent	680	
Supplies	60	
Furniture and equipment	9,500	
Accounts payable		4,135
Long term notes payable		4,000
Beckett-Owner's Equity		22,500
Beckett-withdrawals	5,000	
Sales		210,000
Salaries expense	102,000	
Rent expense	2,400	
Utilities expense	875	
Supplies expense	200	
Depreciation expense	950	
Accumulated depreciation		950
Cost of goods sold	107,000	
	241,585	241,585

The Beckett Company

Income Statement, for the Year January 1, 19X3 to December 31, 19X3.

Sales		210,000
less cost of goods sold		107,000
Gross profit		103,000
Salaries expense	102,000	
Rent expense	2,400	
Utilities expense	875	
Supplies expense	200	
Depreciation expense	950	106,425
Net loss		(3,425)

The Beckett Company

Balance sheet as of December 31, 19X3

Assets		Liabilities	
Current:		Current:	
Cash	$3,920	Acc.payable	4,135

Accounts receivable	3,000	Long-term: notes payable	4,000
Inventory	6,000	Owner's equity	
Prepaid rent	680	Beckett-capital	14,075
Supplies	60	Total claims	22,210
Long-lived assets:			
Furniture & Equipment	9,500		
Less accum. deprec.	950		
	8,550		
Total Assets	22,210		

Ms. Beckett's capital is obtained as follows,

$22,500 - $5,000 (withdrawls) - $3,425 (net loss)

= $14,075.

It was not a good year for the Beckett Company. Note that expense and revenue accounts do not appear on the balance sheet. Instead, the net result of all revenues and expenses is calculated on the income statement. This net result or net income represents a change in owner's equity. Here the net result is a loss, which therefore is subtracted from owner's equity which, in turn, is recorded on the balance sheet.

RATES AND RATIOS

• PROBLEM 16-14

The balance-sheet figures of Mason's Garage (George Mason, owner) for 19X8 and 19X9 are shown below.

19X8	19X9
Cash 1,500	Cash $2,800
Government Bonds $1,000	Government Bonds $2,000
Accounts Receivable $800	Accounts Receivable $1,640
Equipment $5,780	Equipment $7,740
Tools $1,200	Tools $1,670
Notes Payable $950	Notes Payable $600
Accounts Payable $120	Accounts Payable $120
George Mason, Capital $9,210	George Mason, Capital $15,130

Writing lengthwise on your paper, prepare a comparative balance sheet showing (a) the amount of increase or decrease for each item, (b) the percent of increase or decrease for each item, and (c) the percent the following items represent of total assets for 19X9: Total Current Assets, Total Fixed Assets.

Solution: Starting with the assets, have two columns, one for 19X8 and one for 19X9.

Assets	19X8	19X9	Change	% Change
Current Assets				
Cash	1500	2800	+ 1300	86.66 %
Government bonds	1000	2000	+ 1000	100 %
Accounts Receivable	800	1640	+ 840	105 %
Total current assets	3300	6440	+ 3140	95.15 %
Fixed Assets				
Tools	1,200	1670	+ 470	6.73 %
Equipment	5,780	7740	+ 1960	33.91 %
Total fixed assets	6,980	9,410	+ 2430	34.81 %
Total assets (current + fixed)	10,280	15,850	+5,570	54.18 %

The "Change" column was obtained by subtracting the 19X8 column from the 19X9 column. For example, the change in cash from 19X8 to 19X9 is

$$2800 - 1500 = 1300.$$

The " % Change " column is obtained by dividing the "Change" column by the 19X8 column, and multiplying the result by 100%. The percentage increase in cash from 19X8 to 19X9 was

$$\frac{1300}{1500} \times 100\% = 86.66\%$$

to two decimal places. Other entries in the % Change column are found the same way.

Liabilities	19X8	19X9	Change	% Change
Current liabilities				
Notes Payable	950	600	- 350	- 36.84%
Accounts Payable	120	120	0	0
Total Current Liabilities	1070	720	- 350	32.71 %

Total liabilities = Current liabilities same as last line.

Owner's Equity

George Mason, Capital	9210	15,130	+ 5920	64.27 %
Liabilities + Owner's Equity	10,280	15,850	+ 5570	54.18 %

The total current assets compose

of $\frac{3300}{10,280} \times 100\% = 32.1\%$ of all assets in 19X8 and

$\frac{6440}{15,850} \times 100\% = 40.6\%$ of all assets in 19X9.

The percentage of total fixed assets to all assets in 19X8 is

$$\frac{6980}{10,280} \times 100\% = 67.8\%.$$

For 19X9 the total fixed assets to total assets percentage is

$$\frac{9410}{15,850} \times 100\% = 59.8\%.$$

• PROBLEM 16-15

The Gowell Company's Balance Sheet as of December 31 19X7 and its income statement for the period 19X6 to 19X7 are shown. From this data calculate the following items is explain their significance:

1. Ratio of operating income to capital employed.

2. Ratio of net income to net worth.

3. Earnings per share of stock.

4. The turnover of Inventories.

5. The turnover of Accounts Receivable.

6. The average number of days Accounts Receivable are outstanding, if 30 days are allowed for payment.

The Balance Sheet of the Gowell Company on December 31 showed:

Current Assets:

Cash..............................	\$ 21,500
Accounts receivable..............	71,750
Inventories......................	98,225
Total Current...................	\$191,475

Other assets	20,225
Property and equipment	200,000
Total assets	$411,700
Current Liabilities:	
Accounts payable	$ 42,995
Long-term debt	150,000
Total liabilities	$192,995
Net worth:	
Common Stock*	150,000
Retained Earnings	68,705
Total liabilities & worth	$411,700

*25,000 shares

The Gowell Company presents the following Income Statement:

Sales		$645,765
Cost of Goods Sold:		
Beginning Inventory	$ 95,380	
Purchases	398,550	
Total Inventory	$493,930	
Ending Inventory	98,225	
Total		395,705
Gross Profit		$250,060
Selling Expenses:		
Salaries & Commisions	$ 64,325	
Advertising	58,400	
Delivery Expenses	20,340	
Total	143,065	
General and Administrative	45,890	
Total		188,955
Net Income from Operations		$ 61,105
Interest on Long-Term Debt		7,500
Earnings Before Income Tax		$ 53,605
Income Taxes		25,730
Net Income for the Year		$ 27,875

Solution: 1. The operating income is the net income derived from sales, purchasing and administrative activities. Expenses such as interest and taxes which do not directly contribute to a firm's sales are not accounted for in operating income. The income statement gives this income for the period 19X6 - 19X7 as $61,105. Take the total capital employed as being $411,700, i.e., the total assets. Usually we take the average of the total assets for the beginning of the production period 19X6 and at the end of the period 19X7. The reason is that $411,700 is not the amount of capital employed throughout 19X6 - 19X7. It is the capital at the end of the period. Nevertheless using $411,700 gives an idea how much capital was employed in 19X6 - 19X7.

$$\text{ratio} = \frac{61,105}{411,700} = 0.148 .$$

This means that 1 dollar of capital gave 14.8 cents of net income before taxes and interest were deducted.

2. The net income is $27,875. The net worth (or owner's equity) is

$$\$150,000 + \$68,705 = \$218,705.$$

$$\text{ratio} = \frac{27,875}{218,705} = 0.127 .$$

This ratio gives stockholders a measure of the return on their investment. For every dollar invested by the stockholders, 12.7 cents was derived as net income.

3. As of December 31, 19X7 there were 25,000 shares of stock. The net income for the year, i.e., total earnings after taxes were 27,875. The earnings per share are

$$\frac{27,875}{25,000} = 1.115$$

or 1 dollar and 11½ cents per share. This may or may not be the amount declared as dividends. The net income can be divided in two parts. retained earnings and dividends to be paid to shareholders.

4. The inventory turnover is the rate at which the inventory is sold and needs to be replaced. The higher the rate, the faster the inventory is being sold. The average inventory held during the year is

$$(95,380 \text{ (beginning)} + 98,225 \text{ (ending)}) \div 2 = 96,802.$$

The total sales were 645,765.

The inventory turnover is

$$\frac{645,765}{98,802} = 6.67 \text{ times per year.}$$

The inventory turnover becomes useful when we compare it to that of other companies in the same industry. We may be able to relate it to the efficiency of a firm.

5. The turnover of accounts receivable is also a rate. It represents the number of times a year that collections are made on receivables. The balance sheet has the figure for the accounts receivable as of the end of 19X7. It would be preferable to also have the figure from the beginning of 19X7. We would then take the average of the two figures and use that to find the turnover. Since this is unavailable, we must make do with $71,750 as the average amount of accounts receivable held. Net sales were $645,765. This figure could also be seen as the total amount of accounts receivable acquired during the entire year; when a sale is made an account receivable is acquired.

The turnover rate is:

$$\frac{\text{Total accounts receivable acquired}}{\text{Average amount of accounts receivable held}} = \frac{\$645,765}{\$71,750} = 9$$

Receivable debts were collected 9 times during the year.

6. If receivables were collected 9 times during the year, the average length of each collection period is

$$\frac{365 \text{ days}}{9} = 40.5 \text{ days.}$$

If the firm gave a payment period of 30 days, collection was approximately 10 days outstanding.

• PROBLEM 16-16

A company's balance sheet for two consecutive years is shown in table 1. The income statement for these years is given in table 2. Using data from these tables find

1. The ratio of operating expenses to net sales for both years.

2. The ratio of gross profit to net sales.

3. Ratio of operating income to net sales, where the operating income is the profit before taxes, dividends, and interest.

4. Ratio of net income to net sales.

5. Ratio of operating income to the total capital employed where the total capital employed is the average of the capital used for this year and the previous year.

6. Ratio of net income to total stockholder's equity.

7. The current ratio.

8. Earnings per share of stock.

9. Turnover of total capital employed.

10. Turnover of inventories.

11. Turnover of receivables.

Solution: 1. We look at the income statement to find the appropiate data. Label this year 19X1 and last year 19X0.

The net sales for 19X1 were $1,553,862,000 and for 19X0 $1,393,978,000. Fifteen rows below you find the total operating expenses.

19X1: Total operating expenses = 1,452,462,000

19X0: total operating expenses = 1,302,709,000

$$\text{ratio for 19X1} = \frac{1,452,462}{1,553,862} = 0.934$$

$$\text{ratio for 19X0} = \frac{1,302,709}{1,393,978} = 0.934$$

This ratio means that this company had to spend 93.4 cents to get one dollar, leaving a gross profit per dollar of 100 - 93.4 = 6.6 cents. Even though net sales increased, the gross profit per dollar of sales did not(because operating costs increased also).

2. The gross profit is the amount left from the net sales after deducting total manufacturing costs, i.e., costs of goods sold

19X0: net sales	1,393,978,000
less cost of goods sold	1,155,811,000
equals gross profit	238,167,000

$$\text{ratio} = \frac{238,167}{1,393,978} = .1708$$

19X1: net sales	1,553,862,000
- cost of good sold	1,290,102,000
gross profit	263,760,000

$$\text{ratio} = \frac{263,760}{1,553,862} = .1697$$

For every dollar obtained in 19X0, 17.08 cents were left after manufacturing costs were taken from net sales. Selling expenses have still to be taken care of, and taxes, interest, etc.

3. The income from operations is obtained by subtracting total operating expenses from net sales.

19X0: income from operations = 91,269,000
(look below 'Total Operating Expenses' in table 2.)

19X1: income from operations = 101,400,000.

$$\text{19X0: ratio} = \frac{91,269}{1,393,978} = 0.065$$

$$\text{19X1: ratio} = \frac{101,400}{1,553,862} = 0.065$$

This is an important measure which indicates the profitability of the firm. This is just another way of doing part 1, i.e. by saying 100% (Sales) - 93.4% (Operating Expenses) = 6.6% return before taxes. Out of 1 dollar, approximatedly, 6.½ cents are left after production, selling and administrative costs have been deducted. There is a discrepancy between 0.065 here and 0.066 in the first section because of round-off errors.

4. Subtracting taxes and interest due on long term debt and taxes from the operations income yields the net income. This has already been done in table 2.

$$19X0: \quad ratio = \frac{50,918}{1,393,978} = 0.036 \qquad (or\ 3.6\%)$$

$$19X1: \quad ratio = \frac{57,660}{1,553,862} = 0.037 \qquad (or\ 3.7\%)$$

Stockholders are very interested in this ratio. For every dollar received, 3.7 cents are left to be declared as dividends and/or retained earnings. Actually, for 19X0 27,493,000 were declared as dividends which is

$$\frac{27,493}{1,393,978} = 0.019 \quad or \quad 1.9 \text{ cents from the possible}$$

3.6 cents that could have been declared.

5. In 19X0, total assets were worth $785,893,173. In 19X1, total assets were $909,984,240. The average is a measure of the amount on hand during 19X0 - 19X1.

$$\text{The (average) total capital} = \frac{\$785,893,173 + 909,984,240}{2}$$

$$= 847,938,707$$

Operating income divided by this gives,

$$ratio = \frac{101,400,000}{847,938,707} = .1196$$

This is a measure of the productivity of capital i.e. for every dollar of capital used, there was a return of 11.96 cents over the period 19X0 - 19X1. Similar calculations cannot be made for 19X0 because the total assets figure shown in the balance sheet is probably not the definite amount available for production during the period prior to 19X0 - 19X1.

6. The total stockholder's equity is found in table 1. The net incomes for 19X0 and 19X1 were obtained from the income statement, and are 50,918,000 and 57,660,000 respectively.

$$19X0: \quad ratio = \frac{50,918,000}{498,339,134} = 0.102 \qquad (or\ 10.2\%)$$

$$19X1: \quad ratio = \frac{57,660,000}{570,538,739} = 0.101 \qquad (or\ 10.1\%)$$

This gives stockholders an indication of the return on their investments.

7. The current ratio is total current assets over total current liabilities. It is a measure of the liquidity of the firm. Liquidity is the measure of a firm's ability to pay its immediate debts

$$19X0\text{: current ratio} = \frac{350,580,876}{124,065,590} = 2.83$$

$$10X1\text{: current ratio} = \frac{377,427,497}{145,244,778} = 2.59$$

8. The company had 25,658,000 shares outstanding for 19X0 and 27,256,000 shares in 19X1. The net income divided by these figures yield the earning per share.

$$19Xo\text{: Earning per share} = \frac{50,918,000}{25,658,000} = \$1.98$$

$$19X1\text{: Earning per share} = \frac{57,660,000}{27,256,000} = \$2.11$$

This is not the amount paid to stockholders in dividends. In 19X0, $27,493,000 were declared as dividends. In 19X1, $31,978,000 were declared. There were 25,658,000 shares outstanding in 19X0, and $27,493,000 were declared as dividends or

$$\frac{\$27,493,000}{25,658,000} = \$1.07 \text{ per share for 19X0}$$

and $$\frac{31,978,000}{27,256,000} = \$1.17 \text{ per share for 19X1.}$$

9. The turnover of total capital employed is a measure of the rate of utilization of capital during that year's operation in obtaining sales revenue. Turnover could also be looked at as how much each dollar of capital brings in net sales per year. For 19X1, net sales were $1,553,862,000 and the average total capital as obtained in #5. is $847,938,707.

$$\text{capital turnover} = \frac{\$1,553,862,000}{\$847,938,707} = 1.83 \text{ times per year.}$$

This could also mean that $1 in capital yields $1.83 a year. A capital turnover of 2 would mean that capital is more productive.

10. Inventory turnover measures the flow of goods in and out of a business by measuring how many times it was necessary to entirely replace inventory stocks. Turnover is equal to the entire amount sold during the year divided by the average size of one inventory stock.

$$\frac{\text{Total cost of goods sold}}{\text{average inventory}} = \text{Turnover}$$

The beginning inventory at the beginning of 19X1 is the closing inventory at the end of 19X0, or 93,150,860. (This is the finished goods inventory.) The inventory at the end of 19X1 is $118,795,110 so that the average inventory in 19X1 is

$$(118,795,110 + 93,150,860) \div 2 = \$105,972,985.$$

The cost of goods sold in 19X1 is 1,290,102,000.

$$\text{Inventory turnover} = \frac{1,290,102,000}{105,972,985} = 12.17 \text{ times per}$$

year.

Assuming the cost of raw materials remained the same throughout the year, the greater the inventory turnover, the better the firm has done.

11. The turnover of receivables is a measure of how effectively credit is being collected. It is the net sales in 19X1 divided by the receivables at the end of 19X1.

$$\text{receivables turnover} = \frac{1,553,862,000}{150,550,519} = 10.32 \text{ times per}$$

year.

The average collection period had a length of 365 days/10.32 = 35 days. If the firm gives 30 days credit to its customers then it was about 5 days late collecting each time.

TABLE 1

Consolidated Balance Sheet (at December 31)

Assets Current Assets:	This year	Year ago	Increase or Decrease
Cash................................	$48,898,044	$46,294,494	$ 2,603,550
U.S. government and other marketable securities (at lower cost or market)	6,334,637	35,130,885	-28,796,248
Receivables.........................	150,550,519	128,692,913	21,857,606
Inventories (at lower cost or market)			
Finished goods.....................	118,795,110	93,150,860	25,644,250
Materials and supplies................	52,849,187	47,311,724	5,537,463
Total Current Assets..............	377,427,497	350,580,876	26,846,621
Other Assets (At cost):			
Investments and advances			
Foreign subsidiary companies........	18,569,687	16,082,756	2,486,931
Domestic associated companies.......	4,026,916	3,906,063	120,852
Securities on deposit.................	1,569,288	1,570,824	- 1,536
(Pursuant to workmen's compensation Laws, etc.)			
Mortgages, receivables, etc.	13,062,474	12,873,954	188,620
Total other assets..............	37,228,365	34,433,497	2,794,868
Property and Equipment (At cost):			
Land................................	25,044,680	22,785,266	2,259,414
Buildings...........................	169,415,296	154,517,559	14,897,737
Machinery, equipment, etc.	397,146,471	333,689,159	63,457,312
Total property and equipment	591,606,447	510,991,984	80,614,463
Less accumulated depreciation.........	225,281,303	205,426,215	19,855,088
Net property and equipment	366,325,144	305,565,769	60,759,375
Deffered Charges	9,749.247	7,614,625	2,934,612
Intangibles	119,253,987	87,698,396	31,555,591
Total .... $$	909,984,240	785,893,173	124,091,067

TABLE 1 contd.

Liabilities	This year	Year ago	Increase or Decrease
Current Liabilities:			
Payables and accrued liabilities.	$121,015,350	$ 94,969,385	$ 26,045,965
Accrued Taxes..................	24,229,428	29,096,205	- 4,866,777
Total Current liabilities	145,244,778	124,065,590	21,979,188
Long-Term Debt....................	158,526,433	130,277,515	28,248,918
Reserves:			
Deferred federal taxes on income.	28,565,672	25,754,352	2,911,320
Insurance, etc.	7,108,618	7,456,542	- 347,924
Total Reserves..........	25,674,290	33,210,894	2,463,396
Stockholder's Equity:			
Capital stock -par value $3.75 per share			
Authorized 37,000,000 shares			
This year (shares) / Last year (shares)			
Issued 27,427,956 / 25,658,000			
Less treasury stock 171,956 / 154,337			
Outstanding 27,256,000 / 25,658,000	102,210,000	96,217,500	5,992,500
Employee's stock purchase installments	5,795,588	15,922,539	-10,126,951
Capital surplus..................	168,217,496	117,564,991	50,652,505
Retained earnings	294,315,655	268,634,144	25,681,599
Total Stockholder's Equity..	570,538,739	498,339,174	72,199,565
Total....................	$909,984,240	$785,893,173	$124,091,067

TABLE 2

Statement of Operations and Retained Earnings
(Years ended December 31)

(000 omitted)	This Year Per-cent	This Year Amount	Last Year Per-cent	Last Year Amount	Increase or Decrease
Net Sales	100.	$1,553,862	100.	$1,393,978	11.5%
Cost of Goods Manufactured & Sold:					
Raw Materials, Beginning Inventory	3.0	47,312	3.3	45,425	4.2
Raw Materials, Purchases	37.4	582,037	40.0	557,775	4.3
Total Available	40.5	629,349	43.3	603,200	4.3
Raw Materials, ending Inventory	2.1	32,779	3.4	47,312	-3.1
Cost of Materials used	38.4	596,570	39.9	555,888	7.3
Factory Labor	31.5	489,776	30.2	420,324	16.5
Factory Overhead	14.8	229,400	13.1	183,100	25.3
Cost of Goods Manufactured	84,7	1,315,746	83.2	1,959,312	13.5
Finished Goods Beginning Inventory	6.0	93,151	6.4	89,650	3.9
Total Available for Sale	90.7	1,408,897	89.6	1,248,962	12.8
Finished Goods, Ending Inventory	7.6	118,795	6.7	93,151	27.5
Cost of Goods Sold	83.1	1,290.102	82.9	1,155,811	11.6
Selling Expenses	7.1	109,600	7.0	98,215	11.6
General and Administrative Expenses	3.4	52,760	3.5	48,683	8.4
Total Operating Expenses	93.5	1,452,462	93.4	1,302,709	11.5
Income from Operation*	6.5	101,400	6.5	91,269	11.1
Deduct:					
Interest on Long Term Debt	.3	5,343	.3	4,266	25.2
Income before Federal Income Taxes	6.2	96,057	6.2	87,003	10.4
Federal Income Taxes	2.5	38,397	2.6	36,085	6.4
Net Income for the Year	3.7	57,660	3.6	59,918	13.2
Cash Dividend paid on Stock	2.1	31,978	2.0	27,493	16.3
Earnings Retained	1.7	25,682	1.6	23,425	9.6
Retained Earnings, Beginning of Year		268,634		245,209	
Retained Earnings, End of Year		294,316		268,634	
Number of Shares of Stock Outstanding		27,256		25,658	

*Subtract Operating Expenses from Net Sales.

The balance sheet of the Morristown Novelty Store is shown below.

MORRISTOWN NOVELTY STORE
Balance Sheet
June 30, 19X6

Assets		Liabilities	
Current Assets:		Current Liabilities:	
Cash	$ 4,272	Notes Payable	$21,100
Accounts Receivable	16,770	Accounts Payable	20,500
Merchandise Inventory	30,600	Total Current Liab.	$41,600
Total Current Assets	$51,642	Owner's Equity	
Fixed Assets:			
Store Equipment	8,320	J.R.Lunt, Capital	18,362
Total Assets	$59,962	Total Liab.& O.E.	$59,962

Comment on the financial position of the Morristown Novelty Store by finding the working capital, the Current Ratio and the Acid-test Ratio as of 19X6.

Solution: All these tests give an indication of the 'liquidity' of the business, i.e., the firm's ability to pay its current debts and finance current operations, by converting its assets to cash. The working capital is the total current assets minus the total current liabilities. The store's working capital is

$$\$51,642 - \$41,600 = \$10,042.$$

This amount provides a basis on which to make short-time spending decisions. The current ratio is a better indication of the liquidity of a firm than working capital because it shows, how many dollars worth of assets there are to back up each dollar of debt. Two firms can have the same amount of working capital, but one can be healthier because it has more dollars of assets per dollar of debt. The current ratio is found by dividing total current assets by total current liabilities. So let us compare the firm in our example with a much larger firm with current assets of $800,000 and the same working capital as our firm, $10,042. The larger firm's liabilities are assumed to be $789,958; assets-liabilities = working capital, so assets-working capital = liabilities. The current ratio of our firm is

$$\frac{51,642}{41,600} = 1.24$$

and the current ratio of the larger firm is

$$\frac{800,000}{789,958} = 1.01$$

Therefore the store in our example has a greater liquidity since it has more dollars of assets per dollar of current debt than the larger firm, even though both enterprises have the same amount of working capital. A current ratio of 2:1 is considered adequate, so the Morristown Novelty Store may be in a 'tight' situation in financing its current activities with a ratio of 1.24 : 1. We should, however, look at the acid-test ratio to gain a clearer picture of the store's liquidity.

The acid-test ratio is found by dividing cash plus accounts receivable plus any notes receivable the firm may possess by the total current liabilities. Only the most liquid assets are summed and used as the numerator. Inventory is not considered liquid enough to be in the acid-test ratio because it can't be converted to cash until it is sold and this is not always possible.

$$\text{acid-test ratio} = \frac{\text{Cash + Accounts Receivable}}{\text{Total current liabilities}}$$

$$= \frac{4,272 + 16,770}{41,600} = 0.506 .$$

This should be a cause for concern. Usually an acid-test ratio of 1 to 1 is acceptable. The Morristown Novelty Store should aim to remedy this situation by perhaps reducing inventory and holding its assets in a more liquid form.

• PROBLEM 16-18

1. Current Assets: / Current Liabilities:

Current Assets		Current Liabilities	
Cash	$22,150	Accounts Payable	$28,500
Marketable Securities	16,000	Notes Payable	20,000
Accounts Receivable	30,450	Other Bills Payable	10,000
Inventories	25,000		
Total	$93,600	Total	$58,500

From this information compute:

a) The current ratio.
b) The quick asset ratio.
c) The net working capital.

Solution: (a) The current ratio like the quick asset ratio gives an indication of the liquidity of the firm, i.e., its ability to convert its assets into cash when it becomes necessary to do so. It indicates a firm's ability to pay its Current Liabilities. It answers the question "How many dollars of current assets are there for each dollar of current liabilities?"

$$\text{Current ratio} = \frac{\text{Total Current Assets}}{\text{Total Current Liabilities}} = \frac{93,600}{58,500} = 1.6 .$$

For every one dollar of current liabilities there is $1.60 of current assets.

(b) The quick asset ratio is used for the same purpose as the current ratio except that only the current assets that are quickly converted into cash are taken as the numerator. This means for the above that cash, Marketablè Securities and accounts receivable are set against total current liabilities. Inventories are excluded, as they are not quickly turned into cash.

$$\text{Quick asset ratio} = \frac{(22,150)+(16,000)+(30,450)}{58,500} =$$

$$\frac{68,600}{58,500} = 1.17 .$$

The ratio is 1.17 : 1. An acceptable quick asset ratio is 1:1. When the ratio falls below this norm, it may indicate that there are not enough quick assets to pay off current debt. If the ratio is above 1:1 as it is here, a shortage of inventories may be indicated. This means a shortage of goods available for sale and the loss of an opportunity to earn revenue.

(c) The net working capital is found by subtracting total current liabilities from total current assets.

working capital = $93,600 - $58,500 = $35,100.

This working capital may be sufficient, depending on the size of the business. For a firm with total assets of 10 millions, this is a meager sum with which to carry daily transaction. For a smaller firm, this may be adequate.

• PROBLEM 16-19

The entries in the balance sheet for the West Side Hardware Store (L. S. Miller, owner) for December 31, 19X4 and 19X5 are shown below. Prepare a comparative balance sheet, showing the amount of increase or decrease for each item.

19X5

Assets		Liabilities	
Cash	$ 2,600	Notes Payable	$ 1,600

Accounts Receivable	2,100	Accounts Payable	1,900
Merchandise Inventory	6,300	Total Liabilities	$3,500
Store Supplies	700		
Store Equipment	1,800	Owner's Equity	
Office Equipment	600	L.S.Miller,Capital	10,600
Total Assets	$14,100	Total Liab.& O.E.	$14,100

19X4

Assets		Liabilities	
Cash	$ 3,100	Accounts Payable	$ 2,400
Account Receivable	1,400		
Merchandise Inventory	4,900		
Store Supplies	1,100		
Store Equipment	1,500	Owner's Equity	
Office Equipment	300	L.S.Miller,Capital	9,900
Total Assets	$12,300	Total Liab.& O.E.	$12,300

Also give the percentage increase/decrease.

Solution:

West Side Hardware Store

Comparative Balance Sheet 19X4 to 19X5

Assets	19X5	19X4	Change	% Change
Cash	2,600	3,100	(500)	- 16.1%
Accounts Receivable	2,100	1,400	700	50%
Inventory	6,300	4,900	1,400	28.5%
Store Supplies	700	1,100	(400)	- 36.3%
Store Equpment	1,800	1,500	300	20%
Office Equipment	600	300	300	100%
Total Assets	14,100	12,300	1,800	14.6%

Liabilities	19X5	19X4	Change	% Change
Notes payable	1,600	0	1,600	-
Accounts payable	1,900	2,400	(500)	- 20.8%
Total Liabilities	3,500	2,400	1,100	45.8%
Owner's Equity				
L.S. Miller, Capital	10,600	9,900	700	7%

The percentage change is found as follows. Divide the number on the change column, i.e., the increase or the decrease, by the corresponding number in the 19X4 column and multiply by 100%. For example, in cash, there was a decrease of 500 from 19X4 to 19X5. This represents a decrease in percent of

$\frac{500}{3,100} \times 100\% = 16.1\%.$

Note that for'notes payable' we do not find the % Change since we cannot divide by zero and consequentty we can not find what per cent 1600 is of 0.

• PROBLEM 16-20

Thora's Ceramics balance sheet figures for last year are as follows,

Current assets: Cash, \$3,400; Accounts Receivable, \$1,640; Merchandise, \$8,200.

Fixed assets: Store equipment, \$4,640; Office Equipment, \$1,350.

Current Liabilities: Accounts Payable, \$2,700; Notes Payable, \$1,000.

Owner's Equity: Ms. K. Thora, Capital \$15,530.

What percentages of the total assets are the different asset entries?

Solution: Arrange the information given in column form.

Current Assets		
Cash	3,400	
Accounts Receivable	1,640	
Merchandise	8,200	
Total current assets	13,240	13,240
Fixed Assets		
Store equipment	4,640	
Office equipment	1,350	
Total fixed assets	5,990	5,990
Total assets		19,230.

Find the sum of the liabilities and the owner's equity to see that the accounting equation is satisfied. Aside from this check we do not need to arrange the liabilities or owner's equity as shown above in order to solve the problem.

To find the percentage of each item on the asset side, divide the amount of the item by the total assets, 19,230 and multiply by 100%.

Current assets

% Cash : $\frac{3400}{19,230} \times 100\% =$ 17.68 %

% Accounts receivable: $\frac{1640}{19,230} \times 100\% =$ 8.52 %

% Merchandise: $\frac{8,200}{19,230} \times 100\% =$ 42.65 %

% Current assets: 68.85%

Fixed assets

% Store equipment: $\frac{4,640}{19,230} \times 100\% =$ 24.12%

% Office equipment: $\frac{1,350}{19,230} \times 100\% =$ 7.03%

% Fixed assets: 31.15%

Note that Current Assets (68.85%) + Fixed Assets (31.15%) = 100% or Total Assets.

• PROBLEM 16-21

The Crown Development Company presents a comparative balance sheet:

Assets	December 31 This year	December 31 Last Year
Current Assets		
Cash	$ 25,957	$ 23,581
Marketable Securities	1,530	24,096
Accounts Receivable	74,785	66,477
Inventories	108,233	99,109
Prepaid Expenses	10,987	10,825
Total Current	221,492	224,088
Fixed Assets		
Land	78,875	55,998
Building & Equipment	646,632	611,164
Less Accumulated Depreciation .	275,298	267,426
Building & Equip. - Net	371,334	343,738
Total Fixed Assets	450,209	399,736
Other Assets	23,504	17,771
Total	$695,205	$641,595
Liabilities and Net Worth		
Current Liabilities		
Accounts & Notes Payable	$ 76,807	$ 64,479
Long-Term Debt	147,328	133,434
Preferred Stock	31,172	31,158
Common Stock	172,040	171,260
Retained Earnings	267,858	241,264
Total Liabilities & Equity ..	$695,205	$641,595

Find the percentage change (increase or decrease) of all items from last year to this year. Also, find the current ratio and the acid-test ratio for both years.

Solution: After subtracting last year's figure from this year's, divide this difference by the amount the item stood at last year then multiply by 100%. For example, as far as cash is concerned, there was an increase of

($25,957 - $23,581) = $2,376.

This is a percentage change of

$$\frac{2,376}{23,581} \times 100\% = 10\%.$$

Crown Development Company
Comparative Balance Sheet for
Dec. 31 19X6, Dec. 31, 19X7

Assets	19X7	19X6	Change	% Change
Current Assets				
Cash	$25,957	$23,581	$2,376	10%
Marketable Securities	1,530	24,096	(22,566)	(93.6%)
Accounts Receivable	74,785	66,477	8,308	12.5%
Inventories	108,233	99,109	9,124	9.2%
Prepaid expenses	10,987	10,825	162	1.4%
Total current	221,492	224,088	(2596)	(1.1%)
Fixed Assets				
Land	78,875	55,998	22,877	29%
Building, Equipment	646,632	611,164	35,468	5.8%
Less depreciation	275,298	267,426	7,872	2.9%
Building, Equip,-Net	371,334	343,738	27,596	8%
Total fixed	450,209	399,736	50,473	12.6%
Other assets	23,504	17,771	5,733	32.2%
Total Assets	695,205	641,595	53,610	8.3%
Liabilities				
Current Liabilities				
Accounts,notes payable	$ 76,807	$ 64,479	12,328	19.1%

Long term debt	147,328	133,434	13,894	10.4%
Owner's equity				
Preferred Stock	31,172	31,158	14	negligible
Common Stock	172,040	171,260	780	.4%
Retained Earnings	267,858	241,264	26,594	11%
Total Liabilities + Equity	$695,205	$641,595	53,610	8.3%

The current ratio for 19X6 is

$$\frac{224,088}{64,479} = 3.47 \qquad \text{i.e.} \qquad \frac{\text{total current assets}}{\text{total current liabilities}}$$

Current Assets are those assets which are expected to be used or turned into cash within a year or so. Current liabilities are the debts which are to be paid within the year.

For 19X7,

$$\text{current ratio} = \frac{221,492}{78,807} = 2.88$$

$$\text{acid-test ratio} = \frac{\text{quick assets}}{\text{total liabilities current}}$$

For this company the quick assets are composed of Cash, Marketable Securities and Accounts Receivable. Quick assets are those which can be turned into cash within a very short period of time, such as a month, or even less, in order to be used as cash on very short notice. For example, inventories can not be guaranteed to be sold, that is turned to cash, within any period of time. Therefore, they can not be considered "quick" as can marketable securities which can be sold for cash with very little wait.

$$\text{19X6 - acid-test ratio} = \frac{114,154}{64,479} = 1.77$$

$$\text{19X7 - acid-test ratio} = \frac{102,272}{64,479} = 1.58.$$

Management may have considered the current asset figure of 19X6 as too high. By eliminating 93.6% of its marketable securities and using the money elsewhere, the company lowered both ratios.

• PROBLEM 16-22

At the beginning of the 19X1 fiscal year Company X had $28,000 of accounts receivable. At the end of the fiscal year it had $32,000. of accounts receivable. Sales in 19X1 were $850,000. At the end of the 19X2 fiscal year, accounts receivable were $35,000. Sales

in 19X2 were $920,000. Using a 360 day year and given that Company X's desired rate of return is 10%, (a) find the average collection period (in days) for 19X1 and 19X2
(b) find the cost (or saving) in extending (or reducing) the credit period during the two periods.

Solution: It is important for a firm to concern itself with the collection period of its account receivables. A very long collection period may prove to be costly in the sense that the money could have been invested if received sooner. For example, if the collection period is 20 days to begin with and management decides to increase it to 35 days, the payments that would be originally due in 20 days could be earning interest during the fifteen days that we must now wait. On the other hand, a very short collection period can result in a decrease of sales since some customers may not be able to meet the stringent payment dates, and may not be able to pay the finance charges on payments made after the deadline.

(a) The average collection period C_p is given by the formula,

$$C_p = \frac{(\$)\text{ average amount of accounts receivable in period}}{(\$)\text{ average daily sales in period}}$$

For 19X1:

($) average amount of accounts receivables in period

$$= \frac{\$28,000 + \$32,000}{2} = \$30,000$$

($) average daily sales in period

$$= \frac{\$850,000}{360\text{ days}} = \$2,361/\text{day to the nearest dollar.}$$

$$C_p = \frac{\$30,000}{\$2,361/\text{day}} = 12.7\text{ days}$$

For 19X2:

($) average amount of accounts receivables in period

$$= \frac{\$32,000 + 35,000}{2} = \$33,500$$

($) average daily sales in period

$$= \frac{\$920,000}{360\text{ days}} = \$2,555/\text{day}$$

$$C_p = \frac{\$33,500}{\$2,555/\text{day}} = 13.11\text{ days.}$$

The collection period has increased 0.41 days from 19X1 to 19X2.

(b) First find the total number of days in the year that are equivalent to the increase of 0.41 days in the collection period. If the number of days in a collection period is 13.11 (for 19X2) then there are

$$\frac{360 \text{ days}}{13.11 \text{ days/period}} = 27.46 \text{ periods;}$$

the actual increase in collection days is therefore

$$(0.41 \text{ days/period}) \times (27.46 \text{ periods}) = 11.257 \text{ days.}$$

This is the number of days that were given up by Company X in 19X2 in which payments could have been invested at an annual rate of 10%.

Sales per day in 19X2 were found to be $2,555/day The total payments received over 11.257 days is

$$(\$2{,}555/\text{day}) \times (11.257 \text{ days}) = \$28{,}762.28.$$

Now suppose that you could invest $2,555 per day over this 11.257 day period at an annual rate of 10%, the total at the end of the 11.257 days will be greater than $28,762.28 and the difference will represent the cost in extending the collection period 0.41 days from 19X1 to 19X2.

An annual rate of 10% is equivalent to a daily rate of (0.10 ÷ 360) = 0.000278 (i.e. .00278%); the daily payments made are $2,555. The future value of a series of $2,555 payments over 11.257 days at a daily interest rate of 0.00278% is

$$F_{11.257} = \$2{,}555 \left[\frac{(1 + 0.000278)^{11.257} - 1}{0.000278} \right] =$$

$$\$28{,}766.73$$

where in general the future value of a series of equal amounts P over n periods at rate r is

$$F_n = P \left[\frac{(1 + r)^n - 1}{r} \right] .$$

The cost in extending the credit period from 12.7 days to 13.11 days is

$$\$28{,}766.73 - \$28{,}762.28 = \$4.45$$

which is certainly not sufficient cause to set stockholders complaining about inefficient credit management.

CHAPTER 17

FINANCIAL STATEMENTS

RATIOS AND MINOR DOCUMENTS

• PROBLEM 17-1

Mr. Reynolds, owner of Reynold's Auto Service, had a total income from his auto service last year of \$366,000. Included in the \$366,000 was \$732 worth of checks that proved to be worthless. What was his percent of loss from bad checks?

Solution: Mr. Reynolds percent of loss from bad checks is the ratio of the amount of bad checks to the total amount that he received. Since he received \$732 in bad checks out of a total amount of \$366,000, the ratio is

$$\frac{\$732}{\$366,000} = .002,$$

which, as a percent, is .2%.

• PROBLEM 17-2

Which one of the following journals would you expect a small businessman to use?

(A) A sales journal

(B) A wage journal

(C) A petty cash journal

(D) A cash receipts journal

(E) A general journal

Solution: A journal is, by definiton, a record of day-by-day transactions, listing the accounts to be debited and credited. Usually, a small businessman would use a general journal, the simplest and most flexible type of journal, allowing himself the ability to keep track of all transactions.

A sales journal is used to record the customer's name, invoice number, and amount of purchase for each charge sale. The sales are usually recorded daily, with the information about each sale being placed on a separate line.

A wage journal is used to record salaries paid to employees. It shows the payroll date for each employee on a separate line.

Payments for small items such as postage, express charges, telegrams, etc, are generally too small to warrant payment by check. Because of this, a petty cash fund is maintained to cover these expenses. The petty cash journal is the record of this fund. Lastly, a cash receipts journal is used to record all cash receipts. This must be a multicolumn journal, since the cash receipts differ as to source, and consequently, as to the accounts credited when cash is received from different sources.

Sales, wage, petty cash and cash receipts journals are examples of specialized journals, and are usually found in larger businesses. The correct answer is therefore (E).

• PROBLEM 17-3

Acme Lumber Co. estimated that loss from bad debts for the current year would be approximately 3/4% of net credit sales. Net credit sales for the year was $78,600 and the loss from bad debts totaled $820. Did the loss exceed the estimate? By how much?

Solution: Since Acme Lumber expected losses from bad debts to be approximately 3/4% (=.0075) of net credit sales, and the net credit sales for the year was $78,600, they expected

$$.0075 \times \$78,600 = \$589.50$$

in losses from bad debts. They actually experienced $820 in losses, so they exceeded their estimate by

$$\$820 - \$589.50 = \$230.50$$

• PROBLEM 17-4

ABC Plumbing has the following current assets and liabilities: Cash, \$7,300; Marketable Securities, \$14,200, Accounts Receivable, \$2,120; Notes Payable, \$1,400; Accounts Payable, \$1,850. Find the acid-test ratio for ABC, correct to the nearest hundreth.

Solution: The acid-test ratio is the ratio of "quick assets" (current assets that can quickly be turned into cash) to current liabilities. ABC has a total of

$$\$7,300 + \$14,200 + \$2,120 = \$23,620$$

in quick assets, with

$$\$1,400 + \$1,850 = \$3,250$$

in current liabilities. The company's acid-test ratio is therefore

$$\frac{\$23,620}{\$3,250} \text{ which,}$$

to the nearest hundredth, is 7.27.

• PROBLEM 17-5

Find the current ratio for each of the following. Give answers to nearest hundreths.

Company Name	Current Assets	Current Liabilities
1. Brandt Appliances	\$16,660	\$10,330
2. Sip'n Sup Diner	\$ 1,420	\$ 660
3. Avery Department Store	\$21,312	\$11,100
4. Guild Book Co.	\$77,430	\$14,885
5. Wonder-Tread Tire Co.	\$17,240	\$16,300

Solution: The current ratio for each of the companies can be found by dividing the value of the current assets by the value of the current liabilities. For example, the current ratio for Brandt Appliances would be

$$\frac{\$16,660}{\$10,330} \text{ which, to the nearest hundredth,}$$

is 1.61.

Following a similar procedure, the current ratios of each of the companies listed above have been calculated and summarized in the table below:

Company Name	Current Ratio (Rounded)
1. Brandt Appliances	1.61
2. Sip'n Sup Diner	2.15
3. Avery Department Store	1.92
4. Guild Book Co.	5.20
5. Wonder-Tread Tire Co.	1.06

• PROBLEM 17-6

Under the double-entry system, the statement "for every debit there is an equal credit" is

(A) always true

(B) usually true with a few exceptions

(C) never true

(D) makes no sense at all

Solution: Under the double-entry system of bookkeeping, every transaction is recorded in two (or more) accounts with equal debits and credits. This procedure offers a means of proving the accuracy of the ledger, since under the double-entry system the sum of the debits must equal the sum of the credits.

Thus, under the double-entry system the statement "for every debit there is an equal credit" is always true. The correct choice is therefore (A).

• PROBLEM 17-7

From the information given below, prepare a customer account for Ms. Lewis. What is the balance as of March 25?

Customer - Barbara Lewis

March 1 - Purchase	$67.50
8 - Payment Received	$67.50
17 - Purchase	$72.50
22 - Purchase	$37.49
25 - Payment Received	$50.00

Solution: In preparing the balance sheet for Ms. Lewis' account, we should make sure that each purchase increases her balance due, and that each payment decreases the amount she owes. The completed balance sheet is shown below:

Customer's Name	Barbara Lewis		
DATE MARCH	CHARGES	PAYMENTS	BALANCE
1	$67.50		$67.50
8		$67.50	0
17	$72.50		$72.50
22	$37.49		$109.99
25		$50.00	$59.99

Her balance as of March 25 was therefore $59.99.

• PROBLEM 17-8

Sections of six customer accounts are shown below. Check them for missing or incorrect entries. On a separate sheet of paper, show any corrected accounts.

a.

Date May	Charges	Payments	Balance
12	114.00		114.00
27	96.50		210.50
30		114.00	96.50

b.

Date Feb.	Charges	Payments	Balance
6	14.35		14.35
9	143.70		
23		158.05	

c.

Date Oct.	Charges	Payments	Balance
1			200.95
16		100.00	100.95
21	74.20		

d.

Date July	Charges	Payments	Balance
6	432.60		432.60
15		350.00	
19		52.60	

e.

Date Mar.	Charges	Payments	Balance
11	673.95		
11	561.40		
20	428.83		
31		1,500.00	

f.

Date Dec.	Charges	Payments	Balance
1			516.00
5		437.00	
7	721.40		
17	300.00		

Solution: In checking each of the customer accounts, we should make sure that each of the charges listed increase the balance, and that each of the payments decrease the balance, and that the amount of each increase (or decrease) agrees with the amount of the charge (or payment). For example, in problem (a), the May 27 charge of $96.50 should increase the balance from $114 to $114 + $96.50 = $210.50 (which it does), and the May 30 payment of $114 should decrease the balance from $210.50 to $210.50 - $114 = $96.50 (which it does).

Shown below are each of the account statements, with corrections as needed:

Date May	Charges	Payments	Balance
12	114.00		114.00
27	96.50		210.50
30		114.00	96.50

Date Feb.	Charges	Payments	Balance
6	14.35		14.35
9	143.70		158.05
23		158.05	0

Date Oct.	Charges	Payments	Balance
1	200.95		200.95
16		100.00	100.95
21	74.20		175.15

Date July	Charges	Payments	Balance
6	432.60		432.60
15		350.00	82.60
19		52.60	30.00

Date Mar	Charges	Payments	Balance
11	673.95		673.95
11	561.40		1,235.35
20	428.83		1,664.18
31		1,500.00	164.18

Date Dec.	Charges	Payments	Balance
1	516.00		516.00
5		437.00	79.00
7	721.40		800.40
17	300.00		1,100.40

• PROBLEM 17-9

Mr. Williams, upon filing a petition for bankruptcy, stated that he had a total of only \$2,240 in assets, with liabilities amounting to \$5,600. How much money can Mr. Johnson, a creditor, expect to receive if he has a claim of \$1,725?

Solution: Mr. Williams does not have sufficient assets to cover all of his liabilities. In order to be fair to all of his creditors, he pays them all a part of their claims. The amount is found by obtaining the ratio of his assets to his liabilities.

Since Mr. Williams has \$2,240 in assets and \$5,600 in liabilities, his ratio of assets to liabilities is

$$\frac{\$2,240}{\$5,600} = .4.$$

This means that he will be able to pay each of his creditors .4 times the amount of their claim.

Mr. Johnson has a claim for \$1,725, so he can expect to receive

$$.4 \times \$1,725 = \$690$$

from his claim.

INCOME STATEMENTS AND NET PROFITS

• PROBLEM 17-10

From the facts given below, calculate the net profit for the Flamingo Restaurant for the month of October: food on hand as of October 1, \$609.31; purchases during the month, \$1,827.63; sales during the month, \$4,501.16; rent, \$175.00; salaries, \$580.15; supplies, \$89.47; miscellaneous expenses, \$50.83; food on hand as of October 31, \$215.76.

Solution: The net profit for the month will be the difference between income and expenses. The income for the month was \$4,501.16. The expenses for the month can be calculated as follows:

at the beginning of the month, the restaurant had \$609.31 worth of food on hand, and purchased an additional \$1,827.63 in food for a total of

$$\$609.31 + \$1,827.63 = \$2,436.94$$

in food. However, at the end of the month the restaurant still had \$215.76 in food, so the expense for the food used was

$$\$2,436.94 - \$215.76 = \$2,221.18.$$

The restaurant also had operating expenses of \$175 for rent, \$580.15 for salaries, \$89.47 for supplies, and \$50.83 for miscellaneous expenses for total expenses of

$$\$2,221.18 + \$175 + \$580.15 + \$89.47 + \$50.83 =$$

\$3,116.63.

The net profit for the month was therefore

$$\$4,501.16 - \$3,116.63 = \$1,384.53.$$

• PROBLEM 17-11

From the information given below, calculate the net profit for the Spring Hills Bakery for the month ended June 30:

Revenue from Sales	\$4,400
Sales Returns	\$ 140
Merchandise Inventory - June 1	\$6,500

Merchandise Inventory - June 30	$5,900
Purchases during June	$2,200
Salary Expense	$ 750
Telephone Expense	$ 20
Rent Expense	$ 125
Miscellaneous Expenses	$ 45

Solution: The net profit for the bakery for the month of June will be the difference between income and expenses. The bakery received a total income for the month of $4,400. From this we must subtract the total expenses for the month which we can calculate as follows:

The bakery had a June 1 inventory of $6,500, and purchased an additional $2,200 in merchandise for a total of $8,700. At the end of the month, $5,900 in inventory remained, so the cost of goods sold during June was $8,700 - $5,900 = $2,800. Adding to this expenses for returns ($140), salary ($750), telephone ($20), rent ($125) and miscellaneous ($45), we get total expenses for the month of

$2,800 + $140 + $750 + $20 + $125 + $45 = $3,880.

The net profit for the bakery for the month of June was therefore

$4,400 - $3,880 = $520.

• PROBLEM 17-12

Complete the following comparative income statement for Sanford and Grier Electronics:

Sanford and Grier Electronics

Comparative Income Statement for Years Ending June 30, 1972 and 1971

	1972	1971	Increase (or Decrease) Amount	Increase (or Decrease) %	% of Net Sales 1972	% of Net Sales 1971
Income:						
Net Sales	$480,000	$400,000				
Cost of Goods:						
Inventory, July 1	$ 40,000	$ 60,000				
Purchases	320,000	240,000				

Goods available for sale	$______	$______				
Inventory, June 30	60,000	40,000				
Cost of goods sold	______	______				
Gross profit	$______	$______				
Expenses:						
Salaries	$60,000	$48,000				
Occupancy	32,000	28,000				
Promotion	24,000	12,000				
Depreciation	12,000	16,000				
Miscellaneous	12,000	8,000				
Total expenses	______	______				
Net profit on operations	$______	$______				

Solution: In completing the income statement, the amount of increase (or decrease) column is simply the difference between the 1972 and 1971 values. For example, the increase in net sales was $480,000 - $400,000 = $80,000. The % increase (decrease) column is the ratio of the amount of increase (decrease) to the 1971 value, expressed as a percentage. For example, the % increase for net sales was

$$\frac{\$80,000}{\$400,000} = .20 = 20\%.$$

The % of net sales for each of the years is the ratio of each of the items listed for the year to the total net sales for the year, expressed as a percentage. For example, the % of net sales of the July 1 inventory for 1972 was

$$\frac{\$40,000}{\$480,000} = .083 = 8.3\%.$$

Similarly, for 1971 it was

$$\frac{\$60,000}{\$400,000} = .15 = 15\%.$$

The goods available for sale is the sum of the July 1 inventory and purchases. The cost of goods sold is the difference between the goods available for sale and the June 30 inventory. The gross profit is the difference between the net sales and cost of goods sold. The total expenses is the sum of each of the expenses listed, and the net profit on operations is the difference between gross profit and total expenses.

Shown below is the completed income statement:

SANFORD AND GRIER ELECTRONICS

Comparative Income Statement
for Years Ending June 30, 1972 and 1971

	1972	1971	Increase (or Decrease) Amount	%	% of Net Sales 1972	1971
Income						
Net sales	$480,000	$400,000	$80,000	20.0%	100.0%	100.0%
Cost of goods:						
Inventory, July 1	$ 40,000	$ 60,000	($20,000)	(33.3)	8.3%	15.0%
Purchases	320,000	240,000	80,000	33.3	66.7	60.0
Goods available for sale	$360,000	$300,000	$60,000	20.0%	75.0%	75.0%
Inventory, June 30	60,000	40,000	20,000	50.0	12.5	10.0
Cost of goods sold	300,000	260,000	40,000	15.4	62.5	65.0
Gross Profit	$180,000	$140,000	$40,000	28.6%	37.5%	35.0%
Expenses:						
Salaries	$ 60,000	$ 48,000	$12,000	25.0%	12.5%	12.0%
Occupancy	32,000	28,000	4,000	14.3	6.7	7.0
Promotion	24,000	12,000	12,000	100.0	5.0	3.0
Depreciation	12,000	16,000	(4,000)	(25.0)	2.5	4.0
Miscellaneous	12,000	8,000	4,000	50.0	2.5	2.0
Total expenses	140,000	112,000	28,000	25.0	29.2	28.0
Net profit on operations	$ 40,000	$ 28,000	$12,000	42.9	8.3%	7.0%

• PROBLEM 17-13

Prepare a comparative income statement for the Oriental Antiques Mart for the years ended December 31, 1975 and 1976, based on the information given below. In addition, (a) show the amount of increase or decrease of each item in 1976 compared with 1975, and (b) show the percent of increase or decrease for Net Sales, Gross Profit and Net Income. (c) Indicate the percent of Net Sales for the following items for 1976: Purchases, Cost of Goods Sold, Gross Profit, Operating Expenses, Net Income.

	1975	1976
Net Sales	$125,600	$132,700
Merchandise Inventory, Jan. 1	$ 38,450	$ 42,650
Merchandise Inventory, Dec. 31	$ 42,650	$ 46,840
Purchases	$ 92,820	$ 91,820
Salaries Expense	$ 19,480	$ 20,340
Rent Expense	$ 12,400	$ 12,400
Repairs and Maintenance	$ 890	$ 360
Insurance and Office Expense	$ 6,240	$ 4,720

Solution: In preparing the comparative income statement for the Oriental Antiques Mart, we will be computing the differences between income and expenses for the years 1975 and 1976 to arrive at a net income, and comparing the results between the two years. The amount of increase or decrease of each item in 1976 compared with 1975 is the difference between the 1976 and 1975 values, expressed as a ratio to the 1975 value. The percent of net sales for 1976 is the ratio of each of the items listed to the 1976 net sales, expressed as a percentage. The comparative income statement is shown below:

Oriental Antiques Mart
Comparative Income Statement
for the years ended Dec. 31, 19X5 and 19X6

	1975	1976	% Increase (decrease) in 19X6	% of 19X6 net Sales
Net Sales	$125,600	$132,700	5.65%	
Merchandise Inventory Jan.1	$ 38,450	$ 42,650	10.92%	
Add-Purchases	$ 92,820	$ 91,820	(1.08%)	69.19%
Less-Merchand. Inventory Dec.31	$ 42,650	$ 46,840	9.82%	
Cost of Goods Sold	$ 88,620	$ 87,630	(1.12%)	66.04%
Gross profit	$ 36,980	$ 45,070	21.88%	33.96%
Operating Expenses: Salaries Expense	$ 19,480	$ 20,340	4.41%	
Rent Expense	$ 12,400	$ 12,400	0%	
Repairs and Maintenance	$ 890	$ 360	(59.55%)	
Insurance and Office	$ 6,240	$ 4,720	(24.36%)	
Total Operating Expenses	$ 39,010	$ 37,820	(3.05%)	28.50%
Net Income (Loss)	($2,030)	$ 7,250	457.14%	5.46%

• PROBLEM 17-14

Prepare a comparative income statement for Nelson's Cycle Shop for the years ended December 31, 1975 and 1976, based on the information listed. In addition, (a) show the increase or decrease of each item, using 1975 as the base year, and (b) show the percent of increase or decrease in net sales, gross profit, and net income.

	1976	1975
Net sales	$130,000	$116,000
Beg. Inventory	$ 56,000	$ 53,000
Final Inventory	$ 51,000	$ 56,000
Purchases	$ 87,000	$ 79,000
Operating Expenses	$ 14,000	$ 17,000

The comparative income statement is shown below:

NELSON'S CYCLE SHOP - COMPARATIVE INCOME STATEMENT				
	1976	1975	INCREASE (DECREASE)	% INCREASE (DECREASE)
Net sales	$130,000	$116,000	$14,000	12.1%
Beginning Inventory-Jan.1	$ 56,000	$ 53,000	$ 3,000	
Purchases	$ 87,000	$ 79,000	$ 8,000	
Final Inventory Dec. 31	$ 51,000	$ 56,000	($5,000)	
Cost of Goods Sold	$ 92,000	$ 76,000	$16,000	
Gross profit	$ 38,000	$ 40,000	($2,000)	(5.0%)
Operating Expenses	$ 14,000	$ 17,000	($3,000)	
Net income	$ 24,000	$ 23,000	$1,000	4.3%

Solution: In preparing the comparative income statement for Nelson's, we will be computing the differences between income and expenses for the years 1975 and 1976 to arrive at net incomes, and then comparing the results between the two years. The cost of goods sold is the sum of the purchases and the beginning inventory, less the ending (final) inventory. The gross profit is the difference between net sales and cost of goods sold, and the net income is the difference between gross profit and operating expenses. The increase or decrease of each item, using 1975 as a base year is simply the difference between the 1976 and 1975 values for that item. The % of increase or decrease for any item is the difference between the 1976 and 1975 values,expressed as a ratio to the 1975 value.

• PROBLEM 17-15

Prepare the end of year income statement for the Johnson Corporation given the information below.

General and administrative expenses	$54,000
Federal income tax	15,040
Federal income tax on investment income	68,900
Depreciation on plant and equipment	26,900
Merchandise inventory, Jan. 1, 1976	125,000
Merchandise inventory, Dec 31, 1976	99,000
Sales discount	3,545
Net income of minority interest	12,050
Extraordinary gains	82,000
Extraordinary losses	13,950
Purchases	308,120
Non-operating income	12,700
Selling expenses	98,000
Gross sales	595,000

35,000 common shares outstanding.

Solution: First, find the cost of goods sold. The total merchandise handled during the year is 125,000 (inventory at Jan 1, 1976) plus 308,120 (the purchases made during the year).

Total merchandise	$433,120
less merchandise inventory Dec 31, 1976	99,000
Cost of goods sold	$334,120.

Johnson Corporation

Income Statement for the year ended Dec 31, 1976.

Gross sales	$595,000
less sales discount	3,545
Net sales	591,455

Cost of goods sold		334,120
Gross profit		257,335
Selling expenses	$98,000	
Administrative expenses	54,000	
Depreciation on plant, equipment	26,900	178,900
Net operating income		78,435
Non operating income		12,700
Extraordinary gains, losses-net gain		68,050
Net income of minority interests		12,050
Net income before federal taxes		171,235

Federal income taxes:

current	15,040	
deferred................	53,860	68,900
Net income		102,335
Earnings per share		$2.92

The "Extraordinary gain,losses" figure of $68,050 is obtained by subtracting the "Extraordinary losses" from the "Extraordinary gains". Extraordinary gains and losses are changes in number of valuables owned, caused by unusual or unpredictable events. An example of an extraordinary loss would be the destruction of a factory by an earthquake. The total tax paid based on the amount reported in the income statement is 68,900, for tax purposes, $15,040 of this was paid and the rest was deferred.

• PROBLEM 17-16

Company X desires to acquire either Company A or Company B, but not both. The following data is available and covers last year's operation.

	Company A	Company B
Total Assets	$1,000,000	$2,000,000
Sales	3,000,000	5,000,000
Gross profit	300,000	750,000
Net income	96,000	272,000

Which company should Company X acquire if the following conditions are present?

(a) X has a strong administration but weak sales.

(b) X has a strong sales force but a weak administration.

(c) X is looking for short-term improvement in its profits.

Solution: Somehow we must obtain a ratio from the data given which indicates the firms's respective efficiency in obtaining sales and carrying out its administrative duties.

(a) The earning power ratio, defined as

$$\frac{\text{Sales}}{\text{Total Assets}}$$

gives a rough idea of how many dollars in sales are obtained from every dollar of asset. The higher ratio in an inter-firm comparison indicates better marketing.

	Company A	Company B
Earning power	$\frac{\$3,000,000}{\$1,000,000} = 3.00$	$\frac{5,000,000}{2,000,000} = 2.50$

For every dollar of asset, Company A has acquired 3 dollars of sales, whereas Company B has only acquired $2.50. A's sales seem to be stronger than B's, therefore A should be acquired. Company X should look at the earning power ratio over a period of say, 10 years for both companies and decide which company overall has the highest earning power ratio.

(b) A measure of administrative performance is the net earning power ratio defined as

$$\frac{\text{Net income}}{\text{Total Assets}}$$

	Company A	Company B
Net earning power	$\frac{\$96,000}{\$1,000,000} = 0.096$	$\frac{272,000}{2,000,000} = 0.137$

For every dollar in assets Company A earned 9.6 cents. For every dollar in assets Company B earned 13.7 cents. We can say that A's lower earning power is due to higher administrative expenses than B and therefore A has a less efficient administration than B. The reason is that gross profit minus administrative expenses and taxes gives you the net income figure. Assuming that taxes are negligible when compared to administrative expenses, Company B does seem to have a more efficient administration, i.e., its administrative expenses are less than A. As before, comparison over a number of years is best.

(c) The gross earning power ratio defined as

$$\frac{\text{Gross Profit}}{\text{Total Assets}}$$

indicates a firm's ability to generate profits with its given assets.

	Company A	Company B
gross earning power	$\frac{300,000}{1,000,000} = 0.30$	$\frac{750,000}{2,000,000} = 0.375$

For every dollar of assets Company A obtained 30 cents of gross profit. Company B got 37.5 cents and is therefore more desirable than A for short-term profit improvements.

CHAPTER 18

INVENTORY

METHODS OF VALUATION

• **PROBLEM** 18-1

Maxwell's Gift Shoppe computes its inventory at selling price, which represents a 37½ % markon over cost. If the value of the inventory as of December 31 was $5954, what was the value of the inventory at cost?

Solution: Since Maxwell's values its inventory at selling price, which is 37½ % (= .375) higher than cost, the amount of $5954 on December 31 represents 100% of the cost plus 37½ % of the cost, or 137½ % of the cost. Thus, $5954 is 1.375 times the actual cost of the merchandise. We can therefore find the actual cost of the merchandise by dividing $5954 by 1.375. Doing so we obtain an approximate cost of inventory (to the nearest cent) of

$$\frac{\$5954}{1.375} = \$4,330.18.$$

• **PROBLEM** 18-2

The Alfors Company had a beginning inventory of $30,000, Jan 1, 1974. During the year, purchases amounted to $87,500, net sales to $102,000. Assuming that the gross profit rate is 40% of the net sales, what is the ending inventory using the gross profit method of inventory evaluation?

Solution: The key to this method is the equation, gross profits = sales - cost of goods sold. Given that we know the sales and the gross profits, we can solve for the cost of goods sold and then use the equation, end of year inventory = total inventory - cost of goods sold.

Gross profits = 40% of sales = .40 × $102,000 = $40,800

Cost of goods sold = $102,000 - $40,800 = $61,200

Total inventory = $30,000 + $87,500 = $117,500

End of year inventory = $117,500 - $61,200 = $56,300.

• PROBLEM 18-3

Firestone's Clothing Store had an August 1 inventory of $2,300. During August, new merchandise purchases totaled $1,125,and sales were $3,485. If the margin on sales was 18%, estimate the final inventory on August 31.

Solution: Since Firestone's has an 18% margin on sales, 18% (= .18) of the $3,485 represents profit. The profit on the August sales was then .18 × $3,485 = $627.30. This means that the actual cost (to Firestone's) of the goods sold in August was $3,485 - $627.30 = $2,857.70. We can now estimate the final inventory on August 31 by the formula:

Final Inventory = Beginning Inventory + Purchases - Cost of Goods Sold.

Substituting a beginning inventory of $2,300, purchases of $1,125, and cost of goods sold of $2,857.70, we get

Final Inventory = $2,300 + $1,125 - $2,857.70 = $567.30.

• PROBLEM 18-4

Nelson's Cycle Shop had a January 1 inventory of $30,156. During the month, new merchandise purchases totaled $28,300, and sales totaled $72,600. If the margin on sales was 45%, estimate the final inventory.

Solution: Since Nelson's has a 45% margin on sales, 45% (= .45) of the $72,600 in sales represents profit. The profit on sales was therefore

$72,600 × .45 = $32,670.

This means that the actual cost of goods sold was $72,600 - $32,670 = $39,930. We can now estimate the final inventory via the formula:

Final Inventory = Beginning Inventory + Purchases - Cost of Goods Sold.

Substituting a beginning inventory of \$30,156, purchases of \$28,300, and a cost of goods sold of \$39,930, we get:

Final Inventory = \$30,156 + \$28,300 - \$39,930 = \$18,526.

• PROBLEM 18-5

The Motor-Cade Auto Supply Company is taking inventory for the quarter ending June 30. It discovers that it has 150 cans of Q-56 motor oil on hand. Records reveal the following information:

	Quantity	Cost per Can
Inventory, April 1	130	\$.36
Purchase, April 15	100	\$.365
Purchase, May 23	180	\$.40
Purchase, June 29	120	\$.425

Find the value of this item in their inventory, using the average cost method.

Solution: In order to find the value of the 150 cans of motor oil, we must first calculate the average cost per can. We can find this value by taking the ratio of the total purchase price to the total number of units.

The total purchase price is the sum of the cost of each of the purchases, which is quantity purchased times cost per can purchased. The total purchase price is then

$$130 \times \$.36 + 100 \times \$.365 + 180 \times \$.40 + 120 \times \$.425 = \$46.80 + \$36.50 + \$72.00 + \$51.00 = \$206.30.$$

The total quantity is 130 + 100 + 180 + 120 = 530 cans.

The average cost per can is then

$$\frac{\$206.30}{530} = \$.389,$$

so the value of the 150 cans is

$$150 \times \$.389 = \$58.35.$$

• PROBLEM 18-6

The Motorolla Electronics Company, in taking inventory, discovers that it has 30 widgets on hand. Company records reveal the following:

	Quantity	Cost Per Unit
Inventory, Dec. 2	6	$2.30
Purchase, Jan. 15	352	$2.50
Purchase, Feb. 4	101	$2.20
Purchase, Feb. 14	645	$2.00

Find the value of the 30 widgets using the average cost method.

<u>Solution:</u> In order to use the average cost method, we will need to know the total number of widgets purchased during the year, as well as their total cost. The total number purchased was 6 + 352 + 101 + 645 = 1104. We can calculate the total cost by adding together the cost for each purchase, which is quantity times cost per unit. Doing so, we obtain

$$\text{Total Cost} = 6 \times \$2.30 + 352 \times \$2.50 + 101 \times \$2.20 + 645 \times \$2.00 = \$13.80 + \$880 + 222.20 + \$1,290 = \$2,406.$$

The average cost per widget is then total cost divided by total number, which is

$$\frac{\$2,406}{1,104} = \$2.18.$$

The value of the 30 widgets, at $2.18 each, is

$$\$2.18 \times 30 = \$65.40.$$

• PROBLEM 18-7

Given the following units purchased and the cost per unit, find the end of year inventory using weighted averages.

	No. of Units	Cost per Unit
Beginning inventory	2,300	$5.00
First purchase	1,500	5.20
Second purchase	3,400	5.20
Third purchase	3,000	5.20
Fourth purchase	2,500	5.10
Fifth purchase	2,400	5.15
Available for sale	15,100	

Available for sale	15,100
Units sold	12,300
Units left in inventory	2,800

Solution: The average cost per unit for the fifth purchase multiplied by the units left, 2,800 to get the end of year inventory figure. At each step of the calculations, we divide the cumulative total cost of the inventory by the cumulative number of units in inventory to get the average cost per unit. The results are displayed in the table below

	Total number in inventory	Total cost	Average price per unit
Beginning inventory	2,300	$11,500	$5.00
First purchase	3,800	19,300	5.08
Second purchase	7,200	36,980	5.14
Third purchase	10,200	52,580	5.15
Fourth purchase	12,700	65,330	5.14
Fifth purchase	15,100	77,690	5.15

Column 3 is obtained by dividing the second column by the first.

The second entry in the first column, 3,800, is 2,300 (beginning inventory) + 1,500 (first purchase); continuing, the third entry in column 1 is, (beginning inventory) + (first purchase) + (second purchase). The second entry in the second column, $19,300 is, $11,500 (i.e. cost of beginning inventory) + (1,500)($5.20)(i.e., total cost of second purchase). The third entry in column 2, 36,980 is (cost of beginning inventory) + (cost of first purchase) + (cost of second purchase).
The final average price per unit is $5.15.

There are 2,800 units so that the end of year inventory is

$$2{,}800 \times \$5.15 = \$14{,}420.$$

• **PROBLEM** 18-8

The Motorolla Electronics Company is taking inventory. It discovers that it has 30 widgets on hand. Records reveal the following information:

	Quantity	Cost Per Unit
Inventory, Dec. 2	6	$2.30
Purchase, Jan. 15	352	$2.50
Purchase, Feb. 4	101	$2.20
Purchase, Feb. 14	645	$2.00

Find the value of widgets in their inventory using the FIFO method of inventory.

Solution: Under the FIFO (First In, First Out) method it is assumed that the merchandise purchased first is the first to be sold. Therefore, the merchandise on hand at the end of the period is assumed to have been purchased last. The cost of each of the remaining 30 widgets under the FIFO method would therefore be $2.00, so the value of the remaining 30 widget is

$$30 \times \$2.00 = \$60.00 \ .$$

• PROBLEM 18-9

The Motorolla Electronics Company, in taking inventory, discovers that it has 30 widgets on hand. Company records reveal the following information:

	Quantity	Cost Per Unit
Inventory, Dec 2.	6	$2.30
Purchase, Jan 15.	352	$2.50
Purchase, Feb 4.	101	$2.20
Purchase, Feb 14.	645	$2.00

Find the value of the widgets in their inventory under the LIFO method.

Solution: Under the LIFO (Last In, First Out) method it is assumed that the merchandise bought last is sold first. This means that the merchandise on hand at the end of an inventory period is assumed to have been bought first. This means that the remaining 30 widgets are assumed to be the 6 from Dec. 2, along with 24 from the Jan. 15 purchase. Since the 6 Dec. 2 widgets were purchased at $2.30 each and the 24 Jan. 15 widgets were purchased at $2.50 each, the value of the remaining 30 widgets would be

$$\$2.30 \times 6 \ + \ \$2.50 \times 24 = \$13.80 + \$60 = \$73.80.$$

The Morbius Corporation adopted dollar-value LIFO in 1970. Using 1966 as the base year, the price level indexes for each year from 1966 to 1970 are shown below along with the inventory at year end prices.

	Inventory at Year-End Prices	Price Level Index
1966	$126,000	100%
1967	143,000	110%
1968	155,250	115%
1969	165,000	125%
1970	174,000	120%

Compute the dollar-value LIFO cost of inventory held at the end of 1970.

Solution: We first convert the values of inventory given each year to base level prices by dividing the values by the price level index corresponding to each year:

	Inventory		Index		Base-Year Value
1966	$126,000	÷	100%	=	$126,000
1967	143,000	÷	110%	=	130,000
1968	155,250	÷	115%	=	135,000
1969	165,000	÷	125%	=	132,000
1970	174,000	÷	120%	=	145,000

The real changes in inventory that have taken place are as follows:

	Base-Year Value	
1966	$126,000	
		130,000 - 126,000 = 4,000
1967	130,000	
		135,000 - 130,000 = 5,000
1968	135,000	
		132,000 - 135,000 =-3,000
1969	132,000	
		145,000 - 132,000 =13,000
1970	145,000	

These changes must be reconverted to their values of the years in which they occurred by multiplying them by the corresponding index. This is not done for the 1968 - 1969 decrease. We say instead that in 1968 there took place a net increase of $5,000 - $3,000 = $2,000 and use the price index for 1968 to reconvert. Adding all the reconverted changes and the base-year value of inventory, in this case $126,000, gives us the dollar-value LIFO cost of the inventory for 1970.

Making the changes:

$4,000	× 110%	=	$4,400
$2,000	× 115%	=	$2,300
$13,000	× 120%	=	$15,600
			$22,300

plus

$126,000
$148,300

This is the dollar-value LIFO cost of inventory at the end of 1970.

• PROBLEM 18-11

The Cool Hand Luke Corporation adopted the dollar-value LIFO method of inventory evaluation. The price indices were computed using 1969 as the base year. The end of year inventory for each year and the price-level indices are:

	Inventory at Year-End Prices	Price-Level Index
Dec. 31, 1969	$16,400	100%
Dec. 31, 1970	$16,200	96
Dec. 31, 1971	$20,900	104
Dec. 31, 1972	$26,400	110
Dec. 31, 1973	$24,035	115
Dec. 31, 1974	$26,568	108

Change the current ending inventory cost for 1974 to dollar-value LIFO cost.

Solution: Using the dollar-value LIFO method does away with the usual specific identification of batches and batch prices. The year-end inventory prices are adjusted back to the base year value using the indices and the changes in inventory from one year to the next are then readjusted and added to obtain the actual LIFO cost at the end of the current year. To get the figure for the inventory at base-year prices, divide the inventory at year end prices by the decimal equivalent of the indices; e.g., in 1970 the inventory at year end prices is $16,200 and the price-level index is 96% so that the inventory in base year prices is

$$\frac{\$16,200}{0.96} = \$16,875.$$

This represents a real increase in inventory of

$$\$16,875 - \$16,400 = \$475,$$

between 1969 and 1970. The other figures for inventory at base-year prices and the corresponding annual changes are shown below:

	Inventory at base-year prices	Change in inventory
1969	$16,400	
1970	16,875	475
1971	20,096	3221
1972	24,000	3904
1973	20,900	(3100)
1974	24,600	3700

The way to handle the decrease in 1973 is to say that there was a net increase in 1973 of 3904 - 3100 = 804. All these real changes are converted to current prices by multiplying them by the index corresponding to the year the net real change took place. Add up all the net increases to obtain the current dollar-value LIFO cost.

1969:	$16,400 ×	100%	=	$16,400
1970:	475 ×	96%	=	456
1971:	3,221 ×	104%	=	3,350
1972:	804 ×	110%	=	884
1974:	3,700 ×	108%	=	3,996
				$25,086

The current dollar-value LIFO cost of inventory is $25,086.

• PROBLEM 18-12

The Magic-Voice Radio Supply Company is taking inventory at the end of the year. One of the items on stock is their #84A tube. Records for these tubes show the following:

	Quantity	Cost per Tube
Inventory, January 1	800	$.252
Purchase of March 3	2,000	$.247

Purchase of June 5	1,500	$.262
Purchase of October 13	900	$.27
Purchase of November 25	600	$.272

If the quantity of these tubes on hand is 1,700, what would be the value of the inventory using each of the following methods?
a. Average Cost
b. FIFO
c. LIFO

Solution: a. The average cost per tube is the total cost of the tubes divided by the total number of tubes. The total cost is the sum of each of the purchases, which is quantity times cost per tube. The total cost is then

$$800 \times \$.252 + 2,000 \times \$.247 + \$1,500 \times \$.262 + 900 \times \$.27 + 600 \times \$.272 = \$201.60 + \$494 + \$393 + \$243 + \$163.20 = \$1,494.80.$$

The total quantity is

$$800 + 2,000 + 1,500 + 900 + 600 = 5,800.$$

The average cost per tube is then

$$\frac{\$1,494.80}{5,800} = \$.258.$$

The value of the 1,700 tubes, under the average cost method, is therefore

$$1,700 \times \$.258 = \$438.60 .$$

b. Under the FIFO method, the 1,700 tubes remaining are assumed to come from the latest purchases. This means that they include the 600 tubes purchased at $.272, the 900 tubes purchased at $.27 and 200 of the tubes purchased at $.262. Their value under FIFO is therefore

$$600 \times \$.272 + 900 \times \$.27 + 200 \times \$.262 = \$163.20 + \$243 + \$52.40 = \$458.60.$$

c. Under the LIFO method, the 1,700 tubes remaining are assumed to come from the earliest purchases. This means that they include 800 tubes purchased at $.252 and 900 of the tubes purchased at $.247. Their value under LIFO is therefore

$$800 \times \$.252 + 900 \times \$.247 = \$201.60 + \$222.30 = \$423.90 .$$

• PROBLEM 18-13

Using the inventory data shown below, find the (i) FIFO cost of ending inventory (ii) LIFO cost of the ending inventory.

	Units	Cost per Unit
Beginning inventory	10,000	$2.30
First purchase	24,500	2.10
Second purchase	30,000	2.00
Third purchase	9,000	2.50
Fourth purchase	14,000	2.50
Available for sale	87,500	
Units sold	80,000	
Units in ending inventory	7,500	

Solution: (i) We consider, as is the practice of the FIFO system, the 80,000 units that were sold as having been the first 80,000 purchased. Therefore the 7,500 units left in inventory belong to the fourth and last purchase layer that originally had 14,000 units priced at $2.50 each .

The FIFO cost of inventory is

$$7,500 \times \$2.50 = \$18,750.$$

(ii) With LIFO, just the reverse is true - the 7,500 units left in inventory belong to the beginning inventory layer that originally had 10,000 units in it priced at $2.30 per unit.

The LIFO cost of inventory is

$$\$7,500 \times \$2.30 = \$17,250.$$

• PROBLEM 18-14

Pinson's Wholesale Hardware Company is taking a year-end inventory of all merchandise on hand. Among the items to be counted are steel bolts. There are 44,000 of these bolts on hand by actual count on December 31. The purchase and inventory records reveal the following information:

	Quantity	Cost per M
January 1 (beginning inventory)	27,000	$6.00
March 12 purchase	50,000	$6.50

September 11 purchase	35,000	\$7.00
December 3 purchase	40,000	\$7.50

Find the value of the December 31 inventory by (a) the average cost method, (b) the FIFO method, and (c) the LIFO method.

Solution: (a) The average cost per bolt is the total cost of the bolts divided by the total number of bolts. The total cost is the sum of each of the purchases, which is the number of thousands of bolts purchased times the cost per thousand. The total cost is therefore

$$\$6.00 \times 27 + \$6.50 \times 50 + \$7.00 \times 35 + \$7.50 \times 40 = \$162.00 + \$325.00 + \$245.00 + \$300.00 = \$1{,}032.00.$$

The total quantity is

$$27{,}000 + 50{,}000 + 35{,}000 + 40{,}000 = 152{,}000.$$

The average cost per thousand bolts is then

$$\frac{\$1{,}032}{152} = \$6.79,$$

so the value of the remaining 44,000 bolts is

$$44 \times \$6.79 = \$298.76.$$

(b) Under the FIFO method, the 44,000 bolts remaining are assumed to come from the latest purchases. This means that they include the 40,000 bolts purchased at \$7.50 per thousand and 4,000 of the bolts purchased at \$7.00 per thousand. Their value under FIFO is therefore

$$40 \times \$7.50 + 4 \times \$7.00 = \$300 + \$28 = \$328.$$

(c) Under the LIFO method the 44,000 bolts remaining are assumed to come from the earliest purchases. This means that they include 27,000 of the bolts purchased at \$6.00 per thousand and 17,000 of the bolts purchased at \$6.50 per thousand. Their value under LIFO is therefore

$$27 \times \$6.00 + 17 \times \$6.50 = \$162.00 + \$110.50 = \$272.50.$$

• PROBLEM 18-15

The Bears Company had the following inventory data for 19X8.

	Units	Cost per Unit
Beginning inventory	10	\$8.00
First purchase	7	9.00

Second purchase	5	9.00
Third purchase	8	11.00
Fourth purchase	4	10.00
Fifth purchase	10	12.00
Sixth purchase	6	12.50
Units sold	34	

What is the ending inventory using:
(a) weighted average?
(b) LIFO?
(c) FIFO?

Solution: (a) For a weighted average make a table showing the cumulative changes in the inventory units and the total inventory costs. Then after each purchase, divide the total cost of inventory to date by the total number of units in inventory to get the unit average price. After all the purchases have been entered, the ending inventory is obtained by multiplying the number of units left in inventory by the last unit average price.

For example, after the first purchase, the total number of units in inventory is 10 + 7 = 17 since we had 10 units in the beginning. The cost of these 7 added units is 7 × \$9.00 = \$63, i.e., the number of units times the unit price. The total cost of the inventory is now 80 + 63 = \$143 since we had 80 dollars worth to start with. Now the unit average price is

$$\frac{\$143}{17 \text{ units}} = \$8.41 \text{ per unit.}$$

The same procedure follows with the other purchases.

	1 Units	2 Cost per unit	3 Commulative inventory	4 Cost of inventory	5 Units Average Price
Beginning inventory	10	\$ 8.00	10	\$ 80	\$ 8.00
First Purchase	7	9.00	17	143	8.41
Second Purchase	5	9.00	22	189	8.59
Third Purchase	8	11.00	30	277	9.23
Fourth Purchase	4	10.00	34	317	9.32
Fifth Purchase	10	12.00	44	437	9.93
Sixth Purchase	6	12.50	50	512	10.24

Column 5 is obtained by dividing column 4 by column 3.

Since 34 units were sold and there was a total of 50 in inventory, there are 16 units left whose average unit price is $10.24 (last entry in column 5.) The ending inventory using weighted average is

$$16 \times \$10.24 = \$163.84.$$

(b) If there are 16 units left in inventory, using LIFO, these units are found in the beginning inventory layer (10 there) and in the first purchase layer (6 there). This is true since, with LIFO, we establish that the first items to be sold have been the last ones to be purchased by the business and the items remaining are the oldest held in the inventory. In counting which items have been sold, we start with the sixth purchase and work our way back until we come to the 16 units that were not sold.

LIFO value of ending inventory is

10 units @ $8.00 per unit = $80

plus

6 units @ $9.00 per unit = $54

$134

(c) Similarly for FIFO, the 16 units that remain are in the sixth purchase layer (6 there) and in the fifth purchase layer (10 there) instead of the bottom layers as before.

FIFO value of ending inventory is

10 units @ $12.00 per unit = $120

plus

6 units @ $12.50 per unit = $ 75

$195

• PROBLEM 18-16

Corporation Y had the following merchandise transactions in 1977.

	Units	Unit Cost
Beginning inventory	600	$5
February 4 purchase	400	6
July 12 purchase	500	7
August 10 purchase	300	8
November 21 purchase	600	4

Sales

January 15 sale 500

July 15 sale 600

September 15 sale 500

Find the ending inventory for December 31, 1977

(a) Using FIFO system:

(i) Periodic

(ii) Perpetual

(b) Using LIFO policy:

(i) Periodic

(ii) Perpetual

Solution: (a) FIFO

(i) Periodic

Under this method we first add all the sales that took place. Then we take out the costs from the first layers beginning with the 600 units, $5 a unit layer. Each layer must be exhausted before going on to the next one.

Total number of units sold 1,600

Of the 1,600,

600 were sold @ $5 per unit(layer 1) = $3,000

400 were sold @ $6 per unit(layer 2) = 2,400

500 were sold @ $7 per unit(layer 3) = 3,500

100 were sold @ $8 per unit (layer 4) = 800

Cost of goods sold $9,700

To find the total inventory in 1977, add all the purchases.

600 units @ $5 per unit = $3,000

400 units @ $6 per unit = 2,400

500 units @ $7 per unit = 3,500

300 units @ $8 per unit = 2,400

600 units @ $4 per unit = 2,400

Total inventory in 1977 13,700

Less cost of goods sold 9,700

ending inventory 4,000

(ii) Perpetual

Using this method, take out the costs immediately after the date of sale. For the January 15 sale, the 500 units sold are taken out of the first layer (600 units) which leaves us with 100-layer 1 units.

Jan 15: 500 units @ $5 per unit = $2,500

For the July 15 sale, 600 units were sold. One hundred layer 1 units remain, so we take this out:

100 units @ $5 per unit = 500.

There are 500 units left and we must go to the other layers. Layer 2 ($6 per unit) has 400 units which we eliminate:

400 units @ $6 per unit = $2,400.

There are now 100 units remaining in the July 15 sale lot to take care of. We go to the third layer ($7 per unit) because the first two have been exhausted:

100 units @ $7 per unit = $700

The breakdown for the July 15 sale is:

100 units @ $5 per unit =	$500
400 units @ $6 per unit =	2,400
100 units @ $7 per unit =	700
Total cost of July 15 sale lot	3,600

For September 15, the breakdown is

400 units @ $7 per unit =	$2,800
100 units @ $8 per unit =	800
	3,600

Adding all the separate costs, we get that the cost of goods sold is

$2,500 + $3,600 + $3,600 = $9,700

which is the same as before. And the ending inventory is $4,000.

(b) LIFO

(i) Periodic

This is similar to FIFO periodic except that now we begin to take the costs out of the last layer first keeping in mind that 1,600 units were sold.

600 units sold	@ $4 per unit (layer 5)	=	$2,400
300 units sold	@ $8 per unit (layer 4)	=	2,400
500 units sold	@ $7 per unit (layer 3)	=	3,500
200 units	@ $6 per unit	=	1,200
1600			9,500

The cost of goods sold is 9,500 and the end of year inventory is 13,700 - 9,500 = $4,200

(ii) Perpetual

We begin to find the costs soon after the purchase is completed. For the January 15 sale, 500 units were sold and there were 600 units in layer 1 ($5 unit cost) se we take 500 units from this layer

Jan 15 500 units @ $5 per unit = $2,500

By July 15 the inventory has the following composition

	Units	Unit Cost
Beginning inventory	100	$5
February 4 purchase	400	$6
July 12 purchase	500	$7

Six hundred units were sold July 15, therefore we take 500 of these from layer 3 ($7 unit cost) and the remaining 100 from layer 2 ($6 unit cost).

July 15 500 units @ $7 per unit = $3,500

100 units @ $6 per unit = 600

cost of goods sold July 15 . . . . $4,100

By the September 15 sale, the inventory composition is

	Unit	Unit Costs
Beginning inventory	100	$5
February 4 purchase	300	$6
August 10 purchase	300	$8

Five hundred units were sold September 15;

take 300 from the $8 unit cost layer and the remaining 200 from the $6 unit cost layer:

300 units @ $8 per unit = $2,400

200 units @ $6 per unit = 1,200

cost of goods sold September 15.. 3,600

The total cost of goods sold is

$2,500 + $4,100 + $3,600 = $10,200

And the end of year inventory is

$13,700 - $10,200 = $3,500 using this policy.

Note that whatever policy we may be talking about, it has nothing whatsoever to do with the actual physical movement of goods, in other words, we assume that the goods are homogeneous. Management does not set aside a specific location for "layer 1 goods" depending on the time the lot was obtained.

Under the FIFO system the dollar value for ending inventory will be the same whether we use perpetual inventory or periodic inventory. In either case one purchase layer must be exhausted, before the next is used. Therefore the items will be distributed among the layers in the same way in both methods and so will be priced the same way.

• PROBLEM 18-17

Company A's inventory transactions in 19X7 were as follows.

Jan. 1 Beginning inventory: 18,000 units @ $2.00 per unit.

Jan. 20 Sale: 15,000 units @ $5.00 per unit.

April 15 Purchase: 30,000 units @ $2.05 per unit.

May 27 Sale: 25,000 units @ $5.10 per unit.

July 16 Purchase: 20,000 units @ $2.10 per unit.

Oct. 1 Sale: 15,000 units @ $5.15 per unit.

Nov. 14 Purchase: 10,000 units @ $2.10 per unit.

Dec. 2 Sale: 18,000 units @ $5.20 per unit.

(a) Find the cost of goods sold and the gross profit made in 19X7 if FIFO was used on a perpetual inventory basis.

(b) The same as (a) but use the LIFO system

Solution: (a) FIFO

Under FIFO inventory evaluation, the first costs entered are the first taken out. For this problem we have three distinct batches according to whether the units were originally purchased for $2.00 per unit, $2.05 or $2.10. The three batches are shown below along with their corresponding increases (purchases) and decrease (sales), where a decrease is indicated by parenthesis.

	[$2.00]	[$2.05]	[$2.10]
Batch	I	II	III
Jan. 1	18,000		
Jan. 20	(15,000)		
April 15		30,000	
May 27	(3,000)	(22,000)	
July 16			20,000

Oct. 1		(8,000)	(7,000)
Nov. 14			10,000
Dec. 2			(18,000)
	0	0	5,000

Now to get the total cost of goods sold for 19X7, multiply the number of units sold by their respective prices and add.

FIFO cost of goods sold $150,000

15,000 @ $2.00 per unit	=	$30,000
3,000 @ 2.00 per unit	=	6,000
22,000 @ 2.05 per unit	=	45,100
8,000 @ 2.05 per unit	=	16,400
7,000 @ 2.10 per unit	=	14,700
18,000 @ 2.10 per unit	=	37,800
73,000		$150,000

The gross annual profit is obtained by subtracting the cost of goods sold from the total revenue.

Jan. 20	Sale: 15,000 units @ $5.00 per unit =	$75,000
May. 17	Sale: 25,000 units @ $5.10 per unit =	127,500
Oct. 1	Sale: 15,000 units @ $5.15 per unit =	77,250
Dec. 1	Sale: 18,000 units @ $5.20 per unit =	93,600

Total revenue in 19X7 . . . . $373,350

less cost of goods sold 150,000

gross profit for 19X7 $223,350

(b) LIFO

The last costs entered are the first to be taken out. Use the same format as before to note the transactions.

	[$2.00]	[$2.05]	[$2.10]
Batch	I	II	III
Jan. 1	18,000		
Jan. 20	(15,000)		
April 15		30,000	
May. 27		(25,000)	
July 16			20,000

Oct. 1			(15,000)
Nov. 14			10,000
Dec. 2		(3,000)	(15,000)
	3,000	2,000	0

LIFO cost of goods sold $150,400

OPEN-TO-BUY AND STOCKTURN RATE

• **PROBLEM** 18-18

Edward's Electronics had a March 1 inventory of $42,000, with a planned inventory of $36,000 for March 31. The store plans sales for the month of $22,000, with an additional $2,000 in planned markdowns. The store already has a $6,000 commitment to purchase inventory during the month. What is the store's open-to-buy?

Solution: Edward's Electronics open-to-buy will be the difference between the amount of merchandise the store needs for the month and the amount of merchandise that is presently available. Since the store has planned sales of $22,000, with an additional $2,000 in planned markdowns, and desires an end-of-month inventory of $36,000, the amount of merchandise required is

$22,000 + $2,000 + $36,000 = $60,000.

The store presently has $42,000 in inventory, with commitments for an additional $6,000, so the total amount of inventory available is

$42,000 + $6,000 = $48,000.

The store's open-to-buy for the month is therefore

$60,000 - $48,000 = $12,000.

• **PROBLEM** 18-19

On January 17, the shirt buyer for Wellington's Department Store decided to determine his open-to-buy. The following figures were available:

Present inventory at retail (Jan 17)	$12,000
Inventory commitments (Jan 17)	3,000
Planned end-of-month inventory (Jan 31)	15,000

Planned sales	6,000
Actual sales	3,000
Planned markdowns	500
Actual markdowns	200

What is the buyer's open-to-buy?

Solution: The shirt buyer's open-to-buy will be the difference between the amount of merchandise he needs for the month and the amount of merchandise that he presently has available.

Since he has planned sales for the month of \$6,000 and has thus far only \$3,000 in sales, he will require an additional

$$\$6,000 - \$3,000 = \$3,000$$

in merchandise to cover the balance of his planned sales. Similarly, he has \$500 in planned markdowns and has thus far only \$200 in markdowns, so he will require an additional \$500 - \$200 = \$300 in merchandise for markdowns. He also has a planned end-of-month inventory of \$15,000, so the total amount of merchandise that he needs for the month is

$$\$3,000 + \$300 + \$15,000 = \$18,300.$$

He presently has \$12,000 worth of inventory, with commitments for an additional \$3,000, so the total amount of merchandise that he has available is

$$\$12,000 + \$3,000 = \$15,000.$$

His open-to-buy is therefore

$$\$18,300 - \$15,000 = \$3,300.$$

• **PROBLEM 18-20**

Describe a procedure that can be used to determine inventory turnover rate.

Solution: The inventory turnover rate is a measure of the number of times an average inventory is sold during an accounting period. The turnover rate is considered a test of merchandising efficiency - a high turnover rate is considered a mark of good merchandising. Also, from a working capital point of view, a company with a high turnover rate requires a smaller investment in inventory than one producing the same sales with a lower turnover.

During a given period, the cost of goods sold represents the minimum total inventory used to produce the goods. The inventory turnover rate can be calculated by dividing this cost of goods sold by the average inventory.

• PROBLEM 18-21

The following entries appeared in the ledgers of Kane's Record Store:

Beginning Inventory = \$16,000

Purchases = \$58,000

Ending Inventory = \$14,000

Find the store's rate of inventory turnover.

Solution: The rate of inventory turnover is the ratio of cost of goods sold to average inventory. We can use the formulas:

Cost of Goods Sold = Beginning Inventory + Purchases - Ending Inventory and

$$\text{Average Inventory} = \frac{\text{Beginning Inventory} + \text{Ending Inventory}}{2}$$

to calculate these quantities. Substituting a beginning inventory of \$16,000, purchases of \$58,000 and an ending inventory of \$14,000, we get:

Cost of Goods Sold = \$16,000 + \$58,000 - \$14,000 = \$60,000

and

$$\text{Average Inventory} = \frac{\$16,000 + \$14,000}{2} = \frac{\$30,000}{2} = \$15,000$$

Taking the ratio of the two, we now get an inventory turnover rate of

$$\frac{\$60,000}{\$15,000} = 4 \text{ times.}$$

• PROBLEM 18-22

Find the inventory turnover rate for each of the stores listed below:

Store	Average Inventory	Cost of Goods Sold	Merchandise Turnover Rate
1	\$16,000	\$ 48,000	______
2	\$57,500	\$143,750	______
3	\$83,800	\$653,640	______
4	\$27,840	\$125,280	______
5	\$ 6,740	\$ 75,488	______

Solution: The inventory turnover rate is the ratio of the cost of goods sold to the average inventory. It is calculated by dividing the cost of goods sold by the value of the average inventory. For example, store number 1 has a cost of goods sold of \$48,000 and an average inventory of \$16,000, so its inventory turnover rate is

$$\frac{\$48,000}{\$16,000} = 3.$$

Following the same procedure, the inventory turnover rate for each of the stores listed has been calculated, with the results summarized in the following table:

Store Number	Calculation of Inventory Turnover Rate
1	$\frac{\$48,000}{\$16,000} = 3$
2	$\frac{\$143,750}{\$57,500} = 2.5$
3	$\frac{\$653,640}{\$83,800} = 7.8$
4	$\frac{\$125,280}{\$27,840} = 4.5$
5	$\frac{\$75,488}{\$6,740} = 11.2$

• **PROBLEM 18-23**

A business started last year with an inventory of 90,000 items which cost \$60,000 and had a selling price of \$80,000, At the end of the year, the inventory consisted of 70,000 items which cost \$90,000 and had a selling price of \$120,000. Records indicate that, during the year, 360,000 items were sold which cost \$300,000, with net sales of \$380,000. What are the stockturn rates at cost, selling price, and number of units?

Solution: We can calculate the stockturn rates at cost, selling price, and number of units by applying the formulas:

$$\text{Stockturn Rate (at cost)} = \frac{\text{Cost of Goods Sold}}{\text{Average Cost of Inventory}}$$

$$\text{Stockturn Rate (at selling price)} = \frac{\text{Selling price of goods sold}}{\text{Average Selling Price of Inventory}}$$

$$\text{Stockturn Rate (in units)} = \frac{\text{Number of Units Sold}}{\text{Average Number of Units in Inventory}}$$

Since the cost of inventory at the beginning of the year was \$60,000, and the cost at the end of the year was \$90,000, the average cost of inventory during the year was

$$\frac{\$60,000 + \$90,000}{2} = \$75,000.$$

Similarly, the average selling price was

$$\frac{\$80,000 + \$120,000}{2} = \$100,000,$$

and the average number of units was

$$\frac{90,000 + 70,000}{2} = 80,000.$$

Substituting these values, along with cost of goods sold of \$300,000, selling price of goods sold of \$380,000 and number of goods sold of 360,000, we get:

$$\text{Stockturn Rate (at Cost)} = \frac{\$300,000}{\$75,000} = 4.0$$

$$\text{Stockturn Rate (at selling price)} = \frac{\$380,000}{\$100,000} = 3.8$$

$$\text{Stockturn Rate (in units)} = \frac{360,000}{80,000} = 4.5$$

CHAPTER 19

DEPRECIATION

UNITS OF PRODUCTION/USE METHOD AND STRAIGHT LINE METHOD

• **PROBLEM** 19-1

John's-Rent-A-Truck purchased a van for $4,500. The truck is expected to last 100,000 miles, and then have a trade-in value of $500. What is the cost of depreciation per mile?

Solution: We must first find the total amount it will depreciate. This is found by taking the cost of the van, and subtracting the trade-in value from it. Thus, the truck will depreciate $4,500 (cost) - $500 (trade-in) = $4,000. To find the cost of depreciation per mile we divide the total depreciation by the total mileage, giving $4,000 ÷ 100,000 = $.04 per mile. Thus, the depreciation expense is 4 cents for every mile traveled. If we need to find the depreciation for a certain period of time, we simply multiply the cost of depreciation per mile by the number of miles driven in that time period.

• **PROBLEM** 19-2

On January 1, 1964, Stead and Company purchased a delivery truck for $4,000. It is estimated that the truck will have a useful life of four years, and that at the end of that time it will have a salvage value (resale value) of $400. It is expected that the truck will be used for 72,000 miles. Find the depreciation per year, if the truck was used for 20,000 miles during the first year, 25,000 miles during the second year, 18,000 miles during the third year and 9,000 miles during the fourth year. Use the units of production method for determining depreciation.

Solution: When using the units of production method of computing depreciation, you divide the total amount of depreciation by the total number of units, in order to get the cost of depreciation-per-unit. We then multiply each year's number of units by the depreciation-per-unit to get the depreciation for the year. In our problem the total amount of depreciation is found by subtraction, the residual worth (salvage value) from the cost. Thus the total depreciation is $4000 (cost) - $400 (residual worth) = $3600. To calculate the depreciation-per-mile, we divide the total depreciation by the total miles, giving $3,600 ÷ 72,000 (miles) = $.05 per mile. To calculate the depreciation for each year we multiply the depreciation-per-mile, by the number of miles driven in that year.

Year	Number of Miles	Depreciation
1	20,000	$1,000.00 (20,000 × $.05)
2	25,000	$1,250.00 (25,000 × $.05)
3	18,000	$ 900.00 (18,000 × $.05)
4	9,000	$ 450.00 (9,000 × $.05)
Total	72,000	$3,600.00

• PROBLEM 19-3

An electric sign in Times Square cost $4,500. It has an expected life of 11,250 hours after which it will have a scrap value of $450. What is the depreciation charge for a month in which it was used 478 hours?

Solution: When using the units of production method of computing depreciation, you divide the total amount of depreciation by the total number of units in order to get the cost of depreciation-per-unit. To find the depreciation for some time period, we multiply the cost of depreciation per unit by the number of units produced in the time interval. Thus, we first find the total amount of depreciation. It is equal to the cost less the scrap value, giving $4,500 - $450 = $,4,050. Now the cost per hour of use is found by dividing the total depreciation ($4,050) by the total number of hours (11,250), giving $4,050 ÷ 11,250 = $.36. We can now find the amount of depreciation for the month during which 478 hours were used.

$.36 × 478 (hours) = $172.08.

• PROBLEM 19-4

WQLP radio station just purchased a stereo system for $8,400. It has an estimated life of 6 years and a residual value of $1,200. Due to the fast wear of needles, there is an additional 20% depreciation in the first year. Find the total amount the stereo system depreciated in the first year using the straight-line basis.

Solution: The first thing we must do is compute the 20% additional depreciation. It is 20% of the cost, thus it is 20% × $8,400 = .20 × $8,400 = $1,680. Now we must find the rest of the depreciation. It is equal to the cost less the additional depreciation, and less the residual value. Thus, the amount of depreciation is $8,400 (cost) - $1,680 (additional depreciation) - $1,200 (residual value) = $5,520. We now find the annual depreciation by dividing $5,520 by the number of years (6) over which it will be depreciated.

$5,520	(amount it will depreciate)
÷ 6	(years of useful life)
$ 920	(annual ordinary depreciation)

Thus, the total depreciation for the first year is the annual ordinary depreciation plus the first year's depreciation.

$ 920	(annual depreciation)
$1,680	(additional depreciation)
$2,600	(total first year depreciation).

• PROBLEM 19-5

An automobile that cost $3,000 four years ago is now worth $1,000. What is the average yearly depreciation?

Solution: Depreciation is a decrease in value, therefore we are seeking the average yearly decrease in value. We first must find the amount of change or decrease between the original and present value. This is obtained by subtracting $1,000 from $3,000, which yields $2,000. The average yearly depreciation is the fraction

$$\frac{\text{total decrease in value}}{\text{total number of years}} .$$

Therefore we find that the average yearly depreciation

$$= \frac{\$2,000}{4} = \$500.$$

• PROBLEM 19-6

Mr. Preston brought a new car for $4,500. He used the car for eight years and then sold it for $475. (a) What was the total depreciation? (b) What was the average yearly depreciation?

Solution: (a) The total depreciation can be found by subtracting the selling price from the cost of the car. Thus, the total depreciation is

$4,500 (cost) - $475 (selling price) = $4,025.

(b) The average yearly depreciation can be found by dividing the total depreciation by the number of years. Thus the average yearly depreciation is equal to

$4,025 ÷ 8 (years) = $503.125 or $503.13.

• PROBLEM 19-7

Amazing Realty bought an office building for $13,000,000. It is estimated that the building will last 20 years, and have a salvage value of $1,000,000. What is the annual depreciation allowance by the straight-line method?

Solution: The building cost $13,000,000, and has a salvage value of $1,000,000, thus the building will depreciate $12,000,000 in the twenty years. The straight-line method divides the amount that will be depreciated by the number of years, and that number is the annual depreciation allowance. Thus, the depreciation allowance for the building is $12,000,000 (amount of depreciation) ÷ 20 (number of years) = $600,000.

• PROBLEM 19-8

The Global Bus Company purchases a bus for $40,000, and depreciates it on a straight-line basis for five years. What is the book value of the bus after 2 years of service?

Solution: The bus will depreciate $40,000 in the five years, thus by the straight-line basis, it will depreciate $8,000 a year ($40,000 ÷ 5 = $8,000).

The book value of an object is its cost less the accumulated depreciation. Thus, after 2 years the book value of the bus will be $40,000 - $8,000 (first year's depreciation allowance) - $8,000 (second year's depreciation allowance) = $40,000 - $16,000 = $24,000.

• **PROBLEM 19-9**

Mr. Haines bought a tractor for $2,895.00. The estimated salvage value at the end of the 10 years is $495.00. Use the straight-line method to find the depreciation after the first five years.

Solution: With the straight-line method the depreciation is the same for each year. It is found by dividing the total depreciation by the number of years. The total depreciation is equal to the cost less the salvage value.

$2,895	(cost)
- $ 495	(salvage value)
$2,400	(total depreciation)

Thus, the annual depreciation is the total depreciation ($2,400) divided by the number of years (10), giving

$2,400 ÷ 10 = $240 (a year).

After 5 years the tractor has depreciated by 5 · $240 = $1,200.

• **PROBLEM 19-10**

Joe Troy purchased a chain saw for $1,200 for his lumber mill. The saw will last 6 years and have no residual value. Mr. Troy wishes to use the straight-line method of depreciation. Find the depreciation and book value for the first two years.

Solution: The saw will depreciate $1,200 in a 6-year period. The straight-line method is to take an equal amount of depreciation each year. We divide the total amount of depreciation by the number of years it will take. Here, the depreciation is

$1,200 ÷ 6 (years) = $200

a year. The book value of the saw is the cost less the accumulated depreciation.

$1,200	Cost
- $ 200	Depreciation of first year
$1,000	Book value, end of first year

$ 200	Decpreciation of first year
$ 200	Depreciation of second year
$ 400	Accumulated depreciation

$1,200	Cost
- $ 400	Accumulated depreciation
$ 800	Book value, end of second year.

• PROBLEM 19-11

The Business Education Department of Edison High School bought 24 new typewriters at a cost of $350 each. Assuming that the estimated life of the typewriters is four years, after which they are expected to have a disposal value of $75 each, (a) what is the annual depreciation for each typewriter, using the straight-line method (depreciation)? (b) The monthly depreciation for each? (c) The annual rate of depreciation for each during the first year? (d) The book value of each at the end of the third year?

Solution: (a) The annual depreciation for each typewriter is found by dividing the amount that will be depreciated by the number of years it will last. The amount that will be depreciated is found by subtracting the disposal value from the cost.

	$350	(cost)
-	$ 75	(disposal value)
	$275	(amount that will be lost to depreciation)

Now the annual depreciation is equal to

$275.00 ÷ 4 (years of life) = $68.75.

(b) The montly depreciation is found by dividing the annual depreciation by 12 (the number of months in a year). Thus, the monthly depreciation for each typewriter is:

$68.75 ÷ 12 = $5.73.

(c) The annual rate of depreciation is the percent obtained by dividing the annual depreciation by the cost. Thus, the annual rate of depreciation for the typewriters is $68.75 (annual depreciation) ÷ $350 (cost) = .196 = 19.6% (rounded to the nearest 1/10 of 1%).

(d) The book value can be found by subtracting the accumulated depreciation from the cost. When using the straight-line method, we find the accumulated depreciation by multiplying the annual depreciation by the number of years. Thus, the accumulated depreciation of the typewriters after 3 years is 3 × $68.75 = $206.25. Thus, the book value is $350.00 (cost) - $206.25 (accumulated depreciation) = $143.75.

• PROBLEM 19-12

Tom bought a new bicycle for $80. After 4 years of use, he sold it to a second-hand dealer for $15. What was the annual depreciation by the straight line method? What was the annual rate of depreciation?

Solution: Depreciation is the decrease in value of an asset. An asset is any type of product that will benefit the owner. One of the major causes of depreciation is physical deterioration brought on by wear and age. For the straight line method of calculating depreciation, one assumes the $ amount of depreciation per year is the same every year. Annual Depreciation is equal to the fraction $\frac{\text{total depreciation}}{\text{useful lifespan}}$. Total depreciation is the difference between the original value and the scrap or trade-in value. Trade-in value is the amount of money obtained when the the used object is accepted as partial payment for a new object. Scrap value is the amount of money obtained when used object is sold for scrap. The total depreciation = $80 - $15 = $65. The useful life was 4 years. The annual depreciation = $\frac{\$65}{4 \text{ years}}$ = $16.25 per year. The annual rate of depreciation is the $\frac{\text{annual depreciation}}{\text{cost}}$.

$$\text{The annual rate} = \frac{\$16.25}{\$80} = .203 = 20.3\%.$$

• PROBLEM 19-13

Find the annual rate of depreciation of each asset. Round off each amount to the nearest tenth of a percent.

Asset	Original Value	Annual Depreciation	Annual Rate of Depreciation
a	$3,100	$248.00	____ %
b	$2,720	$272.00	____ %
c	$1,100	$ 71.50	____ %
d	$ 650	$ 97.50	____ %
e	$ 325	$ 75.00	____ %
f	$ 975	$128.70	____ %

Solution: To find the annual rate of depreciation, we divide the annual depreciation by the original value. We then multiply by 100%.

Asset	Original Value	Annual Depreciation	Annual Rate of Depreciation
a	$3,100	$248.00	$\frac{248.00}{3100.00}$ = .08 = 8%
b	$2,720	$272.00	$\frac{272.00}{2720.00}$ = .10 = 10%

c	$1,100	$ 71.50	$\frac{71.50}{1100.00} = .065 = 6.5\%$
d	$ 650	$ 97.50	$\frac{97.50}{650.00} = .15 = 15\%$
e	$ 325	$ 75.00	$\frac{75.00}{325.00} = .231 = 23.1\%$
f	$ 975	$128.00	$\frac{128.00}{975.00} = .131 = 13.1\%$.

• PROBLEM 19-14

The New Products Chemical Corporation purchased $350,000 worth of equipment for its new plant. If the equipment will be completely worthless because of obsolescence at the end of eight years, at what annual rate is it depreciating? What is the annual amount of depreciation? What is the book value of the equipment at the end of the second year? Use the straight-line method.

Solution: The equipment will depreciate $350,000 in 8 years, thus it will depreciate $43,750 annually. The rate of depreciation is the annual amount of depreciation divided by the cost, thus it is

$43,750 ÷ $350,000 = .125 = 12.5%.

The book value of the equipment is the cost less the accumulated depreciation. When using the straight line depreciation method, the accumulated depreciation can be found by multiplying the annual amount of depreciation by the number of years. Thus, the accumulated depreciation of the equipment is

2 × $43,750 = $87,500.

The book value is therefore

$350,000 (cost) - $87,500 (accumulated depreciation)

= $262,500.

DECLINING BALANCE METHOD

• PROBLEM 19-15

Ringling Brothers Circus recently purchased a new tiger cage for $1,950. The accountants have decided to depreciate the cage using the declining balance method with a rate of 15%. What will be the book value of the cage in 3 years?

Solution: Book value at the end of 1st year - The amount depreciated will be ($1,950)(0.15) = $292.50, so that at the end of the first year, the cage will have a book value of

$1,950 - $292.50 = $1,657.50.

Book value at the end of 2nd year - The amount depreciated will be ($1,657.50)(0.15) = $248.63. The book value is

$1,657.50 - $248.63 = $1,408.87.

Book value at the end of 3rd year - The amount depreciated will be ($1,408.87)(0.15) = $211.33. The book value is

$1,408.87 - $211.33 = $1,197.54.

Equivalently, we could have used the formula

$P(1 - r)^n$ to find the book value at the end of year 3. Here P is the original cost of the asset, r is the depreciation rate and n is the number of years the asset has been on the books. In our example:

book value after 3 years -

$$\$1,950 (1 - 0.15)^3 = \$1,950 (0.6141) = \$1197.54.$$

In 8 years the book value would be

$$\$1,950 (.85)^8 = \$1,950 (0.2724) = \$531.36.$$

• **PROBLEM 19-16**

The Help-A-Tourist Travel Agency recently purchased a car for $4,000. It is estimated that the car will last for four years and have a trade-in value of $400. During the first year the company made enormous profits and they want to use the maximum rate of depreciation under the declining-balance method, in order to claim higher expenses for the year and pay less taxes. Find the depreciation they will claim for each of the four years they will use the car.

Solution: When using the declining-balance method, we do not take the salvage value into consideration until the last years, when we must be careful not to make the book value less than the residual value. The maximum rate is twice the rate you would get if you used the straight-line method. In the straight-line method the item depreciates equally over a four year period, thus each year depreciates 25% (1/4) of the cost. (Remember we do not take residual value into account.) Thus, the maximum rate for the declining balance method is $2 \times 25\% = 50\%$. The declining-balance method multiplies the rate by the book value in order to get the depreciation for the year. The book value is the cost less the accumulated interest. Note that the book value must never fall below the residual value. We can now find the amount depreciated each year.

Year	Book Value	Depreciation
1	\$4,000 (cost)	\$4,000 × 50% = \$2,000
2	\$2,000 (\$4,000-\$2,000)	\$2,000 × 50% = \$1,000
3	\$1,000 (\$4,000-\$3,000)	\$1,000 × 50% = \$ 500

In the fourth year we can only deduct \$100 for depreciation, for after the third year the book value of the car is \$4,000 - \$3,500 (accumulated depreciation) = \$500, and the residual worth is \$400, and we cannot make the book value for the car lower than the residual value.

• PROBLEM 19-17

A canning company bought a \$15,000 piece of machinery for its vegetable farm. The machinery is expected to last six years at which time it will have no residual value. The company wishes to use the maximum percentage allowable under the declining-balance method for computing the depreciation. Find the depreciation and book value for the first three years of operation.

Solution: The maximum percentage allowable,for tax purposes, is twice the rate one would use under the straight-line method. Under the straight-line method, the amount depreciated each year would be

$$\$15,000 \div 6 \text{ (years)} = \$2,500.$$

The rate is found by depreciation divided by the cost. Thus the rate is

$$\$2,500 \div \$15,000 = \frac{1}{6} = 16\,\frac{2}{3}\,\%.$$

Thus the maximum rate is

$$2 \times 16\,\frac{2}{3}\,\% = 33\,\frac{1}{3}\,\% = \frac{1}{3}\,.$$

To use the declining-balance method, we find the amount depreciated by multiplying the rate (1/3) by the book value. The book value is the cost less the accumulated depreciation. We can now find the depreciation for the first three years.

Year	Depreciation	Book Value at End of Year
1	$\$15{,}000 \times \frac{1}{3} = \$5{,}000$	$10,000
2	$\$10{,}000 \times \frac{1}{3} = \$3{,}333$	$6,667
3	$\$\ 6{,}667 \times \frac{1}{3} = \$2{,}222$	$4,445

• PROBLEM 19-18

The ABC Leasing Co. charges depreciation on its typewriters at the rate of 15% per year on the declining balance method. The customer service department recently purchased ten typewriters for $4,800. What will the book value of each of the typewriters be at the end of three years? What will the depreciation expense be for each of these years?

Solution: Since the customer service department purchased ten typewriters for $4,800, and the depreciation rate is 15% (= .15) of the declining balance, the depreciation expense for the first year was $4,800 × .15 = $720. This leaves a net book value at the end of the first year of $4,800 - $720 = $4,080. The depreciation expense for the second year was $4,080 × .15 = $612, so the net book value at the end of the second year was $4,080 - $612 = $3,468. Finally, the depreciation expense for the third year was $3,468 × .15 = $520.20, so the book value for the ten typewriters at the end of the third year was $3,468 - $520.20 = $2,947.80. Since this represents ten typewriters, the net book value of each of the typewriters at the end of the third year was $\frac{\$2{,}947.80}{10}$ = $294.78.

• PROBLEM 19-19

The Five Star Hotel put down $3,000 worth of carpeting. The carpeting is made to last for five years. The hotel's accountant wishes to use the declining-balance method. What is the depreciation for the second year?

Solution: The declining-balanced method takes a fixed percentage of the book value of the item as its depreciation. This fixed percentage is usually taken to be twice the percentage that would be used if we used the straight-line method. Here, if we used the straight-line method, the depreciation allowance for each year would be the amount depreciated ($3,000) divided by the number of years (5), giving $600. Now the rate is found by dividing the depreciation allowance by the cost, giving 20% ($600 / $3,000 = .20 = 20%). Thus we will use 40% as the declining-balance rate. The cost of the carpeting was $3,000. The depreciation for the first year is 40% of the book-value (or the cost), which is

$$40\% \times \$3,000 = .40 \times \$3,000 = \$1,200.$$

The book value is now the cost less the depreciation, being $3,000 - $1,200 = $1,800. The depreciation for the second year is 40% of the book value ($1,800), or

$$40\% \times \$1,800 = .40 \times \$1,800 = \$720.$$

• PROBLEM 19-20

The Century Shoe Company bought a machine for $1200. Depreciation was charged at the rate of 20% of the declining balance. Find the book value at the end of 3 years.

Solution: The declining balance method takes the given rate and multiplies it by the book value of the machine in order to get its depreciation for that year. The book value of the machine is found by subtracting the accumulated depreciation from the cost.

Year	Book Value	Depreciation
1	$1,200.00 (cost)	20% × $1,200 = $240.00
2	$ 960.00 ($1200 - $240)	20% × $960 = $192.00
3	$ 768.00 ($960 - $192)	20% × $768 = $153.60

Thus the book value at the end of the third year is

$1,200.00 - $585.60 (accumulated depreciation) = $614.40.

• PROBLEM 19-21

Dr. Frankel bought a new X-ray machine for $4,000. It has an estimated life of 5 years, at the end of which its estimated salvage value is $800. Dr. Frankel wishes to use the declining-balance method to compute the machine's depreciation. He will use 40% for his rate of depreciation. Compute the depreciation for each year.

Solution: Using the declining-balance method, we multiply the fixed rate by the current book value of the item in order to get the amount of depreciation for that year. The book value is the cost less the accumulated depreciation up to that point.

Year	Rate		Book Value	Depreciation
1	40%	×	$4,000	= $1,600
2	40%	×	$2,400 ($4,00-$1,600)	= $ 960
3	40%	×	$1,440 ($2,400-$960)	= $ 576

In the fourth year the book value is $1,440 - $576 = $864. Depreciation will not be the usual 40%, or $864 × .40 = $345.60, because $800 must be left over for salvage value. (The salvage value of an asset cannot be depreciated.) Therefore $864 - $800 = $64 will be the depreciation for the fourth year. In the fifth year of the asset's life, it will have no depreciation.

SUM OF THE YEARS' DIGITS METHOD AND COMPREHENSIVE PROBLEM

• PROBLEM 19-22

The Daily Beagle bought a printing press for $4,000; it will depreciate to a scrap value of $500 in 4 years. Find the depreciation charge, and the book value at the end of the second year by the sum-of-the-years'-digits method.

Solution: The first thing we must find is the total depreciation. It is found by subtracting the scrap value from the cost, giving $4,000 (cost) - $500 (scrap value) = $3,500.

We now find each year's depreciation by multiplying the total depreciation by the fraction obtained by dividing the number of years left for the item (including the one you are in) by the sum of the years' digits. Since there are four years, the sum of the digits is 1 + 2 + 3 + 4 = 10.

We can now find the depreciation for the second year.

Year	Depreciation
1	$\frac{4}{10}$ × $3,500 = $1,400
2	$\frac{3}{10}$ × $3,500 = $1,050

The book value at the end of the two years is the cost less the accumulated depreciation.

$1,400	(depreciation for year 1)
+ $1,050	(depreciation for year 2)
$2,450	(accumulated depreciation)

Thus the book value of the printing press after 2 years is $4,000 (cost) - $2,450 (accumulated depreciation) = $1,550.

• PROBLEM 19-23

John Erickson purchased a weaving machine for his factory at a cost of $8,000. The machine will last for four years, and have a salvage value of $800. Find the depreciation for each year using the sum-of-the-years'-digits method.

Solution: First we must find out the total depreciation. It is equal to the cost less the salvage value. Thus, the total amount of depreciation of the weaving machine is $8,000 (cost) - $800 (salvage value) = $7,200.

In the sum-of-the-years'-digits method we find the amount to be depreciated each year by multiplying the total depreciation by the fraction obtained by dividing the number of years left for the machine (including the one you are in) by the sum-of-the-years'-digits. Since the machine will last for four years the sum-of-the-years'-digits is equal to 1 + 2 + 3 + 4 = 10. We can now find the depreciation for each year.

Year	Depreciation
1	$\frac{4}{10} \times \$7,200 = \$2,880$
2	$\frac{3}{10} \times \$7,200 = \$2,160$
3	$\frac{2}{10} \times \$7,200 = \$1,440$
4	$\frac{1}{10} \times \$7,200 = \$\ \ 720$
Total	$7,200

• PROBLEM 19-24

Bob Franklin purchased a new car for $10,000. The car is estimated to last 10 years, and will have no residual value. How much will the car depreciate during the seventh year? He uses the sum of the years' digits method.

Solution: The first thing we must do is to find the sum of the digits of the years. It is 1 + 2 + 3 + 4 + 5 + 6 + 7 + 8 + 9 + 10 = 55. We then find the depreciation of a year by multiplying the amount that will be depreciated ($10,000) by the number of years left (including the year you are in) divided by the sum of the years' digits. Thus the amounts are:

Year	Amount of Depreciation
1	$\frac{10}{55} \times \$10,000 = \$1,818.18$
2	$\frac{9}{55} \times \$10,000 = \$1,636.36$
3	$\frac{8}{55} \times \$10,000 = \$1,454.55$
4	$\frac{7}{55} \times \$10,000 = \$1,272.73$
5	$\frac{6}{55} \times \$10,000 = \$1,090.91$
6	$\frac{5}{55} \times \$10,000 = \$\ \ 909.09$
7	$\frac{4}{55} \times \$10,000 = \$\ \ 727.27$
8	$\frac{3}{55} \times \$10,000 = \$\ \ 545.45$
9	$\frac{2}{55} \times \$10,000 = \$\ \ 363.64$
10	$\frac{1}{55} \times \$10,000 = \$\ \ 181.82$
Total 55	$= \$10,000$

The total row serves as a check for the computations. By looking at the above table we can see that in the seventh year the car depreciated $727.27.

• **PROBLEM** 19-25

A bulldozer that the Columbus Construction Co. purchased for $15,500, will have a trade-in value of $2,600 after five years. What is the book value at the end of the first three years, if the company uses the sum-of-the-years'-digits method?

Solution: The amount the bulldozer will depreciate is equal to the cost less the trade-in value, which is $15,500 - $2,600 = $12,900. The book value of the bulldozer is its cost less the accumulated depreciation. The depreciation, using the sum-of-the-years'-digits method, can be found by multiplying the amount it will depreciate ($12,900) by the number of years left (including the year you are in) divided by the sum-of-the-years'-digits. The sum-of-the-years-digits is 1 + 2 + 3 + 4 + 5 = 15. We can now find the depreciation for each year.

Year	Depreciation
1	$\frac{5}{15} \times \$12,900 = \$4,300$
2	$\frac{4}{15} \times \$12,900 = \$3,440$
3	$\frac{3}{15} \times \$12,900 = \$2,580$
4	$\frac{2}{15} \times \$12,900 = \$1,720$
5	$\frac{1}{15} \times \$12,900 = \$\ \ 860.$

The accumulated depreciation after the first three years is the sum of the depreciation of the first three years.

$ 4,300	(depreciation in year 1)
$ 3,440	(depreciation in year 2)
$ 2,580	(depreciation in year 3)
$10,320	(accumulated depreciation)

Thus, the book value after three years is the cost ($15,500) less the accumulated depreciation ($10,320) = $5,180.

• PROBLEM 19-26

Mr. Casey purchased office furniture for $725. It has an estimated salvage value of $25.00 at the end of 10 years. Using the sum-of-the-years'-digits method, find the depreciation for the fourth year.

Solution: The first thing we must find is the total depreciation. It is found by subtracting the salvage value from the cost. Thus, the salvage value of the furniture is: $725 - $25 = $700. Each year's depreciation is found by multiplying the total depreciation by the number of years left (including the one you are in) divided by the sum of the years' digits. The sum of the years' digits is equal to

$$1 + 2 + 3 + 4 + 5 + 6 + 7 + 8 + 9 + 10 = 55.$$

Thus the depreciation for the fourth year is equal to

$$\frac{7}{55} \times \$700.00 = \$89.09.$$

• PROBLEM 19-27

Hershberg's Accounting Service Inc. bought a computer for $6,300,000. The computer will last 35 years, after which time it will be worthless. Find the amount of depreciation for the first three years, using the sum-of-the-years'-digits method.

Solution: To find the annual depreciation using the sum-of-the-years-digits method, we multiply the amount that will be depreciated by the fraction obtained by dividing the number of years left (including the one you are in) by the sum of the years' digits. Instead of adding the numbers 1 through 35 to find the sum of the years digits, we can use the formula:

$$\text{Sum of 1 through N} = \frac{N \times (N + 1)}{2}.$$

Here we want to add 1 through 35, thus the sum is equal to

$$35 \times (35 + 1) \div 2 = 35 \times 36 \div 2 = 630.$$

Thus the depreciation for the first three years is as follows:

Year	Depreciation
1	$\$6,300.000 \times \frac{35}{630} = \$350,000$
2	$\$6,300,000 \times \frac{34}{630} = \$340,000$
3	$\$6,300,000 \times \frac{33}{630} = \$330,000$

• **PROBLEM 19-28**

Jacob and Sons Plumbing bought a forklift for $10,000. The forklift is expected to last 5 years, and to have a residual value of $3,000. Jacob wishes to use the straight line depreciation method, while his sons wish to use the sum-of-the-years'-digits method. What will the difference in the depreciation allowances be for the third year?

Solution: The forklift cost $10,000 and will have a residual value of $3,000. It will depreciate $10,000 - $3,000 = $7,000, in the 5 years. By the straight line method we divide the amount depreciated by the number of years it will last, and use that as the depreciation allowance each year. Thus, by the straight-line method we would depreciate the forklift by $7,000 ÷ 5 = $1,400 each year. By the sum-of-the-years-digits method we first find the sum of the years digits. Since it is going to last 5 years, then the sum of the digits is equal to 1 + 2 + 3 + 4 + 5 = 15. Now the amount that is depreciated each year is found by multiplying the total depreciation ($7,000) by the fraction of the number of years left for the item,(including the year you are in), divided by the sum of the years digits. Thus, the depreciation allowance will be:

Year	Amount Depreciated
1	$\frac{5}{15} \times \$7,000 = \$2,333.33$
2	$\frac{4}{15} \times \$7,000 = \$1,866.67$
3	$\frac{3}{15} \times \$7,000 = \$1,400.00$
4	$\frac{2}{15} \times \$7,000 = \$\ \ 933.33$
5	$\frac{1}{15}\ \ \$7,000 = \$\ \ 466.67$
Total 15	$7,000.00

Thus, in the third year the depreciation allowance would also be $1,400. The difference in depreciation is zero.

• **PROBLEM 19-29**

Using the sum-of-the-years'-digits method, find the annual depreciation on each of the following assets for the first year.

No.	Cost	Disposal Value	Number of Years Held	First Year
1	$1,200	$300	5	$ ______
2	$1,500	$240	6	$ ______
3	$1,100	$110	9	$ ______
4	$ 600	$125	4	$ ______

Solution: To use the sum-of-the-years-digits method, we find the total amount of depreciation and multiply it by the fraction obtained by dividing the number of years left (including the one you are in) by the sum of the years digits. The total amount of depreciation is found by subtracting the disposal value from the cost. The sum of the year digits is found by adding up all the digits for the years. It can be done faster by using the formula:

$$\text{sum} = \frac{n \times (n + 1)}{2}$$

where n is the number of years it will take for the item to depreciate.

No.	Cost	-	Disposal Value	=	Total depreciation
1	$1,200	-	$300	=	$ 900
2	$1,500	-	$240	=	$1,260
3	$1,100	-	$110	=	$ 990
4	$ 600	-	$125	=	$ 475

No.	Number of years held	Sum of digits	Fraction
1	5	$\frac{5\times(5+1)}{2} = \frac{5\times 6}{2} = 15$	$\frac{5}{15}$
2	6	$\frac{6\times(6+1)}{2} = \frac{6\times 7}{2} = 21$	$\frac{6}{21}$
3	9	$\frac{9\times(9+1)}{2} = \frac{9\times 10}{2} = 45$	$\frac{9}{45}$
4	4	$\frac{4\times(4+1)}{2} = \frac{4\times 5}{2} = 10$	$\frac{4}{10}$

Now we can find the depreciation for the first year

No.	Fraction	×	Total depreciation	=	depreciation, 1st year
1	$\frac{5}{15}$	×	$900	=	$300
2	$\frac{6}{21}$	×	$1,260	=	$360
3	$\frac{9}{45}$	×	$990	=	$198
4	$\frac{4}{10}$	×	$475	=	$190.

• **PROBLEM 19-30**

A tractor that cost $7,600 will be used for 5 years, after which time it will have an expected trade-in value of $1,600. Using the sum-of-the-years'-digits method, find each year's estimated depreciation.

Solution: Many types of equipment are more efficient when new and therefore give better service in the early years of useful life. If we assume the benefits derived from the tractor are greatest in the early years when the asset is new, then the amount of depreciation of the tractor should be greatest in these same years. The sum-of-the-years'-digits method is one of allocating a large part of the depreciation of an asset to the early years of its use. The total depreciation is the difference between the original value and the trade-in value. Here the total depreciation is $7,600 - $1,600 = $5,000.

The rate of depreciation is a fraction whose denominator is the sum of the years of useful life and whose numerator is the remaining years of useful life (as of the beginning of the year). Each year's annual depreciation can be determined as follows: (1) List the number of years of estimated life in decreasing order. Find the sum of the number of years. (2) Set up each year's rate of depreciation. (3) Multiply each year's rate of depreciation by the total amount of depreciation to find each year's annual depreciation.

The sum of the number of years is 15. Therefore, the rate of depreciation for the first year is $\frac{5}{15}$, since there are 5 more years of use (as of the beginning of the year). For the second year, the rate of depreciation is $\frac{4}{15}$, since there are 4 more years of use (as of beginning of the year). Hence, we find the rate of depreciation for the third year is $\frac{3}{15}$, rate of depreciation for the fourth year is $\frac{2}{15}$, and the rate of depreciation for the fifth year is $\frac{1}{15}$. Now we can find each year's annual depreciation with the following formula:

annual depreciation - rate of depreciation × total depreciation

for the first year: depreciation = rate of depreciation × total depreciation

$$= \frac{5}{15} \times \$6,000$$

$$= 2,000$$

for second year: depreciation $= \frac{4}{15} \times \$6,000$

$$= \$1,600.$$

for third year: depreciation $= \frac{3}{15} \times \$6,000$

$$= \$1,200.$$

for fourth year: depreciation $= \frac{2}{15} \times \$6,000$

$$= \$800$$

for fifth year: depreciation $= \frac{1}{15} \times \$6,000$

$$= \$400.$$

• PROBLEM 19-31

The rate department of the Mid-America Freight Company purchases 10-key adding machines for its rate clerks at a cost of \$195 each. At the end of five years, these machines will be traded in for new ones. The disposal value of the old machines will be \$85 each.

(a) Using the straight-line method of depreciation, what is the depreciation on each machine during the first year? the last year?

(b) Using the sum-of-the-years'-digits method of depreciation, what is the depreciation on each machine during the first year? the last year?

(c) Find the book value for each of the five years, assuming depreciation is computed by the declining-balance method and the annual rate is 15.3%.

Solution: (a) The straight-line method finds the amount that will be depreciated, and divides it by the number of years. The result is the depreciation allowance for each year. The amount that will be depreciated over the 5 years is found by subtracting the disposal value (residual worth) from the cost. Thus, the amount that will be depreciated is equal to \$195 - \$85 = \$110. Therefore the depreciation allowance for any year is \$110/5 = \$22.

(b) The sum-of-the-years'-digits method takes the amount that will be depreciated (\$110) and multiplies that by the fraction of the years left (including the one you are in) for the object divided by the sum of the years digits. The sum-of-the-years'-digits = 1 + 2 + 3 + 4 + 5 (because it will depreciate over 5 years) = 15. Another way to compute the sum of the years digits is: if the object will last for n years then the sum-of-the-years'-digits is $\frac{n \times (n + 1)}{2}$.

Here it will last for five years, the sum of the years digits is $\frac{5 \times (5 + 1)}{2} = \frac{5 \times 6}{2} = 15$.

Now we can compute the depreciation allowance for each year.

Year	Depreciation Allowance
1	$\frac{5}{15} \times \$110 = \$36.67$
2	$\frac{4}{15} \times \$110 = \$29.33$
3	$\frac{3}{15} \times \$110 = \$22.00$
4	$\frac{2}{15} \times \$110 = \$14.67$
5	$\frac{1}{15} \times \$110 = \$\ 7.33$
Total 15	$110

The total serves as a check for the computations.

(c) The declining-balance method takes a fixed percentage, here 15.3% = .153, of the book value as the depreciation. The book value is the cost less the accumulated depreciation.

Year	Book Value	Depreciation
1	$195.00 (cost)	$195.00 × .153 = $29.84
2	$165.16 ($195.00 - $29.84)	$165.16 × .153 = $25.27
3	$139.89 ($195.00 - $55.11)	$139.89 × .153 = $21.40
4	$118.49 ($195.00 - $76.51)	$118.49 × .153 = $18.13
5	$100.36 ($195.00 - $94.64)	$100.36 × .153 = $15.36

Book value after the five years is

$195.00 (cost) - $110.00 (accumulated depreciation) = $85 .

CHAPTER 20

OVERHEAD DISTRIBUTION

FLOOR SPACE BASIS

• **PROBLEM** 20-1

Teddy's Auto Parts is renting a warehouse. The lease stipulates that the tenant must pay an annual rent of $2 per square foot, plus taxes and insurance. If the taxes are $12,000 a year, the insurance is $400, and the warehouse contains 62,500 square feet, what is Teddy's cost for the occupancy of the warehouse for one year?

Solution: Teddy must pay an annual rent of $2 per square foot. Since the warehouse contains 62,500 square feet, his annual rent is $2 x 62,500 = $125,000. His cost for occupancy is:

$125,000	annual rent
12,000	taxes
400	insurance
$137,400	total cost

• **PROBLEM** 20-2

Distribution of overhead is based on floor space. Department A occupied 8,100 sq. ft. of the 121,500 sq. ft. of space used by Harrison Manufacturing Company. Find department A's share of overhead based on floor footage for a month in which the total overhead of the Harrison Manufacturing Company was $97,500.

Solution: Find the ratio of overhead cost to the total area, which is the cost per square foot. It is found by dividing overhead by the total area, which equals $97,500 ÷ 121,500 = $.80247, per square foot. To find department A's share of overhead we multiply the cost per square foot by the number of square feet occupied by department A, giving $.80247 x 8,100 = $6,500.

• PROBLEM 20-3

Find the amount of monthly overhead chargeable to each department in the Wonder King Electrical Company, based on the information in the following table. The charges are computed on the basis of square feet of space occupied by each department.

Department	Square Feet of Space Occupied	Percent of Total Space	July $6,400	Aug. $5,700	Sept. $7,200
Raw materials	3,600	____	____	____	____
Parts	1,800	____	____	____	____
Assembly	2,400	____	____	____	____
Finished goods	1,000	____	____	____	____
Office	1,200	____	____	____	____
Totals	10,000	____	____	____	____

Solution: To compute each department's share of overhead, we multiply each department's percentage of the total space occupied by the company's monthly expenses. To get each department's percentage we divide the area occupied by the department by the total area (10,000 square feet).

Department	Area ÷ 10,000	= Percent of Total Space
Raw materials	3,600	.36 = 36%
Parts	1,800	.18 = 18%
Assembly	2,400	.24 = 24%
Finished goods	1,000	.10 = 10%
Office	1,200	.12 = 12%

The overhead cost of each department for July, August and September is:

Department	% of Space	July	August	September
Raw materials	36%	$2,304	$2,052	$2,592
Parts	18%	$1,152	$1,026	$1,296
Assembly	24%	$1,536	$1,368	$1,728
Finished goods	10%	$ 640	$ 570	$ 720
Office	12%	$ 768	$ 684	$ 864
Total	100%	$6,400	$5,700	$7,200

• **PROBLEM 20-4**

Department	Percent of Total Space	Amount of Expense: Rent $3,000	Taxes $300	Maintenance $740	Utilities $240
Finance	12 1/2%	$____	$____	$____	$____
Executive	6 1/4%	$____	$____	$____	$____
Production	25%	$____	$____	$____	$____
Marketing	31 1/4%	$____	$____	$____	$____
Research	18 3/4%	$____	$____	$____	$____
Personnel	6 1/4%	$____	$____	$____	$____
Totals		$____	$____	$____	$____

Find the amount of rent, taxes, maintenance, and utilities expense to be distributed to each department if the company distributes the overhead on a space basis.

Solution: If the company distributes the overhead on a space basis, then we multiply each department's percent of the total space by the expense to distribute the overhead.

Department	% of Space	Rent $3,000	Taxes $300	Maintenance $740	Utilities $240
Finance	12.5%	$375.00	$37.50	$92.50	$30.00
Executive	6.25%	$187.50	$18.75	$46.25	$15.00
Production	25%	$750.00	$75.00	$185.00	$60.00
Marketing	31.25%	$937.50	$93.75	$231.25	$75.00
Research	18.75%	$562.50	$56.25	$138.75	$45.00
Personnel	6.25%	$187.50	$18.75	$46.25	$15.00
Total	100%	$3,000	$300.00	$740.00	$240.00

• **PROBLEM 20-5**

The Johnson Supply Company distributes its $3,160 of overhead on the basis of square feet occupied. Find the amount charged to each of the following departments, given their respective areas.

Department	Area
Raw Materials	2,500 sq. ft.
Manufacturing	5,000 sq. ft.
Storage	2,000 sq. ft.
Administrative	500 sq. ft.

Solution: Find the total area:

	2,500 sq. ft. (Raw Materials)
+	5,000 sq. ft. (Manufacturing)
+	2,000 sq. ft. (Storage)
+	500 sq. ft. (Administrative)
	10,000 sq. ft. (Total Area)

We now find the ratio of the total overhead to the total area, by dividing the total overhead by the total area, giving $3,160/10,000 = $.316. This ratio is the cost per square foot. To find the amount charged to each department we multiply the cost per square foot by the area occupied by each department.

Department	Area	Amount of overhead
Raw materials	2,500 sq. ft.	$790 ($.316 × 2,500)
Manufacturing	5,000 sq. ft.	$1,580 ($.316 × 5,000)
Storage	2,000 sq. ft.	$632 ($.316 × 2,000)
Administrative	500 sq. ft.	$158 ($.316 × 500)
Total	10,000 sq. ft.	$3,160 (overhead)

• PROBLEM 20-6

The Flushing Bicycle Manufacturing Company allocates overhead among its departments on the basis of space occupied. The overhead expenses for one month were:

Rent	$4,000
Taxes	600
Insurance	100
Utilities	250
Cleaning and Maintenance	750

The space occupied by the various departments is as follows:

Raw materials	1,200 square meters (m^2)
Processing	2,400 m^2
Assembling	1,800 m^2
Finishing	2,000 m^2
Storage	3,000 m^2
Offices	1,600 m^2

How much was each department charged for overhead for the month?

Solution: Find the cost per square meter by finding the total overhead expense and dividing it by the total area. We then multiply the cost per square meter by the area occupied by each department.

	$4,000	(rent)
+	600	(taxes)
+	100	(insurance)
+	250	(utilities)
+	750	(cleaning and maintenance)
	$5,700	(total overhead)
	1,200 m^2	(raw materials)
+	2,400 m^2	(processing)
+	1,800 m^2	(assembling)
+	2,000 m^2	(finishing)
+	3,000 m^2	(storage)
+	1,600 m^2	(offices)
	12,000 m^2	(total area)

The cost of overhead per square meter is $5,700 ÷ 12,000 = $.475. We can now see how the overhead was allocated.

Department	Area	Overhead expense
Raw materials	1,200 m^2	$570 ($.475 x 1,200)
Processing	2,400 m^2	$1,140 ($.475 x 2,400)
Assembling	1,800 m^2	$855($.475 X 1,800)
Finishing	2,000 m^2	$950($.475 X 2,000)
Storage	3,000 m^2	$1,425($.475 x 3,000)
Offices	1,600 m^2	$760($.475 x 1,600)
Total	12,000 m^2	$5,700.

COST/PROFIT BASIS

• PROBLEM 20-7

The June sales of the five departments of a retail store were as follows:

Accessories	$15,100
Leather goods	$10,400
Outerwear	$31,500
Sportswear	$25,700
Shoes	$13,300

The overhead expenses for the month was $12,000. If these expenses are allocated to each department on the basis of the sales volume of that department, how much expense will be charged to each department?

Solution: Find the ratio of the total overhead to total sales. Then multiply this ratio by each department's sales in order to distribute the overhead.

Accessories	\$15,100
Leather goods	+ \$10,400
Outerwear	+ \$31,500
Sportswear	+ \$25,700
Shoes	+ \$13,300
Total sales	\$96,000

The ratio of total overhead to total sales is \$12,000 ÷ \$96,000 = .125.

Overhead expense will be charged as follows:

Department	Sales	Overhead expense
Accessories	\$15,100	\$1,887.50 (.125 X \$15,100)
Leather goods	\$10,400	\$1,300.00 (.125 X \$10,400)
Outerwear	\$31,500	\$3,937.50 (.125 x \$31,500)
Sportswear	\$25,700	\$3,212.50 (.125 x \$25,700)
Shoes	\$13,300	\$1,662.50 (.125 x \$13,300)
Total	\$96,000	\$12,000

• PROBLEM 20-8

The Redding Department Store distributes its administrative expenses by the sales ratio method. If the total sales during June were \$408,000, and the administrative expense was \$22,600, find the share of the administrative expenses based on sales of the lingerie department, which had \$10,200 of sales in June.

Solution: Find the ratio of the sales of the lingerie department to the total sales. We then multiply that ratio by the total administrative expense to find out what share of the expense belongs to the lingerie department.

$$\text{Sales ratio} = \frac{\text{Sales of lingerie department}}{\text{total sales}}$$

$$= \frac{\$10,200}{\$408,000} = .025 .$$

The administrative expense of the lingerie department is:

$$\$22,600 \times .025 = \$565.$$

• PROBLEM 20-9

> Johnstown Mills manufactures cotton fabrics. Overhead is allocated to each department according to the ratio of total overhead to the total prime cost. During February, total direct labor costs came to $216,000 and the cost of materials to $84,000. The total overhead for the month was $45,000. Find the overhead percent of prime cost to be charged to each department. Then find the amount of overhead to be charged to the Design Department with a prime cost of $18,500.

Solution: The prime cost is equal to the direct labor cost plus the material cost, or $216,000 (labor) + $84,000 (materials) = $300,000. The overhead percent of prime cost is the ratio of the total overhead to the total prime cost, being $45,000 ÷ 300,000 × 100% = 15%. The overhead charged to each department is calculated by multiplying the department's prime cost by 15%. Thus the Design Department is charged $18,500 × .15 = $2,775.

• PROBLEM 20-10

> The Adam Manufacturing Co. distributes its overhead by using the ratio of total overhead to total prime cost. If the total overhead is $44,733, the total direct labor is $185,600, and the total materials used are $54,900, find (a) the overhead percent of prime cost, (b) the overhead charge to a department with a prime cost of $32.600.

Solution: The company computes the ratio of total overhead to total prime cost, and then multiplies this ratio by the prime cost of each department in order to establish how much overhead will be charged to it. The prime cost is equal to the cost of labor plus the cost of materials used, or total $185,600 (labor) + $54,900 (materials) = $240,500. The ratio of prime cost charged to all departments is:

$$\frac{\text{Total overhead}}{\text{Total Prime Costs}}$$

$$= \frac{\$44,733}{\$240,500} \times 100\% = 18.6\% .$$

(b) To find how much a department will be charged for overhead expense, we multiply its prime cost by the ratio, 18.6%. Thus, a department with a prime cost of $32,600 will be charged $32,600 × 18.6% = $32,600 × .186 = $6,063.60.

• PROBLEM 20-11

> The Extruded Plastics Company distributes overhead to each of its six departments according to the ratio of total overhead to the total direct labor costs. During January, the total overhead for the factory was $20,000; the total direct labor cost $140,000. Find

the ratio to be applied to all departments. Then find the amount to be charged to the Quality Control Department whose direct labor costs for the month were $16,000.

Solution: Find the ratio of total overhead to the total labor costs. Then multiply this ratio by each department's labor costs. The ratio is found by dividing overhead by the labor cost, giving $20,000 ÷ $140,000 = 1/7. This rate is applied to all departments.

Thus, the overhead charged to the Quality Control Department was $16,000 (labor cost) x 1/7 (or $16,000 ÷ 7) = $2,285.71 (rounded to the nearest cent).

• PROBLEM 20-12

A department store distributes its overhead based on the direct labor cost. If the overhead for one month was $4,200, and the direct labor cost of the department store was $35,000, find (a) what percent overhead is of direct labor and (b) the cost of overhead for the housewares department, which has a labor cost of $5,340.

Solution: To allocate overhead the store finds the ratio of the total overhead to the total direct labor costs, and multiplies that by the labor cost of each department.

(a) Overhead is $\frac{\$4,200}{\$35,000} \times 100\% = 12\%$ of the direct labor cost.

(b) The housewares department has a labor cost of $5,340. Thus, overhead expenses are 12% x $5,340 = .12 x $5,340 = $640.80.

CHAPTER 21

PARTNERSHIPS

• PROBLEM 21-1

Jim and Joe are partners who share profits and losses equally. Last year, their firm's net profit was $28,400. What is each partner's profit?

Solution: A partnership is a business organization owned by 2 or more individuals. In a partnership, the profits and losses are shared in a manner to which all the partners have agreed. Here they are shared equally. Since there are two partners, each receives a 1/2 share of the profits or losses. In this case, each partner receives 1/2 of $28,400, or $14,200.

• PROBLEM 21-2

Matthews and Green are partners in a delicatessen. They have agreed that Matthews should receive 60% of the profits or losses, and that Green should receive 40%. If the profits for a year were $10,200, what was each partner's share?

Solution: Matthews received 60% of $10,200 = .60 × $10,200 = $6,120.

Green received 40% of $10,200 = .40 × $10,200 = $4,080.

To check, add the two shares together, to see if the sum is the annual profit.

$6,120	(Matthew's share)
+ $4,080	(Green's share)
$10,200	(annual profit)

• PROBLEM 21-3

Frank Lee and Steve Barnes are partners. Barnes receives a weekly salary of $300, and 1/3 of the remaining net income. The other 2/3 of the remaining income goes to Lee. If the profits are $28,269, how much does each partner receive?

Solution: Barnes' annual salary = \$300/week $\times$ 52 weeks = \$15,600. The balance of the profits is \$28,269 - \$15,600 = \$12,669. Barnes' share of this is 1/3 $\times$ \$12,669 = \$4,223, giving him a total of \$15,600 + \$4,223 = \$19,823. Lee's share of the profits is 2/3 $\times$ \$12,669 = \$8,446. To check:

$$\begin{array}{rl} \$8,446 & \text{(Lee's share)} \\ +\ \$19,823 & \text{(Barnes' share)} \\ \hline \$28,269 & \text{(total profits)} \end{array}$$

• PROBLEM 21-4

Schaeffer, Brown and Smith invested \$10,000, \$15,000 and \$25,000 respectively in a partnership. They share profits and losses in proportion to their investments. Last year, their profit was \$42,000. What was each partner's share of the profit?

Solution: Each partner's share when profits and losses are shared proportionally, is computed by the formula:

$$\frac{\text{partner's investment}}{\text{total investment}} \times \text{profit or loss} .$$

Total investment = \$10,000 + \$15,000 + \$25,000 = \$50,000.

$$\text{Schaeffer's share} = \frac{\$10,000}{\$50,000} \times \$42,000 = \frac{1}{5} \times \$42,000 = \$8,400.$$

$$\text{Brown's share} = \frac{\$15,000}{\$50,000} \times \$42,000 = \frac{3}{10} \times \$42,000 = \$12,600.$$

$$\text{Smith's share} = \frac{\$25,000}{\$50,000} \times \$42,000 = \frac{1}{2} \times \$42,000 = \$21,000.$$

• PROBLEM 21-5

Mr. Joseph Miles and Mr. Gary Rose are partners in a manufacturing company. Mr. Miles receives a salary of \$600 a month, and the balance of the profits is to be divided equally. During their first year, profits were \$6,000. How much did each receive?

Solution: Since there are 12 months in a year, Mr. Miles' salary for the year was 12 $\times$ \$600 = \$7,200. The profits are not large enough to pay his salary.

$$\begin{array}{rl} \$7,200 & \text{(salary)} \\ -\ \$6,000 & \text{(profits)} \\ \hline \$1,200 & \text{(loss)} \end{array}$$

Since both partners share the balance of the profits and losses, they each lost \$1,200 $\div$ 2 = \$600.

Thus, Mr. Miles received \$7,200 (salary) - \$600 (deficit) = \$6,600. Mr. Rose lost \$600.

• PROBLEM 21-6

Evans and King are partners in a copying service. Evans invested \$8,500 and King invested \$6,500. The profits for the year were \$9,600. If the partners agreed to divide profits and losses according to their initial investments, how were the profits divided?

Solution: To find the partners' shares use the formula:

$$\frac{\text{Partner's investment}}{\text{Total investment}} \times \text{profit (or loss)} .$$

The total investment is \$8,500 (Evans' investment) + \$6,500 (King's investment) = \$15,000.

Evans' share of the profits is therefore

$$\frac{\$8,500}{\$15,000} \times \$9,600(\text{profits}) = \frac{17}{30}\left(\frac{8500 \div 500}{15000 \div 500} = \frac{17}{30}\right) \times \$9,600 = \$5,440.$$

King's share of the profits is therefore

$$\frac{\$6,500}{\$15,000} \times \$9,600(\text{profits}) = \frac{13}{30}\left(\frac{6500 \div 500}{15000 \div 500} = \frac{13}{30}\right) \times \$9,600 = \$4,160.$$

To check:

	\$4,160	King's share
+	5,440	Evans' share
	\$9,600	total profits.

• PROBLEM 21-7

Johnson, Morgan and Pierpont are partners who receive monthly salaries of \$600, \$500 and \$400 respectively with the balance of profits shared equally. Last year their profit was \$36,900. What was each partner's profit?

Solution: Each partner's share was equal to (monthly salary × 12) + [(total profit - total salaries)/3], that is, his yearly salary and an equal share (i.e., 1/3) of the balance after salaries were distributed.

Johnson's salary: \$600 × 12 = \$7,200
Morgan's salary : \$500 × 12 = \$6,000
Pierpont's salary: \$400 × 12 = \$4,800
Total salaries = \$18,000

Each partner also got a share of what was left after salaries were paid, equal to

$$\frac{36,900 - 18,000}{3} = \$6,300.$$

Johnson's profit: \$7,200 + \$6,300 = \$13,500
Morgan's profit: \$6,000 + \$6,300 = \$12,300
Pierpont's profit: \$4,800 + \$6,300 = \$11,100
Total profit = \$36,900

Partners 1, 2 and 3 own 3 flower shops and divide the income from all shops according to each partner's investment. Compute each partner's share of net income.

Shop	Partner's Investment 1	2	3	Net Income
A	\$5,000	\$5,000	\$10,000	\$5,200
B	\$7,000	\$9,000	\$ 0	\$4,000
C	\$10,000	\$15,000	\$25,000	\$12,500

Solution: When the net income is to be divided according to each partner's investment, use the formula:

$$\text{Partner's share of net income} = \frac{\text{partner's investment}}{\text{total investment}} \times \text{net income} .$$

Shop A:

\$5,000	(partner 1)
\$5,000	(partner 2)
\$10,000	(partner 3)
\$20,000	(total investment in Shop A)

Thus, Partner 1's share of the net income is $\frac{\$5,000}{\$20,000} \times \$5,200 = 1/4 \times \$5,200 = \$1,300$.

Partner 2's share is $\frac{\$5,000}{\$20,000} \times \$5,200 = 1/4 \times \$5,200 = \$1,300.$

Partner 3's share is $\frac{\$10,000}{\$20,000} \times \$5,200 = 1/2 \times \$5,200 = \$2,600.$

To check the results, add the partners' shares; the sum should equal the net income.

\$1,300	(partner 1's share)
\$1,300	(partner 2's share)
\$2,600	(partner 3's share)
\$5,200	(net income)

Shop B: Total investment = \$7,000 (partner 1) + \$9,000 (partner 2) = \$16,000.

Partner 1's share = $\frac{\$7,000}{\$16,000} \times \$4,000 = 7/16 \times \$4,000 = \$1,750.$

Partner 2's share = $\frac{\$9,000}{\$16,000} \times \$4,000 = \$2,250.$

Check:

\$1,750	(partner 1)
+ \$2,250	(partner 2)
\$4,000	(net income)

Shop C: Total investment = \$10,000 (partner 1) + \$15,000 (partner 2) + \$25,000 (partner 3) = \$50,000.

Partner 1's share = $\frac{\$10,000}{\$50,000} \times \$12,500 = 1/5 \times \$12,500 = \$2,500$.

Partner 2's share = $\frac{\$15,000}{\$50,000} \times \$12,500 = 3/10$ (reduce the fraction by dividing the numerator and denominator by 5,000) $\times \$12,500 = \$3,750.$

$$\text{Partner 3's share} = \frac{\$25,000}{\$50,000} \times \$12,500 = 1/2 \times \$12,500 = \$6,250.$$

Check:

$2,500	(partner 1)
+ $3,750	(partner 2)
+ $6,250	(partner 3)
$12,500	(net income)

• PROBLEM 21-9

Roy Alcott and Jon Buxton are partners in a steel company. They share the net income in proportion to their average investments. On January 1, Alcott invested $4,000 and Buxton invested $5,000. On May 1, Alcott invested an additional $2,000 and Buxton invested $1,750. On September 1, Alcott withdrew $500. On November 1, each partner invested an additional $2,000. The net profit for the year was $8,736. Find each partner's share of the profit.

Solution: To find the average investment, take each investment and multiply it by the number of months it remained unchanged, then add the products, and then divide by 12.

Using the former method:

Alcott

$4,000 × 4 =	$16,000	(Jan.-April)
+ $6,000 × 4 =	$24,000	(May-Aug.)
+ $5,500 × 2 =	$11,000	(Sept.-Oct.)
+ $7,500 × 2 =	$15,000	(Nov.-Dec.)
	$66,000	

Buxton

$5,000 × 4 =	$20,000	(Jan.-April)
+ $6,750 × 6 =	$40,000	(May-Oct.)
+ $8,750 × 2 =	$17,500	(Nov.-Dec.)
	$78,000	

Alcott's average investment = $66,000 ÷ 12 = $5,500
Buxton's average investment = $78,000 ÷ 12 = $6,500

Total average investment = $12,000

Use the following formula to compute each partner's share of the profits:

$$\frac{\text{partner's average investment}}{\text{total average investment}} \times \text{profits}$$

$$\text{Alcott's share: } \frac{5,500}{12,000} \times \$8,736 = \frac{11}{24} \times \$8,736 = \$4,004 .$$

$$\text{Buxton's share: } \frac{6,500}{12,000} \times \$8,736 = \frac{13}{24} \times \$8,736 = \$4,732$$

Total profits $8,736 .

• PROBLEM 21-10

Ms. Susan Wane and Ms. Dolly Watson invested $35,000 and $20,000 respectively, in a corkscrew factory. They decided to share the profits equally, after each receives 8% interest on her investment. Show the distribution of income if the business earns $24,200.

Solution: Susan Wane receives 8% interest on her investment of $35,000, which is $2,800(.08 X 35,000). Dolly Watson receives 8% interest on her investment of $20,000, which is $1,600(.08 X 20,000).

This leaves $24,200 - $1,600 - $2,800 = $19,800 to be divided equally. Thus, each partner also gets $19,800 ÷ 2 = $9,900. Ms. Wane therefore receives $9,900 + $2,800 = $12,700, and Ms. Watson receives $9,900 + $1,600 = $11,500.

• PROBLEM 21-11

Conway and Roberts own a business. Conway has invested $50,000 and Roberts, $40,000. Each partner will receive from the firm's profit 6% interest on his investment and 1/2 of the balance. Last year the firm's profit was $20,000. How much should each partner receive?

Solution: Conway's interest = $50,000 x 6% = $50,000 x.06 = $3,000.
Robert's interest = $40,000 x 6% = $40,000 x .06 = $2,400.
Total interest on investment = $5,400 . After interest was paid, there should be a $20,000 - $5,400 = $14,600 balance. Each partner should receive 1/2 of $14,600, or $7,300.

The profit, therefore, should be shared as follows:

Conway:	$3,000 + $7,300 =	$10,300
Roberts:	$2,400 + $7,300 =	$ 9,700
Total profit	=	$20,000

• PROBLEM 21-12

Ike Waterman and Sean Cole invested $20,000 and $10,000 respectively in a fast food store. Each partner receives 6% of his investment. The remaining profit is to be shared equally. If the profit last year was $10,400, what was each partner's share?

Solution: To find out the interest that each one gets on his investment, multiply the investment by 6% (.06). Waterman received $20,000 x .06 = $1,200, and Cole received $10,000 X .06 = $600. The total interest was $600 + $1,200 = $1,800. The balance of profits, the profits ($10,400) less the total interest ($1,800), is $8,600. Each partner's share of this is $8,600 ÷ 2 = $4,300.

Waterman's share of the profits was therefore $4,300 + $1,200 = $5,500, and Cole's share was $4,300 + $600 = $4,900.

• PROBLEM 21-13

Al and Bob have invested $70,000 and $90,000 respectively, in a business. The profits and losses are shared, so that each partner receives 8% interest on his investment and 1/2 of the balance. If the business earns a $10,000 profit, what is each partner's share?

Solution: Al's interest: $70,000 x 8% = $70,000 X .08 = $5,600.

Bob's interest: $90,000 X 8% = $90,000 X ,08 = $7,200

Total interest income = $12,800

The balance after interest has been allocated is $10,000 - 12,800 = -$2,800. This negative balance is divided equally the same way a positive balance would have been. Therefore, each partner must deduct 1/2 of -$2,800 or -$1,400 from his interest income. If the balance had been positive, each would have added 1/2 of it to his interest income.

Partner's share: interest income - share of negative balance
Al's share: $5,600 - $1,400 = $4,200

Bob's share: $7,200 - $1,400 = $5,800 .
Total profit of business = $10,000.

• PROBLEM 21-14

Bob Gafney and Susan Medina invested $40,000 and $50,000 respectively in a luncheonette. Since Mr. Gafney is the manager of the luncheonette, he gets 4% of the net income. Each partner receives 6% interest on his or her investment. Any remaining net income is divided equally. If the net income for any year is $28,600, how is it divided?

Solution: Mr. Gafney's interest: 4% of net income (.04 × $28,600 = $1,144) + 6% on investment (.06 × $40,000 = $2,400) = $3,544.

Ms. Medina's interest:
6% on investment = .06 x $50,000 = $3,000

Total interest $6,544

There is a $28,600 - 6,544 = $22,056 balance to be divided equally; each partner will receive, in addition to interest income, $22,056 ÷ 2 = $11,028 .

Mr. Gafney's income: $3,544 + $11,028 = $14,572
Ms. Medina's income: $3,000 + $11,028 = $14,028

Total income $28,600

• PROBLEM 21-15

Frank Higgins and Joe Dumont invested $16,000 and $24,000 respectively, in a car wash. Their gross profit last year was $28,500, with expenses of $6,580. Each partner is to receive 6% interest on his investment, and the remaining net income is to be shared equally.

(a) What was the net income of the car wash?

(b) What was each partner's share of the net income.

Solution: (a) Net income = gross profit - expenses
= $28,500 - $6,580
= $21,920 .

(b) Interest on investment:
Higgins: 6% X $16,000 = .06 X $16,000 = $960

Dumont: 6% X $24,000 = .06 X $24,000 = $1,440
Total interest on investment = $2,400

The remainder of the net income to be shared equally was $21,920 - $2,400 = $19,520, of which each partner received half, or $9,760.
Higgins' share of net income: $960 + $9,760 = $10,720

Dumont's share of net income: $1,440 + $9,760 = $11,200
Net income = $21,920

• PROBLEM 21-16

Kirk and Martin are partners and have agreed that, after interest at 6% is allowed on average investment, Kirk will receive one third and Martin two thirds of the remaining profits. On Jan. 1, Kirk's net worth was $72,000 and Martin's was $63,000. Kirk withdrew $3,000 on July 1 and made an additional investment of $1,200 on Nov. 1. On Aug. 1 Martin withdrew $1,800. If profits for the year amounted to $37,080, what was each partner's share?

Solution: If I = an investment held in a company and m = the number of months the investment is held, average investment equals the sum of all I X m held during one year divided by 12.

Kirk started the year with a net worth, or investment of $72,000. On July 1 he withdrew $3,000, changing his net worth to $69,000. Thus he held a $12,000 investment for 6 months. On November 1, he added $1,200 changing his net worth to $70,200. Thus, he held a $69,000 investment for 4 months and a $70,200 investment for 2 months.

$72,000 X 6 months = $432,000
+ $69,000 X 4 months = $276,000
+ $70,200 X 2 months = $140,400
$848,400

His average investment was $848,400 ÷ 12 = $70,700. The interest due him was 6% of $70,700 = .06 X $70,700 = $4,242.

Martin's net worth started at $63,000. He withdrew $1,800 on August 1, changing his net worth to $61,200. Thus he held a $63,000 investment for 7 months, and a $61,200 investment for 5 months.

$$
\begin{array}{lr}
\$63,000 \times 7 \text{ months} = & \$441,000 \\
+ \quad \$61,200 \times 5 \text{ months} = & \underline{\$306,000} \\
 & \$747,000
\end{array}
$$

His average investment was $747,000 ÷ 12 = $62,250. Thus his interest was 6% of $62,250 = .06 x $62,250 = $3,735. The total interest due was $4,242 (Kirk) + $3,735 (Martin) = $7,977. The balance of profits was $37,080 (total profits) - $7,977 (interest due) = $29,103.

Kirk's share of the balance was 1/3 x $29,103 = $9,701. Martin's share of the balance was 2/3 x $29,103 = $19,402.

Kirk's share of total profits: $4,242 + $9,701 = $13,943

Martin's share of total profits: $3,735 + $9,402 = $23,137

Total profits = $37,080

CHAPTER 22

COST ACCOUNTING

STANDARD COSTS

• PROBLEM 22-1

The Ships Ahoy Manufacturing Company, a producer of supplies for both commercial and leisure time fishermen, wants to check on the efficiency of the production of its deluxe net for tuna fishing. It has established standard costs for making one of these fishing nets as shown below:

Deluxe Fishing Net

Direct materials: 15 pounds @ 21¢	$3.15
Direct labor: 6 hours @ $2.00	12.00
Overhead costs	
Variable overhead cost $1.20 per direct labor hour	7.20
Fixed overhead cost: $0.85 per direct labor hour.	5.10
Total costs per net	$27.45

The fixed overhead rate is based on normal monthly activity of 120,000 direct labor hours. Last month 19,500 nets were produced. There had been no inital inventories. The total costs of production were:

Materials used: 296,000 @ 22¢	$65,120
Direct labor: 120,000 hours	252,000
Overhead	
Variable overhead:	$141,000
Fixed overhead:	$103,500

Find the following variances: price, quantity, labor rate, labor, and overhead.

Solution: A variance is the difference between the actual costs and the standard costs of a production process. The actual costs differ from the standard costs either because the inputs (hours of labor or units of material) have a different cost per unit, or because production required a different amount of an input than was specified in the list of standard costs. We must check for both causes of variation.

1) In direct materials used there is obviously a price variance of 1¢ per pound. The total unfavorable price variance is equal to:

(price variance per unit) × (total units used)

$$\$0.01/\text{lb.} \times 296{,}000 \text{ lbs.} = \$2{,}960.$$

i.e., materials cost was $2,960 more than was expected. The price variance can also be calculated by subtracting the total standard cost of materials used from the total actual cost of materials used:

total actual cost of materials used ($296,000 × $.22)	=	$65,120
total standard cost of materials used (296,000 × $.21)	=	$62,160
Price variance of materials used	=	$ 2,960

2) Companies generally calculate their quantity variances in dollars. The standard number of pounds that are expected to make 19,500 nets is

$$19{,}500 \text{ nets} \times 15 \text{ lb/net} = 292{,}500 \text{ lb.}$$

The total number of pounds actually used is 296,000 so that there was an unfavorable quantity variance of

$$296{,}000 - 292{,}500 = 3{,}500$$

pounds. The dollarized quantity variance is this number of pounds times the standard cost of one pound or

$$3{,}500 \text{ lbs.} \times \$0.21/\text{lb.} = \$735$$

3) We calculate the actual labor rate by dividing the total cost of labor by the total hours worked.

$$\text{The actual labor rate} = \frac{\$252{,}000}{120{,}000} = \$2.10/\text{hr.}$$

The standard labor rate is $2.00/hr so that the unfavorable labor rate variance is

$$\$2.10/\text{hr.} - \$2.00/\text{hr.} = \$0.10/\text{hr.}$$

i.e., the labor rate has increased by 10 cents per hour.

4) The standard amount of labor to produce 19,500 nets is

(6 hours/net)×(19,500 nets) = 117,000 hours.

The actual number of hours used is 120,000. There is an unfavorable labor variance of 120,000 - 117,000 = 3,000 hours. At the standard labor rate of $2.00/hr., the unfavorable, dollarized labor variance is 3,000 hrs × $2/hr = $6,000.

5) Variable overhead

There ar two variable overhead variances to consider, the spending variance and efficiency variance.

The standard variable overhead cost for the 120,000 labor hours actually used is

120,000 hrs × $1.20/hr. = $144,000 .

This is the variable overhead we would expect to incur for 120,000 labor hours, where $1.20/hr. is the variable overhead rate. The total actual variable overhead is $141,000 so that the spending variance is

$144,000 - $141,000 = $3,000.

This is a favorable variance. The number of hours that should have been worked in producing 19,500 nets is 19,500 nets × 6 hours/net = 117,000. The actual number of hours worked is 120,000, thus giving the unfavorable labor variance of 3,000 hours.

The dollarized efficiency variance is

3,000 hrs × $1.20/hr. = $3,600.

6) Fixed overhead

The fixed overhead rate of 85¢/hr. is based on a monthly activity of 120,000 labor hours. Therefore total standard fixed overhead is 120,000 × 85¢ = $102,000. There are two fixed overhead variances to consider: the budget variance which refers to differences in cost, and the volume variance which refers to differences in labor hours.

Since actual labor hours worked equals the standard number of labor hours upon which the fixed overhead rate was based, there is no volume variance.

Budget variance is actual fixed overhead minus standard fixed overhead = 103,500 - 102,000 = 1,500. This variance is unfavorable because actual cost exceed standard cost.

• **PROBLEM 22-2**

Analysis of Variances. Chemical, Inc., has set up the following standards for materials and direct labor:

	PER FINISHED UNIT
Materials: 10 lbs. @ \$3.00	\$30.00
Direct labor: 4 hours @ \$2.50	10.00

The number of finished units budgeted for the period was 10,000; 9,810 units were actually produced.

Actual results were:

Materials: 98,073 lbs. used	
Direct labor: 39,300 hrs.	\$98,240

During the month, purchases amounted to 100,000 lbs. at a total cost of \$301,193.

Compute a) the materials price variance, b) the materials quantity variance c) the labor rate variance and d) the labor efficiency variance. Comment on whether each variance is favorable or unfavorable.

Solution: a) The actual cost of one pound of materials is

$$\frac{\text{Actual price}}{\text{Actual purchase size}} = \frac{\$301,193}{100,000 \text{ lbs}} = \$3.01/\text{lb.}$$

The price variance per lb. is \$3.01 - \$3.00 = 1¢
The total variance = Total purchase × variance = 100,000 lbs × 1¢ = \$1,000. This is an unfavorable variance since the actual cost is greater than the standard cost.

b) Materials for 9,810 units should have been 9,810 × 10 lbs. = 98,100 lbs. 98,073 were actually used so the variance was 98,100 - 98,073 = 27 lbs. In dollar terms the variance is 27 lbs × \$3.00 (standard price) = \$81.00. This is a favorable variance since less than the standard amount of materials was used.

c) For 39,300 labor hours the cost should have been \$2.50/hr. × 39,300 = \$98,250. The actual cost was \$98,240. The total labor cost variance was \$98,250 - 98,240 = \$10. This is a favorable variance since less than the standard cost was spent on labor.

d) To produce 9,810 units, 9,810 × 4 hrs./unit = 39,240 hrs. should have been worked. It actually took 39,300 hours to make 9,810 units, so the unfavorable variance is 39,300 hours - 39,240 hours = 60 hours. The variance in dollar terms is 60 hours × \$2.50/labor hour = \$150.

• PROBLEM 22-3

The standard cost card for the Rollins Manufacturing Company's only product is:

STANDARD COST CARD	
Materials	$108
Labor: 4 hours @ $8.00 per hour.....	32
Overhead	
Variable: $3.50 per labor hour....	14
Fixed: $1.00 per labor hour (rate based on normal capacity)	4
Total standard cost per unit......	$158

Other data is as follows:

Normal capacity:	40,000 units
Units produced:	38,000 units
Actual labor hours:	155,000 hours
Actual fixed overhead:	$162,000
Actual variable overhead:	$580,000

Required:

Compute the variable and fixed overhead variances.

Solution: The variable overhead variance consists of two items: the spending variance and the efficiency variance. The spending variance is the difference between the actual variable overhead cost and the product of actual hours worked and the standard variable overhead rate.

Actual variable overhead	$580,000
Actual labor hours at standard variable overhead cost (155,000 @ 3.50)....	542,500
Variable overhead spending variance........	$ 37,500

The efficiency variance is the labor efficiency variance times the standard variable overhead rate per hour. The labor efficiency variance (in hours) is the difference between the actual number of hours it took to complete a given number of units (here, 38,000 units) and the standard time it should take to complete them.

Actual time to finish 38,000 units	155,000
less: Standard time to finish 38,000 units @ 4 hrs.	152,000

Labor efficiency variance (in hours) 3,000

The variable overhead efficiency variance is:

Labor efficiency variance (in hours)	3,000
times: variable overhead rate per hour	×$3.50
	$10,500

The are also 2 fixed overhead variances, the <u>budget variance</u> and the <u>volume variance.</u> The budget variance is the difference between the actual overhead cost and the budgeted overhead cost. Here, the budgeted overhead rate of $1.00 per hour based on a normal capacity of 40,000 units @ 4 hours or 160,000 hours. The budget variance is therefore:

Actual fixed overhead:	$162,000
less: Budgeted overhead:	160,000
	$ 2,000

The volume variance measures, in dollars, the expected number of units to be produced as per normal capacity figures and the actual number produced.

Volume variance is:

Fixed overhead for expected production (40,000 @ $4)	$160,000
less: fixed overhead for actual production (38,000 @ $4)	$152,000
	$ 8,000

• PROBLEM 22-4

The Funtime Toy Company has recently established a standard cost system to control costs. The standard cost per unit have been established as:

Materials: 12 pieces per unit @ 56¢ each
Labor: 2 hours per unit @ $2.75/hour

Last month, the company finished 1,000 units
Actual production costs for the month were:

Materials: 14,000 pieces at a total cost of $7,140

Labor: 2,500 direct labor hours at a total cost of $8,000

There were no beginning or ending inventories. Compute the material price and quantity variances and the labor cost (rate) and efficiency variances. Briefly explain the significance of each variance.

Solution: The material price variance is the difference between the standard and actual cost of the actual amount of materials used.

Actual cost of 14,000 pieces	$7,140
less: Standard cost of 14,000 pieces (14,000 × 56¢/piece)	$7,840
Total material price variance	-$ 700

That the actual cost of materials used is less than the standard cost of materials used is a favorable sign. It shows that the purchasing department has been thrifty and has been taking advantage of available discounts.

The material quantity variance is the difference between the actual and standard quantity of materials needed to produce the actual output (i.e., 1,000 units).

Actual materials for 1,000 units	14,000
less: Standard materials for 1,000 units (1,000 units × 12 pcs/unit)..........	12,000
Materials quantity variance in unit terms	2,000

Materials quantity variance in dollar = variance in units × standard cost per unit

= 2,000 units × 56¢ = $1,120.00 .

If the actual quantity of materials used exceeds the standard quantity, as it does here, it could either mean that labor is wasting and/or stealing the materials, or that management underestimated how much material would be needed.

The labor rate, or cost variance is the difference between the actual labor cost and the standard cost of the actual hours worked.

Actual cost of 2,500 labor hours	$8,000
less: Standard cost of 2,500 labor hours (2,500 hrs × 2.75/hr)	6,875
Total labor rate (cost) variance	$1,125

This variance can also be calculated as:

Actual direct labor hours (actual rate/hr. - standard rate/hours)

$$= 2{,}500 \left(\frac{\$8{,}000}{2{,}500} - \$2.75 \right)$$

$$= 2{,}500\ (\$3.20-2.75) = 2{,}500 \times 0.45 = \$112.5$$

Note: actual rate per hour =

$$\frac{\text{Actual Total Labor Cost}}{\text{Actual Direct Labor Hours}}$$

The actual labor cost is higher than the standard cost. Management may or may not have control over how much it pays labor, depending on the existence of labor, unions, a minimum wage rate, etc.

The labor efficiency variance is the difference between the actual number of labor hours used to produce the actual output and the standard number of labor hours estimated for that output.

Actual labor hours for 1,000 units	2,500
less: Standard labor hours for 1,000 units (1,000 units × 2 hrs/unit)..............	2,000
Labor efficiency variance in hours	500 hrs.

Labor efficiency variance in dollars =

Labor efficiency variance in hours × standard labor rate

= 500 hrs × 2.75/hr. = $1,375.00 .

Once again the actual amount exceeds the standard amount, there is an unfavorable variance. This could either mean that labor is slow and inefficient or that not enough machines and tools are available per worker so that each may produce as many units as possible without having to stop and "share" or rotate use of the equipment.

• PROBLEM 22-5

The Patrick Company has the following standard cost card for one of its products.

Standard Cost Card One Unit of Production	
Materials: 35 lbs. @ $1.20 per lb.........	$42
Labor: 10 hours @ $3.60 per hour......	36
Variable overhead: 1.50 per direct labor hour...........	15
Fixed overhead: 1.00 per direct labor hour	10
Total standard cost per unit............	$103

The actual production data is:

1. 23,800 units were produced

2. Materials:

Actual cost of raw material purchases:	$1,036,029
Units of raw materials purchased	842,300 lbs.
Units of raw materials used:	821,000 lbs.

3. Labor:

Actual labor cost	$ 847,875
Labor hours worked	226,100 hrs.

4. Variable overhead cost: $ 377,022

5. Fixed overhead cost:

Actual cost:	$ 240,000
Budgeted cost:	245,000

Find the following variances.

(a) Material price variance.

(b) Material quantity variance.

(c) Labor rate variance.

(d) Labor efficiency variance.

(e) Variable overhead spending variance.

(f) Variable overhead efficiency variance.

(g) Fixed overhead budget variance.

Solution: (a) The actual cost per unit is

$$\frac{\$1,036,029}{842,300 \text{ lbs.}} = \$1.23/\text{lb.}$$

The difference in price is 1.23 - 1.20 = $0.03/lb. The dollarized material price variance is

$$\$0.03/\text{lb} \times 842,300 \text{ lbs.} = \underline{\underline{\$25,269}} \ .$$

This is a unfavorable variance, which means more than the standard price was spent.

(b) The quantity of materials that should have been used is

23,800 units × 35 lbs./unit = 833,000 lbs.

The quantity variance in units is 821,000 lbs - 833,000 lbs = -12,000 lbs.

Dollarized material quantity variance:

-12,000 × $1.20 = $14,400 (favorable) .

Note that we used the figure for actual materials used and not the figure for actual materials purchased to calculate the quantity variance. This is because the quantity variance deals with the differences in quantities used. The favorable variance means that <u>less</u> than the standard quantity was used.

(c) The actual labor rate is

$$\frac{\$847,875}{226,100 \text{ hrs}} = \$3.75/\text{hr}.$$

Difference in rate: $3.75/hr - $3.60/hr = $0.15/hr.

Dollarized labor rate variance:

$0.15/hr × 226,100 hrs = <u>$33,915</u> (unfavorable).

(d) Hours that should have been worked:

23,800 units × 10 hrs./unit = 238,000 hrs.

Difference in hours: 226,100 - 238,000 = -11,900

Dollarized labor efficiency variance:

-11,900 hrs × $3.60/hr. = <u>$-42,840</u> (favorable).

(e) The actual variable overhead cost is $377,022. At $1.50 per direct labor hour, the budget for 226,100 hours is $1.50/hr. × 226,100 hr. = $339,150. There is an unfavorable spending variance of

$377,022 - 339,150 = <u>$37,872</u>.

(f) In (d) we found there was a favorable labor efficiency of 11,900 hours. At $1.50/hr the dollarized variance is 11,900 hrs. × $1.50/hr. = $17,850.

(g) Budgeted cost: $245,000

Actual cost: 240,000

$ 5,000 (favorable) .

The Sterling Manufacturing Company has the following standard cost card for its main product.

Product Zee-Standard Cost Card

Per unit costs:	
Materials (5 lbs. @ $3/lb)	$ 15
Labor (10 hrs. @ $2/hr.)	20
Variable overhead (70¢ per labor hour)	7
Fixed overhead (30¢ per labor hr.)	3
Standard Cost per unit	$ 45

The fixed overhead rate is based on a normal activity level of 100,000 labor hours per month. Two months ago the actual cost and production data were as follows:

Goods produced: 8,000 units

Materials Purchases: 50,000 lbs. for a total cost of $152,000.

Materials used in production: 46,000 lbs.

Labor hours worked: 85,000 for a total cost of $175,000

Factory overhead incurred: fixed, $31,000; variable $64,000.

Calculate the following variances: (a) materials price (b) materials quantity (c) labor cost (wage rate) (d) labor efficiency (e) variable overhead spending (f) variable overhead efficiency (g) fixed overhead budget (h) fixed overhead volume. State whether each variance is favorable or unfavorable.

Solution: (a) The actual materials cost per pound is

$$\frac{\text{Actual Total Cost}}{\text{Actual total material in pounds}} =$$

$$\frac{\$152{,}000}{50{,}000 \text{ lbs.}} = \$3.04/\text{lb.}$$

The price variance per pound is $3.04 - 3.00 = 4¢/lb.

The total price variance for materials is

$$50{,}000 \times \$0.04 = \$2{,}000.$$

This variance can also be calculated:

Actual cost of 50,000 lbs.	$152,000
less: Standard cost of 50,000 lbs. (@ 3.00/lb.)	150,000
	$ 2,000

This is an unfavorable variance, since the actual cost of materials was greater than the standard cost.

(b) The standard amount of materials to produce 8,000 units is 8,000 × 5 lbs/units = 40,000 lbs. However 46,000 pounds were actually used, which yields an unfavorable quantity variance of 46,000 lbs - 40,000 lbs. = 6,000 lbs, or in dollar terms (6,000 × standard cost $3/lb,) = $18,000.

(c) Actual cost of 85,000 labor hours	$175,000
less: Standard cost of 85,000 labor hours @ $2.00/hr.	170,000
Total labor cost (wage rate) variance (unfavorable)	5,000

(d) Actual hours to complete 8,000 units	85,000
less: Standard hours to complete 8,000 units @ 10 hrs/unit	80,000
Labor efficiency variance in hours	5,000
Labor efficiency variance in dollars (@ 2/hr.)	$10,000

This is an unfavorable variance.

(e) Actual variable overhead for 85,000 labor hours	$64,000
less: Standard variable overhead for 85,000 hrs. @ 70¢/hr.	59,500
Variable overhead spending variable (unfavorable)	$4,500

(f) Variable overhead efficiency variance = labor efficiency variance (in hours) × standard variable overhead rate

= 5,000 hrs. (unfavorable) × 70¢/hr.

= \$3,500 (unfavorable).

(g) Actual Fixed overhead = \$31,000

(g) Actual Fixed overhead =	\$31,000
less: Budget Fixed overhead	30,000
Unfavorable Fixed overhead budget variance	\$ 1,000

(h) Applied Fixed overhead =

Actual labor hours × Fixed overhead rate

85,000 × 30¢/hr. = \$25,500 .

The fixed overhead volume variance is computed as follows:

Budgeted fixed overhead	\$30,000
less: Applied fixed overhead	25,500
	\$ 4,500

or as follows:

(Budgeted normal activity in labor hours - actual activity) × fixed overhead rate

= (100,000 hrs - 85,000) × 30¢

= 15,000 × 30¢ = \$4,500 .

Since this variance indicates that the activity level was less than normal, it is considered an unfavorable variance.

• **PROBLEM 22-7**

The Standwell Company produces a night table for which the standard costs are as follows.

Materials Lumber - 50 board feet @ 10¢	\$5.00
Direct labor 3 hours at \$2.00	6.00
Indirect costs:	
Variable overhead - \$1.00 per direct labor hour	3.00
Fixed overhead - \$0.50 per direct labor hour	1.50
	\$15.50

Last month, 400 night tables were made. There were no initial or ending inventories. The summary of operating costs showed the following variances:

Material price variance	250 (U)
Material quantity variance	100 (U)
Direct labor rate variance	110 (F)
Direct labor efficiency variance	200 (F)
Fixed overhead	
Budget variance	10 (U)
Volume variance	$100 (U)
Variable overhead:	
Efficiency variance	100 (F)
Spending variance	200 (U)

Find for last month's production

(a) Actual materials used (board feet of lumber, and actual cost of materials used.)

(b) Accrued (actual) payroll.

(c) Actual variable overhead incurred.

(d) Normal activity (indirect labor hours).

(e) Actual direct labor hours used.

(f) Actual direct labor rate per hour.

(U) means an unfavorable variance and (F) means a favorable one.

Solution:

a.) The total cost of the actual amount of board, priced at the standard cost of 10¢ per board foot, is the sum of the standard cost of wood for 400 desks and the quantity variance. We add the quantity variance because it is unfavorable. Unfavorable variances mean that what was actually spent or used exceeds the standards set. Total standard cost of wood for 400 desks is 400 × $5.00 = 2,000. ($5.00 is the cost of wood per desk.)

Standard cost of wood	$2,000
Quantity variance	100
Total quantity at standard cost	$2,100

To find total quantity in board feet, let x equal the number of board feet. Since $2,100 is the total cost when each board foot costs 10¢.

$$2,100 = .10x$$

$$21,000 = x$$

21,000 board feet were used to make 400 desks.

The actual cost per board can be determined by calculating the total actual cost of wood and dividing it by total actual amount of wood. Here we are interested in price changes, so we add in the price variance. In computing the actual materials used we added only the quantity variance because we were only interested in the change in quantity. We add both variances rather than subtract because both are unfavorable and therefore cause costs to exceed the standard costs.

Actual total cost of wood = Standard cost + price variance

+ quantity variance

= 2,000 + 250 + 100

= 2,350 .

Cost per unit = $2,350 ÷ 21,000 $\simeq$ 11¢,

b.) Actual accrued payroll is the standard cost of payroll plus, or minus, the variances. Both labor variances were favorable, which means that the actual rate of pay for labor and the actual amount of labor used were less than what the standard cost card had established. Therefore we subtract the variances from total standard labor costs to get the actual labor cost. The total standard cost is standard cost per tables.

Actual labor costs = standard labor costs - (labor rate variance + labor efficiency variance)

= 2,400 - (110+200) = 2,400 - 310

= $2,090 .

c.) Variable overhead is the cost of running an operation that varies directly with the amount of production. The efficiency variance, like the labor efficiency variance, refers to the number of hours needed to produce a given amount. Here, the variable overhead efficiency variance is favorable. This means that less than the standard number of direct labor hours have been used to produce the tables. The spending variance refers to the rate charged per direct labor hour to cover the variable overhead. We add this variance to standard variable overhead, because it is unfavorable. We subtract the favorable efficiency variance. Total standard variable overhead equals the standard cost per direct labor hour times the standard number of labor hours for 400 tables.

Total standard variable overhead for 400 tables =

$$\$1.00 \times 3 \times 400 = \$1,200 \ .$$

Actual variable overhead = standard variable overhead + spending variance - efficiency variance

$$= \$1,200 + 200 - 100 = \$1,300.$$

d.) Normal activity in direct labor hours is

$$= \text{Standard hours per unit} \times \text{number of units}$$

$$= \quad 3 \quad \times \quad 400$$

$$= 1,200 \ .$$

e.) Actual direct labor hours are calculated in the following steps.

1. Calculate standard labor cost for 400 tables. Labor for each table is \$6.00 therefore total standard labor cost is 4 × \$6.00 or 2,400.

2. Subtract the labor efficiency variance from standard labor cost, \$2,400 - 200 = \$2,200. Since we have left the labor rate variance out of our calculations, the number we have, \$2,200, is the cost of total labor hours used priced at the standard rate of \$2.00 per hour.

3. Let x = total labor hours used

$$2,200 = 2x$$

$$x = 1,100 \ .$$

f.) Actual direct labor rate =

$$\frac{\text{Total Actual Labor Cost}}{\text{Actual Labor Hours}} \ .$$

from part (b), labor cost is \$2,090.

$$\text{Labor rate} = \frac{\$2,090}{1,100} = \$1.90 \text{ per hour.}$$

The following data from the records of the Gas-Widget Company for the year ended December 31, 19A, are available:

1) Standard cost card:

Materials	(2 lb. @ $5)	$10
Labor	(5 hr. @ $2)	10
Overhead	(5 hr. @ $1.40)	7
Total		$27

2) Annual flexible overhead budget:

practical capacity = 50,000 direct-labor hours

	Total	Rate
Fixed costs	$25,000	$0.50
Variable costs	45,000	0.90
Total	$70,000	$1.40

3) Equivalent units of product produced for the year: for materials, 8,000; for labor and overhead, 8,500.

4) Direct materials inventory, January 1, 19A (beginning) 3,000 pounds.

5) Purchased materials, 16,000 pounds at average price of $5.02 per pound, $80,320.

6) Direct materials inventory, December 31, 19A (ending), 2,000 pounds.

7) Direct-labor costs: 45,000 hours worked at average labor rate of $2.05 per hours, $92,250.

8) Actual fixed overhead costs incurred, $25,000; actual variable overhead costs incurred $45,000.

9) Sold during 19A, 8,000 units of product at $40 each, $320,000.

10) Finished goods inventory, January 1, 19A (beginning), zero; finished goods inventory, December 31, 19A (ending), 1,000 units.

11) Work in process inventory, January 1, 19A (beginning), 2,000 units-completed as to materials, one-half completed as to labor and overhead.

REQUIRED: 1) How many units were in the work in process inventory, December 31, 19A (ending) (and at what stage of completion were labor and overhead costs?) Materials costs were fully complete in this inventory.

2) Compute the following variations (gain or loss?): (a) materials price, (b) materials usage, (c) labor wage rate, (d) labor efficiency, (e) overhead activity, (f) overhead budget, (g) overhead efficiency.

Solution: 1) Since 8500 units were completed as to labor and overhead while only 8000 were completed as to materials, the labor and overhead were completed for the equivalent of 8500 - 8000 = 500 units beyond the 8000 totally completed during the year. The costs to provide all the labor overhead for 500 units equals the cost of half the labor and overhead for 1000 units. Since the 2000 units in the beginning inventory were half-done as to labor and overhead, the expediture to provide 500 units' worth of labor & overhead had to be made to provide 1000 units' worth of half the labor and overhead; thereby completing 1000 units from the beginning inventory which had been missing ½ the necessary labor and overhead. Therefore 2000 - 1000 = 1000 units half-completed as to labor and overhead were left in the work in process inventory on December 31. 8000 units produced completely within the year and the 1000 finished during the year equal 9000 units to be transferred to the finished goods inventory. Of these 8000 were sold, leaving, as stated in item (10) of the question, 1000 units.

2) (a) The materials price is equal to

(Actual price per pound - standard price per pound) × pounds purchased

= (5.02 - 5.00) × 16,000 = $0.02 × 16,000 = $320.

(b) For the 8000 units completed as to materials, 8000 units × 2 lbs. per unit = 16,000 lbs. is the standard amount of materials used. The actual amount of materials used was:

Beginning inventory: Materials	3,000 lbs.
Purchases	+ 16,000 lbs.
Materials available	19,000 lbs.
less: ending inventory	- 2,000 lbs.
Materials used	17,000 lbs.

Materials usage variance =

(Actual materials used - Standard materials used) × Standard price per pound

(17,000 pounds - 16,000 pounds) × $5.00 per pound

= 1000 pounds × $5.00 = $5,000.

(c) Labor wage rate variance =

(Actual wage rate - standard wage rate) × (direct labor hours)

= ($2.05 - 2.00) × 45,000 hours = $0.05 × 45,000

= $2,250

(d) For the 8,500 units completed as to labor, 8,500 units × 5 labor hours per unit = 42,500 labor hours was the standard number of hours for production. The labor efficiency variance, which measures labor's speed and competence is calculated as follows:

(Actual direct labor hours - standard direct labor hours) × standard wage rate

= (45,000 - 42,500) × $2.00 per hour

= 2,500 hours × $2.00 per hour

= $5,000 .

(e) The activity variance - standard overhead rate × (actual labor hours - standard labor hours) = $1.40 × (45,000 - 50,000) = -$7,000. This negative variance means that less than the standard number of hours were used. Remember, that the labor efficiency variance indicates that more than the standard number of labor hours have been worked, considering the number of units produced.

(f) There is no overhead budget variance;

Budgeted overhead costs		$70,000
Actual fixed costs	$25,000	
Actual variable costs	45,000	70,000
Budget variance		$ 0

(g) The overhead efficiency variance will be the difference between actual overhead hours for 8,500 units and the standard number of hours times the standard overhead rate

Actual overhead hours:	45,000
Standard overhead hours: 8,500 units × 5 hrs. per unit =	42,500
	2,500
Standard overhead rate	×$1.40
Overhead efficiency variance	$3,500

Except for the overhead activity and budget variances,

all the variances indicate that the time and money actually used exceeded the standard amounts. The actual prices of materials and labor were higher than the standard costs and more than the standard amounts of labor and materials were used.

• PROBLEM 22-9

The standard cost of one unit of product of a company is:

Materials (10 pounds @ $2)	$20
Labor (5 hours @ $3)	15
Overhead (5 hours @ $1.20)	6
Standard Cost per Unit	$41

Last month 1,000 units were manufactured, and 800 were sold for $53 per unit. The costs actually incurred were:

Materials (purchased and used, 10,500 lbs.)	$21,525
Labor (5,100 hours)	15,402
Overhead	6,400

1) What is a standard cost? How is it used?

2) Find the 2 materials variances and state whether each is favorable or unfavorable.

3) Find the 2 labor variances and state whether each is favorable or unfavorable.

4) How much is the overhead variance?

Solution: 1) A standard cost is the expected expense of producing an item. Actual expenses incurred are compared to standard costs and differences between the two can be analyzed to detect inefficiency and waste in operations.

2) The price or rate variance is the difference between the standard and actual cost of all materials purchased. A large variance might indicate that the purchasing department has not taken advantage of all available discounts or has not found a dealer who offers the best prices.

Standard Cost of Materials Purchased =

Standard Unit Cost × Actual Materials Purchased

= $2 per pound × 10,500 pounds

= $21,000 .

Actual Cost of Materials Purchased	$21,525
less: Standard Cost of Materials Purchased	(21,000)
Materials Price Variance	$525

This is an unfavorable variance, since the actual cost is greater than the standard cost.

This variance can also be computed by multiplying the difference between the standard and actual unit price by the number of units purchased.

$(\frac{\$21,525}{10,500} - \$2.00) \times 10,500 = (\$2.05/\text{lb.} - \$2.00) \times 10,500 \text{ lbs}$

$= \$0.05$ variance per pound $= \$525$. $2.05 is the actual cost per pound.

The quantity variance measures possible waste or theft of materials.

Actual Materials Used	10,500 lbs.
Standard Materials Used: 10 lbs. per unit × 1,000 units =	(10,000 lbs.)
Material Quantity Variance	500 lbs.
Quantity Variance in dollar terms ($2 per lb;)	$1,000

This variance is unfavorable, as it shows 500 pounds (or $1,000) of materials beyond the standard allowances were used. When considering the rate variance, evaluate it in terms of materials purchased, since this variance helps evaluate the operations of the purchase department. "Materials used" for the quantity variance is used to evaluate the production department.

3) The labor rate variance, which is used to evaluate the wage for which competent help can be hired, can be computed by the same two methods by which the materials variance is computed.

Actual Labor Cost:	$15,402
Standard Labor Cost of 5,100 hours @ $3.00/hour	$15,300
Labor rate variance	$ 102

The actual labor cost is greater than the standard cost. Therefore the variance is unfavorable or,

$(\frac{15,402}{5,100 \text{ hours}} - \$3.00/\text{hour}) \times 5,100 \text{ hours} = (\$3.02/\text{hour} - \$3.00/\text{hour}) \times 5,100 \text{ hours} = \$0.02/\text{hour} \times 5,100 \text{ hours} = \$102.$

$3.02/hour is the actual hourly labor wage and $0.02 is the variance per labor hour.

The efficiency variance measures the speed and competence of labor. It is the difference between the standard cost of actual labor hours and the standard cost of standard labor hours. The standard number of labor hours is (number of units produced) × (standard labor hours per unit) = 1,000 unit × 5 hours/unit = 5,000 hours.

Standard Cost of Actual Labor hours:	
5,100 hours × $3/hr. =	$15,300
Standard Cost of Standard Labor hours:	
5,000 hours × $3/hr. =	$15,000
Labor Efficiency Variance	$ 300

More than the standard number of labor hours have been used; the efficiency variance is unfavorable.

The total labor variance, $15,402 - 15,000 = $402, is equal to the sum of the rate variance, $102, and the efficiency variance $300.

4) Actual overhead cost:	$6,400
Standard overhead cost:	
1,000 unit × $6/unit	$6,000
	$ 400

The actual cost is greater than the standard cost; the variance is unfavorable.

• PROBLEM 22-10

The Keldsen Company uses a standard cost system for its production activity. Standard cost data applicable to 19x1, and actual data for 19x1, are as follows:

Standard Data:

Normal activity: 112,500 units
Materials: 30 lb per unit @ $1.50 per lb
Labor: 8 hours per unit @ $3.00 per hour
Overhead: Fixed, $900,000; Variable, $2.00 per direct labor hours

Actual Data:

Units produced: 120,000 units
Materials requisitioned and used: 3,750,000 lb

Materials inventory data:

Purchases: (A) 80,000 lb @ $1.60
(B) 1,200,000 lb @ $1.40
(C) 1,440,000 lb @ $1.50
(D) 1,100,000 lb @ $1.70

Labor: A total cost of $2,929,500 based on 945,000 hours.
Overhead: Actual total overhead $2,560,000, comprising $850,000 fixed and $1,710,000 variable.

Required:

Compute the material, labor, and overhead variances.

Solution: (1) The material variance can be broken down into two parts, the price variance and the quantity variance.

(a) The price variance measures the total difference between what should have been paid for the amount purchased and what was actually paid for the amount purchased. First we calculate the actual per unit cost of materials purchased.

$$\frac{\text{Actual Total Cost}}{\text{Actual Units Purchased}} =$$

$$= \frac{(80,000\times\$1.60)+(1,200,000\times\$1.40)}{80,000 + 1,200,000 + 1,440,000 + 1,100,000}$$

$$+ \frac{(1,440,000\times\$1.50)+(1,100,000\times\$1.70)}{80,000 + 1,200,000 + 1,440,00 + 1,100,00}$$

$$= \frac{5,838,000}{3,820,000} = \$1.5282722 \text{ per unit}.$$

The unit price variance is equal to

Standard per unit price - Actual per unit price

= 1,5282722 - 1.50 - .0282722.

The total variance is:

Units purchased × unit price variance

= 3,820,000 × .0282722

= $107,999.8 .

The price variance can also be calculated by adding up the variances of each purchase.

Units Purchased	×	Variance per unit	=	Variance for purchase
(A) 80,000	×	(1.60 - 1.50)	= 80,000 × .10 =	$ 8,000
(B) 1,200,000	×	(1.40 - 1.50)	= 1,200,000 ×-.10 =	-120,000
(C) 1,440,000	×	(1.50 - 1.50)	= 1,440,000 × 0 =	0
(D) 1,100,000	×	(1.70 - 1.50)	= 1,100,000 × .20 =	220,000
		Total variance		$108,000

With either method, the result is that approximately $108,000 more than the standard cost has been spent on materials. This is an unfavorable variance.

(b) The quantity variance is the difference between the amount of materials that should have been used to produce the company's actual output and the amount of materials that actually was used.

Actual materials used for 120,000 units....	3,750,000 lbs.
less: Standard materials for 120,000 units @ 30 lbs. per unit.........	3,600,000 lbs.
Quantity variance in units	150,000 lbs.

Quantity variance in dollars = (150,000 × $1.50) =$225,000

150,000 lbs. over the standard amount was used. This is an unfavorable variance.

2. There are two labor variances: the cost variance and the efficiency variance.

(a) The cost variance is the difference between what should have been spent for the actual number of labor hours used and what actually was spent on those labor hours.

$$\text{The actual per hour labor rate} = \frac{\text{Actual total Cost of labor}}{\text{Actual labor hours used}}$$

$$= \frac{\$2,929,500}{945,000 \text{ hrs}} = \$3.10 \text{ per labor hour.}$$ This exceeds the standard labor rate and therefore is unfavorable.

The per labor hour variance = $3.10/hr - $3.00/hr = $0.10 per hour.

The total labor cost variance = actual labor hours × per hour variance

= 945,000 × $0.10

= $94,500 .

(b) The labor efficiency variance is the difference between the amount of labor that should have been used to produce the actual output (120,000 units) and the amount of labor actually used

Actual labor for 120,000 units	945,000 hrs.
less: Standard labor for 120,000 units (120,000 × 8 hrs/units)	960,000 hrs.
Labor efficiency variance in hours	-15,000 hrs.
Labor efficiency variance in dollars (-15,000 × $3.00)	-45,000.00

Less than the standard amount of labor was used. Therefore, this variance is favorable.

3. The total overhead variance is broken into the fixed overhead variance and the variable overhead variance

a) The variable overhead variance is made up of the variable overhead spending variance and the variable overhead efficiency variance.

(i) The spending variance is the difference between the variable overhead that should have been incurred from the actual number of labor hours used and actual variable overhead cost that was incurred from those hours. Note that variable overhead cost is based on direct labor hours. The spending variance is therefore:

Actual variable overhead for 945,000 labor hrs............	$1,710,000
Standard variable overhead (945,000 hrs × $2.00/labor hr.)	$1,890,000
Variable overhead spending variance	-$ 180,000

This is a favorable variable.

(ii) The variable overhead efficiency variable is the difference between the number of labor hours for which variable overhead should have been incurred, and the number of labor hours for which it actually was incurred. This variance is also based on labor hours. Variable overhead efficiency variance equals labor efficiency variance (in hours) × variable overhead per direct labor hour

$$= -15,000 \times \$2.00$$

$$= -\$30,000 .$$

This is a favorable variance, since variable overhead has been incurred for less than the standard number of direct labor hours.

(b) The fixed overhead variance is made up of a fixed overhead budget variance and a fixed overhead volume variance.

(i) The fixed overhead budget variance is calculated as:

Actual fixed overhead costs	\$850,000
less: Standard fixed overhead costs	\$900,000
	-\$50,000

Since the budget variance is used to check on estimations of costs rather than on the level of costs, we cannot interpret the \$50,000 variance as a favorable one; the variance only shows we have not estimated overhead costs accurately.

(ii) The volume variance is the difference between expected volume at a standard fixed overhead cost per unit and the actual volume priced at that standard rate.

Standard fixed overhead cost per unit

$$= \frac{\text{Standard total fixed overhead}}{\text{normal (standard) output}}$$

$$= \frac{\$900,000}{112,500} \text{ units} = \$8.00/\text{unit} .$$

Fixed overhead volume variance is:

Standard output at Standard Cost (112,500 units × \$8)	\$900,000
less: Actual output at Standard Cost (120,000 × \$8.00)	960,000
	-\$60,000

This could be considered a favorable variance since it shows that actual activity is greater than normal activity.

BREAKEVEN ANALYSIS AND PRICING

• PROBLEM 22-11

A company wants a 20 percent return on investment before taxes at a sales volume equal to 80 percent of capacity. Fixed annual costs are \$200,000 and the annual capacity is 200,000 units. If the variable cost per unit is \$9 and the company investment is \$1,400,000, what should be the selling price per unit given that production and sales are 80 percent of capacity?

Solution: This year's production will be 80% of capacity which means that $0.8 \times 200{,}000 = 160{,}000$ units. To get the selling price per unit we have to divide total expected sales revenue by this number of units.

If the fixed costs are set at $200,000 and variable costs are $9/unit, 160,000 units will cost

$$\$200{,}000 + \$(9)(160{,}000) = \$1{,}640{,}000.$$

The return on investment is 20% of 1,400,000 which is $280,000. Total sales revenue must be

$$\$1{,}640{,}000 + \$280{,}000 = \$1{,}920{,}000.$$

Each unit should sell for

$$\$1{,}920{,}000/160{,}000 \text{ units} = \$12.$$

• PROBLEM 22-12

The McDougall Company produces and sells two qualities of carpet. The better quality carpeting sells for $6.00 per yard and has variable costs of 70 percent of sales. The other type costs $3.00 per yard and has variable costs of 60 percent of sales. Total fixed costs of both types of carpet combined are $122,200.

If both carpets have the same dollar sales, how many yards of each must be sold to earn a profit of $50,000?

Solution: Together both products must earn, beyond the variable costs, enough to cover fixed costs and to earn the desired profit, or $122,200 + $50,000 = $172,200. Since dollar sales are the same for each product, each must earn

$$\frac{\$172{,}200}{2} = \text{or } \$86{,}100$$

beyond its own variable costs. In order to calculate the number of yards that must be sold of each product we use the following formula:

$$\frac{\text{Fixed Costs + Profit}}{\text{Contribution margin}} = \text{units to be sold} .$$

The contribution margin is equal to the sales price per unit minus the variable costs per unit. The numerator of the formula, Fixed Cost + Profit will be each product's share of fixed costs and profit, or $86,100.

For the $6.00 carpet:

Contribution margin = \$6.00-.7(6.00) = \$6.00-\$4.20= \$1.80

Units to be sold = $\frac{\$86,100}{\$1.8}$ = 47833.333 or 47833 1/3 yds.

For the \$3.00 carpet:

Contribution margin = \$3.00-.6(3.00)= \$3.00-\$1.80= \$1.20

Units to be sold = $\frac{\$86,100}{\$1.20}$ = 71,750 yards.

These results can be checked as follows:

Gross Sales: X (47833.333 yds × \$6)	=	\$286,999.98
Y (71750 yds × \$3)	=	\$215,250.00
		\$502,249.98
less:Variable costs: X (\$286,999.99 × .7)	=	\$200,899.99
Y (\$215,250 × .6)	=	\$129,150.00
		\$330,049.99
(Gross sales) - (variable costs)	=	\$172,199.99
less: Total fixed costs		\$122,200.00
Profit	=	\$ 50,000.00

• PROBLEM 22-13

The Richland Company sells a single product for which the following data is available:

Current selling price	\$5 per unit
Expected sales volume	300,000 units
Budgeted fixed costs	600,000
Budgeted variable costs	\$2 per unit

The company is contemplating an increase in the selling price of its product to \$6 per unit.

How many units would have to be produced and sold at the new price to produce a 10 percent increase in total net income?

Solution: At the current selling price, total net income would be.

Gross revenue (300,000 units @ \$5)	\$1,500,000
less: Variable costs (300,000 units @ \$2)	(600,000)
Total contribution margin	\$ 900,000

less: Total fixed costs	600,000
Total net profit	$ 300,000

The total contribution margin is the difference between total gross revenue and total variable costs.

A 10 percent increase in net profits would yield a net profit of $300,000 + $30,000 = $330,000. The change in units necessary to make this profit when the unit price is $6.00 is computed by the formula

$$\frac{\text{Total Fixed Costs + Desired Net Profit}}{\text{Contribution margin Per Unit}} .$$

The contribution margin per unit equals the selling price per unit minus variable costs per unit, i.e., $6 - 2 = $4. When the selling price is $6.00, the unit sales necessary for a $330,000 net profit.

$$\frac{\$600{,}000 + \$330{,}000}{\$4}$$

$$= \frac{\$930{,}000}{\$4}$$

$$= 232{,}500 \text{ units.}$$

• PROBLEM 22-14

A Company manufactures a single product and is in a monopoly position with respect to this product.

The company is trying to determine a price that will yield the greatest income to the company. The following data have been developed:

Variable costs per unit of product	$6
Fixed costs per year	$400,000
Practical capacity per year	100,000 units of product

Sales Price per Unit	Estimated Sales and Production Volume per Year (units of product)
$14	60,000
13	70,000
12	80,000
11	90,000
10	100,000

What price should be established for the product? Why? Show computation to support your recommendation.

Solution: Find the sales price for which net profits are highest. (Note that as the sales price increases sales volume decreases). Compute net profit for each price as follows:

Gross Profit: Sales price per unit × units sold

less: Variable cost: unit variable cost × units sold

less: Fixed cost: $400,000

Net Profit

(i) Gross Profits: $14 × 60,000 units		$840,000
less: Variable Costs: $6 × 60,000 =$360,000		
less: Fixed Costs	400,000	760,000
Net Profits		$ 80,000
(ii) Gross Profits:$13 ×70,000 units		$910,000
less: Variable Costs:$6×$70,000= $420,000		
Fixed Costs	400,000	820,000
Net Profits		$ 90,000
(iii) Gross Profits: $12 × 80,000 units		$960,000
less:Variable Costs: $6 × $80,000= $480,000		
Fixed Costs:	400,000	880,000
		$ 80,000
Net Profits		
(iv) Gross Profits: $11 × 90,000 units		$990,000
less: Variable Costs: $6 × 90,000= $540,000		
Fixed Costs:	400,000	940,000
		$ 50,000
(v) Gross Profits: $10 × 100,000 units		$1,000,000
less:Variable Costs: $6 × 100,000=$600,000		
Fixed Costs:	400,000	1,000,000
Net Profits		$ 0

The highest net profit is yielded by a $13 per unit price. Assuming the predictions of sales volume are accurate, $13 should be the established price.

• PROBLEM 22-15

The Experimental Company is now producing and selling 17,000 units of product per year at a sales price of $250 each. It has had a profit objective of 20 percent return on a $2,000,000 investment. Its present cost structure is as follows:

Manufacturing costs:	
Fixed costs	$400,000 per year
Variable costs	$175 per unit produced
Selling and administration expenses:	
Fixed expenses	$135,000 per year
Variable expenses	$25 per unit sold

Ten hours are required to produce a unit of product. The company is interested in pushing its rate of operations to 100 percent of its capacity-20,000 units of product. It believes that it can raise its price by up to 5 percent of the present sales price without cutting its present sales volume. In addition, it believes that it can increase its sales to productive capacity with minor design and quality improvements that will increase variable manufacturing costs by $5 per unit, and with accompanying promotion that will increase its variable selling and administration expenses by $5 per unit for all units sold.

The company would like to achieve a profit objective of 25 percent on its investment.

REQUIRED: 1) Can the company, within the price increase limitation indicated, achieve its new profit objective by reaching full utilization of capacity with the increased variable costs and expenses required?

2) What would the sales price have to be to achieve the new profit objective?

3) What sales price would achieve the old profit objective?

Solution: 1) We must see the net profit that the Experimental Company will earn with its new strategy. The new sales price per unit will be $250 + (.05 × $250) = $262.50. The new variable manufacturing costs will be $175 + $5 = $180 per unit. The new variable selling and administration costs will be $25 + $5 = $30/units. If the company achieves its sales objective of 20,000 units, the net profit will be:

Gross revenue		
20,000 × \$262.50		\$5,250,000
less: Manufacturing costs		
fixed	\$400,000	
variable		
(\$180 × 20,000)	3,600,000	\$4,000,000
		\$1,250,000
less: Sales and administration costs		
fixed	\$135,000	
variable		
(\$30 × 20,000)	600,000	735,000
Net profit		\$ 515,000

Desired net profit was a 25% return on a \$2,000,000 investment or 25% × 2,000,000 = \$500,000. Therefore selling 20,000 at \$262.50 will yield a profit that will exceed the desired profit by \$15,000.

2) To derive the unit sales price that will yield a net profit of \$500,000, we sum the total costs and profits that the sales price would have to cover and divide this sum by the number of units sold

price per unit =

$$\frac{\text{manufacturing costs+selling and administrative cost+net desired profit}}{\text{number of units sold}}$$

Referring back to part 1) of the problem for the cost figures we get:

$$\frac{\$4{,}000{,}000 + \$735{,}000 + 500{,}000}{20{,}000}$$

$$= \frac{5{,}235{,}000}{20{,}000} = \$261.75/\text{unit}.$$

3) The old profit objective was 20% of \$2,000,000 or \$400,000. We can use the same method we used in part 2) to calculate the appropriate selling price for the old profit objective. Note that we use the old variable costs, but that the fixed costs do not change.

price per unit =

$$\frac{400{,}000 + (17{,}000 \times \$175)+\$135{,}000+(17{,}000 \times \$25)+\$400{,}000}{17{,}000}$$

$$= \frac{\$4{,}335{,}000}{17{,}000} = \$255.00/\text{unit}.$$

• PROBLEM 22-16

Lukinswel Clothing Outlets, Inc. is considering opening a store to sell a brand of trousers. All pairs having the same expenses and sales price are as follows

Variable data (per pair of trousers)

Selling Price	$30.00
Cost of Pants	$19.50
Sales commissions	1.50
Total Variable Expenses	$21.00

Annual Fixed Expenses of new store, include items such as salaries and rent, are $360,000.

a) What is the annual break-even point in unit sales?
b) If 32,000 pairs of trousers were sold, what would be the profit or loss?
c) If the store manager were paid 30¢ per pair sold as a commission what would be break-even point in unit sales?
d) Refer to the original figures. What would be the new break-even point units if sales commissions were stopped in favor of an $81,000 increase in fixed salaries?
e) Referring to the original figures, compute the annual net profit if the store manager received 30¢ per pair sold in excess of the break even point and 50,000 pairs of trousers were sold.

Solution:
The break-even point in pairs equals

$$\frac{\text{Total Fixed Expense}}{\text{Contribution margin}}$$

$$= \frac{\$360,000}{\$9/\text{pair}}$$

$$= 40,000 \text{ pairs}.$$

At a unit price of $30 per pair, the break-even point in dollars is

$$40,000 \text{ pairs} \times \$30/\text{pairs}.$$

The contribution margin above is the difference between the selling price and the total variable expenses,

$$\$30 - \$21 = \$9.$$

b) If only 32,000 pairs of pants were sold, the net result would be as follows:

Revenue (32,000 @ \$30)	\$960,000
less: total variable expenses (32,000 @ \$21)	672,000
Total contribution margin	\$288,000
less: total fixed expenses	\$360,000
Net loss	\$ 72,000

c) If variable expense per unit were increased by 30¢, it would equal \$21.00 + 0.30 = \$21.30. Therefore the contribution margin per unit equals \$30.00 - \$21.30 = \$8.70.

As before

$$\text{B.E.P.} = \frac{\text{Total Fixed Expense}}{\text{Contribution margin/pair}}$$

$$= \frac{\$360{,}000}{\$8.7/\text{pair}}$$

$$= 41379.31 \text{ pair,}$$

$$= 41{,}379 \text{ pairs (rounding off to the nearest}$$
whole number)

$$\text{B.E.P. (in \$)} = 41{,}379 \text{ pairs} \times \$30/\text{pair}$$

$$= \$1{,}241{,}370 .$$

d) If sales commissions were discontinued, that would decrease variable expenses per pair by \$1.50 to \$19.50. The contribution margin per pair would then be

(\$30 - \$19.50) or \$10.50.

The increase in fixed salaries of \$81,000 would bring the total fixed expense up to (\$360,000 + \$81,000) or \$441,000.

$$\text{B.E.P. (in units)} = \frac{\text{Total Fixed Expense}}{\text{Contribution margin/pair}}$$

$$= \frac{\$441{,}000}{\$10.50/\text{pair}}$$

$$= 42{,}000 \text{ pairs}$$

$$\text{B.E.P. (in \$)} = \$42{,}000 \text{ pairs} \times \$30/\text{pair}$$

$$= \$1{,}260{,}000 .$$

e) According to the original data, the break-even point in units is 40,000 units. Therefore if 50,000 pairs of trousers were sold, there would be 10,000 pairs in excess of the break-even point and the store manager would receive a bonus commission of (10,000 ×.30) or $3,000. The $3,000 would be an increase in expenses. If 50,000 pairs of trousers were sold, the new store would have a net income calculated as follows:

Revenue (50,000 @ $30,000)	$1,500,000
less: Total variable expenses (50,000 @ $21)	(1,050,000)
Contribution margin (50,000 @ $9)	$ 450,000
less: Total fixed expenses	(360,000)
less: Bonus commission to manager (10,000 @ 30¢)	(3,000)
Net income	$ 87,000

• PROBLEM 22-17

Suppose that a company has the following budget data of 19X1.

	PRODUCT		TOTAL
	X	Y	
Selling price	$3	$6	
Variable expenses	- 1	- 2	
Contribution margin	$2	$4	
Total fixed expenses	$100,000	$120,000	
Number of units to be sold to break even	?	?	?
Number of units expected to be sold	30,000	50,000	80,000

1. Compute the breakeven point for each product.

2. Suppose that Products X and Y were made in the same plant. Assume that a prolonged strike at the factory of the sole supplier of raw materials prevented the production of X for all of 19X1. Suppose also that fixed costs were unaffected.

a. What is the breakeven point for the company as a whole, assuming that no X is produced?
b. Suppose instead that the shortage applied so that only X and no Y could be produced. Then what is the breakeven point for the company as a whole?

3. Draw a breakeven chart for the company as a whole, using an average selling price and an average variable expense per unit. What is the breakeven point under this aggregate approach? What is the breakeven point if you add together the individual breakeven points that you computed in requirement 1? Why is the aggregate breakeven point different from the sum of the individual breakeven points?

Solution: 1. The breakeven point in units is equal to:

$$\frac{\text{Fixed costs}}{\text{contribution margin}}$$

The breakeven point for product X is

$$\frac{\$100{,}000}{\$2} = 50{,}000 \text{ units}$$

and for product Y it is

$$\frac{\$120{,}000}{\$4} = 30{,}000 \text{ units} \quad .$$

2. a.) If no X is produced, but fixed costs do not decrease, the contribution margin of product X must cost all \$100,000 + \$120,000 = \$220,000 in fixed costs. The company's breakeven point will be

$$\frac{\$220{,}000}{\$4} = 55{,}000.$$

b. If no Y is produced the breakeven point will be

$$\frac{\$220{,}000}{\$2} = 110{,}000 \text{ units.}$$

3.

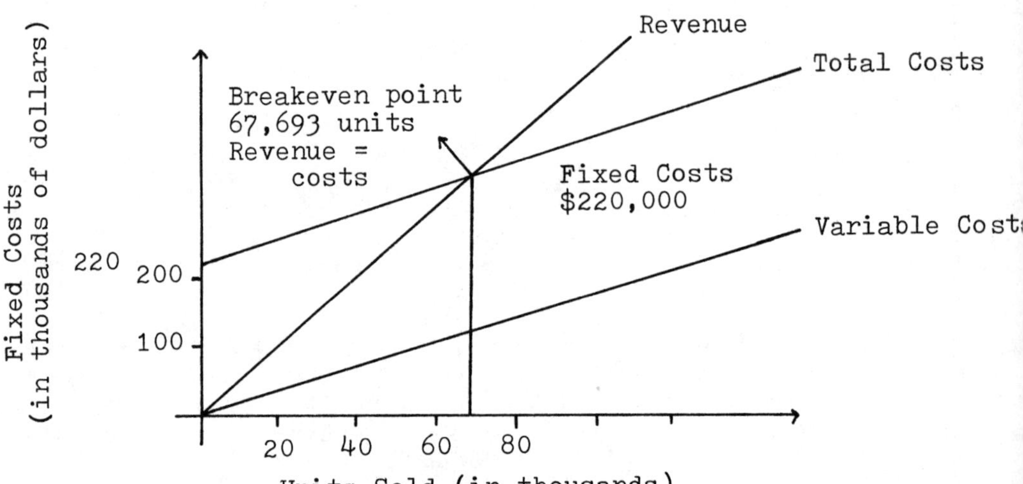

To construct the average breakeven chart for the company, first find the average selling price and variable cost per unit. Since the products do not sell equally well, use the weighted average method to find the averages. Of 80,000 units sold 30,000 or 3/8, are product X and 50,000, or 5/8, are product Y. Therefore, the selling price (and variable cost) will not be (½)(X) + (½)(Y), but (3/8)(X) + (5/8)(Y).

Average unit selling price: (3/8)($3) + (5/8)($6) $\approx$	$4.88
less: Average unit variable cost: (3/8)($1) + (5/8)($2) $\approx$	1.63
Average contribution margin	$3.25

The breakeven point for the company on the whole is

$$\frac{\$220,000}{\$3.25} = 67,692.3$$

or 67,693 units. Round off to the higher figure, because if the company only sells 67,692 units, it will not break even, as it must sell at least 67,692.3 to break even. The break even point is 50,000 + 30,000 = 80,000 units when the 2 points computed in part 1 are added. The aggregrate break even point is different from this because

$$\frac{\$100,000}{\$2} + \frac{\$120,000}{4} \quad \text{does not amount}$$

to the same as adding $100,000 to $120,000 and dividing the sum by $3.25; each part of the fixed cost has been weighted differently in each of the two computations.

• PROBLEM 22-18

Comparison of Two Businesses. Consider two businesses with the following unit prices and fixed and variable costs:

Business A:	
Selling price per unit	$1.00
Variable cost per unit	$ .20
Fixed cost of operations per year	$5,000
Business B:	
Selling price per unit	$1.00
Variable cost per unit	$ .60
Fixed cost of operations per year	$2,500

1. Calculate the breakeven point of each business in units.

2. Compute the profits of each business if sales in units are 10 percent above the breakeven point.

3. Which business would fare better if sales dropped to 5,000 units? Why?

4. Which business would fare better if the market collapsed and the price per unit fell to 50¢? Why?

Solution: 1. The breakeven point in units is the number of units a business needs to sell in order to cover all fixed and variable expenses.
It is calculated as follows:

$$\text{Breakeven point (B.E.P.)} = \frac{\text{Total Fixed Costs}}{\text{Contribution margin (C.M.) per unit}} .$$

The contribution margin per unit = selling price per unit - variable costs per unit.

For business A, C.M. = \$1.00 - 0.20 = \$0.80

$$\text{B.E.P.} = \frac{\$5,000}{\$0.80} = 6,250 \text{ units} .$$

For business B, C.M. = \$1.00 - 0.60 = \$0.40

$$\text{B.E.P.} = \frac{\$2,500}{\$0.40} = 6,250 \text{ units} .$$

2. If sales in units are 10 percent above the breakeven point, then sales for both companies are 6,875 units.

Profits are calculated as:

	A	B
Gross revenue (6,875 × \$1.00)	\$6,875	\$6,875
less:Total variable costs (A-6,875 × 20¢) (B-6,875 × 60¢)	1,375	4,125
Total contribution margin	\$5,500	\$2,750
less: Total fixed costs	5,000	2,500
Net profits	\$ 500	\$ 250

3. If sales dropped to 5,000 units, the net results would be as follows:

	A	B
Gross revenue (5,000 × \$1.00)	\$5,000	\$5,000

less: Total variables costs (A:5,000 × 20¢) (B:5,000 × 60¢)	1,000	3,000
Total contribution margin	$4,000	$2,000
Total fixed costs	5,000	2,500
Net loss	($1,000)	($ 500)

Business B would fare better because it would sustain a smaller loss if sales dropped to 5,000. This would happen because, although business B has a smaller total contribution margin than does business A, it also has smaller fixed costs.

4. Business A would do better if the selling price dropped to 50¢, because it would still have a contribution margin with which to cover its fixed costs. Business B's product could not even cover its 60¢ per unit variable costs with such a selling price. Business A would have to sell 5,000 ÷ (50¢ - 20¢) or 16,667 units to break even, but business B would never be able to break even; no matter how many units it sold, because variable costs would entirely consume whatever revenue was made from sales.

• PROBLEM 22-19

The Flintlock Company makes and sells 500,000 can openers a year fo 50 cents each. The total fixed expenses come to $80,000 a year and variable expenses are 30 cents a unit.

1. a) What is the net profit for a year?
   b) What is the break-even point

      i) in units?
      ii) in dollars?

2. Consider each of the following situations, each time referring back to the original material. Compute the breakeven points in dollars and in units, for all three situations.

(a) The company wishes to use a better metal for the can openers. This will cause variable expense to increase 4¢ per unit.

(b) The fixed expense and selling price decrease by 20 percent, variable expenses decrease by 10 percent and sales go up by 40 percent.

(c) The selling price increases by 10 percent and fixed expenses increase by $20,000.

Solution: (a) The net profit is equal to total revenue minus total costs

Total revenue: (500,000 units @ 50¢)........		$250,000
less: total variable expenses (500,000 × 30¢)	150,000	
Total fixed expenses...........	80,000	230,000
Net profit		$ 20,000

(b)i. The break even point is where the revenue which is left over after variable cost have been deducted is enough to cover all fixed costs. This "leftover" revenue is called the contribution margin. We find the breakeven point (B.E.P.) in by the formula

$$\text{B.E.P. (units)} = \frac{\text{Total Fixed Costs}}{\text{Contribution margin per unit}} .$$

Each unit sold will "contribute" its contribution margin towards covering fixed expenses. With this formula we will find how many units need to be sold so that the sum of all the contribution margins per unit will be equal to fixed costs.

The contribution margin per unit in this problem is:

Revenue per unit	.50¢
Variable cost per unit	.30¢
Contribution margin (C.M.)	.20¢

Therefore,

$$\text{B.E.P. (units)} = \frac{\$80,000}{\$0.20} = 400,000 \text{ units.}$$

(ii) The breakeven point in dollars is equal to

$$\frac{\text{Total Fixed Costs}}{\text{Contribution Margin Ratio (C.M.R.)}}$$

The C.M.R. is the ratio of the contribution margin per unit to the total revenue per unit. Here it is 20¢/50¢ or 0.4

$$\text{B.E.P. (dollars)} = \frac{80,000}{.4} = \$200,000 .$$

The unit figure for the breakeven point corroborates the dollar figure because 400,000 units sold at 50¢ apiece equals $200,000. in revenue .

2.(a) Variable expenses per unit equals 30¢ + 4¢ or 34¢. Therefore the C.M. is 50¢ - 34¢ or 16¢ and the C.M.R. is 16¢/50¢ or .32 .

$$\text{B.E.P. (units)} = \frac{\text{Total Fixed Costs (T.F.C.)}}{\text{C.M.}}$$

$$= \frac{\$80,000}{\$0.16}$$

$$= 500,000 .$$

$$\text{B.E.P.(dollars)} = \frac{\text{T.F.C.}}{\text{C.M.R.}}$$

$$= \frac{\$80,000}{0.32}$$

$$= \$250,000 .$$

Note that when the contribution margin per unit decreases, we need to sell more units to cover fixed costs.

(b) First we must calculate the new figures for sales, selling price, fixed expenses and variable expenses.

New sales(in units) = 500,000 units + (40% × 500,000 units)

= 500,000 + 200,000

= 700,000 units .

New selling price (per unit) = 50¢ - (20% × 50¢)

= 50¢ - 10¢ = 40¢/unit .

New fixed expenses = \$80,000 - (20% × \$80,000)

= \$80,000 - \$16,000 = \$64,000 .

New Variable expenses (per unit) = 30¢ - (10% × 30¢)

= 30¢ - 3¢ = 27¢ .

The new net profit is calculated as follows:

Revenue (700,000 @ 40¢)		\$280,000
less: Total Variable Costs (700,000 @ 27¢)	189,000	
Total Fixed costs	64,000	243,000
Net profit		\$ 37,000

$$\text{B.E.P.(units)} = \frac{\text{T.F.C.}}{\text{C.M. per unit}}$$

$$= \frac{\$64,000}{\$0.40 - \$0.27} = \frac{\$64,000}{.13}$$

$$= 429,307.69$$

$$\approx \quad 492{,}308 \text{ units} .$$

$$\text{B.E.P.(dollars)} = \frac{\text{T.F.C.}}{\text{C.M.R.}}$$

$$= \frac{\$64{,}000}{13¢/40¢} = \frac{\$64{,}000}{.325}$$

$$= \$196{,}923.07 .$$

(c) The new selling price is 50¢ + (10% × 50¢) or 55¢. The new fixed expenses are $80,000 + $20,000 or $100,000.

$$\text{B.E.P.(units)} = \frac{\text{T.F.C.}}{\text{C.M. per unit}}$$

$$= \frac{\$100{,}000}{\$0.55 - \$0.30} = \frac{\$100{,}000}{\$0.25}$$

$$= 400{,}000 \text{ units} .$$

$$\text{B.E.P.(dollars)} = \frac{\text{T.F.C.}}{\text{C.M.R.}}$$

$$= \frac{\$100{,}000}{25¢/55¢} = \frac{\$100{,}000}{.454545}$$

$$= \$220{,}000.22 .$$

• PROBLEM 22-20

Morgan Company sold 100,000 units of its product at $20 per unit. Variable costs are $14 per unit (manufacturing costs of $11 and selling costs of $3). Fixed costs are incurred uniformly throughout the year and amount to $792,000 (manufacturing costs of $500,000 and selling costs of 292,000). There are no beginning or ending inventories.

(i) What is the break-even point for this product in units? What are the costs and sales revenue at this point?

(ii) How many units need to be sold in order to make a profit of $60,000?

(iii) Sketch the break-even chart.

Solution: (i) The total cost equation is

$$Y = 792{,}000 + 14X$$

↑

Fixed cost Variable Cost

where Y is the total cost and X is the number of units sold. Total revenue is \$20X. The break-even point is the point where total cost equals total revenue:

$$20X = 792,000 + 14X$$

$$6X = 792,000$$

$$X = \frac{792,000}{6} = 132,000 \text{ units must be sold}$$

to break-even. The sales revenue at this level is \$(20)(132,000) = \$2,640,000. The total cost is 792,000 + (14)(132,000) = \$2,640,000 as it should be.

(ii) The profit as a function of the number of units sold is

$$P = (20-14)X - 792,000 \qquad \text{i.e.,}$$

Profit = Total Revenue - Total cost

$$(20X) - (14X + 792,000).$$

To find the production level that yield \$60,000 in profits, set this equation equal to \$60,000 and solve for X

$$60,000 = 6X - 792,000$$

$$852,000 = 6X$$

$$X = \frac{852,000}{6} = 142,000 \text{ units have to be}$$

made to obtain a profit of 60,000.

(iii)

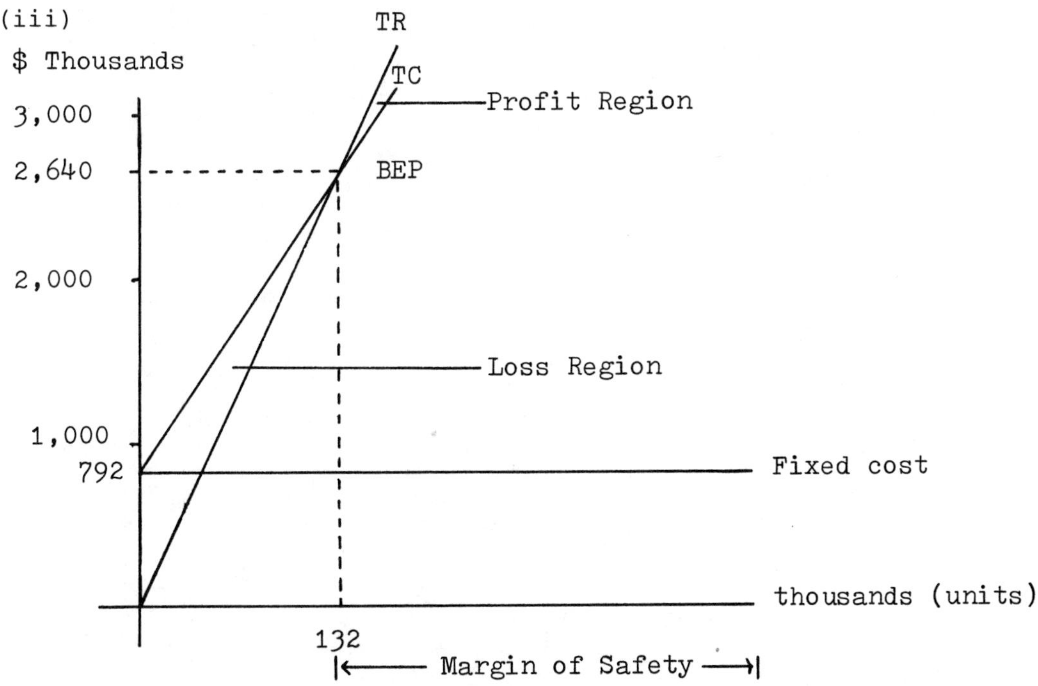

The break-even chart showing revenue and cost functions is shown above.

The margin of safety is the number of units sold in excess of the break even point.

CHAPTER 23

INTEREST

SIMPLE INTEREST

• PROBLEM 23-1

James took a loan of \$240 for 30 days at 6% interest. How much interest did he have to pay?

Solution: Substitution in the formula

$I = P \times R \times T$ yields $I = \$240 \times 6\% \times 1/12$ year $=$

$\$240 \times \frac{6}{100} \times \frac{1}{12} = \$240 \times .01 \times \frac{1}{2} = \$120 \times .01 = \$1.20.$

James paid \$1.20 interest.

• PROBLEM 23-2

What rate of interest would produce \$12 on \$1,200 in 90 days?

Solution: A simple method of finding the rate is to compute the interest at 1%, then divide the total interest (\$12) by that amount.

Interest = Principal × Rate × Time

$= \$1,200 \times 1\%/\text{year} \times \frac{90}{360}\ \text{year} = \$1,200 \times 1\% \times$

$\frac{1}{4} = \frac{\$12}{4} = \$3.$

$\text{Rate} = \frac{\text{total interest}}{\text{interest at } 1\%} = \frac{\$12}{\$3} = 4\%$

• PROBLEM 23-3

How much money must be on deposit for 3 months at an annual interest rate of 3% in order to earn $11.25 in interest. Verify your answer, using the formula

Interest = Principal × rate per year × time (in years)

or $I = Prt$.

Solution: Using the formula

Interest = Principal × rate of interest × time ($I = Prt$),

we can substitute the given values for I, r, and t, and then solve for P. Since we must earn $11.25 in interest, I = $11.25. The rate of interest (r) is 3% or 3/100 per year. The time (which must be expressed in the same unit as the interest rate, i.e. years) is $\frac{3 \text{ months}}{12 \text{ months}}$ or $\frac{1}{4}$ of a year. Substituting in the equation $I = Prt$ we get

$$11.25 = P \times \frac{3}{100} \times \frac{1}{4} \text{ or } 11.25 = \frac{3}{400} \times P.$$

Multiplying both sides by $\frac{400}{3}$ we get

$$\frac{400}{3} \times 11.25 = \frac{400}{3} \times \frac{3}{400} \times P$$

$$\text{or} \quad P = \frac{400}{3} \times \$11.25 = \frac{\$4500}{3} = \$1500.$$

The amount of money that must then be deposited for a period of 3 months at an annual interest rate of 3% in order to earn $11.25 is $1500. This can be verified using the formula $I = Prt$ as follows:

$$P = \$1500, \quad r = 3\% \text{ or } \frac{3}{100}, \text{ and } t = \frac{3}{12} \text{ or } \frac{1}{4} \text{ of a}$$

$$\text{year, so} \quad I = \$1500 \times \frac{3}{100} \times \frac{1}{4} = \frac{\$13{,}500}{1200} = \$11.25.$$

• PROBLEM 23-4

How much interest will Jerry pay on his loan of $400 for 60 days at 6% per year?

Solution: Use the formula:

Interest = Principal × Rate × Time ($I = P \times R \times T$).

$$\$400 \times 6\%/\text{year} \times 60 \text{ days} = \$400 \times .06 \times \frac{1}{6}$$

$$= \$400 \times \frac{1}{100} = \$4.00.$$

Jerry will pay $4.00

• PROBLEM 23-5

> How much interest will George pay on a 6-month loan of $300 at 8% interest?

Solution: Substitution in the formula

Interest = Principal × Rate × Time yields

$$I = \$300 \times 8\% \text{ per year} \times \frac{1}{2} \text{ year}$$

$$= \$300 \times .08 \times .5 = \$12 \text{ interest.}$$

• PROBLEM 23-6

> Paul takes out a loan of $677.21 for 90 days at a rate of 4%. How much interest will he have to pay?

Solution: A period of 90 days is ¼ year, so that 4% per year is 1% per 90 days. Therefore the interest is 1% of

$$\$677.21 = .01 \times \$677.21 = \$6.77.$$

(Note that the Simple - Interest Table gives 1.00 on $100, which is 1%.)

• PROBLEM 23-7

> Paul took a loan of $384.75 for 60 days at 6% interest. How much interest did he pay?

Solution: 60 days is $\frac{1}{6}$ of a year. Thus 6% per year is 1% for 60 days. To find the interest we multiply the principal by 1% = .01.

$$.01 \times \$384.75 = \$3.8475 = \$3.85$$

Thus he paid $3.85 interest.

• PROBLEM 23-8

> How much interest did Paul pay on his loan of \$1,285 for $2\frac{1}{2}$ years, given that the rate of interest was $5\frac{1}{2}$ %?

Solution: Substitution in the formula

$I = P \times R \times T$ yields

$I = \$1,285 \times 5\frac{1}{2}\ \% \times 2.5 = \$1,285 \times .055 \times 2.5$

$= \$176.69$ Paul paid \$176.69 in interest.

• PROBLEM 23-9

> Mr. John Kirk borrowed \$3,000 to pay his bills. He was charged an interest rate of $10\frac{1}{2}$ % for a 180 day period. How much interest will Mr. Kirk have to pay?

Solution: In order to find out how much interest Mr. Kirk will have to pay we use the formula:

$$\text{Interest} = \text{Interest Rate} \times \text{Principal} \times \frac{\text{number of days}}{360}$$

By using the formula we see that the interest he will be charged is equal to

$$10\frac{1}{2}\ \% \times \$3,000 \times \frac{180}{360} = .105 \times \$3,000 \times \frac{180}{360} =$$

$$.105 \times \$3,000 \times \frac{1}{2} = .105 \times \$1,500 = \$157.50.$$

• PROBLEM 23-10

> Mr. Jackson has borrowed \$150 from his bank. The loan must be paid in 90 days and has an interest rate of 6%. Find the amount due at the end of the 90 days.

Solution: The amount due is found by adding the amount of interest to the principal. The amount of interest is found by the following formula:

$\text{Interest} = \text{Principal} \times \text{Rate} \times \text{Time}$

The time is expressed in years, hence for our example the time is 90/360 (360 days in a banker's year) = 1/4 (by reducing the fraction to lowest terms). The principal here is \$150, and the rate is 6% = .06. Thus the interest is equal to

$$\$150 \times .06 \times \frac{1}{4} = \$2.25.$$

Therefore, the amount due is \$150 (the principal) + \$2.25 (the interest) = \$152.25.

• PROBLEM 23-11

Joanna Moorman borrowed \$2,000 from the credit union where she works, agreeing to pay 9% interest for the actual number of days during which the loan was outstanding. The date on which the money was borrowed was April 12, and the full amount, including interest, was paid on July 11.

a. For how many days will Mrs. Moorman pay interest?

b. What is the amount of interest to be paid?

c. What is the total amount due the credit union?

Solution: (a) By using the time table, we see that from April 12 to July 12 is 91 days, thus from April 12 to July 11 is 90 days.

(b) The amount of interest to be paid is found by the following formula:

$$\text{Interest} = \text{Interest Rate} \times \text{Principal} \times \frac{\text{number of days}}{360}$$

The reason we divide the number of days by 360 is, the unit of time used for computing interest is a year, or fraction of one, and thus we divide the number of days by 360 (the number of days in a business year) in order to make the time period in terms of years.

The amount of interest is equal to

$$9\% \times \$2,000 \times \frac{90}{360} = .09 \times \$2,000 \times \frac{90}{360} = \$45.$$

The total amount due is the principal + interest.

\$2,000	principal
+ \$ 45	interest
\$2,045	amount due

• PROBLEM 23-12

The Harbor Lights Boat Company loaned an employee \$3,000 to help toward the down payment on a new house. The employee agreed to pay 9½ % interest for the number of days he owed the money. The date of the loan was September 16, and it was repaid on October 31 of the same year.

a. How many days' interest will the company charge the employee?

b. What is the amount of interest the company will collect?

c. What is the total amount the company received from the employee on October 31?

Solution: (a) From September 16 to October 16 is 30 days, from October 16 until October 31 is 15 days, thus, the number of days is 30 + 15 = 45.

(b) The amount of interest can be found using the following formula.

$$\text{Interest} = \text{Interest rate} \times \text{Principal} \times \frac{\text{number of days}}{360}$$

Thus, the amount of interest is

$$9\tfrac{1}{2}\,\% \times \$3{,}000 \times \frac{45}{360} = .095 \times \$3{,}000 \times \frac{45}{360} =$$

$$\$35.625 = \$35.63$$

(c) The total amount the company received, was the principal + interest.

Principal	$3,000.00
+ Interest	35.63
Total	$3,035.63

• PROBLEM 23-13

How would Jerry use a short-cut method to determine the interest on $671.59 for 18 days at 7½ %?

Solution: The simple - interest table shows that the rate of 6% per year for 6 days yields $.10 on $100. This is equivalent to .001 of $1. Jerry's principal is $671.59. To find the interest on this amount at 6% for 6 days, multiply

$$.001 \times \$671.59 = \$.67159$$

The interest for 18 days = 3 × 6 days is 3 × $.67159 = $2.01477. Jerry has to pay interest at the rate of

$$7\,\frac{1}{2}\% = \frac{15}{2}\%. \quad \frac{\frac{15}{2}\%}{6\%} = \frac{\frac{15}{2}}{\frac{12}{2}} = \frac{15}{12} = \frac{5}{4}$$

Therefore, $7\,\frac{1}{2}\% = \frac{5}{4} \times 6\%$. Paul can compute the interest for 18 days at $7\,\frac{1}{2}\%$ by multiplying

$$\frac{5}{4} \times \text{(interest for 18 days at 6\%)}$$
$$= \frac{5}{4} \times \$2.01477 = \$2.5185 = \$2.52$$

• PROBLEM 23-14

> Jim Murphy wants to compute the simple interest he will have to pay on a loan of $193 at 6% for 38 days. He decides to use the 6%, 60-day method. How much is the interest?

Solution: Using ordinary time, in which a month is 30 days and a year is $12 \times 30 = 360$ days, Jim finds that 6% per year for 60 days is

$$\frac{6}{100}\text{ per year} \times \frac{2}{12}\text{ year} = \frac{1}{100} \cdot \frac{2}{2} = \frac{1}{100}.$$

The interest on $193 is $1.93. For 30 days, the interest is one-half the interest for 60 days:

$$\frac{\$1.93}{2} = .965.$$

To find 6 days' interest, divide $1.93 by 10:

$$\frac{\$1.93}{10} = \$.193.$$

To find 2 days' interest, divide $1.93 by 30:

$$\frac{\$1.93}{30} = .0643.$$

Finally, 38 days' interest is 30 days' plus 6 days' plus 2 days'.

```
$0.965
  .193
+ .0643
$1.2223 = $1.22 = 38 days' interest
```

• PROBLEM 23-15

> Mr. Bancroft of the Second National Bank approved 3 loans today. The first one was to Ms. Atlas for

$1,800 at 6% for a period of 60 days. The second one was to Mr. Johnson for $2,400 at 5% for 3 years. The third one was to Mr. Breakman for $7,000 at 6½ % for 4 years. How much interest will each of them have to pay?

Solution: In order to find the amount of interest that will be paid, we use the following formula:

Interest = Interest Rate × Principal × Time

To use the formula, the time must be in years, because, when an interest rate is given, it is in terms of years. For example a 6% interest rate means the interest will be 6% of the principal for a one year period of time. If the period of the loan is given in days, we must multiply it by the number of days divided by 360, for in business we say there are 360 days in a year. Similarly, if the period is given in months, we must multiply by the number of months and divide by 12. We can now find the interest that will be charged each customer. Ms. Atlas will be charged

$$6\% \times \$1,800 \times 60 \text{ days}/360 = .06 \times \$1,800 \times 60/360 = .06 \times \$1,800 \times 1/6 = \$18.$$

Mr. Johnson will have to pay

$$5\% \times \$2,400 \times 3 \text{ years} = .05 \times \$2,400 \times 3 = \$360.$$

Mr. Breakman will have to pay an interest charge of

$$6\tfrac{1}{2}\% \times \$7,000 \times 4 \text{ years} = .065 \times \$7,000 \times 4 = \$1,820.$$

• PROBLEM 23-16

Find the interest on each of the following loans by using the simple-interest table and the time table. All dates are in the same year.

No.	Principal	Rate	Period of Loan	No. of Days	Interest
1	$ 600.00	4%	April 5 to May 5	_____	$_________
2	$ 900.00	6%	August 17 to September 15	_____	$_________
3	$ 400.00	5%	February 14 to March 15	_____	$_________

4	$ 300.00	4½%	June 12 to August 16	_____	$_________
5	$1,400.00	5½%	March 5 to June 23	_____	$_________
6	$ 350.00	6%	July 24 to November 20	_____	$_________
7	$ 425.00	3½%	May 27 to September 8	_____	$_________
8	$1,275.00	4%	June 10 to November 18	_____	$_________
9	$ 302.50	4½%	March 12 to May 15	_____	$_________
10	$ 451.36	7%	April 9 to July 12	_____	$_________

Solution: The simple-interest table is based on a $100 amount, and the interest rate is based on a 365 day year. To use this table you need to know how many days the interest is based on. You then find the column headed by your interest rate, you then go down the column to the row headed by the correct number of days. You then take the number listed, and multiply by the principal divided by 100, giving the amount of interest.

Examples:

(a) $200 for 20 days at 4%. Find the column lab. led 4%, go down the column until you reach the row labelled 20 days. Take the number from the table (.2222) and multiply it by the principal divided by 100 to get the amount of interest.

.2222 (from table) × $2 ($200 ÷ 100 = $2) =

$.4444.

Thus the interest is $.44 (round to two decimal places).

(b) If the number of days in not listed in the table, we then break 48 into 30 and 18 which are both listed in the table. We then find out how much the inerest will be for 30 days and add it to the amount of interest for 18 days. We can also write 48 = 60 - 12, and subtract the amount of interest for 12 days from the amount of interest for 60 days.

The time table is a quick way to determine the exact number of days from any day in one month to the same day in any other month. To use it, follow the month column downward until the name of the month of the first date is found, we then follow that row across until you reach the column headed by the name of the month of the second date. The number is the number of days from the same day in the first month until the same day in the second month. If we do not wish to go to the same day in the second month, but a different one, we subtract the day of the first month from the day of the second month and add that to the number of days.

Examples:

(a) April 5 to September 17. We find, using the above method, that April 5 to September 5 is 153 days. Then we subtract the day of the first month from that of the second, and add it to the number of days.

17 - 5 = 12, 153 + 12 = 165. So the answer is 165 days.

(b) April 5 to September 2.

April 5 to September 5 153 days

2 - 5 = -3 so add -3 to 153, the result is 150.

Thus there are 150 days between April 5 and September 2.

To solve our problem we must first find the number of days in the period of the loan. We do this by the method described above, using the time table.

No.	Period of loan	No. of Days
1	April 5 to May 5	30
2	August 17 to Sept. 15	29
3	Feb. 14 to March 15	29
4	June 12 to Aug. 16	65
5	March 5 to June 23	110
6	July 24 to Nov. 20	119
7	May 27 to Sept. 8	104
8	June 10 to Nov. 18	161
9	March 12 to May 15	64
10	April 9 to July 12	94

We now find the interest, by following the procedure described above, using the simple-interest table.

(1) .3333 (30 days at 4%) × 6 ($600 ÷ 100) = $2.00

(2) .4833 (29 days at 6%) × $9 ($900 ÷ 100) = $4.35

(3) .4028 (29 days at 5%) × $4 ($400 ÷ 100) = $1.61

(4) .7500 (60 days at 4½ %) × $3 = $2.25
+ .0625 (5 days at 4½ %) × $3 = $ .19
$2.24

(5) 1.3750 (90 days at 5½ %) × $14 = $19.25
+ .3056 (20 days at 5½ %) × $14 = $ 4.28
$23.53

(6) 2.0000 (120 days at 6%) × $3.5 ($350 ÷ 100) = $7.00
- .0167 (1 day at 6%) × $3.5 ($350 ÷ 100) = .06
$6.94

(7) .8750 (90 days at 3½ %) × $4.25 = $3.72
+ .1361 (14 days at 3½ %) × $4.25 = $ .58
$4.30

(8) 1.6667 (150 days at 4%) × $12.75 = $21.25
+ .1222 (11 days at 4%) × $12.75 = $ 1.56
$22.81

(9) .7500 (60 days at 4½ %) × $3.025 ($302.50 ÷ 100) = $2.27
+ .0500 (4 days at 4½ %) × $3.025 ($302.50 ÷ 100) = $ .15
$2.42

(10) 1.7500 (90 days at 7%) × $4,5136 ($451.36 ÷ 100) = $7.90
+ .0778 (4 days at 7%) × $4.5136 ($451.36 ÷ 100) = $ .35
$8.25

• PROBLEM 23-17

$ 7,200.00 San Rafael Ca. May 23 19__

Forty-five days after date I promise to pay

to the order of Allen Furniture Co. Inc.

Seventy-two hundred and no/100------------- Dollars

at Allen Furniture Co. Inc.

Value received with interest at 12%

No 47 Due____ Manu L. Michaels

Find (a) the maturity date

(b) the amount of interest

Solution: (a) To find the maturity date, we subtract the number of days left in the month the note was written, from the number of days you have to pay back the loan. (If not enough days, then just add the number of days to the date it was issued.) Then subtract the number of days in the months following from the total number of days until you do not have enough days for a full month. Then the due date is that number of days in the month following the last one which you had subtracted. Thus if the note for 45 days was issued on May 23, we do the following.

31	total days in May
- 23	date of issue
8	days left in May

Thus, the note is for 45 - 8 = 37 days after May.

37	days left
- 30	days in June
7	days

Since we cannot subtract the full month of July we see that the note is due on July 7.

(b) To find how much interest there will be we use the following formula:

$$\text{Interest} = \text{Interest Rate} \times \text{Principal} \times \frac{\text{number of days}}{360}$$

We divide by 360 because that is how many days there are in a banker's year.

Thus the interest on the note is

$12\% \times \$7,200 \times 45/360 = .12 \times \$7,200 \times 45/360$

$= \$108$

• PROBLEM 23-18

Find the number of days required for $1,640 to produce $6.56 in interest at 4%.

Solution: Compute what the interest would be for one year. Then find the fraction of the annual interest that is $6.56.

$$\$1,640 \times 4\%/\text{year} = \$65.60.$$

$$\frac{\$6.56}{\$65.60} = \frac{1}{10} \text{ year.}$$

Thus we need keep it for 1/10 of a year. Assuming a year is 360 days, we need keep it

$$360 \div 10 = 36 \text{ days.}$$

EXACT INTEREST

• PROBLEM 23-19

Mr. Frankel wants to borrow $2,000 from November 16 for 143 days. The interest rate is 6%. What would the difference in the interest charge amount to if the bank used exact interest instead of bankers' interest?

Solution: When interest is figured by the bankers' method, we use the formula Interest = Principal × Rate × Time where Time is the number of days divided by 360. The exact method uses the same formula, but subsitutes for Time the number of days divided by 365. We can now find the difference in Mr. Frankel's interest charge.

Using Bankers' Interest

$$\text{Interest} = \$2,000 \times .06 \times \frac{143}{360} = \$47.67$$

Using Exact Interest

$$\text{Interest} = \$2,000 \times .06 \times \frac{143}{365} = \$47.01$$

Thus the diffence is $47.67 - $47.01 = $.66.

• PROBLEM 23-20

As a businessman, you need to know what part of a year is the period from July 15 to September 15. How many correct answers are there? How do you determine them?

Solution: There are two answers for exact time and two for approximate time. There are exactly 62 days, as shown in the time table, from July 15 to September 15. Exact interest is determined by considering a year as 365 days. Ordinary interest is based on a 360-day year. Finally, there are approximately 60 days from July 15 to September 15. The four answers are as follows:

Exact Time and Exact Interest

$$T = \frac{62}{365} = .1699$$

Exact Time and Ordinary Interest

$$T = \frac{62}{360} = .1722$$

Approximate Time and Exact Interest

$$T = \frac{60}{365} = .1643$$

Approximate Time and Ordinary Interest

$$T = \frac{60}{360} = .1667$$

• PROBLEM 23-21

How much interest will Paul have to pay on a 60-day loan of \$823 at 4% per year, computed by the exact time method?

Solution: Exact time is based on a 365-day year. We determine what fraction of a year is 60 days by dividing by 365 days. The interest is computed by substituting in the formula I = P × R × T, where R denotes the rate of interest and T denotes the period of time in terms of years. In this problem

$$I = \$823 \times 4\% \times \frac{60}{365} = \$823 \times .04 \times \frac{60}{365} = \$5.41.$$

• PROBLEM 23-22

Paul wants to know how much exact interest he would have to pay if he took a loan of \$720, with interest rate of 5% per year, from April 25 to June 15.

Solution: Exact interest is computed by considering a year to be 365 days. Using the time table, we see that April 15 to June 15 is 61 days, so that April 25 to June 15 is 51 days.

Substitution in the formula I = P × R × T =

$$\$720 \times 5\% \times \frac{51}{365} = \$720 \times \frac{5}{100} \times \frac{51}{365} = \frac{72}{10} \times \frac{1}{73} \times$$

$$51 = \frac{3672}{730} = \$5.03$$

• PROBLEM 23-23

A loan of \$1,262.77 is made on March 15 and repaid on August 12. If the interest rate is

8% per year, what is the amount of interest? (use exact time)

Solution: Exact time is based on a 365-day year. The time table shows that there are 153 days from March 15 to August 15, so that there are 150 days from March 15 to August 12. Using the interest formula

I = Principal × Rate (per year) × Time (fraction of a year), we have

$$I = \$1,262.77 \times 8\% \times \frac{150}{365} = \$41.52$$

COMPOUND INTEREST

• PROBLEM 23-24

Mr. Smith wishes to find out how much interest he will receive on $300 if the rate is 3% compounded annually for three years.

Solution: Compound interest is interest computed on both the principal and the interest it has previously earned. The interest is added to the principal at the end of every year. The interest on the first year is found by multiplying the rate by the principal. Hence, the interest for the first year is

$$3\% \times \$300 = .03 \times \$300 = \$9.00.$$

The principal for the second year is now $309, the old principal ($300) plus the interest ($9). The interest for the second year is found by multiplying the rate by the new principal. Hence, the interest for the second year is

$$3\% \times \$309 = .03 \times \$309 = \$9.27.$$

The principal now becomes $309 + $9.27 = $318.27.

The interest for the third year is found using this new principal. It is

$$3\% \times \$318.27 = .03 \times \$318.27 = \$9.55.$$

At the end of the third year his principal is $318.27 + $9.55 = $327.82. To find how much interest was earned, we subtract his starting principal ($300) from his ending principal ($327.82), to obtain

$$\$327.82 - \$300.00 = \$27.82.$$

• PROBLEM 23-25

> Bill deposits $1,000 for 4 years at 5% interest, compounded annually. What is its accumulated value?

Solution: Use the formula $A = P(1 + i)^n$ where A is the accumulated value, P is the principal, in this case $1,000, i is the interest rate (5%), and n is the number of periods:

$$A = P(1 + i)^n = \$1,000\ (1 + .05)^4$$

$$= \$1,000\ (1.215506) = \$1,215.51$$

• PROBLEM 23-26

> Mr. Beame placed $400 in a bank which pays 3% interest compounded semiannually. How much interest did he get after 2 years?

Solution: Compound interest is interest computed on both the principal and the interest it has previously earned. This interest is added to the principal at regular intervals. Mr. Beame's interest is being compounded semiannually. That means we are adding the interest to the principal twice a year. To compute how much the interest was for a two year period, we must break it up into 4 six month periods, so we can add the interest to the principal every six months. Since the account is earning 3% a year, it is earning 1½ % (3% ÷ 2) for every 6 months (½ year). We did this for we have to compute the interest on a six month basis, and not a yearly one. To find the interest for a period, we simply multiply the principal by the interest rate based on that period. Thus, the interest for the first six months is

$$\$400\ (\text{principal}) \times 1\tfrac{1}{2}\ \% = \$400 \times .015 = \$6.$$

Since we are working with compound interest, the principal now becomes the sum of the old principal ($400) and the interest ($6), which is $406. Thus the interest for the second six months is

$$\$406\ (\text{principal}) \times .015\ (\text{interest rate}) = \$6.09.$$

Thus, the principal for the next period is

$$\$406 + \$6.09 = \$412.09.$$

The interest for the third period is $412.09 (principal) × .015 (interest rate) = $6.18. The new principal for the fourth period is now

$$\$412.09 + \$6.18 = \$418.27.$$

The interest for the fourth period is \$418.27 (principal) × .015 (interest rate) = \$6.27. The principal is now \$418.27 + \$6.27 = \$424.54. To find the compound interest for the two year period, we subtract from the new principal, the starting principal. Thus, the compund interest is

$$\$424.54 - \$400.00 = \$24.54.$$

• PROBLEM 23-27

Mr. Josephson put \$200 in a savings account which receives 4% interest compounded semiannually. Find the present value of his account after 2 years.

Solution: Mr. Josephson receives 4% compounded semiannually, or 2% interest per period. There have been 4 periods (2 years × 2 periods per year). Using the compound interest table we see that at 2% after 4 periods one dollar will become \$1.082432. Thus, \$200 becomes

$$\$200 \times 1.082432 = \$216.49.$$

• PROBLEM 23-28

Nancy Miller deposited \$800 for 3 years. Her interest is compounded semiannually at 5%. How much interest accumulated?

Solution: There are two periods in a year, so there are six periods in 3 years. The semiannual interest rate is

$$\frac{5\%}{2} = 2.5\%.$$

Reading across the line for 6 periods, we find 1.159693 under 2.5%. The principal + interest is

$$1.159693 \times \$800 = \$927.7544.$$

The amount of interest is therefore

$$\$927.75 - \$800.00 = \$127.75.$$

• PROBLEM 23-29

Mrs. Smith deposited \$200 in her savings account at an interest rate of 5%, compounded semiannually. If she leaves the money in the account for 5 years, how much will she have at the end of that period of time? How much interest will she have earned?

Solution: The amount of money that Mrs. Smith will have in the account at the end of the five year period will be her original deposit (called principal) plus any interest that her principal has earned during the five years. Since her money was deposited at compound interest, we can use the Compound Interest table to determine how much she will have. This can be done as follows: her money was invested at the interest rate of 5%, compounded semiannually (two times a year), so the rate for each interest period is

$$\frac{5\%}{2} = 2\frac{1}{2}\%.$$

Also, since there are two interest periods per year, and the money is left on deposit for 5 years, there are 5×2 or 10 interest periods. Using the compound interest table, the factor for 10 interest periods at a per period interest rate of

$$2\frac{1}{2}\% \text{ is } 1.280085.$$

Applying the formula: Amount on Deposit = Principal × Compound Interest Factor, the amount of money that Mrs. Smith will have on deposit is

$$\$200.00 \times 1.280085 = \$256.017$$

which we round to \$256.02. The amount of interest she will have earned is the difference between how much she will have on deposit after the five years and her original principal. This will be

$$\$256.02 - \$200.00 = \$56.02$$

• PROBLEM 23-30

John's \$200 earns interest at the rate of 5% for one year, compounded quarterly. Show how he would calculate the interest without the aid of a formula or a table.

Solution: First compute the simple interest for one year and divide by 4 to find the amount of interest for the first quarter. Add to that the original principal, \$200 and you find the principal for the second quarter. Now we take this and find the simple interest at 5% for a year, so ¼ of it is the interest for the second quarter. Follow the same pattern of operations throughout. The actual computations are as follows:

```
          $200-original principal
            .05-rate of interest
        4 |10.00-annual amount of interest
           2.50-amount of interest at end of first
                quarter
        $200    -original principal
        $202.50-principal at beginning of second
                quarter
            .05-rate of interest
     4 |10.1250 -annual amount of interest
        2.53125-amount of interest at end of second
                quarter
     $202.50    -principal at beginning of second quarter
     $205.03125-principal at beginning of third period
            .05-rate of interest
   4 |10.2515625-annual amount of interest
      2,5628906-amount of interest at end of third
                quarter
   $205.03125   -principal at beginning of third period
   $207.5941406-principal at beginning of fourth period
            .05-rate of interest
4 | 10.379707030-annual amount of interest
  2.5949267575 -amount of interest at end of fourth
                period
$207.5941406    -principal at beginning of fourth period
$210.1890673575-principal and compounded interest for year
        $210.19--principal and compounded interest for year
         200.00--original principal
         $10.19 -compounded interest for year.
```

• PROBLEM 23-31

George put $500 into an account that bears interest at the rate of 8%, compounded quarterly. If he leaves the $500 for five years, how much will he have?

Solution: 8% per year is 2% per quarter. 5 years × 4 periods per year = 20 periods. Using the compound interest table, we find the table value of

$\$1.00 = 1.485947.$

$\$500 \times 1.485947 = \$742.97$ is the amount that George will have.

• PROBLEM 23-32

> James Higley deposits $2,000 for 2 years in an account that pays 4% per year, compounded quarterly. How much will accumulate, assuming James does not withdraw any of the interest?

Solution: 4% per year is equivalent to 1% per quarter. There are 8 quarters in 2 years. Substitution in the formula

$$A = \text{Principal } (1 + \text{Interest Rate})^n,$$

where n is the number of periods, in this case quarters, we have

$$A = 2000\ (1 + .01)^8 = 2000\ (1.01)^8$$

$$= 2000\ (1.0828567) = \$2,165.71$$

This is the accumulated amount that will be on deposit.

• PROBLEM 23-33

> Paul Reilly deposited a $5,000 check in his savings and loan association account, which yields 4% interest. It remained there 3 years. Paul can have his interest compounded semiannually or quarterly. Which way will be more profitable to him?

Solution: If the interest is compounded semiannually, then the rate is 2% per period, where one period is 6 months. Three years is equivalent to 6 periods. In the compound interest table, read across the line for 6 periods and stop under 2%. The entry is 1.126162. The principal plus interest is found by multiplying this factor, which is based on $1.00, by the principal, $5,000.

$$1.126162 \times \$5,000 = \$5,630.81$$

If the interest is compounded quarterly, the rate is

$$\frac{4\%}{4 \text{ quarters}} = 1\%.$$

Since there are 3 years, there are $3 \times 4 = 12$ periods. Reading across the line for 12 periods, we find 1.126825 under 1%.

$$1.126825 \times \$5,000 = \$5,634.13$$

Therefore, Paul will earn $3.32 more if his interest is compounded quarterly.

• PROBLEM 23-34

A savings account containing $2000 earned 4% interest, compounded quarterly for 3 years, and then 5% interest, compounded semiannually, for the next two years. What was the final balance in the savings account? How much interest did it earn? (Use 6 decimals in table factor.)

Solution: Since the $2000 was first deposited at 4% interest compounded quarterly (4 times a year), the rate of interest for each interest period was 1%. Also, 4 interest periods per year for 3 years is a total of 12 periods. Using the Compound Interest Table, the factor for the 12 interest periods at a per period interest rate of 1% (correct to 6 decimals) is 1.126825. Applying the formula:

Amount on Deposit = Principal × Compound Interest Factor,

the amount on deposit at the end of the first three years is

$$\$2000 \times 1.126825 = \$2253.65.$$

For the next two years, the money was deposited at 5%, compounded semiannually. This is equivalent to $2\frac{1}{2}$ % per period for a total of 4 periods. The table factor for $2\frac{1}{2}$ % interest per period for 4 periods (to 6 decimals) is 1.103813. Once again applying the formula:

Amount on Deposit = Principal × Compound Interest Factor

with a principal of $2253.65 and a factor of 1.103813, we obtain a final balance (rounded to the nearest cent) of $2487.61. Since the account originally contained $2000, the amount of interest earned was

$$\$2487.61 - \$2000 = \$487.61$$

• PROBLEM 23-35

How much cash can be obtained now on a \$4,000 loan repayable in three years with interest compounded at ½ % per month?

Solution: We want to find the principal amount that will have an accumulated value of \$4,000 in three years. In order to find the principal, divide both sides of the formula

$$P(1+i)^n = A$$

by $(1+i)^n$ to obtain $P = \dfrac{A}{(1+i)^n}$.

Substitution gives $P = \dfrac{\$4,000}{(1+.005)^{36}}$, since $\frac{1}{2}\% = .005$

and 3 years is 36 months. Using a calculator, we find

$$P = \$4,000 \div 1.1966786 = \$3,342.59.$$

• PROBLEM 23-36

Paul Murphy wants to have \$10,000 in his account after 10 years. If interest is compounded annually at 4%, how much should Mr. Murphy invest now?

Solution: The compound amount formula

$$\text{Accumulated Amount} = \text{Principal} \times (1 + i)^n,$$

where i is the rate of interest and n is the number of periods for which interest will be compounded, can be rearranged to solve for P, the principal amount. We can divide each side by $(1 + i)^n$ as follows:

$$\frac{A}{(1+i)^n} = \frac{P(1+i)^n}{(1+i)^n} = P, \quad \text{since } \frac{(1+i)^n}{(1+i)^n} = 1.$$

By the definiton of negative exponents,

$$(1+i)^{-n} = \frac{1}{(1+i)^n}, \text{ so that } P = A\,(1+i)^{-n}.$$

$(1+i)^{-n}$ is called the present worth factor. Its values are given in Table s. Reading across the line for n=10, we find 0.6756 under 4%. Substitution in

$$P = A(1+i)^{-n} \text{ gives}$$

$$P = \$10,000\ (0.6756) = \$6,756.00$$

• **PROBLEM 23-37**

Jim Smith put \$792.81 in his savings account on April 3. He withdrew \$260 on April 25 and deposited \$200 on May 5. He deposited \$271.50 on June 9 and \$544.53 on June 16. If interest was compounded quarterly at 5% from day of deposit to day of withdrawal, what was the total amount in Jim's account on July 1?

Solution: There are (25 - 3) = 22 days from April 3 to April 25. We use the formula

Interest = Principal × Rate (per year) × Time (fraction of year). Recall that

$$5\% = \frac{5}{100} = .05$$

Thus the interest on the \$792.81 for the 22 days is

$$792.81 \times .05 \times \frac{22}{365}$$ (exact time is based on

a 365-day year) = \$2,389 ≐ \$2.39

The amount on deposit on April 25 is \$792.81 - \$260.00 = \$532.81.

There are 10 days from April 25 to May 5, so that the interest for this period is

$$\$532.81 \times .05 \times \frac{10}{365} = \$.729 = \$.73$$

We compute the interest for the next three periods by the same method. The results are as follows:

April 3	-	April 25	792.81 × .05 × 22/365 =	\$2.39
April 25	-	May 5	532.81 × .05 × 10/365 =	.73
May 5	-	June 9	732.81 × .05 × 35/365 =	3.51
June 9	-	June 16	1004.31 × .05 × 7/365 =	.96
June 16	-	July 1	1548.84 × .05 × 15/365 =	3.18
				\$10.77

EFFECTIVE INTEREST

• **PROBLEM 23-38**

Under the Truth-In-Lending regulations, what must a retailer indicate on the sales contract as the annual interest rate if he charges $1\frac{1}{2}$ % interest per month on the unpaid balance of each customer's account?

Solution: Many retailers, in an effort to sell their goods on the installment plan, have tried to advertise what appears to be a small finance charge on the installment payments. One way of making the finance charge look smaller than it actually is has been to list the interest rate charged on a monthly basis, for example, $1\frac{1}{4}$ % per month. This gives many consumers the mistaken idea that the finance charge is smaller than it actually is, since most consumers are used to seeing interest charges on an annual basis, as opposed to monthly rates. To protect these consumers, the federal Truth-in-Lending regulations require that retailers list the equivalent annual interest rate along with the monthly rate, enabling the consumer to get a better idea of the actual finance charge he is paying. Since there are 12 months in the year, the monthly interest rate of

$$1\tfrac{1}{2}\ \% \ (= 1.5\%) \text{ is}$$

equivalent to an annual rate of

$$1.5\% \times 12 = 18\%$$

• PROBLEM 23-39

Pauline DiLorenzo wishes to purchase a store valued at $26,000. She obtains a mortgage for $23,000 at a rate of 5.5% per annum. If her gross income is $3,500 and her expenses are $1,800, what is the return on her investment?

Solution: Return on investment is the percentage of the investment that is net profit. To find the net profit, we subtract the total expenses from the gross income ($3,500). Total expenses are the sum of expenses ($1,800) and interest on the mortgage

$$5\tfrac{1}{2}\% = .055. \quad \$23,000 \times .055 = \$1,265.$$

Total expenses = $1,800 + $1,265 = $3,065.

Gross income - Total expenses = $3,500 - $3,065 =

$435 = net profit.

$$\frac{\text{net profit}}{\text{investment}} = \frac{\$435}{\$26,000-\$23,000} = \frac{\$435}{\$3,000} = .145 = 14.5\%$$

• PROBLEM 23-40

George Mason bought a new grand piano for $8,650. He made a down payment of $1,000 and paid the balance in 20 equal monthly installments of $425. What rate of interest was he paying (to nearest 10th of 1%)?

Solution: When charges are expressed as a flat fee to be paid in a number of equal installments, the constant ratio formula is used to find the effective annual interest rate. The formula is

$$r = \frac{2 \times m \times I}{P \times (n+1)} .$$

P is balance due = cost - down payment = $8,650 - $1,000 = $7,650. I is finance charge = (total of installment payments) - (balance due) = (20 × $425) - $7,650 = $8,500 - $7,650 = $850

m = number of installments per year = 12

n = number of installment payments = 20

Substitution in the formula gives:

$$r = \frac{2 \times m \times I}{P \times (n+1)} = \frac{2 \times 12 \times \$850}{\$7,650 \times (20+1)}$$

$$= \frac{24 \times \$850}{\$7,650 \times 21} = .127 = 12.7\%$$

• PROBLEM 23-41

Mr. Smith purchased a car for $4250. He was allowed $500 for his old car as a down payment. The balance was paid in 25 equal monthly payments of $180. What was the interest rate (nearest 10th of 1%)? Use the constant ratio formula.

Solution: The constant ratio formula is a method used to find the effective annual interest rate. when the charges are expressed as a flat fee to be paid in a number of equal installments. The formula is:

$$r = \frac{2 \times m \times I}{p \times (n + 1)}$$

where r is the effective annual interest rate, m is the number of installments per year (12 if monthly installments and 52 if weekly installments), I is the finance or credit charge (the flat fee), P is the net amount of credit on an installment loan after the deduction of the down payment or the actual cash received, and n is the number of payments required.

The first thing we will find is the balance due (P in the formula). It is equal to the cost of the car less the down payment. Thus

P = \$4,250 (cost of car) - \$500 (allowance of old car as a down payment) = \$3,750.

In order to find the finance charge (I in the formula) we must first find how much Mr. Smith paid for the car, and then subtract from that his balance due. Mr. Smith paid \$180 a month for 25 months, thus he paid a total of

$$\$180 \times 25 = \$4,500$$

for the car. The balance due was \$3,750, and thus the finance charge was \$4,500 - \$3,750 = \$750. We are now able to find the annual interest rate using the constant ratio formula.

$$r = \frac{2 \times m \times I}{P \times (n + 1)}$$

m = 12 (12 months in a year)

I = \$750 (finance charge)

P = \$3,750 (balance due)

n = 25 (number of payments)

$$r = \frac{2 \times 12 \times \$750}{\$3,750 \times (25+1)} = \frac{2 \times 12 \times \$750}{\$3,750 \times 26} = .1846$$

= 18.46 %, or rounding it to the nearest 10th of 1%, 18.5%.

CHAPTER 24

INSTALLMENT PLANS

INSTALLMENT COST AND FINANCE CHARGES

• PROBLEM 24-1

A \$250 stove can be purchased under the installment plan for a \$25 down-payment and 12 monthly payments of \$20. What is the financing charge?

Solution: The financing charge is the difference between the installment price and the cash price. The installment price requires a \$25 down payment and 12 monthly payments of \$20. The installment payments total \$20 x 12 = \$240, and adding the \$25 down payment, we get a total installment price of \$240 + \$25 = \$265.

The finance charge is, therefore, \$265 - \$250 = \$15.

• PROBLEM 24-2

A television set with a cash price of \$525 is to be paid for on the installment plan with a \$75 down payment and twelve monthly payments of \$42.75. Calculate the carrying charge for the television set.

Solution: The carrying charge is the difference between the amount paid out under the installment plan and the cash price. The twelve monthly payments of \$42.75 total \$42.75 X 12 = \$513. Adding the \$75 down payment, we get a total installment price of \$513 + \$75 = \$588. Since the case price of the television set was \$525, the carrying charge was \$588 - \$525 = \$63.

• PROBLEM 24-3

A bedroom set with a list price of \$1010 was advertised for sale at a \$35 reduction. Using the installment plan, the bedroom set can be purchased for a down payment of \$337.60 and 18 monthly payments of \$43.61. Find the sale price and the finance charge for the furniture.

Solution: Since a $35 discount was offered on the $1010 list price, the sale price of the bedroom set was $1010 - $35 = $975. The cost of the 18 monthly payments of $43.61 is $43.61 × 18 = $784.98. Adding the $337.60 down payment, we get a total installment price of $337.60 + $784.98 = $1122.58. The finance charges which is the difference between installment price and sale price is $1122.58 - $975 = $147.58.

• PROBLEM 24-4

Find the finance charge on each of the purchases in the following table.

No.	Merchandise	Cash Price	Down Payment	No. of Payments	Amount of each Payment	Finance Charge
1.	Jacket	$ 55.00	$ 20.00	8	$ 5.00	$____
2.	Clock radio	$ 30.00	$ 8.00	6	$ 4.00	$____
3.	Bike	$ 47.00	$ 7.50	7	$ 6.00	$____
4.	Ski equipment	$ 62.50	$ 10.50	10	$ 5.50	$____
5.	Typewriter	$112.75	$ 12.75	12	$ 8.75	$____
6.	Tape player	$163.40	$ 25.00	18	$ 8.25	$____

Solution: The finance charge is the difference between the cash price and the installment price. For example, in problem no. 1, the eight payments of $5.00 each total 8 × $5.00 = $40.00. Adding the $20.00 down payments, we get a total installment price of $40.00 + $20.00 = $60.00. The cash price was $55.00, so the finance charge is $60.00 - $55.00 = $5.00 . Following the same procedure, the finance charge for each of the above problems has been calculated and the results are summarized below:

No.	Cash Price	Installment Price	Finance Charge
1.	$ 55.00	$ 60.00	$ 5.00
2.	$ 30.00	$ 32.00	$ 2.00
3.	$ 47.00	$ 49.50	$ 2.50
4.	$ 62.50	$ 65.50	$ 3.00
5.	$112.75	$117.75	$ 5.00
6.	$163.40	$173.50	$10.10

• PROBLEM 24-5

A stereo with a cash price of $895 can be purchased on the installment plan for 15% down and 30 monthly payments of $29.42. What is the finance charge on the installment plan?

Solution: The finance charge is the difference between the installment price and the cash price. Since the stereo requires a down payment of 15% (= .15) of the cash price, the down payment is .15 x $895 = $134.25. Adding the 30 payments of $29.42 for $29.42 x 30 = $882.60, we get a total installment price of $134.25 + $882.60 = $1016.85. The finance charge is therefore $1016.85 - $895 = $121.85.

• PROBLEM 24-6

Mr. Scaccio borrows $100 from his credit union and agrees to pay back $20 a month with interest of 1% per month on the unpaid balance. How much does he pay?

Solution: Since Mr. Scaccio is paying an interest charge of 1% (= .01) per month of the unpaid balance, in the first month he will pay an interest charge of $100 x .01 = $1. Adding this to the $20 in principal he must pay, we get a total payment for the first month of $20 + $1 = $21. His unpaid balance as of the end of the first month is $100 - $20 = $80.

Following a similar procedure, the interest charges and total payments required have been calculated and summarized in the table below:

	Unpaid Balance	*Interest at 1%*	*Payment on Principal*	*Total Payment*
1st. mo.	$100.00	$1.00	$ 20.00	$ 21.00
2nd mo.	80.00	.80	20.00	20.80
3rd mo.	60.00	.60	20.00	20.60
4th mo.	40.00	.40	20.00	20.40
5th mo.	20.00	.20	20.00	20.20

The total amount that Mr. Scaccio must pay is therefore

$21.00 + $20.80 + $20.60 + $20.40 + $20.20 = $103.00.

• PROBLEM 24-7

A radio costing $38.00 plus 3% excise tax and 4% sales tax may be purchased for $10.00 down and 3 payments of $11.60.

(A) What is the cash price of the radio?
(B) What is the installment price of the radio?

Solution: Since there is a 3% (= .03) excise tax on the radio's $38.00 price, the excise tax is $38.00 x .03 = $1.14, bringing the cash price of the radio to $38.00 + $1.14 = $39.14. The sales tax, which is 4% (= .04) of the cash price, is $39.14 x .04 = $1.57, bringing the total cash price of the radio to $39.14 + $1.57 = $40.71.

The cost of the three installment payments of $11.60 each is $11.60 × 3 = $34.80. Adding on a $10.00 down payment, we get a total installment price of $44.80.

• PROBLEM 24-8

Mr. Glass borrowed $250 from the ABC Finance Company. He agreed to repay the $250 in five monthly installments, with interest at 3% a month on the first $150 and 2% a month on any part of the loan over $150. What was his total interest cost?

Solution: Since Mr. Glass has agreed to repay the $250 over five installments, each payment would include a payment of principal for $\frac{\$250}{5} = \$50$. The unpaid balance would therefore decrease after each payment by $50. The interest charge for the first payment, which is 3% (= .03) of the first $150 and 2% (= .02) of the $250 - $150 = $100 over, would be .03 × $150 + .02 × $100 = $4.50 + $2.00 = $6.50. The unpaid balance after the first payment would be $250 - $50 = $200.

Following a similar procedure, the interest charges on the remaining payments have been calculated and summarized in the table below:

	Unpaid Balance	Interest at 3% on $150 or less	Interest at 2% on Amount over $150	Total Interest
1st mo.	$250	$4.50	$2.00	$6.50
2nd mo.	200	4.50	1.00	5.50
3rd mo.	150	4.50	—	4.50
4th mo.	100	3.00	—	3.00
5th mo.	50	1.50	—	1.50

The total interest charge was therefore

$6.50 + $5.50 + $4.50 + $3.00 + $1.50 = $21.

• PROBLEM 24-9

A bicycle selling for $82 can be purchased on the installment plan with no down-payment, but a 10% per year finance charge. How much should each of the monthly payments be to pay off the bicycle in six months?

Solution: Since the finance charge is 10% (= .10) per year, and the bicycle is to be paid for in six months, the finance charge is found by the formula:

Charge = Principal × Time in years.

Substituting we get $\$82 \times .10 \times \frac{6}{12} = \$8.20 \times \frac{6}{12} = \$4.10$. The total amount to be paid is therefore $82 + $4.10 = $86.10. Since this is to be paid over 6 months, each monthly payment should be $86.10 ÷ 6 = $14.35.

• PROBLEM 24-10

Mary Redmond purchased a $28,500 home with 20% down and the balance to be paid by monthly payments over 10 years. In addition, a financing charge of 7% per year of the unpaid balance is to be added to each monthly payment. Calculate the total payment due for the first month.

Solution: Since Ms. Redmond made a down payment of 20% (= .20) of the $28,500 price, her down payment was $28,500 × .20 = $5,700. This leaves an unpaid balance of $28,500 - $5,700 = $22,800.

Over a 10-year period there are 10 × 12 = 120 monthly payments, so the amount of the balance to be paid in each installment is

$$\frac{\$22,800}{120} = \$190.$$

In addition, the finance charge for the first payment is found by the formula:

Charge = Principal × Interest rate × Time in years.

Substituting the numbers we get $\$22,800 \times .07 \times \frac{1}{12} = \$133$. This means that the total amount of the first payment is $190 + $133 = $323.

• PROBLEM 24-11

A new sofa, valued at $547.50 was purchased on the installment plan with a 20% down payment, and the remainder to be paid off in 36 months. If 20% of the unpaid balance was added on as a service charge, what was the amount of each of the monthly payments?

Solution: Since the down payment on the sofa was 20% (= .20) of the $547.50 value, the down payment was $547.50 × .20 = $109.50. The unpaid balance was then $547.50 - $109.50 = $438. A finance charge of 20% was added to the $438. The finance charge was then $438 × .20 = $87.60, resulting in a total balance on installment of $438 + $87.60 = $525.60. Since this is to be paid off in 36 monthly payments, each of the monthly payments should be $525.60 ÷ 36 = $14.60.

• PROBLEM 24-12

An automobile dealer wishes to sell one of his used cars, having a cash price of $1260, on the installment plan. The plan requires no down payment, but a service charge of 6% per year is charged on the unpaid balance. In addition, a charge of \$20 is made to cover legal fees. If the car is to be paid off in 18 monthly payments, how much should each monthly payment be?

Solution: Since the car requires no down-payment, the amount subject to financing is \$1260. There are to be 18 payments, thus the ending principal balance is

$$\frac{\$1260}{18} = \$70.$$

This means that the average principal balance is $\frac{\$1260 + \$70}{2} = \$665.$ The total interest charge to be paid over the 18 month period can now be found via the formula:

Interest Charge = Avg. Principal Balance × Annual Interest Rate × Term.

Substituting an average balance of \$665 an annual rate of 6% (= .06) and a term of 18/12 = 1.5 years, we get:

$$\text{Interest Charge} = \$665 \times .06 \times 1.5 = \$59.85.$$

The total amount to be paid for the car is then principal (\$1260) plus interest charges (\$59.85) plus legal fees (\$20), which is \$1260 + \$59.85 + \$20 = \$1339.85. Since this is to be paid over 18 payments, each payment should be

$$\frac{\$1339.85}{18} = \$74.44\ .$$

• PROBLEM 24-13

A \$225 refrigerator can be purchased on the installment plan for 15% down. The balance due, along with a 7% a year service charge, is to be paid in 18 equal monthly payments. If Mr. Trauten purchased the refrigerator on the installment plan, what was his down-payment? What was the amount of each monthly payment?

Solution: Since a down-payment of 15% (= .15) of the \$225 was made, the down payment was \$225 × .15 = \$33.75. This leaves a balance owed of \$225 - \$33.75 = \$191.25. The service charge, which was 7% (= .07) per year for 18/12 of a year (because he will be paying for 18 months) was \$191.25 × .07 × 18/12 = \$20.08, bringing the total amount due to \$191.25 + \$20.08 = \$211.33. In order to pay this off in 18 monthly payments, each monthly payment should be

$$\$211.33 \div 18 = \$11.74\ .$$

• PROBLEM 24-14

A piano, priced at \$1250, plus 4½% tax, was purchased on the installment plan with a down payment of 10% of the cash value, with 18 months in which to pay the balance. If a service charge of 12% was added to the unpaid balance, what was the monthly installment? What was the total cost of the piano?

Solution: Since sales tax at the rate of $4\frac{1}{2}\%$ (= .045) was charged on the sale, and the piano was priced at $1250, the sales tax was $1250 × .045 = $56.25. This means that the total cost of the piano was $1250 + $56.25 = $1306.25. A down payment of 10% (= .10) of the $1250 cash value, which is $1250 × .10 = $125 was paid, so the unpaid balance on the piano was $1306.25 - $125 = $1181.25. A service charge of 12% (= .12) of this amount was added on as a financing charge. The financing charge was therefore $1181.25 × .12 = $141.75, bringing the total balance due on installment to $1181.25 + $141.75 = $1323. Since this balance is to be paid off in 18 equal payments, each payment would be $1323 ÷ 18 = $73.50 .

The total cost of the piano, which is down payment plus monthly installments, is $125 + $1,323 = $1,448.

• PROBLEM 24-15

Mr. and Mrs. Wilson purchased a $28,500 home for 10% down and financed the balance at 8% over 15 years.

(A) Find the monthly payments.
(B) Find the amount of the first payment applied to principal if the loan was amortized.

Solution: Since the Wilsons made a down payment of 10% (= .10) of the $28,500 purchase price, the down payment was $28,500 × .10 = $2,850. This means that the principal of their loan was $28,500 - $2,850 = $25,650. Over a 15 year period there are 15 × 12 = 180 payments, so the ending principal balance is $25,650 ÷ 180 = $142.50. Amortizing a loan means you pay the loan in equal installments over the years. The average principal balance is therefore

$$\frac{\$25,650 + \$142.50}{2} = \$12,896.25.$$

We can now find the total interest charge by applying the formula:

Interest Charge = Avg. principal balance × annual interest rate × term.

Substituting an average balance of $12,896.25, an interest rate of 8% and a term of 15 years, we get:

Interest Charge = $12896.25 × .08 × 15 = $15,475.50.

The total amount to be repaid is therefore $25,650 + $15,475.50 = $41,125.50. Each of the 180 monthly installments should therefore be

$$\frac{\$41,125.50}{180} = \$228.48 .$$

The amount of the first payment applied to interest is

$$\$25,650 \times .08 \times \frac{1}{12} = \$171 ,$$

so the amount of the first payment applied to principal was $228.48 - $171 = $57.48.

• PROBLEM 24-16

Debra Cole wishes to buy a used car worth $720. She can either pay for the car on the installment plan, with 10% down and 12 monthly payments of $65, or borrow the $720 for the same 12 month period at 8% interest. Which method of financing is more economical? By how much?

Solution: Under the installment plan, Ms. Cole will make a down payment of 10% (= .10) of the $720, which is .10 × $720 = $72. In addition, she must make 12 monthly payments of $65, for 12 × $65 = $780. The total price under the installment plan is therefore

$780 + $72 = $852 .

If she were to borrow the money, Ms. Cole would pay an 8% (= .08) interest charge which is .08 × $720 = $57.60. Adding on the $720 principal, we get a total cost of $720 + $57.60 = $777.60. Comparing this to the $852 cost under the installment plan, it would be more economical to borrow the $720 at 8% interest. The savings would be

$852 - $777.60 = $74.40.

• PROBLEM 24-17

Mr. Ed Williams, owner of a newspaper delivery service, bought a new truck for his business on the installment plan. The pertinent information is given below:

Price of truck	$3,000
Additional equipment	240
Sales tax	5%
Insurance	$ 60
Cash deposit	$ 500
Used car allowance	$ 732

Assume a 5% finance charge, find the amount to be financed, and determine the amount to be paid each month to pay off the truck in one year.

Solution: Since Mr. Williams purchased a $3,000 truck with $240 worth of additional equipment, he spent a total of $3,000 + $240 = $3,240. The sales tax at a 5% (= .05) rate would be .05 × $3,240 = $162. Adding a $60 charge for insurance, we get a total charge of

$3240 + $162 + $60 = $3,462 for the truck.

Mr. Williams gave a $500 cash deposit and was allowed $732 for his used car for a $500 + $732 = $1,232 credit. The net balance on the truck was therefore $3,462 - $1,232 = $2,230. The financing charge, which is 5% (= .05) would be $2,230 × .05 = $111.50 yielding a total amount to be paid of $2,230 + $111.50 = $2,341.50.

In order to calculate how much each of the monthly payments should be, we would divide $2341.50 by 12, which to the nearest dollar is $195. Mr. Williams would therefore make 11 monthly payments of $195 (for a total of 11 × $195 = $2145) and a final 12th payment for the balance of $2341.50 - $2145 = $196.50.

• PROBLEM 24-18

Find the amount to be paid each month in order to pay off the car described below in two years.

Price of car: $5,779.00
Transportation charge: $73.00
Factory-installed equipment:

Radio	$ 95.50
Metallic paint	59.90
Racing stripes	39.50
Power steering	98.00
Wide radial tires	198.10
Air conditioning	429.00

Dealer-installed equipment:

Mirror	$ 8.50
Mats	10.75
Undercoat	35.00

Insurance:

Collision ($100-deductible)	$505.75 for two years
Comprehensive	231.50 for two years

Sales tax: 5%
Cash deposit: $500.00
Cost of financing: 9½% per year for two years
Used car allowance: $370.00

Solution: Since the car has a base price of $5779 and a transportation charge of $73, it has a delivery price of $5852. In addition, the car has $95.50 + $59.90 + $39.50 + $98 + $198.10 + $429 = $920 in factory-installed equipment and $8.50 + $10.75 + $35.00 = $54.25 of dealer-installed equipment bringing the price of the car to

$5852 + $920 + $54.25 = $6826.25.

The sales tax on the car, at a 5% (= .05) rate would be $6826.25 x .05 = $341.31, bringing the total cash price of the car to $7167.56. Allowing $370 for a used car and $500 deposit, we get a total credit of $370 + $500 = $870, bringing the net balance on the car to

$7167.56 - $870 = $6297.56.

Also, the insurance of $505.75 for collision and $231.50 for comprehensive totals $505.75 + $231.50 = $737.25, bringing the amount of money necessary to pay for the car to

$6297.56 + $737.25 = $7034.81.

The finance charge, which is 19% (= .19) of this amount is:

.19 x $7034.81 = $1336.61.

The total balance due is therefore

$7034.81 + $1336.61 = $8371.42.

Dividing $8371.42 by 24, and rounding to the nearest dollar, we get $349. The buyer would therefore pay $349 a month for the first 23 months (for a total of $349 x 23 = $8027), and the balance of $8371.42 - $8027 = $344.42 for the 24th payment.

• PROBLEM 24-19

A motorcycle with a cash price of $275 can be purchased on the installment plan for 10% down and $18.20 per month for 18 months. Find the finance charge and the percent (to the nearest 1/10 %) by which the installment price exceeds the cash price.

Solution: Since the installment plan calls for a down payment of 10% (= .10) of the cash price, the down payment would be .10 x $275 = $27.50. The 18 monthly payments of $18.20 total $18.20 X 18 = $327.60, so the total cost under the installment plan would be $327.60 + $27.50 = $355.10. The finance charge, which is the difference between installment price and cash price, is $355.10 - $275 = $80.10. The amount by which the installment price exceeds the cash price, expressed as a percent, is

$$\frac{\$80.10}{\$275} = .291 = 29.1\%.$$

• PROBLEM 24-20

A used car worth $1650 was purchased on the installment plan with a $50 down payment and a total of $1840 in monthly payments over a period of two years. What was the rate of interest computed on the entire amount paid by the purchaser?

Solution: Since the automobile had a cash price of $1650 and the purchaser paid a total of $50 + $1840 = $1890 in the installment plan, the finance charge over the two year period was $1890 - $1650 = $240. We can now calculate the rate of interest paid by the purchaser by using the formula:

$$\text{Rate of Interest} = \frac{\text{Finance Charge}}{\text{Principal} \times \text{Term of Financing}}.$$

Substituting a finance charge of $240, principal of $1,600, and a term of 2 years, we get

$$\text{Rate of Interest} = \frac{\$240}{\$1,600 \times 2} = \frac{\$240}{\$3200} = .075,$$

which is equivalent to 7.5% per year.

• PROBLEM 24-21

Find the finance charge and the percent by which the installment price exceeds the cash price (to the nearest tenth of a percent) on each purchase.

No.	Merchandise	Cash Price	Down Payment	No. of Payments	Amount of Payment
1	Set of encyclopedias	$350.00	$ 40.00	24	$ 15.00
2	Sewing machine	$225.00	$ 24.00	14	$ 16.50
3	Coat	$ 40.00	$ 11.20	7	$ 5.00
4	Television set	$188.00	$ 44.40	12	$ 13.22
5	Used car	$575.00	$ 57.50	10	$ 63.25
6	Piano	$800.00	$120.00	20	$ 38.48

Solution: The finance charge is the difference between the installment price and the cash price. The percent by which the installment price exceeds the cash price is the ratio of the finance charge to the cash price, expressed as a percentage.

For example, in problem no. 1, the 24 payments of $15 total 24 x $15 = $360. Adding on a $40 down payment, we get a total installment price of $360 + $40 = $400. The finance charge is therefore $400 - $350 = $50, and the percent by which the installment price exceeds the cash price (rounded) is

$$\frac{\$50}{\$350} = .143 = 14.3\%.$$

The same procedure was followed to complete the remaining problems, and the results have been summarized in the table below:

No.	Cash Price	Installment Price	Finance Charge	Percent in Excess
1	$350	$400	$50	14.3%
2	$225	$255	$30	13.3%
3	$ 40	$ 46.20	$ 6.20	15.5%
4	$188	$203.04	$15.04	8.0%
5	$575	$690	$115	20.0%
6	$800	$889.60	$89.60	11.2%

PERCENT OF FINANCE CHARGES

• PROBLEM 24-22

The Charge-It revolving charge card requires payment of one-sixth of the balance each month, along with an interest charge of 1½%. How much must be paid on a balance of $75? What is the new unpaid balance? What is the annual rate of interest charged?

Solution: Since the charge card requires payment of one-sixth of the balance (along with interest), the payment on balance due is $\frac{1}{6} \times \$75 = \$12.50$. In addition, an interest charge of 1½% (= .015), which is .015 x $75 = $1.13 is due, so the total payment due is

$$\$12.50 + \$1.13 = \$13.63.$$

Since $12.50 of the $75 balance was paid, the new unpaid balance would be $75 - $12.50 = $62.50. Also, the interest rate of 1½% per month, over the 12 months in the year is equivalent to an annual interest rate of

$$1\tfrac{1}{2}\% \times 12 = 18\% .$$

• PROBLEM 24-23

Mr. Thomas purchased a \$190 lawn mower on an installment plan. He was charged a flat fee of 8% per year as a service charge. If Mr. Thomas paid for the mower in 6 equal monthly payments, how much was each monthly payment? What was the true interest rate he was charged?

Solution: Since Mr. Thomas was charged a flat fee of 8% (.08) per year for the 6 months (= $\frac{1}{2}$ year), the interest charge (using the formula I = prt) was \$190 × .08 × $\frac{1}{2}$ = \$7.60. This means that his total cost for the mower was \$190 + \$7.60 = \$197.60. Since this was paid off in 6 equal installments, each payment was

$$\frac{\$197.60}{6} = \$32.93.$$

We can calculate the true interest rate via the formula:

$$\text{Rate} = \frac{2 \times \text{no. of payments per year} \times \text{interest charge}}{\text{Cash balance} \times (\text{no. of payments to be made} + 1)}$$

Substituting 12 payments per year, an interest charge of \$7.60, a cash balance of \$190, and 6 + 1 = 7 payments, we get:

$$\text{Rate} = \frac{2 \times 12 \times \$7.60}{\$190 \times 7} = .137, \text{ which is } 13.7\%.$$

• PROBLEM 24-24

Mrs. Reynolds purchased \$450 worth of carpeting on an easy payment plan that required \$70 down, with the balance in 12 monthly payments of \$35 each. What was the annual interest rate she paid?

Solution: Mrs. Reynolds made 12 monthly payments of \$35 each, for a total of 12 x \$35 = \$420, as well as a down payment of \$70. Her total cost for the carpeting was therefore \$420 + \$70 = \$490. Since the carpeting was worth \$450, she paid a financing charge of \$490 - \$450 = \$40. Also, since she paid \$70 down, her cash balance subject to financing was \$450 - \$70 = \$380. We can now find the annual interest rate by applying the formula:

$$\text{Rate} = \frac{2 \times \text{No. of Payments in Year} \times \text{Finance Charge}}{\text{Cash Balance} \times (\text{No. of Payments to be made} + 1)}$$

Substituting 12 payments per year, a finance charge of \$40, a cash balance of \$380, and 12 + 1 = 13 payments, we get:

$$\text{Rate} = \frac{2 \times 12 \times \$40}{\$380 \times 13} = .194 \text{ which is } 19.4\%.$$

• PROBLEM 24-25

Assume that the following charges (flat rates) are made on \$500 for a year and that the loan in each case is to be repaid in 12 equal monthly installments:

(a) 3% , (b) 5%.

What is the monthly payment and the true annual interest rate that the borrower is paying in each case? (Record interest rate correct to the nearest tenth of 1%.)

Solution: (a) At the 3% (= .03) per year rate, the interest charge on \$500 over a period of 12 months (= 1 year) is \$500 x .03 x 1 = \$15. This means that the total amount to be repaid would be \$500 + \$15 = \$515, so each monthly payment would be

$$\frac{\$515}{12} = \$42.92.$$

We can calculate the true annual interest rate via the formula:

$$\text{Rate} = \frac{2 \times \text{No. of Payments in Year} \times \text{Interest Charge}}{\text{Cash balance} \times (\text{No. of Payments to be made} + 1)}\ .$$

Substituting 12 payments per year, an interest charge of \$15 and a cash balance of \$500, we get:

$$\text{Rate} = \frac{2 \times 12 \times \$15}{\$500 \times 13} = .055, \text{ which is } 5.5\%$$

(b) At the 5%)= .05) per year rate, the interest charge on the \$500 is \$500 X .05 X 1 = \$25. The total amount to be repaid would be \$500 + \$25 = \$525, and each of the monthly installments would be

$$\frac{\$525}{12} = \$43.75.$$

Applying the formula for true annual interest rate used before, we get:

$$\text{Rate} = \frac{2 \times 12 \times \$25}{\$500 \times 3} = .092 = 9.2\%.$$

• PROBLEM 24-26

A \$39.90 radio can be purchased on the installment plan for \$5.00 down and \$3.10 a month for a year. What is the annual interest rate for this installment purchase?

Solution: Purchasing the radio on the installment plan requires a \$5.00 down payment, as well as twelve monthly payments of \$3.10. The total cost of the radio under the installment plan is therefore the down payment (\$5.00) plus the monthly payments (12 x \$3.10 = \$37.20) for a total of \$5.00 + \$37.20 = \$42.20. Since the value of the radio is \$39.90, the finance charge for the installment plan is \$42.20 - \$39.90 = \$2.30. Also, since a \$5.00 deposit is required, the cash balance subject to financing is \$39.90 - \$5.00 = \$34.90. We can now find the annual interest rate by using the formula:

$$\text{rate} = \frac{2 \times \text{No. of payments in Year} \times \text{Finance Charge}}{\text{Cash balance} \times (\text{No. of payments to be made} + 1)}$$

Substituting 12 payments per year, a \$2.30 finance charge, a cash balance of \$34.90 and 12 + 1 = 13 payments, we get:

$$\text{rate} = \frac{2 \times 12 \times \$2.30}{\$34.90 \times 13} = .122, \text{ which is } 12.2\%.$$

• PROBLEM 24-27

A water bed sells for $330 cash or $40 down and $10.50 a month for 36 months. Find the annual interest rate charged.

Solution: Since the installment payments of $10.50 a month are for 36 months, their cost is $10.50 x 36 = $378. Adding on the $40 down payment, we get a total cost on the installment plan of $378 + $40 = $418. The bed sells for $330, so the installment charge is $418 - $330 = $88. Also, since a down payment of $40 is required, the cash balance subject to financing charges is $330 - $40 = $290. We can now calculate the annual interest rate by using the formula:

$$\text{rate} = \frac{2 \times \text{no. of payments in year} \times \text{finance charge}}{\text{Cash balance} \times (\text{No. of payments to be made} + 1)}$$

Substituting 12 payments per year, an installment charge of $88, a cash balance of $290 and a total of 36 payments we get:

$$\text{rate} = \frac{2 \times 12 \times \$88}{\$290 \times 37} = .197, \text{ which is } 19.7\% .$$

• PROBLEM 24-28

Ms. Chen purchased a used car, worth $1650, on the installment plan, paying $50 down and $1,840 in monthly installment payments over a period of two years. What annual interest rate did she pay?

Solution: Since Ms. Chen paid $50 down and $1840 in installments, she paid a total of $50 + $1840 = $1890 for the car. It had a cash value of $1660, so she paid $1890 - $1650 = $240 in installment charges. Also, since she paid $50 down, her cash balance subject to installment charges was $1650 - $50 = $1600. We can now find the annual interest rate by applying the formula:

$$\text{rate} = \frac{2 \times \text{no. of payments in year} \times \text{installment charge}}{\text{Cash balance} \times (\text{no. of payments to be made} + 1)} .$$

Substituting 12 payments per year, an installment charge of $240, a cash balance of $1600 and 24 (12 payments per year for 2 years = 12 x 2 = 24) payments, we get:

$$\text{rate} = \frac{2 \times 12 \times \$240}{\$1600 \times 25} = .144, \text{ which is } 14.4\% .$$

• PROBLEM 24-29

A desk valued at $125 can be purchased on the installment plan with a down payment of $16.25 and 16 monthly payments of $7.50. Calculate the interest rate involved.

Solution: Since the installment plan requires 16 monthly payments of $7.50 each, the installment payments total $7.50 x 16 = $120.

Adding the $16.25 down payment, we get a total cost under the installment plan of $120 + $16.25 = $136.25. The desk has a cash value of $125, so the finance charge is $136.25 - $125 = $11.25. Also, since a down payment of $16.25 was made on the $125 cash price, the unpaid balance which was financed was $125 - $16.25 = $108.75. We can now find the interest rate via the formula:

$$\text{rate} = \frac{2 \times \text{no. of payments per year} \times \text{finance charge}}{\text{Unpaid balance} \times (\text{no. of payments to be made} + 1)} .$$

Substituting 12 payments per year, a finance charge of $11.25, an unpaid balance of $108.75, and 16 payments, we get:

$$\text{rate} = \frac{2 \times 12 \times \$11.25}{\$108.75 \times 17} = .146 = 14.6\% .$$

• PROBLEM 24-30

Mrs. Kaplan purchased a $200 coffee table on an installment plan for $35 down and 9 monthly payments of $20. Find the annual interest rate she paid.

Solution: Since Mrs. Kaplan made 9 monthly payments of $20 each (for a total of 9 x $20 = $180), as well as a down payment of $35, her total cost for the coffee table under the installment plan was $180 + $35 = $215. The table was worth $200, so she paid a finance charge of $215 - $200 = $15. Also, since she paid $35 down, her cash balance subject to financing was $200 - $35 = $165. We can now find the annual interest rate by applying the formula:

$$\text{rate} = \frac{2 \times \text{no. of payments in year} \times \text{finance charge}}{\text{Cash balance} \times (\text{no. of payments to be made} + 1)}$$

Substituting 12 payments per year, a finance charge of $15, a cash balance of $165, and 9 payments, we get:

$$\text{rate} = \frac{2 \times 12 \times \$15}{\$165 \times 10} = .218, \text{ which is } 21.8\% .$$

• PROBLEM 24-31

A bedroom set with a cash value of $720 can be purchased on the installment plan for 18 monthly payments of $47.20 each. What is the annual interest rate?

Solution: Since the bedroom set requires 18 monthly payments of $47.20 each, the total cost under the installment plan is $47.20 x 18 = $849.60. The set has a cash value of $720, so the finance charge is $849.60 - $720 = $129.60. Also, since no down payment was made, the unpaid cash balance was the $720 cash value. We can now calculate the annual interest rate by applying the formula:

$$\text{rate} = \frac{2 \times \text{no. of payments per year} \times \text{finance charge}}{\text{Unpaid cash balance} \times (\text{no. of payments to be made} + 1)}$$

Substituting 12 payments per year, a finance charge of \$129.60, an unpaid cash balance of \$720 and 18 payments, we get:

$$\text{rate} = \frac{2 \times 12 \times \$129.60}{\$720 \times 19} = .227, \text{ which is } 22.7\% .$$

• PROBLEM 24-32

A \$98 movie camera can be purchased on the installment plan for 10% down, with the balance over 24 weekly payments of \$4 each. What is the annual interest rate?

Solution: Since the camera can be purchased for 10% (= .10) down, the down payment required is 10% of \$98, which is \$98 x 10 = \$9.80. This leaves a cash balance of \$98 - \$9.80 = \$88.20. The 24 weekly payments total 24 x \$4 = \$96. Along with the \$9.80 down payment, this gives us a total installment price of \$96 + \$9.80 = \$105.80. The camera has a cash value of \$98, so the installment charge is \$105.80 - \$98 = \$7.80. We can now calculate the annual interest rate by applying the formula:

$$\text{rate} = \frac{2 \times \text{no. of payments in year} \times \text{finance charge}}{\text{Cash balance} \times (\text{no. of payments to be made} + 1)}$$

Substituting 52 payments per year, an installment charge of \$7.80, a cash balance of \$88.20, and 24 payments, we get:

$$\text{rate} = \frac{2 \times 52 \times \$7.80}{\$88.20 \times 25} = .368, \text{ which is } 36.8\% .$$

• PROBLEM 24-33

An electric guitar with a cash value of \$90.50, was purchased on the installment plan for \$14.95 down, followed by 8 monthly payments of \$10 each. Calculate the interest rate.

Solution: Since there were 8 monthly payments of \$10 each, the total of the installment payments was 8 x \$10 = \$80. Adding on the \$14.95 down payment, we get a total installment price of \$80 + \$14.95 = \$94.95. The guitar had a cash value of \$90.50, so the finance charge was \$94.95 - \$90.50 = \$ 4.45. Also, since a \$14.95 down-payment was made on the \$90.50 cash price, the unpaid balance subject to financing was \$90.50 - \$14.95 = \$75.55. We can now find the interest rate by applying the formula:

$$\text{rate} = \frac{2 \times \text{no. of payments per year} \times \text{finance charge}}{\text{Unpaid balance} \times (\text{no. of payments to be made} + 1)}$$

Substituting 12 payments per year, a finance charge of \$4.45, an unpaid balance of \$75.55 and 8 payments, we get:

$$\text{rate} = \frac{2 \times 12 \times \$4.45}{\$75.55 \times 9} = .157 = 15.7\% .$$

CHAPTER 25

BANKING

BANK STATEMENTS AND DEPOSIT ACCUMULATION

• **PROBLEM** 25-1

On September 1, Mr. Blake received a statement for his checking account. The closing balance on the statement was $1,810.50. Mr. Blake's checkbook shows a balance of $1,685.75. In comparing his check stubs to the statement, he notices that checks for amounts of $60.80 $40.30, and $25.00 did not appear on the statement. Also, the statement lists a service charge of $1.35 which does not appear on his checkbook stubs. Prepare a reconciliation statement for Mr. Blake.

Solution: Since not all the checks listed on his checkbook stubs are included on his bank statement, and since he hasn't yet deducted the bank's service charge from his checkbook balance, the bank statement that Mr. Blake received on September 1, has a different balance from his checkbook. A reconciliation between the bank statement and the checkbook will serve two purposes. First, it will verify that neither Mr. Blake nor his bank made any mistakes in processing the checks he has written, and second, it tells Mr. Blake what the latest balance in his checkbook is. We can prepare a reconciliation as follows:

Begin with the balance in Mr. Blake's checkbook of $1,685.75. Deduct from it the service charge of $1.35 which did not appear on his checkbook stubs. The result of $1,684.40 is what Mr. Blake believes to be his latest checkbook balance. We will now check this with the balance in the bank statement. From a statement balance of $1,810.50, we must subtract the value of the three checks that Mr. Blake has issued but have not been received by the bank. The total of the three checks

= $60.80 + $40.30 + $25.00 = $126.10.

The adjusted bank statement balance is

$1,810.50 - $126.10 = $1,684.40,

which agrees with the adjusted checkbook balance. The reconciliation procedure used has been summarized in the reconciliation statement below.

Gerald Blake Reconciliation Statement Sept. 1, 19-			
Balance per checkbook:	$1685.75	Balance per bank statement:	$1810.50
Deduct:		Deduct:	
Service charges	$1.35	Checks outstanding	
		#23	$60.80
		#26	40.30
		#32	25.00
		Total	$126.10
Adjusted checkbook Balance	$1684.40	Available bank Balance	$1684.40

• PROBLEM 25-2

Fig. 1 Checks and Deposits from Checkbook

Check No. 106 ...	$ 7.50	Check No. 114 ...	$ 22.50
Check No. 107 ...	3.25	Check No. 115 ...	1.50
Check No. 108 ...	18.69	Check No. 116 ...	8.98
Check No. 109 ...	1.25	Check No. 117 ...	16.74
Check No. 110 ...	25.00	Check No. 118 ...	10.00
Deposit	138.75	Check No. 119 ...	35.00
Check No. 111 ...	6.15	Deposit	282.72
Check No. 112 ...	5.00	Check No. 120 ...	1.67
Check No. 113 ...	15.00	Check No. 121 ...	125.00

Fig. 2

Statement of Account with

CITY NATIONAL BANK
OF NORTHHAMPTON
Northhampton, Massachusetts

Alfred C. Staples
Alice E. Staples
2245 West Cedar Street
Northhampton, MA 02357

Checks	Checks	Deposits	No. of checks	Date	Balance
		Balance forward		FEB 1	358.26
1.25	3.25		2	FEB 3	353.76
7.50			3	FEB 4	346.26
18.69			4	FEB 5	327.57
5.00		138.75	5	FEB 7	461.32
15.00			6	FEB 9	446.32
8.98	16.74		8	FEB 10	420.60
22.50		282.72	9	FEB 12	680.82
1.50			10	FEB 18	679.32
1.63 SC			10	FEB 20	677.69
1.67			11	FEB 23	676.02
25.00			12	FEB 25	651.02

Key
CC-Certified check
CM-Credit memo.
DM-Debit memo.
EC-Error Corrected
LST-List
OD-Overdraft
RT-Return
SC-Service Charge for Preceding Month

PLEASE EXAMINE STATEMENT AT ONCE
If no errors are reported in ten days the account will be considered correct

The last amount in the above column is your balance

Shown above (Figure 1) are a list of the checks and deposits from Mr. and Mrs. Staples' checkbook. Figure 2 shows their bank statement corresponding to the checks and deposits listed in Figure 1. The balance in their checkbook is $476.50. Prepare a bank reconciliation statement for them.

Solution: Mr. and Mrs. Staples checkbook shows a balance of $476.50. Not included in this figure, however, is a bank service charge of $1.63. Deducting this service charge from the balance as shown in the checkbook we obtain an adjusted checkbook balance of $476.50 - $1.63 = $474.87.

The bank statement shows a closing balance of $651.02.

However, comparing the checks listed on the bank statement against the record in the Staples' checkbook, we see that checks # 111, 118, 119 and 121 have not yet been received by the bank, and so are not reflected on the bank statement. The total of these checks = $6.15 + $10.00 + $35.00 + $125.00 = $176.15 should be subtracted from the balance on the bank statement, resulting in an adjusted balance of $651.02 - $176.15 = $474.87, which agrees with the adjusted checkbook balance. The reconciliation procedure has been summarized in Figure 3 below.

Figure 3.

THIS FORM IS PROVIDED TO HELP YOU BALANCE YOUR BANK STATEMENT

Date *Today*, 19 —

Balance shown on BANK STATEMENT $ *651.02*	Balance shown in Your CHECK BOOK $ *476.50*
Add deposits not on STATEMENT $ ______	Add any deposits not already entered in CHECKBOOK: $ ______
Total. .$ *651.02*	
Subtract Checks Issued but Not on Statement:	Total . .$ *476.50*
No. *111* $ *6.15*	
118 *10.00*	
119 *35.00*	
121 *125.00*	Subtract Service Charges and other Bank charges not in Check book:
	$ *1.63*
Total. . . .$ *176.15*	Total. . . .$ *1.63*
Balance. . . . . $ *474.87*	Balance. . . . . $ *474.87*

These totals should agree with your check book. Any difference should be reported to the bank within ten days after the receipt of your statement.

• PROBLEM 25-3

Mr. Williams has $20 deducted from his paycheck every month and automatically deposited in his savings account. If the savings account declares interest at 5 3/4 %, how much will these monthly deposits add to his account in 3 months?

Solution: Since Mr. Williams is making three separate deposits at different points in time, each deposit will earn a different amount of interest. We can calculate how much interest each of the three deposits will earn, and then add the three amounts to determine the total interest that the three monthly installments will receive. We can use the formula:

Interest = Principal × Rate of Interest × Term (in years)

to calculate each of the amounts of interest.

The first of the monthly deposits of $20 will be in the account for the full 3 months, so it will have a term of $\frac{3}{12} = \frac{1}{4}$ of a year at an interest rate of $5\frac{3}{4}\% = .0575$ per year. The interest on this deposit is calculated as follows:

$$\text{Interest} = \$20 \times .0575 \times \frac{1}{4} = \frac{\$1.15}{4} = 0.2875.$$

Since the bank retains fractions of a cent on the interest from savings accounts, this amount is to be rounded down to $0.28.

The second $20 deposit will not be made until the second month of the three month period, so it will have a term of only $\frac{2}{12} = \frac{1}{6}$ of a year. Using the same rate of interest (.0575), the interest earned will be

$$\$20 \times .0575 \times \frac{1}{6} = \frac{\$1.15}{6},$$

which the bank will round to $.19.

Finally, the interest on the third deposit, which will have a term of only $\frac{1}{12}$ of a year, will be

$$\$20 \times .0575 \times \frac{1}{12} = \frac{\$1.15}{12},$$

which the bank will round to $.09.

The total interest for the three installments will therefore be

$$\$.28 + \$.19 + \$.09 = \$56.$$

Adding this to the $60 Mr. Williams will have deposited over the three month period, we get a total increase in his account of

$$\$60 + \$.56 = \$60.56.$$

BANK NOTES AND MORTGAGES

• PROBLEM 25-4

John Backus will pay the Third National Bank $342.65 on July 1. Find the amount he borrowed, given the interest is $17.25.

Solution: The amount due on a loan is the principal plus the interest charge. Thus the principal is equal to the amount due less the interest charge. Hence the amount Mr. Backus borrowed is equal to $342.65 (amount due) - $17.25 (interest) = $325.40.

• PROBLEM 25-5

What is the date of maturity of a note dated January 30 with a term of one month?

Solution: The date of maturity of a note is the date at which a note achieves its full value. This occurs at the end of the term of the note. Since the note in the problem was dated January 30 and had a term of one month, its date of maturity would be one month from January 30. January 30 plus one month is either February 29 or February 28 (depending on whether or not it is a leap year), since there is no February 30.

• PROBLEM 25-6

Mr. Carson signed a note as payment for a debt on March 15. If the note had a term of two months, what was its maturity date?

Solution: When Mr. Carson signed the note on March 15, he promised to repay his debt on the date of maturity of the note. Since the note had a term of two months, and was dated March 15, its date of maturity was two months after March 15, or May 15.

• PROBLEM 25-7

In order to help finance his new home, Mr. Hendricks borrowed \$5,000 from a bank under a fixed mortgage, agreeing to pay 5% interest yearly, in semiannual installments with the mortgage to fall due in twenty years. How much interest is due every six months?

Solution: The amount of interest that Mr. Hendricks must pay every 6 months is the interest on the \$5,000 mortgage at the interest rate of 5% per year. We can calculate the amount of interest he must pay each period by using the formula:

$$\text{Interest} = \text{Principal of Loan} \times \text{Rate of Interest} \times \text{Term (in years)}$$

Substituting \$5,000 for the amount, or principal, of the loan, 5%, or .05, per year for the interest rate, and $\frac{6}{12}$ or $\frac{1}{2}$ of a year for the term of each payment period, we obtain

$$\text{Interest} = \$5,000 \times .05 \times \frac{1}{2} = \frac{\$250}{2} = \$125.$$

The amount of interest due every six months is therefore $125.

• PROBLEM 25-8

> Mr. Rose is buying a house with an appraised value of $16,500. He has applied for a FHA loan for 20 years at an interest rate of 7 ½ %. The property tax on the house is $264 per year, and fire and tornado insurance runs $18 per year. (a) What is the amount of his mortgage if he makes the minimum down payment of 3%? (b) What is his total monthly payment?

Solution: The amount of Mr. Rose's mortgage will be the appraised value of the house less any down payment that he makes. Since the FHA requires a minimum down payment of 3% on the first $25,000 of appraised value, Mr. Rose will have to put down 3% of the appraised value of the house. This is calculated as follows:

3% of $16,500 = .03 × $16,500 = $495.

The amount Mr. Rose's mortgage would then be

$16,500 - $495 = $16,005.

Using the partial payment tables, we can determine the monthly payment necessary to pay off the $16,005 mortgage. At an interest rate of 7 ½ % per year for a term of 20 years, we see from the partial payments table in order to pay off the $16,005, Mr. Rose will have to make a monthly payment of $129. In addition, his taxes and insurance will be $264 + $18 = $282 per year. To find out what this expense is on a monthly basis, we simply divide by 12:

$$\frac{\$282}{12} = \$23.50 \quad \text{per month.}$$

Mr. Rose's total monthly payment will then be mortgage plus taxes and insurance, for a total of

$129 + $23.50 = $152.50.

LOANS AND NOMINAL VS. TRUE INTEREST RATE

• PROBLEM 25-9

A sum of money is borrowed for a term of 1 year, discounted at the rate of 6%. What is the true rate of interest charged? What would the true rate of interest be for the same sum of money discounted at an 8% rate? (Record answers to the nearest tenth of 1%.)

Solution: When a loan is discounted, the interest charges are deducted in advance. As a result, the amount you actually receive is always less than the amount of the loan. Because the interest charges are deducted in advance, the discounted rate of interest is not the true rate of interest on the loan. One way to determine the true rate of interest is to use the formula:

True Interest Rate =

$$\frac{\text{Discounted Interest Rate}}{1 - \text{Discounted Interest Rate} \times \text{Term of Loan (in Years)}}$$

Substituting a discounted interest rate of 6% (.06) per year and a term of 1 year into the equation, we get

$$\text{True Interest Rate} = \frac{.06}{(1 - .06) \times 1}$$

$$= \frac{.06}{1 - .06} = \frac{.06}{.94}$$

which, to the nearest tenth of 1%, is 6.4%.

Following the same procedure for the 8% discount rate we obtain:

$$\text{True Interest Rate} = \frac{.08}{1 - .08 \times 1} = \frac{.08}{1 - .08} = \frac{.08}{.92}$$

which rounds to 8.7%.

• PROBLEM 25-10

Mrs. Davis takes out a 12 month loan for $150, discounted at 6%. How much did she actually receive? What are her monthly payments?

Solution: Since the loan is discounted, the amount that Mrs. Davis actually received was the amount of the loan less interest charges. The interest charged to her can be calculated using the formula

$$\text{Interest} = \text{Principal of Loan} \times \text{Interest Rate} \times \text{Term of Loan}.$$

In this problem, the amount of the loan is \$150, the interest rate is 6% (or .06) per year and the term is $\frac{12}{12}$ or 1 year. Substituting in the formula, we get

$$\text{Interest} = \$150 \times .06 \times 1 = \$9.$$

Since Mrs. Davis was charged \$9 interest, the amount she actually received was

$$\$150 - \$9 = \$141.$$

Since she has to pay back \$150 over 12 payments, each payment should be $\frac{1}{12}$ of \$150, which is

$$\frac{\$150}{12} = \$12.50 \text{ per month}.$$

• PROBLEM 25-11

Mrs. Kane has decided to buy a new stereo that costs \$150. She wants to take out a loan from her bank to pay for it. If the bank agrees to give her a 12 months loan at a 6% rate of interest, deducted in advance, how much should she ask for to actually receive the \$150? What will her monthly payment be?

Solution: When a bank deducts the interest on a loan in advance, the amount of money you receive is always less than the amount you asked for. The percentage will vary, depending on the rate of interest and the term of the loan. Using the formula

$$\text{Interest} = \text{Principal} \times \text{Rate} \times \text{Time } (I = Prt),$$

we can determine what percentage of the principal will be deducted as interest. For example, Mrs. Kane has agreed to an interest rate of 6% (or .06) per year for a period of 1 year. Substituting into the formula $I = Prt$ we get

$$I = P \times .06 \times 1 \quad \text{or} \quad I = .06 \times P.$$

In other words, no matter how much she borrows, 6% of it will be deducted in advance, so Mrs. Kane will actually receive 100% - 6% or 94% of the total amount she borrows. Since she wants to receive $150, we must find what amount $150 is 94% of. This can be done as follows: $\$150 = .94 \times P$. Dividing both sides by .94 we obtain

$$\frac{\$150}{.94} = P, \text{ so } P \text{ is approximately } \$159.58.$$

This is the total amount she should ask for. In order to pay back the loan, she must pay back the $159.58 over a period of 12 payments. Each payment should then be $\frac{1}{12}$ of $159.58 or $\frac{\$159.58}{12}$, which rounds to $13.30.

• PROBLEM 25-12

> Mr. Stone decides to take a loan from his bank to purchase a new car. If he borrows $4,000 for ninety days at 6 percent discount, how much will he actually receive?

Solution: When you borrow money from the bank, you are charged interest on it. With a discounted loan the interest is always deducted in advance, so the amount you actually receive is the amount of the loan minus any interest charges. To find out how much Mr. Stone actually will receive, we must first find out how much interest he is being charged. Since

Interest = Principal of Loan × Rate of Interest × Length of Time Money is Borrowed

and Mr. Stone will borrow $,4000 at a normal (annual) interest rate of 6% $\left(\text{or } \frac{6}{100}\right)$ for a period of $\frac{90}{360}$ or $\frac{1}{4}$ of a year, the amount of interest he will be charged is

$$\$4,000 \times \frac{6}{100} \times \frac{1}{4} = \frac{\$4000 \times 6}{100 \times 4} = \frac{\$24000}{400} = \$60.$$

Mr. Stone will actually receive

$$\$4,000 - \$60 = \$3,940.$$

• PROBLEM 25-13

> The Last National Bank has just approved a loan at an interest rate of 6% for 90 days. If the interest charge on the loan is $36, how much is the principal of the loan?

Solution: Using the formula

Interest = Principal × Rate of Interest × Time (I = Prt),

we can substitute the values of I, r, and t and solve for P. I = \$36, since the interest charge was \$36. The rate of interest (r) is 6% $\left(\text{or } \frac{6}{100}\right)$ per year and the length of time is $\frac{90}{360}$ or $\frac{1}{4}$ of a year. Substituting

we get $\$36 = P \times \frac{6}{100} \times \frac{1}{4}$ or $\$36 = \frac{6}{400} \times P$. Multiplying

both sides by $\frac{400}{6}$ we get $\frac{400}{6} \times \$36 = P$ or $P = \$2400$.

• PROBLEM 25-14

Mr. White received the sum of \$972.50 from ABC Loan Company. If he signed a loan agreement to pay \$1000 to the loan company at the end of 180 days, what is the discount rate of the loan?

Solution: When a bank or loan company discounts a loan, they deduct the interest charges in advance. In this problem, since Mr. White agreed to repay \$1000 while he received only \$972.50, he was charged \$1000 - 972.50 = \$27.50 in interest.

Knowing the interest, amount of the loan and term of the loan we can use the formula:

Interest = Principal of Loan × Interest Rate × Term of Loan

to find the interest rate that the loan was discounted at. Substituting \$27.50 for Interest, \$1,000 for the amount of the loan and $\frac{180}{360} = \frac{1}{2}$ of a year for the term of the loan we get

$$\$27.50 = 1000 \times \text{Interest Rate} \times \frac{1}{2}$$

or $\$27.50 = 500 \times \text{Interest}$.

Dividing both sides by 500 we get $\frac{\$27.50}{500} = .055$ = Interest Rate. The discount rate of the loan was, therefore, .055 or 5.5% per year.

• PROBLEM 25-15

Find the interest charge on a \$600 loan at 6% for 60 days. Find the total amount due.

Solution: Interest is the charge made for borrowing money. When you pay back the money, you pay back the amount borrowed plus the interest. Interest is dependent on three things; the principal, the rate of interest, and the length of the time, or term, of the loan. The principal is the original amount that you borrow. The rate of interest is the percentage of the money you borrow that you must pay for the use of the money. Therefore, we can derive an equation for the interest due:

$$\text{Interest due} = \text{Principal} \times \underset{\text{(per year)}}{\text{rate of interest}} \times \underset{\text{(in years)}}{\text{time}}$$

When determining the length of time one assumes that in a year there are 360 days. Therefore, we can say that 60 days $= \frac{1}{6}$ of a year. The rate of interest, 6%, can be expressed as a fraction. Because % means parts per hundred, $6\% = \frac{6}{100}$.

Therefore,

$$\text{Interest due} = \text{amount of money} \times \text{rate of interest} \times \text{length of time}$$

$$= \$600 \times \frac{6}{100} \text{ per year} \times \frac{1}{6} \text{ year}$$

$$\text{The total amount due} = \text{principal} + \text{interest due}$$

$$= \$600 + \$6 = \$606.$$

• PROBLEM 25-16

Mr. Langham decides to take a loan from his bank for \$60 at a nominal rate of 6%. If he agrees to repay the loan in equal installments over a period of 15 months, how much will each of the monthly payments be?

Solution: Mr. Langham has taken out a loan which he will have to repay in 15 equal installments. Before we can figure out how much each of these payments will be, we must first know the total amount that he will have to pay to his bank, which is the amount of the loan plus the interest that the bank is charging him. Using the formula

Interest = Principal of Loan × Interest Rate × Length of Time Money is Borrowed

with a principal of \$60, rate of interest of 6% or $\frac{6}{100}$ and a length of time of $\frac{15}{12}$ of a year, the interest to be paid is

$$\$60 \times \frac{6}{100} \times \frac{15}{12} = \frac{\$5400}{1200} = \$4.50.$$

The total amount he will have to pay back is then \$60 + \$4.50 or \$64.50. Since he will pay this in 15 equal payments, each payment will be

$$\frac{1}{15} \text{ of } \$64.50 = \frac{\$64.50}{15} = \$4.30.$$

• PROBLEM 25-17

> Mr. and Mrs. Golden have just purchased a new home. After selling their own house, they find that they still need an additional \$18,000 to pay for the new house. They borrow the \$18,000 at 6% for a term of 20 years. What is the first monthly payment of their loan?

Solution: Mr. and Mrs. Golden have taken out a loan for \$18,000 at 6% for 20 years. Using the partial payments table, which tells how much must be paid in order to pay off a given principal with a given interest charge in a given number of payments, we see that the monthly payment necessary to pay off a loan of \$18,000 at 6% for 20 years is \$128.96.

The \$128.96 that Mr. and Mrs. Golden will pay every month is separated into payment of interest charges and reduction of the principal of the loan. We can use the formula

Interest = Principal of loan × Interest Rate × Term of Period

to calculate how much interest is charged in any period. To find out how much the interest charge will be on their first monthly payment, we substitute a principal of \$18,000, an interest rate of 6% = .06 per year for a period of 1/12 of a year. We obtain:

$$\text{Interest} = \$18{,}000 \times .06 \times \frac{1}{12} = \frac{\$1080}{12} = \$90 \text{ interest.}$$

Since they will make a payment of \$128.96, and \$90 of it will be interest, the remaining \$128.96 - \$90 = \$38.96 will be payment on the principal. This leaves a balance of the principal of \$18,000 - \$38.96 = \$17,961.00.

• PROBLEM 25-18

Mr. Davis purchased a car for \$6250, paying 20% down and financing the balance with a loan. The loan was to be paid back in regular monthly installments of \$50 plus interest at 6% on the unpaid balance. (a) Find the amount of the loan. (b) Find the amount of each of the first three monthly payments. (c) What was the balance of the loan after the third monthly payment was made?

Solution: (a) Since Mr. Davis paid 20% down, the amount he put down was .20 × \$6250 = \$1250.

The amount of the loan was therefore \$6250 - \$1250 = \$5000.

(b) Each of the monthly payments was \$50 plus 6% of the unpaid loan. We can calculate the interest charge by using the formula:

Interest = Principal of Loan × Interest Rate × Term of Period

To calculate the interest charge for the first payment we would substitute a principal of \$5000, an interest rate of rate of 6% = .06 per year for a term of $\frac{1}{12}$ of a year. Substituting, we obtain

$$\text{Interest} = \$5000 \times .06 \times \frac{1}{12} = \frac{\$300}{12} = \$25.$$

The total of the first payment was then

$$\$50 + \$25 = \$75.$$

Also, since \$50 of the first payment was principal, the balance of the loan after the first payment was

$$\$5000 - \$50 = \$4950.$$

Using the same formula as before with the same interest rate and term, and a principal of \$4950, the interest charge for the second payment was

$$\$4950 \times .06 \times \frac{1}{12} = \frac{\$297}{12} = \$24.75.$$

The total of the second payment was then

$$\$50 + \$24.75 = \$74.75,$$

and the balance of the principal after the second payment was

$$\$4950 - \$50 = \$4900.$$

Using the same formula, with the same interest rate and term, and a principal of \$4900, the interest charge for the third payment would be

$$\$4900 \times .06 \times \frac{1}{12} = \frac{\$294}{12} = \$24.50.$$

The total for the third payment was

$$\$50 + \$24.50 = \$74.50.$$

Also, since \$50 of the third payment was principal, the balance of the loan after the third payment was

$$\$4900 - \$50 = \$4850.$$

CHAPTER 26

STOCKS

COST

• **PROBLEM 26-1**

The cost of a stock was $4,200. If its selling price was 85% percent of the total cost, find the selling price.

Solution: Since the selling price of the stock was 85% of the total cost, all we need to do to find the selling price is to find 85% of $4,200. This can be done as follows:

85% of $4,200 = .85 × $4,200 = $3,570.

The selling price was therefore $3,570.

• **PROBLEM 26-2**

State transfer taxes for stocks in New York are as follows:

$ .01¼ a share for stocks under $5 a share par value

$ .02½ a share for stocks from $5-$10 a share par value

$ .03¾ a share for stocks from $10-$20 a share par value

$ .05 a share for stocks over $20 a share par value

Mr. Carr sold 300 shares of stock having a par value of $50 per share. What was the New York State transfer tax?

Solution: Since the par value of the stock that Mr. Carr sold was over $20 per share, the New York State transfer tax is $.05 per share. He sold 300 shares, so the total tax was

300 × $.05 = $15.

• PROBLEM 26-3

Mr. Wills buys 100 shares of stock at 19 7/8. Using the Commission Table listed below, calculate the commission he paid on the purchase.

BROKERAGE RATES ON ROUND LOTS

Amount of Purchase	Commission
\$ 100 - \$ 799	2.0% plus \$6.40 up to \$65
\$ 800 - \$2499	1.3% plus \$12 up to \$65
\$2500 and above	.9% plus \$22.00 up to \$65

Solution: Mr. Wills purchased 100 shares of stock at 19 7/8 (= 19.875). The amount of his purchase was therefore

$$100 \times 19.875 = \$1,987.50.$$

Consulting the Brokerage Rates on Round Lots (100 shares) tables, we see that the commission is 1.3% (= .013) of purchase price plus \$12. The commission was then

$$.013 \times \$1,987.50 + \$12 = \$25.84 + \$12 = \$37.84.$$

• PROBLEM 26-4

Mrs. Rosen purchased 500 shares of stock at 44 1/8 per share. Using the Brokerage Rates on Multiple Round Lots tables below. calculate the commission charged by the broker on her purchase.

BROKERAGE RATES ON MULTIPLE ROUND LOTS

Amount of Purchase	Commission
\$100 - \$2,499	1.3% plus \$12 plus \$6 per round lot
\$2,500 - \$19,999	.9% plus \$22 plus \$6 per round lot
\$20,000 - \$29,999	.6% plus \$82 plus \$6 per round lot
\$30,000 - \$500,000	.4% plus \$142 plus \$6 per round lot

Solution: Since Mrs. Rosen purchased 500 shares of stock at 44 1/8 (= 44.125) per share, the amount for her purchase was

$$500 \times \$44.125 = \$22,062.50.$$

Consulting the table listed above, we see that the commission on her purchase is .6% (= .006) of purchase price plus \$82 plus \$6 per round lot. She purchased 500 shares of stock, and a round lot is equivalent to 100 shares, so she purchased 5 round lots. The additional charge of $6 per round lot was therefore $6 × 5 lots = $30. We can calculate the total commission as follows:

.6% of purchase price plus $82 plus $6 per round lot =

.006 × $22,062.50 + $82 + $30 = $132.38 + $82 + $30 = $244.38.

The total brokerage fee was therefore $244.38.

• PROBLEM 26-5

Mr. Samuels purchased 50 shares of stock when the round lot price was 146 1/8. The odd-lot differential on the sale is 1/4 of a point. Using the table of Brokerage Rates below, calculate the Commission on the sale.

BROKERAGE RATES ON ODD LOTS

Amount of Purchase	Commission
$100 - $799	2.0% plus $4.40 up to $65
$800 - $2,499	1.3% plus $10 up to $65
$2,500 and above	.9% plus $20 up to $65

Solution: Since Mr. Samuels purchased the stock with an odd-lot differential of 1/4 (= .25), the adjusted price per share for calculating the broker's fee is

146.125 + .25 = 146.375 per share.

Mr. Samuels purchased 50 shares, so the adjusted amount of purchase was

146.375 × 50 = $7,318.75.

Consulting the Odd-Lot table above, we see that the commission on a purchase above $2,500 is .9% (= .009) of the purchase price plus $20 up to $65. Calculating the commission we get

.009 × $7,318.75 + $20 = $65.87 + $20 = $85.87.

Since this amount is larger than the $65 limit, the broker's commission on the purchase would be $65.

• PROBLEM 26-6

On July 7, Magee Data stock sold at a high of 23 1/8 and a low of 22 5/8. Giant Industrials sold for a high of 24 1/4 and a low of 23 1/2. Mr. Taylor purchased 300 shares of Magee Data at the high of the day and 400 shares of Giant Industrials at the low of the day. What was the cost of his purchase?

Solution: Since Mr. Taylor purchased the Magee Data stock at its high for the day, he paid 23 1/8 (= 23.125) per share. The cost for the 300 shares was therefore

$$300 \times 23.125 = \$6,937.50$$

Mr. Taylor purchased the Giant Industrials at the low of 23 1/2 (= 23.5) per share. His cost for the 400 shares of Giant Industrials was

$$400 \times 23.5 = \$9,400.$$

The total cost of Mr. Taylor's purchase was then

$$\$6,937.50 + \$9,400 = \$16,337.50.$$

• PROBLEM 26-7

Using the table of stock quotations below, find the cost of each of the following:

Stock Name	Number of Shares	Purchase Price
Gerardi Moving	300	Opening
Interstate RR	100	Opening
Giant Aircraft	700	Opening
Moss Insurance	100	Low
Gendreau Films	600	Low
Hoyer Chemicals	300	Low
Geiger Baking	900	Last
Gilbreth Computers	2,300	Last
Lyden Steel	2,700	Last

19x4 High	19x4 Low	Stocks and Div. in dollars	Sales 100s	Open	High	Low	Last	Chg.
$16\frac{7}{8}$	$11\frac{1}{4}$	Geiger Bak	44	$15\frac{3}{4}$	$15\frac{3}{4}$	$14\frac{1}{4}$	$14\frac{7}{8}$	$-\frac{5}{8}$
$16\frac{1}{2}$	11	Gendr-Films 1.16..	69	12	$12\frac{1}{4}$	12	$12\frac{1}{8}$	$+\frac{3}{8}$
$60\frac{5}{8}$	$27\frac{7}{8}$	Gerar Mov 1.20..	34	$45\frac{7}{8}$	46	$45\frac{5}{8}$	$45\frac{5}{8}$	$+\frac{7}{8}$
$34\frac{3}{4}$	20	Giant Air .20..	1	$21\frac{1}{2}$	$21\frac{1}{2}$	$21\frac{1}{2}$	$21\frac{1}{2}$	$+\frac{1}{2}$
$65\frac{3}{4}$	$47\frac{1}{2}$	Gilb Comp 2.....	20	$47\frac{3}{4}$	$47\frac{3}{4}$	47	$47\frac{1}{2}$	$-\frac{3}{4}$

$119\frac{1}{4}$	$97\frac{1}{2}$	Hoyer Chem 2.....	54	109	$110\frac{3}{8}$	$108\frac{1}{2}$	$108\frac{5}{8}$	$-\frac{3}{8}$
$27\frac{1}{4}$	$22\frac{1}{4}$	Inter RR 1.10..	36	$25\frac{3}{8}$	$25\frac{3}{8}$	$25\frac{1}{4}$	$25\frac{1}{2}$	$-\frac{1}{8}$
$28\frac{1}{8}$	20	Lyden Steel .70..	22	27	27	$26\frac{5}{8}$	$26\frac{5}{8}$	...
$10\frac{5}{8}$	8	Moss Ins 2.....	8	10	10	$9\frac{7}{8}$	$9\frac{7}{8}$	$-\frac{1}{8}$

Solution: Consulting the table of stock quotations, we see that Gerardi Moving (Gerar Mov) had an opening price of 45 7/8 (= 45.875). Since the stock was purchased at the opening price, it was purchased for $45,875 per share. Three hundred shares were purchased, so the cost was

300 × $45,875 = $13,762.50

for the Gerardi stock.

Following a similar procedure, we can calculate the cost of the remaining stocks. The results have been summarized in table form:

Stock	Number of Shares	Purchase Price	Cost
Gerardi Moving	300	Open = 45 7/8 = 45,875	300 × 45.875 = $13,762.50
Interstate RR	100	Open = 25 3/8 = 25.375	100 × 25.375 = $2,537.50
Giant Aircraft	700	Open = 21 1/2 = 21.5	700 × 21.5 = $15,050
Moss Insurance	100	Low = 9 7/8 = 9.875	100 × 9.875 = $987.50
Gendreau Films	600	Low = 12	600 × 12 = $7,200
Hoyer Chemicals	300	Low = 108 1/2= 108.5	300 × 108.5 = $32,550
Geiger Baking	900	Last = 14 7/8 = 14.875	900 × 14.875 = $13,387.50
Gilbreth Computers	2,300	Last = 47 1/2 = 47.5	2300 × 47.5 = $109,250
Lyden Steel	2,700	Last = 26 5/8 = 26.625	2700 × 26.625 = $71,887.50

• PROBLEM 26-8

Amalgamated Corp. offered one of its Vice Presidents an option to purchase 1000 shares of its common stock on June 21 at 95% of its average price for the day. If

Amalgamated's high for the day was 19 3/8 and its low was 18 3/4, at what price per share was the option awarded?

Solution: Since Amalgamated had a daily high of 19 3/8 (= 19.375) and a low of 18 3/4 (= 18.75), its average for the day was

$$\frac{19.375 + 18.75}{2} = \frac{38.125}{2} = \$19.0625 \text{ per share.}$$

The vice president was offered an option at 95% of the average price of $19.0625, so his option price would be 95% of

$$\$19.0625 = .95 \times \$19.0625 = \$18.109375 \text{ per share.}$$

• PROBLEM 26-9

ABC Corporation shows total assets of $75,000 and total liabilities of $52,000. If the Corporation has only 500 shares of stock outstanding, what is the book value per share?

Solution: The book value per share of the ABC stock is the total capital divided by the number of shares of outstanding stock. The total capital, which is total assets less total liabilities, is

$$\$75,000 - \$52,000 = \$23,000.$$

Since there are 500 shares outstanding, the book value per share is therefore

$$\frac{\$23,000}{500} = \$46 \text{ per share.}$$

YIELD RATE AND INCOME FROM STOCKS

• PROBLEM 26-10

Mr. Darnell purchased 20 shares of American Telephone and Telegraph common stock at $182.50 per share. Two months later, he sold the stock at $168.75 per share. What was his loss per share? Total loss?

Solution: Since Mr. Darnell purchased the stock at $182.50 per share and sold it at $168.75 per share, his loss per share was

$$\$182.50 - \$168.75 = \$13.75.$$

He had 20 shares, so his total loss was

$$20 \times \$13.75 = \$275.00$$

• PROBLEM 26-11

Velco Corporation shows a profit to common shareholders of $5,250. If the corporation has 1,250 shares of stock outstanding, what is Velco's earnings per share?

Solution: We can calculate Velco's earnings per share using the formula:

$$\text{Earnings per Share} = \frac{\text{Profits to Common Shareholders}}{\text{Number of Shares of Stock Outstanding}}$$

Substituting a profit to common shareholders of $5,250 and 1,250 for the number of shares outstanding, we get an earnings per share of

$$\frac{\$5,250}{1,250} = \$4.20.$$

• PROBLEM 26-12

What are the earnings per share of a company showing a profit to common shareholders of $4,750, if the company has 1,000 shares of stock outstanding.

Solution: The earnings per share of a company can be computed using the formula:

$$\text{Earnings per Share} = \frac{\text{Profits to stockholders}}{\text{Number of Shares Outstanding}}$$

Subtituting a profits to stockholders of $4,750 and 1,000 for the number of shares outstanding, we get:

$$\text{Earnings per Share} = \frac{\$4,750}{1,000} = \$4.75$$

• PROBLEM 26-13

What is the effective rate of yield of a stock selling for $60 and paying an annual dividend of $2?

Solution: The effective rate of yield, or the rate of return, is the percentage of the price paid as a dividend. We can calculate the effective yield of the stock using the formula:

$$\text{Effective Yield} = \frac{\text{Dividends for Year}}{\text{Market Price}}$$

Substituting a yearly dividend of \$2 and a market price of \$60, we get

$$\text{Effective Yield} = \frac{\$\ 2}{\$60}\text{, which is } 3\ 1/3\%.$$

• PROBLEM 26-14

What is the rate of return on a 5½ % preferred stock having a par value of \$50 and selling for 52 3/4. Give answer to nearest 1/10%.

Solution: Since the stock pays a 5½ % (.055) dividend, and has a par value of \$50, the annual dividend is

$$.055 \times \$50 = \$2.75.$$

The rate of return, which is annual dividend divided by investment, is

$$\frac{\$2.75}{\%52\ 3/4} = \frac{\$2.75}{\$52.75}\text{, which rounds to } 5.2\%.$$

• PROBLEM 26-15

Last year, Mr. Donald received dividends from his stocks of \$48, \$64, \$82.50, and \$90. If his total investment was \$12,450, what was the rate of return on Mr. Donald's investment for the year? Give answer to nearest 1/10%.

Solution: The total amount he received in dividends was

$$\$48 + \$64 + \$82.50 + \$90 = \$284.50.$$

We can use the formula

$$\text{Rate of Return} = \frac{\text{Dividends}}{\text{Investment}} \text{ to}$$

compute the rate of return. Substituting dividends of \$284.50 for an investment of \$12,450, we get a rate of return of

$$\frac{\$284.50}{\$12,450}\text{, which to the nearest } 1/10\% \text{ is } 2.3\%.$$

• PROBLEM 26-16

Find the rate of return (to the nearest tenth of a percent) on each of the following:

Stock Number	Purchase Price Per Share	Yearly Dividend
1	$75	$2.50
2	$19	$1.25
3	$58 1/2	$3.35
4	$16 3/4	$1.20
5	$18 1/8	$1.60
6	$12 3/8	$1.00
7	$8 7/8	$ .60
8	$62 5/8	$ .90

Solution: We can use the formula:

$$\text{Rate of Return} = \frac{\text{Yearly Dividend}}{\text{Purchase Price}}$$

to calculate the rate of return for each of the stocks listed. For example, substituting a yearly dividend of $2.50 and a purchase price of $75 for stock number 1, we obtain a rate of return of

$$\frac{\$2.50}{\$75}\text{, which rounds to 3.3\%.}$$

Following the same procedure, the rates on the remaining stocks have been calculated and are summarized in the below table:

Stock Number	Purchase Price	Yearly Dividend	Rate of Return
1	$75	$2.50	$\frac{\$2.50}{\$75} = 3.3\%$
2	$19	$1.25	$\frac{\$1.25}{\$19} = 6.6\%$
3	$58 1/2 = $58.50	$3.35	$\frac{\$3.35}{\$58.50} = 5.7\%$
4	$16 3/4 = $16.75	$1.20	$\frac{\$1.20}{\$16.75} = 7.2\%$
5	$18 1/8 = $18.125	$1.60	$\frac{\$1.60}{\$18.125} = 8.8\%$
6	$12 3/8 = $12.375	$1.00	$\frac{\$1.00}{\$12.375} = 8.1\%$
7	$8 7/8 = $8.875	$ .60	$\frac{\$.60}{\$8.875} = 6.8\%$
8	$62 5/8 = $62.625	$ .90	$\frac{\$.90}{\$62.625} = 1.4\%$

The following information is found in the stock table of the daily newspaper

Stocks and Div. in Dollars		Open	High	Low	Last
Gem Instr pf	3.50	56	56	56	56
Gerar Mov.	1.20	45 3/8	46	45 5/8	45 5/8
Harrig Tir.	1.20	36 5/8	36 5/8	35 1/4	35 7/8
Hygrade Bro	1.20	25 1/8	25 3/8	25 1/4	25 1/2
Ivy-Dolman	.30	8	8 1/8	8	8
Lyden Steel	.70	27	27	26 5/8	26 5/8

Find the rate of return to the nearest tenth of a percent of each of the following:

	Company	Purchase Range
(A)	Ivy-Dolman	Low
(B)	Gem Instr	Low
(C)	Lyden Steel	First
(D)	Hygrade Bro	High
(E)	Gerar Mov	Low
(F)	Harrig Tir	High

Solution: We can use the formula:

$$\text{Rate of Return} = \frac{\text{Annual Dividend}}{\text{Purchase Price}}$$

to determine the rate of return of each of the stocks listed. Consulting the table of stock quotations, we see that Ivy-Dolman pays an annual dividend of \$.30. Also, since the stock was purchased at the daily low, it was purchased at a price of \$8. The rate of return for the Ivy-Dolman stock was then

$$\frac{\$.30}{\$8} = .0375, \text{ which rounds to } 3.8\%.$$

Following a similar procedure, we can calculate the rates of return on each of the remaining stocks. The calculations have been summarized in the below table:

Stock	Dividend	Price		Rate of Return
Ivy-Dolman	\$.30	\$8	$\frac{\$.30}{\$8}$	which rounds to 3.8%

Gem Instr	\$3.50	\$56	$\frac{\$3.50}{\$56}$	which rounds to 6.3%
Lyden Steel	\$.70	\$27	$\frac{\$.70}{\$27}$	which rounds to 2.6%
Hygrade Bro	\$1.20	\$25 3/8 = \$25.375	$\frac{\$1.20}{\$25.375}$	which rounds to 4.7%
Gerar Mov	\$1.20	\$45 5/8 = \$45.625	$\frac{\$1.20}{\$45.625}$	which rounds to 2.6%
Harrig Tir	\$1.20	\$36 5/8 = \$36.625	$\frac{\$1.20}{\$36.625}$	which rounds to 3.3%

• PROBLEM 26-18

Mr. Torres owns 350 shares of Kresco stock paying a quarterly dividend of \$1.20 per share, with an extra year-end dividend of \$.30 per share. What was his total income from the stock for the year?

Solution: Since the stock paid a quarterly dividend of \$1.20 per share, and it was paid 4 times during the year, the quarterly dividends yielded \$1.20 × 4 = \$4.80 per share in income. Adding the year-end dividend of \$.30 per share, we get a total of

$\$4.80 + \$.30 = \$5.10$

per share in income for the year.

Since Mr. Torres owns 350 shares of stock, his total income was

$350 \times \$5.10 = \$1,785$ for the year.

• PROBLEM 26-19

Mr. Williams owns 75 shares of Mid-Atlantic common stock paying a dividend of \$.35 per share, and 135 shares of its 5% \$50 par-value preferred stock. How much in dividends does he receive?

Solution: Since Mr. Williams owns 75 shares of the common stock paying a dividend of \$.35 per share, he received a dividend of

$\$.35 \times 75 = \$26.25$

for the common stock. Preferred stock receives a dividend

as a set percentage of its par value. The par value is an amount set by the company before selling the stock. Thus, the preferred stock pays

$$\$50 \times .05 = \$2.50$$

per share as a dividend. The dividend for the 135 shares of the preferred stock is then

$$135 \times \$2.50 = \$337.50.$$

The total dividend Mr. Williams received was therefore

$$\$26.25 + \$337.50 = \$363.75.$$

• PROBLEM 26-20

The Neighborhood Cooperative Market declared a 6% dividend on investment and a 4½ % dividend on patronage. If Mr. Schwartz owns 5 shares with a par value of $50 each, and $983 in receipts for the year, what will his total dividend be?

Solution: Mr. Schwartz's total dividend will be the sum of the dividend on his shares and the dividend on his patronage receipts.

Since his stock has a par value of $50 and pays a 6% (= .06) dividend, the dividend per share is

$$\$50 \times .06 = \$3 \text{ per share.}$$

Mr. Schwartz owns 5 shares, so the dividend on his stock is $\$3 \times 5 = \$15$.

The dividend on patronage is 4½ % (= .045) and Mr. Schwartz has $983 in receipts, so his dividend on patronage is

$$\$983 \times .045 = \$44.235, \text{ which rounds to } \$44.24.$$

Mr. Schwartz's total dividend will then be

$$\$15 + \$44.24 = \$59.24.$$

• PROBLEM 26-21

Reeves Corporation is going to pay a total dividend of $50,000 for the year. The Corporation has 1,000 shares of 6%, $50 par value preferred stock outstanding, as well as 5,000 shares of common stock outstanding. Find the dividends per share for each class of stock.

Solution: Since the Reeves preferred stock has a par value of \$50, and pays a dividend of 6% (=.06), the dividend per share for the preferred stock is

$$\$50 \times .06 = \$3 \text{ per share.}$$

There are 1,000 shares of preferred stock outstanding, so the total dividend for the preferred stock was

$$1{,}000 \times \$3 = \$3{,}000.$$

This leaves \$50,000 - \$3,000 = \$47,000 in dividends for the common stockholders. Since there are 5,000 shares of common stock outstanding, the dividend per share to the common stockholders is

$$\frac{\$47{,}000}{5{,}000} = \$9.40 \text{ per share.}$$

• PROBLEM 26-22

The Novelco Corporation has 1,000 shares of cumulative preferred stock outstanding, as well as 20,000 shares of common stock. The preferred stock has a par value of \$100 per share, and pays dividends at the rate of 6%. During the first two years of operation, Novelco had the following amounts available for dividends:

First year - None
Second year - \$14,000

Find the dividends per year for each class of stock.

Solution: Since the preferred stock had a par value of \$100 and paid a dividend of 6% (= .06), the dividend per share for the preferred stock was

$$\$100 \times .06 = \$6 \text{ per share.}$$

There are 1,000 shares of preferred stock, so the total annual dividend for the preferred stock is

$$1{,}000 \times \$6 = \$6{,}000.$$

In the first year of operation, there were no funds available for dividends, so none were paid. However, the deferred dividends on cumulative preferred stock must be paid before common stock dividends, and so a total of

$$\$6{,}000 + \$6{,}000 = \$12{,}000$$

in preferred dividends must be paid in the second year. Since a total of \$14,000 was allocated for dividends, and \$12,000 went for preferred dividends, the remaining

$$\$14,000 - \$12,000 = \$2,000$$

went for dividends for the common stock.

• PROBLEM 26-23

Janet Firestone purchased an option on a stock for $175 giving her the right to buy 100 shares at 14½ within 90 days. One month later, she exercised her option and then sold the stock on the same day for 17. What was her profit on the stock?

Solution: Her profit on the sale of the stock will be the amount she received for the 100 share less her costs to obtain it. Janet paid $175 for the option plus $14½ per share for 100 shares. The $14½ (= 14.5) per share for 100 shares comes to

$$14.5 \times 100 = \$1,450.$$

Adding to this her cost of $175, we see that her total cost was

$$\$1,450 + \$175 = \$1,625.$$

When she sold the stock, she received $17 per share for the 100 shares for a total of

$$\$17 \times 100 = \$1,700.$$

Her profit was then

$$\$1,700 - \$1,625 = \$75.$$

CHAPTER 27

BONDS

CHARACTERISTICS OF BONDS

• PROBLEM 27-1

Which of the following is the owner of a bond entitled to?

A) one voting right for each bond held.
B) one share of ownership in the company.
C) 1,000 shares of ownership in the company.
D) repayment of the face value by a specified date plus interest.
E) repayment of the maturity value by a specified date plus interest.

Solution: The correct answer is (E).

A bond is a written agreement to repay a fixed amount, known as the bond's maturity or redemption value, along with interest at a specific rate on specific dates in the future.

• PROBLEM 27-2

In the event of bankruptcy, what is the order of payment of bonds, common stock, and preferred stock?

Solution: Since a bond represents a written guarantee to repay a debt, while a share of stock represents part ownership of a company, all bondholders must be paid first.

The preferred stockholders comes next, since his claim on profits and assets, by law, is prior to the claim of the common stockholder.

• PROBLEM 27-3

Which is usually the least expensive way to raise capital?
A) Common stocks
B) Preferred stock
C) Convertible preferred stock
D) Secondary offering
E) Bonds

Solution: The two principal classes of securities are stocks and bonds. The major difference between the two is that, while a stock owner is a part-owner of the company that issues the stock, and receives dividends from the profits that the company earns, the bond owner is guaranteed repayment of the maturity value of the bond, as well as fixed interest payments on specified dates. As a result, if a venture is successful, bonds will be the least expensive way to raise capital, since the return is fixed and not effected by increased profits. The correct answer is therefore E.

• PROBLEM 27-4

Which of the following would yield the greatest net return to a corporation in the 50% tax bracket
(A) 5% certificate of deposit
(B) 5% government bond
(C) 5% corporate bond
(D) 5% treasury bond
(E) 4% municipal bond

Solution: Of all the investments listed above, only municipal bonds are tax free. Therefore, a corporation in the 50% tax bracket, and investing in a taxable bond paying 5% interest could only keep ½, or 2½%, of the 5% interest.

The corporation could keep the entire 4% yield on a municipal bond. The correct choice is therefore (E).

• PROBLEM 27-5

Mr. James is in the 50% income tax bracket. He can either buy, at par value, corporate bonds which yield 8% interest, or municipal bonds which yield 4½% interest. Which is the wiser investment?

Solution: The interest on municipal bonds is tax-exempt; Mr. James could keep the entire 4½% interest he would earn on municipal bonds.

Mr. James would have to pay 50% taxes on the 8% interest from corporate bonds; he could only keep ½ or 4% of the interest.

The municipal bonds are therefore the wiser investment, assuming no further tax complications.

COST AND FACE VALUE

• PROBLEM 27-6

A bond yielding 5% interest pays annual interest of $2.50. What is the face value of the bond?

Solution: We can calculate the face value of the bond by using the formula

$$\text{Interest} = \frac{\text{Face Value} \times \text{Interest Rate}}{\text{Number of Interest Payments Per Year}} .$$

Substituting interest of $2.50, an interest rate of 5% = .05 per year, and 1 for the number of interest payments per year, we get:

$$\$2.50 = \frac{\text{Face Value} \times .05}{1} ,$$

so .05 x Face Value = $2.50. Dividing both sides by .05 we get

$$\text{Face Value} = \frac{\$2.50}{.05} = \$50.$$

• PROBLEM 27-7

On October 17, Thomas Long purchased two $1,000 bonds, bearing 6% interest payable January 1 and July 1, at 98. Find his total cost, and the net proceeds to the seller. Assume a brokerage fee of $5 per bond.

Solution: Mr. Long's total cost for the two bonds was the market price plus brokers fees plus accrued interest. Since the bonds were purchased at 98, the market price of each of the bonds was 98% of $1,000 = .98 x $1,000 = $980 per bond. The market price for the two bonds were therefore $980 x 2 = $1,960. The total brokers fee was $5 x 2 = $10. The accrued interest on each of the bonds can be calculated using the formula:

$$\text{Interest} = \text{Face Value of Bond} \times \text{Interest Rate} \times \text{Term}$$

Substitute a face value of $1,000, an interest rate of 6% = .06 per year and a term of 108/360 of a year (since the period of time from July 1 to October 17 is the remaining 30 days of July plus the 31 days of August plus the 30 days of September plus the 17 days of October, which is 30 + 31 + 30 + 17 = 108 days).

$$\text{Interest Per Bond} = \$1{,}000 \times .06 \times \frac{108}{360} = \frac{\$6{,}480}{360} = \$18 \text{ per bond.}$$

The total accrued interest for the two bonds was therefore $\$18 \times 2 = \$36$. The total cost to Mr. Long was therefore

$$\$1,960 + \$10 + \$36 = \$2,006.$$

The net proceeds to the seller were market price plus accrued interest less brokers fees. The market price plus accrued interest was $1,960 + $36 = $1,996. The brokers fees, was $10. The proceeds to the seller were therefore $1,996 - $10 = $1,986.

• PROBLEM 27-8

What was the cost, including accrued interest, of three $1,000 bonds bearing 6% interest payable January 1 and July 1 and purchased on August 30 at 102. Assume a brokerage fee of $5 a bond.

Solution: The cost of the three bonds is determined by market price plus broker's fees plus accrued interest. Since the bonds were purchased at 102, the market price of each of the bonds was 102% of $1,000. The market price for the three bonds was $\$1,020 \times 3 = \$3,060$. The broker's fee for the three bonds was $3 \times \$5 = \$15$. The accrued interest on each of the bonds can be calculated as

$$\text{Interest} = \text{Face Value of Bond} \times \text{Interest Rate} \times \text{Term}.$$

Substitute a face value of $1,000, an interest rate of 6% = .06 per year, and a term of 60/360 = 1/6 of a year (the period of time from July 1, the last interest date, to August 30, the date of purchase, is 60 days).

$$\text{Accrued Interest per Bond} = \$1,000 \times .06 \times \frac{1}{6} = \frac{\$60}{6} = \$10.$$

The accrued interest for 3 bonds was $3 \times \$10 = \$30$. The total cost for the three bonds was $3,060 + $15 + $30 = $3,105.

• PROBLEM 27-9

How much must be invested in $1,000 5% bonds to have an annual income from interest of $3,000 if the bonds sell at $74\frac{7}{8}$?

Assume a brokerage fee of $5 a bond.

Solution: In order to calculate how many bonds are needed to generate a yearly income from interest of $3,000, we must first know what the annual interest payment per bond is. We can calculate this using the formula:

$$\text{Interest} = \frac{\text{Face Value} \times \text{Interest Rate}}{\text{Number of Interest Payments Per Year}}.$$

Substituting a face value of $1,000, an interest rate of 5% = .05 per year, and 1 for the number of interest payments per year, we get:

$$\text{Interest} = \frac{\$1,000 \times .05}{1} = \$50 \text{ interest per bond.}$$

Since each bond generates a yearly interest of $50, the number of bonds necessary to generate an annual interest payment of $3,000 is $3,000/$50 = 60 bonds. The total cost per bond is market price plus broker's fees. The market price is

$$74\frac{7}{8}\% \text{ of } \$1,000 = .74875 \times \$1,000 = \$748.75.$$

The broker's fee is $5 per bond. The cost of each bond is therefore $748.75 + $5 = $753.75 per bond. The total cost for the 60 bonds is $753.75 x 60 = $45,225.

INTEREST RATES

• PROBLEM 27-10

Mr. Burke purchased three $5\frac{1}{4}\%$ bonds with par values of $1,000 each, and interest paid semiannually. How much interest will he receive?

Solution: To calculate the amount of interest that Mr. Burke will receive on one bond use the formula:

$$\text{Interest} = \frac{\text{Par Value} \times \text{Rate of Interest}}{\text{Number of Interest Payments Per Year}} .$$

Substitute a par value of $1,000, an interest rate of $5\frac{1}{4}\%$ = .0525 per year, and two interest periods per year.

$$\text{Interest} = \frac{\$1,000 \times .0525}{2} = \frac{\$52.50}{2} = \$26.25.$$

The total interest he will receive on three bonds will then be $26.25 x 3 = $78.75

• PROBLEM 27-11

Mrs. Valdez owns six $9\frac{1}{8}\%$ coupon bonds, with a par value of $500 each, on which she receives annual interest. On the date that the annual interest falls due, she clips the coupons from the bonds and presents them at her bank for payment. How much does she receive?

Solution: To compute the interest on one bond, use the formula:

$$\text{Interest} = \frac{\text{Par Value} \times \text{Rate of Interest}}{\text{Number Interest Payments Per Year}} .$$

If par value is $500, the interest rate $9\frac{1}{8}\%$ equals .09125, and the number of payments per year is 1,

$$\text{Interest} = \frac{\$500 \times .09125}{1},$$

which equals \$45.625. On six bonds Mrs. Valdex receives

$$\$45.625 \times 6 = \$273.75$$

in interest.

• PROBLEM 27-12

For each bond, compute the interest for the period shown.

No.	Par Value	Interest Rate	Period
1.	\$1,000	5%	Annually
2.	\$1,000	7%	Annually
3.	\$ 500	$8\frac{1}{4}$%	Annually
4.	\$1,000	6%	Semiannually
5.	\$ 500	$9\frac{1}{2}$%	Semiannually
6.	\$1,000	$4\frac{1}{4}$%	Semiannually
7.	\$1,000	5 3/4%	Semiannually
8.	\$ 500	5%	Quarterly
9.	\$1,000	$6\frac{1}{4}$%	Quarterly
10.	\$1,000	5 3/4%	Quarterly

Solution: The interest paid on a bond for each interest period can be calculated using the formula:

$$\text{Interest} = \frac{\text{Par Value of Bond} \times \text{Interest Rate}}{\text{Number of Interest payments per year}}$$

For example, for Bond 1, par value = \$1,000, interest rate = 5% = .05 and the number of payments per year = 1. The interest on Bond 1 each interest period is

$$\frac{\$1,000 \times .05}{1} = \frac{\$50}{1} = \$50.$$

Below are the interest calculations on the remaining bonds in table form:

Bond	Par Value	Interest Rate	No. of Interest periods per year	Interest Calculation
2.	\$1,000	.07	1	$\frac{\$1000 \times .07}{1} = \$70$
3.	\$ 500	.0825	1	$\frac{\$500 \times .0825}{1} = \$41.25$
4.	\$1,000	.06	2	$\frac{\$1000 \times .06}{2} = \$30$
5.	\$ 500	.095	2	$\frac{\$500 \times .095}{2} = \$23.75$
6.	\$1,000	.0425	2	$\frac{\$1000 \times .0425}{2} = \$21.25$
7.	\$1,000	.0575	2	$\frac{\$1000 \times .0575}{2} = \$28.88$
8.	\$ 500	.05	4	$\frac{\$500 \times .05}{4} = \$6.25$
9.	\$1,000	.0625	4	$\frac{\$1000 \times 0625}{4} = \$15.63$
10.	\$1,000	.0575	4	$\frac{\$1000 \times .0575}{4} = \$14.38$

• PROBLEM 27-13

Find the interest for the period shown on each bond.

No.	Par Value	Interest Rate	Period
1.	$1,000	4 %	Annually
2.	$1,000	$4\frac{1}{2}$%	Semiannually
3.	$1,000	3 3/4 %	Quarterly

Solution: The interest paid on a bond each interest period is:

$$\frac{\text{Par value} \times \text{interest rate}}{\text{Number of interest payments per year}}\,.$$

For Bond 1, par value = $1,000, the interest rate = 4% = .04, and number of payments per year = 1. The interest paid each interest period is

$$\frac{\$1,000 \times .04}{1} = \$40.$$

For Bond 2 there are 2 interest payments per year, and the interest rate = $4\frac{1}{2}$% = .045. The interest per payment period is

$$\frac{\$1,000 \times .045}{2} = \$22.50.$$

For Bond 3, there are 4 payments per year and the interest rate = 3 3/4 % = .0375. The interest per payment period is

$$\frac{\$1,000 \times .0375}{4} = \$9.38\,.$$

• PROBLEM 27-14

What is the effective yield of a $6\frac{1}{2}$% bond with a face value of $1,000 purchased at $87\frac{1}{4}$? Give the answer to the nearest 1/10%.

Solution: We calculate the effective yield of a bond by using the formula:

$$\text{Effective Yield} = \frac{\text{Nominal Interest Rate} \times \text{Face Value}}{\text{Market Price}}$$

Substituting a $6\frac{1}{2}$% interest rate, which is equivalent to .065 per year; a face value of $1,000, and a market price of $872.50 ($87\frac{1}{4}$% of $1,000 x .8725 = $872.50), we get

$$\text{Effective Yield} = \frac{.065 \times \$1,000}{\$872.50} = \frac{\$65}{\$872.50} = 7.4\%$$

to the nearest 1/10%.

• PROBLEM 27-15

What is the effective yield of a 6 $\frac{3}{4}$ % bond ($1,000 face value), purchased at 88 3/4 ? Give answer to nearest 1/10%.

Solution: The effective yield of a bond can be calculated using the formula:

$$\text{Effective Yield} = \frac{\text{Nominal Interest Rate} \times \text{Face Value}}{\text{Market Price}}$$

Substituting a nominal interest rate of 6 3/4 % = .0675 per year, a face value of $1,000, and a market price of $887.50 (88 3/4 % of $1,000 = $1,000 x .8875.50), we get

$$\text{Effective Yield} = \frac{.0675 \times \$1,000}{\$887.50} = \frac{\$67.50}{\$887.50}, \text{ which}$$

rounds to 7.6%.

• PROBLEM 27-16

What is the effective yield of a $1,000 bond, maturing in one year, and purchased for $960, if it earns a nominal annual interest rate of 6% ? Give answer to nearest 1/10% .

Solution: The effective yield of the bond is the income generated by the bond divided by the cost of the bond. The total income generated by the bond is the interest earned, plus the difference between the face and purchase values of the bond. We can calculate the interest earned by the bond by using the formula:

$$\text{Interest} = \frac{\text{Face Value} \times \text{Interest Rate}}{\text{Number of Interest Periods per Year}}$$

Substituting a face value of $1,000, an interest rate of 6% = .06 per year and one for the number of interest periods, we get interest = $1,000 x .06/1 = $60. The difference between the face and purchase values is $1,000 - $960 = $40.

The effective yield is thus $\frac{\text{income}}{\text{cost}} = \frac{\$60 + \$40}{\$960} = \frac{\$100}{\$960}$, which rounds to 10.4%.

• PROBLEM 27-17

Mr. Dominguez purchased a $1,000 bond at par on which the nominal interest rate was 5%. He then agreed to accept an effective rate of interest of 4½% on the bond. What is the bond's new market price?

Solution: Since Mr. Dominguez purchased the bond at par, he paid $1,000 for it. However, when he agreed to accept an effective rate of interest of only 4½%, the market price of the bond increased. We can determine how much it increased by using the formula:

$$\text{Effective Yield} = \frac{\text{Nominal Interest Rate} \times \text{Face Value}}{\text{Market Price}}$$

Substituting 4½% = .045 for the effective yield, 5% = .05 for the nominal interest rate, and $1,000 for the face value, we get:

$$.045 = \frac{.05 \times \$1,000}{\text{Market price}} ; \quad \frac{.05 \times \$1,000}{.045} = \frac{\$50}{.045} ;$$

market price = \$1,111.11 .

• PROBLEM 27-18

> Mr. Simmons has the choice of buying a $6\frac{1}{4}\%$, \$1,000 bond at 98, or 10 shares of 6% preferred stock, par valued at \$100 per share, at 101. Which investment gives the greater effective yield? By how much? Perform all calculations to the nearest 1/10 %.

Solution: We can calculate the effective yield of each of the investments by using the formula:

$$\text{Effective Yield} = \frac{\text{Nominal Interest Rate} \times \text{Face Value}}{\text{Market Price}}$$

Substituting for the bond, a nominal interest rate of $6\frac{1}{4}\% = .0625$ per year, a face value of \$1,000, and a market price of \$980 (98% of \$1,000 = \$1,000 × .98 = \$980), we get:

$$\text{Effective Yield} = \frac{.0625 \times \$1,000}{\$980} = \frac{\$62.50}{\$980} \text{, which}$$

rounds to 6.4%.

Substituting for the stocks a nominal interest of 6% = .06 per year, a face value of \$1,000 (10 shares at \$100 each), and a market price of \$1010 (101% of \$1,000 = \$1,000 × 1.01 = \$1010), we get:

$$\text{Effective Yield} = \frac{.06 \times \$1,000}{\$1010} = \frac{\$60}{\$1010} \text{, which}$$

rounds to 5.9%. The greater effective yield is therefore derived from the bond. The difference in yields is 6.4% - 5.9% = .5%.

REDEMPTION OF BONDS

• PROBLEM 27-19

> Mr. Arno has a special payroll deduction plan at work which allows him to invest \$7.50 a week in Series E bonds. How much will his weekly savings be worth at the end of three years? Use the table.

Weekly Savings	Accumulated value at end of: 1 yr.	3 yrs.	5 yrs. 10 mos.	15 yrs. 10 mos.
$ 1.25	$ 66	$ 205	$ 429	$ 1,600
$ 2.50	$131	$ 412	$ 861	$ 3,211
$ 3.75	$197	$ 618	$1,295	$ 4,824
$ 5.00	$263	$ 825	$1,726	$ 6,432
$ 6.25	$328	$1,031	$2,160	$ 8,047
$ 7.50	$395	$1,237	$2,593	$ 9,657
$12.50	$657	$2,063	$4,323	$16,103
$18.75	$987	$3,095	$6,489	$24,167

Solution: Look down the weekly savings column to $7.50, and then across to the accumulated value at the end of three years, $1,237.

• PROBLEM 27-20

SERIES E SAVINGS BONDS

Monthly Savings	Accumulated value at end of: 1 yr.	3 yrs.	5 yrs. 10 mos.	15 yrs. 10 mos.
$ 3.75	$ 45	$ 142	$ 296	$ 1,102
$ 6.25	$ 76	$ 237	$ 494	$ 1,842
$ 7.50	$ 91	$ 284	$ 595	$ 2,212
$12.50	$151	$ 474	$ 993	$ 3,689
$18.75	$228	$ 714	$1,493	$ 5,556
$25.00	$303	$ 951	$1,987	$ 7,398
$37.50	$455	$1,428	$2,986	$11,112
$56.25	$683	$2,142	$4,480	$16,669
$75.00	$910	$2,856	$5,973	$22,225

(A) John Zimmer has been investing $6.25 a month in Series E bonds. If he holds the bonds until maturity, how much cash will he need to convert to a $500 denomination Series H bond?

(B) Ted Logan and his wife Sue each buy a $100 Series E bond every month. How much will they have accumulated in three years?

Solution: (A) $6.25 a month, accumulated at the end of 5 years 10 months (maturity period for Series E bonds), will have a value of $494. Since Mr. Zimmer wishes to purchase a $500 Series H bond and the Series H bonds are sold at par (i.e., at the $500 face value), he would need an additional $500 - $494 = $6 to convert to a Series H bond.

(B) Since Ted and Sue each buy a $100 bond every month, and a $100 Series E bond has a purchase price of $75, each one is investing $75 a month in the bonds. A monthly $75 investment has, over 3 years, an accumulated value of $2,856. Since each of them will have accumulated $2,856, together they will have accumulated

$$\$2,856 \times 2 = \$5,712.$$

• PROBLEM 27-21

Find the redemption value of each of the following Series E bonds, using the table:

(A) A $25 denomination bond if redeemed within 3½ to 4 years.
(B) A $75 denomination bond if held to maturity.
(C) A $50 denomination bond if cashed within 5 to 5½ years.
(D) A $200 denomination bond if redeemed within 6 months after purchase.
(E) A $100 denomination bond if held to maturity.

REDEMPTION VALUE OF BONDS BEARING ISSUE DATES BEGINNING 6/1/70

Period After Issue Date	Redemption values during each ½ year period						Annual Interest
	($25 Bond)	($50 Bond)	($75 Bond)	($100 Bond)	($200 Bond)	($500 Bond)	
First ½ year	$18.75	$37.50	$56.25	$75.00	$150.00	$375.00	0.00%
½ to 1 year	$19.05	$38.10	$57.15	$76.20	$152.40	$381.00	3.20%
1 to 1½ years	$19.51	$39.02	$58.53	$78.04	$156.08	$390.20	4.01%
1½ to 2 years	$19.95	$39.90	$59.85	$79.80	$159.60	$399.00	4.18%
2 to 2½ years	$20.40	$40.80	$61.20	$81.60	$163.20	$408.00	4.26%
2½ to 3 years	$20.88	$41.76	$62.64	$83.52	$167.04	$417.60	4.35%
3 to 3½ years	$21.39	$42.78	$64.17	$85.56	$171.12	$427.80	4.44%
3½ to 4 years	$21.93	$43.86	$65.79	$87.72	$175.44	$438.60	4.53%
4 to 4½ years	$22.53	$45.06	$67.59	$90.12	$180.24	$450.60	4.64%
4½ to 5 years	$23.16	$46.32	$69.38	$92.64	$185.28	$463.20	4.75%
5 to 5½ years	$23.82	$47.64	$71.46	$95.28	$190.56	$476.40	4.84%
5½ years to 5 years and 10 months	$24.51	$49.02	$73.53	$98.04	$196.08	$490.20	4.93%
MATURITY VALUE (5 yrs. & 10 mos. from issue date)	$25.73	$51.46	$77.19	$102.92	$205.84	$514.60	5.50%

Solution: To find the redemption value of a bond, look down the left-hand column of the above figure (Period After Issue Date) to locate the length of time between the bond's issue and the redemption date. Then look across the top to find the entry under the appropriate denomination. For example, the redemption value of a $25 bond redeemed within 3½ to 4 years would be $21.93. Using the same procedure, we can summarize the remaining redemption values as follows:

Period After Issue Date	Denomination	Redemption Value
b. until maturity	$75	$77.19
c. 5 to 5½ years	$50	$47.64
d. within 6 months (½ year)	$200	$150.00
e. until maturity	$100	$102.92

Consider a year to have 360 days.

(A) Mr. King purchased a $100 Series E savings bond and held it until maturity. Mr. Dean purchased a $75 bond at the same time and held it until maturity. How much more is Mr. King's bond worth? How much of this difference is additional interest?

(B) What is the difference in redemption value between keeping a $100 Series E bond for 5 years instead of cashing it in after 4 years?

REDEMPTION VALUES OF BONDS BEARING ISSUE DATES BEGINNING JUNE 1, 1970

Period After Issue Date	Redemption values during each ½ year period						Annual Interest
	($25 Bond)	($50 Bond)	($75 Bond)	($100 Bond)	($200 Bond)	($500 Bond)	
First ½ year	$18.75	$37.50	$56.25	$75.00	$150.00	$375.00	0.00%
½ to 1 year	$19.05	$38.10	$57.15	$76.20	$152.40	$381.00	3.20%
1 to 1½ years	$19.51	$39.02	$58.53	$78.04	$156.08	$390.20	4.01%
1½ to 2 years	$19.95	$39.90	$59.85	$79.80	$159.60	$399.00	4.18%
2 to 2½ years	$20.40	$40.80	$61.20	$81.60	$163.20	$408.00	4.26%
2½ to 3 years	$20.88	$41.76	$62.64	$83.52	$167.04	$417.60	4.35%
3 to 3½ years	$21.39	$42.78	$64.17	$85.56	$171.12	$427.80	4.44%
3½ to 4 years	$21.93	$43.86	$65.79	$87.72	$175.44	$438.60	4.53%
4 to 4½ years	$22.53	$45.06	$67.59	$90.12	$180.24	$450.60	4.64%
4½ to 5 years	$23.16	$46.32	$69.38	$92.64	$185.28	$463.20	4.75%
5 to 5½ years	$23.82	$47.64	$71.46	$95.28	$190.56	$476.40	4.84%
5½ years to 5 years and 10 months	$24.51	$49.02	$73.53	$98.04	$196.08	$490.20	4.93%
MATURITY VALUE (5 yrs. & 10 mos. from issue date)	$25.73	$51.46	$77.19	$102.92	$205.84	$514.60	5.50%

Solution: (A) Using the tables for the Redemption Values of Bonds, we can determine the maturity values of Mr. King's and Mr. Dean's bonds. A $100 bond, held til maturity, has a redemption value of $102.92. A $75 bond, held for the same period of time, is worth $77.19. The difference between maturity values of the two bonds is therefore $102.92 - $77.19 = $25.73. Mr. King's bond is therefore worth $25.73 more than Mr. Dean's is. Also, since Mr. King originally spent $75 for his bond, and Mr. Dean spent $56.25, Mr. King originally spent $75 - $56.25 = $18.75 more for his bond. This means that out of the $25.73 of additional worth, $25.73 - $18.75 = $6.98 is additional interest.

(B) Using the same tables, we see that a $100 Series E bond held for 5 years has a redemption value of $95.28, while the same bond held for 4 years has a value of $90.12. The difference in value is therefore $95.28 - $90.12 = $5.16.

The ABC Corporation has issued 200 bonds, each with a $1,000 face value, redeemable at par after 15 years. In order to accumulate the funds required for redemption, ABC has established a fund of annual deposits earning 4% interest per year. What will be the principal in the fund at the end of 12 years? Round your answer to the nearest dollar.

Solution: Since the ABC Corporation will be required to redeem 200 bonds at $1,000 each, they will need 200 x $1,000 = $200,000 at the end of fifteen years.

Using the Annuity tables amount on the 4% compound interest factors table, note that a deposit of $1 per period at an interest rate of 4% per period will yield $20.024 after 15 periods. Therefore, the amount that must be deposited each period in order to yield the sum of $200,000 after 15 periods is

$$\frac{\$200,000}{20.024} = \$9,988.01.$$

Using the same table, note that a deposit of $1 per period at 4% for a total of 12 periods yields $15.026, therefore a deposit of $9,988.01 per period for 12 periods at 4% will yield a total of $150,079.83. Thus, to the nearest dollar, the principal in the fund at the end of 12 years will be approximately $150,080.

CHAPTER 28

NOTES AND DRAFTS

NOTES

• **PROBLEM** 28-1

What is the date of maturity of a 60-day note dated March 15?

Solution: Since the note has a term of 60 days and was dated March 15, its date of maturity will be 60 days from March 15. We can figure out the date of maturity of the note as follows: since the note was signed March 15, and there are 31 days in March, 31 - 15 = 16 days of the term of the note will have expired as of the end of March. Since there are 30 days in April, an additional 30 days of the term will have expired as of the end of April, for a total of 16 + 30 = 46 days. The note has a total term of 60 days, and only 46 will have expired as of the end of April, so in order to reach the date of maturity of the note, we will require an additional 60 - 46 = 14 days in May. This makes the date of maturity of the note May 14.

• **PROBLEM** 28-2

Max Flaum had a note for $2400. He discounted it 30 days before it was due. The bank paid him $2389, find the discount rate.

Solution: To find the rate we start with the formula for the charge.

$$\text{Charge} = \text{Rate} \times \frac{\text{days left to maturity}}{\text{360 days}} \text{ (Time)} \times \text{worth of note.}$$

If we divide both sides of the formula by Time and worth of note we arrive at the formula

$$\text{Rate} = \text{Charge} \div \text{(Time)} \times \text{Worth of note.}$$

We now find the charge by subtracting the proceeds from the worth of the note. The worth of the note is the face value since it was a non-interest-bearing note. Hence the charge is equal to $2400 - $2389 = $11. We can now find the rate by substituting the correct figures into the formula.

Rate = $11 ÷ (30/360 × $2400) = $11 ÷ 199.99 = .055

= 5 1/2% .

• PROBLEM 28-3

James Parcer discounted a customer's $500 note on April 25. The note was dated March 1. and must be paid within 3 months of the day issued. What is the term of discount?

Solution: The term of discount here refers to the number of days left between the time the discount was given and the last day it could be paid.

From March 1 to April 25 there are (30 + 25) or 55 days, using time table to find it. The three month period March to April, April to May, and May to June has (31 + 30 + 31) or 92 days. And 92 days - 55 days = 37 days is the period covering the time the discount was given and the maturity day of June 1.

(March 1 + 3 months = June 1).

The terms of discount is 37 days.

• PROBLEM 28-4

Record the maturity date for a draft dated (a) November 12 and payable 60 days after date, (b) June 10 and payable 3 months after date, (c) March 3 and payable 30 days after sight if it is accepted March 15, and (d) October 4 and payable 6 months after sight if it is accepted October 25.

Solution: (a) This draft is payable 60 days after date. By using the time table we see from November 12 to January 12 is 61 days, thus the draft is due on January 11.

(b) This draft is payable 3 months after date. Since it was dated on June 10, it is payable on September 10.

(c) This draft is payable 30 days after sight. It was accepted on March 15. Since March has 31 days, the draft is payable on April 14.

(d) This draft is payable 6 months after sight. Being that it was accepted on October 25 it is due on April 25 (six months later).

• PROBLEM 28-5

Mann Bros. accepted a 3-months note, dated November 11, for $500 at 6% from Mr. Hope in payment of a debt. On January 2, it was discounted at the First National Bank at 5 1/2%. Furnish the following information: maker of note, payee, maturity date, maturity value, term of discount, bank discount, and proceeds.

Solution: The maker of the note is the person who wrote the note to be used as a payment. Hence the maker is Mr. Hope. The payee of the note is the "person" who receives the note as payment, and will collect from it. Here the payee is Mann Bros. The maturity date of the note is 3 months from November 11, the date it was written, or February 11. The maturity value is the worth of the note at the maturity date. It is the face value of the note ($500) plus the earned interest. The amount of interest can be computed from the formula

Interest = Principal × Rate × Time in years, giving

$$\$500 \times .06 \times 3/12 = \$500 \times .06 \times 1/4 = \$7.50.$$

Hence, the maturity value is $500 + $7.50 = $507.50. The term of discount is the number of days the note was discounted before it becomes due. By using the time table we find this to be 40 days. The bank discount is the amount charged by the bank for discounting the note. It can be found by the following formula:

Charge = Rate × (number of days to maturity) × worth of

note, giving $.055 \times 40/360 \times \$507.50 = \$3.10$.

The proceeds of the note can be found by subtracting the discounting charge ($3.10) from the worth of the note ($507.50) giving $504.40.

• PROBLEM 28-6

Jacob gave the Franklin Mint a 90-day note for $1250 on October 10. If it was discounted at the bank on November 15 at 6 1/2%, what were the proceeds?

Solution: The note is due in 90 days from October 10. By using the time table, we see that it is due on January 8. It was discounted on October 10. Hence it was discounted for 54 days. The proceeds of this note are found by subtracting the discounting charge from the worth of the note (its face value). The discounting charge is found by the following formula:

Charge = Rate × (days left to maturity ÷ 360 days) × worth of note.

Hence the charge is equal to

$$.065 \times 54/360 \times \$1250 = \$12.19.$$

Thus the proceeds can be found.

$$\text{Proceeds} = \text{worth} - \text{discounting charge} = \$1250 - \$12.19 = \$1,237.81.$$

• PROBLEM 28-7

Jane Carpov held a 60-day note for $4200 bearing interest at 5%. This note was discounted 25 days before maturity at 6%. Find the proceeds.

Solution: The proceeds can be found by subtracting the discounting charge from the worth of the note. The worth of the note is the face value of $4200 plus the interest that it earned in the 60 days. The amount of interest can be computed by the formula

Interest = Principal × Rate × Time (in years), giving

$$\$4,200 \times .05 \times 60/360 = \$35.$$

Hence, the worth of the note is $4200 + $35 = $4235. The discounting charge can be found using the following formula:

$$\text{Charge} = \text{Rate} \times \frac{\text{days to maturity}}{\text{360 days}} \text{(days in a year)} \times \text{worth}$$

of note. Hence, the discounting charge is equal to

$$.06 \times 25/360 \times \$4235 = \$17.65.$$

We can now find the proceeds.

	Worth of note	$4235.00
Less	discounting charge	$ 17.65
	proceeds of note	$4217.35

• PROBLEM 28-8

Mr. Atlas had a note for $45,000. He discounted it at his bank 120 days before it was due. The bank's discount rate was 6%. Find Mr. Atlas' proceeds.

Solution: The proceeds of the note can be found by subtracting the charges for the bank's discounting from the worth of the note. Here the worth of the note is its face value of $45,000. The discounting charge can be found by the following formula:

Charge = Rate × (days to maturity ÷ 360 business days in a year) × worth of note. Hence, the charge is

$$.06 \times 120/360 \times \$45,000 = .06 \times 1/3 \times \$45,000 = \$900.$$

The proceeds can now be computed.

	Worth of note	$45,000
Less	discounting charge	$ 900
	proceeds of note	$44,100

• PROBLEM 28-9

Find the proceeds on each of the following noninterest-bearing notes.

	Face of Note	Time to Run	Date of Note	Discount Date	Rate of Discount
(a)	$350.00	60 days	July 17	Aug. 16	$4\frac{1}{2}$%
(b)	1450.00	3 months	Oct. 11	Nov. 23	8%
(c)	653.00	90 days	Mar. 26	May 15	$5\frac{1}{2}$%
(d)	800.50	5 months	Jan. 5	Mar. 4	6%

Solution: The proceeds are found by subtracting the discounting charge from the worth of the note. In these noninterest-bearing notes, the worth is the face value. The discounting charge is found using the following formula:

Charge = Rate × (days discounted ÷ 360 days) × worth.

(a)

Date of Note	Time to Run
July 17	60 days

Due Date	Discount Date	# of days discounted
September 15	August 16	30

Charge = .045 × 30/360 × $350 = $1.31

Proceeds = $350 - $1.31 = $348.69

(b)

Date of Note	Time to Run
October 11	3 months

Due Date	Discount Date	# of days discounted
January 11	November 23	49

Charge = .08 × 49/360 × $1450 = $15.79

Proceeds = $1,450 - $15.79 = $1432.21

(c)

Date of Note	Time to Run
March 26	90 days

Due Date	Discount Date	# of days discounted
June 24	May 15	40

Charge = .055 × 40/360 × $653 = $3.99

Proceeds = $653 - $3.99 = $649.01

(d)

Date of Note	Time to Run
January 5	5 months

Due Date	Discount Date	# of days discounted
June 5	March 4	93

Charge = .06 × 93/360 × $800.50 = $12.41

Proceeds = $800.50 - $12.41 = $788.09

• PROBLEM 28-10

Mrs. Reeves accepted a note for $815.50 at 6% with a four month term on December 10. On January 10 she had it discounted at 6 1/2%. A 1/8% charge for collection when due was also made. How much did she receive?

Solution: Since the note earned interest, we can use the formula

Interest = Principal of Note × Rate of Interest × Term of Note

with an amount of $815.50, interest rate of 6% = .06 per year, and term of

$$\frac{4}{12} = \frac{1}{3} \text{ of a year to calculate interest of}$$

$$\$815.50 \times .06 \times \frac{1}{3} = \frac{\$48.93}{3} = \$16.31 \text{ in interest.}$$

The maturity value of her note was therefore

$$\$815.50 + \$16.31 = \$831.81.$$

The note had a term of 4 months, but was held for one month by Mrs. Reeves (from December 10 to January 10), so the term of the discount was 4 - 1 = 3 months. Using the formula:

Interest = Principal of Note × Rate of Interest × Term of Discount,

we can calculate the interest deducted when the note was discounted. Substituting $831.81 for the maturity value of the note, 6 1/2% = .065 per year for the interest rate, and

$$\frac{3}{12} = \frac{1}{4} \text{ of a year for the term of the discount,}$$

we obtain

$$\text{Interest} = \$831.81 \times .065 \times \frac{1}{4} = \frac{\$54.06765}{4}, \text{ which}$$

rounds to $13.52. Also, a fee of $\frac{1}{8}\%$ = .00125 for collection was charged. This can be calculated as follows:

$\frac{1}{8}\%$ of $831.81 = .00125 × $831.81, which rounds to $1.04. The total charges were therefore interest plus collection = $13.52 + $1.04 = $14.56.

Mrs. Reeves therefore received

$$\$831.81 - \$14.56 = \$817.25.$$

• PROBLEM 28-11

Mr. Samuels signed a 120-day note for $300, discounted at 6%. What are the proceeds of the note?

<u>Solution:</u> The amount Mr. Samuels will receive (proceeds of the note) will be the amount of the note less interest charges. We can find the interest charges

using the formula:

Interest = Principal of Note × Rate of Interest × Term of Discount.

Substituting $300 for the amount of the loan, 6% = .06 per year for the interest rate, and

$\frac{120}{360} = \frac{1}{3}$ of a year for term we get

$$\text{Interest} = \$300 \times .06 \times \frac{1}{3} = \$18 \times \frac{1}{3} = \$6 \text{ interest.}$$

The amount Mr. Samuels will receive (proceeds of the note) is then

$$\$300 - \$6 = \$294.$$

• PROBLEM 28-12

Mr. Johnson discounted a non-interest bearing draft for $850 due July 12 on July 1 at a discount rate of 5%. Assuming a 365-day year, what were his proceeds?

Solution: Since Mr. Johnson's draft was due on July 12 and he discounted it on July 1, the term of the discount was 11 days. We can find out how much was deducted from the value of the draft as interest by using the formula:

Interest = Principal of Note × Rate of Interest × Term of Discount.

Substituting an amount of $850 at an interest rate of 5% = .05 per year for a term of

$\frac{11}{365}$ of a year we obtain:

$$\text{Interest} = \$850 \times .05 \times \frac{11}{365} = \frac{\$467.50}{365},$$

which rounds to $1.28. Since $1.28 was deducted as an interest charge, Mr. Johnson's proceeds were

$$\$850 - \$1.28 = \$848.72.$$

• PROBLEM 28-13

A $925 noninterest bearing note dated June 15 with a term of 120 days was discounted August 24 at the interest rate of 5%. What were the proceeds?

Solution: Since the note was noninterest bearing, its maturity valve was $925. Also, since the note was dated June 15 and discounted on August 24, the remaining 15 days of June plus the 31 days of July plus 24 days of August for a total of 15 + 31 + 24 = 70 days elapsed between the date of the note and the date that the note was discounted on. The note had a total term of 120 days, so the term of the discount was 120 - 70 = 50 days. Using the formula:

Interest = Principal of Note × Interest Rate × Term of Discount

we can calculate the amount of interest that was deducted from the maturity value of the note. Substituting $925 for the amount of the note, 5% (or .05) per year for the interest rate, and

$$\frac{50}{360} = \frac{5}{36}$$ for the term of the discount, we obtain:

$$\text{Interest} = \$925 \times .05 \times \frac{5}{36} = \frac{\$231.25}{36},$$

which rounds to $6.42. The proceeds were therefore

$$\$925 - \$6.42 = \$918.58.$$

• PROBLEM 28-14

A noninterest-bearing note with a face value of $600 and a term of 30 days dated April 5 was discounted April 15 at a rate of 5%. What were the proceeds?

Solution: Since the note was issued on April 5, and was not discounted until April 15, a period of 10 days elapsed between the date of the note and the day it was discounted. The note had a term of 30 days, so the term of the discount was 30 - 10 = 20 days. We can use the formula:

Interest = Principal of Note × Rate of Interest × Term of Discount

to determine how much interest was deducted from the value of the note. Substituting $600 for the amount, 5% = .05 per year for the interest rate and

$$\frac{20}{360} = \frac{1}{18}$$ of a year for the term, we obtain:

$$\text{Interest} = \$600 \times .05 \times \frac{1}{18} = \frac{\$30}{18},$$

which rounds to \$1.67. The proceeds were therefore

$$\$600 - \$1.67 = \$598.33$$

• PROBLEM 28-15

> Mr. Firestone signed a 90-day note for Ace Lending Company for \$1,250 on October 10, 1976. On November 15, 1976, Ace had the note discounted at the bank at 6 1/2%. What were the proceeds?

Solution: Mr. Firestone signed the note on October 10, 1976, and it was discounted on November 15, 1976. Since there are a total of 31 days in October, 21 days elapsed between the date that the note was signed and the month ended. Since an additional 15 days elapsed in November until the note was discounted, a total of 21 + 15 = 36 days elapsed between the date the note was signed and the date that it was discounted. Also, since the note was for 90 days, and it was discounted after 36 days of its term, the remaining term on the note as of the date it was discounted was 90 - 36 = 54 days. In order to determine the proceeds as of the date the note was discounted, we should subtract the interest charged from the face value of the note. We can calculate the interest charged using the formula:

Interest = Principal of Note × Rate of Interest × Term of Discount.

Substituting \$1,250 for the amount of the loan, 6 1/2% (or .065) per year for the rate of interest, and $\frac{54}{360}$ of a year for the term we get

$$\text{Interest} = \$1,250 \times .065 \times \frac{54}{360} = \$81.25 \times \frac{54}{360},$$

which rounds to \$12.19. The proceeds of the note were then

$$\$1,250 - \$12.19 = \$1,237.81 .$$

• PROBLEM 28-16

> On April 1, Douglas, Inc. received a 6% note with a 90 day term for \$800. On May 1, the note was discounted at 6%. How much did Douglas, Inc. actually receive?

Solution: Since the note earned interest at 6% for 90 days, its maturity value would be \$800 plus the interest on \$800 for 90 days at 6%. We can calculate the interest using the formula:

Interest = Principal of Note × Interest Rate × Term of Note

Substituting \$800 for the amount, 6% (or .06) per year for the interest rate, and

$\frac{90}{360} = \frac{1}{4}$ of a year for term we obtain

$$\text{Interest} = \$800 \times .06 \times \frac{1}{4} = \frac{\$48}{4} = \$12 \text{ interest.}$$

The maturity value of the note was the \$800 + \$12 = \$812. Now, since the note was dated April 1 and discounted May 1, a total of 30 days elapsed between the date of the note and the date it was discounted. The note had a term of 90 days, so the term of the discount was 90 - 30 = 60 days. Using the formula:

Interest = Principal of Note × Interest Rate × Term of Discount,

we can calculate the amount of interest discounted from the maturity value of the note. Substituting \$812 for the maturity value of the note, 6% (.06) per year for the interest rate and

$\frac{60}{360} = \frac{1}{6}$ of a year for the term, we obtain:

$$\text{Interest} = \$812 \times .06 \times \frac{1}{6} = \frac{\$48.72}{6} = \$8.12 \text{ interest.}$$

The amount that Douglas, Inc. actually received was then

$$\$812 - \$8.12 = \$803.88 .$$

• PROBLEM 28-17

Mr. Allyn received a note for \$1800 bearing interest at 6% for 90 days, dated March 31 and due June 29. On April 20, his bank discounted the note at 6%. What were the proceeds?

Solution: Since the note received interest at 6% for 90 days, we can use the formula:

Interest = Principal of Note × Rate of Interest × Term of Note with an amount of \$1800, interest rate of 6% (.06) per year, and term of

$\frac{90}{360} = \frac{1}{4}$ of a year to calculate interest of

$\$1800 \times .06 \times \frac{1}{4} = \frac{\$108}{4} = \$27$ interest.

The maturity value of the note was then \$1800 + \$27 = \$1827. Since the note was dated March 31 and discounted on April 20, a total of 20 days lapsed between the date the note was issued and the day it was discounted. The term of the note was 90 days, so the term of the discount was 90 - 20 = 70 days. To calculate the amount of the discount, we can use the formula

Interest = Principal of Note × Rate of Interest × Term of Discount.

Substituting \$1827 for the maturity value of the note at an interest rate of 6% (.06) per year for a term of

$\frac{70}{360}$ of a year, we obtain

$$\text{Interest} = \$1827 \times .06 \times \frac{70}{360} = \$109.62 \times \frac{70}{360} = \frac{\$7673.40}{360},$$

which the bank rounded to \$21.32. The proceeds were then

\$1827 - \$21.32 = \$1805.68.

• PROBLEM 28-18

Ms. Baden has just signed a 90-day note with a face value of \$350, discounted at 6%. How much will she actually receive from the note?

Solution: With discounted loans, the interest charges are deducted in advance. The amount that Ms. Baden will actually receive is therefore the face value of the note less the interest charged on it. Since we already know what the face value of the note is, once we know what the interest charge is, we can determine the amount she actually received. We can determine the interest using the formula:

Interest = Principal of Note × Rate of Interest × Term of Discount.

Substituting \$350 for the amount of loan, 6% or .06 per year for rate of interest, and

$\frac{90}{360}$ or $\frac{1}{4}$ of a year for term we get

$$\text{Interest} = \$350 \times .06 \times \frac{1}{4} = \frac{\$21}{4} = \$5.25 \text{ interest.}$$

The amount Ms. Baden actually received is then

$$\$350 - \$5.25 = \$344.75.$$

• PROBLEM 28-19

> The Amalgamated Loan Company received a 6-months note for $1,500, bearing 6% interest and dated May 17, 1976. On September 22, 1976, the note was discounted at 8%. What were the proceeds?

Solution: Since the note was earning 6% interest for a period of six months, its total value would be $1,500 plus the interest that it earned. We can calculate the amount of interest that the note earned using the formula:

Interest = Principal of Note × Interest Rate × Term of Note

Substituting an amount of $1,500, at an interest rate of 6% (.06) per year, for a term of

$\frac{6}{12}$ or $\frac{1}{2}$ year, we obtain

$$\text{Interest} = \$1,500 \times .06 \times \frac{1}{2} = \$90 \times \frac{1}{2} = \$45 \text{ interest.}$$

The total value of the note would then be $1,500 + $45 = $1,545. The note was originally issued on May 17, with a term of 6 months. This means that the date at which the note attained its full value of $1,545 was 6 months after May 17, that is, Nov 17.

Since the note was discounted on September 22, and it did not reach its full value until Nov. 17, it was discounted for a period of 56 days (the 8 remaining in September, plus 31 in October and 17 in November). In order to determine how much the discount on the note was, we can use the formula:

Interest = Principal of Note × Interest Rate × Term of Discount.

Substituting an amount of $1,545 at an interest rate of 8% (.08) per year for a term of

$\frac{56}{360}$ of a year, we obtain:

$$\text{Interest} = \$1,545 \times .08 \times \frac{56}{360} = \$123.60 \times \frac{56}{360} = \frac{\$6921.60}{360},$$

which rounds to $19.23.

Since a discount of \$19.23 was deducted from the total value of the note, the proceeds were

$$\$1,545 - \$19.23 = \$1,525.77 .$$

• PROBLEM 28-20

On April 17, Mr. Hicky received a three-month note for \$800 bearing interest at 4%. On May 17, his bank discounted the note at a 6% interest rate. Find his proceeds.

Solution: Mr. Hicky's note received interest at 4% for three months. We can calculate how much interest that was using the formula:

Interest = Principal of Note × Rate of Interest × Term of Note.

Substituting an amount of \$800 at an interest rate of 4% = .04 per year for a term of

$\frac{3}{12} = \frac{1}{4}$ of a year, we obtain:

$$\text{Interest} = \$800 \times .04 \times \frac{1}{4} = \frac{\$32}{4} = \$8 \text{ interest.}$$

The maturity value of the note was therefore \$808. The note had a term of three months, but Mr. Hicky held it for one month (from April 17 to May 17) so the term of the discount was 3 - 1 = 2 months. Using the formula:

Interest = Principal of Note × Rate of Interest × Term of Discount

with a maturiy value of \$808, rate of interest of 6% = .06 per year, and term of

$\frac{2}{12} = \frac{1}{6}$ of a year, we can calculate the interest charged as

$$\$808 \times .06 \times \frac{1}{6} = \frac{\$48.48}{6} = 8.08.$$

His proceeds were therefore

$$\$808 - \$8.08 = \$799.92.$$

• PROBLEM 28-21

A note bearing interest at 7% for 60 days with a face value of \$3,000 was issued on September 25. On November

1, the note was discounted at 5 1/2%. What were the proceeds?

Solution: The note earned interest for 60 days at 7%. Using the formula

Interest = Principal of Note × Rate of Interest × Term of Note,

and substituting \$3,000 for the amount, 7% = .07 per year for the interest rate, and

$\frac{60}{360} = \frac{1}{6}$ of a year for the term, we obtain

$$\text{Interest} = \$3,000 \times .07 \times \frac{1}{6} = \frac{\$210}{6} = \$35.$$

The maturity value of the note was therefore \$3,000 + \$35 = \$3,035. Since the note was issued on September 25, 5 days in September, 31 in October, and 1 day in November, for a total of 5 + 31 + 1 = 37 days elapsed between the date the note was issued and the day it was discounted. The note had a term of 60 days, so the term of the discount was 60 - 37 = 23 days. In order to find out how much interest was deducted, we can use the formula:

Interest = Principal of Note × Rate of Interest × Term of Discount.

Substituting \$3,035 for the maturity value of the note, $5\frac{1}{2}\% = .055$ per year for the interest rate, and $\frac{23}{360}$ of a year for the term, we obtain:

$$\text{Interest} = \$3,035 \times .055 \times \frac{23}{360} = \$166.925 \times \frac{23}{360} =$$

$$\frac{\$3839.275}{360}, \text{ which rounds to } \$10.66.$$

The proceeds were therefore

$$\$3,035 - \$10.66 = \$3024.34$$

• PROBLEM 28-22

Beinstock Inc. received a 6-months note on May 17 for \$1500 bearing interest at 6%. It was discounted at 8% on September 22. What were the proceeds?

Solution: The note comes due on November 17, six months after May 17. The worth of the note is its face value + interest. The interest is computed by the formula

Interest = Principal × Rate × Time (in years), giving

$1500 × .06 × 1/2 (six months = 1/2 year) = $45.

Thus, the worth of the note is $1500 + $45 = $1545. The proceeds of the note are found by subtracting the discounting charge from the worth of the note. The note was discounted on September 22, or 56 days before it was due (use the time table to compute this). The discounting charge is found by the following formula:

Rate × (days to maturity ÷ 360 days) × worth of note.

Hence, the charge is

.08 × 56/360 × $1545 = $19.23.

We can now compute the proceeds.

	Worth of note	$1545.00
Less	Discounting charge	$ 19.23
	proceeds of note	$1525.77

• PROBLEM 28-23

A 3-month note for $850, bearing interest at 6% was discounted at 6% a month after it was issued. What were the proceeds?

Solution: Since the note earned interest for 3 months at the rate of 6%, its maturity value would be the $850 plus the interest it earned. We can calculate the interest it earned using the formula:

Interest = Principal of Note × Interest Rate × Term of Note

Substituting an amount of $850, at an interest rate of 6% (.06) per year for a term of

$\frac{3}{12} = \frac{1}{4}$ of a year, we obtain:

Interest = \$850 × .06 × $\frac{1}{4} = \frac{\$51}{4}$ = \$12.75 interest.

Therefore, the full maturity value of the note was $850 + $12.75 = $862.75. Now, since the note had a 3 month term and it was discounted 1 month after it was issued, it was discounted for a period of 3 - 1 = 2 months. In order to determine what the proceeds of the note were, we must determine how much interest was deducted from the full maturity value of the note. We can use the formula:

Interest = Principal of Note × Interest Rate × Term of Discount.

Substituting an amount of $862.75 at a rate of 6% (.06) per year for a period of

$$\frac{2}{12} = \frac{1}{6} \text{ of a year we obtain:}$$

Interest = $\$862.75 \times .06 \times \frac{1}{6} = \frac{\$51.765}{6}$, which rounds to $8.63. The proceeds were then

$$\$862.75 - \$8.63 = \$854.12.$$

DRAFTS

• PROBLEM 28-24

Jane Morrow gave a 60-day sight-draft dated May 5 for $255 to Jason Bros. Inc. It was accepted by Jason Bros. on June 1. If it was discounted on July 1 for 5%, what were the proceeds?

Solution: A 60-day sight-draft is one which starts the count of days after it has been accepted, not after the date on it. In order to compute the proceeds, we must find out the discounting charge. The charge, is found by the formula,

$$\text{Charge} = \text{Rate} \times \frac{\text{days to maturity}}{360 \text{ days}} \times \text{Principal},$$

where time is expressed in terms of a 360 day year. Since the draft was discounted on July 1, it was discounted 30 days after sight (after it was accepted). Thus, the charge is equal to

$$.05 \times 30/360 \times \$255 = \$1.06.$$

The proceeds are

$$(\$255.00 - \$1.06) = \$253.94.$$

• PROBLEM 28-25

Mr. Owens accepted a draft dated July 11 for $544.20 at 4% with a term of 3 months. He discounted it August 2 at 5%. The bank charged a 1/8% collection fee. What were the proceeds?

Solution: We can calculate the interest that the draft received by using the formula:

Interest = Principal of Note × Rate of Interest × Term of Note

Substituting \$544.20 for the amount of the note, 4% = .04 per year for the interest rate, and

$\frac{3}{12} = \frac{1}{4}$ of a year for the term, we obtain:

$\$544.20 \times .04 \times \frac{1}{4} = \frac{\$21.768}{4}$, which rounds to \$5.44

The maturity value of the draft was therefore \$544.20 + \$5.44 = \$549.64.

The draft was dated July 11, and had a term of 3 months, so its maturity date was October 11. Since it was discounted on August 2, the term of the discount was from August 2 to October 11. This includes 29 days in August, 30 days in September, and 11 days in October, for a total of 29 + 30 + 11 = 70 days. We can calculate the interest discounted using the formula:

Interest = Principal of Note × Rate of Interest × Term of Discount.

Subtituting a maturity value of \$549.64, an interest rate of 5% = .05 per year, and a term of

$\frac{70}{360}$ of a year, we obtain

Interest = $\$549.64 \times .05 \times \frac{70}{360} = \frac{\$1923.74}{360}$, which rounds to \$5.34. Also, a collection fee of 1/8% = .00125 was charged. This can be calculated as follows:

$\frac{1}{8}\%$ of \$549.64 = .00125 × \$549.64,

which rounds to \$.69. The total charges were therefore

\$5.34 + \$.69 = \$6.03, so the proceeds were

\$549.64 - \$6.03 = \$543.61 .

• PROBLEM 28-26

A draft for \$350 dated October 15 and due in 60 days was discounted on November 12 at 5% with collection fee of 1/5%. Find the proceeds.

Solution: Since the draft was dated October 15 and had a term of 60 days, it was due 60 days after October 15. This includes the remaining 16 days of October, as well as the 30 days of November and an additional 14 days in December. The maturity date of the draft was therefore December 14. Since the date that the draft was discounted was November 12, the term of the discount was from November 12 to December 14. This includes the remaining 18 days of November, and December 1 to 14 for a total of 32 days. We can use the formula:

Interest = Principal of Note × Rate of Interest × Term of Discount

to determine the interest charge on the draft. Substituting an amount of \$350 at an interest rate of 5% = .05 per year for a term of

$\frac{32}{360}$ of a year, we obtain:

$$\text{Interest} = \$350 \times .05 \times \frac{32}{360} = \frac{\$560}{360}$$, which rounds to \$1.56.

An additional fee of $\frac{1}{5}\%$ = .002 was charged for collection.

This can be calculated as follows: $\frac{1}{5}\%$ of

$$\$350 = \$350 \times .002 = \$.70.$$

The total charges were therefore

$$\$1.56 + \$.70 = \$2.26,$$

so the proceeds were

$$\$350 - \$2.26 = \$347.74.$$

• PROBLEM 28-27

James Owen accepted a draft, dated December 9, drawn by Parker Bros, for \$815.50 at 6% payable 4 months after date. Parker Bros. had the draft discounted at the bank on January 9 at 6 1/2%. A charge of 1/8% for collecting it when due was also charged. What were the proceeds?

Solution: The first thing we must do to solve this problem, is to find out how much the draft will be worth on April 9, four months from December 9. To find this, we use the formula:

Interest = Principal × Rate × Time (in years).

Since the draft is for four months, or one-third of a

year, the interest is equal to

$$\$815.50 \times .06 \times 1/3 = \$16.31.$$

Thus, the worth of the draft is

$$\$815.50 + \$16.31 = \$831.81.$$

The draft was discounted on January 9, by using the time table, we see that the number of days until April 9 is 90. We can now find the cost of the discounting by the formula

Charge = Rate × Time (in a 360 day year) × Principal

(worth of draft). Thus, the charge for discounting the draft is

$$.065 \times 90/360 \times \$831.81 = \$13.52 .$$

The collection fee is 1/8%. To find this we take 1% of the worth of the draft and divide it by 8.

Collection fee = \$831.81 × 1% ÷ 8 = \$1.04.

To find the proceeds we subtract the collection fee and the discount charge from the worth of the draft.

	worth of draft	\$831.81
Less	discounting charge	\$ 13.52
Less	collection fee	\$ 1.04
	draft's proceeds	\$817.25

• PROBLEM 28-28

Friedman Brothers accepted a 60-day sight draft on April 10, for \$562.50. It was discounted on April 15 at 6%, find the proceeds.

Solution: The draft was discounted five days after it was accepted, thus it still has 55 days to maturity. The proceeds of the draft is the amount of the draft less the discounting charge. The discounting charge is found by the formula:

$$\text{Charge} = \text{Rate} \times \frac{\text{days to maturity}}{\text{360 days}} \text{ using a 360 day year}$$

$$\times \text{ Principal (amount of draft).}$$

Thus, the charge is equal to

$$.06 \times 55/360 \times \$562.50 = \$5.16$$

Hence, the proceeds of the draft are

$$\$562.50 - \$5.16 = \$557.34.$$

• PROBLEM 28-29

Bennet Bros. accepted a draft for $3000, dated March 15, and due in 2 months after sight on March 30. They had it discounted on April 15 at 6%. Find the proceeds.

Solution: Being that this draft is due two months after sight, and it was accepted on March 30, it is due on May 30. Thus, by using a time table, we see that it was discounted 45 days before it becomes due i.e. number of days between April 15 and May 30. To find the discounting charge, we use the formula

$$\text{Charge} = \text{Rate} \times \frac{\text{days to maturity}}{360 \text{ days}} \times \text{Principal}$$

(For computing the charge we assume that a year has 360 days.)
Hence the charge is

$$.06 \times 45/360 \times \$3000 = \$22.50.$$

Thus, the proceeds of the draft is the draft's worth minus the discounting charge.

	draft's worth	$3000.00
Less	discounting charge	$ 22.50
	proceeds	$2977.50

• PROBLEM 28-30

Parker Bros. accepted a draft for $3500 bearing interest at 6%, dated April 5 and due in 6 months after date. It was discounted on August 20 at 6 1/2%. If the bank charged a 1/3% collection fee, what were the proceeds?

Solution: The first thing we must do is compute how much the draft will be worth at the date of maturity. Since it bears 6% interest, we can find the amount of interest by the formula

$$\text{Interest} = \text{Principal} \times \text{Rate} \times \text{Time (in years)}.$$

Since the time of the loan is six months, or one-half of a year, we see that the amount of interest is equal to $\$3500 \times .06 \times 1/2 = \$105$. Hence the draft is worth

$3500 + $105 = $3605 at its maturity date. The draft was dated on April 5, and is due six months later, thus it is due on October 5. By using a time table we see that the draft was discounted for 46 days. The charge for the discounting is found by the formula:

$$\text{Charge} = \text{Rate} \times \frac{\text{days to maturity}}{360} \times \text{Principal.}$$

Thus, the charge

$$.065 \times 46/360 \times \$3605 = \$29.04.$$

(The charge is based on a 360 day year.) Finally, the bank charges a collection fee of 1/3%. To find this we take 1% of the principal and divide it by 3 getting 1/3%.

Collection fee = ($3605 × 1%) ÷ 3 = $36.05 ÷ 3 = $12.02.

The proceeds of the draft is its worth minus all the fees.

	Draft's worth	$3605.00
Less	discounting charge	$ 29.94
Less	collection fee	$ 12.02
	draft's proceeds	$3563.04

• PROBLEM 28-31

Holmes Bros. accepted a draft dated July 10 for $326.80 at 5%, payable 90 days after date. (a) How much was paid if Homes Bros. paid it when due? (b) If this draft had been discounted at 5 1/2% 30 days before maturity and a 1/4% collection fee was charged, what were the proceeds? (Assume a 360 day year.)

Solution: (a) The draft is worth its face value plus the interest. The amount of interest is found by the formula

Interest = Principal × Rate × Time

the note is held. (Use 360 day year)

Interest = $326.80 × .05 × 90/360 = $4.09

Thus, the worth is $326.80 + $4.09 = $330.89.

(b) The proceeds is the worth less the collection fee and the charge for discounting. The discounting charge is found by the following formula:

$$\text{Charge} = \text{Rate} \times \frac{\text{days to maturity}}{\text{360 days}} \times \text{Principal (draft's}$$

worth) = $.055 \times 30/360 \times \$330.89 = \$1.52$.

The collection fee is one-quarter of 1% of the worth of the draft, being

$$\$330.89 \times 1\% \times 1/4 = \$0.83.$$

Thus, the proceeds are

$$\$330.89 - \$1.52 - \$0.83 = \$328.54.$$

• PROBLEM 28-32

On October 25 Ralph Muffet accepted a draft for $620 that was dated October 10 and due 3 months after sight. It was discounted on November 16 at 4 1/2%. The bank charges 1/8% collection fee. Find the proceeds of the draft.

Solution: The draft was due 3 months after the date of sight, 3 months after Oct. 25 is Jan.25. It was discounted on November 16 which is, using the time table, 70 days before Jan. 25. To find the discount charge we use the formula

$$\text{Charge} = \text{Rate} \times \frac{\text{days to maturity}}{360} \times \text{Principal} =$$

$$.045 \times 70/360 \times \$620 = \$5.43.$$

The collection fee is 1/8 of 1% of $620 or

$$1/8 \times 1\% \times \$620 = \frac{\$6.20}{8} = \$.78.$$

Thus the proceeds are:

	Worth of draft	$620.00
Less	Collection fee	$ .78
Less	Charge for discounting	$ 5.43
	Proceeds	$613.79

• PROBLEM 28-33

Finkel Company accepted a 90 day after sight draft for $850 on May 10. It was discounted on July 1 at 5%. If the bank charges a 1/4% collection fee, what are the proceeds?

Solution: The draft is due 90 days after May 10. By using the time table, we see that it is due on Aug.

8. This draft was discounted on July 1. Using the time table we see that the date to maturity is 38 days, i.e., July 1 to August 8. We can now find the discounting charge. It is found by the formula:

$$\text{Charge} = \text{Rate} \times \frac{\text{days to maturity}}{360 \text{ days}} \times \text{Principal} = .05 \times$$

$$38/360 \times \$850 = \$4.49.$$

The collection fee is 1/4 of 1% of $850, or

$$1/4 \times .01 \times \$850 = \$2.13.$$

The proceeds of the draft can be found by subtracting the collection fee, and the discounting charge from the value of the draft.

	Value of the draft	$850.00
Less	Charge for discounting	$ 4.49
Less	Collection fee	$ 2.13
	Proceeds of the draft	$843.38

• PROBLEM 28-34

Owens Company accepted a draft, 90-day sight, amounting to $560 drawn on them by Watts Bros. Watts Bros. had the draft discounted 34 days before the due date at 6%. What were the proceeds?

Solution: The proceeds will be the $560 face value, less the discounting charge. The discounting charge is equal to the rate times the principal (face value) times the number of days before maturity divided by 360 days where a year is taken to have 360 days. Hence the discount rate =

$$.06 \times \$560 \times 34/360 = \$3.17.$$

Therefore the proceeds are $560 - $3.17 = $556.83.

• PROBLEM 28-35

Florsheim and Co. accepted a 90-day sight draft for $425.00 on October 10. It was discounted on November 1 at 5%. If their bank charged a 1/3% collection fee, what were the proceeds?

Solution: The draft was accepted on October 10. Using the time table, we find that it is due on January 8 (90 days later). The proceeds of the draft is the face value of $425 less the collection fee of 1/3% and the discounting charge. The discounting charge can be found by the following formula:

$$\text{Charge} = \text{Rate} \times \frac{\text{days to maturity}}{360 \text{ days}} \times \text{worth (face value)}.$$

Being that it was discounted on November 1, by using the Time table we see that the discounting period is 68 days. i.e. the days between November 1 and January 8. Hence the charge is equal to

$$.05 \times 68/360 \times \$425 = \$4.01.$$

The collection fee is 1/3%. To convert that we take 1% of the face value and divide it by three. Thus the collection fee is

$$(\$425 \times .01) \div 3 = \$4.25 \div 3 = \$1.42.$$

The proceeds now can be found.

	Face value	$425.00
Less	Collection fee	$ 1.42
Less	Discounting charge	$ 4.01
	Proceeds	$419.57

• PROBLEM 28-36

A draft for $800, due in 3 months and bearing interest at 4 1/2%, was discounted 60 days before it was due. If the discount rate was 5%, what were the proceeds?

Solution: The proceeds of this draft are the face value plus the interest, and less the discounting charge. The interest is found by the formula

Interest = Principal × Rate × Time (in years), being

$$\$800 \times .045 \times 90/360 = \$800 \times .045 \times 1/4 = \$9.$$

Thus, the worth of the draft is $800 (face value) + $9 (interest) = $809. The discounting charge is found by the following formula:

$$\text{Charge} = \text{Rate} \times \frac{\text{days to maturity}}{360} \times$$

worth of the draft. Hence the charge is

$$.05 \times 60/360 \times \$809 = \$6.74.$$

The proceeds can now be found.

	Worth of draft	\$809.00
Less	Discounting charge	\$ 6.74
	proceeds of draft	\$802.26

• PROBLEM 28-37

J. Robertson and Co. sold furniture to Haverson Stores in the amount of \$13,560. A draft dated July 10 was submitted in payment with terms of "90 days after date," bearing interest at 6%. If the draft was discounted on August 30 at 6 1/2% and the bank charged a collection fee of 1/10%, find the proceeds.

Solution: The draft is due 90 days after the date, of July 10, being October 8. (Use the time table.) This draft bears interest at the rate of 6%, hence its worth is its face value (\$13,560) plus the interest that is earned. The amount of interest can be computed by the formula

Interest = Principal × Rate × Time in years, giving

$$\$13,560 \times .06 \times \frac{90}{360} = \$203.40.$$

The worth of the draft is therefore

$$\$13,560 + \$203.40 = \$13,763.40 .$$

The draft was discounted on August 30, using the time table we see that this is 39 days before the draft is due. The charge for the discounting is found by the following formula:

Charge = Rate × (days to maturity date ÷ 360 days a year) × worth of draft. Hence the charge is

$$.065 \times \frac{39}{360} \times \$13,763.40 = \$96.92.$$

The bank charges a collection fee of 1/10 of 1%. To find out how much this amounts to we multiply the worth of the draft by .001 (.1% = 1/10%) and get \$13.76. The proceeds of the draft can be found by subtracting the collection fee and the discounting charge from the worth of the draft.

Worth of the draft	\$13,763.40
Less collection fee	\$ 13.76
Less Discounting charge	\$ 96.92
Proceeds of draft	\$13,652.72

CHAPTER 29

PERSONAL FINANCE

EXPENDITURES AND CHOICES

• PROBLEM 29-1

If Mr. Hammer's disposable income last year was $5,000 and his total expenditures were 4,600, what was his propensity to save?

Solution: The propensity to save is the amount of money saved divided by total disposable income. If Mr. Hammer had $5,000 and consumed $4,600, then he has $400 left to save. The propensity to save is

$$\frac{400}{5,000} = 0.08 \text{ or } 8\%.$$

If we were told that Mr. Hammer's propensity to save remained constant for any income above $4,000, then if he made 6,700 in one year this means that he saved

$$(\$6,700)(0.08) = \$536.$$

• PROBLEM 29-2

Suppose you are offered a used car for $2,500, less 15%. Then a second dealer offers to sell you a similar car for $2,350 less 10%, plus a $25 tune-up charge. Which is the lower offer? How much less is it?

Solution: The first offer is

$$\$2,500 - (15\% \times \$2,500) = \$2,500 - \$375 = \$2,125.$$

The second is

$$\$2,350 - (10\% \times \$2,350) + \$25 = \$2,350 - \$235 + \$25 = \$2,140.$$

The first offer is $15 less than the second.

• PROBLEM 29-3

Mr. Tencer has a $10,000 mortgage at a rate of 6% payable in 10 years. After five years, Mr. Tencer owes $7,000 and decides to pay the total amount remaining. If there is a 3% prepayment penalty, what is the total amount Mr. Tencer has to pay?

Solution: The 3% charge is calculated from the balance due, i.e., the penalty is

$$(0.03)(7{,}000) = \$210.$$

The total amount paid by Mr. Tencer is

$$\$7{,}000 + \$210 = \$7{,}210.$$

• PROBLEM 29-4

If two friends have an equal sum to invest, and one invests in bonds and the other in real estate, which represents an advantage to the real estate investor?

(i) Simpler management
(ii) Easier liquidation
(iii) Tax regulations
(iv) Greater diversification

Solution: (iii) The depreciation allowance for buildings represents a major advantage in real estate investment. It is more important when the value of the building is high, relative to land value. The advantage of the depreciation allowance is that it isn't necessary to continously make direct cash payments to benefit from the tax deduction.

• PROBLEM 29-5

You are hired to paint the walls and ceiling of a room 14'× 12' × 8½'. You know that paint cost $6.50 per gallon which will cover 425 sq.ft. or $1.85 per quart. How do you find the cost of the paint?

Solution: We need to know the number of square feet to be covered. The total area of the walls is (total length of walls) (height of walls) =

$(14' + 14' + 12' + 12') \times (8\frac{1}{2}') = 442$ sq. ft.

The ceiling area is (length = 14') × (width = 12') = 168 sq.

Total sq. ft. to be painted is 442 + 168 = 610 sq. ft. One gallon will cover 425 sq. ft., so that 2 gallons will cover 2 × 425 = 850 sq. ft. The cost of 2 gallons is 2 × $6.50/gallon = $13.00. Since 1 gallon covers 425 sq.ft.,

$$1 \text{ quart} = \frac{1}{4} \text{ gallon covers } \frac{425}{4} = 106.25 \text{ sq. ft.}$$

To economize, we can buy a gallon to cover 425 feet.

610 - 425 = 185 sq. ft. will be left. We can use 2 quarts, which will cover 2 x 106.25 = 212.25 sq. ft., with 212.5 - 185 = 27.5 sq. ft. left over. The cost of 2 quarts is 2 x $1.85/quart = $3.70. The gallon cost $6.50, so our total cost is $3.70 + $6.50 = $10.20. In this way we will save

$13.00 - $10.20 = $2.80

over the cost of 2 gallons.

• PROBLEM 29-6

James Taggert wishes to paint the walls of his storage room. The room's dimensions are 14' by 10' by 8½'. One quart of paint costing $9.80 will cover 36 sq. ft. Labor costs is $5 per quart or fraction there of. Find his cost for painting the room.

Solution: To find the cost we must find the area of the room's walls and then find out how many quarts are necessary to cover the area.

The area of the room's walls is found by adding the area of each of the four walls. The area of each wall is found by multiplying its height by its width.

8½' × 14'	=	119 sq. ft.
+ 8½ × 10'	=	85 sq. ft.
+ 8½ × 14'	=	119 sq. ft.
+ 8½ × 10'	=	85 sq. ft.
Area of walls	=	408 sq. ft.

A quart of paint will cover 36 sq. ft., thus in order to find the number of quarts required we divide the area (408) by the area a quart covers (36), giving

$$408 \div 36 = 11\frac{1}{3} \text{ quarts.}$$

Thus he must pay for 12 quarts of paint.

	$9.80 × 12 = $117.60	Cost of paint
+	$5.00 × 12 = $ 60.00	Cost of labor
	$177.60	Total cost

• PROBLEM 29-7

During a 6-month heating season, a homeowner expects to average $40 a month for fuel oil. He has purchased the following amounts to date: $37.50, $42.60, $39.80, $40.75, $44.10. What amount will he spend during the last month to maintain the expected average?

Solution: To do the problem one must first understand what the term average means. If you have a group of numbers, the average can be found by adding all the numbers in the group and then dividing the sum by the number of members of the group. Here we are told the average and are expected to maintain it by finding a suitable value for the last month. First, we find the amount already spent by adding the amounts to date:

$37.50 + $42.60 + $39.80 + $40.75 + $44.10 = $204.75.

Next calculate the amount expected to be spent. This equals the (expected average per month) × (total number of months) = 40 × 6 = $240.

If the homeowner expects to spend $240, and has already spent $204.75, then he would spend the difference between the two during the last month to maintain the expected average. Therefore he must spend

($240 - $204.75 =) $35.25

during the last month.

• PROBLEM 29-8

A building contractor agrees to build a home on the basis of cost plus 10% of the cost. Expenses include the following: excavating, $1,354; masonry, $1,551; carpentry and mill work, $11,525; plastering, painting and papering, $3,413; roofing, $1,259; plumbing, $3,307, wiring and fixtures, $926; linoleum, tiling and landscaping, $1,785. What must the buyer pay for the house?

Solution: The cost of the house is the sum of the expenses. When we have added all the expenses, we will then take 10% of the total. The total expenses plus 10% of that number is the cost to the buyer.

Excavating	\$1,354	
Masonry	1,551	
Carpentry	11,525	
Plastering	3,413	
Roofing	1,259	
Plumbing	3,307	
Electrical	926	
Other	1,785	
	25,120.00	expenses
	2,512.00	10% fee cost to buyer
	27,632.00	cost to buyer

• PROBLEM 29-9

A man buys a house and lot for \$35,000, paying \$12,000 down and borrowing the balance on a 6% mortgage due in 10 years. He pays real-estate taxes of \$240, a water tax of \$30, and insurance premiums of \$70 a year. Allowing 4% interest on his investment, and 2% depreciation on the house valued at \$25,000, what is the cost per month of owning the home if repairs average \$120 a year?

Solution: We compute depreciation, interest on the mortgage and interest on the investment for the year. Then we add all the expenses for a year and divide by 12 to find the monthly cost.

Depreciation= 2% × \$25,000 = \$500. 6% of the mortgage

is 6% × \$23,000 = \$1,380. 4% of the \$12,000 down payment

is 4% × \$12,000 = \$480.

Their sum is \$2,360. To this we add repairs (\$120) + insurance (\$70) + combined taxes (\$240 + 30 = \$270).

The total annual cost is \$2,360 + (\$120 + 70 + 270) =

\$2,360 + \$460 = \$2,820.

The monthly cost, therefore, is

$$\frac{\$2{,}820 \text{ per year}}{12 \text{ months}} = \$235 \text{ per month.}$$

• **PROBLEM 29-10**

Suppose that your utility bill for July states that you used 328 kw-hrs of electricity and 1400 cu.ft. of natural gas. There is a flat rate of $1.70 for the first 15 kw-hours. Different rates are set for daytime, evening and late-evening to 8 A.M. You used 45 hours at .043 per hour, 140 hours at $.0318 per hour, and 128 hours at .0179 per hour. The charges for gas are: 600 cu. ft. ($3.20 flat charge) plus 800 cu. ft. at $.253 per 100 cu. ft. Your phone bill, subject to a 10% federal tax, has a basic charge of $6.27, plus long distance calls at $1.36 and $3.45. Electric, gas, and phone bills are subject to a 6% city tax. What is the total amount of each bill?

Solution: The total electric bill is the sum of the individual charges, which we must compute, plus the 6% tax.

Electricity

Number of kw-hours	Rate	Price
15	(basic)	$1.70
45	.043	1.94
140	.0318	4.45
128	.0179	2.29
328		10.38

.06 × 10.38 = $.62 tax. $10.38 + .62 = $11.00

Gas

Cubic Feet	Rate per 100	Price
600	(basic)	$3.20
800	$.253	2.02
1400 cu. ft.		5.22

.06 × 5.22 = $.31 tax. $5.22 + $.31 = $5.53 total gas bill.

Telephone

The telephone bill is the sum of the basic charge, federal and city taxes plus the sum of the long distance calls and their taxes. We have:

$6.27 + (.10 × 6.27) + (.06 × 6.27)

= 6.27 + .63 + .38 = $7.28 basic + taxes

Tolls: $1.36 + 3.45 = 4.81 $4.81 + (.10× 4.81) +

(.06 × 4.81) = 4.81 + .48 + .29 = $5.58 toll calls + taxes.

The total is $7.28 + 5.58 = $12.86

• PROBLEM 29-11

How much will it cost to cover a floor 13'6" × 18'8" with asphalt tile if the price is 9 3/4¢ per 9" tile?

Solution: Our method is to convert the dimensions of the floor to inches and divide each dimension by 9" (tiles are 9" square) to find the number of tiles needed for the width of the room and for the length of the room. The number of tiles needed to cover the floor will be the product of the number of tiles for the length and width. When we know the total tiles needed, we multiply by price per tile ($.09 3/4) to find cost.

Following our procedure,

13'6" = 13' × 12"/foot + 6" = 162"

Tiles for width of room: 162" ÷ 9" = 18 tiles

18'8" = 18'× 12"/foot + 8" = 224"

Tiles for length: 224" ÷ 9" = 25 tiles

Tiles for entire room: 25 × 18 = 450.

Cost: 450 tiles × ($.09$\frac{3}{4}$ per tile) = $43.875 = $43.88

• PROBLEM 29-12

You have just redesigned your kitchen. The new floor dimensions are 7'6" × 11'8". Now you want to cover the floor with linoleum, which sells for $1.79 per running foot in 6' width. What is the best way to cover the floor? How much will it cost?

Solution: $1.79 per running foot in 6' width means the roll of linoleum is 6' wide, and each foot of this roll costs $1.79. Notice that the length of the room is almost 12' - just 4 inches short. If we buy two pieces 6' wide and 7½' long, we will be able to cover the floor with only 4 inches on one side wasted.

The total cost is (2 pieces) × 7½" × ($1.79 per foot) = $26.85

• PROBLEM 29-13

> You wish to carpet a room 13' by 18' with a roll of carpet that is 12' wide. Carpeting costs \$13.50 per square yard, and there is an installation charge of \$1.50 per square yard. How much will it cost?

Solution: First we must determine how to cut the carpet to cover the room. A length of 13' of a 12'-wide roll will cover 2/3 of the floor. This will leave an area 6' × 13' to be covered. Another length of 6½' of the 12'-wide roll can be cut in half lengthwise and pieced together to cover the 6'× 13' area, as the diagram shows:

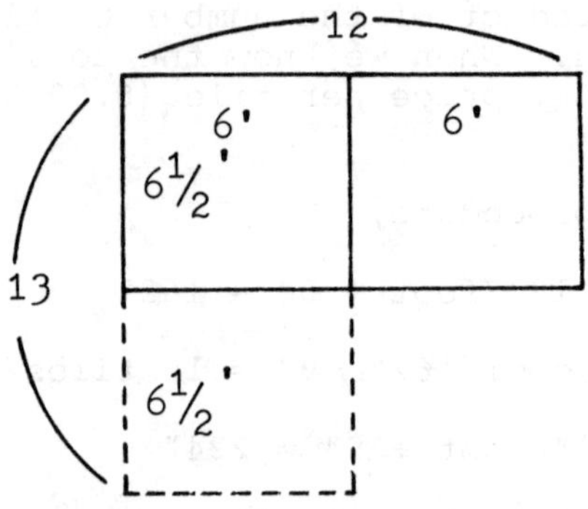

The total length cut from the 12' roll is 13' + 6½'. Thus total area = 12' × 19½' = 234 sq. ft.

$$\frac{234 \text{ sq. ft}}{9 \text{ sq. ft/yard}} = 26 \text{ sq. yards}$$

Total cost per square yard is \$13.50 + \$1.50 = \$15.00. Therefore total cost is

(\$15/sq. yard)× 26 sq. yds. = \$390.

• PROBLEM 29-14

> You are planning to carpet a room 14'6" by 11'3". The price is \$11.95 per sq. yd. Assuming that available widths are 15' and 12'. which is more economical? What is the cost?

Solution: If we use a width of 15', we will need a length of 11'3". This gives

$$15' \times 11\frac{1}{4}' = 168\frac{3}{4} \text{ sq. ft.}$$

$$= \frac{168\frac{3}{4} \text{ sq. ft.}}{9 \text{ sq.ft/sq.yd.}} = 18\frac{3}{4} \text{ sq. yd.}$$

If we use a width of 12', we will need a length of 14'6" = 14½'. The area will be 12' × 14½' = 174 sq.ft.

$$= 19\frac{1}{3} \text{ sq.yd.}$$

The 15' width requires less yardage; therefore it is more economical. The cost of

$$18\frac{3}{4} \text{ sq.yd. is } 18\frac{3}{4} \times \$11.95 \text{ per sq.yd} = \$224.06 =$$

cost of carpeting.

SAVINGS AND FUNDS

• PROBLEM 29-15

What is the amount that must be deposited annually at 6% over ten years to yield $300,000?

Solution: Find the sinking fund factor in the 6% compound interest table corresponding to n = 10. The factor is 0.07587. Multiplying the future value, $300,000 by this factor, obtain

$$(\$300{,}000)(0.07587) = \$22{,}761 \quad \text{as}$$

the amount that must be deposited annually for 10 years to yield $300,000.

If we did not have a 6% table, we would use the formula

$$P = \frac{Ri}{(1+i)^n - 1} \quad \text{where } n = 10,\ i = 0.06,$$

R = $300,000 the value of the sinking fund, and P is annual payment made.

$$P = \frac{(\$300{,}000)(0.06)}{(1 + 0.06)^{10} - 1} = \$22{,}760.39$$

This answer is extremely close to the figure from the table.

• PROBLEM 29-16

You plan to by a house,priced at $24,000, so you apply at a bank for a mortgage. The loan officer informs you that a 25% down-payment is required and that the interest rate is 7½ %. Property taxes are $30 per $1,000 and homeowner's insurance cost $5.50 per $1,000 each year. What is the amount of the mortgage and the interest charge? How much property tax will you have to pay? What will your insurance premium be?

MONTHLY PAYMENTS PER $1,000 ON 20-YEAR MORTGAGE

Interest Rate	Monthly Payments
5 %	$6.60
5½%	6.88
6 %	7.17
7 %	7.76
7½%	8.06
8 %	8.37
8½%	8.68

Solution: We know that the house costs $24,000 and that the down payment is 25% of the cost, or

$$.25 \times \$24,000 = \$6,000$$

A mortgage is a loan made by a bank to help an individual purchase property. The amount of a mortgage for a house is the difference between the price and the amount that the buyer can invest. In this problem the buyer can only invest the down payment, which is $6,000. Thus the mortgage is price - downpayment =

$$\$24,000 - \$6,000 = \$18,000.$$

Checking the table, we see that for a 7½ % interest rate, the monthly payment is $8.06 per $1,000.

Property taxes will be ($30 per $1,000)× $24,000 =

$$\frac{30}{1,000} \times 24,000 = 30 \times 24 = \$720.$$

Homeowner's insurance may provide "protection" against fire and water damage and theft. The premium is the cost of coverage. Your rate is $5.50 per $1,000 each year, so that the premium is $5.50 × 24 = $132.00.

• PROBLEM 29-17

What is the future value obtained when \$5,000 is saved annually for 20 years at 5% compounded quarterly.

Solution: The above is the same as asking, "What is the future value obtained when

$$\$1,250 \quad \left(\text{i.e. } \frac{5,000}{4}\right) \text{ is saved at } 1\ 1/4\% \ (\text{i.e. } \frac{5\%}{4})$$

interest over 4(20) = 80 periods?"

The important thing to realize is that the interest is compounded quarterly. Four equal payments of \$1,250 represents \$5000 annually. The interest rate for each period is 1¼ %, over four periods gives 5% annual interest.

Finally, if payments are made over 20 years, there will be 80 payments made, i.e. there are 4 × 20 = 80 quarters (three month periods) in 20 years.

To obtain the future value of \$1,250 at 1¼ % over 80 periods we look in the 1¼ % compound interest table for n = 80 periods and under the column named, "compound amount factor." This factor is 136.119.

The future value of a uniform series of payments, each \$1,250 over 80 periods at 1¼ % is

$$(\$1,250)(136.119) = \$170,148.75.$$

• PROBLEM 29-18

The Argo Scholarship Fund consists of twenty scholarships of \$1,000 each. If this fund is to last for twenty years and the annual rate of interest is 5%, what is the amount needed to establish the fund?

Solution: This is the same as asking, "what is the present value of a uniform annual series of payments \$1,000 each, made over 20 years if the rate of return is 5%?"

Look in the Compound Interest Table. In the uniform annual series section under the present worth factor column find 12.462 for n=20 years. Multiplying this factor by \$1,000. gives you the present value of a uniform series of annual payments made over 20 years. The amount needed to set up the fund is

$$(\$1,000.)(12.462) = \$12,462.$$

• **PROBLEM 29-19**

Mrs. Hilton wishes to save \$10,000 to purchase a new car 10 years from now. If she can get 5% per year compounded quarterly in her savings account, what must her quarterly deposits be?

Solution: Mrs. Hilton wants to have \$10,000 by the end of 10 years. Since her account is compounded quarterly, there are 4 payments in a year, resulting in a total of 40 payments. In each period the interest is 5% per year/4 periods per year = 1¼ % per period. To find out how much is needed, we look for the compound amount factor. This factor tells how much we shall have from a \$1 per period deposit. We look in the table labeled 1¼ %, and the row labeled 40, and we go across to the column of Uniform Annual Series Compound Amount Factors. We find the number 51.490. Hence, for every dollar that is deposited quarterly the result is \$51.49 in ten years. To find how many dollars are required to total \$10,000, we simply divide 10,000 by 51.49, giving 194.21. Hence Mrs. Hilton must deposit \$194.21 each quarter to end up with \$10,000 at the end of the 10 years.

• **PROBLEM 29-20**

Mrs. Ash wants to set up a savings account for her daughter's education. What is the amount she has to deposit annually for 17 years at a rate of 5% to yield \$20,000?

Solution: If R is the amount deposited in n periods at a rate of interest i, then at the end of the n periods you have

$$Q = \frac{R(1 + i)^n - 1}{i} \text{ dollars.}$$

We solve this problem using this formula. The expression

$$\frac{(1 + i)^n - 1}{i} \text{ is the uniform annual}$$

series compound factor. The same amount will be deposited annually over n periods at a rate of i percent.

As far as the formula above is concerned,

$n = 17$ years $i = 5\%$ and Q is 20,000.

The question is, what R will yield Q?

$$20{,}000 = R\,\frac{(1 + 0.05)^{17} - 1}{0.05}$$

Solving for R:

$$(20,000)(0.05) = R\left[(1 + 0.05)^{17} - 1\right]$$

$$R = \frac{(20,000)(0.05)}{(1.05)^{17} - 1}$$

Using a calculator, we find R = 773.98. \$773.98 over 17 years at 5% interest will yield \$20,000.

• PROBLEM 29-21

Mr. Stade set up a sinking fund which requires \$1000 deposits made over 20 years at an annual rate of 3½ percent. What is the value of the fund at the end of fifteen years?

Solution: Clearly, the value of the fund is 1,000 the first year. For any year between 1 and 20, find the corresponding compound amount factor in the 3½ % compound interest factors table and multiply it by \$1,000.

From the 3½ % table, get 28.280 as the factor for n = 20 years, so that the final value of the sinking fund is

$$(\$1,000)(28.280) = \$28,280.$$

For n = 15, the compound amount factor is 19.296. By the end of the fifteenth year, the fund is worth

$$(\$1,000)(19.296) = \$19,296.$$

If we did not have a table for a specific rate of interest, we would use the formula,

$$S = R\ \frac{(1 + i)^n - 1}{i} \qquad \text{where}$$

R is the annual deposit made, n is the number of years, i is the interest rate and S is the value of the sinking fund. If interest was compounded quarterly, n would then represent the periods in which deposits were made. For this case, interest compounded quarterly means that

$$n = (4)(20) = 80 \text{ periods},\ i = \frac{3.5\%}{4} = 0.88\%$$

(or 0.0088 in decimals), and R would be $\frac{\$1,000}{4} = \$250$

Since there is no table for 0.88%, we must use the given formula.

$$S_{20} = \$250 \; \frac{(1.0088)^{80} - 1}{0.0088}$$

$$= \$250 \; \frac{1.0156}{0.0088} = \$28,852.$$

This is the value of the sinking fund at the end of 20 years (80 quarters), when interest is compounded quarterly. At the end of 15 years (60 quarters), the value of the fund interest compounded quarterly is

$$S_{15} = \$250 \; \frac{(1.0088)^{60} - 1}{0.0088} = \$19,648$$

• PROBLEM 29-22

> Minnie Morello is considering investing $5,000. in 5 year savings bonds at 5½ %. Broker Ted Turpid is advising her to purchase mutual funds. Ms. Morello would have to pay a fee of 5 8/10% of the amount invested, to acquire the funds. How much interest must the fund pay to match the projected return from savings bonds?

Solution: This question is solved in three parts.

(I) Total amount from savings bonds after 5 years $= \$5,000.(1.055)^5$

$= \$6,535$

(II) Where we use the simple interest formula,

$P = R\,(1 + i)^n$; R is the amount saved, i is the interest rate and n is the number of periods interest accrues. Principal to be invested in mutual funds

is $= \$\,x. \; - \;$ Fee

$= \$5,000. - 0.058\,(5,000.)$

$= \$5,000 - 290. = \$4,710.$

(III) To find the proper interest rate, we must set the mutual fund amount equal to the mature bond,

$$\$4,710\,(1 + i)^5 = 6,535$$

where we have to solve for i.

$$(1 + i)^5 = \frac{6,535}{4,710} = 1.38$$

$$1 + i = \sqrt[5]{1.3874}$$

and $i = \sqrt[5]{1.3874} - 1 = 0.0677$ or

approximately 6.77%.

• **PROBLEM 29-23**

1

Monthly Savings Needed to Yield $1,000 (Interest Compounded Quarterly)

Time	4%	5%	6%	7%
5 years	$15.05	$14.70	$14.40	$13.95
10 years	$ 6.80	$ 6.45	$ 6.10	$ 5.80
15 years	$ 4.10	$ 3.75	$ 3.45	$ 3.15
20 years	$ 2.75	$ 2.45	$ 2.20	$ 1.95

2

No.	Amount Desired	Years	Annual Rate Interest	Monthly Savings Required
1	$2,000	5	5%	$________
2	$1,500	10	4%	$________
3	$3,000	5	6%	$________
4	$2,500	15	4%	$________

Use table 1 to complete table 2. Table 1 gives the amount of each monthly deposit needed to yield $1,000 at the end of n years where n varies from 5 to 20 years. For example, if you wanted to know how much to save each month to have 1,000 after 10 years, given an interest rate of 6%, the second row (n = 10) and third column(6%) give the amount $6.10.

<u>Solution:</u> 1. $2,000 in 5 years at 5% interest: Table 1 tells us that to have $1,000 in 5 years at 5% interest, we must make monthly deposits of $14.70. It follows that if we want $2,000 at the end of the five years we must deposit 2 × $14.70 = $29.40 each month.

2. $1,500 in 10 years at 4% interest: Find the monthly deposits that yield 1,000 in 10 years at 4% interest. The amount from table 1 is $6.80. One thousand dollars goes into $1,500,

$\frac{1500}{1000} = 1\frac{1}{2}$ times. The necessary monthly deposit is

$(1\frac{1}{2})(\$6.80) = \$10.20$

3. $3,000 in 5 years at 6% interest: Monthly payments of $14.40 yield 1,000 in 5 years at a rate of 6%. To have three times that much, make monthly deposits of 3($14.40) = $43.20.

4. \$2,500 in 15 years at 4% interest:
Monthly deposit for \$1,000 in 15 years at 4% is \$4.10. To yield 2½ times 1,000, i.e., 2,500 you need.

$$\left(2\ \frac{1}{2}\right)(\$4.10) = \$10.25 \text{ in monthly deposits.}$$

• PROBLEM 29-24

COMPOUND INTEREST
Amount on \$1 Compounded Annually

Periods	1%	1¼%	1½%	2%	2¼%	2½%	3%	3½%	4%	5%	5½%	6%
1	1.0100	1.0125	1.0150	1.0200	1.0225	1.0250	1.0300	1.0350	1.0400	1.0500	1.0550	1.0600
2	1.0201	1.0252	1.0302	1.0404	1.0455	1.0506	1.0609	1.0712	1.0816	1.1025	1.1130	1.1236
3	1.0303	1.0380	1.0457	1.0612	1.0690	1.0769	1.0927	1.1087	1.1249	1.1576	1.1742	1.1910
4	1.0406	1.0509	1.0614	1.0824	1.0931	1.1038	1.1255	1.1475	1.1699	1.2155	1.2388	1.2625
5	1.0510	1.0641	1.0773	1.1041	1.1177	1.1314	1.1593	1.1877	1.2167	1.2763	1.3070	1.3382
6	1.0615	1.0774	1.0934	1.1262	1.1428	1.1597	1.1941	1.2293	1.2653	1.3401	1.3788	1.4185
7	1.0721	1.0909	1.1098	1.1487	1.1685	1.1887	1.2299	1.2723	1.3159	1.4071	1.4547	1.5036
8	1.0829	1.1045	1.1265	1.1717	1.1948	1.2184	1.2668	1.3168	1.3686	1.4775	1.5347	1.5938
9	1.0937	1.1183	1.1434	1.1951	1.2217	1.2489	1.3048	1.3629	1.4233	1.5513	1.6191	1.6895
10	1.1046	1.1323	1.1605	1.2190	1.2492	1.2801	1.3439	1.4106	1.4802	1.6289	1.7081	1.7908
11	1.1157	1.1464	1.1779	1.2434	1.2773	1.3121	1.3842	1.4600	1.5395	1.7103	1.8021	1.8983
12	1.1268	1.1608	1.1956	1.2682	1.3060	1.3449	1.4258	1.5111	1.6010	1.7959	1.9012	2.0122
13	1.1381	1.1753	1.2136	1.2936	1.3354	1.3785	1.4685	1.5640	1.6651	1.8856	2.0058	2.1329
14	1.1495	1.1900	1.2318	1.3195	1.3655	1.4130	1.5126	1.6187	1.7317	1.9799	2.1161	2.2609
15	1.1610	1.2048	1.2502	1.3459	1.3962	1.4483	1.5580	1.6753	1.8009	2.0789	2.2325	2.3966
16	1.1726	1.2199	1.2690	1.3728	1.4276	1.4845	1.6047	1.7340	1.8730	2.1829	2.3553	2.5404
17	1.1843	1.2351	1.2880	1.4002	1.4597	1.5216	1.6528	1.7947	1.9479	2.2920	2.4848	2.6928
18	1.1961	1.2506	1.3063	1.4282	1.4926	1.5597	1.7024	1.8575	2.0258	2.4066	2.6215	2.8543
19	1.2081	1.2662	1.3270	1.4568	1.5262	1.5987	1.7535	1.9225	2.1068	2.5270	2.7656	3.0256
20	1.2202	1.2820	1.3469	1.4859	1.5605	1.6386	1.8061	1.9898	2.1911	2.6533	2.9178	3.2071
21	1.2324	1.2981	1.3671	1.5157	1.5956	1.6796	1.8603	2.0594	2.2788	2.7860	3.0782	3.3996
22	1.2447	1.3143	1.3876	1.5460	1.6315	1.7216	1.9161	2.1315	2.3699	2.9253	3.2475	3.6035
23	1.2572	1.3307	1.4084	1.5769	1.6682	1.7646	1.9736	2.2061	2.4647	3.0715	3.4262	3.8197
24	1.2697	1.3474	1.4295	1.6084	1.7085	1.8087	2.0328	2.2833	2.5633	3.2251	3.6146	4.0489
25	1.2824	1.3642	1.4509	1.6406	1.7441	1.8539	2.0938	2.3632	2.6658	3.3864	3.8134	4.2919

Using the compound interest table shown above, find the amount of money in a savings account at the end of x years if interest is compounded quarterly or semiannually at the rates shown below:

Deposit	Interest rate	Compounded	Period of deposit
1 \$3,600	4%	Semiannually	2 yrs.
2 \$4,000	5%	Quarterly	2½ yrs.
3 \$4,500	4½ %	Quarterly	3 yrs.

Solution: 1. \$3,600 at 4% compounded semiannually for 2 years means that \$3,600 is compounded at 2% over 2(2) = 4 periods. When it is said that the interest rate is i, this means specifically refers to the annual interest rate. Interest compounded semiannually means that the rate is

$\frac{i}{2}$ over two six-month periods.

Interest compounded quarterly means that there is a rate of

$\frac{i}{4}$ over four, three-month periods.

A rate of four percent annually is the same as

$\frac{4}{2} = 2\%$ semiannually.

A rate of four percent is the same as $\frac{4}{4} = 1\%$ over 4 periods (quarterly).

The factor corresponding to n=4 periods and i=2% is 1.0824. The amount after 2 years is

($3,600)(1.0824) = $3,896.64

2. An annual rate of 5% is the same as $\frac{5}{4} = 1\frac{1}{4}\%$ quarterly.
In 2½ years there are 4(2½) = 10 periods in which interest is compounded at a rate of 1¼ %; i.e., there are 10 three-month periods (quarters) in 2½ years.

The factor for n=10 periods and i=1¼ % is 1.1323. After 2½ years there will be

(1.1323)($4,000) = $4,529.20 in the account.

3. An annual rate of 4½ is equal to a quarterly rate of (4½ %) ÷ 4 = 1.125%.
In three years you have 4 × 3 = 12 quarters.

There is a problem in that there is no column for 1.125% ($1\frac{1}{8}\%$), but we can take the average of the factors corresponding to n=12, 1% and n=12, 1¼ %.

n = 12, 1% : 1.1268

n = 12, 1¼ % : 1.1608

Estimate of n = 12, $1\frac{1}{8}\%$: $\frac{1.1268 + 1.1608}{2} = 1.1438$.

The balance at the end of five years is

($4,500)(1.1438) = $5,147.10.

• PROBLEM 29-25

Mrs. Etelman plans a sinking fund for her daughter's education. She will make a series of equal annual payments from the first year of the fund up to the seventeenth. The fund will yield $2,000 at the beginning of the 18th, 19th, 20th and 21st year. If the rate of interest is 2%, what will be the annual payment made?

Solution: The series of equal payments 18, 19, 20, 21 years from now has to be converted to an equivalent present value for today.

The question is, "How much does the series of $2,000 payments represent in terms of present dollars?"

Look in the table of 2% compound interest factors under the present worth factor. The factor corresponding to n = 18 periods (which are years in this case) is 0.7002. A $2,000 payment 18 years from now at 2% is

($2,000)(0.7002) = $1,400.40.

Similarly, we find the present worth factors corresponding to years 19, 20, 21. They are 0.6864, 0.6730, and 0.6598. The present value of $2,000 paid each year is

19th year: ($2,000)(0.6864) = $1,372.80

20th year: ($2,000)(0.6730) = $1,346

21th year: ($2,000)(0.6598) = $1,319.60

Add all the present values to get a total present value of $5,438.80. This is the amount that has to be available by the end of the 17th year, in terms of present value. The future value of this amount must now be calculated. This is done by multiplying the single-payment compound amount factor corresponding to n = 17, in the 2% compound interest table by $5,438.80. The amount that has to be available at 2% interest in 17 years is

($5,438.80)(1.4002) = $7,615.40 or just

$7,615 to the nearest dollar.

The question is now, "What is the annual payment that has to be made at 2% interest to yield $7,615 in 17 years?"

The sinking fund factor corresponding to n = 17 is 0.04997. This is found under the uniform annual series payments section. The annual payment is

($7,615)(0.04997) = $380.52

Mrs. Etelman has to deposit this much annually for 17 years to obtain the series of $2,000 payments over a four year period beginning on the 18th year.

CHAPTER 30

LINEAR PROGRAMMING

MAXIMIZATION AND MINIMIZATION PROBLEMS

• PROBLEM 30-1

A man operates a pushcart. He sells hotdogs and sodas. His cart can support 200 lbs. A hotdog weighs 2 ounces a soda weighs 8 ounces. He knows from experience that he must have at least 60 sodas and at least 80 hotdogs. He also knows that for every two hotdogs he sells, he needs at least one soda. Given he makes 8¢ profit on a hotdog and 4¢ profit on a soda, find how many sodas and hotdogs he must have in order to maximize profits.

Solution: This is a linear programming problem. To solve we make a graph of hotdogs versus soda and find the point that gives the maximum profit.

The formula for profit is

$$\$.08 \cdot X + \$.04 \; Y = \text{profit},$$

where X is the number of hotdogs and Y is the number of sodas.

We maximize the profits under the following constraints:

(1) $\quad 1/2 \cdot Y + 1/8 \cdot X \le 200$

(2) $\quad Y \ge 60$

(3) $\quad X \ge 80$

(4) $\quad 2Y - X \ge 0$.

The meaning of the constraints is:

(1) a soda weighs 1/2 of a pound, and a hotdog weighs 1/8 of a pound and the maximum weight the cart can support is 200 pounds

(2) he must have at least 60 sodas

(3) he must have at least 80 hotdogs

(4) he must have at most twice as many hotdogs as sodas (or in other terms at least half as many sodas as hotdogs).

We now put the restraints into a graph, and by the theory of linear programming we know that the maximum profit can be found on a corner of the region determined by the constraints.

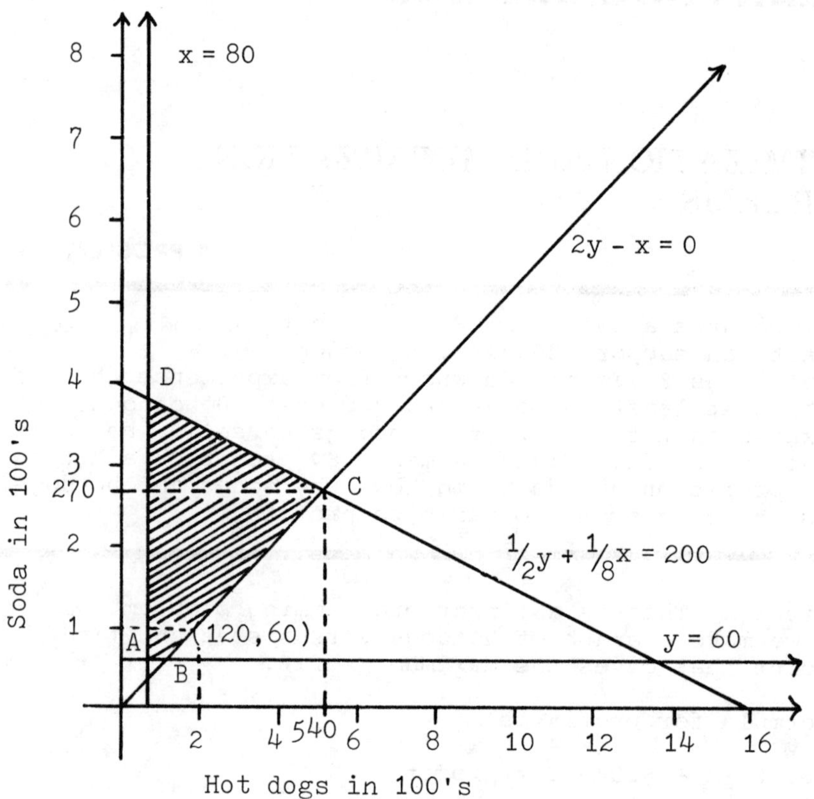

The shaded region on the above graph is the region which is determined by the constraints. The corners of the region are:

A)	X = 80	Y = 60
B)	X = 120	Y = 60
C)	X = 540	Y = 270
D)	X = 80	Y = 375 .

We can now find the maximum profit by substituting the points into the profit formula.

A) $\$.08 \cdot 80 + \$.04 \cdot 60 = \$\ 8.80$

B) $\$.08 \cdot 120 + \$.04 \cdot 60 = \$12.00$

C) $\$.08 \cdot 540 + \$.04 \cdot 270 = \$54.00$

D) $\$.08 \cdot 80 + \$.04 \cdot 375 = \$21.40$.

By inspection we see that maximum profit is obtained at point C. He will take 540 hotdogs and 270 sodas to make the maximum profit of $54.

• PROBLEM 30-2

A company makes desk organizers. The standard model requires 2 hours of the cutter's and one hour of the finisher's time. The deluxe model requires 1 hour of the cutter's time and 2 hours of the finisher's time. The cutter has 104 hours of time available for this work per month , while the finisher has 76 hours of time available for work. The standard model brings a profit of $6 per unit, while the deluxe one brings a profit of $11 per unit. The company, of course, wishes to make the most profit. Assuming they can sell whatever is made, how much of each model should be made in each month?

Solution: The company wishes to make the most profit within the given constraints. We graph the constraints and within the defined region we pick the point with the most profit. The profit is found by the formula:

$$\text{Profit} = \$6\,X + \$11\,Y$$

where X stands for the number of standard desk organizers and Y stands for the number of deluxe ones.

The constraints for this problem are:

(1) $X \geq 0$; we cannot have a negative number of standard units.

(2) $Y \geq 0$; we cannot have a negative number of deluxe units.

(3) The finisher has only 76 hours of time available. Since a standard model takes one hour of the finisher's time, and a deluxe model takes 2 hours of the finisher's time, we get the constraint

$$X + 2\,Y \leq 76.$$

(4) The cutter has only 104 hours of time available. A standard unit takes two hours of the cutter's time, and a deluxe unit takes one hour of the cutter's time, thus, we get the constraint

$$2\,X + Y \leq 104.$$

We can now graph these constraints to get the region in which we can choose our point of maximum profit.

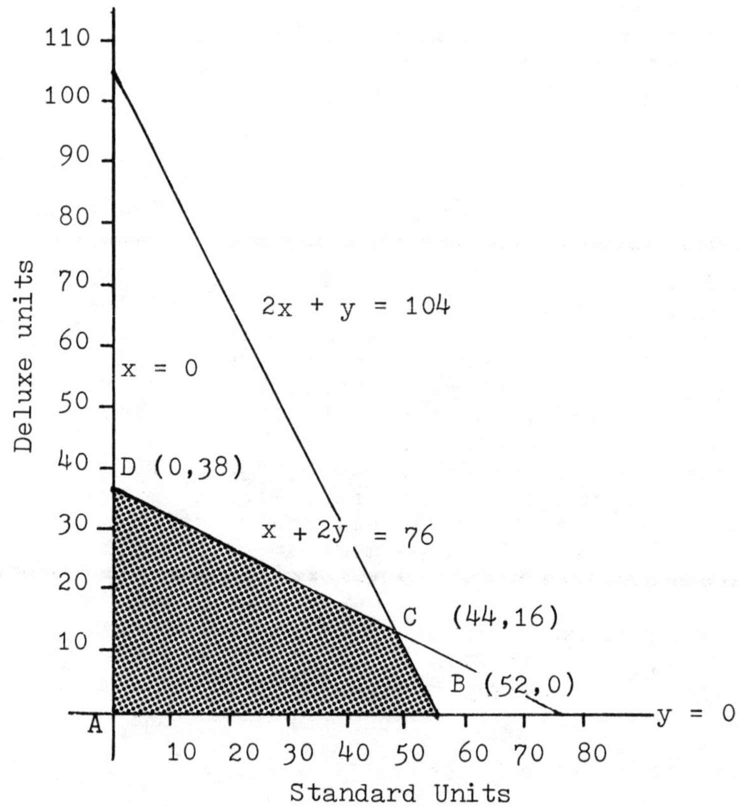

The shaded area of the graph is the area which conforms to the constraints. Within this region we must pick the point with the maximum profit. By a theorem of linear programming we know that the point of maximum profit occurs at a corner of the region. Thus, we need only check the corners and take the point with the most profit.

A)	(0,0)	Profit = \$6 (0)	+	\$11 (0)	= \$0
B)	(52,0)	Profit = \$6 (52)	+	\$11 (0)	= \$312
C)	(44,16)	Profit = \$6 (44)	+	\$11 (16)	= \$440
D)	(0,38)	Profit = \$6 (0)	+	\$11 (38)	= \$418

By observation, we note that the point with the largest profit is (44,16) (Point C). Thus, for the company to make the maximum profit of \$440, they must produce 44 standard units and 16 deluxe ones.

• PROBLEM 30-3

A company wishes to bottle 2 different drinks. It takes 2 hours to can one gross of drink A, and it takes 1 hour to label the cans. It takes 3 hours to bottle one gross of drink B, and it takes 4 hours to label the cans. The company makes $10 profit on one gross of drink A and $20 profit on one gross of drink B. Given that the bottling department has 20 hours available, and the labelling department has 15 hours available, find out how many gross of drink A and drink B must be packaged in order to maximize the profit.

Solution: The company wishes to use their time remaining for the most profit. To do this we graph the constraints and get the area of points one of which will yield, the maximum profit. If we let X be the number of gross of drink A and Y be the number of gross of drink B, then the profit can be found via the formula:

$$\text{Profit} = \$10 \cdot X + \$20 \cdot Y .$$

The constraints in the problem are:

(1) $X \geq 0$

(2) $Y \geq 0$.

These must be because you can have no negative number of gross of a drink.

(3) We have a constraint due to the canning department. Because each gross of drink A takes 2 hours to can and each gross of drink B takes 3 hours to can, we see that the number of hours is 2X + 3Y. But they only can work 20 hours or less, thus the constraint is

$$2X + 3Y \leq 20 .$$

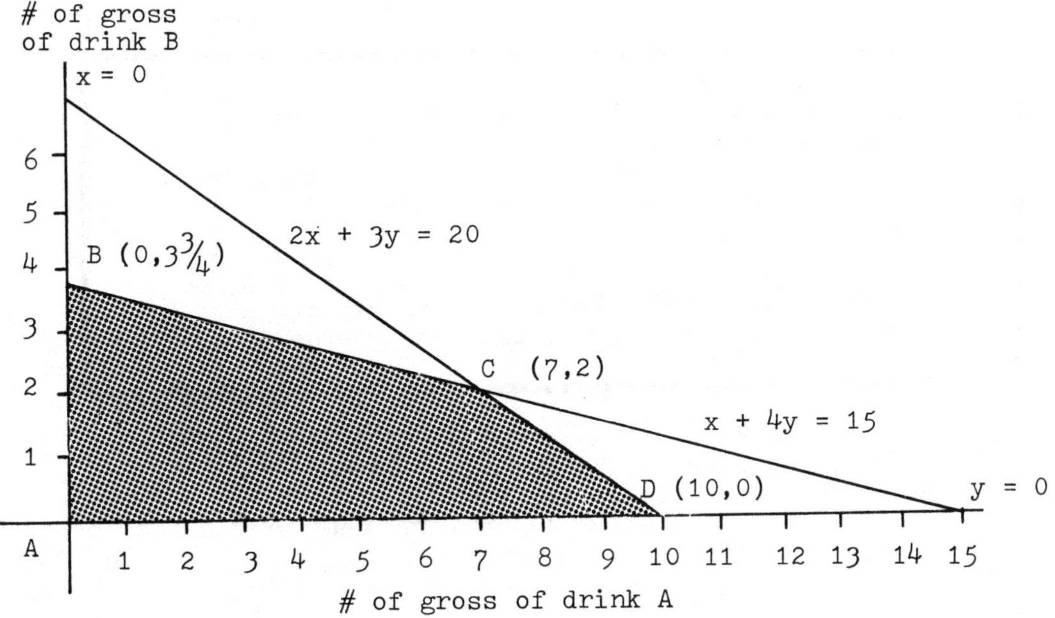

(4) We similarly have a constraint due to the labelling department. Since they have only 15 hours, and one gross of drink A takes 1 hour to label and one gross of drink B takes 4 hours to label, we get the constraint

$$X + 4Y \leq 15.$$

We now place these constraints on a graph, and the region defined by them is the region in which the number of gross of drinks A and B meet the constraints. We must then find the point in that region which yields the maximum profit.

In the graph, the shaded area is the region described by the four constraints. By a theorem of linear programming, the point of maximum profit must occur at a corner of the region. It is also true that the minimum profit will be found on a corner. This is understandable, since the corners represent the places with the most or least number of gross of drinks that are produced. Thus, to find the point with the maximum profit we need only check the four corner points and take the corner with the most profit.

A) (0,0) Profit = \$10(0) + \$20(0) = 0

B) (0,3 3/4) Profit = \$10(0) + \$20(3 3/4) = \$75

C) (7,2) Profit = \$10(7) + \$20(2) = \$110

D) (10,0) Profit = \$10(10) + \$20(0) = \$100

Thus, the point with the most profit is (7,2). The company must package 7 gross of drink A and 2 gross of drink B yielding a profit of \$110.

• PROBLEM 30-4

A publisher is printing a new book. This book may be either a hard cover book or a paperback. They get \$4 profit on each hard cover and \$3 profit on each paperback. It takes them 3 minutes to bind a hard covered book and 2 minutes to bind a paperback. The total available time for binding is 800 hours. By previous experience the publisher knows that he needs at least 10,000 hard covered editions and not more than 6,000 paperbacks. Find the number of paperbacks and hard covered editions that must be printed in order to yield the maximum profit.

Solution: We make a graph of the constraints, and from the region thus defined we take the point yielding the maximum profit. If we let X = number of hard covered books and Y = the number of paperbacks, the formula to find the profit is:

$$\text{Profit} = \$4X + \$3Y.$$

We wish to maximize the profits given the following constraints:

(1) The number of minutes to bind a hard cover book is 3 and the minutes to bind a paperback is 2; since the total number of minutes available is 48,000; (800 hours × 60 min./hr.); we have the constraint

$$3X + 2Y \leq 48,000 .$$

(2) The minimum number of hard covered editions is 10,000, thus we get the constraint

$$X \geq 10,000.$$

(3) The maximum number of paperbacks is 6,000 thus we get the constraint

$$Y \leq 6,000 .$$

(4) Obviously we have the constraint $Y \geq 0$ because you can't publish a negative number of books.

We can now draw the graph of these constraints, and the region defined by these constraints is the region

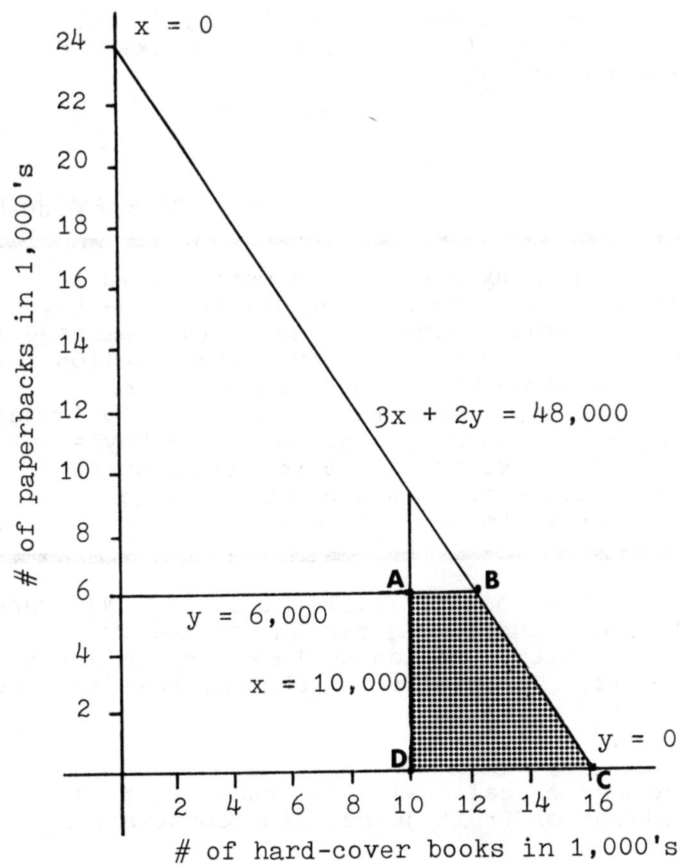

from which the publisher must choose a point in order to publish the books by his specifications. From this region we must find the point which yields the maximum profit.

The shaded region in the graph is the region in which the number of hard covered and paperback editions meet the specified constraints. From this region we need to find the point which yields the maximum profit. By a theorem of Linear Programming we know that the points which yield the maximum and minimum profits are on the corners of the region defined by the constraints. This seems likely because the corners represent the points in which the minimum and maximum number of books of each type are produced, meeting the constraints.

Thus we need only check which of the four corners yields the most profit, by applying the formula.

A) (10000, 6000) Profit = \$4 (10,000)+ \$3(6,000)= \$58,000

B) (12000, 6000) Profit = \$4 (12,000)+ \$3(6,000)= \$66,000

C) (16000, 0) Profit = \$4 (16,000)+ \$3(0) = \$64,000

D) (10000, 0) Profit = \$4 (10,000)+ \$3(0) = \$40,000

By inspection we can see that the maximum profit occurs at point B; the maximum profit of \$66,000 will be obtained if the company publishes 6,000 paperbacks and 12,000 hard covered editions.

• PROBLEM 30-5

A boy wants to open a drink stand. His mother said he cannot sell more than four gallons of drinks. The boy sells lemonade and a fruit juice. He sells the lemonade for \$2 a gallon and the fruit juice for \$1.50 a gallon. The lemonade uses 30 lemon slices per gallon and one pound of sugar per gallon. The fruit juice uses 10 lemon slices and two pounds of sugar per gallon. The boy's mother has only 90 lemon slices and 6 pounds of sugar. Find out how many gallons of each type of beverage the boy should make in order to make the most money.

Solution : To find the most profitable solution, we graph the boy's constraints, and find a region defined by these constraints. In this region we look for the point with the most profit. The profit is found by the formula:

$$\text{Profit} = \$2X + \$1.50Y$$

where X is the number of gallons of lemonade and Y is the number of gallons of fruit juice. The constraints are:

(1) $X \geq 0$ The boy either makes lemonade or not.

(2) $Y \geq 0$ The boy either makes fruit juice or not.

(3) The boy's mother only allows him to make 4 or less gallons. Thus we get the constraint

$$X + Y \leq 4.$$

(4) The lemonade takes 30 lemon slices, and the fruit juice takes 10 lemon slices per gallon. Since the boy's mother has only 90 lemon slices, we have the constraint

$$30X + 10Y = 90.$$

(5) The lemonade takes one pound of sugar, while the fruit juice takes two pounds of sugar per gallon. Thus, we have the constraint

$$X + 2Y \leq 6.$$

We now graph these constraints and find the "feasible region", i.e., the region where the constraints are met. Within this region we will look for the point yielding the maximum profit.

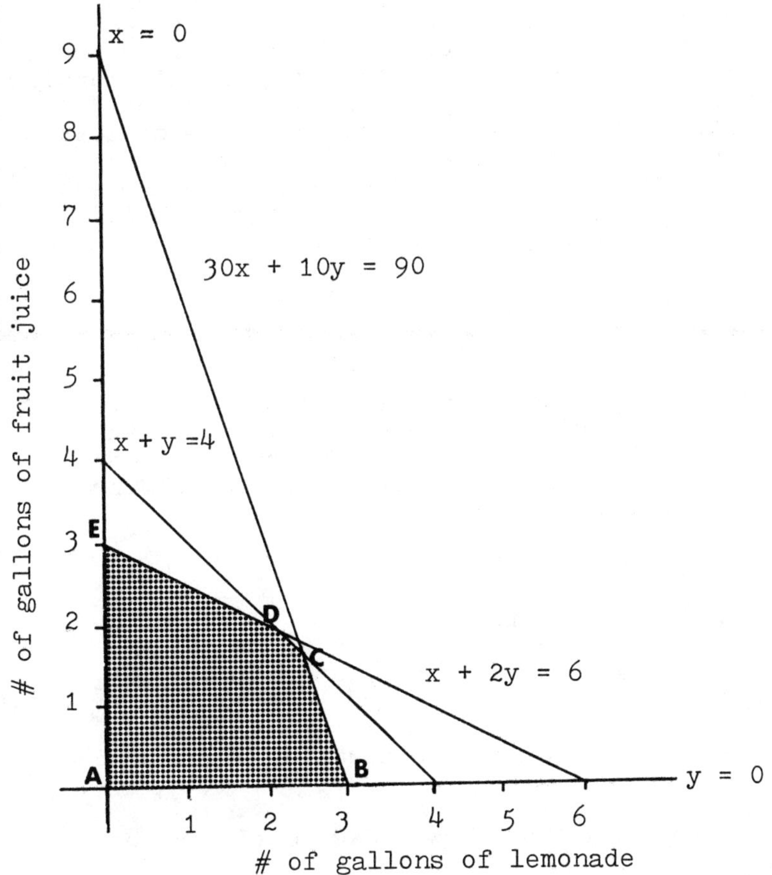

The shaded area on the graph is the "feasible region". To find the point with the maximum profit, we use a theorem of Linear Programming that states that the point of maximum profits is an interection of two of the constraint lines. Thus we need only apply the profit formula to each of the region's corners, and choose the one giving the most profit.

A) (0,0) Profit = \$2 (0) + \$1.50 (0) = \$0

B) (3,0) Profit = \$2 (3) + \$1.50 (0) = \$6.00

C) (2.5,1.5) Profit = \$2 (2.5) + \$1.50 (1.5) = \$7.25

D) (2,2) Profit = \$2 (2) + \$1.50 (2) = \$7.00

E) (0,3) Profit = \$2 (0) + \$1.50 (3) = \$4.50

We observe that the maximum profit of \$7.25 occurs when the boy makes, and sells, 2½ gallons of lemonade, and 1.5 gallons of fruit juice. (Point C on the graph).

• PROBLEM 30-6

A company produces two types of mopeds. The low speed moped is produced at their New Jersey plant which can only handle 1,000 mopeds per month. The high speed moped is produced at their Maryland plant which can only handle 850 mopeds per month. The company has a sufficient supply of parts to build 1,175 low speed mopeds or 1,880 high speed mopeds. They also have sufficient labor to build 1,800 low speed mopeds or 1,080 high speed mopeds. A low speed moped yields \$100 profit while a high speed moped yields \$125 profit. Find what combination of high and low speed mopeds should be produced in order to achieve the maximum profit for one month.

Solution: We take the constraints, and we graph them, thus defining a region in which they are satisfied. From this region we then choose the point which yields the maximum profits. If we let Y = the low speed mopeds and X = the high speed mopeds, the profit can be found by applying the following formula:

$$\text{Profit} = \$100Y + \$125X .$$

We now will find the constraints.

(1) $Y \geq 0$ because you can't have negative low speed mopeds.

(2) $X \geq 0$ because you can't have negative high speed mopeds.

(3) $Y \leq 1{,}000$ for only 1,000 low speed mopeds can be accommodated.

(4) $X \leq 850$ for the plants can only accommodate 850 high speed mopeds.

(5) They have sufficient parts for 1,175 low speed mopeds, or for 1,880 high speed mopeds. Thus if we add together the ratios of the number of high and low speed mopeds produced divided by their maximum number that can be produced, the result must be not greater than 1 (because if it were greater than 1, we would be using more parts than we have ---1 = 100%)
Thus we have the constraint

$$\frac{Y}{1,175} + \frac{X}{1,880} \leq 1 \; .$$

(6) Similarly, since we have labor sufficient for either 1,800 low speed moped or 1,080 high speed mopeds, we have the constraint

$$\frac{Y}{1,800} + \frac{X}{1,080} \leq 1 \; .$$

We now graph these constraints to find the region defined by them.

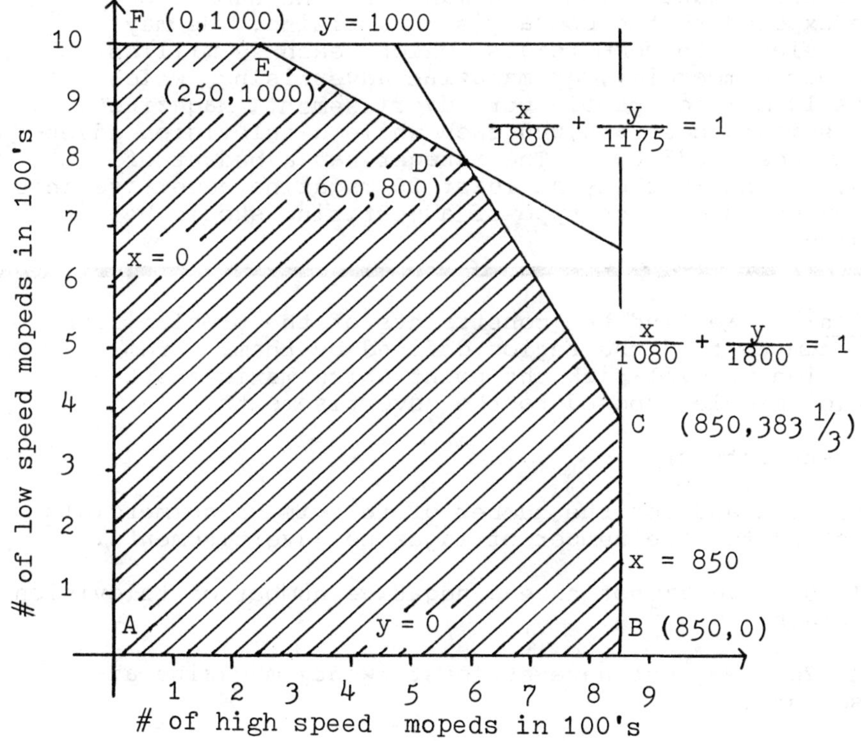

The shaded area of the graph is the area which conforms with the constraints. We now wish to find the point in this region which gives the maximum profit. By a theorem of Linear Programming, the maximum profit will occur at a corner of the region. Thus we need only check each corner and find which one yields the maximum profit.

A) (0,0) Profit = \$125(0) + \$100(0) = \$0.00

B) (850,0) Profit = \$125(850)+\$100(0) = \$106,250.00

C) (850,383 1/3) Profit = \$125(850)+\$100($383\frac{1}{3}$)= \$144,583.33

D) (600,800) Profit = \$125(600)+\$100(800) = \$155,000.00

E) (280,1000) Profit = \$125(280)+\$100(1,000)=\$135,000.00

F) (0,1000) Profit = \$125(0) +\$100(1,000)=\$100,000.00

Thus, the maximum profit, following the constraints, is \$155,000 which is attained at point D on the graph. In order to achieve the maximum profit of \$155,000, the company must produce 800 low speed mopeds and 600 high speed mopeds.

• PROBLEM 30-7

A marketing manager wishes to maximize the number of people exposed to the company's advertising. He may choose television commercials, which reach 20 million people per commercial, or magazine advertising, which reaches 10 million people per advertisement. Magazine advertisements cost \$40,000 each while a television advertisement costs \$75,000. The manager has a budget of \$2,000,000 and must buy at least 20 magazine advertisements. How many units of each type of advertising should be purchased?

Solution: We find the constraints of the problem, and graph them to find the region defined by them. From this region we will pick the point which maximizes the number of people exposed to the advertisements.

The constraints are:

Let T stand for the number of television commercials and M stand for the number of magazine advertisements.

(1) $T \geq 0$ We cannot have a negative number of television commercials

(2) $M \geq 20$ We must have at least twenty magazine advertisements.

(3) This constraint comes from the costs. In thousands the cost of a television commercial is \$75 and the cost of a magazine advertisement is \$40. He is budgeted to \$2,000,000 so we get the constraint

$$40M + 75T \leq 2,000.$$

We now graph these constraints to find the region which is defined by them.

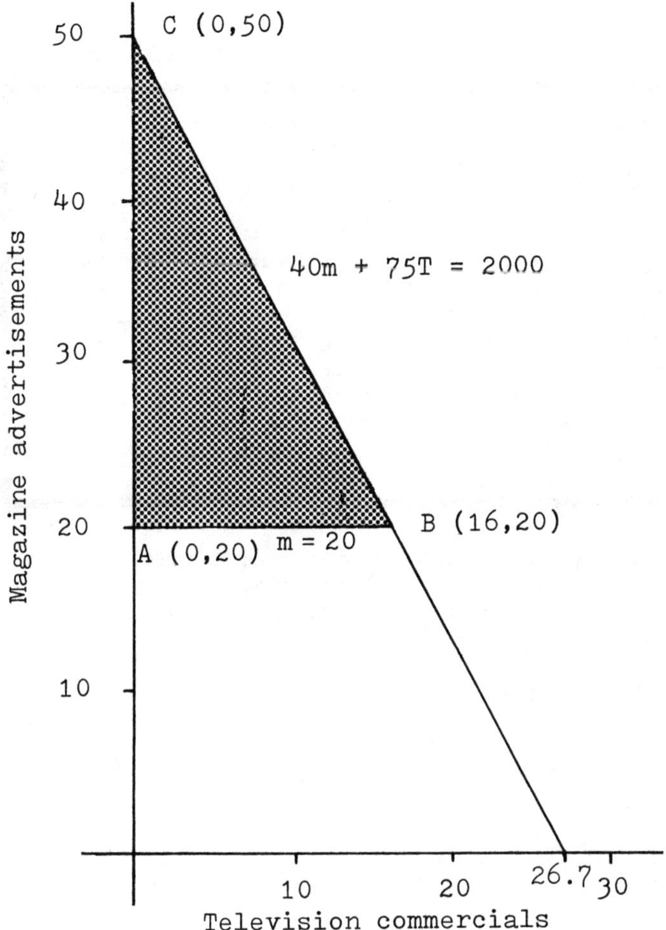

The shaded area is the region which is defined by the constraints. To find the point which yields the highest number of people exposed to the advertisement can be found by a theorem of linear programming which states that the point must be one of the corners of the region.

A) (0,20) number of people = 20 million × T + 10 million × M = 20 million × 0 + 10 million × 20 = 200 million.

B) (16,20) number of people = 20 million × 16 + 10 million × 20 = 520 million.

C) (0,50) number of people = 20 million × 0 + 10 million × 50

$$= 500 \text{ million.}$$

Thus, the best thing for the manager to do is have 16 television commercials and 20 magazine advertisements.

• PROBLEM 30-8

The Marvel Toy Company wishes to make three models of boats for the most profit. They found that a model of a steamship takes the cutter one hour, the painter 2 hours, and the assembler 4 hours of work. It produces $6 of profit. Their model of a four-mast sailboat takes the cutter 3 hours, the painter 3 hours, and the assembler 2 hours. It produces $3 of profit. Their model of a two-mast sailboat takes the cutter one hour, the painter three hours, and the assembler one hour. It produces $2 of profit. The cutter is only available for 45 hours, the painter for 50 hours, and the assembler for 60 hours. Assuming that they can sell all the models that are built, find the constraints of the problem and describe how you would obtain the solution,

Solution: To find the constraints for this problem, let X be the number of models of steamships, Y be the number of models of four-mast sailboats, Z be the number of two-mast sailboats. The constraints are:

(1) $X \geq 0$ We cannot have a negative number of models of steamships.

(2) $Y \geq 0$ We cannot have a negative number of models of four-mast sailboats.

(3) $Z \geq 0$ We cannot have a negative number of models of two-mast sailboats.

(4) A steamship takes one hour of the cutter's time, a four-mast sailboat takes three hours of the cutter's time, and a two-mast sailboat takes one hour of the cutter's time. Since the cutter has only 45 hours available we get the constraint

$$X + 3Y + Z \leq 45.$$

(5) A steamship takes two hours of the painter's time, a four-mast sailboat takes three hours of the painter's time, and a two-mast sailboat takes three hours of the painter's time. Since the painter has only 50 hours of time available, we get the constraint

$$2X + 3Y + 3Z \leq 50.$$

(6) A steamship takes four hours of the assembler's time, a four-mast sailboat takes 2 hours of the assembler's

time, and a two-mast sailboat takes one hour of the assembler's time. Since the assembler can work only 60 hours, we get the constraint

$$4X + 2Y + Z \leq 60.$$

Since there are three unknowns, we would require a three dimensional graph to plot the constraints. However, we know from a theorem of Linear Programming that the point of maximum profit lies on the intersection of three lines of constraints (the same number of constraints as the number of unknowns). Thus, to solve this we break up the six constraints into all groups of three that are possible. We then solve each group of three equations for the three unknowns. We now have a group of points. We take from that group of points those that meet the conditions set by all of the constraints. We then take from that new group the point which yields the most profit. That point is the solution to our problem. To find which point yields the most profit, we use the following equation for the profit:

$$\text{Profit} = \$6X + \$3Y + \$2Z.$$

After following the above procedure we find that, in order to make the most profit, the company should produce 13 steamships, no four-mast sailboats, and 8 two-mast sailboats. This will yield a profit of $94.

• PROBLEM 30-9

A commercial dairy farmer is interested in feeding his cattle at minimum cost, subject to meeting some constraints. The cattle are fed two feeds: oats and NK-34, a commercial preparation. The constraints are that each cow must get at least 400 grams per day of protein, at least 800 grams per day of carbohydrates, and no more than 100 grams per day of fat. Oats contains 10 percent protein, 80 percent carbohydrates, and 10 percent fat. NK-34 contains 40 percent protein, 60 percent carbohydrates, and no fat. Oats cost $0.20 per 1000 grams, and NK-34 cost $0.50 per 1000 grams.

a. Write a linear programming formulation to solve for the optimal amounts of each type of feed.

b. Solve the problem graphically.

c. Check your solution by finding the three corner points of interest and evaluating the objective function.

Solution: If we let X stand for the amount of oats (in 1000 gram units), and Y stand for the amount of NK-34 (in 1000 gram units), then we wish to minimize the cost function

$\$.20X + \$.50Y.$

The constraints are the following:

(1) $X \geq 0$ you either buy oats or you don't.

(2) $Y \geq 0$ you either buy NK-34 or you don't.

(3) $.1X \leq .1$ This is because there is 10% fat in oats, and they must have not more than 100 grams (.1 × 1000) of fat.

(4) Oats are 80% carbohydrates, NK-34 is 60% carbohydrates, and they need at least 800 grams (80% of 1,000 grams), thus we have the constraint

$$.8X + .6Y \geq .8 \quad .$$

(5) Oats are 10% protein and NK-34 has 40% protein. The cattle require at least 400 grams (40% of 1,000) of protein, giving us the constraint

$$.1X + .4Y \geq .4 \; .$$

We now graph these constraints to find the region described by them.

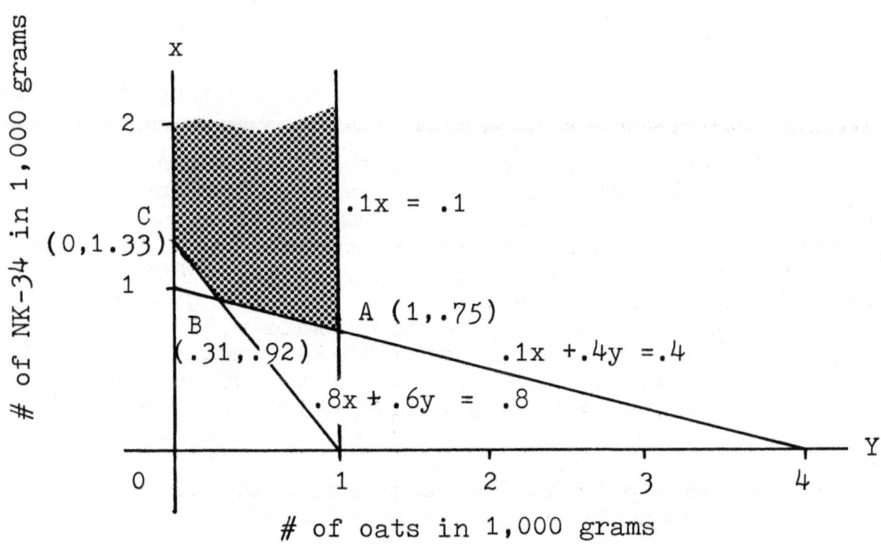

The shaded area in the graph is the region defined by the constraints. The point of minimum cost is known by the theory of linear programming to lie on a corner of the region. Thus, we need only check the corners to find the one with the least cost.

A) (1,.75) Cost = $.20(1) + $.50(.75) = $.575

B) (.31,.92) Cost = \$.20(.31)+\$.50(.92) = \$.522

C) (0,1.33) Cost = \$.20(0) +\$.50(1.33)= \$.67

Thus, the cheapest is point B, .31 kilograms of oats and .92 kilograms of NK-34

• PROBLEM 30-10

A businessman needs 5 cabinets, 12 desks, and 18 shelves cleaned out. He has two part time employees Sue and Janet. Sue can clean one cabinet, three desks and three shelves in one day, while Janet can clean one cabinet, two desks and 6 shelves in one day. Sue is paid \$25 a day, and Janet is paid \$22 a day. In order to minimize the cost how many days should Sue and Janet be employed?

Solution: The businessman wishes to minimize the cost of cleaning out the office. To do this we must graph the constraints, and take the point which gives the minimum cost. To find the cost we use the formula

$$\text{Cost} = \$25\,X + \$22\,Y,$$

where X is the number of days Sue is employed and Y is the number of days Janet is employed. We now will find the constraints.

(1) Since Sue can do a cabinet in one day, and Janet can do a cabinet in one day, and we must have at least 5 cabinets cleaned, we get the constraint

$$X + Y \geq 5.$$

(2) Since Sue can do 3 desks in one day, and Janet can do 2 desks in one day, and we require 12 desks to be cleaned, we have the constraint

$$3X + 2Y \geq 12.$$

(3) Similarly the constraint $3X + 6Y \geq 18$ comes from Sue being able to clean 3 shelves and Janet being able to clean 6 shelves in one day.

(4) $X \geq 0$ Sue cannot work a negative number of days

(5) $Y \geq 0$ Janet cannot work a negative number of days.

We now graph the constraints to find the region described by them.

The shaded area is the region described by the constraints. Note that this is an infinite region, because they can work more days than is needed. To

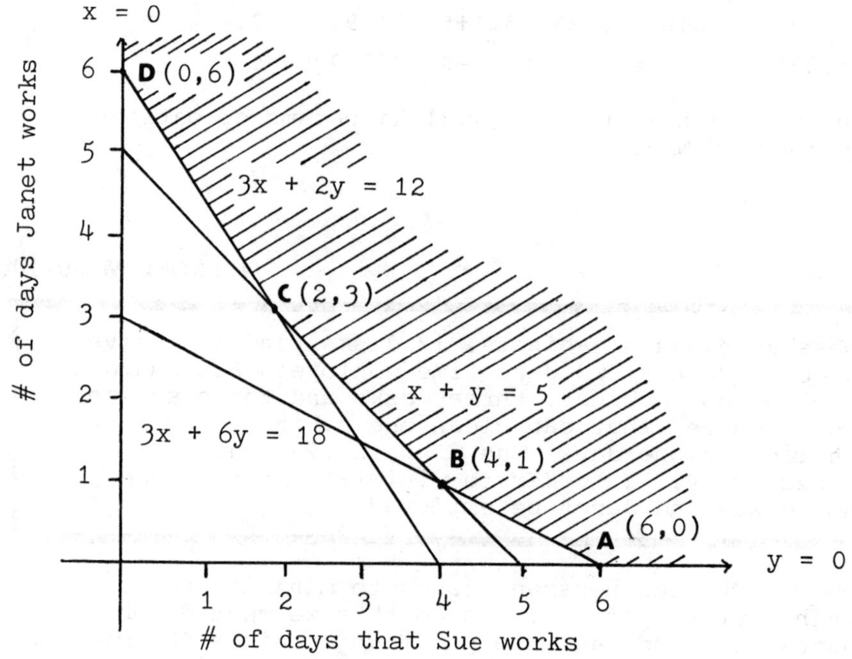

find the minimum point, we refer to a theorem of linear programming which states that a minimum cost must occur in one of the corners. Thus, we need only check which of the four corners has the smallest cost, and we will have the answer.

A)	(6,0)	\$25 (6)	+	\$22 (0)	=	\$150
B)	(4,1)	\$25 (4)	+	\$22 (1)	=	\$122
C)	(2,3)	\$25 (2)	+	\$22 (3)	=	\$116
D)	(0,6)	\$25 (0)	+	\$22 (6)	=	\$132

We can now see that the minimum cost is, with Janet working 3 days and Sue working 2 days, equal to \$116. (Point C on the graph.)

• PROBLEM 30-11

An office is willing to hire up to ten temporary employees to help them with their mail. They have found that a male employee can handle 300 letters and 80 packages per day, and a female employee can handle 400 letters and 50 packages in one day. They expect to have no less than 3,400 letters and no less than 680 packages in a day. A male employee receives \$25 and a female employee receives \$22 per day. How many male and female helpers should they hire to keep the payroll at a minimum?

Solution: The office wishes to minimize their expenses while meeting their constraints. To do this we graph the constraints, and we choose the point with the minimum cost from the region described by them. The cost is found by the formula

$$\$25X + \$22Y = \text{Cost},$$

where X is the number of male employees, and Y is the number of female employees. The constraints are the following:

(1) $X \geq 0$ You cannot have a negative number of male employees.

(2) $Y \geq 0$ You cannot have a negative number of female employees.

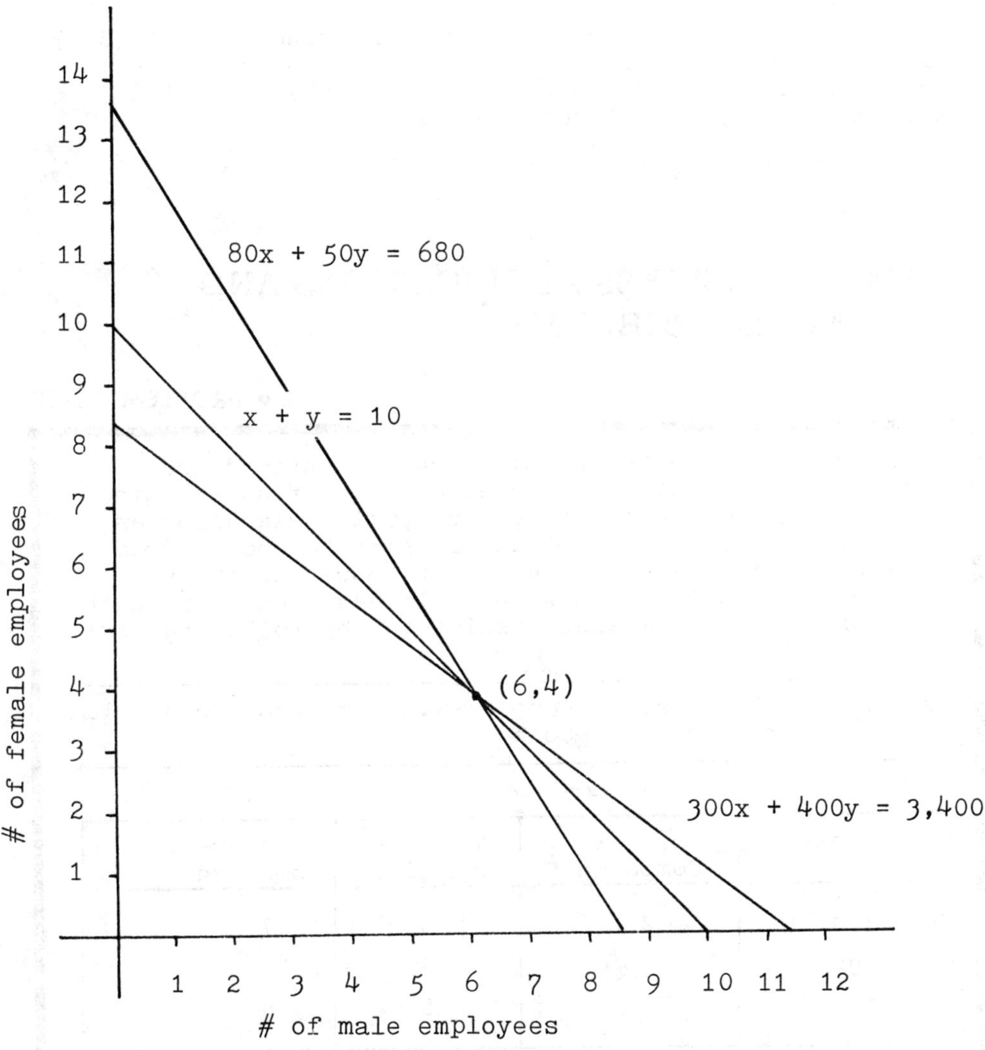

(3) Since the office will only hire up to ten temporary employees we get the constraint

$$X + Y \leq 10.$$

(4) A male employee can handle 300 letters a day, and a female employee can handle 400 letters a day. Since they expect at least 3,400 letters, we have the constraint

$$300X + 400Y \geq 3,400 .$$

(5) A male employee can handle 80 packages a day, and a female employee can handle 50 packages in one day. Since they expect at least 680 packages we have the constraint

$$80X + 50Y \geq 680.$$

We now graph these constraints to find the region which is defined by them. From this region we choose the point with the least cost.

The region in this problem is only the single point (6,4). All other points fail to meet at least one of the constraints. Thus the minimum cost is the cost of 6 male and 4 female employees, being

$$\$25(6) + \$22(4) = \$238.$$

GAMES, BUSINESS APPLICATIONS AND ADVANCED PROBLEMS

• PROBLEM 30-12

A new soda company, Super-Cola, recently entered the market. This company has three choices of advertising campaigns. Their major competitor, Cola-Cola, also has three counter campaigns of advertising to choose from in order to minimize the number of people switching from their soda to the new one. It has been found that their choices of campaign results in the following pay-off matrix:

Number, in 10,000's, of people switching from Cola-Cola to Super-Cola.			
	Cola-Cola		
Super-Cola	Counter-Compaign 1	Counter-Compaign 2	Counter-Compaign 3
Campaign 1	2	3	7
Campaign 2	1	4	6
Campaign 3	9	5	8

Find the best strategies for Super-Cola and Cola-Cola.

Solution: Each company wishes the strategy that is best for them. Super-Cola wishes to get the maximum amount of people from Cola-Cola, and Cola-Cola wishes to minimize their losses to Super-Cola. To do this, we use the minimax procedure. Super-Cola realizes that Cola-Cola will always look for the minimum losses, thus Super-Cola considers the minimum of what will happen for each choice of campaign. Super-Cola notices that the minimum gain for campaign 1 is 20,000 people, the minimum gain for campaign 2 is 10,000 people, but the minimum gain for campaign 3 is 50,000 people. Thus, Super-Cola will choose campaign 3 - the maximum of the minimums. Similarly Cola-Cola realizes that Super-Cola will want to choose the maximum for each of Cola-Cola's counter-campaigns. Thus;Cola-Cola only looks at the maximums. For counter-campaign 1 the maximum loss is 90,000 people, for counter-campaign 2 the maximum loss is 50,000 people, and for counter-campaign 3 the maximum loss is 80,000 people. Thus, Cola-Cola will choose counter-campaign 2 which is the minimum of the maximums. In this way they will minimize the losses. The point on the payoff matrix which they both choose is called the "saddle point". At this point neither company will change it's strategy for they are doing the best that they can. This type of a "game" is called a two-player zero-sum game, because whatever one player wins, the other player loses. Thus,the algebraic sum of the two is zero. Another way of looking at this problem is "pure-strategy". Super-Cola will look at the matrix and note that campaign 3 contains the largest numbers in each column. Thus, campaign 3 is the best choice regardless of which counter-campaign Cola-Cola chooses. Cola-Cola will notice this also. They will choose counter-campaign 2,for that one contains the minimum of all their choices, given Super-Cola will choose campaign 3.

• PROBLEM 30-13

Two land agents are interested in purchasing land for their competing companies. Company A has three options on how to buy its land, and Company B has four options on how to buy its land. They found that depending on how each company chooses the way they purchase their land, they will take some of the other company's business. They found the amounts to be as in the following payoff matrix.

Percent of business going from Company B to Company A (Note: A negative percent goes from Company A to Company B).

Company B options					
		B_1	B_2	B_3	B_4
Company A options	A_1	-2	3	-3	2
	A_2	-1	-3	-5	12
	A_3	9	5	8	10

Find the best strategy for the two companies.

Solution: Each land agent realizes that the other land agent will choose the best strategy for his company. Company A will want the highest number it can get from the matrix, while company B will try to get the smallest number from the matrix (recall that a negative number means that percent goes to company B). Since each land agent will not underestimate their opponent, they will assume that their opponent will make the best choices. Using "pure strategy", the agent for Company B will never choose plan B_4, because independent of Company A's choice, B_1's entries are smaller than B_4's.

Similarly, Company A will never choose plan A_1, because independent of Company B's choice, A_3 has larger entries than A_1. Thus, in reality the matrix is reduced to:

	B_1	B_2	B_3
A_2	-1	-3	-5
A_3	9	5	8

By looking at the above matrix, Company A will surely choose plan A_3 because independent of Company B's choice, the entries in A_3 are larger than those in A_2. Noting that, Company B will choose plan B_2 which is the minimum of the choices left to it. Thus, Company A will take 5% of Company B's business. This point (A_3, B_2) is called the "saddle-point". It is the point where both companies must operate, otherwise they will lose more in the long run, for the other company will choose a better strategy. This type of "game" is called a two person zero-sum game, because whatever one "person" loses the other "person" gains. Thus, if we add the gains and losses, we get zero. Another way of determining the best move is called the "minimax" procedure. In this procedure, Company A's agent realizes that Company B will always pick the minimum number, thus they will look at the minimum of each choice. The minimum for choice A_1 is -3, the minimum for choice A_2 is -5, and the minimum for choice A_3 is 5. Now Company A will choose plan A_3 which is the maximum of the minimums, guaranteeing a gain of at least 5% of Company B's business. Similarly, Company B realizes that Company A will take the maximum of their choice. Thus, they will consider only the maximum for each plan. If they choose plan B_1 the maximum is 9, B_2 the maximum is 5, B_3 the maximum is 8, B_4 the maximum is 12. Thus, they will choose the minimum of those maximums, namely B_2 and only lose 5% of their business. Note that either procedure will result in the same play for each agent.

• PROBLEM 30-14

Country A is a member of OPEC, the cartel which fixes the price of oil. Country A's economists realized that if they cheat on the cartel, they could make more money. Meanwhile the head of OPEC was warned by his informants that country A has intentions of cheating. OPEC now wishes to lower their prices to induce country A not to cheat, but they still wish to make an exorbitant profit. It has been found that the following payoff matrix comes about as a result of their choices.

Profit to Country A (in billions of dollars) Country A			
OPEC price per barrel	cheats slightly	cheats moderately	cheats heavily
$20	4	15	35
$15	5	10	12
$13	4	5	-5

Find the best strategy, for OPEC and for Country A.

Solution: Country A wants to make the most profit that they can. OPEC on the other hand wants to minimize Country A's profits in order to increase their own. Country A realizes that OPEC wants to minimize Country A's profits; when they consider their plan of action they look at the minimum amounts for each choice. The minimum for cheating a little is $4 billion, for cheating moderately it is $5 billion, and a $5 billion loss for cheating heavily. Therefore, Country A chooses the maximum of the minimums, so they will cheat moderately. OPEC meanwhile knows that Country A wants the maximum amount, so they will look at the maximum amounts for each of their choices. For a $20 price the maximum profit to Country A is $35 billion, for a $15 price it is $12 billion, and for a $13 price it is $5 billion.

Thus, OPEC will choose the minimum of the maximums, namely they will have a \$13 per barrel price so that Country A will get a \$5 billion profit. This point is called the "saddle point". Both OPEC and Country A have an interest in remaining at this point.

• PROBLEM 30-15

Two competing ice cream chains,Kool Ice and Ice Kold, want to hold ice cream sales in order to capture some extra business from each other.

They each have the option of having a sale either on their most popular flavors or on all their ice cream. They found the following payoff matrix to show which way the business is turning for each of their choices.

Number of customers of Kool Ice switching to Ice Kold (in hundreds of people). Note that a negative number means they are switching from Ice Kold to Kool Ice.

	Kool Ice	
Ice Kold	Sale on All	Sale on Popular
Sale on All	4	-3
Sale on Popular	-3	2

Find the best strategy for each of them.

Solution: Kool Ice wants to sell to the most people, thus they want the smallest number (negative means consumers switching to Kool Ice). Ice Kold also wants the most people, thus they want the largest number. If we use the minimax procedure, we will end up with two different points. Kool Ice will want -3 and Ice Kold will want 2. Thus, there is no saddle point in this problem. The best strategy to get the best results is to choose one approach with a certain probability. Assuming Ice Kold has a sale on all the ice cream with probability p, then it has a sale on the popular ice cream with probability 1-p. To find p, we find the expected values of the two columns. Expected value is the value of the box times it s probability, summed up. So we now have

		C_1	C_2
Ice Kold	p	4	-3
	1 - p	-3	2

Thus, the expected value of column C_1 is

$$4p + (-3)(1-p) = 7p - 3.$$

The expected value against a sale of popular flavors by Kool Ice is

$$(\text{Column } C_2)\quad (-3)\,p + 2\,(1-p) = -5p + 2.$$

To solve for p we set the two equations equal to each other:

$$7p - 3 = -5p + 2 \quad \text{or} \quad 12p - 3 = 2 \quad \text{or}$$

$$12p = 5 \quad \text{or } p = 5/12$$

The reason we do this is that we want the same result to occur independently of the other company's choice. Hence we set the expected values of each column equal to each other. Therefore, Ice Kold should have a sale on their most popular ice cream 7/12 of the time and a sale on all of their ice cream 5/12 of the time. This gives an expected value of

$$-5\,(5/12) + 2 = -1/12,$$

or Kool Ice acquires an expected 8 people ($1/12 \times 100$) of Ice Kold's clientele. Similarly, the probabilities for Ice Kold are the same. So they should have a sale on all of their ice cream 5/12 of the time and the rest of the time a sale on their popular ice cream. This also yields an expected loss of 8 people to Kool Ice.

• PROBLEM 30-16

The Brown Company has two warehouses and three retail outlets. Warehouse number one (which will be denoted by W_1) has a capacity of 12 units; warehouse number two (W_2) holds 8 units. These warehouses must ship the product to the three outlets, denoted by O_1, O_2, and O_3. O_1 requires 8 units. O_2 requires 7 units, and O_3 requires 5 units. Thus, there is a total storage capacity of 20 units, and also a demand for 20 units. The question is, which warehouse should ship how many units to which outlet? (The objective being, of course, to accomplish this at the least possible cost.)

Costs of shipping from either warehouse to any of the outlets are known and are summarized in the following table, which also sets forth the warehouse capacities and the needs of the retail outlets:

	O_1	O_2	O_3	Capacity
W_1	$3.00	$5.00	$3.00	12
W_2	2.00	7.00	1.00	8
Needs (units)	8	7	5	

Solution: This seems to be a linear programming problem with three variables. However, the third variable can be computed from the previous two. Let X be the number of units sent from warehouse 1 to outlet 1. Since outlet 1 requires only 8 units, we have the constraint $X \leq 8$. Obviously $X \geq 0$ means youeither ship one or you don't. Let y be the number of units shipped from warehouse 1 to outlet 2. Similarly,

$$0 \leq y \leq 7$$

is another constraint. Because there are 12 units in warehouse 1, the number of units sent to outlet 3 is

$$12 - X - y.$$

Obviously, this must be larger or equal to zero. Thus,

$$12 - X - y \geq 0 \quad \text{or} \quad X + y \leq 12$$

is a constraint.

The amount of units sent from warehouse 2 to outlet 1 is the original eight less the X that was sent from warehouse 1, or 8 - X. Similarly we find all of the others.

	O_1	O_2	O_3
W_1	x	y	12 - x - y
W_2	8 - x	7 - y	x + y - 7

Note that the quantities shipped from both warehouses to Outlet 3 have been determined by simply subtracting the quantities shipped to Outlets 1 and 2 from the total capacities of the warehouses.

So we have the following constraints:

(1) $X \geq 0$

(2) $y \geq 0$

(3) $X \leq 8$

(4) $y \leq 7$

(5) $X+y \leq 12$

(6) $X+y \geq 7$ (from $O_3-W_2 \geq 0$) .

We wish to minimize the cost function. It can be found by multiplying the number of units sent by their costs. We get

$$\text{Cost} = 3X + 5y + 3(12-X-y) + 2(8-X) + 7(7-y) + 1(X+y-7) = 94 - X - 4y.$$

To minimize this we plot the constraints to find the region that is defined by them.

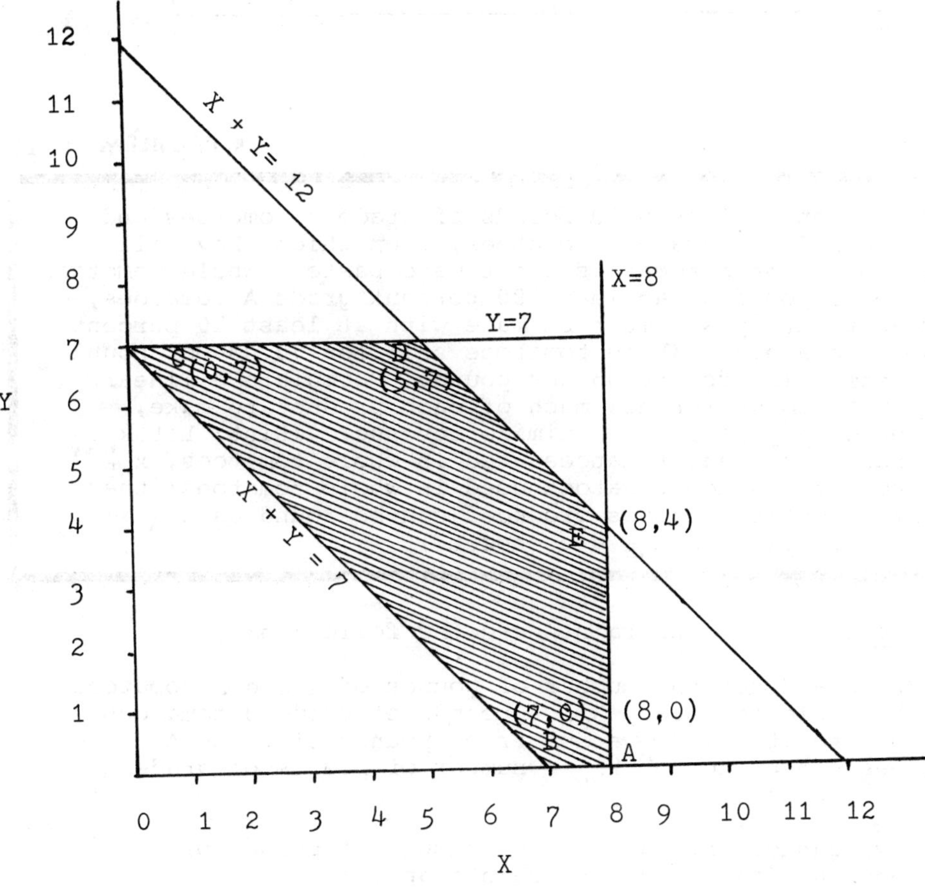

The shaded region is the area that is defined by the constraints. By linear programming we know the minimum cost will appear at a corner of this region. We need only check these corners to pick the best point.

A	(8,0)	$94 - 8 = \$86$
B	(7,0)	$94 - 7 = \$87$
C	(0,7)	$94 - 0 - (4 \times 7) = \$66$

D	(5,7)	$94 - 5 - (4 \times 7) = \$61$
E	(8,4)	$94 - 8 - (4 \times 4) = \$70$

Thus the point with the least cost is point D. So for the lowest cost the shipping schedule should be

	O_1	O_2	O_3	
W_1	5	7	0	12
W_2	3	0	5	8
	8	7	5	

• PROBLEM 30-17

A tomato cannery has 5000 pounds of grade A tomatoes and 10,000 pounds of grade B tomatoes, from which they will make whole canned tomatoes and tomato paste. Whole tomatoes must be composed of at least 80 percent grade A tomatoes, whereas tomato paste must be made with at least 10 percent grade A tomatoes. Whole tomatoes sell for \$0.08 per pound and paste sells for \$0.05 per pound. Formulate a linear program to solve for how much of each product to make, if the company wants to maximize revenue. (Hint: Let x_{WA} = pounds of A grade tomatoes used in whole tomatoes, x_{WB} = pounds of B grade tomatoes used in whole tomatoes; the amount of whole tomatoes produced can be found as $x_{WA} + x_{WB}$ after x_{WA} and x_{WB} are chosen.)

Solution: The constraints are the following:

Let X_{WA} stand for the number of pounds of grade A tomatoes used in whole tomatoes, X_{WB} = pounds of grade B tomatoes in whole tomatoes, X_{PA} = number of pounds of grade A tomatoes in paste, X_{PB} = number of pounds of grade B tomatoes in paste.

Since we cannot have a negative number of pounds of tomatoes the following constraints apply:

(1) $X_{WA} \geq 0$

(2) $X_{WB} \geq 0$

(3) $X_{PA} \geq 0$

(4) $X_{PB} \geq 0$.

Since there are 5,000 pounds of grade A tomatoes, we have the constraint

$$(5) \qquad X_{WA} + X_{PA} \leq 5{,}000 .$$

Since there are 10,000 pounds of grade B tomatoes, we have the constraint

$$(6) \qquad X_{WB} + X_{PB} \leq 10{,}000 .$$

We know that whole tomatoes must be composed of at least 80% grade A tomatoes. The amount of whole tomatoes is $X_{WA} + X_{WB}$, thus we have the constraint

$$(7) \qquad \frac{X_{WA}}{X_{WA} + X_{WB}} \geq .80 \quad \text{or rewriting we have}$$

$$X_{WA} \geq .80\, X_{WA} + .80\, X_{WB} \quad \text{or}$$

$$X_{WA} - .80\, X_{WA} \geq .80\, X_{WB} \geq 0 \quad \text{or finally}$$

$$.2\, X_{WA} - .8\, X_{WB} \geq 0.$$

The last constraint is found from knowing that grade A tomatoes must be at least 10% of the paste. Being that the total number of pounds of paste is

$$X_{PA} + X_{PB},$$

we have the constraint

$$\frac{X_{PA}}{X_{PA} + X_{PB}} \geq .10 \quad \text{or rewriting we have}$$

$$X_{PA} \geq .1\, X_{PA} + .1\, X_{PB} \quad \text{or finally}$$

$$(8) \qquad .9\, X_{PA} - .1\, X_{PB} \geq 0.$$

Given these constraints we wish to maximize the revenue. The formula of the revenue is

$$\$.08\,(X_{WA} + X_{WB}) + \$.05\,(X_{PA} + X_{PB}).$$

We then would use more advanced linear programming techniques to solve this problem.

• PROBLEM 30-18

For its Sanford to Marksville short run, Sutland Airlines has first class, tourist class, and coach accommodations.

Packets of three tickets each, called 3-Paks, are available at a special discount. If tickets are sold in accordance with seating capacity, because of "no shows" it often happens that flights are not made at full capacity, thus losing money for Sutland. If Sutland oversells a flight and there are not enough cancellations or "no shows" to balance the oversubscription, then some passengers are going to be inconvenienced until new arrangements are made. It has been found that passengers thus inconvenienced exhibit essentially three kinds of reaction: I. The passenger who heartily curses Sutland and then forgets all about his ordeal after new arrangements have been made; II. The passenger who becomes so angry that he never flies Sutland again; and III. The passenger whose anger is so great that he never flies Sutland again and campaigns to stop other people from flying Sutland.

The effects of these reactions have been thoroughly studied, and an annoyance scale has been developed so that these effects can be described in quantitative terms. For a given flight 15 points of reaction I (measured on the annoyance scale), 12 points of reaction II, and 9 points of reaction III can be tolerated at most. Table 1 was developed and distributed to the executives of Sutland who are involved in customer relations. From an analysis of the past earnings of Sutland Airlines, the expected profit on a 3-Pak of first class tickets is \$10, the expected profit on a 3-Pak of tourist class tickets is \$12, and a 3-Pak of coach tickets nets \$14.

Table 1: Number of points of reaction for different classes of 3-Paks as measured on the annoyance scale.

	First Class	Tourist Class	Coach
Reaction I	1	1	5
Reaction II	2	3	1
Reaction III	2	2	1

Of concern to Sutland Airlines is the question: By how many 3-Paks of each type of accommodation should a flight be oversold if the tolerance levels on the annoyance scale are not to be exceeded and the largest possible profit is to be obtained? Of course, Sutland will break up a 3-Pak when necessary. Find the constraints, and explain how the problem should be solved.

Solution: To find the constraints for this problem, let X be the number of oversold first class "3-Paks", let Y be the number of oversold tourist class "3-Paks", and let Z be the number of oversold coach "3-Paks". The constraints are:

(1) $X \geq 0$ Either they overbook first class or they don't.

(2) $Y \geq 0$ Either they overbook tourist class or they don't.

(3) $Z \geq 0$ Either they overbook coach or they don't.

(4) First class has one point for Reaction I, tourist class has one point for Reaction I, and coach has 5 points for Reaction I. Since the maximum tolerable limit is 15 points for Reaction I, we have the constraint

$$X + Y + 5Z \leq 15.$$

(5) First class has 2 points for Reaction II, tourist class has three points for reaction II, and coach has one point for Reaction II. Since the maximum tolerable limit is 12 points for Reaction II, we have the constraint

$$2X + 3Y + Z \leq 12.$$

(6) First class has two points for Reaction III, tourist class has two points for Reaction III, and coach has one point for Reaction III. Since the maximum tolerable limit is 9 points for Reaction III, we have the constraint

$$2X + 2Y + Z \leq 9.$$

We cannot plot these constraints, for there are three unknown quantities and we would therefore require a three-dimensional graph. However, we know from a theorem of Linear Programming, that the point of maximum profit lies on the intersection of three constraints (the same number of constraints as the number of unknowns). Thus, to solve this problem we break up the six constraints into all the possible groups of three constraints. We then solve each group of three equations (taken from the three constraints) for the three unknowns. We now have a group of points. We take from that group of points those that meet the conditions set by all of the constraints. We then apply the profit formula to that set of points to obtain the point yielding the highest profit. The profit formula is:

$$\text{Profit} = \$10X + \$12Y + \$14Z.$$

After following the above procedure we find that in order to make the most profit, the company should overbook 1/3 of a first-class "3-Pak", 3 tourist class "3-Paks", 7/3 of coach "3-Paks" (1 first class ticket, 9 tourist tickets, and 7 coach tickets). This yields the maximum profit of

$$\$10(1/3) + \$12(3) + \$14(7/3) = \$10/3 + \$36 + \$98/3$$

$$= \$108/3 + \$36 = \$36 + \$36 = \$72.$$

CHAPTER 31

DATA PROCESSING

• **PROBLEM 31-1**

An economist wants the computer to produce tables that give the present value of $1 over a certain time given a fixed rate of inflation. The present value of $1 at the end of the ith period is

$$P_i = P_{i-1} / (1 + r),$$

where r is the constant rate of inflation (in decimals) and P_{i-1} (for i = 1, 2, 3 ..., n) is the present value of the dollar at the end of the previous time period. The value of Po is equal to 1. The algorithm's inputs should consist of the inflation rate r and the number of time periods N to be included in the table. Construct

(i) a descriptive flowchart,

(ii) and an algorithm flowchart.

(iii) Trace the program flow with an inflation rate of 5½% and N = 5 years.

Solution: (i) The descriptive flowchart gives a rough conceptual sketch of the sequence of steps to be carried out. The descriptive flowchart resembles the algorithm flowchart in that the steps are placed in blocks. Arrows leading to and emerging from blocks indicate the sequence of operations. Be sure to place in both types of charts a "start" block and at least one "stop" block to end the computation. The "decision" block will be a diamond. This block asks a question and transfers program flow to different places in the program depending on the answer to the question.

The descriptive flowchart is shown on the next page.

There is nothing unique about descriptive or algorithm flowcharts. Their construction is mostly a matter of personal style and perhaps a reflection of the programming languages into which the algorithm will eventually be "coded".

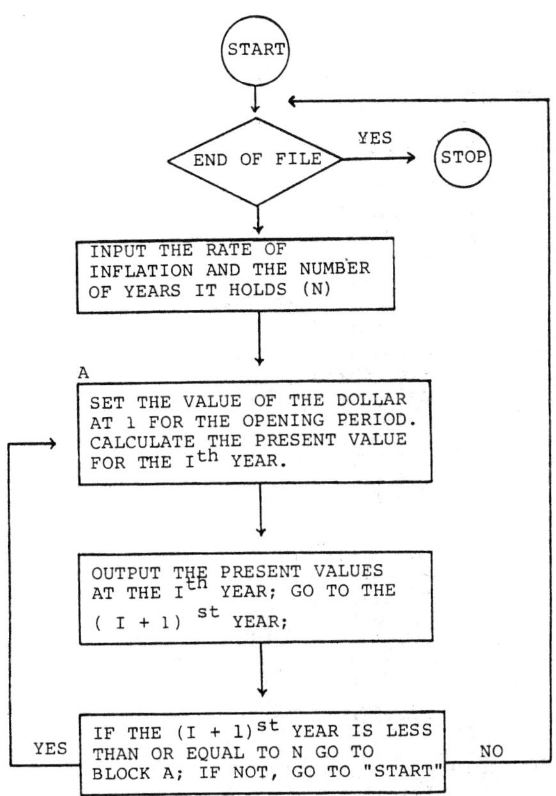

Descriptive flowchart.

(ii) First in constructing the algorithm flowchart, we assign specific labels to the quantities we will input, calculate, and output.

Let N = the number of years over which to find the present value for 1 dollar,

R = the inflation rate (in decimals),

PVAL = the present value of the dollar,

Q = a dummy variable that serves as a counter and index for the year.

The algorithm flowchart is shown on the next page.

In block 4 we assign the value 1 to dummy variable Q. Call the present year 1. Note that given R, 1/(R+1) is a constant e.g., R = 0.055 then 1/(R+1)= 1/1.055 = 0.9479, to four decimal places. Define the constant K as 1/(R+1). Initially in year 1 the present value of the dollar is 1. Block 5 gives the first line of the output. In block 6 the next line (year) is calculated and the year is updated. Since the first time Q is greater than N - 1, it actually equals N (the last year) we print

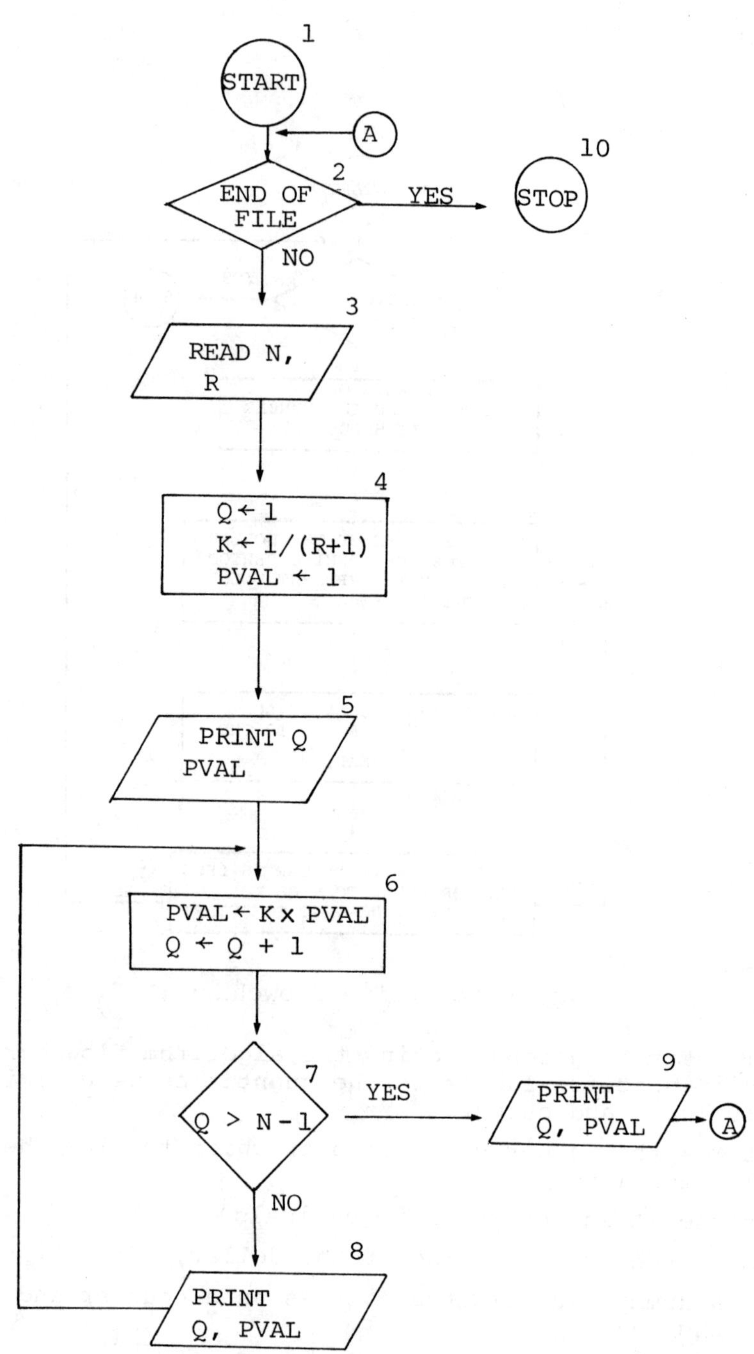

ALGORITHM FLOWCHART

the final line (block 9) and go to the beginning for new data. If Q is less than or equal to N - 1, we print the result in block 8 and return to 6 for the next line. The trace of the program flow is as follows for N = 5, R = 0.055.

(iii) N=5, R = 0.055

Block number		Instruction/Decision
1		START
2		not END OF FILE; continue to 3
3		N= 5, R=0.055
4		Q ← 1, K ← 0.9479, PVAL ← 1
5	1	1
6		PVAL ← 0.9479 × 1 $\approx$ 0.95
		Q ← 1 + 1 = 2
7		Q=2 is not greater than N-1=4
		go to 8
8	2	0.95
6		PVAL ← 0.9479 × 0.95 = 0.90
		Q ← 2 + 1 = 3
7		Q=3 is not greater than 4
		go to 8
8	3	0.90
6		PVAL ← 0.9479 × 0.90 = 0.85
		Q ← 3+1 = 4
7		Q=4 is not greater than 4
		go to 8
8	4	0.85
6		PVAL ← 0.9479 × 0.85 = 0.81
		Q ← 4 + 1 = 5
7		Q=5 is greater than 4
		go to 9
9	5	0.81
2		END OF FILE: YES
10		STOP

Note that when actually translating this algorithm to a specific computer language, we want the printout to look readable with headings and column labels.

Table giving the present value of 1 dollar during the I-th year at the given rate of inflation:

N = 5 years   Rate = 0.055

Year	Present value
1	1.00
2	0.95
3	0.90
4	0.85
5	0.81

Other details, like rounding off, and memory assigment, are left to the programmer.

• PROBLEM 31-2

An investor wants the computer to produce tables of the value of a fixed investment at each time period, where the investment accrues interest that is compounded at a fixed rate. The value of the compounded investment at the end of the jth period can be computed as $(1 + r) \cdot I_{j-1}$ where r is the interest rate per period and I_{j-1} (for j = 1, 2, 3 ... n) is the investment value at the end of the previous period. The value of I_0 is equal to the initial investment. The algorithm inputs should consist of the initial investment, the constant interest rate, and the number of time periods for which the investment has been made.

Construct

(i) a descriptive flowchart,

(ii) an algorithm flowchart,

(iii) Trace the program flow with the following data: initial investment is $7,000, rate is 0.055 (i.e., 5½%), over five years.

Solution: (i) The descriptive algorithm giving a rough sketch of the sequence of operations is shown.

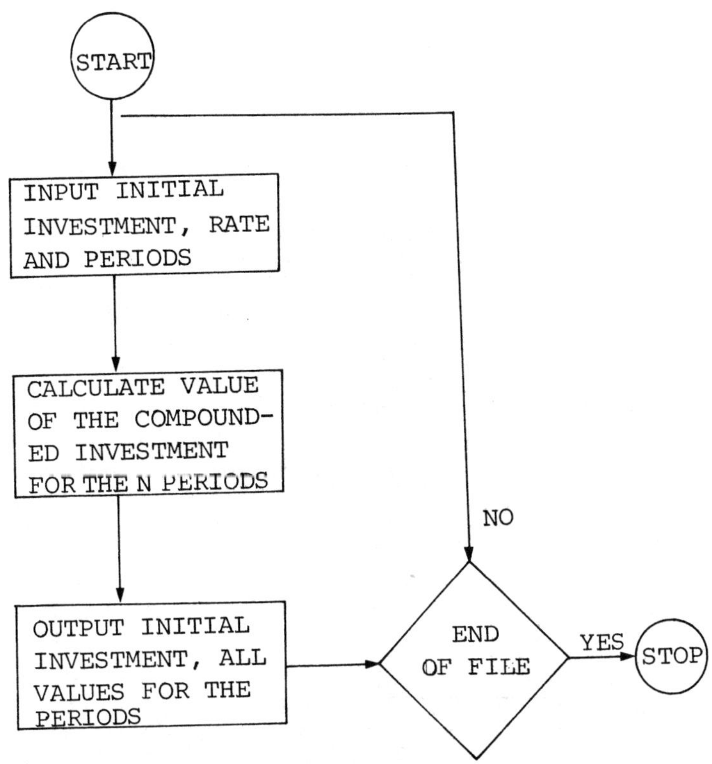

DESCRIPTIVE FLOWCHART

(ii) Before making the algorithm flowchart, assign specific names to the quantities needed to complete the computations:

initial investment = INV, intrest rate = R value of the investment = VAL, Q = dummy variable used as an index, N = number of periods over which the investment is made. (It is not obvious where we get Q from. Actually we know when to use a dummy variable only by starting the flowchart and seeing the need to create the dummy variable.) We call the first year, year 0 and the value of the investment, VAL is just the amount of the investment INV. This is the reason for block 3. In block 4, zero and VAL = INV would be printed as the first line of output. For each set of data, this is done only once. Block 6 uses the compound interest factor to calculate the value of the investment at the end of the Qth year. The reason this works is that if the compounded investment at the end of the Qth period is $(1+r) \cdot I_{Q-1}$ then $(1+r) \cdot I_{Q-1} = (1+r)(1+r) \cdot I_{Q-2} = \dots =$

$$\underbrace{(1+r)(1+r) \cdots (1+r)}_{Q \text{ times}} I_o = (1+r)^Q I_o .$$

So that in this algorithm, instead of finding I_{K-1} for all periods $K > 2$, storing it, then multiplying it by $(1+r)$ to get I_K, we simply use the compound interest formula

$$I_Q = (1+r)^Q I_o$$

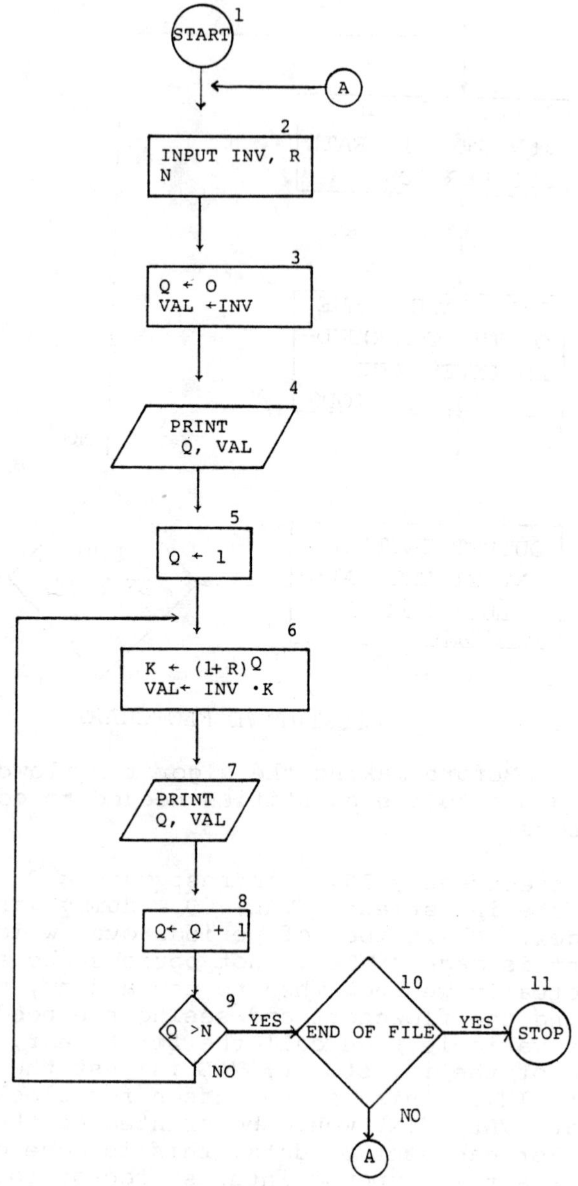

Algorithm Flowchart

where I_0 is the initial investment. Block 7 immediately prints line Q of the program which has the value of the investment at the end of the Qth year. Block 8 goes to the next year and block 9 asks if this year is greater than the last one we specified. If it is, then line N (for the last year) was printed and the task has been completed. We go to block 10 to see if the end of file has been reached. If "no" then go to A (START) to get a table for the new data.

(iii) initial investment = $7,000   R = 0.055   N = 5 years

1 START

2 INV = 7,000;   R = 0.055;   N = 5.

3 Q = 0;   VAL = 7,000

4 0   7,000.00   ← BEGINNING YEAR

5 Q = 1

6 K = $(1.055)^1$ = 1.055;   VAL = (7000)(1.055) = 7,385.00

7 1   7,385.00   ← FIRST YEAR

8 Q = 2

9 2 is not greater than 5 : <u>go to 6.</u>

6 K = $(1.055)^2$ = 1.1130   (to four places)

VAL = (7,000)(1.1130) = 7,791.00

7 2   7,791.00

8 Q = 3

9 3 is not greater than 5 : <u>go to 6.</u>

6 K = $(1.055)^3$ = 1.1742; VAL = (7,000)(1.1742) = 8,219.69

7 3   8,219.69

8 Q = 4

9 4 is not greater than 5 : <u>go to 6.</u>

6 K = $(1.055)^4$ = 1.2388;   VAL = (7,000)(1.2388) = 8,671.77

7 4   8,671.77

8 Q = 5

9 5 is not greater than 5 : <u>go to 6.</u>

6 K = $(1.055)^5$ = 1.3070;   VAL=(7,000)(1.3070) = 9,148.72

7 5   9,148.72

8 Q = 6

9 6 is greater than 5 : <u>go to 10.</u>

10 END OF FILE, YES :   GO TO 11

11 STOP

The actual output would be as shown below:

0	7,000.00
1	7,385.00
2	7,791.00
3	8,219.69
4	8,671.77
5	9,148.72

• PROBLEM 31-3

A marketing manager wants to know the breakeven point of a product. She wants a table made for each product that has five columns labeled,

PRODUCTION_LEVEL TOTAL COST_ TOTAL_REVENUE

TOTAL PROFIT_(LOSS) PROFIT_(LOSS) / UNIT

The inputs are defined as follows:

PPU = price per unit

NUM = total number of units to be made

FC = fixed cost

VC = variable cost

The output figures for the columns above are given the following labels,

PLEVEL = production level TC = total cost

TR = total revenue PL = total profit or loss

PLU = profit or loss per unit.

Develop

(i) A descriptive flowchart.

(ii) An algorithm flowchart.

(iii) Give a sample output giving the following data.

Product 1:

Maximum units to be made = 25

Price per unit = \$40

Fixed cost = \$400

Variable cost = \$20 / unit

i.e., if x units are produced, the variable cost is 20x dollars.

Solution: The mathematics of the problem are as follows.

TOTAL COST = FIXED COST + VARIABLE · QUANTITY

TOTAL REVENUE = QUANTITY · PRICE PER UNIT

TOTAL PROFIT = TOTAL REVENUE - TOTAL COST

PROFIT PER UNIT = TOTAL PROFIT ÷ QUANTITY.

(i) The descriptive flowchart orients us before making the algorithm flowchart. It summarizes in words what steps are to be taken to solve the problem.

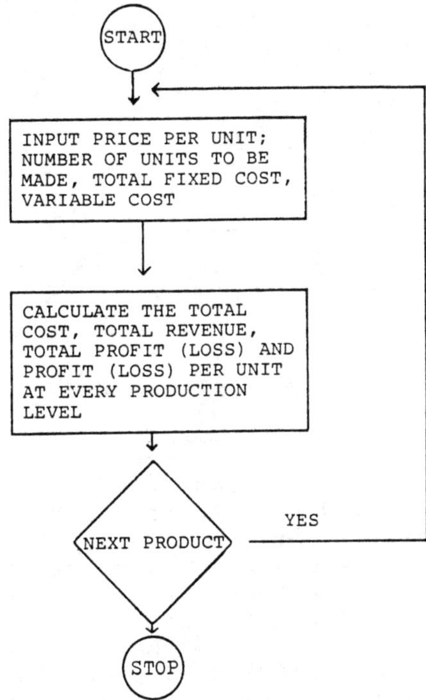

Descriptive Flowchart

For each product there will be one and only one table.

(ii)

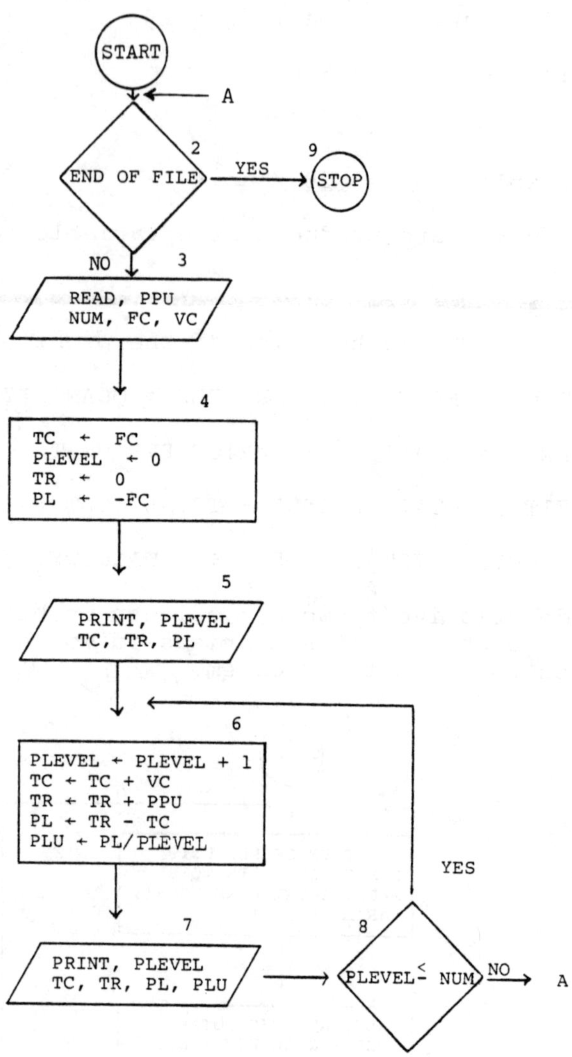

Algorithm Flowchart

The END OF FILE block checks to see if there is any data to be evaluated. If there is then block 3 reads these data. In block 4 we are setting up the first line of the output for the case where the production level, PLEVEL is set at zero, total revenue, TR is also 0, the total cost is just the fixed cost since there is no variable cost and the loss is - (total cost) since the revenue is zero. With every set of data, block 4 will only be passed through once. In block 5, the first line of output is printed. Note that PLU, profit (loss) per unit is not defined for the first line of output because we cannot divide by zero. Block seven computes the second line of output. The total cost TC is always incremented by a fixed amount VC which is the variable cost.

We know that previously the fixed cost was also the total cost. So that saying TC ← TC + VC is actually the same as saying TC ← FC + VC. Since the cost is cumulative, by the time we come to calculate line 3 of the output, all we do is add the increment cost VC. This will become clearer in section (iii). The total revenue is also cumulative and the increment here is the price per unit made. Block 7 prints the line of output just calculated and block 8 checks to see if all lines have been printed, i.e., printed for all production levels 0, 1, 2, . . . , NUM where we previously entered NUM. Once PLEVEL is greater than NUM, we go to the beginning to get a new set of data.

<u>Program Trace</u>

(iii)

1 START

2 NOT END OF FILE; GO TO 3

3 PPU = 40 NUM = 25 FC = 400 VC = 20

4 TC = 400; PLEVEL = 0; TR = 0; PL = -400

5 o 400 o -400

6 PLEVEL = 1; TC = 400 + 20 = 420;

TR = 0 + 40 = 40; PL = 40 - 420 = -380;

PLU = -380/1 = -380

7 1 420 40 -380 -380

8 1 ≤ 25 : true; GO TO 6

6 PLEVEL = 2; TC = 420 + 20 = 440;

TR = 40 + 40 = 80; PL = 80 - 440 = -360;

PLU = -360/2 = -180

7 2 440 80 -360 -180

Continuing likewise we get the remaining lines:

3	460	120	-340	-113.33
4	480	160	-320	- 80.00
5	500	200	-300	- 60.00
6	520	240	-280	- 46.67
7	540	280	-260	- 37.14
8	560	320	-240	- 30.00

9	580	360	-220	- 24.44
10	600	400	-200	- 20.00
11	620	440	-180	- 16.36
12	640	480	-160	- 13.33
13	660	520	-140	- 10.77
14	680	560	-120	- 8.57
15	700	600	-100	- 6.67
16	720	640	- 80	- 5.00
17	740	680	- 60	- 3.53
18	760	720	- 40	- 2.22
19	780	760	- 20	- 1.05
20	800	800	0	0
21	820	840	20	0.95
22	840	880	40	1.81
23	860	920	60	2.61
24	880	960	80	3.33
25	900	1000	100	4.00

When PLEVEL is 26, block 8 transfers us to the beginning where we get the next product data.

• PROBLEM 31-4

Given the following input values of Principal, Interest Rate, and Payment Amount develop an algorithm that will give an amortization table with the columns arranged as shown below.

Beginning Balance	Payment	Interest Payment	Principal Payment	Ending Balance

(i) Develop a descriptive flowchart.

(ii) Write the algorithm flowchart.

(iii) Describe the program flow through the algorithm flowchart with the data shown below.

	Principal	Rate	Payment
Set 1	1000.00	0.06	300.00
Set 2	500.00	0.12	3.00

Solution: An amortization table gives the balance on a loan on a period-by-period basis. The balance at the beginning of the first period is called the principal. Before reducing the balance for the next period, we must

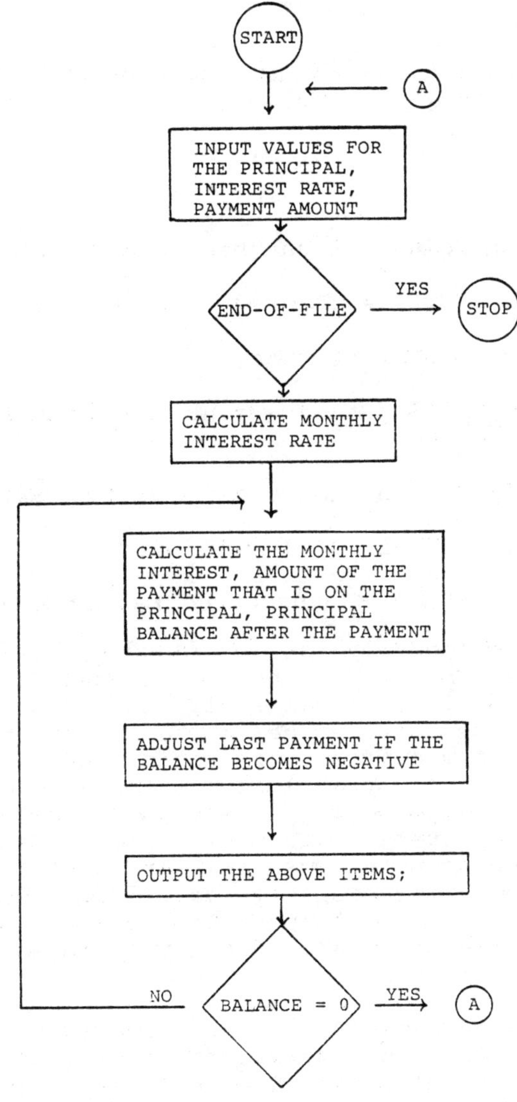

Descriptive Flowchart

deduct the interest from the payment made. Suppose that the principal is $1000 at the beginning of the first period; if the interest rate is $7\frac{1}{2}\%$, then the interest is $1000 × .075 = $75. If we pay $200, the balance will be reduced by $200 - $75 = $125. The beginning balance at the second period is $1,000 - $125 = $875. The interest for this second period is $(875)(0.075) = $65.63, and given that the payment for this second period is also 200, the principal balance is reduced by $200 - $65.63 = $134.37. The balance at the beginning of the third period is now

$875 - $134.37 = $740.63.

For this problem assume that the payment each period is constant except perhaps for the last period.

(i) The descriptive flowchart shown on the previous page gives a conceptual summary of the procedure.

(ii) Let

PRIN = the principal at the beginning of the period.

PAY = payment INTER = interest RATE = interest rate

MRATE = monthly interest rate.

PRINAMT = the part of the payment that is subtracted from the beginning balance

ENDBAL = is the balance at the end of the period

i.e., ENDBAL = PRIN - PRINAMT.

The algorithm flowchart is shown on the following page.

In block 4 the monthly rate is found by dividing the given annual rate by 12 (months/yr.). Also, the dummy variable A is initially set equal to 1. It is not clear just by looking at the arithmetical mechanics of the problem where this variable comes from. The use of dummy variables and indices is determined by decisions to be made during the execution of the algorithm. As soon as we see the need to repeat a number of steps as part of a program there must be a way to tell the computer when to stop. Setting a certain variable J equal to 1, successively adding after completing each "loop", and telling the computer to leave the loop after number N has been reached, effectively repeats the sequence of steps N times.

In this case variable A does not have this use. It serves as an indicator to direct program flow depending on some test condition encountered. The first time block 6 is tested A equals 1 and the response to "A does not equal 1" is no; we go to block 7 where the statement made is "The interest is less than the payment". If yes, then we go to

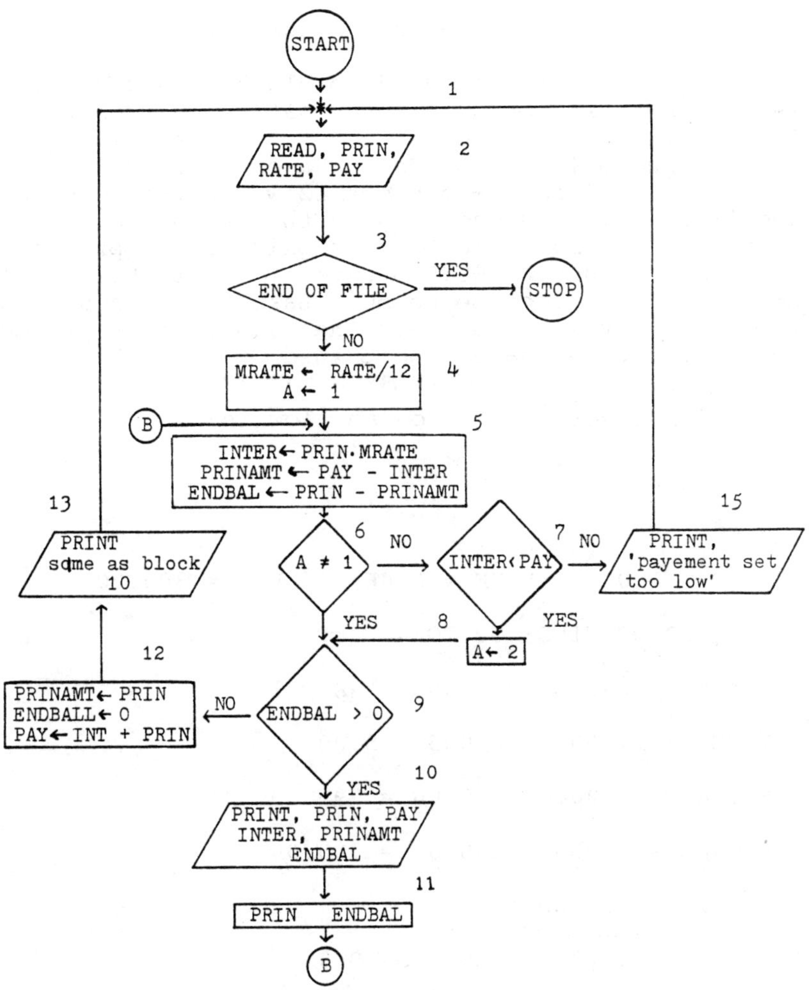

Algorithm Flowchart

block 8 and continue from there. If the interest is greater than the payment then block 15 gives an error message and returns to the beginning to obtain new data. In block 8, (interest is less than the payment) A is given the value 2; actually any number other than 1 is acceptable. The idea is to go directly on the next round to block 9 since by that time it is already known that the interest is less than the payment.

Block 9 tests to see if the ending balance is positive; if "yes" then the following are printed,

PRIN = the balance at the beginning of the period

PAY = the payment for the period

INTER = interest paid for the period

PRINAMT = the payment made to the reduce the beginning balance

ENDBAL = the balance at the end of the period.

Program flow is directed to block 5 to calculate the values for the next period. Note that we go from block 6 to block 9 since 2, the new value of A, is not equal to 1. When the ending balance is less than or equal to zero, program flow is directed to block 12 where the adjustment for the last period is made. Here the ending balance is set at zero, the amount left to be paid of the principal balance is also the "PRINCIPAL PAYMENT", but this is not the amount we pay, because we must take into account the interest for that last period. The last line is printed in block 13; the new data is obtained in block 2.

Using the first set given program flow is:

(iii)

1 START

2 PRIN = 1000; RATE = 0.06; PAY = 300.00

3 NOT END OF FILE; GO TO 4

4 MRATE = 0.06/12 = 0.005; A = 1

5 INTER = 1,000 $\times$ 0.005 = 5.00

PRINAMT = 300.00 - 5.00 = 295.00

ENDBAL = 1,000 - 295.00 = 705.00

6 1 $\neq$ 1 : NO; GO TO 7

7 5.00 $<$ 300.00 : YES; GO TO 8

8 A = 2

9 705 $>$ 0 : YES; GO TO 10

10 PRIN = 1000 PAY = 300.00 INTER = 5.00

PRINAMT = 295.00 ENDBAL = 705.00

11 PRIN = 705.00

5 INTER = 705.00 $\times$ 0.005 = 3.53

PRINAMT = 300.00 - 3.53 = 296.47

ENDBAL = 705.00 - 296.47 = 408.53

6 2 $\neq$ 1 : YES; GO TO 9

9 408.53 $>$ 0 : YES; GO TO 10

```
10    PRIN = 705.00  PAY = 300   INTER = 3.53
      PRINAMT = 296.47    ENDBAL = 408.53
11    PRIN = 408.53
5     INTER = 408.53 × 0.005 = 2.04
      PRINAMT = 300.00 - 2.04 = 297.96
      ENDBAL = 408.53 - 297.96 = 110.57
6     2 ≠ 1 : YES;  GO TO 9
9     110.57 > 0 : YES;  GO TO 10
10    PRIN = 408.53   PAY = 300.00    INTER = 2.04
      PRINAMT = 297.96    ENDBAL = 110.57
11    PRIN = 110.57
5     INTER = 110.57 × 0.005 = 0.55
      PRINAMT = 300.00 - 0.55 = 299.45
      ENDBAL = 110.57 - 299.45 = -188.88
6     2 ≠ 1 : YES;  GO TO 9
9     -188.88 > 0 : NO; GO TO 12
12    PRINAMT = 110.57;    ENDBAL = 0;
      PAY = 0.55 + 110.57 = 111.12
13    PRIN = 110.57    PAY = 111.12    PRINAMT = 110.57
      ENDBAL = 0;   GO TO 2
```

(Summary: Table for the first data set is

Beginning Balance	Payment	Interest Payment	Principal Payment	Ending Balance
1,000.00	300.00	5.00	295.00	705.00
705.00	300.00	3.53	296.47	408.53
408.53	300.00	2.04	297.96	110.57
110.57	111.12	0.55	299.45	0)

2	PRIN = 500.00	RATE = 0.12	PAY = 3.00
3	NOT END OF FILE; GO TO 4		
4	MRATE = 0.12/12 = 0.01; A = 1		
5	INTER = 500.00 × 0.01 = 5.00		
6	1 ≠ 1 : NO; GO TO 7		
7	5.00 < 3.00 : NO; GO TO 15		
15	"PAYMENT SET TOO LOW".		
2	o	o	o
3	END OF FILE : YES; GO TO 14		
14	STOP		

• PROBLEM 31-5

A loan company manager wants the computer to be able to generate an amortization table for the case in which the amount of the periodic payment is not given. That is, algorithm input will be the interest rate for the period, the principal amount and the number of months over which the loan is to be repaid. The amount of each payment will be calculated using the formula

$$\text{Payment} = \frac{\text{Prin} \cdot \text{Mrate} \cdot (1 + \text{Mrate})^N}{(1 + \text{Mrate})^N - 1}$$

where Prin is the principal amount, Mrate is the monthy interest rate, and N is the number of months over which the loan is to be repaid.

(i) Draw the descriptive flowchart.

(ii) Draw the algorithm flowchart.

(iii) Describe the program flow with the following data:

Amount of loan	period rate	months
800	0.075	12

Solution: The payment each month is different and determined by the formula given for only N-1 months, where N is the total number of months in which to pay the loan. In month N, the payment will consist of (1) the remaining balance and (2) the interest for that last month. The interest in month i is found by multiplying the remaining balance in month i-1 by the fixed monthly rate.

In the formula

$$\text{Payment} = \frac{\text{Prin} \cdot \text{Mrate} \cdot (1+\text{Mrate})^N}{(1 + \text{Mrate})^N - 1}$$

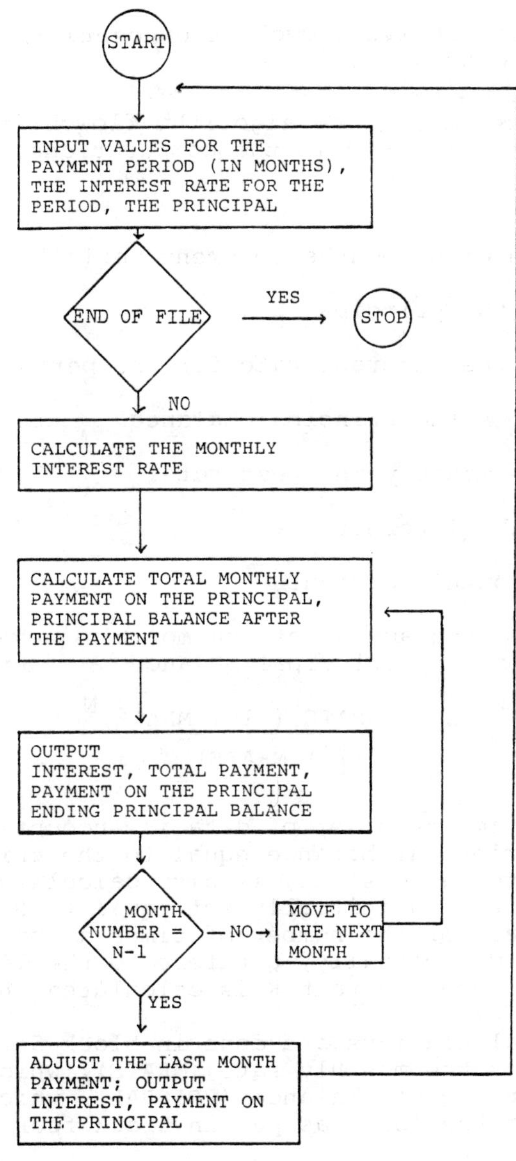

Descriptive flowchart

Prin refers to the principal balance of the previous month. The formula can be stated as

$$(\text{Payment})_i = (\text{Prin})_{i-1} \cdot K,$$

where the constant K equals

$$\frac{\text{Mrate} \cdot (1 + \text{Mrate})^N}{(1 + \text{Mrate})^N - 1} .$$

Having found the principal balance in the period i-1, multiply it by K to get the payment in period i.

(i) The descriptive flowchart conceptually summarizes the sequence of steps.

(ii) Before making the algorithm flowchart, label the quantities to be used in the computations.

Let

N = number of months (payment period)

PRIN = the principal

RATE = the interest rate for the period.

PRINBAL = the principal balance

MRATE = monthly interest rate.

INT = the interest

PAY = monthly payment

PAYBAL = the amount of the monthly payment which is deducted from the principal balance. And as before let

$$K = \frac{\text{MRATE} \; (1 + \text{MRATE})^N}{(1 + \text{MRATE})^N - 1} .$$

The first time each set of data is encountered, block 4 sets the principal balance equal to the principal; the monthly rate, a constant, is also calculated in block 4. The variable Q is initially set equal to 0 and will serve to keep track of the number of times a loop has been executed. Conceptually, Q refers to the line of the output table. The constant K is calculated in block 4.

The calculations are done in block 5 : the interest (INT) equals the monthly rate (MRATE), which is fixed, times the principal balance (PRINBAL), which for the first run through the loop was put in block four to be the principal.

The payment (PAY) equals the principal balance times the constant K. The part of the payment that goes to

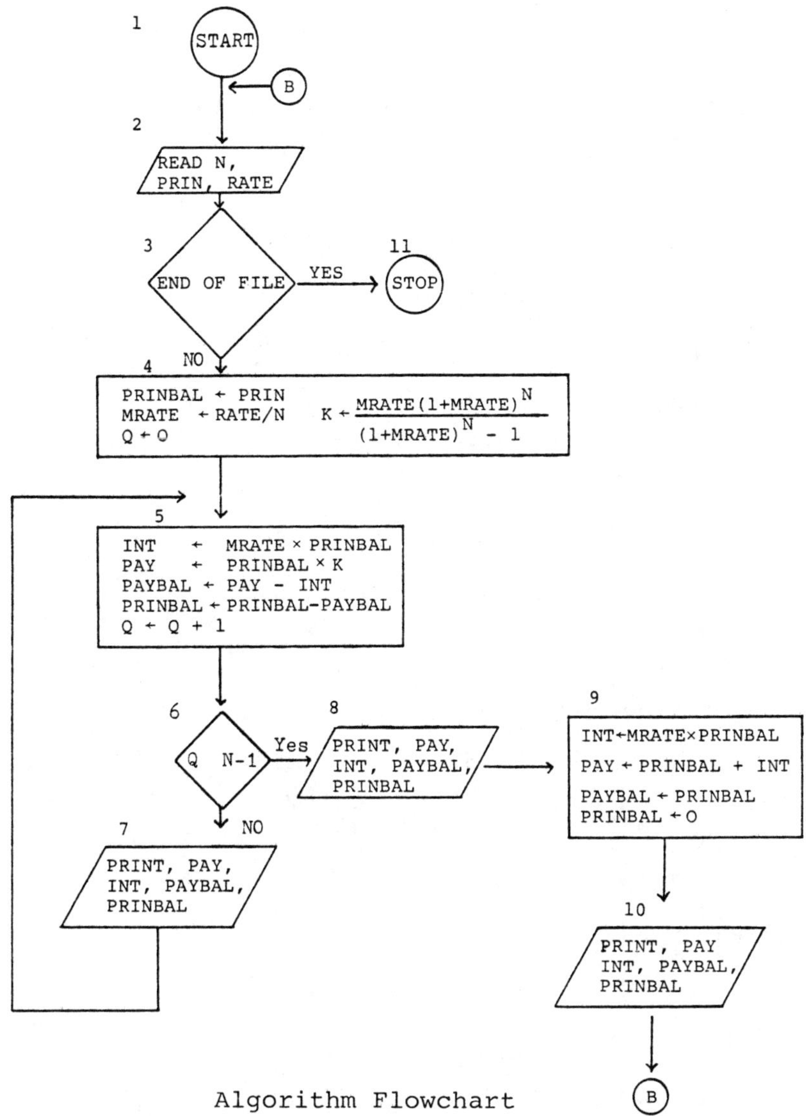

Algorithm Flowchart

reduce the principal balance is PAYBAL and equals the payment (PAY) less the interest (INT). The principal balance for this period equals the principal balance for the previous period less PAYBAL. By incrementing Q as the last instruction in block 5, we actually refer to the line of the output table that has just ben calculated. If this line is the next to last, program flow is directed to block 8 which prints this next-to-last line. Block 9 makes the adjustments for the last line. Here again the interest equals the monthly rate times the principal balance; the payment for the last month equals the principal balance plus the interest due. The amount that goes to reduce the principal balance is just the principal balance for this last period. Block 10 prints the last line and returns to obtain the new set of data.

Going back to block 6, if the line just calculated is less than the next to last line, it is printed in block seven and returns to block five where the next line is calculated. The program trace will clarify the sequence of steps.

(iii) Program trace with the following data: principal = \$800 period rate = 0.075 months = 12

1 START

2 N=12, PRIN = 800, RATE = 0.075

3 NOT END OF FILE; GO TO 4

4 PRINBAL = 800 MRATE = 0.075/12 = 0.00625

$$K = \frac{0.00625(1.00625)^{12}}{(1.00625)^{12}-1} = 0.08676 \quad \text{(to five places)}$$

Q = 0

5 INT = 0.00625 × 800 = 5 PAY = 800 × 0.08676 = 69.41

PAYBAL = 69.41 -5 = 64.41 PRINBAL = 800-64.41=735.59

Q = 1

6 1 = 11 : no; go to 7

7 69.41 5.00 64.41 735.59 (line 1)

5 INT = 0.00625 × 735.59 = 4.60

PAY = 735.59 × 0.0867 = 63.78

PAYBAL = 63.78 - 4.60 = 59.18

PRINBAL = 735.59 - 59.18 = 676.41

Q = 2

6 2 = 11 : NO; go to 7

7 63.78 4.60 59.18 676.41 (2)

5 . . .

Continuing likewise we find the following results up to line 10:

58.64	4.23	54.41	622.00	(3)
53.93	3.89	50.04	571.96	(4)
49.59	3.57	46.02	525.94	(5)
45.60	3.29	42.31	483.63	(6)
41.93	3.02	38.91	444.72	(7)
38.56	2.78	35.78	408.94	(8)
35.46	2.56	32.90	376.04	(9)

```
        32.63        2.35      30.28      345.76          (10)
5       INT = 0.00625  × 345.76 = 2.16
        PAY = 0.0867   × 345.76 = 30.00
        PAYBAL = 30.00 - 2.16 = 27.84
        PRINBAL = 345.76 - 27.84 = 317.92
        Q = 11
6       11 = 11 : YES; go to 8
8       30.00        2.16      27.84      317.92          (11)
9       INT = 0.00625 × 317.92 = 1.99
        PAY = 317.92 + 1.99 = 319.91
        PAYBAL = 317.92
10      319.91       1.99      317.92                     0
2 . . . 3 END OF FILE
```

The actual output should include the proper labels

AMORTIZATION TABLE			
PRINCIPAL = 800 — MONTHLY RATE = $0.6\frac{1}{4}\%$ — MONTHS = 12			
Payment	Interest	Payment on the balance	Principal balance
1 69.41	5.00	64.41	735.59
2 63.78	4.60	59.18	676.41
3 58.64	4.23	54.41	622.00
4 53.93	3.89	50.04	571.96
5 49.59	3.57	46.02	525.94
6 45.60	3.29	42.31	483.63
7 41.93	3.02	38.91	444.72
8 38.56	2.78	35.78	408.94
9 35.46	2.56	32.90	376.04
10 32.63	2.35	30.28	345.76
11 27.84	2.16	27.84	317.92
12 319.91	1.99	317.92	0

CHAPTER 32

STATISTICS

• **PROBLEM 32-1**

When BankAmericard became VISA, the vice president of a small branch bank compiled the following data:

Accounts Outstanding ($)	Number of Accounts
Less than 100	28
100 - 200	32
200 - 300	17
300 - 400	9
400 - 500	6
500 - 600	1
	93

Draw a histogram for this data.

Solution: We first apportion the x-axis into equal intervals corresponding to the above account divisions. Above each division, we put a block with the same width as the division. The height of the block will correspond to the number of people in that division.

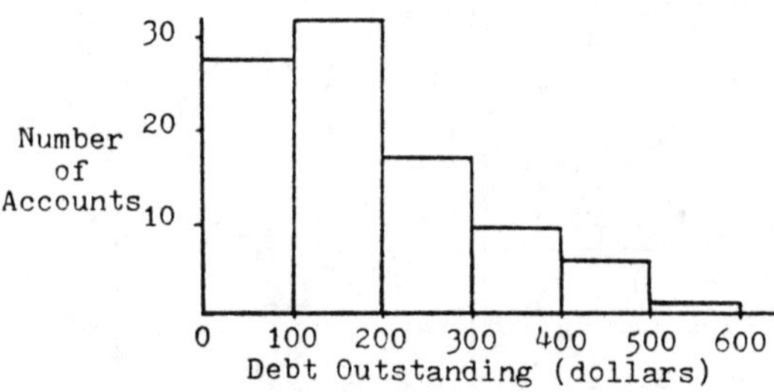

• **PROBLEM 32-2**

The following table represents a distribution of the number of shares (in thousands) of common stock in the Micheli corporation traded during the trading days of August 1976 and for 1976 altogether. Prepare cumulative frequency distributions for both.

Number of Shares	August 1976 Number of Days	Year 1976 Number of Days
0 - 10	6	60
11 - 20	12	168
21 - 30	4	64
31 - 40	1	12
41 - 60	1	8
	24	312

Solution: We first convert all our data into percentages by dividing in each case by the total number of days (24 or 312) and multiplying by 100%. This results in the following table:

Number of Shares	% (August)	% (1976)
0 - 10	25	19
11 - 20	50	54
21 - 30	17	20
31 - 40	4	4
41 - 60	4	3
	100	100

We have produced a relative frequency table for both data sets. Direct comparison is now possible, yet the relationship within and between each group has been maintained. Note that 6:12:4:1:1 is almost the same as 25:50:17:4:4, the difference being due only to rounding.

The cumulative frequency table gives what percentage of the observations lie at or below a certain value. We compute the values for the table by adding each successive frequency figure to the previous cumulative total. Using the above relative frequency distribution:

	Number of Days 1976 - August	1976 - Year
Number of Shares	% Cumulative Frequency	% Cumulative Frequency
0 - 10	25	19
11 - 20	75	73
21 - 30	92	93
31 - 40	96	97
41 - 60	100	100

• PROBLEM 32-3

Plot the following time series. Use percentages for convenience.

Year	British GNP (1958 constant prices) (millions of £)	British GNP percentage change compared with 1958.
1958	21,768	0
1959	22,628	4.0
1960	23,719	9.0
1961	24,517	12.6
1962	24,762	13.8
1963	25,911	19.0
1964	27,289	25.4

Solution: The x-axis contains the years of interest. It is the time axis. The y-coordinate will be the GNP percentage change compared with 1958. We connect the points in order to visualize the trend.

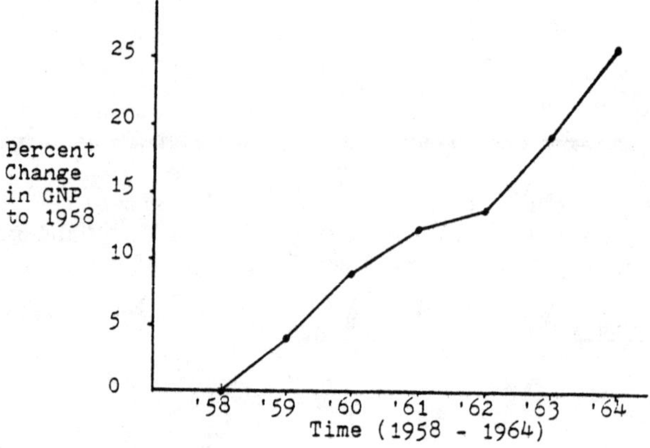

• **PROBLEM 32-4**

Graph the following time series

Year	Soap Purity as Percentage of Total
1955	99.0
1956	99.0
1957	98.3
1958	98.1
1959	98.2
1960	98.6
1961	98.8
1962	98.3
1963	98.0

Solution: Plotting this in a conventional manner (below) produces a graph of dubious value. It is almost impossible to detect the changes in soap purity.

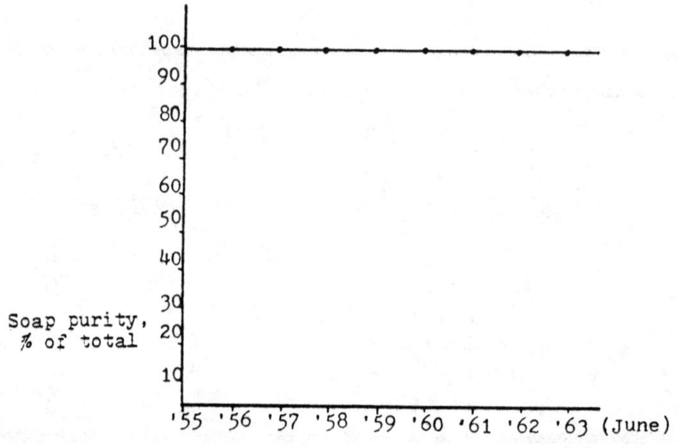

In the following graph the origin is suppressed.

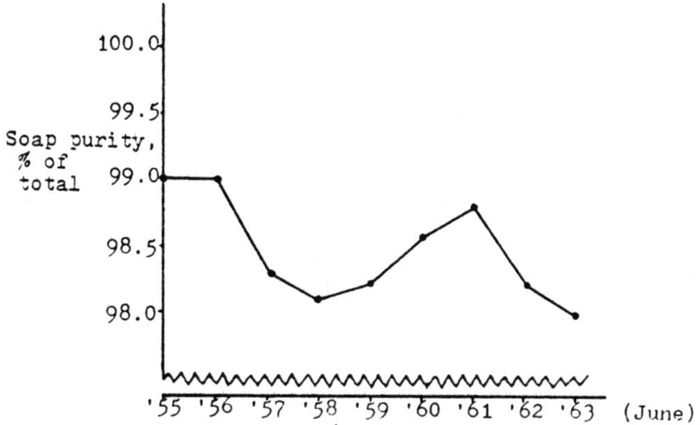

This is indicated by a jagged edge at the bottom (representing a tear). Any suitable device may be employed to illustrate the omission of a section of the vertical axis.

• PROBLEM 32-5

Plot the following two time series on the same graph and compare.

Coal production Tons (millions)	Year	Wage earners in industry Number (thousands)
210.8	1952	706.2
211.5	1954	701.8
207.4	1956	697.4
198.8	1958	692.7
183.9	1960	602.1
176.8	1962	531.0

Solution: There is no natural relationship between the units of measurement and thus no obvious basis of comparison. We resolve this difficulty with the use of index numbers. The index numbers used here are the percentage changes in each year of the series as compared with 1952. For example, the index number for coal production in 1954 is

$$\frac{211.5}{210.8} \times 100 = 100.3 .$$

Similarly,

Year	Coal Production Index	Wage Earners Index
1952	$\frac{210.8}{210.8} \times 100 = 100$	$\frac{706.2}{706.2} \times 100 = 100.0$
1954	$\frac{211.5}{210.8} \times 100 = 100.3$	$\frac{701.8}{706.2} \times 100 = 99.4$
1956	$\frac{207.4}{210.8} \times 100 = 98.4$	$\frac{697.4}{706.2} \times 100 = 98.8$
1958	$\frac{198.8}{210.8} \times 100 = 94.3$	$\frac{692.7}{706.2} \times 100 = 98.1$
1960	$\frac{183.9}{210.8} \times 100 = 87.2$	$\frac{602.1}{706.2} \times 100 = 85.3$
1962	$\frac{176.8}{210.8} \times 100 = 83.9$	$\frac{531.0}{706.2} \times 100 = 75.2$

We now have a basis of comparison. For each category we place the years on the x-axis and index numbers on the y-axis. We plot the above points and connect them with straight lines.

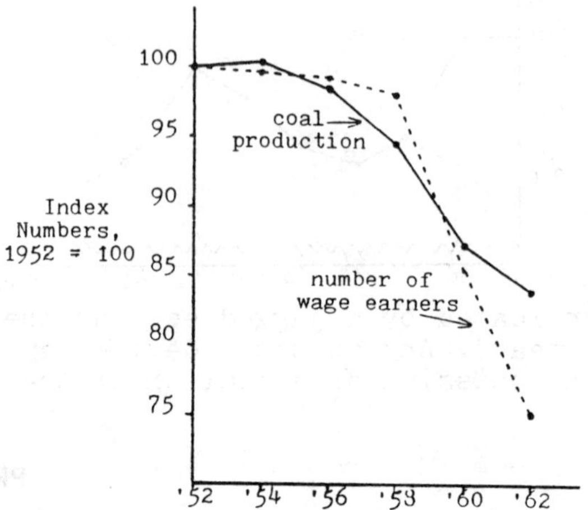

• PROBLEM 32-6

Plot the following data on one chart. Make sure cumulative effects are shown.

British Current Expenditure on the Social Services (millions of £'s)

	1954-5	Cumulative total	1956-7	Cumulative total	1958-9	Cumulative total	1960-1	Cumulative total
Benefits and assistance	909-9	909-9	1063-1	1063-1	1383-7	1383-7	1494-7	1494-7
Health and welfare	631-0	1540-9	750-4	1813-5	825-1	2208-8	982-3	2477-0
Education	432-0	1972-9	546-4	2359-9	669-9	2878-7	811-7	3288-7
Housing	103-9	2076-8	103-8	2463-7	110-7	2989-4	121-5	3410-2
	2076-8		2463-7		2989-7		3410-2	

Solution: Begin by placing the time periods along the x-axis. The scale for the vertical axis is in millions of pounds.

First plot the series representing benefits and assistance. Shade the area under the line. Now consider the series of health and welfare. Add each observed value of this series to the corresponding value of the benefits and assistance series in each time period. The height of the point should be the cumulative height for benefits and assistance and health and welfare expenditures. Connect the points to form a line. The newly constructed area represents health and welfare. Repeat this procedure for education and housing.

The final graph is shown below.

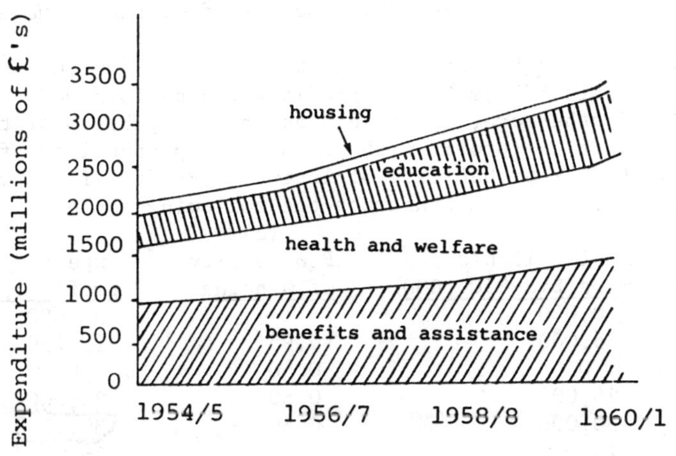

• PROBLEM 32-7

Contractor Dittmar is bidding on a job that he expects will cost him $500,000 to complete. Dittmar has excess capacity and can take on the new job. Several other contractors, including the firm of Causey and Grasso, are bidding on the same job. Dittmar has bid against this company in the past and feels that he has some knowledge about how they are likely to bid. In the following table, Dittmar has estimated the subjective probabilities of winning for any bid he makes.

PROBABILITIES OF VARIOUS BIDS

Possible Bid	Cumulative Probability of Winning with Bid
$450,000	1.00
475,000	0.95
500,000	0.90
525,000	0.80
550,000	0.60
575,000	0.35
600,000	0.20
625,000	0.10
650,000	0.05
675,000	0.02

a) Sketch a graph of these probabilities.
b) What should Dittmar's optimal strategy be?

Solution: a)

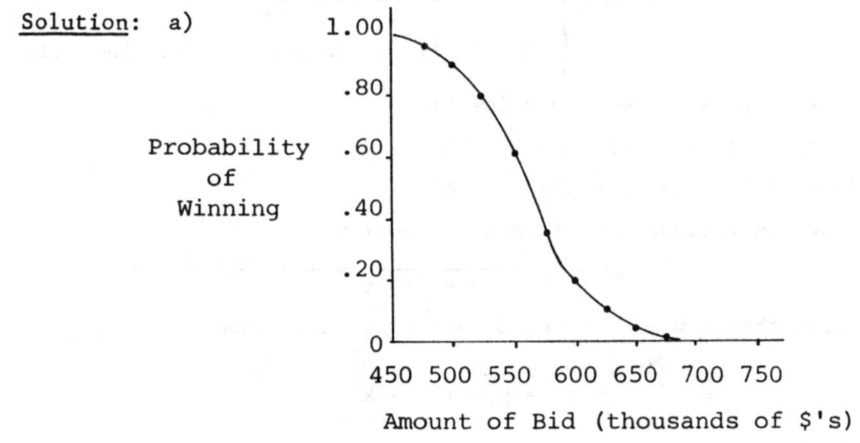

b) The situation Dittmar is in is very common. The contract is to be awarded to the lowest bidder. The higher the contractor raises his bid, the more his profit, but the less his chances of winning. He must find some balance.

Dittmar's profit if his bid wins is his bid less the \$500,000 cost. For example, if his bid is \$575,000, his profit would be \$575,000 - \$500,000 = \$75,000. Furthermore, if his bid doesn't win, his profit is zero. Hence E(profit) = (profit with given bid x probability of winning at that bid) + (0 x probability of losing) = Profit if bid wins x probability of winning. We can construct the following table

Bid	(1) Profit if bid wins(Bid-\$500,000)	(2) Probability of winning	(3) Expected profit[(1)x(2)]
450,000	-50,000	1	-50,000
475,000	-25,000	0.95	-23,750
500,000	0	0.90	0
525,000	25,000	0.80	20,000
550,000	50,000	0.60	30,000
575,000	75,000	0.35	26,250
600,000	100,000	0.20	20,000
625,000	125,000	0.10	12,500
650,000	150,000	0.05	7,500
675,000	175,000	0.02	3,500

We now assume that Dittmar wants to maximize his expected profit. The above table shows he should bid \$550,000.

• PROBLEM 32-8

A contractor has found through experience that the low bid for a job (excluding his own bid) is a random variable that is uniformly distributed over the interval $(3c/4, 2c)$ where c is the contractor's cost estimate (no profit or loss) of the job. If profit is defined as zero if the contractor does not get the job (his bid is greater than the low bid) and as the difference between his bid and the cost estimate c if he gets the job, what should he bid, in terms of c, in order to maximize his expected profit?

Solution: Let k be the contractor's bid. Profit π is defined as follows:

$$\pi = \begin{cases} k - c & \text{if } k \text{ is less than lowest bid by competition} . \\ 0 & \text{if } k \text{ is greater than low bid.} \end{cases}$$

$$E(\pi) = (k - c)\cdot\Pr(k \text{ is less than low bid}) + 0\cdot\Pr(k \text{ is greater than low bid}) = (k - c)\cdot\Pr(k \text{ is less than low bid}) .$$

But the low bid follows a uniform distribution.

$$F(\text{low bid}) = \frac{1}{2c - 3/4\ c} = \frac{4}{5c},\quad 3c/4 < \text{low bid} < 2c.$$

Pr (k is less than low bid) = Pr (low bid is greater than k)

$$= \int_k^{2c} \frac{4}{5c}\,dx = \left[\frac{4}{5c}\right](2c - k) .$$

Now $E(\pi) = (k - c)\frac{4}{5c}(2c - k) = \frac{4}{5c}(2ck - 2c^2 + kc - k^2)$.

To maximize, we set $\frac{dE(\pi)}{dk} = 0$.

$$\frac{dE(\pi)}{dk} = \frac{4}{5c}[2c + c - 2k] = 0$$

or

$$3c - 2k = 0 \ .$$

Thus the optimal bid is

$$k = \frac{3c}{2} \ .$$

We now need to check that we have a maximum. We do this by showing $\frac{d^2E(\pi)}{dk^2} < 0$:

$$\frac{d^2E(\pi)}{dk^2} = \frac{d}{dk}\left[\frac{4}{5c}(3c - 2k)\right]$$

$$= -\frac{8}{5c} < 0.$$

• PROBLEM 32-9

You are the president of a company that makes wrist watches. The prestige line of watches, Chronomatrix 1536 is waterproof, shockproof, dustproof and features anti-magnetic movement. This watch is sold to distributors for \$25 apiece. Your vice-president suggests that a guarantee to replace watches that fail within two years of purchase would allow a price increase of \$2.00 per watch without a decrease in demand.

The engineering department assures you that the lifetimes of the Chronomatrix 1536 follow some unknown probability distribution with mean $\mu = 3.5$ years and $\sigma = 0.5$ years. If sales remain constant at 100,000 watches per year and a replacement watch would cost \$15.00, is this a profitable policy for your company?

Solution: We wish to find the expected profit of these ventures. Let X be the lifetime of one of these watches.

From Chebyshev's inequality, which is valid for any random variable with a mean and variance,

$$\Pr(|X - \mu| \geq k\sigma) \leq 1/k^2$$

for some constant k.

Equivalently, this inequality states that

$$\Pr(X \geq k\sigma) + \mu \ , \ X \leq \mu - k\sigma) \leq 1/k^2.$$

The region, $X \geq k\sigma + \mu$, $X \leq \mu - k\sigma$ is shown in the figure below:

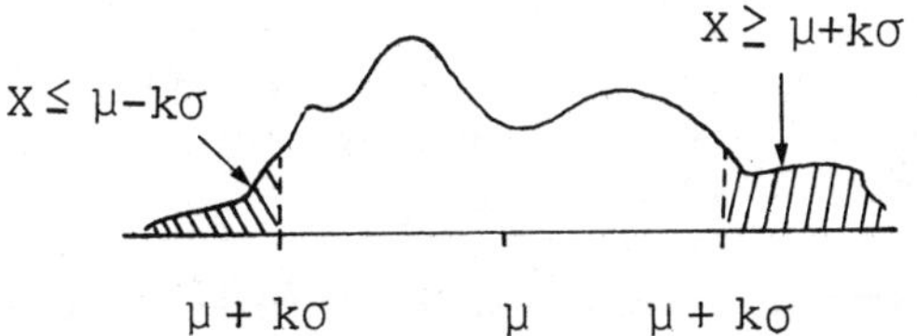

The probability of this event, $X \geq \mu + k\sigma$ or $X \leq \mu - k\sigma$, is the combined area of the two shaded regions. Because the two regions are disjoint,

$$Pr(X \geq \mu + k\sigma \,,\ X \leq \mu - k\sigma)$$
$$= Pr(X \geq \mu + k\sigma) + Pr(X \leq \mu - k\sigma) < 1/k^2 \,.$$

Substituting for μ and σ gives

$$Pr(X \geq 3.5 + k/2) + Pr(X \leq 3.5 - k/2) < 1/k^2 \,.$$

We are interested in the probability that a watch lasts for less than 2 years. If k is chosen to be 3, then the inequality becomes

$$Pr(X \geq 3.5 + 3/2) + Pr(X \leq 3.5 - 3/2) < 1/3^2$$

or

$$Pr(X \geq 5) + Pr(X \leq 2) < 1/9 \,.$$

We do not know anything about the $Pr(X \geq 5)$ except that it is a positive number between zero and 1. Because of this,

$$Pr(X \leq 2) \leq Pr(X \geq 5) + Pr(X \leq 2) < 1/9$$

or

$$Pr(X \leq 2) < 1/9 \,.$$

Thus by the use of Chebyshev's inequality, we have derived an inequality about the probability that one watch will fail in 2 years or less.

Out of 100,000 watches sold we would expect that $(100,000)\ Pr(X \leq 2)$ of them will fail.

By Chebyshev's inequality

$$(100,000)\ Pr(X \leq 2) \leq (100,000) \cdot 1/9$$

or expected number of watches that fail in two years or less $\leq 11,111.11$.

The expected cost of replacing the watches under the proposed guarantee would be

$$\$15 \times (\text{Expected \# of watches that fail})$$

which is less than

$$\$15 \times 11,111.11 = \$166,666.67.$$

Thus the expected cost of guarantee < \$166,666.67. The company will gain \$2.00 on every watch sold with an entire gain of \$100,000 $\times$ \$2.00 = \$200,000.00 gain. Thus the expected profit is

$$\$200,000 - \text{expected cost} \geq \$200,000 - \$166,666.67 \geq \$33,333.33$$

In summary, the company's profit will be on the average greater than \$33,333.34 per year. The president should conclude that the guarantee is a profitable policy and adopt it.

• PROBLEM 32-10

The marketing research firm of Burrows, Heller and Larimer wants to estimate the proportions of men and women who are familiar with a shoe polish. In a sample (random) of 100 men and 200 women it is found that 20 men and 60 women had used this particular shoe polish. Compute a 95% confidence interval for the difference in proportions between men and women familiar with the product. Use this to test the hypothesis that the proportions are equal.

Solution: Some quantities necessary for solution to this problem are:

$$\hat{p}_1 = \frac{x_1}{n_1} = \left(\frac{60}{200}\right) = 0.3 = \text{the proportion of women familiar with the product}$$

$$\hat{p}_2 = \frac{x_2}{n_2} = \left(\frac{20}{100}\right) = 0.2 = \text{the proportion of men familiar with the product}$$

and

$$\sqrt{\frac{\hat{p}_1(1-\hat{p}_1)}{n_1} + \frac{\hat{p}_2(1-\hat{p}_2)}{n_2}} = \sqrt{\frac{.3(.7)}{200} + \frac{.2(.8)}{100}} = 0.0515 = \text{the estimated}$$

standard deviation of $\hat{p}_1 - \hat{p}_2$.

n_1 and n_2 are sufficiently large to apply the Central Limit Theorem to $x_1/n_1 - x_2/n_2 = \hat{p}_1 - \hat{p}_2$.

$$\text{Thus} \quad E(\hat{p}_1 - \hat{p}_2) = E(\hat{p}_1) - E(\hat{p}_2) = p_1 - p_2 .$$

We can justify the use of the above estimated standard deviation by noting that we have a large sample and the Law of Large Numbers applies; hence

$$Z = \frac{(\hat{p}_1 - \hat{p}_2) - (p_1 - p_2)}{\sqrt{\frac{\hat{p}_1(1-\hat{p}_1)}{n_1} + \frac{\hat{p}_2(1-\hat{p}_2)}{n_2}}}$$

is approximately standard normal. With our values.

$$Z = \frac{(0.3-0.2) - (p_1-p_2)}{.0515} \quad \text{is} \quad N(0,1) .$$

Therefore,

$$(0.1-(1.96)(0.0515), 0.1+(1.96)(0.0515))$$
$$=(-0.00094, 0.20094)$$

The required confidence interval is

$$(-.00094, .20094).$$

Since equal proportions mean that $p_1 - p_2 = 0$, we see that this confidence interval covers this difference and so we conclude that the true proportions of women and men do not differ significantly, i.e., the proportions are equal.

• PROBLEM 32-11

A research worker was interested in racial differences in the standard of living of farm operators in the southeastern United States. He used the presence of running water in farm dwellings as a crude index of the standard of living. For each of 31 economic areas in North Carolina, South Carolina, and Georgia in 1945, he calculated two measures: X = farms operated by nonwhites per 100 white farm operators and Y = percent of farms having running water in dwellings. The following values were obtained:

$$\Sigma X = 1,860 \qquad \Sigma Y = 465 \qquad \Sigma XY = 23,400$$

$$\Sigma X^2 = 201,600 \quad \Sigma Y^2 = 7,925 \qquad n = 31$$

Compute the regression line and the correlation of X and Y.

Solution: The regression line is $Y = a + bX$ where a and b are found by the computation formulae

$$b = \frac{\Sigma XY - n\bar{X}\bar{Y}}{\Sigma X^2 - n\bar{X}^2}$$

$$a = \bar{Y} - b\bar{X} \ .$$

$$\bar{Y} = \frac{\Sigma Y}{n} \quad \text{and} \quad \bar{X} = \frac{\Sigma X}{n} \ .$$

$$\bar{Y} = \frac{465}{31} = 15 \quad \text{and} \quad \bar{X} = \frac{1860}{31} = 60 \ ,$$

Using the formula above

$$b = \frac{23{,}400 - 31 \cdot 60 \cdot 15}{201{,}600 - 31(60)^2} = \frac{23{,}400 - 27{,}900}{201{,}600 - 111{,}600} = \frac{-4500}{90{,}000}$$

$$= -.05.$$

And

$$a = \bar{Y} - b\bar{X} = 15 - (-0.05)60 = 18.$$

The least-squares regression line is

$$Y = 18 - 0.05\,X \ .$$

The computational formula for r, the correlation between x and y is:

$$r = \frac{n\Sigma XY - (\Sigma X)(\Sigma Y)}{\left(\sqrt{n\Sigma X^2 - (\Sigma X)^2}\right)\left(\sqrt{n\Sigma Y^2 - (\Sigma Y)^2}\right)}$$

In our case

$$r = \frac{(31)(23{,}400) - (1860)(465)}{\sqrt{31(201{,}600) - (1860)^2}\ \sqrt{31(7925) - (465)^2}}$$

$$= \frac{725{,}400 - 864{,}900}{\sqrt{6{,}249{,}600 - 3{,}459{,}600}\ \sqrt{245{,}675 - 216{,}225}}$$

$$= \frac{-139{,}500}{\sqrt{2{,}790{,}000}\ \sqrt{29{,}450}}$$

$$= -.4867.$$

• PROBLEM 32-12

The following data pertains to presidential elections of the past

Year	New York City Registration (in 1000's)	New York State Vote (in 1000's)
1924	1500	3246
1928	2030	4406
1932	2340	4689
1936	2900	5596
1940	3390	6302
1944	3218	6317
1948	3316	6177

Compute the regression line with New York City registration as the independent variable. Compute the correlation.

Solution: Letting X be the registration and Y the vote we can expand the table as follows.

Year	X	X^2	Y	Y^2	XY
1924	1500	2,250,000	3246	10,536,516	4,869,000
1928	2030	4,120,900	4406	19,412,836	8,944,180
1932	2340	5,475,600	4689	21,986,721	10,972,260
1936	2900	8,410,000	5596	31,315,216	16,228,400
1940	3390	11,492,100	6302	39,715,204	21,363,780
1944	3218	10,355,524	6317	39,904,489	20,328,106
1948	3316	10,995,856	6177	38,155,329	20,482,932
Totals	18694	53,099,980	36,733	201,026,311	103,188,658

Note first that

$$\bar{X} = \frac{\Sigma X}{N} = \frac{18694}{7} = 2670.57$$

and

$$\bar{Y} = \frac{\Sigma Y}{N} = \frac{36,733}{7} = 5247.57.$$

We now use the computational formulae

$$b = \frac{\Sigma XY - n\bar{X}\bar{Y}}{\Sigma X^2 - n\bar{X}^2}$$

$$a = \bar{Y} - b\bar{X} .$$

Here

$$b = \frac{103,188,658 - 7\cdot(2670.57)(5247.57)}{53,099,980 - 7(2670.57)^2}$$

$$= \frac{5,090,558}{3,176,318} = 1.603$$

$$a = 5247.57 - (1.603)(2670.57) = 967.553$$

The line is: $Y = 967.553 + 1.603X$

This line is plotted below.

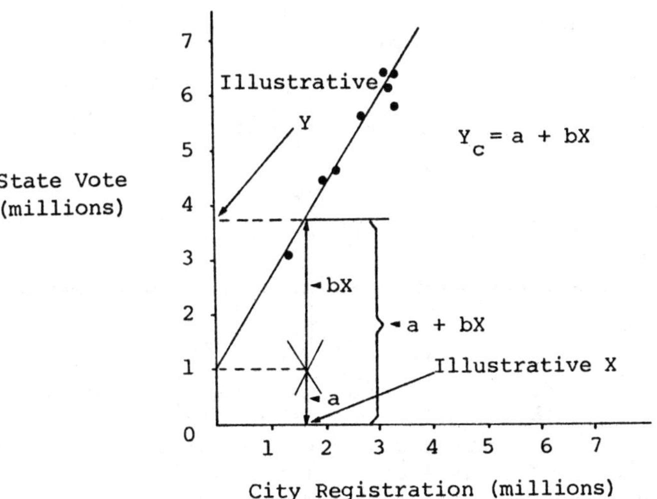

Our sample points seem to provide a good approximation to our line. Intuition tells us the correlation should be close to one. Calculating r:

$$r = \frac{n\Sigma XY - (\Sigma X)(\Sigma Y)}{(\sqrt{n\Sigma X^2 - (\Sigma X)^2})(\sqrt{n\Sigma Y^2 - (\Sigma Y)^2})}$$

$$= \frac{7(103,188,658) - (18,694)(36,733)}{\sqrt{7(53,099,980) - (18,694)^2}\sqrt{7(201,026,311) - (36,733)^2}}$$

$$= \frac{35,633,904}{(4715.32)(7607.29)}$$

$$= .993.$$

Our suspicions are confirmed.

• PROBLEM 32-13

The following table contains time series observations on per capita consumption of beef and the retail price of beef deflated by a consumer price index:

Year	Consumption per Capita Q Pounds	Retail Price P cents/lb.
1949	63.9	67.2
1950	63.4	73.3
1951	56.1	79.5
1952	62.2	76.3
1953	77.6	60.4
1954	80.1	59.7
1955	82.0	59.0
1956	85.4	56.8
1957	84.6	58.7
1958	80.5	65.6
1959	81.4	66.4
1960	85.2	63.8

a) Why is a deflated price used?
b) Find the regression line $Q = f(P)$.

Solution: a) According to consumer theory, an equal percentage change in the prices of all commodities and in money income should not disturb the pattern of quantities demanded or consumed. Hence, during a period such as 1949-1960 in which the consumer price index rose more than 20 percent, we would expect that the actual price of beef would be less closely associated with changes in its per capita consumption than would the deflated price, which shows changes in the price of beef relative to the average price level for all consumer goods and services.

b) We now expand the previous table.

Year	Q	Q^2	P	P^2	PQ
1949	63.9	4083.21	67.2	4515.84	4294.08
1950	63.4	4019.56	73.3	5372.89	4647.22
1951	56.1	3147.21	79.5	6320.25	4459.95
1952	62.2	3868.84	76.3	5821.69	4745.86
1953	77.6	6021.76	60.4	3648.16	4687.04
1954	80.1	6416.01	59.7	3564.09	4781.97
1955	82.0	6724.00	59.0	3481.00	4838.00
1956	85.4	7293.16	56.8	3226.24	4850.72
1957	84.6	7157.16	58.7	3445.69	4966.02
1958	80.5	6480.25	65.6	4303.36	5280.80
1959	81.4	6625.96	66.4	4408.96	5404.96
1950	85.2	7259.04	63.8	4070.44	5435.76
Totals	902.4	69,096.16	786.7	52,178.61	58,392.38

The regression line will be of the form

$$Q = a + bP$$

where

$$b = \frac{\Sigma PQ - N\bar{P}\,\bar{Q}}{\Sigma P^2 - N\bar{P}^2}$$

and

$$a = \bar{Q} - b\bar{P} .$$

First $N = 12$, $\bar{P} = \frac{\Sigma P}{N} = \frac{786.7}{12} = 65.56$, and $\bar{Q} = \frac{\Sigma Q}{N} = \frac{902.4}{12} = 75.2$.

Now

$$b = \frac{58,392.38 - 12(\,65.56)(75.2)}{52,178.61 - 12(65.56)^2}$$

$$= \frac{-768.96}{601.25} = -1.28$$

and

$$a = 75.2 - (-1,28)(65.56) = 159.12.$$

Therefore $Q = 159.12 - 1.28P$.

The slope coefficient, -1.28, implies that a 1.28 pound decrease in predicted per capita consumption is associated with every one-cent increase in the deflated retail price of beef.

• PROBLEM 32-14

Suppose a pilot plant is run for 30 weeks in order to establish costs of production. In each period, a rate of output is established and the corresponding total costs are found. The resulting data is plotted in a scatter diagram.

Microeconomic theory and empirical investigations suggest that a linear relationship might not be best. Sketch possible linear, quadratic, and cubic regression lines.

Solution:

(1) linear
(2) quadratic
(3) cubic

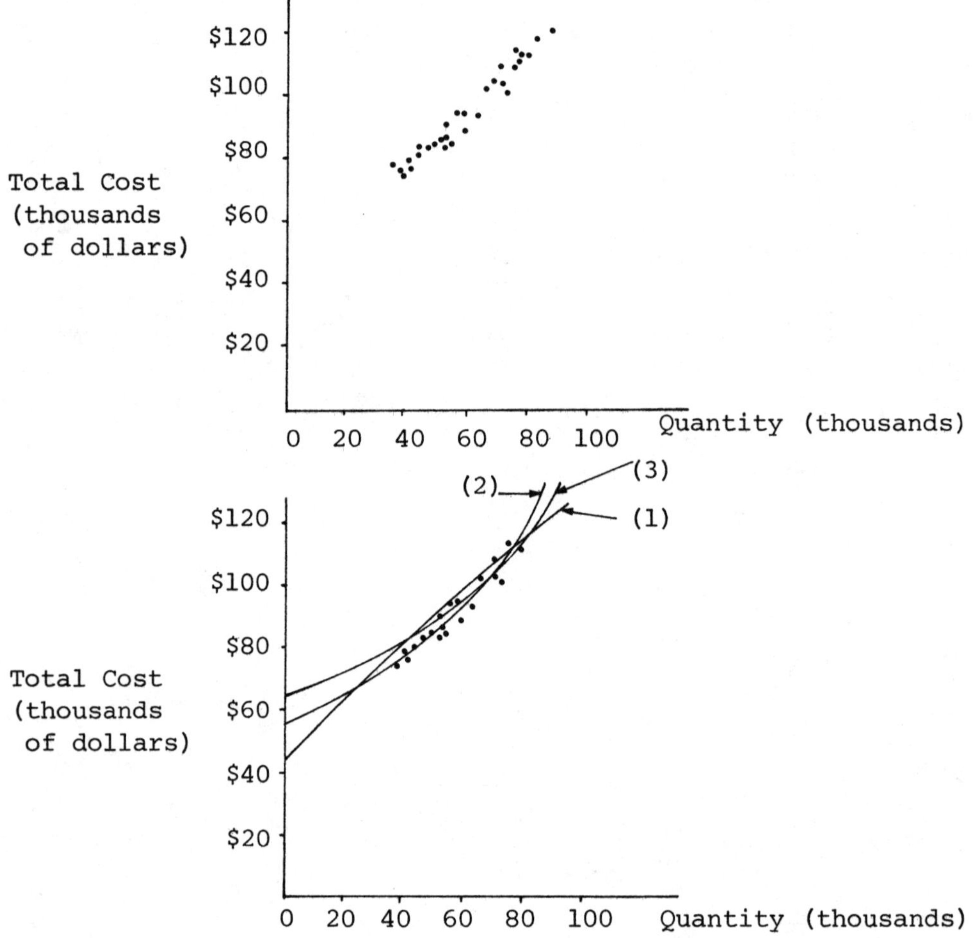

• PROBLEM 32-15

Suppose Q is a measure of output, K is a measure of capital stock in use, and L is a measure of the size of the employed labor force. Then

$$Q = AK^{\beta}L^{\gamma}$$

is a much used form of production function. When $\beta + \gamma = 1$, it is known as a Cobb-Douglas production function.

This function has many convenient properties: Marginal products of both labor and capital are positive if β and γ are. If $\beta + \gamma = 1$, the function has constant returns to scale. That is, if both inputs are increased in like proportion, output will increase in that same proportion. A doubling of both inputs, for example, will result in doubled output. Discuss how the concept of linear regression might be applied to estimate β and γ.

Solution: Notice that this is a problem with two independent variables, K and L. Multiple regression is called for. But first we must obtain a linear form. We have

$$Q = AK^{\beta}L^{\gamma} .$$

Taking the natural log of both sides, we obtain

$$\ln Q = \ln (AK^{\beta}L^{\gamma})$$

or

$$\ln Q = \ln A + \beta \ln K + \gamma \ln L$$

$\ln Q$, $\ln K$, and $\ln L$ are observable.

Let $$\underset{-}{Y} = \begin{bmatrix} \ln Q_1 \\ \ln Q_2 \\ \cdot \\ \cdot \\ \cdot \\ \ln Q_n \end{bmatrix}$$ and

$$\underset{-}{X} = \begin{bmatrix} 1 & \ln K_1 & \ln L_1 \\ \cdot & \ln K_2 & \ln L_2 \\ \cdot & \cdot & \cdot \\ \cdot & \cdot & \cdot \\ \cdot & \cdot & \cdot \\ 1 & \ln K_n & \ln L_n \end{bmatrix} .$$

Then by our analysis of multiple regression in an earlier chapter, we have estimates of:

$$\begin{bmatrix} \widehat{\ln A} \\ \hat{\beta} \\ \hat{\gamma} \end{bmatrix} = [\underset{-}{X}'\underset{-}{X}]^{-1} \underset{-}{X}' \underset{-}{Y} .$$

Our final production function would be $Q = e^{\ln A} K^{\beta}L^{\gamma}$.

• PROBLEM 32-16

XYZ Company is considering digging an oil well. The cost of the well is $50,000. If the well is successful XYZ will make a profit of $400,000, otherwise zero. The probability of the well being successful is 0.1. Is it worthwhile to dig the well?

Solution: We have the following choice :

We will choose the alternative with the higher expected profit. If we don't dig, our expected profit is zero. If we dig, we have the following uncertainty:

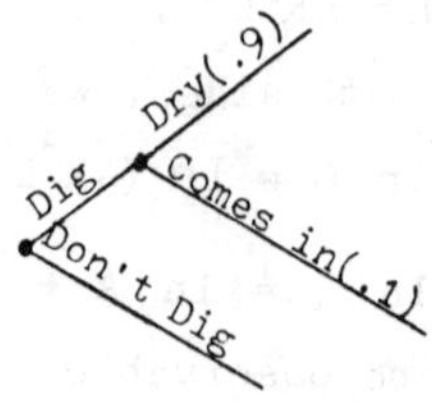

If there is oil, our profit is $400,000 - $50,000 = $350,000. If there isn't we loose the $50,000 cost of the well. Therefore our expected profit is $350,000·P (oil) + (-$50,000)·P (dry) = 350,000(.1) - 50,000(.9) = -$10,000. If we dig, our expected profit is less than zero. Our best bet is not to dig.

We can summarize the solution in a decision tree with the profit shown.

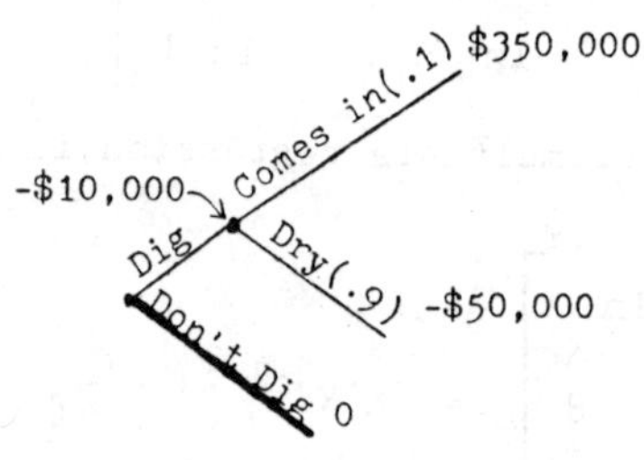

The optimal decision is indicated by the darkened line.

• PROBLEM 32-17

Suppose in the previous problem, the probability of striking oil if the well is dug is 0.2. Would the decision still be the same?

Solution: Our decision tree will be of the same form only with different probabilities.

The new expected profit if we dig is ($350,000)·P(oil) + (-$50,000)·P(dry) = 350,000(.2) - 50,000(.8) = $30,000.

Our expected profit is now higher if we dig. We might now chose to dig. However, there are other sides to this problem; if the president of XYZ is adverse to risk, he still might not want to dig. For our decision, we would say the Expected Profit Criterion indicates that the firm should dig the well.

• PROBLEM 32-18

The Kannan Manufacturing Company is going to build a new plant. Kannan can either build a large plant or a small one with the option of expanding the small one if feasible. Kannan is uncertain of the demand for his product, but he does know that it will be high with a probability of 0.6 and low with a probability of 0.4. For a large plant and high demand net profit is $6 million; and if the demand is low, the payoff is $1 million. Similarly, if a small plant is built initially and no expansion is made the net profits are $4 million (high demand) and $3 million (low demand). There is a net profit of $5 million with expansion of a small plant in the face of high demand. This is determined as follows:

Profit from high demand (with production ability to meet demand)		$10 million
Less: Cost of building small plant	$2 million	
Cost of expanding	3 million	
Total cost		5 million
Payoff		$ 5 million

Similarly, expanding in the face of low demand costs the $5 million as above and only has a profit of $5 million. The net profit is zero.

Should Kannan build a large or a small plant?

Solution: We use a decision tree to analyze this problem.

Starting at the left, the first two lines or branches of the decision tree represent the alternative actions for the first decision - either build a large or a small plant. At the end of each of the decision branches comes a fork with two branches representing the events high and low demand for the product. It is unknown at the time of the first decision (size of plant) which of these events will actually occur.

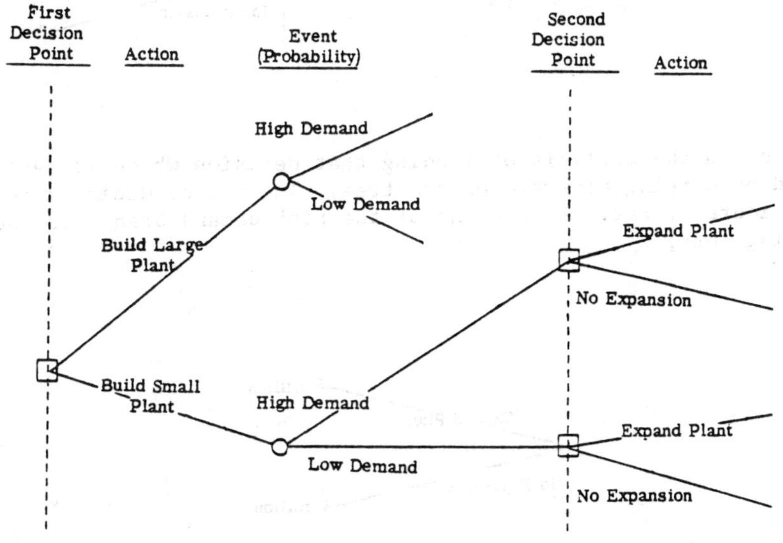

For the "build large plant" action, the tree ends after the event branches. However, for the "build small plant" action a second decision point is reached after the demand events. The decision-maker can choose between the actions expand and no expansion after he knows the market demand. These actions are represented as branches on the decision tree. Including both branches at this point may seem unnecessary at first. One would generally expect to expand the plant in response to a high demand and not to expand if a low demand occurred. But we cannot be sure of this until we include the economic information in the tree. There is always the possibility that the expansion will cost more than the additional revenue. Hence, we should retain both action alternatives at each of the second decision points.

We now augment the original decision tree with the probabilities and payoffs given in the problem,

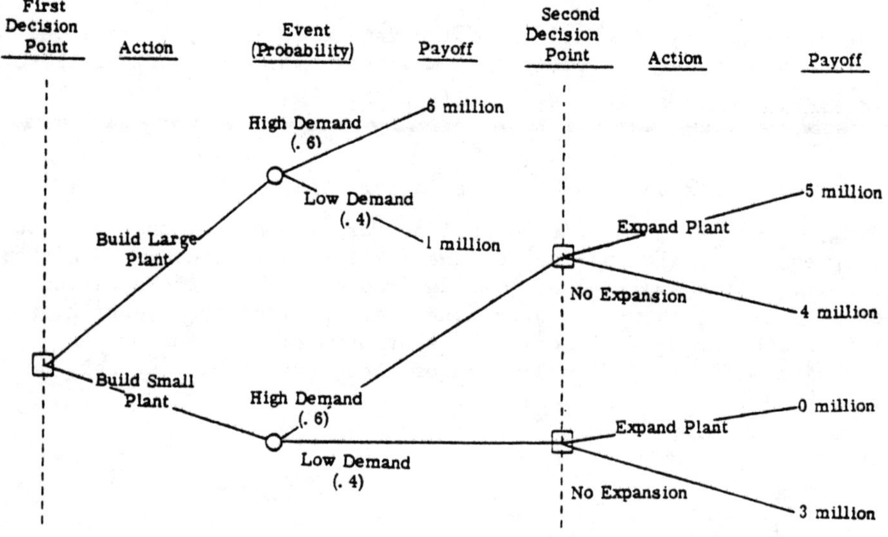

We now begin the analysis of finding that decision which is best. We proceed by working backward on the tree. The second decision point is considered first. At the end of the high demand branch is the following fork,

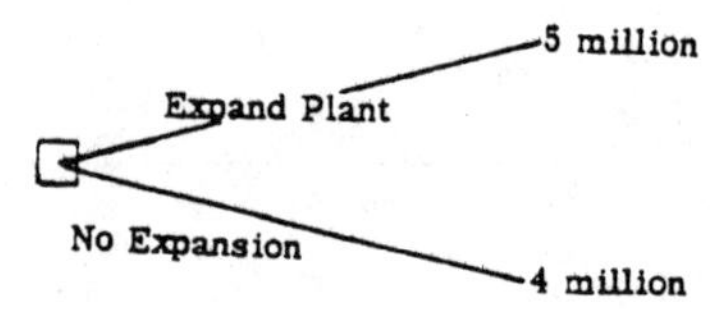

Since the action "expand the plant" leads to $5 million net profit as opposed to only $4 million for no expansion, that alternative is selected and the "no expansion" branch is removed from further consideration. Similarly, we remove the "expand plant" option at the end of the low demand branch. Our result is the following reduced decision tree.

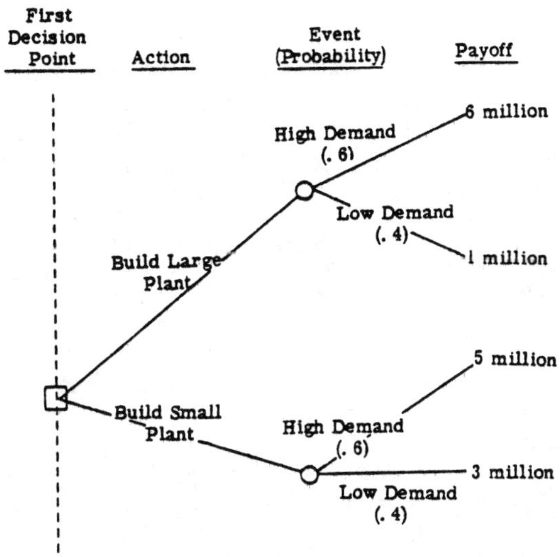

We now back up to the event forks, with branches labeled "high demand" and "low demand", respectively. At each of these forks an expected value if taken using the payoffs at the ends of the branches and the probabilities shown. For the fork at the end of the "Build Large Plant" action the expected value is $4.0 million ($6 million x .6 + .4 x $1 million). For the fork at the end of the "Build Small Plant" branch, the expected value is $4.2 million ($5 million x 0.6 + $3 million x 0.4). By replacing the event forks by their expected values, the final reduced form of the decision tree is obtained.

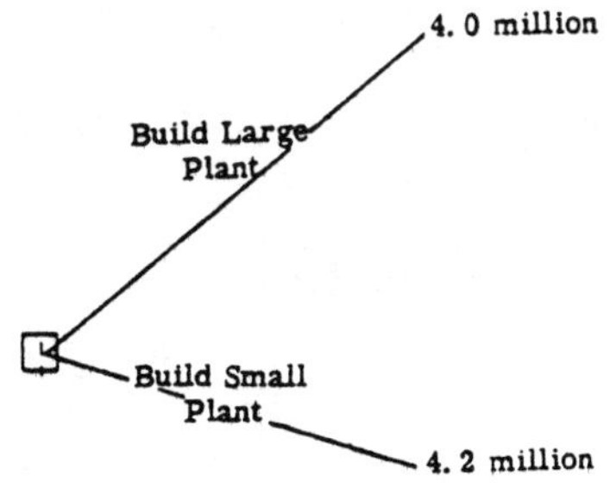

Seeing this, Kannan decides to build the small plant.

Flapjack Computers is interested in developing a new tape drive for a proposed new computer. Flapjack does not have research personnel available to develop the new drive itself and so is going to subcontract the development to an independent research firm. Flapjack has set a fee of $250,000 for developing the new tape drive and has asked for bids from various research firms. The bid is to be awarded not on the basis of price (set at $250,000) but on the basis of both the technical plan shown in the bid and the firm's reputation.

Dyna Research Institute is considering submitting a proposal (i.e., a bid) to Flapjack to develop the new tape drive. Dyna Research Management estimated that it would cost about $50,000 to prepare a proposal; further they estimated that the chances were about 50-50 that they would be awarded the contract.

There was a major concern among Dyna Research engineers concerning exactly how they would develop the tape drive if awarded the contract. There were three alternative approaches that could be tried. One involved the use of certain electronic components. The engineers estimated that it would cost only $50,000 to develop a prototype of the tape drive using the electronic approach, but that there was only a 50 percent chance that the prototype would be satisfactory. A second approach involved the use of certain magnetic apparatus. The cost of developing a prototype using this approach would cost $80,000 with 70 percent chance of success. Finally, there was a mechanical approach with cost of $120,000, but the engineers were certain of success.

Dyna Research could have sufficient time to try only two approaches. Thus, if either the magnetic or the electronic approach tried and failed, the second attempt would have to use the mechanical approach in order to guarantee a successful prototype.

The management of Dyna Research was uncertain how to take all this information into account in making the immediate decision-whether to spend $50,000 to develop a proposal for Flapjack. Can you help?

Solution: Since this decision seems complex, we will build the decision tree in steps. The first decision facing Dyna Research involves the actions "Prepare a Proposal" and "Do not Prepare a Proposal". If a proposal is developed and submitted to Flapjack, then either of the events "Contract Awarded to Dyna" or "Dyna Loses Contract". Each event has probability 0.5. These choices are shown below:

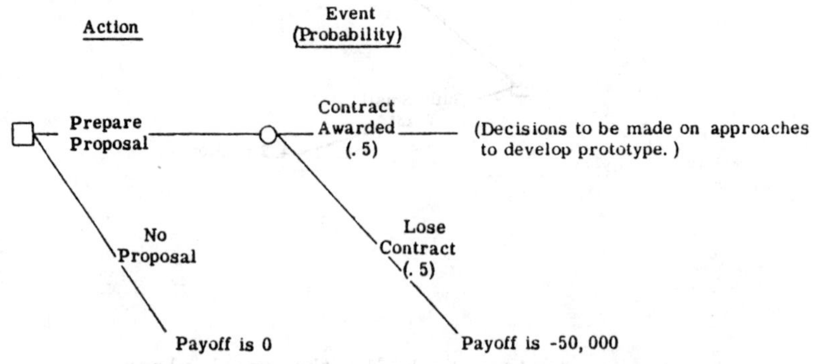

If Dyna Research decides not to prepare a bid, the net payoff is zero. If a bid is prepared but the contract is lost, Dyna Research loses the $50,000 cost of preparing the bid (i.e., the payoff is -$50,000). If the contract is awarded to Dyna, then the next decision, the choice between alternative methods of developing a successful tape drive, must be made.

In the second decision, Dyna Research must decide which of the three approaches - mechanical, electronic, or magnetic - to try first. This decision is shown below:

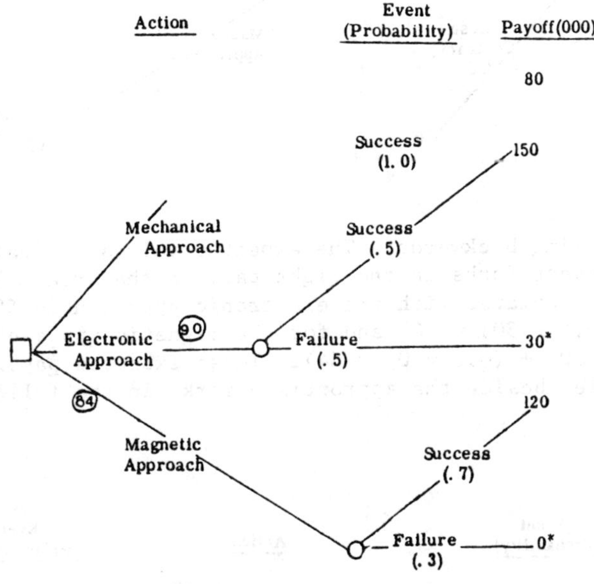

*Mechanical Approach must be used.

The payoffs in the above diagram are calculated as shown below:

			Payoff(thousands of dollars)					
End of Branch	Fee		Cost of Proposal		Cost of Prototype Indicated		Cost of Mechanical Prototype	
Electronic Approach								
Success..................	250	-	50	-	50			= 150
Failure..................	250	-	50	-	50	-	120	= 30
Magnetic Approach								
Success..................	250	-	50	-	80			= 120
Failure..................	250	-	50	-	80	-	120	= 0

For the mechanical approach we take

Fee - Cost of Proposal - Cost of Mechanical Prototype

= 250 - 50 - 120 = 80.

The complete decision tree is shown as follows:

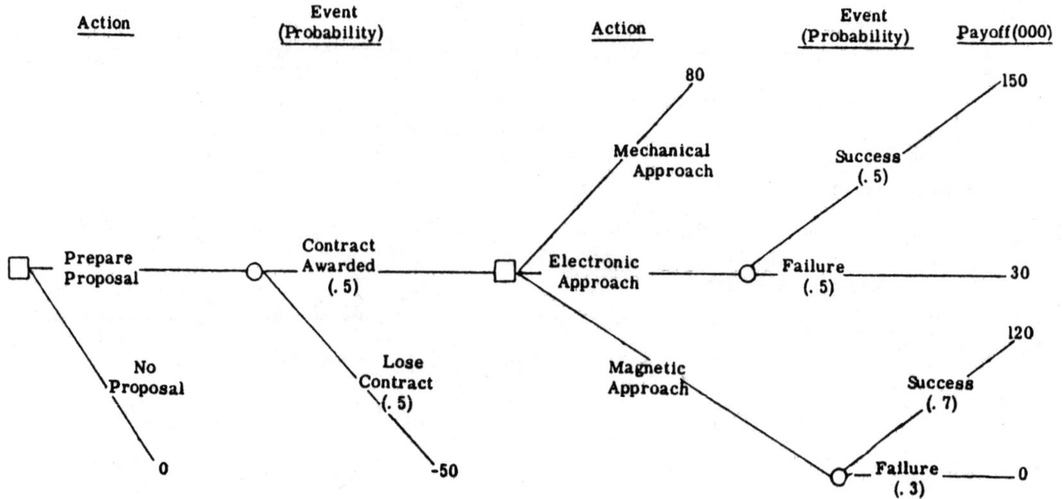

We proceed by working backwards. The expected values are calculated for each of the event forks in the right part of the tree. Thus the expected payoff associated with the electronic approach is \$90,000 ((0.5 x 150) + (0.5 x 30) = 90) and for the magnetic approach, it is \$84,000 ((0.7 x 120) + (0.3 x 0) = 84). These expected payoffs are inserted in circles beside the appropriate forks in the following figure:

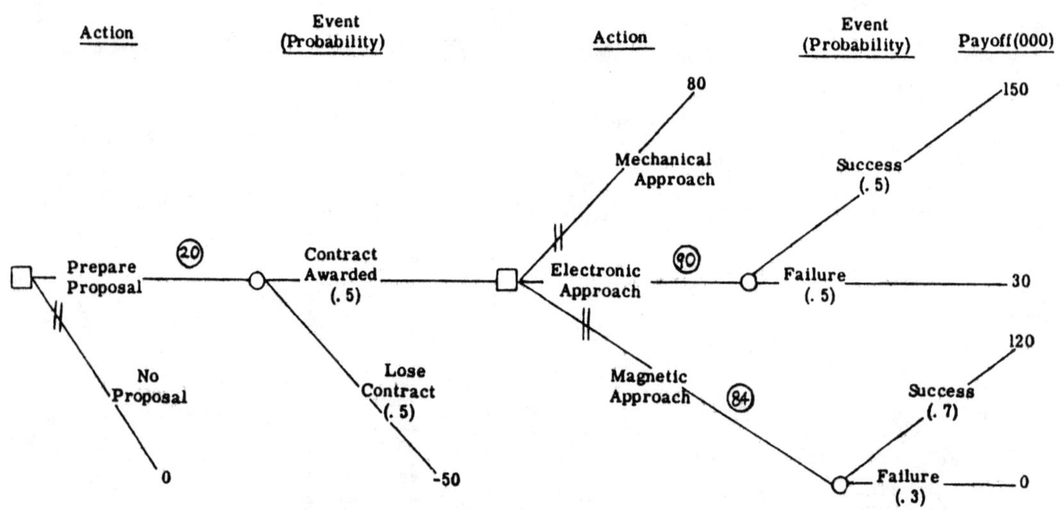

Moving left to the second decision point, we see that the electronic approach offers the highest expected payoff (\$90,000) and is the best choice. The value \$90,000 is written (circled) beside the decision point and the nonpreferred approaches are indicated by drawing || on the branches.

The tree now has a payoff of +\$90,000 if the contract is awarded and -\$50,000 if not. The expected value of preparing a proposal is \$20,000 ((0.5 x 90) + (0.5 x (-50)) = 20). This is written in a circle beside the event fork.

Finally, the choice must be made between the expected profit of \$20,000 for preparing the proposal and zero if the proposal is not prepared. The first course is selected, and the mark "||" drawn through the "No Proposal" branch.

In summary, Dyna Research should prepare the proposal. If the contract is awarded, the electronic approach should be tried first; but if this fails, the mechanical approach should be used.

• PROBLEM 32-20

World-Wide Vacuums Inc., the nation's largest producer of central vacuuming systems, has 5 training centers for its service personnel. Upon completion of a 10 week training session, each employee is given a competency exam and rated on a scale of 1 to 20. A random sample of size four is selected from each training center and the results of their exams given below.

Center 1	Center 2	Center 3	Center 4	Center 5
9	5	11	9	16
11	6	14	10	15
12	8	15	7	19
7	8	10	9	14

Test the hypothesis:

H_0: $\mu_1 = \mu_2 = \mu_3 = \mu_4 = \mu_5$ against the alternative

H_A: the means are not all equal.

Use $\alpha = .01$.

Solution: We first note that because all samples contain the same number of observations, (a situation known as a balanced design) there are simplifications in the formulas for the sums of squares needed for the ANOVA table.

The summary statistics are

$$k = 5, \quad n = n_1 = n_2 = n_3 = n_4 = n_5 = 4$$

$$\sum_{i=1}^{4} Y_{i1} = 39 \qquad \sum_{j=1}^{5}\sum_{i=1}^{4} Y_{ij}^2 = 2575$$

$$\sum_{i=1}^{4} Y_{i2} = 27$$

$$\sum_{i=1}^{4} Y_{i3} = 50 \qquad \sum_{j=1}^{5}\sum_{i=1}^{4} Y_{ij} = 215 .$$

$$\sum_{i=1}^{4} Y_{i4} = 35$$

$$\sum_{i=1}^{4} Y_{i5} = 64$$

Computing the sums of squares:

$$SSTO = \sum_{j=1}^{5} \sum_{i=1}^{4} (Y_{ij} - \bar{Y}_{..})^2 = \sum_{j=1}^{5} \sum_{i=1}^{4} Y_{ij}^2 - 4 \cdot 5 \cdot \bar{Y}_{..}^2$$

$$= 2575 - 20\left(\frac{215}{20}\right)^2$$

$$= 2575 - \frac{(215)^2}{20} = 2575 - 2311.25$$

$$= 263.75 .$$

$$SSTR = \sum_{j=1}^{5} n_j(\bar{Y}_{.j} - \bar{Y}_{..})^2 = 4\left(\sum_{j=1}^{5} \bar{Y}_{.j}^2 - 5 \cdot \bar{Y}_{..}^2\right)$$

$$= 4\left(\sum_{j=1}^{5} \bar{Y}_{.j}^2\right) - 20 \cdot \bar{Y}_{..}^2$$

$$= 2517.75 - 2311.25$$

$$= 206.5 .$$

Thus

$$SSE = SSTO - SSTR = 263.75 - 206.5 = 57.25 .$$

The ANOVA table is thus

Source of Variation	Sum of Squares	Degrees of Freedom	Mean Square
Between training centers	206.5	k-1=5-1=4	51.625
Within training centers (error)	57.25	rk-k=k(r-1)=5.3=15	3.817
Total	263.75	20-1 = 19	

The F-statistic for testing the hypothesis that $\mu_1 = \mu_2 = \ldots = \mu_5$ is $F = \frac{MSTR}{MSE} = \frac{51.625}{3.817} = 13.52$. The 99th percentile of the F distribution with 4 and 15 degrees of freedom is

$$F(.99, 4, 15) = 4.8932 .$$

$$F = 13.52 > F(.99, 4, 15) = 4.8932$$

thus we reject H_0 and accept that the population means are not all equal.

• PROBLEM 32-21

The largest manufacturer of cold breakfast cereal in Spokane, Washington notices that sales of its hottest selling cereal, Crispy Crunchy **Sugar-Coated Corn Chips** , are slipping. In a marketing research study, the company experiments with three new package designs in the hope of finding one that will reverse this trend. The company thinks that the area in which the cereal is marketed will have an effect on sales and thus divides the state into 4 geographical areas. Five nearly identical stores are selected in each area to be used for the experiment. After a month sales in each store are recorded and an analysis of variance table is constructed. No interactions between package design and geographical area are found. Thus the ANOVA table is

Source of Variation	Sum of Squares	Degrees of Freedom	Mean Square
Package Design	154.24	3-1=2	77.12
Geographical Area	218.00	4-1=3	72.66
Error	746.01	29-2-3=24	31.08

Test at the .025 level, for significant differences in sales due to differences in package designs and geographical area.

Solution: We first test the hypothesis that there is no effect on sales due to differences in package design.

The test for significant differences in sales between the 3 designs is carried out in the following manner:

1) Compute $F = \dfrac{\text{Mean Square due to Package Design}}{\text{Mean Square Error}}$.

2) Under the null hypothesis that there is no difference between designs, F is distributed with an F-distribution having 2 and 24 degrees of freedom.

3) Set the level of significance of the test at α . We are given $\alpha = .025$. Now find $F(1-\alpha, 2, 24) = F(.975, 2, 24)$ the 97.5 percentile of the F-distribution with 2 and 24 degrees. From a table, we see that $F(.975, 2, 24) = 4.3187$.

4) If $F > 4.3187$, reject the null hypothesis, otherwise accept. We see that

$$F = \frac{77.12}{31.08} = 2.48 < 4.3187 ,$$

thus accept that there is no significant effect on sales due to package design.

Similarly, we reject

H_0: no effect due to geographical area

if $\quad F = \dfrac{\text{Mean Square Due to Geographical Area}}{\text{Mean Square Error}}$

is less than $F(.975, 3, 24) = 3.7211$. $F = \dfrac{72.66}{31.08} = 2.34 < 3.7211$

therefore accept the null hypothesis that there is no effect on sales due to the geographical location.

An economist wishes to estimate the relationship between the quantity demanded of a good, its price, the price of a substitute and disposable personal income. Thus he hypothesizes the following linear relationship

$$Q_i = \beta_0 + \beta_1 P_i + \beta_2 P_i' + \beta_3 Y_i + u_i \, , \tag{1}$$

where Q is the quantity demanded, P is the price of the good, P' is the price of a substitute and Y is the disposable income. β is the regression coefficient and the u_i are random disturbances.

He obtains, using a sample of 30 successive time periods, the following results:

$$Q = 67,900 - 14,870P - 4,986P' + 146.7Y \tag{2}$$
$$(20,004) \quad (1,594) \quad (4,141) \quad (25.8) \tag{3}$$

$$R^2 = 0.7729 \qquad \bar{R}^2 = 0.7467$$

$$F = 29.50 \qquad S_e = 5646 \, .$$

Interpret the above results.

Solution: Let us first clarify the relationship (1). Since quantity demanded varies inversely with price, we expect $\beta_1 < 0$. On the other hand $\beta_2 > 0$ since the quantity demanded of a good varies proportionately with the price of a substitute good. Finally, under normal conditions $\beta_3 > 0$.

The random disturbances, u_i, are assumed to be independently distributed. Furthermore, they are identically distributed, the form of the distribution being

$$u_i \sim N(0,\sigma_u^2) \, .$$

This is the assumption of homoskedasticity. With this assumption one can prove that the least squares estimators are linearly unbiased with minimum variance.

Next, we turn to an interpretation of the regression results. First consider (2). The estimate of the intercept (i.e., when P = P' = Y = 0) is $\beta_0 = 67,900$. The three regression coefficients are

$$\beta_1 = -14,870 \, , \; \beta_2 = -4,986 \; \text{and} \; \beta_3 = 146.7 \, .$$

The set of numbers in (3) gives the standard error of estimates of the regression coefficients. We use these errors to calculate confidence intervals and the significance levels of the β_i. To do this for β_1 set up the null and alternative hypotheses.

$$H_0: \; \beta_1 = 0$$

$$H_1: \; \beta_1 \neq 0 \, .$$

Using the t-test, (since the variance of the β_s is unknown)

$$\frac{\hat{\beta} - \beta_0}{s_{\hat{\beta}}} \sim t(\alpha/2, \, n-k) \tag{4}$$

where k denotes the number of parameters being estimated, α is the significance level desired, and $n-k$ are the degrees of freedom. Substituting the given results into (4),

$$\frac{-14,870 - 0}{1594} = -9.33 .$$

Since 4 parameters are being estimated $t(\alpha/2,n-k) = t(.025,26)$. From a table of t-values we find

$$t(.025,26) = 2.056 .$$

Since the calculated value of the t-statistic is much less than -2.056, we reject the null hypothesis $\beta_1 = 0$ and conclude, in accordance with economic theory, that $\beta_1 < 0$.

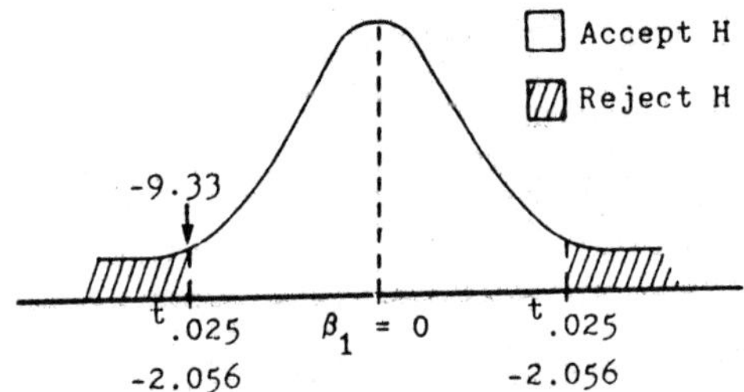

Similarly, we find that

$$\frac{\hat{\beta}_3}{s_{\hat{\beta}_3}} = \frac{146.7}{25.8} = 5.69 ,$$

leading us to the conclusion that $\beta_3 > 0$. But $\frac{\hat{\beta}_2}{s_{\hat{\beta}_2}} = \frac{-4986}{4141} = -1.20,$

indicating that we should accept the null hypothesis $\beta_2 = 0$.

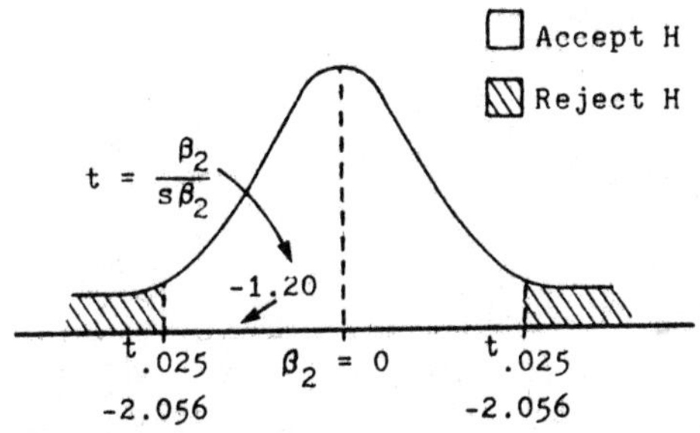

We now examine the coefficient of determination, R^2, and the corrected coefficient of determination, $\bar{R}^2$. Let $\hat{Y}_i$ denote the ith value on the regression line and $\bar{Y} = \frac{1}{n}\sum_{i=1}^{n} Y_i$ the mean of the observed values of the explained variable. Then R^2 is defined to be

$$R^2 = \frac{\sum_{i=1}^{n} (\hat{Y}_i - \bar{Y})^2}{\sum_{i=1}^{n} (Y_i - \bar{Y})^2} . \tag{5}$$

Since $Y_i-\bar{Y}=(Y_i-\hat{Y}_i)+(\hat{Y}_i-\bar{Y})$, then, $0 \le R^2 \le 1$. Since $R^2=0.7729$, we suspect that the hypothesis $\beta_1 = \beta_2 = \beta_3 = 0$ must be rejected.

If the null-hypothesis is true,

$$\frac{\sum_{i=1}^{n} (\hat{Y}_i - \bar{Y})^2/(k-1)}{\sum_{i=1}^{n} (Y_i - \hat{Y})^2/(n-k)} \sim F_{k-1,n-k} \tag{6}$$

where $F_{k-1,n-k}$ denotes a member of the family of F distributions with parameters k-1, n-k. Define

$$SSR = \sum_{i=1}^{n} (\hat{Y}_i - \bar{Y})^2$$

$$SSE = \sum_{i=1}^{n} (Y_i - \hat{Y})^2$$

$$SST = SSR + SSE \ .$$

Then (6) may be written,

$$\frac{SSR/(k-1)}{SSE/(n-k)} = \left[\frac{n-k}{k-1}\right]\left[\frac{SSR/SST}{1 - SSR/SST}\right] \tag{7}$$

But, from (5), $R^2 = SSR/SST$. Hence (7) becomes

$$\left[\frac{n-k}{k-1}\right]\left[\frac{R^2}{1 - R^2}\right] \tag{8}$$

In the present problem, n = 30, k = 4. Hence, (8) becomes

$$\left(\frac{26}{3}\right)\left(\frac{0.7729}{0.2271}\right) = 29.50 \ .$$

This is the calculated F statistic. From (6),

$$F_{.01,3,26} = 4.64.$$

Since $F_{calculated} > F_{test}$, we reject $H_0: \beta_1 = \beta_2 = \beta_3 = 0$.

Quite frequently we desire a value of R^2 that is adjusted for the degrees of freedom lost in attempting to estimate the required parameters. Define

$$\bar{R}^2 = R^2 - \frac{(k-1)}{n-k}(1 - R^2) \tag{9}$$

where n is the number of observations, and k is the number of parameters estimated.

(9) is called the corrected coefficient of determination. In the present problem, we find

$$\bar{R}^2 = .7729 - \frac{3}{26}(.2271)$$

$$= .7467 \ .$$

CHAPTER 33

USING OPERATIONS RESEARCH FOR BUSINESS, MANAGEMENT, & FINANCE

• PROBLEM 33-1

A small plant makes two types of automobile parts. It buys castings that are machined, bored, and polished. The data shown in Table 1 are given.

Castings for Part A cost $2 each; for Part B they cost $3 each. They sell for $5 and $6, respectively. The three machines have running costs of $20, $14, and $17.50 per hour. Assuming that any combination of Parts A and B can be sold, what product mix maximizes profit?

TABLE 1

	Part *A*	Part *B*
Machining capacity	25 per hour	40 per hour
Boring capacity	28 per hour	35 per hour
Polishing capacity	35 per hour	25 per hour

Solution: The first step is to calculate the profit per part. This is done in Table 2. From the results shown, if on the average x of Part A and y of Part B per hour is made, the net profit is

$$Z = 1.20x + 1.40y. \qquad (1)$$

Because there is no meaning for negative x and y,

$$x \geq 0, \qquad y \geq 0. \qquad (2)$$

TABLE 2

	Part A	Part B
Machining	20/25 = 0.80	20/40 = 0.50
Boring	14/28 = 0.50	14/35 = 0.40
Polishing	17.50/35 = 0.50	17.50/25 = 0.70
Purchase	2.00	3.00
Total cost	3.80	4.60
Sales price	5.00	6.00
Profit	1.20	1.40

x and y cannot be chosen freely, because the capacity limits have to be taken into account. These yield the following results:

Machining $\frac{x}{25} + \frac{y}{40} \leq 1$

Boring $\frac{x}{28} + \frac{y}{35} \leq 1$

Polishing $\frac{x}{35} + \frac{y}{25} \leq 1$

Multiply through to clear fractions and obtain:

$$\begin{aligned} &\text{Machining} \quad 40x + 25y \leq 1000 \\ &\text{Boring} \quad 35x + 28y \leq 980 \\ &\text{Polishing} \quad 25x + 35y \leq 875 \end{aligned} \tag{3}$$

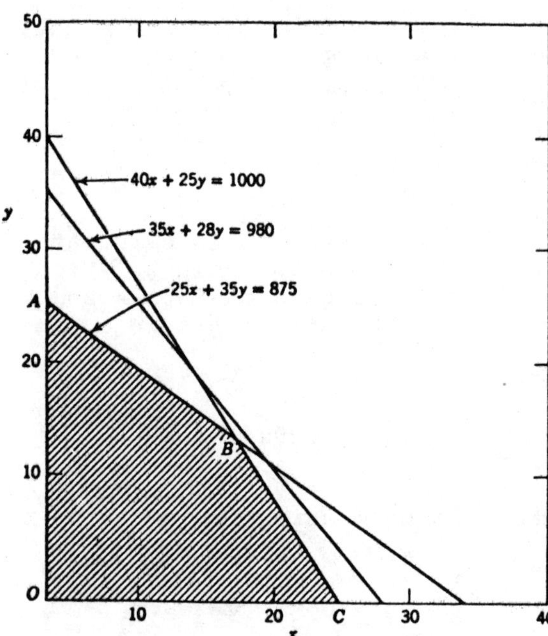

Fig. 1

When the equation 40x + 25y = 1000 is plotted, a line that divides the plane into two regions is obtained (Figure 1). In the region that includes the origin $40x + 25y < 1000$; in the other region $40x + 25y > 1000$. The other two inequalities in (3) divide the plane in a similar fashion. Thus if one regards the decision about the values of x and y as selecting a point in a plane, one sees that the point must lie within or on the boundaries of the region OABC. Because the line $35x + 28y = 980$ lies outside this region, the boring constraint is redundant. In other words, any combination of x and y that satisfy the machining and polishing constraints will automatically be within the boring capacity.

The point (x,y) for which profits attain their maximum must lie at one of the corners of OABC. The possible maximizing values are O(0,0), A(0,25), B(16.93,12.90), and C(25,0). The corresponding profits are $Z_0 = 0$, $Z_A = 35$, $Z_B = 38.39$, and $Z_C = 30$, so that the best production plan is 16.93 of A per hour and 12.90 of B per hour. It is not hard to see why the maximizing point (x,y) must lie at a corner. Consider the geometric interpretation of equation 1. If Z is kept fixed (say Z = 20), then as x and y vary, (1) must be represented by a line of equal profit. If one chooses another value of Z (say Z = 25), one shall obtain a parallel line further away from the origin O. As one increases Z, one obtains a family of parallel lines. Clearly, Z is maximized by finding the line of the family furthest from the origin which has at least one point within or on the boundary of OABC. Such a line passes through B. Thus, no matter what boundary figure one draws, the maximizing line must pass through a corner.

• PROBLEM 33-2

A machine shop has one drill press and five milling machines, which are to be used to produce an assembly consisting of two parts, 1 and 2. The productivity of each machine for the two parts is given below:

Production Time in minutes per piece

Part	Drill	Mill
1	3	20
2	5	15

It is desired to maintain a balanced loading on all machines such that no machine runs more than 30 minutes per day longer than any other machine (assume that the milling load is split evenly among all five milling machines).

Formulate a linear program to divide the work time of each machine to obtain the maximum number of completed assemblies assuming an 8-hour working day.

Solution: Let x_1 = number of Part 1 produced per day,

and

x_2 = number of Part 2 produced per day.

The load on each milling machine (in minutes) =

$$\frac{20x_1 + 15x_2}{5} = 4x_1 + 3x_2,$$

whereas the load on the drill press (in minutes) = $3x_1 + 5x_2$. Thus the time restriction on each milling machine is:

$$4x_1 + 3x_2 \leqq (8)(60) = 480.$$

Similarly, for the drill press

$$3x_1 + 5x_2 \leqq 480.$$

The machine balance constraint can be represented by

$$|(4x_1 + 3x_2) - (3x_1 + 5x_2)| \leqq 30$$

or

$$|x_1 - 2x_2| \leqq 30.$$

This is a nonlinear constraint which can be replaced by the following two linear constraints:

$$x_1 - 2x_2 \leqq 30$$

$$-x_1 + 2x_2 \leqq 30.$$

The number of completed assemblies cannot exceed the smaller value of Part 1 and Part 2 produced. Thus, the objective function is to maximize Z = minimum (x_1, x_2). This is again a nonlinear function. However, another trick can be used to represent it as a linear function. Let y = minimum of (x_1, x_2) where y represents the number of completed assemblies.

This means that:

$$x_1 \geq y$$

$$x_2 \geq y$$

and the objective is to maximize Z = y. Thus, the complete linear programming formulation becomes:

$$\text{Maximize: } Z = y$$

$$\begin{aligned} \text{Subject to: } 4x_1 + 3x_2 &\leq 480 \\ 3x_1 + 5x_2 &\leq 480 \\ x_1 - 2x_2 &\leq 30 \\ -x_1 + 2x_2 &\leq 30 \\ x_1 \quad -y &\geq 0 \\ x_2 - y &\geq 0 \end{aligned}$$

$$x_1 \geq 0, \quad x_2 \geq 0, \quad y \geq 0.$$

• **PROBLEM 33-3**

The Red Tomato Company operates two plants for canning their tomatoes and has three warehouses for storing the finished products until they are purchased by retailers. The Company wants to arrange its shipments from the plants to the warehouses so that the requirements of the warehouses are met and so that shipping costs are kept at a minimum. The schedule below represents the per case shipping cost from plant to warehouse: (Table a).

Each week, plant I can produce up to 850 cases and plantII can produce up to 650 cases of tomatoes. Also, each week warehouse A requires 300 cases, warehouse B, 400 cases, and warehouse C, 500 cases. If the number of cases shipped from plant I to warehouse A is represented by x_1, from plant I to warehouse B by x_2, and so on, the above data can be represented by the table: (Table b).
Solve by the Simplex Method.

TABLE (a)

	A	B	C
Plant I	\$.25	\$.17	\$.18
Plant II	\$.25	\$.18	\$.14

TABLE (b)

	Warehouse A	B	C
Plant I	x_1	x_2	x_3
Plant II	x_4	x_5	x_6
Total Demand	300	400	500

Solution: The linear programming problem is stated as follows: Minimize the cost function:

$$C = .25x_1 + .17x_2 + .18x_3 + .25x_4 + .18x_5 + .14x_6$$

subject to the conditions:

$$x_1 + x_2 + x_3 \leq 850 \qquad x_1 \geq 0,\ x_2 \geq 0$$

$$x_4 + x_5 + x_6 \leq 650 \qquad x_3 \geq 0,\ x_4 \geq 0 \qquad (1)$$

$$x_1 + x_4 = 300 \qquad x_5 \geq 0,\ x_6 \geq 0$$

$$x_2 + x_5 = 400$$

$$x_3 + x_6 = 500$$

Before finding a solution, notice that the linear objective function contains six variables. Also, the number of constraints is eleven. The simplex method requires that the constraints of a linear programming problem be given as linear equations, not as linear inequalities. Thus, before proceeding further, change the inequalities of (1) to equalities. To do this, introduce slack variables. For example, since $x_1 + x_2 + x_3 \leq 850$, there is some nonnegative real number x_7, so that $x_1 + x_2 + x_3 + x_7 = 850$, $x_7 \geq 0$. Here x_7 is a slack variable. Similarly, there is a nonnegative integer x_8 so that $x_4 + x_5 + x_6 + x_8 = 650$, $x_8 \geq 0$.

Thus, by introducing slack variables, the linear programming problem can be restated as: Minimize the cost function:

$$C = .25x_1 + .17x_2 + .18x_3 + .25x_4 + .18x_5 + .14x_6$$

subject to the conditions:

$$x_1 + x_2 + x_3 + x_7 = 850, \quad x_1 \geq 0,\ x_2 \geq 0$$

$$x_4 + x_5 + x_6 + x_8 = 650, \quad x_3 \geq 0,\ x_4 \geq 0$$

$$x_1 + x_4 = 300, \quad x_5 \geq 0,\ x_6 \geq 0 \qquad (2)$$

$$x_2 + x_5 = 400, \quad x_7 \geq 0,\ x_8 \geq 0$$

$$x_3 + x_6 = 500 .$$

Now the constraints have been expressed as linear equalities. Physically, the two slack variables x_7 and x_8 can be interpreted as cases of tomatoes produced at plant I and plant II, respectively, but not shipped to any warehouse. It is clear that the shipping cost of not shipping is zero so that the slack variables introduced cannot affect the objective (cost) function to be minimized . From the system of equations (2) there is:

$$x_1 = 300 - x_4$$

$$x_2 = 400 - x_5$$

$$x_6 = 500 - x_3$$

Now, $x_1 = 850 - x_2 - x_3 - x_7$ but $x_1 = 300 - x_4$, $x_2 = 400 - x_5$. Therefore, $x_7 = 850 - 300 + x_4 - 400 + x_5 - x_3$ so, $x_7 = 150 - x_3 + x_4 + x_5$. Also, $x_8 = 650 - x_4 - x_5 - x_6$ but $x_6 = 500 - x_3$, thus,

$$x_8 = 650 - x_4 - x_5 - 500 + x_3$$

$$x_8 = 150 + x_3 - x_4 - x_5 .$$

The cost function C then becomes $C = .25x_1 + .17x_2 + .18x_3 + .25x_4 + .18x_5 + .14x_6$ but $x_1 = 300 - x_4$, $x_2 = 400 - x_5$, and $x_6 = 500 - x_3$. Therefore $C = .25(300 - x_4) + .17(400 - x_5) + .18x_3 + .25x_4 + .18x_5 + .14(500 - x_3)$. $C = 75 - .25x_4 + 68 - .17x_5 + .18x_3 + .25x_4 + .18x_5 + 70 - .14x_3$. $C = 213 + .04x_3 + .01x_5$. Therefore, minimize $C = 213 + .04x_3 + .01x_5$ subject to:

$$x_1 = 300 - x_4$$

$$x_2 = 400 - x_5$$

$$x_6 = 500 - x_3$$

$$x_7 = 150 - x_3 + x_4 + x_5$$

$x_8 = 150 + x_3 - x_4 - x_5$ in which each variable is ≥ 0. The matrix representing the linear programming problem is:

	1	x_3	x_4	x_5
$-C$	-213	-.04	0	-.01
x_1	300	0	-1	0
x_2	400	0	0	-1
x_6	500	-1	0	0
x_7	150	-1	1	1
x_8	150	-1	-1	-1

in which -C is to be maximized. Since every entry in the -C row is negative or zero, go no further. The maximum value for -C is -213. The minimum cost C is then $213. The values x_1, x_2, x_3, x_4, x_5, x_6 giving the minimum cost of $213 are:

$$x_1 = 300$$

$$x_2 = 400$$

$$x_3 = 0$$

$$x_4 = 0$$

$$x_5 = 0$$

$$x_6 = 500 .$$

A small-trailer manufacturer wishes to determine how many camper units and how many house trailers he should produce in order to make optimal use of his available resources. Suppose he has available 11 units of aluminum, 40 units of wood, and 52 person-weeks of work. (The preceding data are expressed in convenient units. Assume that all other needed resources are available and have no effect on his decision.) The table below gives the amount of each resource needed to manufacture each camper and each trailer.

	Aluminum	Wood	Person-weeks
Per camper	2	1	7
Per trailer	1	8	8

Assume further that based on his previous year's sales record the manufacturer has decided to make no more than 5 campers. If the manufacturer realized a profit of $300 on a camper and $400 on a trailer, what should be his production in order to maximize his profit?

Solution: Letting x_1 represent the number of camper units, and x_2 the number of house trailers, consider first the constraints. From the table note that the manufacturer uses 2 units of aluminum per camper and 1 unit of aluminum per trailer. Thus he needs a total of $2x_1 + x_2$ units of aluminum. This fact, along with the fact that he has available only 11 units of aluminum, gives the inequality $2x_1 + x_2 \leq 11$. Similarly, he needs a total of $x_1 + 8x_2$ units of wood. And since he has available only 40 units of wood, $x_1 + 8x_2 \leq 40$ is obtained. The total number of person-weeks needed to build x_1 campers and x_2 trailers is $7x_1 + 8x_2$. Since only 52 weeks are available, $7x_1 + 8x_2 \leq 52$. He wants to produce no more than 5 campers, therefore, $x_1 \leq 5$. Finally, there exists a constraint that is unrelated to the numbers actually appearing in the statement of the problem. Certainly it is physically impossible for the manufacturer to produce a negative number of campers or trailers, thus $x_1, x_2 \geq 0$. It is desired to maximize the total profit attained from x_1 campers and x_2 trailers, namely $300x_1 + 400x_2$. Thus, the problem is reduced to the following:

Maximize $300x_1 + 400x_2$ subject to the conditions that:

$$\begin{aligned} 2x_1 + x_2 &\leq 11 \\ x_1 + 8x_2 &\leq 40 \\ 7x_1 + 8x_2 &\leq 52 \\ x_1 &\leq 5 \\ x_1, x_2 &\geq 0. \end{aligned} \qquad (1)$$

Now, determine the extreme points of the feasible solution set. One way to make the process of finding the extreme points efficient is to introduce slack variables. The purpose is to convert the inequalities of (1) to equalities.

Specifically, let $x_3 = 11 - (2x_1 + x_2)$, $x_4 = 40 - (x_1 + 8x_2)$, $x_5 = 52 - (7x_1 + 8x_2)$, and $x_6 = 5 - x_1$, and consider the system of equations:

$$\begin{aligned}
2x_1 + x_2 + x_3 &= 11 \\
x_1 + 8x_2 + x_4 &= 40 \\
7x_1 + 8x_2 + x_5 &= 52 \\
x_1 + x_6 &= 5
\end{aligned} \qquad (2)$$

and still requiring that $x_1, x_2 \geq 0$. Moreover, the original inequality constraints will be satisfied if $x_3, x_4, x_5, x_6 \geq 0$ is also required. Observe, for example, that $x_3 = 11 - (2x_1 + x_2) \geq 0$ if and only if $2x_1 + x_3 \leq 11$. First form the augmented matrix for (2). The function written below the matrix is a reminder for what must be maximized:

$$\begin{bmatrix} 2 & 1 & 1 & 0 & 0 & 0 & 11 \\ 1 & 8 & 0 & 1 & 0 & 0 & 40 \\ 7 & 8 & 0 & 0 & 1 & 0 & 52 \\ 1 & 0 & 0 & 0 & 0 & 1 & 5 \end{bmatrix}$$

$$300x_1 + 400x_2 + 0x_3 + 0x_4 + 0x_5 + 0x_6 .$$

Thus the starting tableau is:

	x_1	x_2	x_3	x_4	x_5	x_6		
x_3	2	1	1	0	0	0	11	11/1 = 11
x_4	1	(8)	0	1	0	0	40	40/8 = 5
x_5	7	8	0	0	1	0	52	52/8 = 6.5
x_6	1	0	0	0	0	1	5	
	-300	-400	0	0	0	0	0	

To determine the pivot element: The elements of the last row of the tableau are called indicators. Begin by finding the negative indicator having the largest absolute value. In the tableau above the indicator is clearly -400, which appears in the second column. Therefore, call the second column the pivot column. Now consider the ratio of each element in the last column to the corresponding element in the pivot column, if the pivot column is positive. The row associated with the smallest of these ratios is called the pivot row. The pivot column contains three positive elements: a 1 in the first row, an 8 in the second row, and an 8 in the third row. Thus the ratios that must be compared are 11/1 = 11, 40/8 = 5 and 52/8 = 6.5. Since 5 is the smallest of the ratios, the second row is the pivot row. The pivot element is the element common to the pivot column and the pivot row, namely the 8 that is circled in the tableau above. Now, use elementary row operations to transform the tableau into one having a 1 in the place of the pivot element and 0's elsewhere in the pivot column. To accomplish this, first multiply each element in the pivot row by the reciprocal of the pivot element to get:

	x_1	x_2	x_3	x_4	x_5	x_6	
x_3	2	1	1	0	0	0	11
x_4	1/8	1	0	1/8	0	0	5
x_5	7	8	0	0	1	0	52
x_6	1	0	0	0	0	1	5
	-300	-400	0	0	0	0	0

Then, multiply the pivot row by -1 and add it to the first row, by -8 and add it to the third row, and by 400 and add it to the fifth row. The result is:

	x_1	x_2	x_3	x_4	x_5	x_6		
x_3	15/8	0	1	-1/8	0	0	6	$6/\frac{15}{8} = 16/5$
x_2	1/8	1	0	1/8	0	0	5	$5/\frac{1}{8} = 40$
x_5	6	0	0	-1	1	0	12	$12/6 = 2$
x_6	1	0	0	0	0	1	5	$5/1 = 5$
	-250	0	0	50	0	0	2000	

In the tableau the x_4 in the notation column is replaced by x_2 . This replacement indicates that the x_2 variable was brought into the solution and the x_4 variable was eliminated. Now, examine the last row of the tableau above. Since -250 is the only negative indicator, the first column is the pivot column. Comparing:

$$6\Big/\frac{15}{8} = \frac{16}{5},\ 5\Big/\frac{1}{8} = 40,\ \frac{12}{6} = 2,\text{ and } 5/1 = 5,$$

see that the third row is the pivot row. Thus the pivot element is 6, which is circled in the tableau above. First multiply the pivot row by 1/6 so a 1 appears in the pivot position. Then, multiply this new pivot row by -15/8, -1/8, -1, and 250, adding the results to the first, second, fourth, and fifth rows, respectively, to get the following tableau:

	x_1	x_2	x_3	x_4	x_5	x_6	
x_3	0	0	1	3/16	-5/16	0	9/4
x_2	0	1	0	7/48	-1/48	0	19/4
x_1	1	0	0	-1/6	1/6	0	2
x_6	0	0	0	1/6	-1/6	1	3
	0	0	0	25/3	125/3	0	2500

Note in the tableau above: Since the pivot element was in the first column and third row, x_1 is placed in the third row of the notation column. Since the tableau above include no negative indicators, it is done. Thus, $x_1 = 2$, $x_2 = 19/4$ is the point at which the function assumes its maximum value, namely, 2500.

A company owns mines A and B. Mine A is capable of producing 1 ton of high-grade ore, 4 tons of medium-grade ore, and 6 tons of low-grade ore per day. Mine B can produce 2 tons of each of the three grades ore per day. The company requires at least 60 tons of high-grade ore, 120 tons of medium-grade ore, and 150 tons of low-grade ore. If it costs $200 per day to work mine A and $300 per day to work mine B, how many days should each mine be operated if the company wishes to minimize costs? Solve the dual problem by the Dual Simplex method.

Solution: The primal problem is

$$\text{Minimize} \quad w = 200y_1 + 300y_2$$
$$\text{subject to} \quad y_1 + 2y_2 \geq 60$$
$$4y_1 + 2y_2 \geq 120$$
$$6y_1 + 2y_2 \geq 150$$

and $\quad y_1, y_2 \geq 0$

The corresponding dual problem is

$$\text{Maximize} \quad u = 60x_1 + 120x_2 + 150x_3$$
$$\text{subject to} \quad x_1 + 4x_2 + 6x_3 \leq 200$$
$$2x_1 + 2x_2 + 2x_3 \leq 300$$

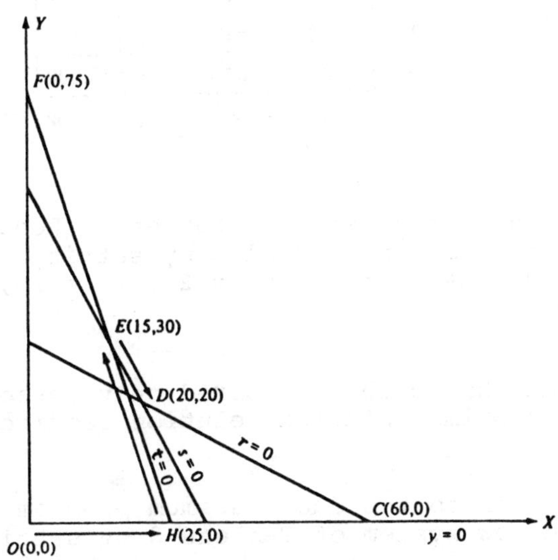

Basic point path (indicated by arrows) $r = 0$ is also $x + 2y = 60$. $s = 0$ is also $4x + 2y = 120$. $t = 0$ is also $6x + 2y = 150$.

Initial tableau for the dual problem is

	x_1	x_2	x_3	1	
y_1	1	4	6	−200	$= -t_1$
y_2	2*	2	2	−300	$= -t_2$
−1	60	120	150	0	$= u$
	$= v_1$	$= v_2$	$= v_3$	$= -w$	

(T.1)

Choosing column 1 as the pivot column leads to $a_{21} = 2$ as the pivot element. Pivoting then results in Tableau 2:

	t_2	x_2	x_3	1	
y_1	$-\frac{1}{2}$	3*	5	−50	$= -t_1$
v_1	$\frac{1}{2}$	1	1	−150	$= -x_1$
−1	−30	60	90	9000	$= u$
	$= y_2$	$= v_2$	$= v_3$	$= -w$	

(T.2)

Note that y_2 and v_1 were interchanged simultaneously with x_1 and t_2. Tableau 2 corresponds to the point on the vertical axis of the Figure shown where $x = 0$ ($y_1 = 0$) and $r = 0$ ($v_1 = 0$). Choosing column 2 as the pivot column yields $a_{12} = 3$ as the pivot element in T.2. Pivoting then results in Tableau 3:

	t_2	t_1	x_3	1	
v_2	$-\frac{1}{6}$	$\frac{1}{3}$	$\frac{5}{3}$	$-\frac{50}{3}$	$= -x_2$
v_1	$\frac{2}{3}$	$-\frac{1}{3}$	$-\frac{2}{3}$	$-\frac{400}{3}$	$= -x_1$
−1	−20	−20	−10	10,000	$= u$
	$= y_2$	$= y_1$	$= v_3$	$= -w$	

(T.3)

This tableau is a terminal tableau. Read off the solution of this minimum problem by setting $v_1 = v_2 = 0$. Thus, one gets $y_1 = 20$, $y_2 = 20$, $v_3 = 10$, and Min $w =$ \$10,000.

Note that this method required only three tableaus, while the primal simplex solution requires four tableaus.

The solution to the dual maximum problem is read off from the row system of Tableau 3 by setting the nonbasic variables equal to zero. Thus, $x_1 = \frac{400}{3}$, $x_2 = \frac{50}{3}$, $x_3 = 0$, $t_1 = t_2 = 0$ and Max $u =$ \$10,000.

Study Table 1

Consider the shipment of steel from two warehouses W_1 and W_2 to two markets M_1 and M_2. The cost of shipping from warehouse W_i to market M_j is given in the ith row and jth column of the table. For example, the cost of shipping from W_1 to M_2 is $c_{12} = 8$ \$/ton. The supplies (a_i) at the warehouses are listed at the right of the table; thus, the supply at W_1 is $a_1 = 15$ tons. The demands (b_j) at the markets are listed at the bottom of the table; thus, the demand at M_1 is $b_1 = 12$ tons. Note that the sum of the supplies equals the sum of the demands:

$$a_1 + a_2 = 20 = b_1 + b_2.$$

Transportation problems in which total supply equals total demand are called balanced.

Let x_{ij} be the amount in tons to be shipped from warehouse W_i to market M_j. The problem is to ship the steel in the least expensive (minimum cost) way and in so doing completely exhaust the supplies at the warehouses and exactly satisfy the demands at the markets.

First, set up the problem in linear programming form and solve it by employing the simplex algorithm. Then, solve by the least cost method.

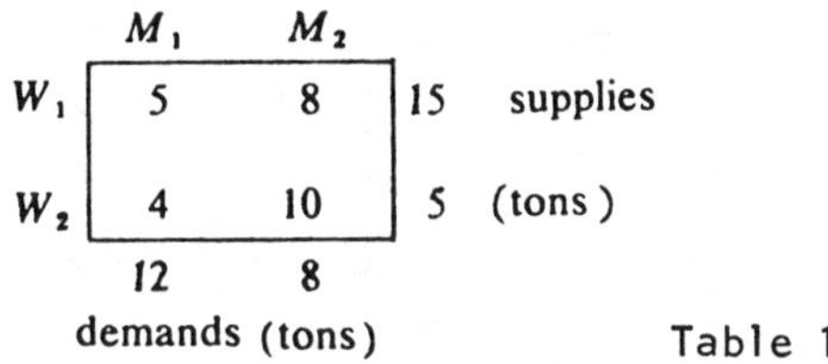

	M_1	M_2	supplies (tons)
W_1	5	8	15
W_2	4	10	5
demands (tons)	12	8	

Table 1

Solution: The cost in dollars in shipping x_{11} tons from W_1 to M_1 is five times x_{11}, i.e., $5x_{11}$. Thus, express the total shipping cost u in the following way:

$$u = 5x_{11} + 8x_{12} + 4x_{21} + 10x_{22} \quad \text{(to be minimized).} \qquad (1)$$

The requirements pertaining to the warehouses and markets are equation constraints (see the next-to-last paragraph of the problem statement):

$$x_{11} + x_{12} = 15 \qquad (2)$$

$$x_{21} + x_{22} = 5 \qquad (3)$$

$$x_{11} + x_{21} = 12 \qquad (4)$$

$$x_{12} + \quad + x_{22} = 8 \qquad (5)$$

and

$$x_{11} \geq 0 \tag{6}$$

$$x_{12} \geq 0 \tag{7}$$

$$x_{21} \geq 0 \tag{8}$$

$$x_{22} \geq 0. \tag{9}$$

Of the four equation constraints, one is redundant. For example, the sum of (2) and (3) minus (4) yields (5). Thus, eliminate (5) as a constraint (any other would do equally as well as the one to be eliminated). This ability to eliminate one of the constraints is a direct consequence of the balanced nature of the problem.

The initial tableau corresponding to (1), (2), (3), and (4) is thus

x_{11}	x_{12}	x_{21}	x_{22}	1	
1*	1	0	0	−15	= −0
0	0	1	1	−5	= −0
1	0	1	0	−12	= −0
5	8	4	10	0	= u

(T.1)

Now replace the zeros in the right-hand margin by basic variables. This is done in Tableaus 2, 3, and 4. In each of these, delete the column with the zero in the top margin. These tableaus, which are very easy to calculate, are as follows:

0	x_{12}	x_{21}	x_{22}	1	
	1	0	0	−15	= $-x_{11}$
0	0	1	1	−5	= −0
−1	−1	1*	0	3	= −0
−5	3	4	10	75	= u

(T.2)

x_{12}	0	x_{22}	1	
1	0	0	−15	= $-x_{11}$
1	−1	1*	−8	= −0
−1		0	3	= $-x_{21}$
7	−4	10	63	= u

(T.3)

x_{12}	0	1	
1	0	−15	= $-x_{11}$
1		−8	= $-x_{22}$
−1*	0	+3	= $-x_{21}$
−3	−10	143	= u

(T.4)

Tableau 4 has the appearance of a standard tableau; there are three basic variables and one nonbasic variable. Since $-b_3 = +3$, this tableau is ready for the next stage. Obtain Tableau 5:

x_{21}	1	
1	−12	$= -x_{11}$
1*	−5	$= -x_{22}$
−1	−3	$= -x_{12}$
−3	134	$= u$

(T.5)

Tableau 5 corresponds to a b.f.p. tableau because all the entries in the right-hand column are negative. This leads to the solution tableau for this minimum problem:

x_{22}	1	
−1	−7	$= -x_{11}$
1	−5	$= -x_{21}$
1	−8	$= -x_{12}$
+3	119	$= u$

(T.6)

Read off the optimal solution as:

$$x_{22} = 0,\ x_{11} = 7,\ x_{21} = 5,\ x_{12} = 8,\ \text{and Min } u = \$119.$$

Check out the solution by substituting the above x_{ij} values into the original equation for u:

$$u = 5.7 + 8.8 + 4.5 = 119 \quad \text{(check)}.$$

The supply and demand requirements also check out.

Now apply the least Cost Method to the initial table. The calculations and the resulting table are indicated as follows: Locate the least cost option of the initial table. It is 4. Allocate as much units as possible to this option. This amount is smaller than the supply and demand quantities corresponding to the option: min (12, 5) = 5. Subtract 12 - 5 = 7. One still requires to satisfy 7 tons of demand of M_1. Cross out the W_2 row since all its supply is allocated. Now search for the next least cost option and continue this way until all allocations are made.

	√2	√3	
	(5)[7]	(8)[8]	~~15~~ ~~8~~ 0
√1	(4)[5]	10	~~5~~ 0
	~~12~~ ~~7~~ 0	~~8~~ 0	

(T.7)

The only relevant cycle is that corresponding to cell (2, 2); the value of cycle is 10 - 4 + 5 - 8 = +3. Thus, the b.f.s. pertaining to Table 7 is an optimal solution. The solution values for the x_{ij}'s are $x_{11} = 7$, $x_{12} = 8$, $x_{21} = 5$, and $x_{22} = 0$. The amount of effort involved in finding the optimal solution is much smaller in the current approach.

A company has four warehouses and six stores. The four warehouses altogether have a surplus of 22 units of a given commodity, divided among them as follows:

Warehouse	Surplus
1	5
2	6
3	2
4	9

The six stores altogether need 22 units of the commodity. Individual requirements are:

Store	Requirements
1	4
2	4
3	6
4	2
5	4
6	2

Costs of shipping one unit of the commodity from warehouse i to store j are displayed in the following matrix:

		Store					
		1	2	3	4	5	6
Warehouse	1	9	12	9	6	9	10
	2	7	3	7	7	5	5
	3	6	5	9	11	3	11
	4	6	8	11	2	2	10

Find feasible (not necessarily optimal) solutions, and the cost associated with each:

a) by the Northwest Corner Method and

b) by the Penalty Method.

Solution: a) Northwest Corner Method:

The first step is to draw up a blank m-by-n matrix complete with row and column requirements, as follows:

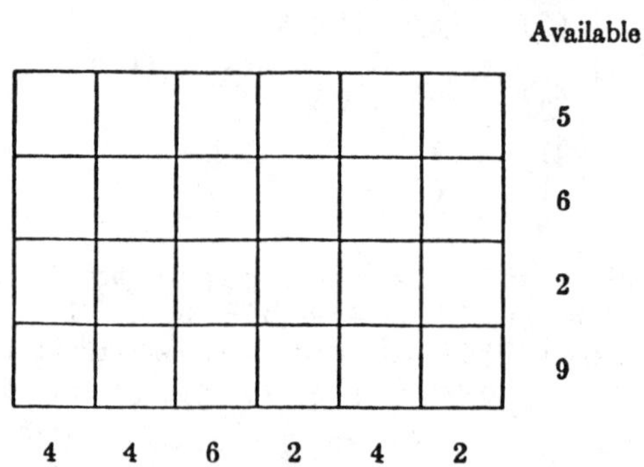

Put a set of allocations in the cells so that row totals and column totals will be as indicated.

Start at the upper left-hand corner, which is cell (1,1), and allocate as much as possible there: in other words, 4. This satisfies the requirement for column 1, and leaves a surplus of 1 unit for row 1; so allocate 1 to cell (1,2). Now the allocations are complete for column 1 and row 1; and there is a remaining deficiency of 3 in column 2. Allocate 3 in position (2,2); now columns 1 and 2 are complete and there is a surplus of 3 in row 2. Continuing in this way, from left to right and top to bottom, eventually complete all the requirements by an allocation in the lower right-hand corner. The resulting feasible solution is:

							Available
	4	1					5
		3	3				6
			2				2
			1	2	4	2	9
Required	4	4	6	2	4	2	

To obtain the cost for the feasible solution, multiply each individual allocation by its corresponding unit cost, and add. The resulting cost is 139.

b) Penalty Method is a better method of finding a feasible solution, in that it usually gives a lower beginning cost. First write down the cost matrix, together with row and column identifications and row and column requirements:

		Store						
		1	2	3	4	5	6	Available
Warehouse	1	9	12	9	6	9	10	5
	2	7	3	7	7	5	5	6
	3	6	5	9	11	3	11	2
	4	6	8	11	2	2	10	9
Required		4	4	6	2	4	2	

The next step is to enter the difference between the smallest and second smallest elements in each column beneath the corresponding column, and the difference between the smallest and second smallest elements of each row to the right of the row. These differences are the numbers in parentheses in the matrix following this paragraph. The first individual allocation will be to the smallest cost of a row or the smallest cost of a column; choose that one for which there is the greatest penalty for not choosing it. That is, choose the minimum cost location in that row or column whose corresponding number in parentheses is the largest. As 5 is the largest number in parentheses, choose column 6 as the line for the first individual allocation, and allocate as much as possible to location (2,6), the minimum cost location in this column. Thus 2 units are allocated to location (2,6) as indicated by the small numeral in the upper left corner of that cell; and this completes the allocations for column 6, so that the other allocations in this column are zero.

Warehouse \ Store	1	2	3	4	5	6	Available
1	9	12	9	6	9	^{0}10	5 (3)
2	7	3	7	7	5	^{2}5	6 (2)
3	6	5	9	11	3	^{0}11	2 (2)
4	6	8	11	2	2	^{0}10	9 (0)
Required	4 (0)	4 (2)	6 (2)	2 (4)	4 (1)	2 (5) ↑	

Completes column 6

The next step is to write down the shrunken cost matrix comprising the rows and columns whose allocations are not yet determined, including revised row and column totals which take into account the allocations already made. Now 4 is the largest unit penalty; this leads to an allocation in the corresponding minimum cost location in column 4: namely cell (4,4). The maximum possible allocation is 2; so allocate 2 units to cell (4,4), and 0 units to the remaining cells in column 4.

Warehouse \ Store	1	2	3	4	5	Available
1	9	12	9	^{0}6	9	5 (3)
2	7	3	7	^{0}7	5	4 (2)
3	6	5	9	^{0}11	3	2 (2)
4	6	8	11	^{2}2	2	9 (0)
Required	4 (0)	4 (2)	6 (2)	2 (4) ↑	4 (1)	

Completes column 4

Next, write down the new cost matrix with column 4 also deleted, and proceed as before. The successive resulting matrices are set down below.

Warehouse \ Store	1	2	3	5	Available
1	9	12	9	^{0}9	5 (0)
2	7	3	7	^{0}5	4 (2)
3	6	5	9	^{0}3	2 (2)
4	6	8	11	^{4}2	7 (4) ←
Required	4 (0)	4 (2)	6 (2)	4 (1)	

Completes column 5

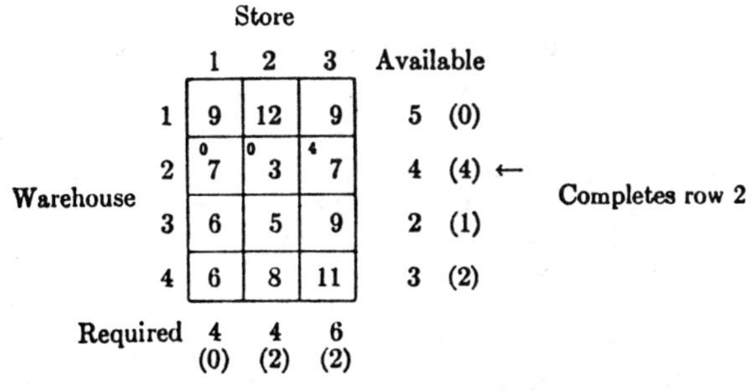

Store

Warehouse	1	2	3	Available	
1	9	12	9	5 (0)	
3	^{0}6	^{2}5	^{0}9	2 (1)	Completes row 3
4	6	8	11	3 (2)	
Required	4 (0)	4 (3) ↑	2 (0)		

Store

Warehouse	1	2	3	Available	
1	9	^{0}12	9	5 (0)	
4	6	^{2}8	11	3 (2)	Completes column 2
Required	4 (3)	2 (4) ↑	2 (2)		

Store

Warehouse	1	3	Available	
1	^{3}9	^{2}9	5 (0)	
4	^{1}6	^{0}11	1 (5) ←	Completes matrix.
Required	4 (3)	2 (2)		

Copying the various positive allocations as they occur in the successive stages, one obtains as the feasible solution:

Store

Warehouse	1	2	3	4	5	6
1	3		2			
2			4			2
3		2				
4	1	2		2	4	

The cost for this solution turns out to be 127.

• PROBLEM 33-8

A manufacturer of a certain good owns three warehouses and supplies three markets. Each warehouse contains known quantities of the good and each market has known demands. In addition, the unit shipping costs from each warehouse to each market are known. These data are best exhibited in the table of Figure 1:

Note that the total supplies in the warehouse add up to 140 tons, which is equal to the sum of the demands at the markets. How shall the manufacturer ship his goods to the markets from the warehouses so that the total transportation cost will be a minimum? Apply Vogel's approximation method to find a feasible solution.

	Market 1	*Market 2*	*Market 3*	*Supplies*
Warehouse 1	3 $/Ton	2 $/Ton	3 $/Ton	50 T
Warehouse 2	10 $/Ton	5 $/Ton	8 $/Ton	70 T
Warehouse 3	1 $/Ton	3 $/Ton	10 $/Ton	20 T
Demands	50 T	60 T	30 T	140

Fig. 1

Solution: The VAM (Vogel Approximation Method) for obtaining an initial basic solution proceeds as follows.

(1) Compute the difference of the two smallest entries in each row and each column and mark this difference opposite each row and column. (In case there is just one entry in a row or a column, mark that entry.)

(2) Choose the largest difference so marked and utilize the smallest entry in that row or column to empty a warehouse or completely fulfill a market demand.

(3) Delete the line (row or column) corresponding to the used-up warehouse or fully supplied market; in case both of these happen simultaneously (the degenerate case) cross out either the row or the column unless there is exactly one row remaining, in which case cross out the column. Circle or otherwise designate the cost used and mark above the circle the amount shipped by that route. Reduce the supplies and demands in the lines containing the cost used.

(4) If all lines are crossed out, stop; otherwise, return to 1.

	2	1	5	
1	3	2	3	50
3	10	5	8	70
2	1	3	10	20
	50	60	30	

Fig. 2

Consider Figure 1. The row and column differences (of the smallest and next smallest entries) are included in Figure 2. Note that the maximum difference is the 5 in the third column. Hence ship as much as possible using the minimum entry, which is $c_{13} = 3$, in the third column.

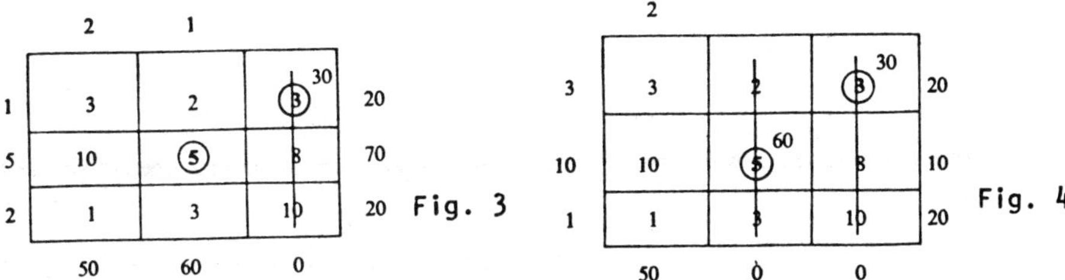

The rationale behind this choice is clear; if one doesn't ship via the smallest entry in the third column, at a cost of 3 $/ton, then one will have to use the next higher cost, which is 8 (or perhaps even the cost of 10 eventually); the amount of the difference between the smallest and next smallest cost is a measure of the "regret" one has for not making use of the smallest cost in that column. Now carry out steps (3) and (4), at the same time recomputing the row differences; since a column was struck out on the previous step, the remaining column differences in columns 1 and 2 will be the same. The result is shown in Figure 3. Now the maximum difference occurs in the second row, so ship as much as possible using the minimum-cost entry, namely $c_{22} = 5$. It turns out that one can ship 60 to M_2 from W_2 and completely satisfy its demand. The result is in Figure 4. Since only the first column remains, list it as instructed in (1). The next step is to bring in the 10 entry, followed by the 3 entry and the 1 entry. The final basic solution is displayed in Figure 5. Verify that it is a basis. Its cost is

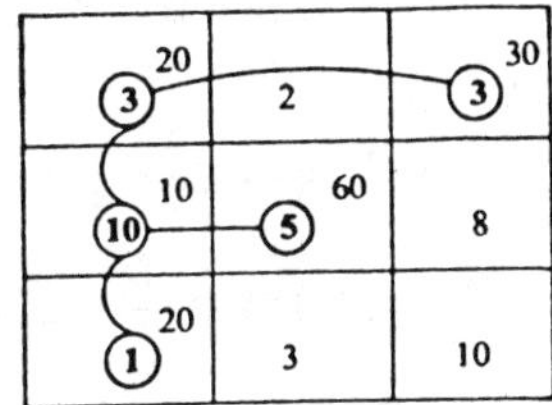

Fig. 5

$$20 \cdot 3 + 30 \cdot 3 + 10 \cdot 10 + 60 \cdot 5 + 20 \cdot 1 = \$570.$$

• PROBLEM 33-9

An excursion company is considering adding small boats to their fleet. The company has $200,000 to invest in this venture. At present there is an estimated maximum demand of 6,000 customers per season for these tours. The company does not wish to provide capacity in excess of the estimated maximum demand. The basic data are given below for the two types of available boats. The company will make an estimated seasonal profit of $4,000 for each boat of Type 1 and $7,000 for each boat of Type 2. How many boats of each type should the company use to maximize profit?

	Type 1	Type 2
capacity, $\frac{\text{customers}}{\text{season}}$	1,200	2,000
initial cost, $\frac{\$}{\text{boat}}$	25,000	80,000

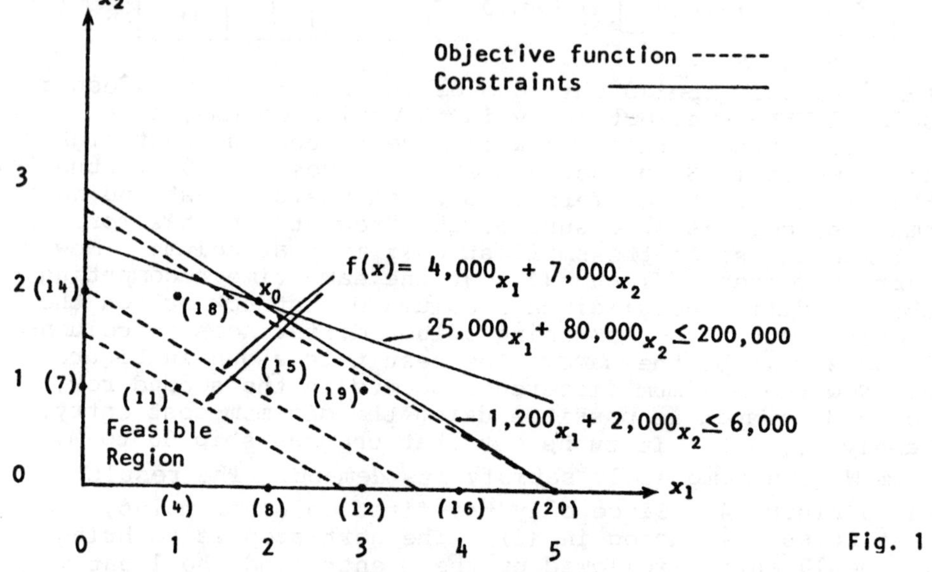

Fig. 1

• Feasible continuations of decision variable values

( ) The value of the objective function in thousands of $

Solution: The linear programming problem (illustrated in Figure 1) is:

$$\text{Maximize} \quad 4{,}000\,x_1 + 7{,}000\,x_2$$

$$\text{Subject to} \quad 1{,}200\,x_1 + 2{,}000\,x_2 \le 6{,}000$$

$$25{,}000\,x_1 + 80{,}000\,x_2 \le 200{,}000$$

$$x_1,\ x_2 \ge 0;\ x_1\ x_2 \text{ are integers.}$$

Constraints in the original problem formulation should be transformed so that all coefficients are integers. This is done to facilitate solution of the integer programming problem. No transformation is required in this problem. If there were a constraint such as $(3/4)x_1 + (6/4)x_2 \le 48/10$, both sides must be multiplied by 20 so that it becomes $15x_1 + 30x_2 \le 96$. To simplify notation, divide the first constraint by 100 and the objective function and second constraint by 1000 and construct the initial tableau (Tableau 1).

Tableau 1

c_i	BASIS	V_1	V_2	V_3	V_4	b_i
0	x_3	12	20	1	0	60
0	x_4	25	80	0	1	200

The final tableau in the Simplex solution is:

Tableau 2

c_i	BASIS	V_1	V_2	V_3	V_4	b_i	f_{i0}
4	x_1	1	0	0.1739	-0.0435	1.739	0.739
7	x_2	0	1	-0.0543	0.0261	1.956	0.956
Solution (x_0)		0	0	-0.3155	-0.0087	20.65	

Since the solution is noninteger, add cutting planes to reduce the feasible region until an integer solution is obtained. The following steps will be used to develop new cutting planes (or constraints).

1. Add a new column to the final Simplex tableau. This is the f_{i0} column in Tableau 2. For each b_i value associated with a basic variable determine an f_{i0} value, where f_{i0} is a nonnegative fraction greater than or equal to zero but less than one, which when subtracted from a given noninteger will convert to an integer (e.g. 0.739 subtracted from 1.739 will convert it to an integer; 0.25 subtracted from -6.75 will convert it to an integer).

2. The largest f_{io} value will determine the row of the tableau to be used in constructing a cutting plane. In the above tableau $f_{20} = 0.956$ designates the second row to be used for this purpose since $0.956 > 0.739$ (i.e. $f_{20} > f_{10}$). When ties occur, an arbitrary choice among tied rows is made. For each a_{ij} coefficient in this row determine an f_{ij} value, just as f_{i0} was determined for b_i.

	x_1	x_2	x_3	x_4	b_i
Row 2	0	1	-0.0543	0.0261	1.956
f_{2j} values	0	0	0.9457	0.0261	0.956
Integer value	0	1	-1	0	1

The f_{2j} values give a new constraint

$$0x_1 + 0x_2 + 0.9457x_3 + 0.0261x_4 \geq 0.956.$$

Adding a surplus variable x_5 gives:

$$0x_1 + 0x_2 + 0.9457x_3 + 0.0261x_4 - x_5 = 0.956.$$

Tableau 3

c_i	BASIS	V_1	V_2	V_3	V_4	V_5	b_i	
4	x_1	1	0	0.1739	-0.0435	0	1.739	
7	x_2	0	1	-0.0543	0.0261	0	1.956	
0	x_3	0	0	0.9457	0.0261	-1	0.956	→

3. The new constraint is added to the final Simplex tableau. The incoming variable is the one that will cause the smallest decrease in the objective function as indicated by the x_{0j} values of the final Simplex tableau. An alternative rule (sometimes more efficient) is to select the incoming variable as that having the maximum quotient of x_{0j}/a_{ij} for nonbasic variable j, where $a_{ij} < 0$. The incoming variable will be x_4 with a x_{04} of -0.0087. The outgoing variable, x_5, is always that associated with the constraint just annexed (in this case, row 3).

Apply the Simplex procedure to get the following tableau:

Tableau 4

c_i	BASIS	V_1	V_2	V_3	V_4	V_5	b_i	f_{io}
4	x_1	1	0	1.750	0	-1.667	3.333	.332
7	x_2	0	1	-1	0	1	1.000	.000
0	x_4	0	0	36.234	1	-38.3142	-0.333	- -
	x_0	0	0	0	0	-0.333	20.333	

In the new solution X = (3.333, 1.000). Since x_1 has the maximum f_{i0}, it is used to determine the next cutting plane. Upon adding another column V_6, and another constraint, the next tableau becomes:

Tableau 5

c_i	BASIS	V_1	V_2	V_3	V_4	V_5	V_6	b_i	
4	x_1	1	0	1.750	0	-1.667	0	3.333	
7	x_2	0	1	-1.	0	1	0	1.000	
0	x_4	0	0	36.234	1	-38.3142	0	36.628	
0	x_6	0	0	.750	0	0.333	-1	0.333	→
						↑			

Apply the Simplex procedure to obtain:

Tableau 6

c_i	BASIS	V_1	V_2	V_3	V_4	V_5	V_6	b_i
4	x_1	1	0	5.5	0	0	5	5
7	x_2	0	1	-325.	0	0	3	0
0	x_4	0	0	122.44	1	0	-114.94	74.94
0	x_5	0	0	2.25	0	1	-3	1.00
	x_{0j}	0	0	-2197	0	0	-41	20

Tableau 6 gives the optimum integer solution. X* = (5,0).

A manufacturer makes three products. The sale volume of each product is dependent on its price, and in one case, product 3, sales volume is also dependent on the price of another product. The market forecasting division estimated the following relationship between monthly sales volume x_j (thousands of units) and unit price p_j for each product:

$$x_1 = 10 - p_1$$

$$x_2 = 16 - p_2 \qquad (1)$$

$$x_3 = 6 - \frac{1}{2}p_3 + \frac{1}{4}p_2$$

The variable costs for the three products are \$6, \$7, and \$10 per unit, respectively. Production is limited by available resources, manpower, and machine time.

Each month 1000 machine hours and 2000 man hours are available. Product 1 uses 0.4 machine hour and 0.2 man hour per unit, product 2 uses 0.2 machine hour and 0.4 man hour per unit, and product 3 uses 0.1 hour of each per unit. The manufacturer wishes to find the monthly sales schedule that will maximize profits.

Solution: Total profit for each product is equal to total revenue minus total variable cost for the product. For product 1, total revenue is

$$R_1 = p_1x_1 .$$

From (1),

$$p_1 = 10 - x_1 ,$$

so

$$R_1 = p_1x_1 = 10x_1 - x_1^2 .$$

Total variable cost for product 1 is $V_1 = 6x_1$. So the total profit for product 1 is

$$\pi_1 = R_1 - V_1 = 10x_1 - x_1^2 - 6x_1 = 4x_1 - x_1^2$$

For product 2 the total revenue amounts to

$$R_2 = p_2x_2 = 16x_2 - x_2^2,$$

and the total variable cost $V_2 = 7x_2$, with the difference of

$$\pi_2 = R_2 - V_2 = 16x_2 - x_2^2 - 7x_2 = 9x_2 - x_2^2$$

Product 3 presents a new problem, since x_3 depends on p_2 as well as p_3. Total revenue is

$$R_3 = p_3x_3 = 2(6 - x_3 + \frac{1}{4}p_2)\ x_3$$

Using $p_2 = 16 - x_2$ from expressions (1), obtain

$$R_3 = 2(6 - x_3 + \frac{1}{4}(16 - x_2))x_3 = 20x_3 - 2x_3^2 - \frac{1}{2}x_2x_3$$

Variable cost is $V_3 = 10x_3$. Hence total profit for product 3 is

$$\pi_3 = R_3 - V_3 = 20x_3 - 2x_3^2 - \frac{1}{2}x_2x_3 - 10x_3$$

$$= 10x_3 - 2x_3^2 - \frac{1}{2}x_2x_3$$

Summing π_1, π_2, and π_3, obtain the total profit function

$$\pi = f(x_1,x_2,x_3) = 4x_1 - x_1^2 + 9x_2 - x_2^2 + 10x_3 - 2x_3^2 - \frac{1}{2}x_2x_3 \qquad (2)$$

It is necessary to find values for x_1, x_2, and x_3 that maximize expression (2) within the monthly machine time and man hour restrictions imposed:

$$4x_1 + 2x_2 + x_3 \le 10 \text{ (units of 100 machine hours)}$$

$$2x_1 + 4x_2 + x_3 \le 20 \text{ (units of 100 man hours)}$$

Summarizing, the following programming problem is obtained.

maximize

$$f(x_1,x_2,x_3) = 4x_1 - x_1^2 + 9x_2 - x_2^2 + 10x_3 - 2x_3^2 - \frac{1}{2}x_2x_3$$

subject to

$$4x_1 + 2x_2 + x_3 \le 10 \quad \text{(machine time)} \qquad (3)$$

$$2x_1 + 4x_2 + x_3 \le 20 \quad \text{(man hours)}$$

$$x_1 \ge 0,$$

$$x_2 \ge 0, \quad \text{(nonnegativity conditions)}$$

$$x_3 \ge 0$$

Problem (3) is a nonlinear programming problem, since some of its functional relationships are nonlinear.

• PROBLEM 33-11

A manufacturer uses large quantities of a purchased part in his assembly operations. He wants to use a constant purchase lot size, and he specifies that no shortages be planned. The following data are relevant to the problem of determining the optimal lot size:

a. Annual requirements -- 300,000 units, uniformly required over the year.

b. Manufacturer's fixed cost of placing an order -- $80.

c. Annual cost of interest, insurance, and taxes on average inventory investment -- 20 percent of the value of average inventory.

d. Cost of storage -- 10 cents per month, based on average quantity stored.

e. Vendor's price schedule -- a fixed charge of $20 per order, plus a charge per unit determined according to the following schedule:

ORDER SIZE	UNIT VARIABLE COST
$0 < Q < 10{,}000$	\$1.00
$10{,}000 \le Q < 30{,}000$	0.98
$30{,}000 \le Q < 50{,}000$	0.96
$50{,}000 \le Q$	0.94

Find the optimal lot size.

Suppose the price schedule above had been of the incremental discount type. Calculate the optimal lot size, for this case.

Solution: For the All Units Discounts schedule, suppose that the procurement cost for a lot size Q is $A + C_jQ$. if $N_{j-1} \le Q < N_j$, $j = 1,2,\ldots,J$, where $C_j < C_{j-1}$. N_0 is the minimum quantity that can be ordered and N_J is the maximum order size, usually unlimited.
Let

$$K_j(Q) = \frac{AD}{Q} + C_jD + iC_j\frac{Q}{2}\,. \qquad (1)$$

K is a mathematical function of Q, which over the range $N_{j-1} \le Q < N_j$ gives the average annual cost of an order of size Q. The average annual cost function is then written as

$$K(Q) = K_j(Q),\ \text{if } N_{j-1} \le Q < N_j, \qquad (j = 1,2,\ldots,J)$$

To find the optimal value of Q, find the minimum cost point on each segment of K and compare the costs at these points to determine the global minimum. This procedure can be stated more precisely as follows: Let Q_j^* be the value of Q that minimizes $K_j(Q)$ in the range $N_{j-1} \le Q_j < N_j$, and define Q^* as the overall optimal lot size. Then $K(Q^*) = \min_j K_j(Q_j^*)$.

To find the minimum cost value, $K_j(Q_j^*)$, in each segment, first find Q_j^*. Let Q_j^0 be the minimum point of the mathematical function $K_j(Q)$,

$$Q_j^0 = \sqrt{\frac{2AD}{iC_j}}\,. \qquad (2)$$

Then if Q_j^0 is in the range $[N_{j-1}, N_j)$, $Q_j^* = Q_j^0$. If

$$Q_j^0 < N_{j-1}, \quad Q_j^* = N_{j-1};$$

and if

$$Q_j^0 \geq N_j, \; Q_j^* = N_j.$$

In the latter case of $Q_j^0 \geq N_j$, the overall optimal lot size cannot lie in the region $Q < N_j$. This follows from the facts that

$$Q_j^0 < Q_{j+1}^0$$

and

$$K_j(Q_j^*) > K_{j+1}(Q_j^*).$$

Thus, begin with the K_J segment and proceed to find Q_J^*, $Q_{J-1}^*, \ldots,$ until reaching an interval, say k, where $Q_k^* = Q_k^0$. The optimal solution must be one of the values $Q_k^0, Q_{k+1}^*, \ldots, Q_J^*$.

To solve this problem, first write the total annual cost function, noting that the fixed cost per order is $100, the sum of the manufacturer's internal cost and the vendor's fixed charge, and that there is a storage cost charge of $1.20 per year per unit of average inventory. For $N_{j-1} \leq Q < N_j$, the price is C_j and the average annual cost is (from (1))

$$K_j(Q) = \frac{(80 + 20)(300{,}000)}{Q} + (300{,}000)C_j$$

$$+ [(0.20)C_j + 1.20]\frac{Q}{2}; \qquad j = 1,2,3,4.$$

The values of C_j, N_{j-1}, and N_j are given in the price schedule. The minimum point on the entire K_j curve is at

$$Q_j^0 = 1000\sqrt{\frac{60}{1.20 + 0.2C_j}}$$

from (2).

For j = 4, C_4 = $0.94 and $Q_4^0 = 6580 < N_3 = 50{,}000$, so the minimum cost point on the K_4 segment occurs at $Q_4^* = 50{,}000$.

For j = 3, C_3 = $0.96 and $Q_3^0 = 6570 < N_2 = 30{,}000$, so $Q_3^* = 30{,}000$. (Obvious, actually, since $Q_3^0 < Q_4^0$.)

For j = 2, C_2 = $0.98 and $Q_2^0 = 6560 < N_1 = 10{,}000$, so $Q_2^* = 10{,}000$. (Again obvious from knowledge that

$Q_2{}^0$ will be less than $Q_4{}^0$.)

For $j = 1$, $C_1 = \$1$ and $Q_1{}^0 = 6550$. This value is in the range for which C_1 applies; therefore $Q_1{}^* = 6550$.

The costs must be calculated for $Q_1{}^*$, $Q_2{}^*$, $Q_3{}^*$, and $Q_4{}^*$:

$K(6550) = \$309{,}155$

$K(10{,}000) = \$303{,}980$ -- minimum

$K(30{,}000) = \$309{,}880$

$K(50{,}000) = \$317{,}500$.

The optimal lot size is $Q^* = 10{,}000$ units. The average time between orders is 0.033 year. The total cost curve is shown in Figure 1.

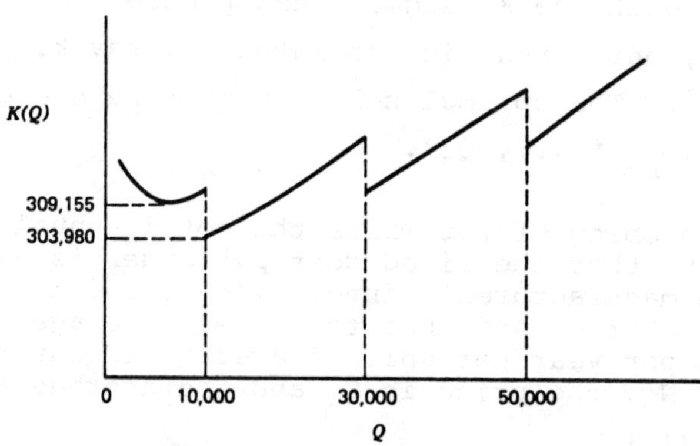

Cost function for all-units-discounts schedule.

Fig. 1

In the Incremental Discount Schedule, the price associated with an interval applies only to the units within that interval. Assuming $N_0 = 0$, the first N_1 units would cost C_1 each, the next $(N_2 - N_1)$ units, C_2 each; the next $(N_3 - N_2)$ units, C_3 each, and so on.

The procurement cost of Q units would be $A + V(Q)$, where $V(Q)$ is the total variable cost of the lot and is given by

$$V(Q) = \sum_{k=1}^{j-1} C_k (N_k - N_{k-1}) + C_j (Q - N_{j-1}),$$

$$N_{j-1} \le Q < N_j$$

$$= V(N_{j-1}) + C_j (Q - N_{j-1}), \quad N_{j-1} \le Q < N_j. \qquad (3)$$

The average annual cost is

$$K(Q) = K_j(Q), \text{ if } N_{j-1} \le Q < N_j$$

where

$$K_j(Q) = [A + V(Q)]\frac{D}{Q} + i\left(\frac{V(Q)}{Q}\right)\frac{Q}{2}$$

$$= [A + V(N_{j-1}) + C_j(Q - N_{j-1})]\frac{D}{Q} + \frac{i}{2}[V(N_{j-1})$$

$$+ C_j(Q - N_{j-1})]. \qquad (4)$$

The term V(Q)/Q in Equation 4 represents the average price per unit and is used to find the dollar value of average inventory. Optimal lot size will never equal the quantity defining a price break.

To find the optimal lot size, compute for j = 1,2,...,J,

$$Q_j^0 = \sqrt{\frac{2D[A + V(N_{j-1}) - C_jN_{j-1}]}{iC_j}} \qquad (5)$$

If $N_{j-1} \leq Q_j^0 < N_j$, compute $K_j(Q_j^0)$. Choose lot size Q* as the value of Q_j^0 yielding the minimum $K_j(Q_j^0)$.

Thus from (4)

$$K_j(Q) = [100 + V(N_{j-1}) + C_j(Q - N_{j-1})]\frac{300,000}{Q}$$

$$+ \frac{(0.20)}{2}[V(N_{j-1}) + C_j(Q - N_{j-1})] + (1.20)\frac{Q}{2}$$

j	C_j	N_j	$V(N_j)$	$V(Q) = V(N_{j-1}) + C_j(Q - N_{j-1})$
1	\$1.00	10,000	\$10,000	Q
2	0.98	30,000	29,600	$200 + 0.98Q$
3	0.96	50,000	48,800	$800 + 0.96Q$
4	0.94	—	—	$1800 + 0.94Q$

from Equation 3.

Using the values given,

$$K(Q) = \begin{cases} K_1(Q) = \dfrac{30 \times 10^6}{Q} + 300,000 + 0.70Q, & 0 < Q < 10,000 \\ K_2(Q) = \dfrac{90 \times 10^6}{Q} + 294,020 + 0.698Q, & 10,000 \leq Q < 30,000 \\ K_3(Q) = \dfrac{270 \times 10^6}{Q} + 288,080 + 0.696Q, & 30,000 \leq Q < 50,000 \\ K_4(Q) = \dfrac{570 \times 10^6}{Q} + 282,180 + 0.694Q, & 50,000 \leq Q. \end{cases}$$

The minimum points on curves K_1, K_2, K_3, and K_4 are obtained using Equation 5 , with the denominator including the storage cost component, 1.20.

$$Q_1^0 = 6550$$

$$Q_2^0 = 11,360$$

$$Q_3^0 = 19,660$$

$$Q_4^0 = 28,700.$$

The values Q_3^0 and Q_4^0 are not in the range where K_3 and K_4 apply, respectively; therefore they are not considered further. The optimal lot size is either Q_1^0 or Q_2^0. To determine which, one must calculate average annual costs. It turns out that K(6550) = \$309,360 and K(11,360) = \$309,860, so the optimal lot size is 6550 units. The optimal time between orders is 0.022 year. This is illustrated in Figure 2.

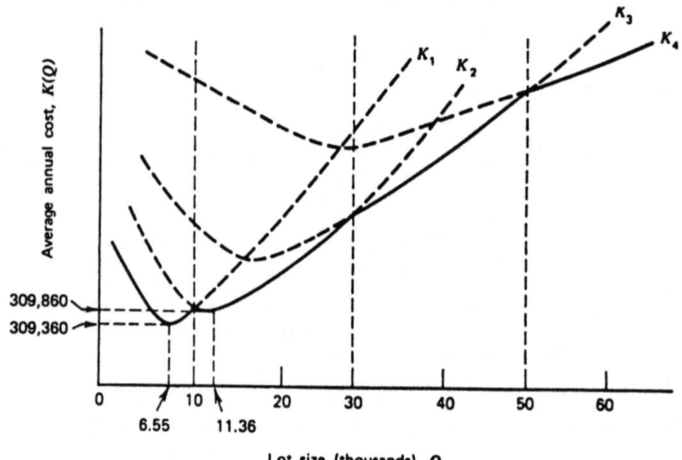

Cost function for incremental discount schedule. Fig. 2

Comparing the solution with that of the previous, where the price schedule was interpreted as an all units discount, note that the optimal lot size is 6550 here versus 10,000 there. This reduction in lot size is to be expected because with the incremental discount where the price discount does not apply to all units, there is less incentive to order to large lots.

CHAPTER 34

USING COMPUTERS FOR BUSINESS APPLICATIONS

DEPRECIATION, INTEREST AND COMMISSION PROBLEMS

• **PROBLEM 34-1**

Write a FORTRAN program to calculate depreciation by the sum of the years digits method.

Solution: The Internal Revenue Service allows various methods for calculating the depreciation on a piece of machinery. The simplest is the straight-line method. According to this method, if an article costs $1000, has an estimated life of 10 years and $0 scrap value, the depreciation per year will be $100 for 10 years. The straight-line method assumes that machines wear out at a constant rate. The sum of the years digit method on the other hand, is used to compute the depreciation on articles that have the greatest rate of depreciation during the first few years of use.

For example, suppose a drilling machine costing $15,000, has a useful life of five years and can be resold for $5,000. The total depreciation is:

15,000	cost
- 5,000	trade-in
10,000	depreciation

The sum of the years 1 through 5 is 1+2+3+4+5 = 15. Thus, the depreciation for the first year is 5/15, for the second year, 4/15, etc.

Year	Depreciation	Book value at end of year
1	5/15 of 10,000 = 3333.33	15,000 - 3333.33 = 11666.67
2	4/15 of 10,000 = 2666.67	11,666.67 - 2666.67 = 9000.00
3	3/15 of 10,000 = 2000	9000 - 2000 = 7000.00
4	2/15 of 10,000 = 1333.33	7000 - 1333.33 = 5666.67
5	1/15 of 10,000 = 666.67	5666.67 - 666.67 = 5000

The program follows:

```
      DIM V(100)
      READ IYR, COST, SAL
      TDEP = COST - SAL
      KSUM = 0
      JTIME = IYR
 20   KSUM = KSUM + JTIME
      IF (JTIME.EQ.0) GOTO 50
      JTIME = JTIME - 1
      GOTO 20
 50   DO 60 I = 1,IYR
      J = IYR - I + 1
      FRA = J/KSUM
      V(I) = COST - FRA * TDEP
 60   CONTINUE
      STOP
      END
```

Program Comments: The READ statement reads in the number of years, the cost of the item, and the salvage value, respectively. TDEP stores the total value to be depreciated. The loop starting at statement 20 calculates the sum of the years. If the number of years IYR, equals 5, then JTIME = 5,4,3,2,1,0 and KSUM = 5+4+3+2+1 = 15.

When JTIME = 0, signifying that the sum of years has been calculated, the program jumps to statement 50. This loop first calculates the FRA, the fractional amount of depreciation for each year, and V(I), the book value for each year.

• PROBLEM 34-2

An item worth $30,000 initially and having a life of 15 years is depreciated according to the double declining balance method. Calculate the amount of depreciation in each of the first five years.

Solution: The depreciation during the nth year can be expressed as

$$D = \frac{2C}{N}\left(1 - \frac{2}{N}\right)^{n-1} \quad \text{where}$$

D is the depreciation for a particular year.
C is the original cost.
N is the life span of the machine.
n is the particular year for which we are calculating the depreciation.

Hence we can write a statement function to compute D. Values of D for n = 1,2,3,4,5 will be stored in an array A.

```
      DIMENSION A (5)
      REAL D,C,N,K
      DO 100 J = 1,5
      A (J) = D (30000., 15., J)
100   CONTINUE
      END
```

```
      FUNCTION D (C,N,K)
      D = 2*C/N*(1.-2./N)**(K-1.)
      RETURN
      END
```

• PROBLEM 34-3

Write a FORTRAN program to read in an initial cost, salvage value, expected lifetime, number of years to be depreciated, and a code. The code indicates the function to be performed, namely

1 - straight-line depreciation
2 - declining balance depreciation
3 - sum-of-the-years-digits depreciation

The program will calculate the depreciation in accordance with the code number you choose.

Solution: To do this problem, we assume the cost is not equal to $999.99. (We use the value of $999.99 to indicate that there are no more DATA cards to be read, and the program should be terminated.) We can set up a DO-WHILE construct here: processing will continue until all the cards are read in. Input values as well as the output statements have been omitted so that you may come up with your own ideas on that.

```
      DIMENSION VALUE (100)
15    READ (3,100) COST, SALV, EXLIFE, IYRS, ICODE
      IF (COST.EQ. 999.99) GO TO 99
      IF (ICODE.EQ.1) GO TO 50
      IF (ICODE.EQ.2) GO TO 70
C     BY DEFAULT, THIS SECTION TAKES CARE OF ICODE = 3
      DEP = COST - SALV
      JSUM = 0
      KT = EXLIFE
20    JSUM = JSUM + KT
      IF (KT.EQ.0) GO TO 30
      KT = KT - 1
      GO TO 20
30    DO 40 M = 1,IYRS
      J = IYRS - 1
      FRA = J/IYRS
      VALUE (M) = FRA*DEP
40    CONTINUE
      GO TO 15
C     THIS SECTION TAKES CARE OF ICODE = 1
50    ANNDEP = DEP/ELIFE
      DO 60 K = 1,IYRS
      COST = COST - ANNDEP
60    VALUE(K) = COST
      GO TO 15
C     THIS SECTION TAKES CARE OF ICODE = 2
      DO 80 I = 1,IYRS
      DEP = VALU*.1667
      VALU = VALU - DEP
      VALUE(I) = VALU
80    CONTINUE
      GO TO 15
99    STOP
      END
```

• PROBLEM 34-4

Write a BASIC program to calculate the principal after N years on a balance (original principal) of B at time 0. Assume that interest is compounded yearly at 5% effective yield. Print the results for N = 1,3,5.

Solution: The formula we need is $P = P_o(Hi)^N$ where $P_o = B$, $i = 0.05$, and N takes on values 1,3, and 5. This program introduces the STEP option in a FOR-NEXT loop. Data of $P_o = B = 200$ is used.

```
 1Ø REM CALCULATES PRINCIPAL ON
 2Ø REM A BALANCE AT 5% INTEREST
 3Ø REM B = ORIGINAL BALANCE, P = PRINCIPAL
 4Ø READ B
 5Ø PRINT "PRINCIPAL", "BALANCE", "YEARS"
 6Ø FOR N = 1 TO 5 STEP 2
 7Ø LET P = B*1.05↑N
 8Ø PRINT P, B, N
 9Ø NEXT N
1ØØ DATA 2ØØ
11Ø END
```

• PROBLEM 34-5

For principal P, a bank pays R interest compounded annually. Define a function in FORTRAN which calculates the deposit at the end of n years. Use the formula

$$\text{NEW DEPOSIT} = P((1+R)^n - 1)/R$$

Solution: Let P be the original principal. After 1 year, the new principal will be

$$P_1 = P(1+R).$$

After two years, it will be

$$P_2 = P_1(1+R) = P(1+R)(1+R) = P(1+R)^2.$$

After n years, it will be

$$P_n = P(1+R)^n.$$

By NEW DEPOSIT is understood the amount in the bank after n years less the original principal.

In FORTRAN we can write

```
FUNCTION ND (P,R,N)
ND = P*(((1.+R)**N) - 1.)/R
RETURN
END
```

[Note: Remember to declare variables as INTEGER or REAL in the main program.]

Write a program in FORTRAN to prepare a payroll for a business employing N workers. The following computations must be performed: 1) regular hours and overtime must be totaled. 2) wages equal to regular rate times regular hours plus overtime rate times overtime hours. 3) Deductions must be made for insurance taxes, and government income tax. 4) Net wages are printed for each worker. Assume that tax schedules can be accessed from secondary memory.

Solution: In preparing a payroll register, the first step is collecting and processing the time cards. The items 1) - 3) are entered by reading a card. This information is then used in calculating gross and net pay. Since the wages values require the accuracy of only two decimal places (cents), while the FORTRAN calculations are much more accurate, the rounding should be made by asking for only two places in the FORMAT statement. If the computer uses truncation as the approximation routine, .005 should be added to each value before truncating.

To calculate the taxes, a table look-up routine must be performed. Assume that Table 1 has already been loaded into an array.

Each time a card is read it will give the salary and number of exemptions.

```
10    FORMAT (F 6.2,I2)
15    DIMENSION A(28,8)
C     READ SALARY AND EXEMPTIONS
20    READ (3,10) S,E
C     EX INDICATES WHERE THE TAX WILL BE
      EX = E + 2
C     C INDICATES ROW OF THE TAX
      C = 1
C     R IS THE LOWEST TAXABLE SALARY
      R = 80
C     TAX NOT IN TABLE
      IF (S.LT.78) GO TO 140
C     CHECKING FOR PROPER ROW
100   IF (S.LT.R) GO TO 110
C     ADVANCING TO NEXT SALARY STEP
      R = R + 2
C     ADVANCING TO NEXT ROW IN TABLE
      C = C + 1
      GO TO 100
C     PRINTS SALARY AND TAX
110   WRITE (4,120)S,A(C,EX)
120   FORMAT (F6.2,5X,F5.2)
      GO TO 20
140   WRITE (4,150)
150   FORMAT ("TAX NOT IN TABLE")
      GO TO 20
      STOP
      END
```

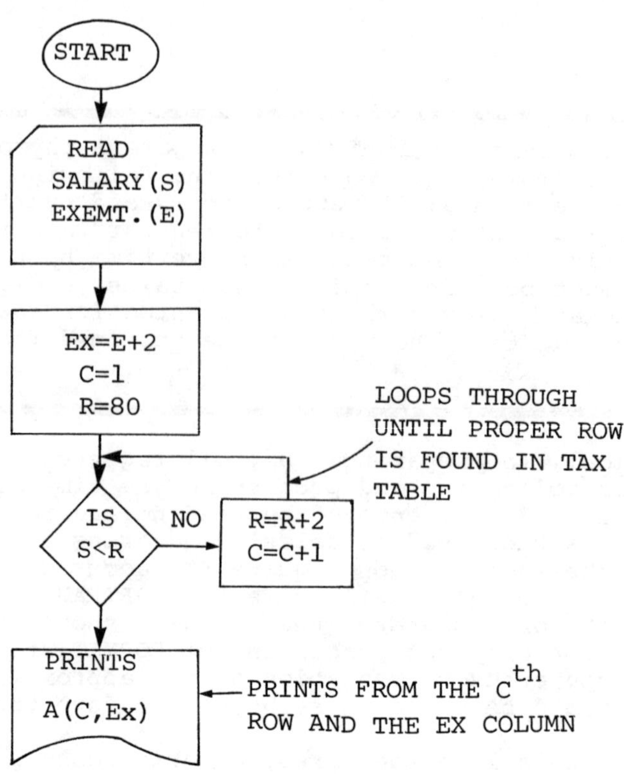

Married Persons ***Weekly Payroll Period***

The wages are		*The number of withholding exemptions claimed*						
At least	*But less than*	*0*	*1*	*2*	*3*	*4*	*5*	*6*
		The amount of tax to be withheld shall be						
$ 78	$ 80	$11.10	$ 9.10	$ 7.00	$ 5.00	$ 3.00	$ 1.10	$ 0.00
80	82	11.40	9.40	7.30	5.30	3.40	1.40	0.00
82	84	11.70	9.70	7.60	5.60	3.60	1.70	0.00
84	86	12.00	10.00	7.90	5.90	3.90	1.90	0.10
86	88	12.30	10.30	8.20	6.20	4.20	2.20	0.30
88	90	12.70	10.60	8.50	6.50	4.50	2.50	0.60
90	92	13.00	10.90	8.80	6.80	4.80	2.80	0.90
92	94	13.30	11.20	9.10	7.10	5.10	3.10	1.20
94	96	13.70	11.50	9.40	7.40	5.40	3.40	1.50
96	98	14.00	11.80	9.70	7.70	5.70	3.70	1.70
98	100	14.40	12.10	10.00	8.00	6.00	4.00	2.00
100	105	15.00	12.70	10.60	8.50	6.50	4.50	2.50
105	110	15.80	13.50	11.30	9.30	7.30	5.30	3.20
110	115	16.70	14.40	12.10	10.00	8.00	6.00	4.00
115	120	17.50	15.20	12.90	10.80	8.80	6.80	4.70
120	125	18.40	16.10	13.80	11.50	9.50	7.50	5.50
125	130	19.20	16.90	14.60	12.30	10.30	8.30	6.20
130	135	20.10	17.80	15.50	13.20	11.00	9.00	7.00
135	140	20.90	18.60	16.30	14.00	11.80	9.80	7.70
140	145	21.80	19.50	17.20	14.90	12.60	10.50	8.50
145	150	22.60	20.30	18.00	15.70	13.50	11.30	9.20
150	160	23.90	21.60	19.30	17.00	14.70	12.40	10.40
160	170	25.60	23.30	21.00	18.70	16.40	14.10	11.90
170	180	27.50	25.00	22.70	20.40	18.10	15.80	13.60
180	190	29.50	26.80	24.40	22.10	19.80	17.50	15.30
190	200	31.50	28.80	26.10	23.80	21.50	19.20	17.00
200	210	33.50	30.80	28.10	25.50	23.20	20.90	18.70

Note that FORTRAN is not the best choice of language for this type of problem as evidenced by the numerous unconditional GO TO statements scattered throughout the program. If the program had been written in COBOL, the structure would have been easier to follow.

• PROBLEM 34-7

Write a BASIC program which keeps track of the numbers of items in stock for four different classes of items. To be specific, let the four classes of items be denoted by 1ØØ1, 1ØØ2, 1ØØ3 and 1ØØ4. Consider the case where the following 7 (seven) items are in stock: 1ØØ1, 1ØØ2, 1ØØ2, 1ØØ3, 1ØØ4, 1ØØ3, 1ØØ1.

Solution: It is convenient to introduce separate counters K1, K2, K3, and K4 for the four classes. It is also convenient to utilize the ON-GO TO statement. Thus if we say

```
50 ON X GO TO 9Ø, 7Ø, 11Ø
```

control will be transferred to statements 9Ø, 7Ø, or 11Ø if the truncated value of X is 1, 2, or 3 respectively.

```
1Ø   REM INVENTORY PROGRAM FOR 4 CLASSES
2Ø   REM K1, K2, K3, K4 ARE THE COUNTERS
3Ø   DATA 1ØØ1, 1ØØ2, 1ØØ2, 1ØØ3, 1ØØ4, 1ØØ3, 1ØØ1
4Ø   LET K1 = K2 = K3 = K4 = Ø
5Ø   FOR I = 1 TO 7
6Ø   READ X
7Ø   ON X - 1ØØØ GO TO 8Ø, 1ØØ, 12Ø, 14Ø
8Ø   LET K1 = K1 + 1
9Ø   GO TO 16Ø
1ØØ  LET K2 = K2 + 1
11Ø  GO TO 16Ø
12Ø  LET K3 = K3 + 1
13Ø  GO TO 16Ø
14Ø  LET K4 = K4 + 1
15Ø  GO TO 16Ø
16Ø  NEXT I
17Ø  PRINT "ITEM 1ØØ1;"; K1; "IN STOCK"
18Ø  PRINT "ITEM 1ØØ2;"; K2; "IN STOCK"
19Ø  PRINT "ITEM 1ØØ3;"; K3; "IN STOCK"
2ØØ  PRINT "ITEM 1ØØ4;"; K4; "IN STOCK"
21Ø  END
```

Some computers do not accept multiple assignment statements. In that case, in statement 40 each variable should be initialized to zero separately.

OPTIMIZING PRODUCTION

• PROBLEM 34-8

A steel producer uses three different processes to produce different qualities of steel. It takes three tons of raw material (iron, coal, oil and minor trace elements) to produce a ton of steel in any process. The percentages of iron, coal and oil used in each process vary and are given below:

	Process A	Process B	Process C
Iron	40	45	25
Coal	50	25	60
Oil	10	30	15

Write a program in Basic to print the number of tons of raw material needed to make 100, 150, 200, 250, 300 tons of steel if the ratio of process usages A to B to C is as 1:3:6.

Solution: We can treat the composition of each process as a column in an input matrix. The input matrix is therefore

$$\begin{bmatrix} 40 & 45 & 25 \\ 50 & 25 & 60 \\ 10 & 30 & 15 \end{bmatrix} \qquad (1)$$

The ratio of processes A, B, C is always 1 to 3 to 6. This means that for 100 tons of steel, Method A produces 10 tons, Method B 30 tons, and Method C 60 tons. In fact, since the ratios total 10, A will always be 10%, B 30%, and C 60% of total output.

To find the number of tons of iron, coal and oil used in the three processes we post multiply (1) by the column vector $\begin{bmatrix} A \\ B \\ C \end{bmatrix}$ where A, B, C, will vary according to total tonnage of output (100, 150, 200, 250).

A coarse flow-chart for the program is as shown in Fig. 1.

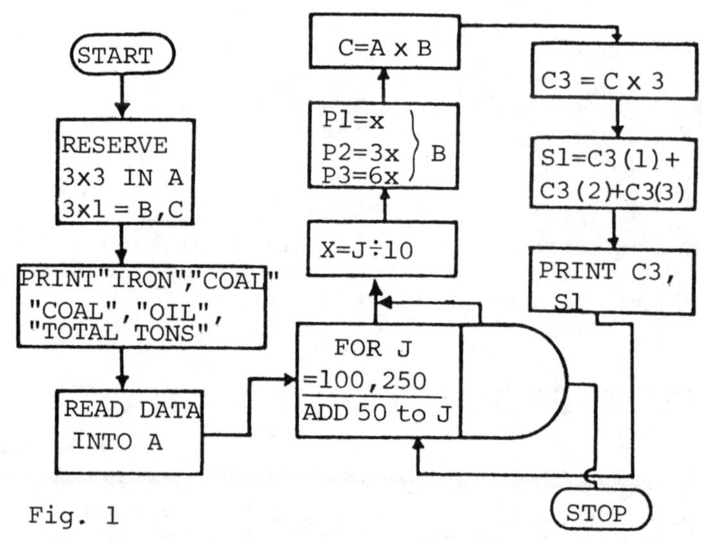

Fig. 1

```
10   PRINT "STEEL PROCESSING"
20   DIM A(2,2) B(2,0) C(2,0)
30   PRINT:  PRINT "IRON," "COAL," "OIL," "TOTAL TONS"
40   MAT READ A
50   FOR J = 100 TO 250 STEP 50
60   X = J/10
70   LET B(0,0) = X
80   LET B(1,0) = 3*X
90   LET B(2,0) = 6*X
100  MAT C = A*B
110  MAT C = (3/100)*C
120  LET S1 = C(0,0) + C(1,0) + C(2,0)
130  PRINT C (0,0), C(1,0), C(2,0), S1
140  NEXT J
150  STOP
160  DATA 40, 45, 25, 50, 25, 60, 10, 30, 15
170  END
```

• **PROBLEM 34-9**

A book publisher is in the business of producing volumes in mathematics, science and the humanities. He basically uses two kinds of labor

a) skilled for writing the books
b) unskilled to correct the completed volumes.

His average costs per book for each type of labor and each type of book is given below:

Expenses	Mathematics	Science	Humanities
Skilled	17.00	16.00	12.00
Unskilled	6.00	5.00	4.00

Write a program in Basic to print the costs of skilled and unskilled labor needed to produce M books in math, S books in science, and H books in humanities, if M = 1, 2, 3, 4, 5; S = 2M + 1; H = 2M - 2.

Solution: We can use matrices to facilitate the solution of this problem. The command MAT X tells the compiler to operate with X according to the rules of matrix algebra.

Form the costs' matrix

$$\begin{bmatrix} 17.00 & 16.00 & 12.00 \\ 6.00 & 5.00 & 4.00 \end{bmatrix} \qquad (1)$$

If we multiply (1) by the vector

$$\begin{bmatrix} M \\ 2M+1 \\ 2M-2 \end{bmatrix}$$ we obtain:

$$\begin{bmatrix} 17500 & 16200 & 12400 \\ 6200 & 5500 & 4900 \end{bmatrix} \begin{bmatrix} M \\ 2M+1 \\ 2M-2 \end{bmatrix}$$

$$= \begin{bmatrix} 17500M + 16200(2M+1) + 12400(2M-2) \\ 6200M + 5500(2M+1) + 4900(2M-2) \end{bmatrix} \quad (2)$$

Adding the two rows of (2) together gives the total cost of skilled and unskilled labor. Note that costs of skilled labor comprise the first row of the result in (2), while costs of unskilled labor comprise the second row.

```
10   DIM A(1,2), B(2,0), C(1,0)
15   PRINT "MATHEMATICS", "SCIENCES", "HUMANITIES",
     "SKILLED LABOR", "UNSKILLED LABOR"
20   PRINT REM L1, L2 DENOTE SKILLED AND UNSKILLED LABOR
25   LET L1 = 0
30   LET L2 = 0
35   FOR M = 0 TO 5
40   LET B(0,0) = M + 1
45   LET B(1,0) = 2*M + 1
50   LET B(2,0) = 2*M + 5
55   MAT C = A*B
60   PRINT
65   PRINT B(0,0), B(1,0), B(2,0), C(0,0), C(1,0)
66   PRINT "TOTAL COSTS", L1, L2
70   LET L1 = L1 + C(0,0)
75   LET L2 = L2 + C(1,0)
80   NEXT M
85   PRINT
90   STOP
95   DATA 17, 16, 12, 6, 5, 4
100  END
```

• PROBLEM 34-10

An economist suspects that a leading indicator in the business cycle has the form xcosx. He wishes to know when the indicator will peak, i.e. achieve a maximum, in different time intervals. Write a FORTRAN program to find the maximum of xcosx in interval [a,b].

Solution: There are many methods of computing the maximum of a function over its domain or a subset of its domain (local maximum). A method particularly suited for computer applications is the elimination scheme. To illustrate the method, let a=o, b=π and suppose we wish to

$$\text{Max } x\cos x \qquad x \in [o,\pi]. \quad (1)$$

1) Place two search points close together at the centre of the interval. Let the distance between the points be $\varepsilon > o$.

2) Evaluate f(x) at X_L and X_R and call the results $f(X_L)$, $f(X_R)$. If $f(X_L) \geq f(X_R)$ Max f(X) lies between o and X_R and the segment $[X_R, \pi]$ can be discarded.

3) Place two search points close together at the center of

the remaining interval and repeat step (2).

4) Suppose $f(X_{R_1}) \geq f(X_{L_1})$. Then Max f(X) lies in the interval $[X_{L_1}, X_R]$ and the segment $[0, X_{L_1}]$ can be discarded.

5) The process continues until an interval less than 2ε is obtained. Since the search cannot continue, the maximum is assumed to occur at the center of this interval.

In the program, a statement function is used to define xcosx so that it can be referred to at any further point in the program. Also, if the search points pass a tolerance limit, the program halts.

```
C     DEFINE THE FUNCTION Y(X)
      Y(X) = X*COX(X)
      READ XL, XR, EPSI
      I = 1
C     CALCULATE INTERIOR POINTS
10    XL1 = XL + .5*(XR - XL - EPSI)
      XR1 = XL1 + EPSI
      YL1 = Y(XL1)
      YR1 = Y(XR1)
      PRINT YL1, YR1, XL, XL1, XR1, XR
      IF (YL1 - YR1) 20, 50, 30
20    XL = XL1
      GO TO 40
30    XR = XR1
C     TEST FOR END OF SEARCH
40    IF (I.GE.100) GO TO 60
      I = I + 1
      IF (XR - XL.GT.3*EPSI) GO TO 10
50    XMAX = .5*(XL1 + XR1)
      YMAX = .5*(YL1 + YR1)
      PRINT YMAX, XMAX
      GO TO 70
C     PRINT OUTPUT TERMINATED BECAUSE OF MAX-
C     IMUM ITERATION COUNT
60    WRITE (6, 300)
300   FORMAT (54HO THE SOLUTION HAS NOT CONVERGED AFTER
      100 ITERATIONS.  TERMINATE PROGRAM
70    STOP
      END
```

• PROBLEM 34-11

A firm is considering investing $75,000 in a new venture. Its economists have projected the following returns over the next five years.

Year		Return
1		20,000
2		30,000
3		35,000
4		40,000
5		50,000
	Total	$175,000

Describe how the discounted cash flow interest rate would be found, given a current interest rate of 10%.

Solution: From the given table we observe that the gross return from the investment is \$175,000 - \$75,000 = \$100,000. However, this is assuming that the money invested has no alternative uses, e.g. it could not be invested in a bank at 10% interest. Taking the time value of money into account, to obtain \$20,000 after 1 year we would have to invest

$$\$20,000 = X + .1X$$

now. Thus, $X = \frac{20,000}{1.1} = \$18182$

Similarly, \$30,000 two years from now is worth

$$\$30,000 = (X+.1X)(1+.1)$$
$$= X(1+.1)(1+.1)$$
$$= X(1.1)^2$$

or, $X = \frac{\$30,000}{(1.1)^2} = \$24,794.$

Applying the same analysis to the remaining returns:

Year	Return	Present Value
1	20,000	$20,000/1.1 = 18,182$
2	30,000	$30,000/(1.1)^2 = 24,794$
3	35,000	$35,000/(1.1)^3 = 26,296$
4	40,000	$40,000/(1.1)^4 = 27,321$
5	50,000	$50,000/(1.1)^5 = 31,047$

Adding the present values of returns over the five years gives the present value of returns from the investment. PV = \$127,640. The net present value of the investment when the current interest rate is 10% is therefore NPV = PV - I = \$127,640 - \$75,000 = \$52,640. This means that the \$100,000 return over five years is actually worth \$52,640 to the firm now. Note that as the interest rate changes continuously from 0% to 100%, the NPV changes continuously from \$100,000 (the gross return becomes the net present value when the interest rate is 0%) to \$-59,063. Thus, there must be an interest rate at which the NPV equals zero. This interest rate value is called the DISCOUNTED CASH FLOW interest rate.

A graph of the NVP versus interest rate might look as shown in Fig. 1.

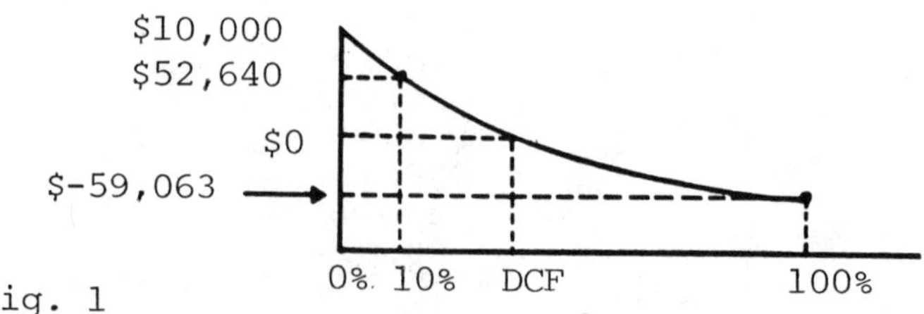

Fig. 1

To actually compute the DCF we must find a root of the equation f(r) = 0 where NVP = f(r). We cannot use the Newton-Raphson method because the functional relationship is not in polynomial form. The bisection method, however, may be applied.

The procedure is as follows: We know that f(.10) = 52,640 and f(1.00) = -$59,063. Compute the value of f at the mid-point of the interval [.10, 1.00], f(.55). If f(.55) ≥ 0 the root must lie in the interval [.55, 1.00] (since f(.10) is positive and f(1.00) is negative). If f(.55) <0, then the root lies in the interval [.10, .55]. In either case the interval of search has been reduced by 1/2.

Repeat the above procedure with the new interval i.e. take the mid-point and evaluate f at this point.

A flowchart for computing the DCF is as shown in Fig. 2

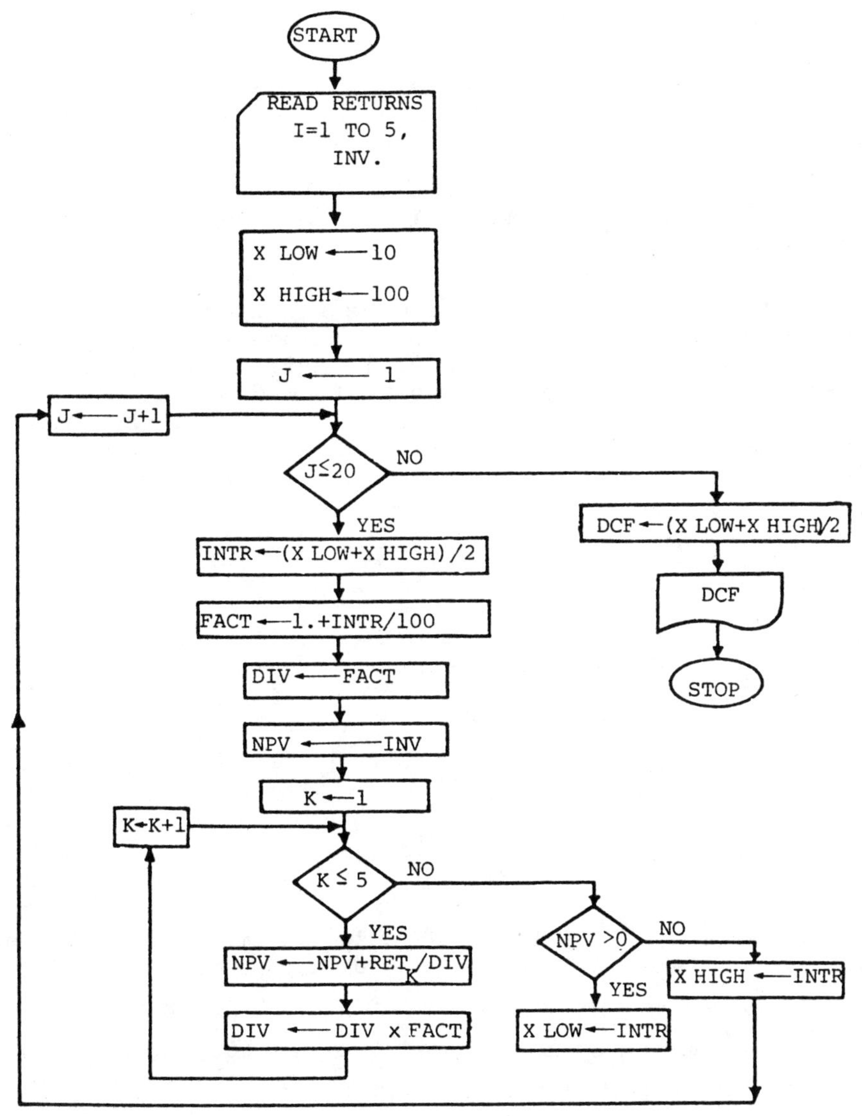

• PROBLEM 34-12

A manufacturer can produce X units of an item at a cost given by the following equation:

$$\text{Cost} = C = 15 + 0.001X^2$$

The relationship between the number of units and price is given by $P = 35 - .1X$ (the producer is a monopolist).

How many units should the monopolist produce in order to maximize his total return?

Solution: The maximization problem may be written as follows:

$$\max_X \{X.(P-C)\}$$

where $P = 35 - 0.1X$
$C = 15 + 0.001X^2,\ X \geq 0$

When X, the quantity produced is zero, there is zero profit. Similarly, when the price of X equals the cost of X, profits are zero. This occurs when $P = C$ or,

$$35 - 0.1X = 15 + 0.001X^2$$

Solving for X gives $X = 100$. Thus profits are zero when $X = 0$ and $X = 100$.

Assuming profit is a continuous function of output Rolle's theorem may be applied to conclude that the maximum profit point lies in the interval (0,100). Numerical approximation of this maximum is performed on the computer using the GOLDEN SECTION method. To illustrate the method, suppose the graph of profit versus production looks as follows:

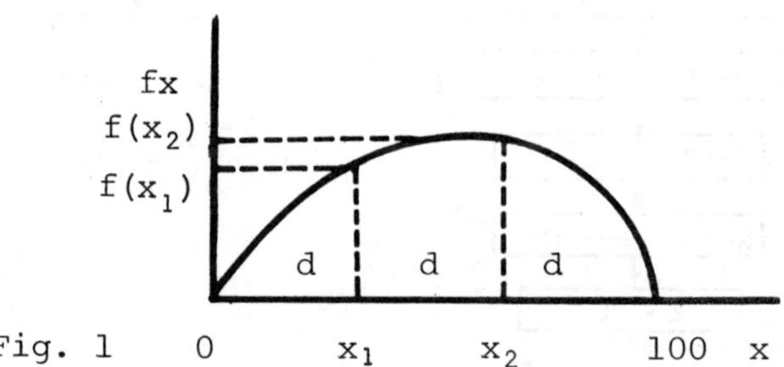

Fig. 1

In the interval [0,100] there is only one maximum. Suppose we pick two points, X_1 and X_2 in that interval and find their ordinates on the curve. If $f(X_2) > f(X_1)$, then the interval of search may be reduced from [0,100] to $[X_1, 100]$ and the interval $[0, X_1]$ can be eliminated.

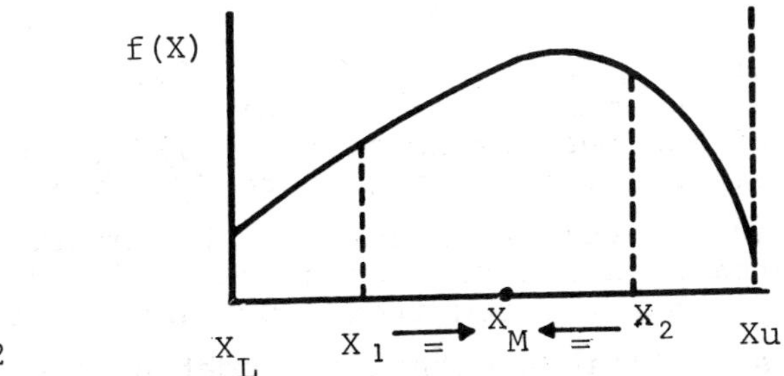

Fig. 2

The original interval $[X_L, X_u]$ is equal to 1 (Fig. 2). Let τ equal the ratio of the long subinterval to the total interval, i.e.

$$\frac{X_2 - X_L}{X_u - X_L} = \tau.$$

Since X_1 and X_2 have been located symmetrically about the center of the interval, the distance between X_1 and X_u is also τ. From Fig. 2, the interval $[X_L, X_1]$ will be eliminated after the first iteration since $f(X_2)>f(X_1)$. In order for X_2 to be properly located within the interval $[X_1, X_u]$ for the next iteration, the following must be true:

$$\frac{X_u - X_2}{X_u - X_1} = \tau$$

But, from Fig. 2, $X_u - X_2 = 1 - \tau$ and $X_u - X_1 = \tau$. Thus,

$$\frac{1-\tau}{\tau} = \tau, \text{ or}$$

$$\tau^2 + \tau - 1 = 0. \tag{1}$$

Solving (1) for τ we obtain $\tau = \frac{\sqrt{5} - 1}{2} = 0.618$. Thus, according to the GOLDEN SECTION rule, X_2 should be 0.618 from X_L and X_1 should be 0.618 from X_u.

For the given problem, the selection of points in the search interval would proceed as follows:

$$X_1 = 100 - 0.618 \times 100 = 100 - 61.8 = 38.2;$$

$X_2 = 0.618 \times 100 = 61.8$. From Fig. 1, $f(X_2) > f(X_1)$ so the interval [0,38.2] is eliminated. The next point is located at 0.618 x (length of interval) = 0.618 x (61.8) = 38.2 from the left end of the interval, or $X_3 = 38.2 + 38.2 = 76.4$. Since $f(X_2) > f(X_3)$, [76.4,100] is eliminated.

X_4 is located at 0.618 x (length of interval) = 0.618 x (38.2) = 23.6 from the right end or 76.4 - 23.6 = 52.8. After three iterations the interval within which the optimum is located has been reduced from [0,100] to [52.8]. These values are now assigned to X_L and X_u. The process is continued until the length of the interval is less than some preassigned $\varepsilon>0$. The average of f(X) at final X_L and X_u is then the required approximation to the optimum. The most efficient method of locating the points is the GOLDEN SECTION technique.

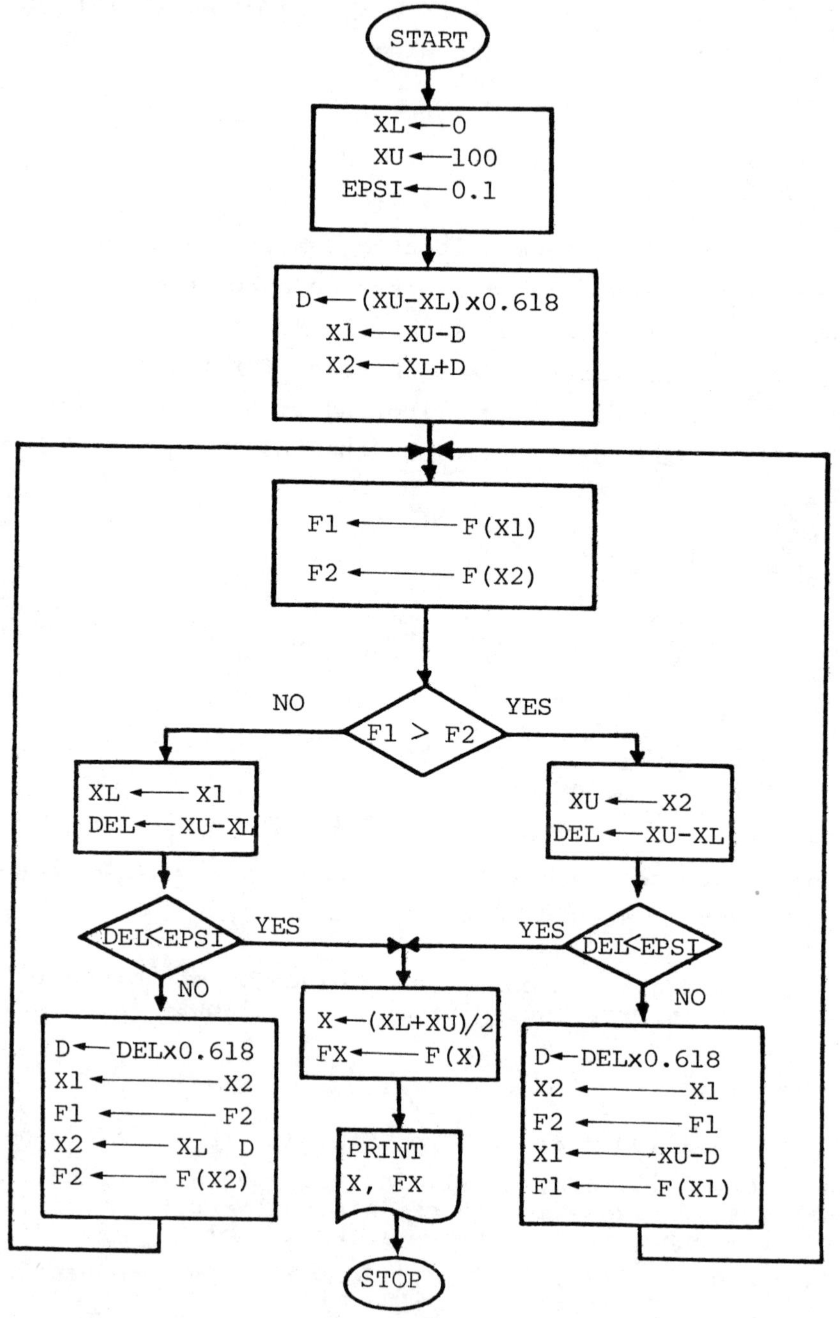

• PROBLEM 34-13

Suppose there are three typists in a typing pool. Each typist can type an average of 6 letters/hr. If letters arrive to be typed at the rate of 15 letters/hr.,

a) What fraction of the time are all three typists busy?

b) What is the average number of letters waiting to be typed?

c) What is the average time a letter spends in the system (waiting and being typed)?

d) What is the probability of a letter taking longer than 20 min. waiting to be typed and being typed?

e) Suppose each individual typist receives letters at the average rate of 5/hr. Assume each typist can type at the average rate of 6 letters/hr., what is the average time a letter would spend in the system (waiting and being typed)?

Solution: a) The following information is given

λ = 15 letters/hr.
μ = 6 letters/hr.
S = 3

Thus, we want $P(n \geq 3)$. To obtain this, we need Po, the probability of no customers in the system given by the equation:

$$Po = \frac{1}{\left\{\left[\sum_{n=0}^{S-1} \frac{1}{n!}\left(\frac{\lambda}{\mu}\right)^n\right] + \frac{1}{S!(1-\lambda/\mu S)}\left(\frac{\lambda}{\mu}\right)^S\right\}}$$

Substituting the given values into the above equation we have the following:

$$Po = \frac{1}{\left[1 + \left(\frac{\lambda}{\mu}\right) + \frac{1}{2}\left(\frac{\lambda}{\mu}\right)^2 + \frac{1}{6}\left(\frac{\lambda}{\mu}\right)^3\left(\frac{1}{\left(1-\frac{\lambda}{3\mu}\right)}\right)\right]}$$

$$= \frac{1}{\left[1 + \frac{15}{6} + \frac{1}{2}\left(\frac{15}{6}\right)^2 + \frac{1}{6}\left(\frac{15}{6}\right)^3\left(\frac{1}{1 - \frac{15}{18}}\right)\right]}$$

$= 0.044944$

Therefore, $P(n \geq S)$ = probability of the arrived letter waiting for service
= probability of at least S customers in the system

$$P(n \geq 3) = \frac{\left(\frac{15}{6}\right)^3 (0.044944)}{6\left(1 - \frac{15}{18}\right)}$$

$$= 0.70225$$

b) L_q = average # of customers in queue

$$= \frac{\left(\frac{\lambda}{\mu}\right)^{S+1} Po}{S \cdot S!(1 - \lambda/\mu S)^2}$$

$$= \frac{\left(\frac{15}{6}\right)^4 (0.044944)}{(3)\ (6)\left(1 - \frac{15}{18}\right)^2}$$

$$= 3.51124$$

c) We first need the average number of letters in the system.

$$L = L_q + \frac{\lambda}{\mu}$$

$$= 3.51124 + \frac{15}{6}$$

$$= 6.01124$$

W = average time a customer spends in a system

$$= \frac{L}{\lambda}$$

$$= \frac{6.01124}{5}$$

$$= 0.40075 \text{ hr.}$$

$$\simeq 24 \text{ min.}$$

d) The probability of a letter taking longer than 20 min. waiting to be typed and being typed

$$P(T>t) = e^{-\mu t}\left\{1 + \frac{(\lambda/\mu)^S Po\ [1 - e^{-\mu t(S-1-\lambda/\mu)}}{S!\ (1 - \lambda/\mu S)(S - 1 - \lambda/\mu)}\right\}$$

Therefore,

$$P(T>\tfrac{1}{3}\text{hr}) = e^{-6(1/3)}\left[1 + \frac{\left(\frac{15}{6}\right)^3 (0.044944)(1-e^{-6(1/3)\left(3-1-\frac{15}{6}\right)}}{6\left(1 - \frac{15}{18}\right)\left(3 - 1 - \frac{15}{6}\right)}\right]$$

$$= 0.46198$$

e) Each queue and server can be treated as a separate single queue, single-server system so that

$$W = \frac{1}{\mu - \lambda}$$

$$= \frac{1}{6 - 5}$$

$$= 1 \text{ hr.}$$

```
** QUEUING PROGRAM **
** INFINITE SOURCE, INFINITE QUEUE, MULTIPLE SERVERS **

WE ASSUME
    ARRIVALS FORM A SINGLE QUEUE
    INFINITE SOURCE AND INFINITE QUEUE
    FIFO QUEUE DISCIPLINE
    THERE ARE MULTIPLE SERVERS WITH EXPONENTIAL SERVICE
    TIME
    DEPARTURES FROM SYSTEM OCCUR COMPLETELY AT RANDOM
    REAL*4TITLE(20), LAMBDA, MU, N, L, LQ, NFACT
5   READ(5, 10, END = 2000) TITLE
10  FORMAT (20A4)
    WRITE (6, 11) TITLE
11  FORMAT ('1', 20A4,//)
    READ (5,20) LAMBDA MU
20  FORMAT (3F10.0)
    READ (5, 20) N, S, T
    IF (LAMBDA. GE. S*MU) GO TO 700
C   ****************************************************
C   *     CALCULATE PZERO                              *
C   ****************************************************
    NS=S
    SUM=0.0
    DO 205 NK=1, NS
    SK=NK-1
    CALL FACT(SK, NFACT)
    SUM=SUM+(1/NFACT)*(LAMBDA/MU)**SK
205 CONTINUE
    CALL FACT(S, SFACT)
    PZERO=1/(SUM+(1/(SFACT*(1-LAMBDA/(MU*S))))*(LAMBDA/MU)
    **S)
C   ****************************************************
C   *     CALCULATE PN                                 *
C   ****************************************************
    IF(N.GE.S) GO TO 210
    CALL FACT(N, NFACT)
    PN=(1/NFACT)*((LAMBDA/MU)**N)*PZERO
    GO TO 215
210 CALL FACT(S, SFACT)
    PN=(1/(SFACT*S**(N-S)))*((LAMBDA/MU)**N)*PZERO
C   ****************************************************
C   *     CALCULATE PS, PT, L, LQ, W, WQ               *
C   ****************************************************
215 CALL FACT(S, SFACT)
    PS=(((LAMBDA/MU)**S)*PZERO)/(SFACT*(1-LAMBDA/(MU*S)))
    PTN=((LAMBDA/MU)**S)*PZERO*(1-EXP(-MU*T*(S-1-LAMBDA/
    MU)))
    PTD=SFACT*(1-LAMBDA/MU*S))*(S-1-LAMBDA/MU)
    PT=EXP(-MU*T)*(1+PTN/PTD)
    LQ=(((LAMBDA/MU)**(S+1))*PZERO)/(S*SFACT*(1-LAMBDA/
    (MU*S))**2)
    L=LQ+LAMBDA/MU
    W=L/LAMBDA
    WQ=LQ/LAMBDA
```

```
C     ****************************************************
C     *     PRINT RESULTS                                *
C     ****************************************************
      WRITE (6,100) LAMBDA, MU, N, S, T, L, LQ, W, WQ, PT,
      PN, PZERO, PS
100   FORMAT(' LAMBDA = ', F10.5/' MU   =',F10.5/' N
      =',F10.5/' S
      * =',F10.5/'T     =',F10.5/' L   =',F10.5/' LQ
      =',F10.5
      */' W  =',F10.5/' WQ   =',F10.5/' PT   =',F10.5/' PN
      ='*,F10.5/' PZERO  =',F10.5/' PS   =',F10.5)
      GO TO 5
700   WRITE(6, 705)
705   FORMAT('QUEUING SYSTEM NOT VALID BECAUSE LAMBDA
      ≤ S*MU')
      GO TO 5
2000  STOP
      END

      SUBROUTINE FACT(P, PROD)
      NUM=P
      PROD=1.
      IF (NUM.EQ.0) GO TO 20
      DO 10 K=1, NUM
10    PROD=PROD*K
20    RETURN
      END
/DATA
      SINGLE QUEUE - MULTIPLE SERVER MODEL
      15.   6.
      1.    3.    .3333
      SINGLE QUEUE - MULTIPLE SERVER MODEL
LAMBDA = 15.00000
MU     =  6.00000
N      =  1.00000
S      =  3.00000
T      =  0.33330
L      =  6.01124
LQ     =  3.51124
W      =  0.40075
WQ     =  0.23408
PT     =  0.46198
PN     =  0.11236
PZERO  =  0.04494
PS     =  0.70225
```

• PROBLEM 34-14

A two-person barbershop has five chairs to accommodate waiting customers. Potential customers arrive at the average rate of 3.7634/hr. and spend an average of 15 min. in the barber's chair.

Assume

M = 7 (total number of persons in the system including the two barbers.)

$\lambda = 3.7634/\text{hr.}$

$\mu = 4/\text{hr.}$

$S = 2$ servers.

a) What is the probability of a customer getting directly into the barber's chair upon arrival?

b) What is the expected number of customers waiting for a haircut?

c) What is the effective arrival rate assuming Pn = 1?

d) How much time can a customer expect to spend in the barbershop?

e) What fraction of potential customers are turned away?

Solution: a) The probability of a customer getting directly into the barber's chair upon arrival is the same as in the case of no customers in the system. This is computed as follows:

$$Po = \frac{1}{\sum_{n=0}^{S} (1/n!)(\lambda/\mu)^n + (1/S!)(\lambda/\mu)^S \sum_{n=S+1}^{M} (\lambda/\mu S)^{n-S}}$$

$$= \frac{1}{\sum_{n=0}^{2} (1/n!)(3.7634/4)^n + \frac{1}{2}(3.7634/4)^2 \sum_{n=3}^{7} (3.7634/4.2)^{n-2}}$$

$= 0.36133$

b) The expected number of customers waiting for a haircut:

$$L_q = \left[\frac{Po(\lambda/\mu)^S(\lambda/\mu S)}{S!(1-\lambda/\mu S)^2}\right]\left[1 - \left(\frac{\lambda}{\mu S}\right)^{M-S} - (M-S)\left(\frac{\lambda}{\mu S}\right)^{M-S}\left(1 - \frac{\lambda}{\mu S}\right)\right]$$

$$= \left[\frac{(0.36133)(3.7634/4)^2(3.7634/4\times 2)}{2![1-(3.7634/4\times 2)]^2}\right]$$

$$\times \left[1 - \left(\frac{3.7634}{4\times 2}\right)^{7-2} - (7-2)\left(\frac{3.7634}{4\times 2}\right)^{7-2}\left(1 - \frac{3.7634}{4\times 2}\right)\right]$$

$= 0.2457$

c) The effective arrival rate

$$\lambda eff = \mu\left[S - \sum_{n=0}^{S-1} (S-n)Pn\right]$$

$$\text{where } P_n = \begin{cases} \frac{1}{n!}\left(\frac{\lambda}{\mu}\right)^n P_o & \text{for } n \le S \\ \frac{1}{S!S^{n-S}} \left(\frac{\lambda}{\mu}\right)^n P_o & \text{for } S < n \le M \\ 0 & \text{for } n > M \end{cases}$$

S = number of servers
M = maximum number of persons in the system

Therefore, since $n \le S$,

$$P_n = \frac{1}{n!}\left(\frac{\lambda}{\mu}\right)^n P_o = \frac{1}{1}\left(\frac{3.7634}{4}\right)^1 P_o$$

$$= \frac{1}{1}\left(\frac{3.7634}{4}\right)(.36133)$$

$$= .2457$$

$$\lambda_{eff} = \mu\left[S - \sum_{n=0}^{S-1} (S-n)\, P_n\right]$$

$$= 4[2 - 2(0.36133) - 0.339957]$$

$$= 3.7495$$

d) The time a customer is expected to spend in the barbershop,

$$W = \frac{L}{\lambda_{eff}} = \frac{L_q + (2 - 2P_o - P_1)}{\lambda_{eff}}$$

$$= \frac{1.183083}{3.7495}$$

$$= 0.3155 \text{ hr}$$

$$\cong 19 \text{ min}$$

e) Fraction of potential customers that will be turned away

$$P(7 \text{ in the system}) = P_7 = \frac{1}{S!S^{n-S}} \left(\frac{\lambda}{\mu}\right)^n P_o$$

since $S < n \le M = 2 < 7 = 7$

$$= \frac{1}{2!2^{7-2}} \left(\frac{3.7634}{4}\right)^7 (0.36133)$$

$$= 0.00368$$

$$= 0.3 \text{ percent}$$

Thus, only 0.3 percent of the potential customers will be turned away.

The Fortran program for the problem follows:

```
** INFINITE SOURCE, FINITE QUEUE, MULTIPLE SERVERS **
** QUEUING PROGRAM **

WE ASSUME
     ARRIVALS TO SYSTEM ARE COMPLETELY AT RANDOM - POISSON
     INPUT
     ARRIVALS FORM A SINGLE QUEUE
     INFINITE SOURCE AND FINITE QUEUE
     FIFO QUEUE DISCIPLINE
     THERE ARE MULTIPLE SERVERS WITH EXPONENTIAL SERVICE
     TIME
     DEPARTURES FROM SYSTEM OCCUR COMPLETELY AT RANDOM

TO CALCULATE AND PRINT
     L        AVERAGE # OF CUSTOMERS IN THE SYSTEM
     LQ       AVERAGE # OF CUSTOMERS IN QUEUE
     PN       PROBABILITY OF N CUSTOMERS IN SYSTEM AT ANY
              POINT IN TIME
     PZERO    PROBABILITY OF NO CUSTOMERS IN THE SYSTEM

     W        AVERAGE TIME CUSTOMER SPENDS IN SYSTEM
     WQ       AVERAGE TIME CUSTOMER SPENDS IN QUEUE
     LAMEFF   OVERALL EFFECTIVE ARRIVAL RATE FOR FINITE
              QUEUE WITH INFINITE SOURCE

      REAL*4 TITLE(20), LAMBDA, MU, N, M, L, LQ, LAMEFF
5     READ(5, 10, END=2000) TITLE
10    FORMAT (20A4)
      WRITE (6, 11) TITLE
11    FORMAT ('1',20A4,//)
      READ (5, 20) LAMBDA, MU
20    FORMAT (3F10.0)
      READ (5, 20) N, M, S
C     ****************************************************
C     *     CALCULATE PZERO                              *
C     ****************************************************
      IS=S+1
      SUM=0.0
      DO 405 NK=1, IS
      SK=NK-1
      CALL FACT (SK, TFACT)
      SUM=SUM+(1/TFACT)*(LAMBDA/MU)**SK
405   CONTINUE
      SUM2=0.0
      NM=M
      DO 410 NK=IS, NM
      SUM2=SUM2+(LAMBDA/(MU*S))**(NK-S)
410   CONTINUE
      CALL FACT(S, SFACT)
      PZERO=1/(SUM+(1/SFACT)*((LAMBDA/MU)**S)*SUM2)
C     ****************************************************
C     *     CALCULATE PN AND LQ                          *
C     ****************************************************
      IF(N.LE.S) GO TO 415
      IF (N.GT.M) GO TO 420
      PN=(1/(SFACT*S**(N-S)))*((LAMBDA/MU)**N)*PZERO
      GO TO 425
415   CALL FACT(N, TFACT)
      PN=(1/TFACT)*((LAMBDA/MU)**N)*PZERO
      GO TO 425
```

```
 420   PN=0.0
 425   LQ=(((LAMBDA/MU)**(S+1)*PZERO)*(1-(LAMBDA/(MU*S))**
       (M-S)-(M-S)*((LAMBDA/(MU*S))**(M-S))*(1-LAMBDA/(MU*S
       ))))/(S*SFACT*(1-LAMBDA/(MU*S))**2)
C      ***************************************************
C      *      CALCULATE LAMEFF, L, W, WQ                 *
C      ***************************************************
       NS=S
       SUM=0
       DO 560 NK=1,NS
       KK=NK-1
       SKK=KK
       CALL FACT(SKK,AFACT)
       SUM=SUM+(S-KK)*PZERO*(1/AFACT)*(LAMBDA/MU)**KK
 560   CONTINUE
       LAMEFF=MU*(S-SUM)
       L=LQ+LAMEFF/MU
       W=L/LAMEFF
       WQ=LQ/LAMEFF
C      ***************************************************
C      *      PRINT RESULTS                              *
C      ***************************************************
       WRITE (6,810) LAMBDA, MU, L, LQ, N, PN, PZERO, W,
       WQ, LAMEFF
 810   FORMAT(' LAMBDA =',F10.5/' MU   =',F10.5/' L
       =',F10.5/' LQ   =',F10.5/' N   =',F10.5/' PN
       =',F10.5/' PZERO  =',F10.5/' WQ  =',F10.5/' LAMEFF
       =',F10.5)
       GO TO 5
2000   STOP
       END

       SUBROUTINE FACT(P, PROD)
       NUM=P
       PROD=1.
       IF (NUM.EQ.0) GO TO 20
       DO 10 K=1, NUM
10     PROD=PROD*K
20     RETURN
       END

/DATA
      WITH N=1
      3.7634      4.
      1.          7.          2.

      WITH N=1

LAMBDA = 3.76340
MU     = 4.00000
L      = 1.18309
LQ     = 0.24571
N      = 1.00000
PN     = 0.33996
PZERO  = 0.36133
W      = 0.31553
WQ     = 0.06553
LAMEFF = 3.74953
```

• **PROBLEM 34-15**

Suppose a one-person tailor shop is in the business of making men's suits. Each suit requires four distinct tasks to be performed before it is completed. Assume all four tasks must be completed on each suit before another suit is started. Assume also that the time to perform each task has an exponential distribution with a mean of 2 hours. Determine

(a) Average number of customers in the system.

(b) Average number of customers in the queue.

(c) Average time a customer spends in the system.

(d) Average time customer spends in the queue.

(e) Probability of no customers in the system.

Solution: (a) The average number of customers in the system equals

$$L = \frac{\lambda}{\mu} + \frac{\lambda^2(1/K\mu^2) + (\lambda/\mu)^2}{2(1 - \lambda/\mu)}$$

$$= \frac{\lambda}{\mu} + \frac{[(K + 1)/K](\lambda^2/\mu^2)}{[2(\mu - \lambda)]/\mu}$$

$$= \left(\frac{K + 1}{2K}\right)\left(\frac{\lambda^2}{\mu(\mu - \lambda)}\right) + \frac{\lambda}{\mu}$$

where K is the number of stations in the service facility, where the service time T_1 at each station is independent on the service times at the other stations and has an exponential distribution with mean $1/K\mu$. Therefore, the service time for each task is

$$\frac{1}{4\mu} = 2 \text{ hr}$$

$$\mu = \frac{1}{8} \text{ order/hr}$$

$$L = \frac{5}{8}\,\frac{(5.5/48)^2}{\left(\frac{1}{8}\right)\left(\frac{1}{8} - 5.5/48\right)} + \frac{(5.5/48)}{\frac{1}{8}}$$

$$= 7.2188$$

(b) Average number of customers in the queue

$$L_q = \left(\frac{K + 1}{2K}\right)\left(\frac{\lambda^2}{\mu(\mu - \lambda)}\right)$$

$$= \left[\frac{4 + 1}{(2)(4)}\right]\left[\frac{\left(\frac{5.5}{48}\right)^2}{\frac{1}{8}\left(\frac{1}{8} - \frac{5.5}{48}\right)}\right]$$

$$= 6.30185$$

(c) Average time customer spends in the system

$$W = \frac{L}{\lambda}$$

$$= \frac{7.2188}{5.5/48}$$

$$= 63 \text{ hr.}$$

$$\tilde{-} \ 1.3 \text{ weeks}$$

(d) $$L_q = \left(\frac{K + 1}{2K}\right)\left(\frac{\lambda^2}{\mu(\mu - \lambda)}\right)$$

$$W_q = \frac{L_q}{\lambda}$$

$$L_q = \left[\frac{4 + 1}{2(4)}\right]\left[\frac{(5.5/48)^2}{\frac{1}{8}\left(\frac{1}{8} - 5.5/48\right)}\right]$$

$$W_q = \frac{\left[\frac{5}{8}\right]\left[\frac{(5.5/48)^2}{\frac{1}{8}\left(\frac{1}{8} - 5.5/48\right)}\right]}{\frac{5.5}{48}}$$

$$= 54.99812$$

(e) Probability of no customers in the system,

$$P_o = 1 - \lambda E(T)$$

where $E(T) = \frac{1}{\mu}$

$$P_o = 1 - \left(\frac{5.5}{48}\right)(8)$$

$$= 0.08334$$

```
C                 **   QUEUING PROGRAM  **
C        **  ARBITRARY DISTRIBUTION OF SERVICE TIME  **
C
C      WE ASSUME
C         ARRIVALS TO SYSTEM ARE COMPLETELY AT RANDOM - POISSON
C         INPUT
C         ARRIVALS FORM A SINGLE QUEUE
C         INFINITE SOURCE AND INFINITE QUEUE
C         FIFO QUEUE DISCIPLINE
C         THERE IS A SINGLE SERVER IN THE SERVICE FACILITY
C         SERVICE TIME (T) HAS AN ARBITRARY DISTRIBUTION
C                  WITH MEAN ETIM AND VARIANCE VARTIM
C         1/LAMBDA > ETIM

      REAL *4 TITLE(20),L,LQ,LAMBDA
    5 READ(5,10,END=2000)TITLE
   10 FORMAT(20A4)
      WRITE(6,11)TITLE
   11 FORMAT('1',20A4,//)
      READ(5,20)LAMBDA,ETIM,VARTIM
   20 FORMAT(3F10.0)
      IF(1/LAMBDA.LE.ETIM) GO TO 40
C     ******************************************************
C     *  CALCULATE QUANTITIES AND PRINT RESULTS            *
C     ******************************************************
      PROD=LAMBDA*ETIM
      PZERO=1-PROD
      L=PROD+(LAMBDA*LAMBDA*VARTIM+PROD*PROD)/(2*PZERO)
      LQ=L-PROD
      W=L/LAMBDA
      WQ=LQ/LAMBA
      WRITE(6,30)LAMBDA,ETIM,VARTIM,L,LQ,W,WQ,PZERO
   30 FORMAT(' LAMBDA =',F10.5/' ETIM  =',F10.5/' VARTIM =',
         F10.5/' L
          =',F10.5/' LQ    =',F10.5/'   W   =',F10.5/' WQ
                  =',F10.5*
       /' PZERO  =',F10.5)
      GO TO 5
   40 WRITE(6,45)
   45 FORMAT(' PROBLEM NOT VALID BECAUSE 1/LAMBDA > ETIM')
      GO TO 5
 2000 STOP
      END


      /DATA

      ERLANG SERVICE TIME
      .114583    8.    16.


      LAMBDA = 0.11458
      ETIM   = 8.00000
      VARTIM = 16.00000
      L      = 7.21852
      LQ     = 6.30185
      W      = 62.99812
      WQ     = 54.99812
      PZERO  = 0.08334
```

Mrs. Jones has some money which she wants to invest in a number of activities (investment programs) in such a way that the total return is maximized.

Assume that she has \$8,000 for allocation and that the investments can only be integral multiples of \$1000. Three investment programs are available. The return function for each program is tabulated below:

Return Functions $h_i(x)$

X(000)	0	1	2	3	4	5	6	7	8
$h_1(x)$	0	5	15	40	80	90	95	98	100
$h_2(x)$	0	5	15	40	60	70	73	74	75
$h_3(x)$	0	4	26	40	45	50	51	52	53

Using the principles of dynamic programming, how would the optimal investment in each program be determined so as to maximize total return?

Solution: The problem can be solved recursively, i.e., the optimal solution for one stage is used as input for the next stage.

Step 1: Assume that program 3 is the only program. Then the optimal return from investing

$$X = 0,1,2,\ldots,8$$

in $h_3(x)$ is given by the last row of the table above. In particular, $h_3(8) = 53$ is the optimal return.

Step 2: Now assume only programs 2 and 3 are available and that $d_2(x)$, $d_3(y)$ can be invested in programs 2 and 3, where

$$x = 0,1,\ldots,8 \quad y = 0,1,2,\ldots,8 \text{ and } x + y = 0,1,2,\ldots,8$$

Thus, with 8 we can invest 0 in 2 and 8 in 3, with 5 3 in 2 and 2 in 3 and so on. Find the optimum of all these choices for each x in 0,1,2,..,8. The functional equation is

$$f_2(x) = \max_{\substack{y = 0,1,\ldots,8-x \\ x = 0,1,\ldots,8}} \left[g_2(y) + f_3(x) \right]$$

Step 3: The final stage is the same as the original problem. We now assume all three programs are available. We examine the results of investing z in program 1 and 8 - z units in programs 2 and 3 (the optimal amounts for each 8 - z (z = 0,1,2,..,8) have already been found in Step 2).

The functional equation for the last stage is

$$f_i(x) = \max [g_i(z) + f_{i+1}(x - z)$$

$$x = 0,\ldots,8$$

$$z = 0,1,\ldots,x$$

$$d_i(x) = \text{value of } z \text{ that yields } f_i(x)$$

where $f_i(x)$ is the optimal return from investing x units in programs i, i + 1,..,3 and $d_i(x)$ is the optimal amount to invest in program i when x units are available to invest in programs i, i + 1,...,3 for i = 1,2,3.

• PROBLEM 34-17

Consider an elementary inventory control system where there is no delay between the ordering of goods and their receipt into inventory. Suppose the order rate is directly proportional to the difference between desired inventory and actual inventory, with proportionality constant 1/A, where A is the time that would be required to correct the inventory if the order rate were constant. Write a FORTRAN program to simulate this system, using modified Euler's method (the method is fully explained, and the subroutine for it is given in the SIMULATION chapter) from time t=0 to $t=t_f$ if I(t) is the inventory level at time t and $I(0)=I_0$.

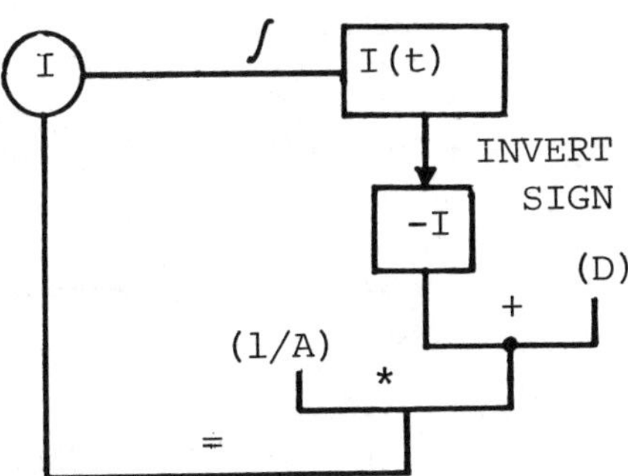

Solution: Clearly, the goal of this system is to maintain the desired inventory, D. If $\dot{I}$ is the order rate (and hence, the rate of change in inventory, since there is no delay), we can write:

$$\dot{I} = 1/A(D - I) \qquad (1)$$

with block diagram as follows:

Note that this model "fills to capacity" using negative feedback control. That is, knowledge of the present system state is used to determine the future system state. If change in inventory is done continuously, the exact solution to equation (1) would be:

$$I(t) = D - (D - I_\emptyset)e^{-t/A}$$

Note, that as $t \to \infty$, I(t) approaches D, which is the steady state solution, the program looks as follows:

```
    DATA T/Ø , Ø/
    COMMON D, A
    INPUT N, TFIN, ACCUR, D, A, IØ
    OUTPUT T, I
    SPACE = D - IØ
    REALN = N
    DT = TFIN/REALN
    I = IØ
    DO 1Ø J = 1, N
        T = T + DT
        CALL MEULER (T, I, ACCUR, DT)
        EXACT = D - SPACE * EXP(-T/A)
        ERROR = ABS((EXACT - I)/EXACT)*1ØØ.
        OUTPUT T, I, EXACT, ERROR
1Ø  CONTINUE
    STOP
    END
    FUNCTION G (W)
    COMMON, D, A
    G = (D - W)/A
    RETURN
    END
```

• **PROBLEM 34-18**

Draw and explain a system dynamics diagram of a market model.

Solution: System dynamics analyzes the forces operating in a system in order to determine their influence on the stability or growth of the system. Here, stability is determined by the rates of changes of different variables.

Consider the following system dynamics diagram of a market model.

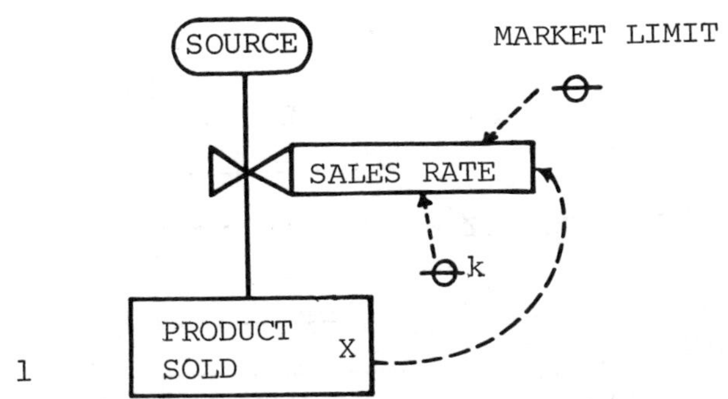

Fig. 1

This diagram depicts a modified exponential growth model in which a variable increases in value at first at an increasing rate and then later at a decreasing rate until it reaches an upper limit. This corresponds to a typical marketing situation. At first, as the product is introduced into the market, sales will increase rapidly. Later as the saturation point is approached, the increase in sales will gradually taper off. Next, consider the various symbols used in the System Dynamics model. The number of products sold can be viewed as a level in a reservoir of products. Levels are represented by boxes. Rates are represented by boxes with valves attached. The constants of the system are indicated by the symbol $\ominus$.

The differential equation corresponding to the system diagram is:

$$\dot{x} = k(X - x) \tag{4}$$

with initial condition $x(o) = 0$

The solution is $x = X(1 - e^{-kt})$ which is known as a modified exponential curve.

A computer simulation model would solve (4) for various values of k, the sales rate constant, and X, the market limit.

• PROBLEM 34-19

Consider a market model showing a positive relationship between number of new houses sold and washing machines sold. Assuming that the number of households increases exponentially and that washing machines break down, draw a system dynamics model for the above system.

<u>Solution</u>: Let H be the number of households, y - the number of houses sold and x - the number of washing machines installed. Since the number of houses sold increases exponentially, the differential equation that gives the rate of change of houses sold over time is

$$\dot{y} = k(H - y). \tag{1}$$

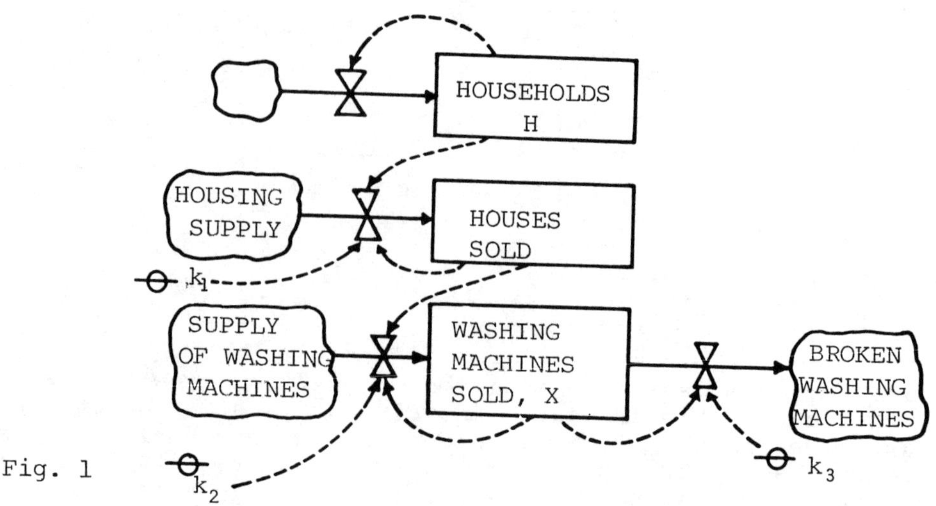

Fig. 1

If the washing machines, once installed, never broke down, the rate of growth of washing machines would be $\dot{x} = k_2(y - x)$.

But washing machines do break down. This means that x, the number of washing machines in use should fall, for every level of x. A new equation needs to be given for x. Assuming that the number of breakdowns is proportional to the level of x, we have

$$\dot{x} = k_2(y - x) - k_3x. \tag{2}$$

Next, the number of households increases exponentially. This is a more realistic assumption regarding the number of households than assuming that H is constant. The new equation for H is

$$\dot{H} = k_4H. \tag{3}$$

A systems diagram for the decay model would trace the interdependencies in the equation system (1) - (3).

DISCOUNT TABLES

DISCOUNT TABLE— Net Decimal Equivalents
(Net Value of $1 00 after Discounts Have Been Deducted)

Rate (%)	5	7½	10	12½	15
Net	.95	.925	.90	.875	.85
2½	.92625	.90188	.8775	.85313	.82875
5	.9025	.87875	.855	.83125	.8075
5, 2½	.87994	.85678	.83363	.81047	.78731
5, 5	.85738	.83481	.81225	.78969	.76713
5, 5, 2½	.83594	.81394	.79194	.76995	.74795
7½	.87875	.85563	.8325	.80938	.78625
7½, 2½	.85678	.83423	.81169	.78914	.76659
7½, 5	.83481	.81284	.79088	.76891	.74694
10	.855	.8325	.81	.7875	.765
10, 2½	.83363	.81169	.78975	.76781	.74588
10, 5	.81225	.79088	.7695	.74813	.72675
10, 5, 2½	.79194	.7711	.75026	.72942	.70858
10, 7½	.79088	.77006	.74925	.72844	.70763
10, 10	.7695	.74925	.729	.70875	.6885
10, 10, 5	.73103	.71179	.69255	.67331	.65408
10, 10, 5, 2½	.71275	.69399	.67524	.65648	.63772
10, 10, 10	.69255	.67433	.6561	.63788	.61965
10, 10, 10, 10	.62330	.60689	.59049	.57409	.55769

Rate %	16 ⅔	20	25	30	33 ⅓
Net	.83333	.80	.75	.70	.66667
2½	.8125	.78	.73125	.6825	.65
5	.79167	.76	.7125	.665	.63333
5, 2½	.77187	.741	.69469	.64838	.6175
5, 5	.75208	.722	.67688	.63175	.60167
5, 5, 2½	.73328	.70395	.65995	.61596	.58663
7½	.77083	.74	.69375	.6475	.61667
7½, 2½	.75156	.7215	.67641	.63131	.60125
7½, 5	.73229	.703	.65906	.61513	.58583
10	.75	.72	.675	.63	.6
10, 2½	.73125	.702	.65813	.61425	.585
10, 5	.7125	.684	.64125	.5985	.57
10, 5, 2½	.69469	.6669	.62522	.58354	.55575
10, 7½	.69375	.666	.62438	.58275	.555
10, 10	.675	.648	.6075	.567	.54
10, 10, 5	.64125	.6156	.57713	.53865	.513
10, 10, 5, 2½	.62522	.60021	.5627	.52518	.50018
10, 10, 10	.6075	.5382	.54675	.5103	.486
10, 10, 10, 10	.54675	.52488	.49208	.45927	.4374

DISCOUNT TABLE — Net Decimal Equivalents (continued)
(Net Value of $1. 00 after Discounts Have Been Deducted)

Rate %	35	37½	40	45
Net	.65	.625	.60	.55
2½	.63375	.60938	.585	.53625
5	.6175	.59375	.57	.5225
5, 2½	.60206	.57891	.55575	.50944
5, 5	.58663	.56406	.5415	.49638
5, 5, 2½	.57196	.54996	.52796	.48397
7½	.60125	.57813	.555	.50875
7½, 2½	.58622	.56367	.54113	.49603
7½, 5	.57119	.54922	.52725	.48331
10	.585	.5625	.54	.495
10, 2½	.57038	.54844	.5265	.48263
10, 5	.55575	.53438	.513	.47025
10, 5, 2½	.54186	.52102	.50018	.45849
10, 7½	.54113	.52031	.4995	.45788
10, 10	.5265	.50625	.486	.4455
10, 10, 5	.50018	.48094	.4617	.42323
10, 10, 5, 2½	.48767	.46891	.45016	.41264
10, 10, 10	.47385	.45563	.4374	.40095
10, 10, 10, 10	.42647	.41006	.39366	.36086

Rate %	50	60	62½	66⅔
Net	.50	.40	.375	.33333
2½	.4875	.39	.36563	.325
5	.475	.38	.35625	.31666
5, 2½	.46313	.3705	.34734	.30875
5, 5	.45125	.361	.33844	.30083
5, 5, 2½	.43997	.35198	.32998	.29331
7½	.4625	.37	.34688	.30833
7½, 2½	.45094	.36075	.3382	.30062
7½,-5	.43938	.3515	.32953	.29292
10	.45	.36	.3375	.3
10, 2½	.43875	.351	.32906	.2925
10, 5	.4275	.342	.32063	.285
10, 5, 2½	.41681	.33345	.31261	.27788
10, 7½	.41625	.333	.31219	.2775
10, 10	.405	.324	.30375	.27
10, 10, 5	.38473	.3078	.28856	.2565
10, 10, 5, 2½	.37513	.30011	.28135	.25009
10, 10, 10	.3645	.2916	.27338	.243
10, 10, 10, 10	.32805	.26244	.24604	.2187

AUTOMOBILE INSURANCE

BASE PREMIUM SCHEDULE

Terr.	Age Group	Comprehensive Symbol Group 1	2	3	4	5	$50 Deductible Symbol Group 1	2	3	4	5	$100 Deductible Symbol Group 1	2	3	4	5
01	0-1	$29	$38	$48	$ 65	$ 84	$116	$132	$155	$186	$217	$ 71	$ 81	$ 95	$114	$133
	2-3	22	29	36	48	63	87	99	116	140	163	53	61	71	86	100
	4-5	16	21	26	36	46	76	85	101	121	141	47	52	62	74	86
	6	13	17	22	29	38	64	73	85	102	119	39	45	52	63	73
02	0-1	44	59	74	100	130	159	180	212	254	297	108	122	144	173	202
	2-3	33	44	56	75	97	119	136	159	191	223	81	92	108	130	151
	4-5	24	33	41	55	71	104	117	138	165	193	71	79	94	112	131
	6	20	27	33	45	58	87	100	117	140	163	59	68	79	95	111
03	0-1	15	20	25	34	44	81	92	108	130	151	69	78	92	110	129
	2-3	11	15	19	25	33	60	69	81	97	113	52	59	69	83	97
	4-5	8	11	14	19	24	53	59	70	84	98	45	51	60	72	84
	6	7	9	11	15	20	44	51	59	71	83	38	43	51	61	71
04	0-1	19	25	31	42	54	102	115	136	163	190	67	76	89	107	125
	2-3	14	19	23	31	41	76	87	102	122	143	50	57	67	80	93
	4-5	10	14	17	23	30	67	75	88	106	124	44	49	58	69	81
	6	8	11	14	19	24	56	64	75	90	105	36	42	49	59	69
05	0-1	20	27	34	46	60	80	91	107	128	150	68	77	91	109	127
	2-3	15	20	26	34	45	60	68	80	96	112	51	58	68	82	96
	4-5	11	15	19	25	33	52	59	70	83	97	45	50	59	71	83
	6	9	12	15	21	27	44	50	59	71	82	37	43	50	60	70
06	0-1	22	29	36	49	63	86	98	115	138	161	74	83	98	118	137
	2-3	16	22	27	36	47	64	74	86	104	121	55	63	74	88	103
	4-5	12	16	20	27	35	56	63	75	90	105	48	54	64	76	89
	6	10	13	16	22	28	47	54	63	76	89	40	46	54	65	75

BASE PREMIUM SCHEDULE

Terr.	Bodily Injury 10-20	25-50	50-100	100-300	Property Damage $5,000	$10,000	$25,000	Medical Payments $500	$1,000	$2,000	$5,000
01	$42	$52	$57	$63	$45	$47	$49	$6	$8	$10	$13
02	$53	$65	$72	$79	$45	$47	$49	$7	$9	$11	$14
03	$31	$38	$42	$46	$41	$43	$44	$4	$6	$ 8	$11
04	$30	$37	$41	$45	$39	$41	$42	$4	$6	$ 8	$11
05	$41	$50	$55	$61	$41	$43	$44	$6	$8	$10	$13
06	$40	$49	$54	$60	$35	$37	$38	$6	$8	$10	$13

AUTOMOBILE INSURANCE

FACTORS FOR YOUTHFUL OPERATOR

Age	Not Owner or Principal Operator: Pleasure or Farm Use	Not Owner or Principal Operator: Drive to Work or Business use*	Owner or Principal Operator: Pleasure or Farm Use	Owner or Principal Operator: Drive to Work or Business Use*	
	Unmarried Male, Under 21				
17 or less	2.75	2.90	3.50	3.65	Without Driver Training
18	2.55	2.70	3.30	3.45	
19	2.40	2.55	3.10	3.25	
20	2.25	2.40	2.85	3.00	
17 or less	2.30	2.45	3.10	3.25	With Driver Training
18	2.15	2.30	2.90	3.05	
19	2.05	2.20	2.70	2.85	
20	1.95	2.10	2.55	2.70	
	Unmarried Male, 21 and Over				
21	1.90	2.05	2.50	2.65	With or Without Driver Training
22	1.70	1.85	2.35	2.50	
23	1.55	1.70	2.20	2.35	
24	1.35	1.50	2.05	2.20	

Factors for no Youthful Operator

Age and Other Factors	Pleasure	Business	Farm	Drives to or from Work (miles): Less than 10	Drives to or from Work (miles): 10 or More
Only operator is female, age 30-64	.90	1.35	.75	1.05	1.30
Principal operator is 65 or over	.95	1.40	.80	1.10	1.35
All other	1.00	1.45	.85	1.15	1.40

*Ten miles or less

FACTORS FOR YOUTHFUL OPERATOR			
	Age	Pleasure or Farm Use	Drive to Work or Business Use*
	Female (Married or Unmarried), Under 21		
WITHOUT DRIVER TRAINING	17 or less	1.75	1.90
	18	1.60	1.75
	19	1.50	1.65
	20	1.25	1.40
WITH DRIVER TRAINING	17 or less	1.60	1.75
	18	1.50	1.65
	19	1.40	1.55
	20	1.20	1.35
	Female (Married or Unmarried), 21 and Over		
WITH OR WITHOUT DRIVER TRAINING	21	1.15	1.30
	22	1.10	1.25
	23	1.05	1.20
	24	1.00	1.15
	Married Male, Under 21		
WITHOUT DRIVER TRAINING	17 or less	1.95	2.10
	18	1.85	2.00
	19	1.75	1.90
	20	1.65	1.80
WITH DRIVER TRAINING	17 or less	1.70	1.85
	18	1.65	1.80
	19	1.60	1.75
	20	1.55	1.70
	Married Male, 21 and Over		
WITH OR WITHOUT DRIVER TRAINING	21	1.50	1.65
	22	1.40	1.55
	23	1.30	1.45
	24	1.20	1.35

*Less than 10 miles

AUTOMOBILE INSURANCE

Premium Charges for Cancelled Policies					
Days Policy in Force	Percent of one year Premium	Days Policy in Force	Percent of one year Premium	Days Policy in Force	Percent of one year Premium
1	5	95–98	37	219–223	69
2	6	99–102	38	224–228	70
3– 4	7	103–105	39	229–232	71
5– 6	8	106–109	40	233–237	72
7– 8	9	110–113	41	238–241	73
9–10	10	114–116	42	242–246 (8 months)	74
11–12	11	117–120	43	247–250	75
13–14	12	121–124 (4 months)	44	251–255	76
15–16	13	125–127	45	256–260	77
17–18	14	128–131	46	261–264	78
19–20	15	132–135	47	265–269	79
21–22	16	136–138	48	270–273 (9 months)	80
23–25	17	139–142	49	274–278	81
26–29	18	143–146	50	279–282	82
30–32 (1 month)	19	147–149	51	283–287	83
33–36	20	150–153 (5 months)	52	288–291	84
37–40	21	154–156	53	292–296	85
41–43	22	157–160	54	297–301	86
44–47	23	161–164	55	302–305 (10 months)	87
48–51	24	165–167	56	306–310	88
52–54	25	168–171	57	311–314	89
55–58	26	172–175	58	315–319	90
59–62 (2 months)	27	176–178	59	320–323	91
63–65	28	179–182 (6 months)	60	324–328	92
66–69	29	183–187	61	329–332	93
70–73	30	188–191	62	333–337 (11 months)	94
74–76	31	192–196	63	338–342	95
77–80	32	197–200	64	343–346	96
81–83	33	201–205	65	347–351	97
84–87	34	206–209	66	352–355	98
88–91 (3 months)	35	210–214 (7 months)	67	356–360	99
92–94	36	215–218	68	361–365 (12 months)	100

Multi-Year Policy Table	
Term (Years)	Annual Rate Factor
2	1.85
3	2.70
4	3.55
5	4.40

Accident Factors	
Number of Accidents	Factor
0	.00
1	.40
2	.90
3	1.50
4	2.20

FIRE INSURANCE

ANNUAL PREMIUM RATES FOR FIRE INSURANCE										
	Brick One-Family Dwellings					Frame One-Family Dwellings				
	Class of Town					Class of Town				
Amount of Insurance	A	B	C	D	E	A	B	C	D	E
$ 5,000	$16.65	$18.35	$20.35	$ 25.35	$ 28.85	$19.10	$20.60	$24.10	$ 29.60	$ 32.60
$ 6,000	$18.15	$19.95	$22.35	$ 38.35	$ 32.55	$20.50	$22.30	$26.50	$ 33.10	$ 36.70
$ 7,000	$19.45	$21.55	$24.35	$ 31.35	$ 36.25	$21.90	$24.00	$28.90	$ 36.60	$ 40.80
$ 8,000	$20.75	$23.15	$26.35	$ 34.35	$ 39.95	$23.30	$25.70	$31.30	$ 40.10	$ 44.90
$ 9,000	$22.05	$24.75	$28.35	$ 37.35	$ 43.65	$24.70	$27.40	$33.70	$ 43.60	$ 49.00
$10,000	$23.35	$26.35	$30.35	$ 40.35	$ 47.35	$26.10	$29.10	$36.10	$ 47.10	$ 53.10
$11,000	$24.65	$27.95	$32.35	$ 43.35	$ 51.05	$27.50	$30.80	$38.50	$ 50.60	$ 57.20
$12,000	$25.95	$29.55	$34.35	$ 46.35	$ 54.75	$28.90	$32.50	$40.90	$ 54.10	$ 61.30
$13,000	$27.25	$31.15	$36.35	$ 49.35	$ 58.45	$30.30	$34.20	$43.30	$ 57.60	$ 65.40
$14,000	$28.55	$32.75	$38.35	$ 52.35	$ 62.15	$31.70	$35.90	$45.70	$ 61.10	$ 69.50
$15,000	$29.85	$34.35	$40.35	$ 55.35	$ 65.85	$33.10	$37.60	$48.10	$ 64.60	$ 73.60
$20,000	$36.35	$42.35	$50.35	$ 70.35	$ 84.35	$40.10	$46.10	$60.10	$ 82.10	$ 94.10
$25,000	$42.85	$50.35	$60.35	$ 85.35	$102.85	$47.10	$54.60	$72.10	$ 99.60	$114.60
$30,000	$49.35	$58.35	$70.35	$100.35	$121.35	$54.10	$63.10	$84.10	$117.10	$135.10
For each $100 not shown add:	$ .13	$ .16	$ .20	$ .30	$ .37	$ .14	$ .17	$ .24	$ .35	$ .41

LIFE INSURANCE

ORDINARY LIFE POLICY					
CASH SURRENDER VALUE PER $1000					
End of year	Age when Insurance was Purchased				
	20	30	40	50	60
5	52.55	70.66	94.57	124.70	159.82
10	125.80	163.73	211.47	268,20	329.62
15	193.44	251.18	318.94	393.47	469.42
20	268.93	340.58	422.95	509.42	588.55

FIVE-YEAR TERM INSURANCE			
PREMIUMS PER $1000			
Age	Annual Premium	Semi-annual Premium	Quarterly Premium
20	4.75	2.42	1.22
30	6.46	3.29	1.66
40	10.22	5.21	2.63
50	18.69	9.53	4.81

ORDINARY LIFE POLICY			
PREMIUMS PER $1000			
Age	Annual Premium	Semi-annual Premium	Quarterly Premiums
20	17.12	8.73	4.41
30	22.48	11.46	5.79
40	30.84	15.73	7.94
50	44.52	22.71	11.46
60	68.23	34.80	17.57

ORDINARY LIFE PAID-UP-AT-AGE-65 POLICY			
PREMIUMS PER $1000			
Age	Annual	Semi-annual	Quarterly
20	19.54	9.97	5.03
30	26.70	13.62	6.88
40	39.40	20.09	10.15
50	67.18	34.26	17.30

RETIREMENT INCOME

RETIREMENT-INCOME POLICY PREMIUMS PER $10 MONTHLY INCOME BEGGINNING AT AGE 60			
Age	Annual	Semi-annual	Quarterly
20	35.86	18.29	9,23
30	53.67	27.37	13.82
40	86.75	44.24	22.34
50	188.61	96.19	48.57

ANNUAL PREMIUMS PER $1000 OF LIFE INSURANCE

Age at Issue	Term 10-yr	Term 15-yr	Whole Life	Limited Payment 20-yr	Limited Payment 30-yr	Endowment 20-yr	Endowment 30-yr
15	$ ...	$ ...	$10.11	$17.97	$13.80	$42.47	$25.90
20	4.99	5.42	11.55	19.84	15.26	42.55	26.15
25	5.19	5.63	13.35	22.07	17.03	42.69	26.50
30	5.77	6.20	15.65	24.73	19.20	43.01	26.92
35	7.09	7.42	18.61	27.93	21.93	43.63	27.50
40	9.18	9.67	22.55	31.80	25.38	44.76	29.95
45	12.74	13.44	27.58	36.49	29.79	46.67	33.33
50	18.59	19.03	33.61	42.19	35.52	49.65	37.77
55	24.89	...	41.57	42.25	...	54.14	...
60	...	...	52.71	58.68	...	61.26	...

PERIODIC PREMIUM TABLE

If period is:	Multiply Annual Premium by:
Semi-annual	.51
Quarterly	.26
Monthly	.087

FURTHER EXAMPLES OF ECONOMY STUDIES

Minimum-Cost Point in the Selection of the Size of a Manufacturing Lot— Comparision of Annual Costs Variable with Lot Size

(1) Lot size........	Q	100	200	300	400	500	600
(2) Lots manufactured per year...	$\frac{NU}{Q}$	30	15	10	7½	6	5
(3) Maximum inventory-pieces......	$Q\left(1-\frac{U}{P}\right)$	90	180	270	360	450	540
(4) Investment (variable) in maximum inventory..	$CQ\left(1-\frac{U}{P}\right)$	$ 39.60	$ 79.20	$118.80	$158.40	$198.00	$237.60
(5) Interest on investment in average inventory....	$\frac{ICQ}{2}\left(1-\frac{U}{P}\right)$	3.96	$ 7.92	$ 11.88	$ 15.84	$ 19.80	$ 23.76
(6) Book value of maximum inventory...........	$TQ\left(1-\frac{U}{P}\right)$	$ 50.40	$100.80	$151.20	$201.60	$252.00	$302.40
(7) Taxes and insurance on average inventory.......	$\frac{BTQ}{2}\left(1-\frac{U}{P}\right)$	$ 0.38	$ 0.76	$ 1.14	$ 1.51	$ 1.89	$ 2.27
(8) Storage cost.....	$AQ\left(1-\frac{U}{P}\right)$	$ 3.60	$ 7.20	$ 10.80	$ 14.40	$ 18.00	$ 21.60
(9) Total annual cost of carrying inventory.........	$\frac{IC+BT+2A}{2}Q\left(1-\frac{U}{P}\right)$	$ 7.94	$ 15.88	$ 23.82	$ 31.75	$ 39.69	$ 47.63
(10) Annual preparation cost........	$\frac{SNU}{Q}$	$138.00	$ 69.00	$ 46.00	$ 34.50	$ 27.60	$ 23.00
(11) Total annual cost variable with lot size............	(9) + (10)	$145.94	$ 84.88	$ 69.82	$ 66.25	$ 67.29	$ 70.63

INTEREST TABLES

1% Compound Interest Factors

n	Single Payment		Uniform Annual Series				n
	Compound Amount Factor	Present Worth Factor	Sinking Fund Factor	Capital Recovery Factor	Compound Amount Factor	Present Worth Factor	
	Given P To find S $(1+i)^n$	Given S To find P $\frac{1}{(1+i)^n}$	Given S To find R $\frac{i}{(1+i)^n-1}$	Given P To find R $\frac{i(1+i)^n}{(1+i)^n-1}$	Given R To find S $\frac{(1+i)^n-1}{i}$	Given R To find P $\frac{(1+i)^n-1}{i(1+i)^n}$	
1	1.010	0.9901	1.00000	1.01000	1.000	0.990	**1**
2	1.020	0.9803	0.49751	0.50751	2.010	1.970	**2**
3	1.030	0.9706	0.33002	0.34002	3.030	2.941	**3**
4	1.041	0.9610	0.24628	0.25628	4.060	3.902	**4**
5	1.051	0.9515	0.19604	0.20604	5.101	4.853	**5**
6	1.062	0.9420	0.16255	0.17255	6.152	5.795	**6**
7	1.072	0.9327	0.13863	0.14863	7.214	6.728	**7**
8	1.083	0.9235	0.12069	0.13069	8.286	7.652	**8**
9	1.094	0.9143	0.10674	0.11674	9.369	8.566	**9**
10	1.105	0.9053	0.09558	0.10558	10.462	9.471	**10**
11	1.116	0.8963	0.08645	0.09645	11.567	10.368	**11**
12	1.127	0.8874	0.07885	0.08885	12.683	11.255	**12**
13	1.138	0.8787	0.07241	0.08241	13.809	12.134	**13**
14	1.149	0.8700	0.06690	0.07690	14.947	13.004	**14**
15	1.161	0.8613	0.06212	0.07212	16.097	13.865	**15**
16	1.173	0.8528	0.05794	0.06794	17.258	14.718	**16**
17	1.184	0.8444	0.05426	0.06426	18.430	15.562	**17**
18	1.196	0.8360	0.05098	0.06098	19.615	16.398	**18**
19	1.208	0.8277	0.04805	0.05805	20.811	17.226	**19**
20	1.220	0.8195	0.04542	0.05542	22.019	18.046	**20**
21	1.232	0.8114	0.04303	0.05303	23.239	18.857	**21**
22	1.245	0.8034	0.04086	0.05086	24.472	19.660	**22**
23	1.257	0.7954	0.03889	0.04889	25.716	20.456	**23**
24	1.270	0.7876	0.03707	0.04707	26.973	21.243	**24**
25	1.282	0.7798	0.03541	0.04541	28.243	22.023	**25**
26	1.295	0.7720	0.03387	0.04387	29.526	22.795	**26**
27	1.308	0.7644	0.03245	0.04245	30.821	23.560	**27**
28	1.321	0.7568	0.03112	0.04112	32.129	24.316	**28**
29	1.335	0.7493	0.02990	0.03990	33.450	25.066	**29**
30	1.348	0.7419	0.02875	0.03875	34.785	25.808	**30**
31	1.361	0.7346	0.02768	0.03768	36.133	26.542	**31**
32	1.375	0.7273	0.02667	0.03667	37.494	27.270	**32**
33	1.389	0.7201	0.02573	0.03573	38.869	27.990	**33**
34	1.403	0.7130	0.02484	0.03484	40.258	28.703	**34**
35	1.417	0.7059	0.02400	0.03400	41.660	29.409	**35**
40	1.489	0.6717	0.02046	0.03046	48.886	32.835	**40**
45	1.565	0.6391	0.01771	0.02771	56.481	36.095	**45**
50	1.645	0.6080	0.01551	0.02551	64.463	39.196	**50**
55	1.729	0.5785	0.01373	0.02373	72.852	42.147	**55**
60	1.817	0.5504	0.01224	0.02224	81.670	44.955	**60**
65	1.909	0.5237	0.01100	0.02100	90.937	47.627	**65**
70	2.007	0.4983	0.00993	0.01993	100.676	50.169	**70**
75	2.109	0.4741	0.00902	0.01902	110.913	52.587	**75**
80	2.217	0.4511	0.00822	0.01822	121.672	54.888	**80**
85	2.330	0.4292	0.00752	0.01752	132.979	57.078	**85**
90	2.449	0.4084	0.00690	0.01690	144.863	59.161	**90**
95	2.574	0.3886	0.00636	0.01636	157.354	61.143	**95**
100	2.705	0.3697	0.00587	0.01587	170.481	63.029	**100**

$2\frac{1}{2}\%$ Compound Interest Factors

n	Single Payment: Compound Amount Factor — Given P To find S $(1+i)^n$	Single Payment: Present Worth Factor — Given S To find P $\frac{1}{(1+i)^n}$	Uniform Annual Series: Sinking Fund Factor — Given S To find R $\frac{i}{(1+i)^n-1}$	Uniform Annual Series: Capital Recovery Factor — Given P To find R $\frac{i(1+i)^n}{(1+i)^n-1}$	Uniform Annual Series: Compound Amount Factor — Given R To find S $\frac{(1+i)^n-1}{i}$	Uniform Annual Series: Present Worth Factor — Given R To find P $\frac{(1+i)^n-1}{i(1+i)^n}$	n
1	1.025	0.9756	1.00000	1.02500	1.000	0.976	1
2	1.051	0.9518	0.49383	0.51883	2.025	1.927	2
3	1.077	0.9286	0.32514	0.35014	3.076	2.856	3
4	1.104	0.9060	0.24082	0.26582	4.153	3.762	4
5	1.131	0.8839	0.19025	0.21525	5.256	4.646	5
6	1.160	0.8623	0.15655	0.18155	6.388	5.508	6
7	1.189	0.8413	0.13250	0.15750	7.547	6.349	7
8	1.218	0.8207	0.11447	0.13947	8.736	7.170	8
9	1.249	0.8007	0.10046	0.12546	9.955	7.971	9
10	1.280	0.7812	0.08926	0.11426	11.203	8.752	10
11	1.312	0.7621	0.08011	0.10511	12.483	9.514	11
12	1.345	0.7436	0.07249	0.09749	13.796	10.258	12
13	1.379	0.7254	0.06605	0.09105	15.140	10.983	13
14	1.413	0.7077	0.06054	0.08554	16.519	11.691	14
15	1.448	0.6905	0.05577	0.08077	17.932	12.381	15
16	1.485	0.6736	0.05160	0.07660	19.380	13.055	16
17	1.522	0.6572	0.04793	0.07293	20.865	13.712	17
18	1.560	0.6412	0.04467	0.06967	22.386	14.353	18
19	1.599	0.6255	0.04176	0.06676	23.946	14.979	19
20	1.639	0.6103	0.03915	0.06415	25.545	15.589	20
21	1.680	0.5954	0.03679	0.06179	27.183	16.185	21
22	1.722	0.5809	0.03465	0.05965	28.863	16.765	22
23	1.765	0.5667	0.03270	0.05770	30.584	17.332	23
24	1.809	0.5529	0.03091	0.05591	32.349	17.885	24
25	1.854	0.5394	0.02928	0.05428	34.158	18.424	25
26	1.900	0.5262	0.02777	0.05277	36.012	18.951	26
27	1.948	0.5134	0.02638	0.05138	37.912	19.464	27
28	1.996	0.5009	0.02509	0.05009	39.860	19.965	28
29	2.046	0.4887	0.02389	0.04889	41.856	20.454	29
30	2.098	0.4767	0.02278	0.04778	43.903	20.930	30
31	2.150	0.4651	0.02174	0.04674	46.000	21.395	31
32	2.204	0.4538	0.02077	0.04577	48.150	21.849	32
33	2.259	0.4427	0.01986	0.04486	50.354	22.292	33
34	2.315	0.4319	0.01901	0.04401	52.613	22.724	34
35	2.373	0.4214	0.01821	0.04321	54.928	23.145	35
40	2.685	0.3724	0.01484	0.03984	67.403	25.103	40
45	3.038	0.3292	0.01227	0.03727	81.516	26.833	45
50	3.437	0.2909	0.01026	0.03526	97.484	28.362	50
55	3.889	0.2572	0.00865	0.03365	115.551	29.714	55
60	4.400	0.2273	0.00735	0.03235	135.992	30.909	60
65	4.978	0.2009	0.00628	0.03128	159.118	31.965	65
70	5.632	0.1776	0.00540	0.03040	185.284	32.898	70
75	6.372	0.1569	0.00465	0.02965	214.888	33.723	75
80	7.210	0.1387	0.00403	0.02903	248.383	34.452	80
85	8.157	0.1226	0.00349	0.02849	286.279	35.096	85
90	9.229	0.1084	0.00304	0.02804	329.154	35.666	90
95	10.442	0.0958	0.00265	0.02765	377.664	36.169	95
100	11.814	0.0846	0.00231	0.02731	432.549	36.614	100

5% Compound Interest Factors

n	Single Payment		Uniform Annual Series				n
	Compound Amount Factor	Present Worth Factor	Sinking Fund Factor	Capital Recovery Factor	Compound Amount Factor	Present Worth Factor	
	Given P To find S $(1+i)^n$	Given S To find P $\frac{1}{(1+i)^n}$	Given S To find R $\frac{i}{(1+i)^n-1}$	Given P To find R $\frac{i(1+i)^n}{(1+i)^n-1}$	Given R To find S $\frac{(1+i)^n-1}{i}$	Given R To find P $\frac{(1+i)^n-1}{i(1+i)^n}$	
1	1.050	0.9524	1.00000	1.05000	1.000	0.952	**1**
2	1.103	0.9070	0.48780	0.53780	2.050	1.859	**2**
3	1.158	0.8638	0.31721	0.36721	3.153	2.723	**3**
4	1.216	0.8227	0.23201	0.28201	4.310	3.546	**4**
5	1.276	0.7835	0.18097	0.23097	5.526	4.329	**5**
6	1.340	0.7462	0.14702	0.19702	6.802	5.076	**6**
7	1.407	0.7107	0.12282	0.17282	8.142	5.786	**7**
8	1.477	0.6768	0.10472	0.15472	9.549	6.463	**8**
9	1.551	0.6446	0.09069	0.14069	11.027	7.108	**9**
10	1.629	0.6139	0.07950	0.12950	12.578	7.722	**10**
11	1.710	0.5847	0.07039	0.12039	14.207	8.306	**11**
12	1.796	0.5568	0.06283	0.11283	15.917	8.863	**12**
13	1.886	0.5303	0.05646	0.10646	17.713	9.394	**13**
14	1.980	0.5051	0.05102	0.10102	19.599	9.899	**14**
15	2.079	0.4810	0.04634	0.09634	21.579	10.380	**15**
16	2.183	0.4581	0.04227	0.09227	23.657	10.838	**16**
17	2.292	0.4363	0.03870	0.08870	25.840	11.274	**17**
18	2.407	0.4155	0.03555	0.08555	28.132	11.690	**18**
19	2.527	0.3957	0.03275	0.08275	30.539	12.085	**19**
20	2.653	0.3769	0.03024	0.08024	33.066	12.462	**20**
21	2.786	0.3589	0.02800	0.07800	35.719	12.821	**21**
22	2.925	0.3418	0.02597	0.07597	38.505	13.163	**22**
23	3.072	0.3256	0.02414	0.07414	41.430	13.489	**23**
24	3.225	0.3101	0.02247	0.07247	44.502	13.799	**24**
25	3.386	0.2953	0.02095	0.07095	47.727	14.094	**25**
26	3.556	0.2812	0.01956	0.06956	51.113	14.375	**26**
27	3.733	0.2678	0.01829	0.06829	54.669	14.643	**27**
28	3.920	0.2551	0.01712	0.06712	58.403	14.898	**28**
29	4.116	0.2429	0.01605	0.06605	62.323	15.141	**29**
30	4.322	0.2314	0.01505	0.06505	66.439	15.372	**30**
31	4.538	0.2204	0.01413	0.06413	70.761	15.593	**31**
32	4.765	0.2099	0.01328	0.06328	75.299	15.803	**32**
33	5.003	0.1999	0.01249	0.06249	80.064	16.003	**33**
34	5.253	0.1904	0.01176	0.06176	85.067	16.193	**34**
35	5.516	0.1813	0.01107	0.06107	90.320	16.374	**35**
40	7.040	0.1420	0.00828	0.05828	120.800	17.159	**40**
45	8.985	0.1113	0.00626	0.05626	159.700	17.774	**45**
50	11.467	0.0872	0.00478	0.05478	209.348	18.256	**50**
55	14.636	0.0683	0.00367	0.05367	272.713	18.633	**55**
60	18.679	0.0535	0.00283	0.05283	353.584	18.929	**60**
65	23.840	0.0419	0.00219	0.05219	456.798	19.161	**65**
70	30.426	0.0329	0.00170	0.05170	588.529	19.343	**70**
75	38.833	0.0258	0.00132	0.05132	756.654	19.485	**75**
80	49.561	0.0202	0.00103	0.05103	971.229	19.596	**80**
85	63.254	0.0158	0.00080	0.05080	1245.087	19.684	**85**
90	80.730	0.0124	0.00063	0.05063	1594.607	19.752	**90**
95	103.035	0.0097	0.00049	0.05049	2040.694	19.806	**95**
100	131.501	0.0076	0.00038	0.05038	2610.025	19.848	**100**

7% Compound Interest Factors

n	Single Payment: Compound Amount Factor. Given P To find S $(1+i)^n$	Single Payment: Present Worth Factor. Given S To find P $\frac{1}{(1+i)^n}$	Uniform Annual Series: Sinking Fund Factor. Given S To find R $\frac{i}{(1+i)^n-1}$	Uniform Annual Series: Capital Recovery Factor. Given P To find R $\frac{i(1+i)^n}{(1+i)^n-1}$	Uniform Annual Series: Compound Amount Factor. Given R To find S $\frac{(1+i)^n-1}{i}$	Uniform Annual Series: Present Worth Factor. Given R To find P $\frac{(1+i)^n-1}{i(1+i)^n}$	n
1	1.070	0.9346	1.00000	1.07000	1.000	0.935	**1**
2	1.145	0.8734	0.48309	0.55309	2.070	1.808	**2**
3	1.225	0.8163	0.31105	0.38105	3.215	2.624	**3**
4	1.311	0.7629	0.22523	0.29523	4.440	3.387	**4**
5	1.403	0.7130	0.17389	0.24389	5.751	4.100	**5**
6	1.501	0.6663	0.13980	0.20980	7.153	4.767	**6**
7	1.606	0.6227	0.11555	0.18555	8.654	5.389	**7**
8	1.718	0.5820	0.09747	0.16747	10.260	5.971	**8**
9	1.838	0.5439	0.08349	0.15349	11.978	6.515	**9**
10	1.967	0.5083	0.07238	0.14238	13.816	7.024	**10**
11	2.105	0.4751	0.06336	0.13336	15.784	7.499	**11**
12	2.252	0.4440	0.05590	0.12590	17.888	7.943	**12**
13	2.410	0.4150	0.04965	0.11965	20.141	8.358	**13**
14	2.579	0.3878	0.04434	0.11434	22.550	8.745	**14**
15	2.759	0.3624	0.03979	0.10979	25.129	9.108	**15**
16	2.952	0.3387	0.03586	0.10586	27.888	9.447	**16**
17	3.159	0.3166	0.03243	0.10243	30.840	9.763	**17**
18	3.380	0.2959	0.02941	0.09941	33.999	10.059	**18**
19	3.617	0.2765	0.02675	0.09675	37.379	10.336	**19**
20	3.870	0.2584	0.02439	0.09439	40.995	10.594	**20**
21	4.141	0.2415	0.02229	0.09229	44.865	10.836	**21**
22	4.430	0.2257	0.02041	0.09041	49.006	11.061	**22**
23	4.741	0.2109	0.01871	0.08871	53.436	11.272	**23**
24	5.072	0.1971	0.01719	0.08719	58.177	11.469	**24**
25	5.427	0.1842	0.01581	0.08581	63.249	11.654	**25**
26	5.807	0.1722	0.01456	0.08456	68.676	11.826	**26**
27	6.214	0.1609	0.01343	0.08343	74.484	11.987	**27**
28	6.649	0.1504	0.01239	0.08239	80.698	12.137	**28**
29	7.114	0.1406	0.01145	0.08145	87.347	12.278	**29**
30	7.612	0.1314	0.01059	0.08059	94.461	12.409	**30**
31	8.145	0.1228	0.00980	0.07980	102.073	12.532	**31**
32	8.715	0.1147	0.00907	0.07907	110.218	12.647	**32**
33	9.325	0.1072	0.00841	0.07841	118.933	12.754	**33**
34	9.978	0.1002	0.00780	0.07780	128.259	12.854	**34**
35	10.677	0.0937	0.00723	0.07723	138.237	12.948	**35**
40	14.974	0.0668	0.00501	0.07501	199.635	13.332	**40**
45	21.002	0.0476	0.00350	0.07350	285.749	13.606	**45**
50	29.457	0.0339	0.00246	0.07246	406.529	13.801	**50**
55	41.315	0.0242	0.00174	0.07174	575.929	13.940	**55**
60	57.946	0.0173	0.00123	0.07123	813.520	14.039	**60**
65	81.273	0.0123	0.00087	0.07087	1146.755	14.110	**65**
70	113.989	0.0088	0.00062	0.07062	1614.134	14.160	**70**
75	159.876	0.0063	0.00044	0.07044	2269.657	14.196	**75**
80	224.234	0.0045	0.00031	0.07031	3189.063	14.222	**80**
85	314.500	0.0032	0.00022	0.07022	4478.576	14.240	**85**
90	441.103	0.0023	0.00016	0.07016	6287.185	14.253	**90**
95	618.670	0.0016	0.00011	0.07011	8823.854	14.263	**95**
100	867.716	0.0012	0.00008	0.07008	12381.662	14.269	**100**

10% Compound Interest Factors

n	Single Payment: Compound Amount Factor — Given P To find S $(1+i)^n$	Single Payment: Present Worth Factor — Given S To find P $\frac{1}{(1+i)^n}$	Uniform Annual Series: Sinking Fund Factor — Given S To find R $\frac{i}{(1+i)^n-1}$	Uniform Annual Series: Capital Recovery Factor — Given P To find R $\frac{i(1+i)^n}{(1+i)^n-1}$	Uniform Annual Series: Compound Amount Factor — Given R To find S $\frac{(1+i)^n-1}{i}$	Uniform Annual Series: Present Worth Factor — Given R To find P $\frac{(1+i)^n-1}{i(1+i)^n}$	n
1	1.100	0.9091	1.00000	1.10000	1.000	0.909	1
2	1.210	0.8264	0.47619	0.57619	2.100	1.736	2
3	1.331	0.7513	0.30211	0.40211	3.310	2.487	3
4	1.464	0.6830	0.21547	0.31547	4.641	3.170	4
5	1.611	0.6209	0.16380	0.26380	6.105	3.791	5
6	1.772	0.5645	0.12961	0.22961	7.716	4.355	6
7	1.949	0.5132	0.10541	0.20541	9.487	4.868	7
8	2.144	0.4665	0.08744	0.18744	11.436	5.335	8
9	2.358	0.4241	0.07364	0.17364	13.579	5.759	9
10	2.594	0.3855	0.06275	0.16275	15.937	6.144	10
11	2.853	0.3505	0.05396	0.15396	18.531	6.495	11
12	3.138	0.3186	0.04676	0.14676	21.384	6.814	12
13	3.452	0.2897	0.04078	0.14078	24.523	7.103	13
14	3.797	0.2633	0.03575	0.13575	27.975	7.367	14
15	4.177	0.2394	0.03147	0.13147	31.772	7.606	15
16	4.595	0.2176	0.02782	0.12782	35.950	7.824	16
17	5.054	0.1978	0.02466	0.12466	40.545	8.022	17
18	5.560	0.1799	0.02193	0.12193	45.599	8.201	18
19	6.116	0.1635	0.01955	0.11955	51.159	8.365	19
20	6.727	0.1486	0.01746	0.11746	57.275	8.514	20
21	7.400	0.1351	0.01562	0.11562	64.002	8.649	21
22	8.140	0.1228	0.01401	0.11401	71.403	8.772	22
23	8.954	0.1117	0.01257	0.11257	79.543	8.883	23
24	9.850	0.1015	0.01130	0.11130	88.497	8.985	24
25	10.835	0.0923	0.01017	0.11017	98.347	9.077	25
26	11.918	0.0839	0.00916	0.10916	109.182	9.161	26
27	13.110	0.0763	0.00826	0.10826	121.100	9.237	27
28	14.421	0.0693	0.00745	0.10745	134.210	9.307	28
29	15.863	0.0630	0.00673	0.10673	148.631	9.370	29
30	17.449	0.0573	0.00608	0.10608	164.494	9.427	30
31	19.194	0.0521	0.00550	0.10550	181.943	9.479	31
32	21.114	0.0474	0.00497	0.10497	201.138	9.526	32
33	23.225	0.0431	0.00450	0.10450	222.252	9.569	33
34	25.548	0.0391	0.00407	0.10407	245.477	9.609	34
35	28.102	0.0356	0.00369	0.10369	271.024	9.644	35
40	45.259	0.0221	0.00226	0.10226	442.593	9.779	40
45	72.890	0.0137	0.00139	0.10139	718.905	9.863	45
50	117.391	0.0085	0.00086	0.10086	1163.909	9.915	50
55	189.059	0.0053	0.00053	0.10053	1880.591	9.947	55
60	304.482	0.0033	0.00033	0.10033	3034.816	9.967	60
65	490.371	0.0020	0.00020	0.10020	4893.707	9.980	65
70	789.747	0.0013	0.00013	0.10013	7887.470	9.987	70
75	1271.895	0.0008	0.00008	0.10008	12708.954	9.992	75
80	2048.400	0.0005	0.00005	0.10005	20474.002	9.995	80
85	3298.969	0.0003	0.00003	0.10003	32979.690	9.997	85
90	5313.023	0.0002	0.00002	0.10002	53120.226	9.998	90
95	8556.676	0.0001	0.00001	0.10001	85556.760	9.999	95
100	13780.612	0.0001	0.00001	0.10001	137796.123	9.999	100

Capital Recovery Factors for Interest Rates from 0% to 25%

n \ i	0%	2%	4%	6%	8%	10%	12%	15%	20%	25%
1	1.00000	1.02000	1.04000	1.06000	1.08000	1.10000	1.12000	1.15000	1.20000	1.25000
2	0.50000	0.51505	0.53020	0.54544	0.56077	0.57619	0.59170	0.61512	0.65455	0.69444
3	0.33333	0.34675	0.36035	0.37411	0.38803	0.40211	0.41635	0.43798	0.47473	0.51230
4	0.25000	0.26262	0.27549	0.28859	0.30192	0.31547	0.32923	0.35027	0.38629	0.42344
5	0.20000	0.21216	0.22463	0.23740	0.25046	0.26380	0.27741	0.29832	0.33438	0.37184
6	0.16667	0.17853	0.19076	0.20336	0.21632	0.22961	0.24323	0.26424	0.30071	0.33882
7	0.14286	0.15451	0.16661	0.17914	0.19207	0.20541	0.21912	0.24036	0.27742	0.31634
8	0.12500	0.13651	0.14853	0.16104	0.17401	0.18744	0.20130	0.22285	0.26061	0.30040
9	0.11111	0.12252	0.13449	0.14702	0.16008	0.17364	0.18768	0.20957	0.24808	0.28876
10	0.10000	0.11133	0.12329	0.13587	0.14903	0.16275	0.17698	0.19925	0.23852	0.28007
11	0.09091	0.10218	0.11415	0.12679	0.14008	0.15396	0.16842	0.19107	0.23110	0.27349
12	0.08333	0.09456	0.10655	0.11928	0.13270	0.14676	0.16144	0.18448	0.22526	0.26845
13	0.07692	0.08812	0.10014	0.11296	0.12652	0.14078	0.15568	0.17911	0.22062	0.26454
14	0.07143	0.08260	0.09467	0.10758	0.12130	0.13575	0.15087	0.17469	0.21689	0.26150
15	0.06667	0.07783	0.08994	0.10296	0.11683	0.13147	0.14682	0.17102	0.21388	0.25912
16	0.06250	0.07365	0.08582	0.09895	0.11298	0.12782	0.14339	0.16795	0.21144	0.25724
17	0.05882	0.06997	0.08220	0.09544	0.10963	0.12466	0.14046	0.16537	0.20944	0.25576
18	0.05556	0.06670	0.07899	0.09236	0.10670	0.12193	0.13794	0.16319	0.20781	0.25459
19	0.05263	0.06378	0.07614	0.08962	0.10413	0.11955	0.13576	0.16134	0.20646	0.25366
20	0.05000	0.06116	0.07358	0.08718	0.10185	0.11746	0.13388	0.15976	0.20536	0.25292
25	0.04000	0.05122	0.06401	0.07823	0.09368	0.11017	0.12750	0.15470	0.20212	0.25095
30	0.03333	0.04465	0.05783	0.07265	0.08883	0.10608	0.12414	0.15230	0.20085	0.25031
40	0.02500	0.03656	0.05052	0.06646	0.08386	0.10226	0.12130	0.15056	0.20014	0.25003
50	0.02000	0.03182	0.04655	0.06344	0.08174	0.10086	0.12042	0.15014	0.20002	0.25000
100	0.01000	0.02320	0.04081	0.06018	0.08004	0.10001	0.12000	0.15000	0.20000	0.25000
∞		0.02000	0.04000	0.06000	0.08000	0.10000	0.12000	0.15000	0.20000	0.25000

Single Payment Present Worth Factors for Interest Rates from 0% to 25%

n \ i	0%	2%	4%	6%	8%	10%	12%	15%	20%	25%
1	1.0000	0.9804	0.9615	0.9434	0.9259	0.9091	0.8929	0.8696	0.8333	0.8000
2	1.0000	0.9612	0.9246	0.8900	0.8473	0.8264	0.7972	0.7561	0.6944	0.6400
3	1.0000	0.9423	0.8890	0.8396	0.7938	0.7513	0.7118	0.6575	0.5787	0.5120
4	1.0000	0.9238	0.8548	0.7921	0.7350	0.6830	0.6355	0.5718	0.4823	0.4096
5	1.0000	0.9057	0.8219	0.7473	0.6806	0.6209	0.5674	0.4972	0.4019	0.3277
6	1.0000	0.8880	0.7903	0.7050	0.6302	0.5645	0.5066	0.4323	0.3349	0.2621
7	1.0000	0.8706	0.7599	0.6651	0.5835	0.5132	0.4523	0.3759	0.2791	0.2097
8	1.0000	0.8535	0.7307	0.6274	0.5403	0.4665	0.4039	0.3269	0.2326	0.1678
9	1.0000	0.8368	0.7026	0.5919	0.5002	0.4241	0.3606	0.2843	0.1938	0.1342
10	1.0000	0.8203	0.6756	0.5584	0.4632	0.3855	0.3220	0.2472	0.1615	0.1074
11	1.0000	0.8043	0.6496	0.5268	0.4289	0.3505	0.2875	0.2149	0.1346	0.0859
12	1.0000	0.7885	0.6246	0.4970	0.3971	0.3186	0.2567	0.1869	0.1122	0.0687
13	1.0000	0.7730	0.6006	0.4688	0.3677	0.2897	0.2292	0.1625	0.0935	0.0550
14	1.0000	0.7579	0.5775	0.4423	0.3405	0.2633	0.2046	0.1413	0.0779	0.0440
15	1.0000	0.7430	0.5553	0.4173	0.3152	0.2394	0.1827	0.1229	0.0649	0.0352
16	1.0000	0.7284	0.5339	0.3936	0.2919	0.2176	0.1631	0.1069	0.0541	0.0281
17	1.0000	0.7142	0.5134	0.3714	0.2703	0.1978	0.1456	0.0929	0.0451	0.0225
18	1.0000	0.7002	0.4936	0.3503	0.2502	0.1799	0.1300	0.0808	0.0376	0.0180
19	1.0000	0.6864	0.4746	0.3305	0.2317	0.1635	0.1161	0.0703	0.0313	0.0144
20	1.0000	0.6730	0.4564	0.3118	0.2145	0.1486	0.1037	0.0611	0.0261	0.0115
25	1.0000	0.6095	0.3751	0.2330	0.1460	0.0923	0.0588	0.0304	0.0105	0.0038
30	1.0000	0.5521	0.3083	0.1741	0.0994	0.0573	0.0334	0.0151	0.0042	0.0012
40	1.0000	0.4529	0.2083	0.0972	0.0460	0.0221	0.0107	0.0037	0.0007	0.0001
50	1.0000	0.3715	0.1407	0.0543	0.0213	0.0085	0.0035	0.0009	0.0001	...
100	1.0000	0.1380	0.0198	0.0029	0.0005	0.0001	...	...	...	...

INDEX

Numbers on this page refer to PROBLEM NUMBERS, not page numbers

Absolute dollar profit, 15-21
Acid-test (quick) ratio, 16-4, 16-17, 16-18, 16-21, 17-4
Account receivable turnover, 16-15, 16-16
Accounting:
  accrual basis, 15-27
  balance sheet, 16-2 to 16-4, 16-12 to 16-14, 16-19, 16-21
  cost accounting, 15-26, 22-1 to 22-20
  double-entry system, 17-6
  journal, 16-9 to 16-11, 16-13, 17-2
  ledgers, 16-11, 16-13
  trial balance, 16-11 to 16-13
Accrual basis of accounting, 15-27
Accumulated value of savings bonds, 27-19, 27-20
Actual costs, 22-1
Addition and subtraction, 1-1 to 1-17
  dollar amounts, 1-1, 1-11 to 1-13, 1-15, 1-16
Adjusted gross income, 2-18 to 2-21
Advertisement, 9-1 to 9-10
  agate line, 9-7 to 9-10
  cost per thousand, 9-1
  line rate, 9-5
  milline rate, 9-7 to 9-10
  one-time basis, 9-2, 9-4
  open rate, 9-5
  rate schedule, 9-2 to 9-4
  six-time basis, 9-2, 9-3, 9-6
  twelve-time basis, 9-6
  volume discount, 9-5
Agate line, 9-7 to 9-10
Algebraic expressions, 4-1 to 4-13, 4-15, 4-16, 4-18 to 4-21, 4-24, 4-25, 4-27, 4-28
Algorithm flowchart, 31-1 to 31-5
Algorithm for:
  amortization table, 31-4, 31-5
  break-even point of a product, 31-3
present value, 31-1
  present value, 31-1
  value of a fixed investment, 31-2
Allowance for waste, 1-28, 1-29
Amortization:
  algorithm, 31-4, 31-5
  of loan, 24-15
Annual earnings, 1-46, 7-7
Annual percentage rate, 11-39
Annual return, 1-53
Annuities, 27-24, 29-18 to 29-21, 29-25
Approximate average sales value, 15-14
Area, 1-25, 1-27 to 1-29
Assessed value of property, 2-30 to 2-34, 2-40 to 2-43, 2-46
  how to calculate with tax rate formula, 2-37, 2-38
Assessed value (property taxes), 2-22, 2-23, 2-44
  of property improvements, 2-46
Assessment rate of property, 2-24, 2-26 to 2-29, 2-36, 2-45
Assets, 26-9
  and fire insurance, 3-42
  current, 16-20
  defined, 16-1
  fixed, 16-20
Automobile insurance, 3-20 to 3-34
Average amount of work completed, 1-38
Average cost, 1-39 to 1-41, 29-7,

Numbers on this page refer to PROBLEM NUMBERS, not page numbers

29-9
per month, 1-41
per unit, 4-14, 4-24, 4-27
Average cost curves, 5-18, 5-19, 5-21, 5-22
derivation, 5-20
Average cost method of inventory, 18-5, 18-6, 18-12, 18-14
Average income, 7-3, 7-4
for social security, 3-13 to 3-15, 3-17
Average Investment by partners, 21-9 to 21-16
Average mileage, 1-35
per gallon, 1-35
Average product curves, 5-16, 5-17
Average rate of change:
of cost, 4-26
Average salary, 1-71
Average speed, 1-37
Average unit cost, 4-14, 4-24, 4-27
Averages, 1-37 to 1-41

Bad debt loss, 17-1, 17-3
Balance of the profits, 21-3, 21-5, 21-7, 21-11 to 21-13, 21-16
Balance sheet:
classification of accounts, 16-2
evaluating account changes over time, 16-14, 16-19, 16-21
preparing a balance sheet, 16-3, 16-4, 16-12, 16-13
Bank discount, 28-5
Bank reconciliation, 25-1, 25-2
Banking, 25-1 to 25-18
Bankruptcy, 1-67, 17-9, 27-2
Bar graph, 5-25
Base pay rate, 7-2, 7-5, 7-9
Board feet, 1-26
Bonds, 14-14, 27-1 to 27-23
coupon bonds, 27-11
effective yield, 27-14 to 27-16, 27-18
interest, 27-9, 27-10, 27-12, 27-13
maturity, 27-1
municipal bonds, 27-4, 27-5
savings bonds, 27-19 to 27-22
tax-free bonds, 27-4, 27-5
Bonds and stocks, differences between, 27-3
Bonus, 7-6, 7-22, 7-23
Book value, 19-8, 19-10, 19-11, 19-14 to 19-22, 19-31
for stock, 26-9
Break-even chart, 15-9, 22-17, 22-20
Break-even point, 4-7, 4-10, 4-21, 4-25, 6-7, 15-6, 15-7, 15-9, 15-11, 22-16 to 22-20
aggregate beak-even point, 22-17
algorithm for: 31-3
Brokerage fee, 27-7 to 27-9
for stocks, 26-4, 26-5
Brokerage rates, 26-3, 26-4
Budget, 2-40, 2-41
from tax revenue, 2-43
Business decisions, 13-1 to 13-16

Cancellation, insurance:
auto, 3-33, 3-34
fire, 3-37, 3-56 to 3-61
Capital (owner's equity), 15-30, 16-20
cost of capital, 15-28
defined, 16-1
total, 26-9
Capital recovery:
cost, 13-2, 13-4 to 13-6, 13-9 to 13-11, 13-13, 13-14, 13-16
factor, 14-2 to 14-4, 14-6, 14-7, 14-10, 14-13
plan, 16-8
Capital, working, 16-4, 16-17, 16-18
ratio, 15-29
sources and uses, 16-7
Carrying charge, 24-2
Cash discount, 1-9, 11-29, 11-30, 11-33 to 11-39

Numbers on this page refer to PROBLEM NUMBERS, not page numbers

Cash surrender value, 3-1
Ceiling price, 5-12
Central Limit Theorem, 32-10
Charges:
  carrying, 24-2
  finance, 24-1, 24-3 to 24-5, 24-9, 24-10, 24-17, 24-19, 24-21
  interest, 24-6, 24-8
  service, 24-11 to 24-14, 24-23
  shipping, 10-1, 10-2
Chebyshev's inequality, 32-9
Circulation, 9-1, 9-7 to 9-10
Coefficient of regression, 32-22
Collection charge, discounting notes, 28-10, 28-25 to 28-27, 28-30 to 28-33, 28-35, 28-37
Collection fee, 2-23, 2-38
Commission, 8-1 to 8-23
  monthly, 1-13
  on stock purchases, 26-3, 26-4
  rate of, 8-10
  salary-plus, 8-13 to 8-16, 8-18
Common stock, 26-10, 26-19, 26-21
Comparative income statement, 17-12 to 17-14
Competition, 5-24
  monopoly, 5-23
  pure, 5-13
Compound-amount factor, 29-19, 29-20
  single payment, 14-1 to 14-3
  uniform series, 14-2, 14-3
Compound interest, 29-17, 29-18, 29-22 to 29-24
Computer science applications, 34-1 to 34-19
Confidence internal, 32-10
Constant ratio formula, 23-41
Constraints, 30-1 to 30-11, 30-16 to 30-18
Consumption curve, 5-30
Contribution margin, 22-12, 22-13, 22-16 to 22-20
  ratio, 22-19
Conversion:
  decimals to percents, 1-45
  fractions to percents, 1-17, 1-46
  metric, 1-73 to 1-75
  to monthly sales, 1-7
Correlation, 32-11, 32-12
Cost accounting, 15-26, 22-1 to 22-20
  variance, 22-1 to 22-10
Cost, 1-16, 4-3 to 4-5, 4-10, 4-12, 4-21
  actual, 22-1
  average rate of change, 4-26
  average unit, 4-14, 4-24, 4-27
  capital recovery, 13-2, 13-4 to 13-6, 13-9 to 13-11, 13-13, 13-14, 13-16
  direct, 15-3
  fixed, 4-3, 4-6, 4-13, 4-17, 4-20, 4-23, 5-22, 15-10
  indirect, 15-3
  mailing, 10-3
  material, 6-14
  minimization, 4-17, 4-22, 6-9 to 6-14, 30-5, 30-7, 30-10, 30-15
  net, 11-1
  occupancy, 20-1
  of labor, 6-14
  of stocks, 26-1 to 26-9
  overhead, 4-7
  per thousand, 9-1
  percentage selling, 8-12
  prime, 20-9, 20-10
  production, 4-25
  rate of change within ranges, 4-4, 4-18, 4-21, 4-22, 4-26
  rental, 10-4 to 10-7
  standard, 22-1 to 22-10
  systems (PERT), 15-26
  to store, 1-6
  total, 1-25, 1-26, 1-41, 4-6, 4-7, 4-10, 4-13, 4-14, 4-16, 4-17, 4-19, 4-24, 4-25, 6-12 to 6-14, 15-20, 15-33,
  unit, 1-30, 1-32 to 1-34, 4-14, 4-20, 4-24, 4-27
  variable, 4-6, 4-13, 4-17, 4-23, 15-10
Cost, average, 1-39 to 1-41, 29-7, 29-9

Numbers on this page refer to PROBLEM NUMBERS, not page numbers

per month, 1-41
per unit, 4-14, 4-24, 4-27
Cost curves:
average cost, 5-18, 5-19, 5-21, 5-22
derivation of marginal and average cost, 5-20
marginal cost, 5-15
total cost, 5-15, 5-19, 5-21
Cost function, 4-3, 4-4, 4-8, 4-12, 4-13, 4-18, 4-20, 4-25 to 4-28, 6-9 to 6-14, 6-18, 6-26, 6-30, 6-31, 15-33
cost linear, 4-3, 4-8, 4-12, 4-18, 4-20
derivation, 4-28
productivity, 15-33
Cost of capital, 15-28
Cost of goods sold, 15-8, 15-16, 15-32, 16-5, 18-7
Cost per thousand, 15-2
Cost-plus pricing, 29-8
Counting:
change, 1-2
days, 1-10
Coupon bonds, 27-11
Creditors, 1-67
Critical point, 4-23
Grossfoot check, 7-26
Cumulative frequency distribution, 32-2
Cumulative stock, 26-22
Current assets, 16-20
Current liabilities, 16-20
Current ratio, 15-29, 16-4, 16-16 to 16-18, 16-21, 17-5
Customer account, 17-7, 17-8

Date of maturity, 23-17, 25-6
bonds, 27-1
defined, 25-5
notes and drafts, 28-1, 28-4, 28-5
Decimals, conversion to percents, 1-45
rounding numbers, 1-72
Decision tree, 32-16 to 32-19
Declining-balance method of depreciation, 19-15 to 19-21, 19-31
Deductions, from earnings, 7-9, 7-25 to 7-30
itemized, 2-16, 2-17, 2-20, 2-21
partial table, 2-18
standard deduction, 2-12, 2-18, 2-19
Deflationary gap, 5-34, 5-35
Demand, 4-16, 4-23, 4-24
curve analysis, 5-4, 5-5
elasticity, 5-6 to 5-10
function, 4-23, 4-24, 6-6, 6-26,
graphing curves, 5-9, 5-10
Demand deposits, 5-39
Deposit slip preparation, 1-4
Depreciation, 14-7, 14-12, 14-13, 19-1 to 19-31, 29-9
allowance in real estate, 29-4
declining balance method, 19-15 to 19-21, 19-31
straight-line method, 19-4 to 19-14, 19-28, 19-31
sum-of-the-year's digits method, 19-22 to 19-31
units of production method, 19-1 to 19-3
Derivation:
cost function, 4-28
linear cost function, 4-18
production function, 4-15, 4-17, 4-24, 4-27
revenue function, 4-23, 4-24
Descriptive flowchart, 31-1 to 31-5
Differential pricing, 15-5
Direct costs, 15-3
labor costs, 20-11, 20-12
Disbursements, 14-8, 14-12, 14-13
Discount, 12-6
bank discount, 28-5
cash, 1-9, 11-29, 11-30, 11-33 to 11-39
on fire insurance premiums, 3-41

Numbers on this page refer to PROBLEM NUMBERS, not page numbers

percentage, 2-9
single discount equivalent, 11-16, 11-17, 11-27
term of, 11-29 to 11-39
trade of, 11-29
trade, 11-3, 11-4, 11-9, 11-36, 12-1, 12-4
with a sales tax, 2-6 to 2-9
Discount rate, 11-7, 11-8, 11-10, 28-2
Discount series, 11-12 to 11-22, 11-24 to 11-28, 11-32, 11-35
fractional, 11-26
Discount table, 11-11
Discounting loans, 25-9 to 25-12, 25-14
Discounting notes and drafts, 28-2, 28-3, 28-5 to 28-37
collection charge, 28-10, 28-25 to 28-27, 28-30 to 28-33, 28-35, 28-37
discount rate, 28-2
interest-bearing notes and drafts, 28-7, 28-10, 28-16, 28-17, 28-19 to 28-23, 28-25, 28-27, 28-30, 28-31, 28-36, 28-37
non-interest-bearing notes and drafts, 28-6, 28-8, 28-9, 28-11 to 28-15, 28-18, 28-24, 28-26, 28-28, 28-29, 28-32 to 28-35
terms of discount, 28-3, 28-5
Distribution:
cumulative frequency, 32-2
uniform, 32-8
Distribution of overhead, 20-1 to 20-12
Dividends, stock, 13-3, 26-13 to 26-17, 26-19 to 26-22
on investment, 26-20
on patronage, 26-20
quarterly, 26-18
return per annum, 1-53
Division, 1-30 to 1-36
Dollar-value LIFO, 18-10, 18-11
Dollar-value, total, 1-23
Double-entry system, 17-6
Double time, 7-5, 7-10 to 7-12, 7-17, 7-18
Drawing account, 8-20

Earning power ratio, 17-16
Earnings:
annual, 1-46, 7-7
gross, 7-9 to 7-11, 7-16, 7-17, 7-26, 7-27, 7-29
net, 7-29
per share, 16-15, 16-16, 26-11, 26-12
total, 1-13, 7-13, 7-14, 7-18, 7-21
Earnings, deductions, 7-9, 7-25 to 7-30
income tax deductions, 2-20, 2-21
Educational budget, 2-43
Effective annual return, 14-5
Effective rate of interest, 27-17
Effective yield:
bonds, 27-14 to 27-16, 27-18
stock, 26-13
Elasticity of demand, 5-6 to 5-10
Ending inventory, estimation of, 18-2 to 18-4
EOM (end-of-month), 11-31, 11-32
Equilibrium level of income, 5-33, 5-34
Equilibrium price, 4-16, 5-12
Estimated expenses, 1-12
Estimated future sales, 15-12, 15-13
Evaluating the better buy, 1-32
Excise tax, 2-5
Exemptions, 2-11, 2-12, 2-14, 2-16, 2-18, 2-19, 2-21, 7-25, 7-27 to 7-30
Expected market value, 2-36
Expected profit, 32-7 to 32-9, 32-16 to 32-19
Expected values, 30-15

Numbers on this page refer to PROBLEM NUMBERS, not page numbers

Face value, 27-6
Factoring, 4-16, 4-21
Factors, auto insurance, 3-20 to 3-23, 3-25 to 3-27
Federal Reserve Board, 5-38
Federal withholding tax, 2-14, 7-26 to 7-28, 13-3
  partial table, 2-14
FHA loan, 25-8
FICA, 7-26 to 7-29
FIFO, 18-8, 18-12 to 18-17
Filing status, 2-11
  marital status, 2-12 to 2-14, 2-16 to 2-18
  single, 2-9
Finance charge, 24-1, 24-3 to 24-5, 24-9, 24-10, 24-17, 24-19, 24-21
Finding percents, 1-49 to 1-51, 1-55, 1-61, 1-63, 1-64, 1-68 to 1-71
Fire insurance, 3-35 to 3-61
  and assets, 3-42, 3-45
  discount on premium, 3-41
Fixed assets, 16-20
Fixed cost, 4-3, 4-6, 4-13, 4-17 4-20, 4-23, 5-22, 15-10
Floor price, 5-12
Floor space, 20-2 to 20-6
Flowchart, algorithm, 31-1 to 31-5
  descriptive, 31-1 to 31-5
Fractional discount series, 11-26
Fractions:
  conversion to percents, 1-17, 1-46
  fractional percents, 1-43
  subtraction, 1-17
Frequency distribution, cumulative, 32-2
Functions:
  cost, 4-3, 4-4, 4-8, 4-12, 4-13, 4-18, 4-20, 4-25 to 4-28, 6-9 to 6-14, 6-18, 6-26, 6-30, 6-31, 15-33
  demand, 4-23, 4-24, 6-6, 6-26
  derivation, 4-2, 4-3
  gross profit, 4-6
  limits of, 4-4
  linear cost, 4-3, 4-8, 4-12, 4-18, 4-20
  linear revenue, 4-20
  marginal cost, 6-7
  output, 4-15
  price, 4-27
  production, 4-15, 4-17
  profit, 6-7, 6-15, 6-16, 6-18, 6-20, 6-24 to 6-26, 6-28, 6-30, 6-31
  revenue, 4-21, 4-23, 4-24, 4-27, 6-6, 6-8, 6-17 to 6-19, 6-21 to 6-24, 6-26 to 6-31
Funds:
  sources, 16-6
  uses, 16-6
Future sales, estimated, 15-12, 15-13
Future value, 29-17

Government market regulations:
  ceiling price, 5-12
  floor price, 5-12
Grand total, 1-14
Graphing:
  alternative investments, 13-10
  bar graph, 5-25
  demand curves, 5-9, 5-10
  statistical data, 32-3 to 32-7
Gross earning power ratio, 17-16
Gross earnings, 7-9 to 7-11, 7-16, 7-17, 7-26, 7-27, 7-29
Gross income, 2-10
  adjusted, 2-18 to 2-21
Gross markdown, 12-7
Gross National Product (GNP), 5-31, 5-33, 5-34
  lower-loop method, 5-28
  upper-loop method, 5-28
Gross profit, 4-6, 12-24, 15-16 to 15-19, 18-17, 21-15
  method of inventory, 18-2
Gross revenue, 6-8, 7-19
Gross wages, 7-28

Numbers on this page refer to PROBLEM NUMBERS, not page numbers

Head of household, filing status, 2-19
Health and welfare budget, 2-43
Health insurance, 3-18, 3-19
Histogram, 32-1
Homogenous product, 5-13
Homoskedasticity, 32-22

Income:
  adjusted gross, 2-18 to 2-21
  before taxes, 2-10
  defined, 16-1
  equilibrium level, 5-33, 5-34
  gross, 2-10
  net, 1-42, 2-10, 7-27, 15-18, 15-19. 21-14, 21-15
  percentage uses of, 1-69, 1-71
  total taxable, 2-20
Income, average, 7-3, 7-4
  for social security, 3-13 to 3-15, 3-17
Income statement, 15-32, 16-2
  comparative, 17-12 to 17-14
  preparing an income statement, 16-12, 16-13
  year end income statement, 17-15
Income taxes, 2-10 to 2-21, 7-25 to 7-30
  itemized deductions, 2-16, 2-17, 2-20, 2-21
Index numbers, 32-5
Indifference curves, 5-1, 5-2
Indirect costs, 15-3
Inflation, 5-36
Installment plan, 24-1 to 24-33
Installment price, 24-7, 24-21
Insurance, auto, 3-20 to 3-34
  accident history, 3-20 to 3-23, 3-25 to 3-27
  age of driver, 3-20, 3-21, 3-25
  age of vehicle, 3-21, 3-26
  base premium schedule, 3-20, 3-21, 3-23, 3-25 to 3-27
  bodily injury, 3-20, 3-22, 3-24, 3-25, 3-27, 3-31, 3-32
  calculation of payment, 3-30 to 3-32
  cancellation, 3-33, 3-34
  car symbol number, 3-21, 3-23, 3-26
  collision, 3-21, 3-23, 3-24, 3-26
  comprehensive, 3-21, 3-24, 3-26
  deductible, 3-21, 3-23, 3-24, 3-26, 3-28, 3-29
  driver history, 3-20, 3-23
  factor, 3-20 to 3-23, 3-25 to 3-27
  group symbol number, 3-21, 3-26
  marital status, 3-20, 3-21, 3-25, 3-26
  medical payments coverage, 3-20, 3-24, 3-27
  payment, 3-27, 3-28, 3-30 to 3-32
  premiums, 3-20 to 3-27
  property damage, 3-20, 3-22, 3-25, 3-27, 3-30
  refund, 3-33
  sex of driver, 3-20, 3-21
  tables, 3-23, 3-25, 3-27, 3-33
  territory, 3-20, 3-21, 3-23 to 3-27
  training of driver, 3-20, 3-21, 3-25
  uninsured motorist, 3-24
  use of car, 3-20, 3-21, 3-23, 3-25, 3-26
Insurance, fire, 3-35 to 3-61
  assets, 3-42, 3-45
  cancellation of policy, 3-37, 3-56 to 3-61
  coinsurance clause, 3-51 to 3-55
  coinsurance perentage formula, 3-51 to 3-55
  decreasing term insurance, 3-45
  deductible clause, 3-41
  distributed coverage, 3-46, 3-48 to 3-50
  face value of policy, 3-40, 3-50

Numbers on this page refer to PROBLEM NUMBERS, not page numbers

fixed total loss coverage, 3-45
increasing principle coverage, 3-45
land worth, 3-35
location, 3-39
multi-year policies, 3-42 to 3-44
payments on loss computation, 3-46 to 3-55
premium, 3-36 to 3-44, 3-47, 3-56 to 3-61
premiums and discounts, 3-41
property owner's loss, 3-50, 3-51, 3-53, 3-55
rates per dollar, 3-36 to 3-38
rates per $100, 3-39 to 3-41, 3-47
rates per $1000, 3-43, 3-44
tables, 3-36, 3-37, 3-42, 3-56 to 3-58, 3-60, 3-61
terms of policy, 3-40

Insurance, health, 3-18, 3-19
age related, 3-18
annual rates for children, 3-18
annual rates for husband and wife, 3-18
annual rates for individual, 3-18
deductible, 3-18
insurance company and payment of medical expenses, 3-19
medical insurance charge schedule, 3-19
medicare coverage, 3-19
premiums, 3-18

Insurance, life, 3-1 to 3-12
age of purchaser, 3-3 to 3-11
beneficiary, 3-3
cash surrender value, 3-1
death of insured, 3-10
endowment policy, 3-4 to 3-6, 3-9, 3-11, 3-12
face value, 3-4, 3-5
frequency of payments, 3-5 to 3-7 3-7
limited payment policy, 3-9
longevity of insured, 3-11
ordinary, 3-1, 3-2, 3-10
premium, 3-1 to 3-8, 3-10, 3-11
retirement income policy, 3-11
tables, 3-5 to 3-7
term insurance, 3-3, 3-4
twenty-payment policy, 3-7, 3-10
type of policy, 3-9, 3-11, 3-12
whole life (insurance), 3-4

Insurance, social security, 3-13 to 3-17

Interest:
annual, 24-24 to 24-33
effective rate, 27-17
nominal annual, 27-14 to 27-16, 27-18
on loans, 25-4, 25-15
on mortagages, 25-7
on savings accounts, 25-3
true rate, 24-23, 25-9

Interpolation, 14-10, 14-13, 14-14

Inventory, estimation of ending, 18-2 to 18-4

Inventory methods:
average cost, 18-5, 18-6, 18-12, 18-14
cost, 18-1
dollar-value LIFO, 18-10, 18-11
FIFO, 18-8, 18-12 to 18-17
gross profit, 18-2
LIFO, 18-9, 18-12 to 18-17
periodic, 18-16
perpetual, 18-16
weighted average, 18-7, 18-15

Inventory turnover, 16-15, 16-16, 16-22, 18-20 to 18-23

Inversions, of proportions, 4-2

Investment:
average investment by partners, 21-9 to 21-16
choice between alternative, 13-1, 13-2, 13-4 to 13-10, 13-12, 13-13, 13-15
graphing alternatives, 13-10
in partnerships, 21-4, 21-6,

Numbers on this page refer to PROBLEM NUMBERS, not page numbers

21-8 to 21-15
percentage of initial investment, 15-24
plans, 14-12
tax considerations, 13-7
total annual costs, 13-14 to 13-16

Invoice, 1-9, 11-32
Isoquant, 5-15
Itemized deductions, 2-16, 2-17, 2-20, 2-21

Joint tax return, 2-13, 2-18, 2-21
partial tax rate schedule, 2-16
Journals, 17-2
classification of transactions, 16-9 to 16-11, 16-13
posting of journal entries, 16-11, 16-13
payroll, 7-26

Labor:
cost, 6-14
standard cost, 7-6
Labor-intensive activity, 15-4
Labor variance:
efficiency, 22-1, 22-2, 22-4 to 22-10
rate, 22-1, 22-2, 22-4 to 22-10
Law of large numbers, 32-10
Ledgers, 16-11, 16-13
Liabilities, 26-9
current, 16-20
defined, 16-1
Life insurance, 3-1 to 3-12
LIFO, 18-9, 18-12 to 18-17
Limits of function, 4-4
Line rate, 9-5
Linear functions, 4-9, 4-11
cost, 4-3, 4-8, 4-12, 4-18, 4-20
revenue, 4-20
Linear programming, 5-26
Linear regression, 32-15
Liquidity, 16-4
Loans, 14-4
amortized, 24-15
counting days included, 1-8
discounting, 25-9 to 25-12, 25-14
FHA, 25-8
interest, 25-4, 25-15
monthly payments, 25-10, 25-11, 25-16, 25-18
principal, 25-13, 25-18
Long-run strategy, 5-14
Loss, net, 22-16, 22-18

Mailing cost, 10-3
Margin on sales, 18-3, 18-4
Marginal cost curves, 5-15
derivation, 5-20
Marginal cost function, 6-7
Marginal physical product, 5-25
Marginal product curves, 5-16, 5-17, 5-23
Marginal propensity to consume, 5-29, 5-30
Marginal propensity to save, 5-29, 5-30
Marginal rate of product transformation (MRPT), 5-3
Marginal rate of substitution (MRS), 5-3
Marginal revenue, 4-17, 5-11, 6-7, 6-23
product, 5-11
Markdown, 12-2, 12-3, 12-5, 12-7
gross, 12-7
net, 12-7
Market environment, 5-24
Market price, 11-3
Market regulations:
ceiling price, 5-12
floor price, 5-12
Market survey, 4-23
Market value:
expected, 2-36
of property, 2-26 to 2-29, 2-45

Numbers on this page refer to PROBLEM NUMBERS, not page numbers

Markup:
averaging, 12-27, 12-28, 12-30
comparing cost and selling price percentages, 12-11, 12-19, 12-25
finding dollar values, 12-8, 12-9, 12-13, 12-17, 12-18, 12-20 to 12-23, 12-26
finding percentage values, 12-10, 12-12, 12-14 to 12-16, 12-29
Married filing status, 2-19
joint return, 2-17, 2-21
Material cost, 6-14
Material variance:
price, 22-1, 22-2, 22-4 to 22-10
quantity, 22-1, 22-2, 22-4 to 22-10
Matrix, payoff, 30-12 to 30-15
Maturity date, 23-17, 25-6
bonds, 27-1
defined, 25-5
notes and drafts, 28-1, 28-4, 28-5
Maturity value, 28-5, 28-31
Maximization of profits, 4-17, 4-23, 4-24, 4-27, 6-15, 6-16, 6-18, 6-20, 6-23 to 6-26, 6-28, 6-30, 6-31, 30-1 to 30-6, 30-8, 30-18
Maximization of revenue, 6-19, 6-21, 6-22, 6-27, 6-29, 30-17
Maximum number of persons, 30-7
Mean, 32-9, 32-20, 32-21
Metric conversion, 1-73 to 1-75
Milline rate, 9-7 to 9-10
Mills, 2-26, 2-35, 2-39
Minimax procedure, 30-13
Minimization of cost, 4-17, 4-22, 6-9 to 6-14, 30-5, 30-7, 30-10, 30-15
Minuend, 1-3
Money:
types of, 5-37
uses of, 5-37
Money supply, 5-39
regulation of, 5-38
Monopoly, 5-23
price setting, 22-14
Monthly commissions, 1-13
Monthly increases, 1-5
Mortgages, 25-8, 29-3, 29-16
interest on mortgages, 25-7
monthly payments, 25-8, 25-17
prepayment penalty, 29-3
Multiple regression, 32-15
Multiplication, 1-18 to 1-29, 29-5, 29-6, 29-10 to 29-14
Multiplier theory, 5-31, 5-32, 5-35
Municipal bonds, 27-4, 27-5

Net cost, 11-1
Net decimal equivalent, 11-11, 11-23, 11-24
Net earning power ratio, 17-16
Net earnings, 7-29
Net income, 1-42, 2-10, 7-27, 15-18, 15-19, 21-14, 21-15
profit objective (based on), 22-12 to 22-14, 22-20
Net loss, 22-16, 22-18
Net markdown, 12-7
Net National Product (NNP), 5-28
Net price, 11-2 to 11-6, 11-13 to 11-15, 11-20 to 11-22
Net profit, 12-24, 15-22, 15-23, 16-8, 17-10, 17-11, 22-14, 22-16, 22-18, 22-19
Net sales, 1-64
Net wages, 7-26, 7-27
Nominal annual interest, 27-14 to 27-16, 27-18
Nominal rate of interest, 25-16
Note proceeds, 28-5
Notes and drafts, 28-1 to 28-37
date of maturity, 28-1, 28-4, 28-5
discounting, 28-2, 28-3, 28-5 to 28-37
maker of note, 28-5

Numbers on this page refer to PROBLEM NUMBERS, not page numbers

maturity value, 28-5, 28-31
payee of note, 28-5
Number of units purchased, 1-34

Occupancy cost, 20-1
Odd lot, 26-5
One-time basis, in advertisement, 9-2, 9-4
Open rate, 9-5
Open-to-buy, 18-18, 18-19
Operations research applications, 33-1 to 33-11
Optimal strategy, 30-12 to 30-15
Option stock, 26-8, 26-23
price, 26-8
Output, 4-14, 4-15, 4-17, 4-18
Outstanding shares, stock, 26-9
Overhead:
cost, 4-7
distribution, 20-1 to 20-12
Overhead variance, 22-1, 22-3 to 22-10
fixed overhead, 22-1
budget, 22-3, 22-5 to 22-8, 22-10
volume, 22-3, 22-6, 22-7, 22-10
variable overhead, 22-1
efficiency, 22-1, 22-3, 22-5 to 22-8, 22-10
spending, 22-1, 22-3, 22-5, 22-7, 22-10
Overtime, 7-2, 7-5, 7-8, 7-11 to 7-15, 7-18, 7-27, 7-29
Owner's equity (capital), 15-30, 16-20
defined, 16-1

Par-value, stocks, 26-2, 26-14, 26-19 to 26-22
Partial table for standard deduction, four exemptions, 2-18
Partial table of federal withholding tax, 2-14
Partial tax rate schedule, joint return, 2-16
Partnerships, 21-1 to 21-16
defined, 21-1
investment in, 21-4, 21-6, 21-8 to 21-15
profit sharing, 1-66
proportional shares, 21-4, 21-6, 21-8, 21-9, 21-16
salary, 21-3, 21-5, 21-7
Pay rate, base, 7-2, 7-5, 7-9
Payoff matrix, 30-12 to 30-15
Payroll, 7-1 to 7-30
journal, 7-26
tax deductions, 7-25 to 7-30
exemptions, 7-25, 7-27 to 7-30
marital status, 7-26
Percentage:
discount, 2-9
gain, 1-57, 1-71
increase, 1-54, 1-56 to 1-60 1-62, 1-71, 15-15
of initial investment, 15-24
selling cost, 8-12
uses of income, 1-69, 1-71
Percents and ratios, 1-42 to 1-71
finding, 1-49 to 1-51, 1-55, 1-61, 1-63, 1-64, 1-68 to 1-71
fractional percents, 1-43
Periodic inventory, 18-16
Perpetual inventory, 18-16
PERT cost systems, 15-26
Piece-rate, 7-21
Posting journal entries, 16-11, 16-13
Preferred stock, 26-14, 26-19, 26-21
cumulative, 26-22
Premiums, 7-23
auto insurance, 3-20 to 3-27
fire insurance, 3-36 to 3-44, 3-47, 3-56 to 3-61
health insurance, 3-18
life insurance, 3-1 to 3-8, 3-10, 3-11
Prepayment penalty, mortagages, 29-3
Present-value, 13-1, 13-5 to 13-9,

13-13, 13-14, 13-16, 14-4 to 14-9, 14-13, 14-14, 29-15
algorithm for, 31-3
Present-worth factor: 29-18
single payment, 14-2, 14-8
uniform series, 14-2 to 14-5, 14-11
Price:
ceiling, 5-12
equilibrium, 4-16, 5-12
floor, 5-12
function, 4-27
installment, 24-7, 24-21
market, 11-3
net, 11-2 to 11-6, 11-13 to 11-15, 11-20 to 11-22
per C, 1-18
per cwt, 1-18
per M, 1-18, 1-19
per square yard, 1-23
per unit, 1-17
selling, 1-6
Price reduction, effect on revenue, 15-1
Price setting, 22-11, 22-15
monopoly, 22-14
Price, stocks, 26-5 to 26-7
average, 26-8
high, 26-6, 26-8, 26-17
last, 26-7, 26-17
low, 26-6 to 26-8, 26-17
market, 26-13
opening, 26-7, 26-17
option, 26-8
purchase, 26-7, 26-16
selling, 26-1, 26-13, 26-14
Pricing, cost-plus, 29-8
differential, 15-5
Prime cost, 20-9, 20-10
Principal (of loan), 25-13, 25-18
Probability, 32-7 to 32-9, 32-16 to 32-19
Proceeds, from note, 28-5
Product curves:
average, 5-16, 5-17
marginal, 5-16, 5-17, 5-23
total, 5-16
Product mix possibilities, 22-12, 22-17
Production, 4-14, 4-15
budget, 4-14
costs, 4-25
function, 4-15, 4-17, 4-24, 4-27
quota, 4-14
total, 1-24
Production-possibility curves, 5-26, 5-27
optimization, 5-26
Profit, 1-6, 4-13, 4-23
absolute dollar, 15-21
balance of the profits, 21-3, 21-5, 21-7, 21-11 to 21-13, 21-16
desired and necessary sales levels, 4-13
expected, 32-7 to 32-9, 32-16 to 32-19
function, 6-7, 6-15, 6-16, 6-18, 6-20, 6-24 to 6-26, 6-28, 6-30, 6-31
gross, 4-6, 12-24, 15-16 to 15-19, 18-17, 21-15
maximization, 4-17, 4-23, 4-4-24, 4-27, 6-15, 6-16, 6-18, 6-20, 6-23 to 6-26, 6-28, 6-30, 6-31, 30-1 to 30-6, 30-8, 30-18
net, 12-24, 15-22, 15-23, 16-8, 17-10, 17-11, 22-14, 22-16, 22-18, 22-19
sharing, 21-1 to 21-16
total, 15-20
Profit objective:
based on net income, 22-12 to 22-14, 22-20
based on return-on-investment, 22-11, 22-15
Programming, linear, 5-26
Propensity to consume, marginal, 5-29, 5-30
Propensity to save, 29-1
marginal, 5-29, 5-30
Property, assessed value, 2-30 to

Numbers on this page refer to <u>PROBLEM NUMBERS,</u> not page numbers

2-34, 2-40 to 2-43, 2-46
how to calculate with tax rate formula, 2-37, 2-38
Property, assessment rate, 2-24, 2-26 to 2-29, 2-36, 2-45
expected market value, 2-26 to 2-29, 2-45
Property taxes, 2-22 to 2-46
assessed value, 2-22, 2-23, 2-44
for college fund, 2-45
for community construction, 2-45, 2-46
for education, 2-45, 2-46
for health and welfare, 2-45
for special projects, 2-46
how to calculuate, 2-44 to 2-46
property improvements, 2-46
tax rate formula, 2-22, 2-43
Proportional shares (in partnerships), 21-4, 21-6, 21-8, 21-9, 21-16
Proportions, 4-2, 4-19
and inverse proportions, 4-2
Purchase, 1-22
Pure competition, 5-13
Pure strategy, 1-13, 1-14, 30-13

Quadratic formula, 4-28
Quantitative analysis, 32-1 to 32-22
Quick (acid test) ratio, 16-4, 16-17, 16-18, 16-21, 17-4
Quota, 1-7, 7-22
bonus method, 7-22
production, 4-14
sales, 8-14

Random variable, 32-8
Rate of change, 6-1 to 6-8
of cost within ranges, 4-4, 4-18, 4-21, 4-22, 4-26
Rate of discount, 11-7, 11-10, 28-2
Rate of return, 14-9 to 14-14
stocks, 26-14 to 26-17
Rate schedule (in advet
Rate schedule (in advertising), 9-2 to 9-4
Ratios, 1-52, 1-65, 1-66
acid-test, 16-4, 16-17, 16-18, 16-21, 17-4
contribution margin, 22-19
current, 15-29, 16-4 to 16-18, 16-21, 17-5
earning power, 17-16
gross earning power, 17-16
net earning power, 17-16
reserve requirement, 5-38, 5-39
working capital, 15-29
Ratios and percents, 1-42 to 1-71
Receipt of goods (R. O. G.), 11-37, 11-38
Redemption value, 27-1, 27-21, 27-23
Regression:
linear, 32-15
multiple, 32-15
Regression coefficient, 32-22
Regression line, 32-11 to 32-13
cubic, 32-14
linear, 32-14
quadratic, 32-14
Regular pay, 7-12 to 7-14, 7-18, 7-27, 7-29
Reimbursement, 1-40
Rental, 4-12
car, 10-6, 10-7
cost, 10-4 to 10-7
truck, 10-4, 10-5
Reserve requirement ratio, 5-38, 5-39
Retained earnings, 15-31
Return on invested capital, 15-25
Return on investment (ROI), 13-2, 13-4 to 13-6, 13-9 to 13-11, 13-13, 13-14, 13-16
profit objective, 22-11, 22-15
Return, rate of, 14-9 to 14-14
Revenue, 4-13, 4-20, 4-25

Numbers on this page refer to PROBLEM NUMBERS, not page numbers

effect of price reduction on, 15-1
gross, 6-8, 7-19
linear functions, 4-20
marginal, 4-17, 5-11, 6-7, 6-23
maximization, 6-19, 6-21, 6-22, 6-27, 6-29, 30-17
total, 4-6, 4-7, 4-17, 5-9, 5-10
Revenue function, 4-21, 4-23, 4-24, 4-27, 6-6, 6-8, 6-17 to 6-19, 6-21 to 6-24, 6-26 to 6-31
derivation of, 4-23, 4-24
R. O. G. (receipt of goods), 11-37, 11-38
Round lots, 26-3
multiple, 26-4
Rounding numbers, decimals, 1-72

Saddle point, 30-12 to 30-15
Salary, 7-7, 7-9, 7-15, 7-16, 7-30
average, 1-71
in partnerships, 21-3, 21-5, 21-7
Salary-plus commission, 8-13 to 8-16, 8-18
Sales, 20-7, 20-8
future estimated, 15-12, 15-13
margin on, 18-3, 18-4
net, 1-64
quota, 8-14
total, 1-21
Sales tax, 2-1 to 2-9
city, 2-4, 2-6, 2-7
discount, 2-6 to 2-9
state, 2-4, 2-6, 2-7
Savings account interest, 25-3
Savings bonds, 27-19 to 27-22
accumulated value, 27-19, 27-20
Schedule of rates, 9-2 to 9-4
Selling price, 1-6
Series discount, 11-12 to 11-22, 11-24 to 11-28, 11-32, 11-35
fractional, 11-26
Service charge, 24-11 to 24-14, 24-23
Settling debts, ("cents on the dollar"), 1-67
Shipping charge, 10-1, 10-2
Short-run strategy, 5-14
Sight draft, definition of, 28-24
Simultaneous equations, 4-8, 4-11
Single discount equivalent, 11-16, 11-17, 11-27
Single filing status, 2-9
Single payment compound-amount factor (SPCA), 14-1 to 14-3
Single payment present-worth factor (SPPW), 14-2, 14-8
Sinking fund, 29-15, 29-21, 29-25
Sinking fund payment factor (SFP), 14-2, 14-3
Six-time basis in advertising, 9-2, 9-3, 9-6
Social security, 3-13 to 3-17
age of retirement, 3-13, 3-14
annual covered earnings, 3-17
average yearly earnings, 3-13 to 3-15, 3-17
benefits to worker's spouse, 3-13 to 3-15
contribution table, 3-16
fund, 3-16
monthly cash benefit, 3-13, 3-14
Sources of funds, 16-6
Standard cost of labor, 7-6
Standard costs, 22-1 to 22-10
Standard deduction, 2-12, 2-18, 2-19
table, 2-13, 2-18
Standard deviation, 32-10
State withholding tax, 7-26
Statistics, 32-1 to 32-22
Chebyshev's inequality, 32-9
confidence interval, 32-10
correlation, 32-11, 32-12
cumulative frequency distribution, 32-2
graphing data, 32-3 to 32-7
homoskedasticity, 32-22
mean, 32-9, 32-20, 32-21
probability, 32-7 to 32-9, 32-16 to 32-19
random variable, 32-8
regression, 32-11 to 32-15, 32-22

Numbers on this page refer to PROBLEM NUMBERS, not page numbers

standard deviation, 32-10
T-test, 32-22
uniform distribution, 32-8
variance, 32-9, 32-20 to 32-22
Stocks, 26-1 to 26-23
average price, 26-8
book value per share, 26-9
brokerage fee, 26-4, 26-5
commission, 8-1 to 8-23
common, 26-10, 26-19, 26-21
cost of, 26-1 to 26-9
cumulative, 26-22
dividends, 13-3, 26-13 to 26-17, 26-19 to 26-22
earnings per share, 16-5, 16-16, 26-11, 26-12
effective rate of yield, 26-13
high price, 26-6, 26-8, 26-17
last price, 26-7, 26-17
low price, 26-6 to 26-8, 26-17
market price, 26-13
opening price, 26-7, 26-17
option, 26-8, 26-23
option price, 26-8
par value, 26-2, 26-14, 26-19 to 26-22
preferred, 26-14, 26-19, 26-21
purchase, 26-7, 26-16
quarterly dividends, 26-18
quotation, 26-7
rate of return, 26-14 to 26-17
selling price, 26-1, 26-13, 26-14
shares outstanding, 26-9
state transfer taxes, 26-1
Stocks and bonds, differences between, 27-3
Stockturn rate, 18-23
Straight-line depreciation, 19-4 to 19-14, 19-28, 19-31
Strategy:
long-run, 5-14
optimal, 30-12 to 30-15
pure, 1-13, 1-14, 30-13
short-run, 5-14
Subtrahend, 1-3
Sum-of-the-years' digits depreciation, 19-22 to 19-31
Supply, 4-16
analysis, 5-12

T-test, 32-22
Tables:
annual insurance premiums, 3-4, 3-8 to 3-11
auto insurance -accident factor tables, 3-23, 3-25, 3-27
auto insurance-premium charge for cancelled policies, 3-33
brokerage rate for round lots, 26-3, 26-4
federal withholding tax, 7-25 to 7-30
fire insurance-annual premiums, 3-36
fire insurance-multiyear policies, 3-42
fire insurance-premium charge for cancelled policies, 3-37, 3-56 to 3-58, 3-60, 3-61
monthly cash payments, 3-13
odd-lot, 26-5
periodic life insurance premium, 3-5 to 3-7
social security contribution, 3-16
Task rate, 7-24
Tax:
considerations in investment, 13-7
excise, 2-5
exemptions, 2-11, 2-12, 2-14, 2-16, 2-18, 2-19, 2-21, 7-25, 7-27 to 7-30
state transfer on stocks, 26-2
water, 2-25
Tax, federal, 13-3
unemployment insurance, 2-15
withholding, 2-14, 7-26 to 7-28, 13-3
Tax-free bonds, 27-4, 27-5
Tax, income, 2-10 to 2-21, 7-25 to 7-30
joint tax return, 2-13, 2-18, 2-21
Tax rate, 2-23, 2-33, 2-34, 2-44

Numbers on this page refer to PROBLEM NUMBERS, not page numbers

calculating, 2-39 to 2-42
per $100. 00, 2-24, 2-27 to 2-33, 2-36, 2-45
Tax rate formula, 2-37 to 2-42
property taxes, 2-22, 2-43
Tax revenue, budget, 2-43
Tax table, 2-19
schedules, 2-12, 2-20
Taxable income, total, 2-20
Terms of discount, 11-29 to 11-39
Time-and-a-half, 7-2, 7-5, 7-9 to 7-15, 7-17, 7-18, 7-29
Time, measuring:
counting days, 1-10
days included in loan, 1-8
Time periods, 23-20
Time series, 32-3 to 32-6, 32-13
Total capital, computation of, 26-9
Total cost, 1-25, 1-26, 1-41, 4-6, 4-7, 4-10, 4-13, 4-14, 4-16, 4-17, 4-19, 4-24, 4-25, 6-12 to 6-14, 15-20, 15-33
Total cost curves, 5-15, 5-19, 5-21
Total dollar-value, 1-23
Total earnings, 1-13, 7-13, 7-14, 7-18, 7-21
Total expenses, 1-15, 1-40
Total income, 15-20
Total product curve, 5-16
Total production, 1-24
Total profit, 15-20
Total revenue, 4-6, 4-7, 4-17, 5-9, 5-10
Total sale, 1-21
Total taxable income, 2-20
Total units needed, 1-25, 1-27 to 1-29
Trade discount, 11-3, 11-4, 11-9, 11-36, 12-1, 12-4
Transportation, 10-1 to 10-7
car rental, 10-6, 10-7
flat rate, 10-1
railway express charges, 10-2
registered mail, 10-3
shipping charge, 10-1, 10-2
truck rental, 10-4, 10-5
vehicle rental cost, 10-4 to 10-7
Trial balance:
adjusted, 16-12, 16-13
preliminary, 16-11 to 16-13
True rate of interest, 24-23, 25-9
Truth-in-lending regulations, 23-38
Twelve-time basis, in advertisement, 9-6

Unemployment insurance tax, 2-15
Uniform distribution, 32-8
Uniform series compound-amount factor (USCA), 14-2, 14-3
Uniform series present-worth factor (USPW), 14-2 to 14-5, 14-11
Unit cost, 1-30, 1-32 to 1-34, 4-14, 4-20, 4-24, 4-27
average, 4-14, 4-24, 4-27
Units-of-production method of depreciation, 19-1 to 19-3
Uses of funds, 16-6

Variable cost, 4-6, 4-13, 4-17, 4-23, 15-10
Variance (cost accounting):
defined, 22-1
dollar terms, 22-2
favorable, 22-2, 22-6, 22-9
unfavorable, 22-2, 22-6, 22-9
Variance, labor:
efficiency, 22-1, 22-2, 22-4 to 22-10
rate, 22-1, 22-2, 22-4 to 22-10
Variance, material:
price, 22-1, 22-2, 22-4 to 22-10
quantity, 22-1, 22-2, 22-4 to 22-10
Variance, overhead, 22-1, 22-3 to 22-10
fixed overhead, 22-1
budget, 22-3, 22-5 to 22-8, 22-10
volume, 22-3, 22-6, 22-7, 22-10
variable overhead, 22-1
efficiency, 22-1, 22-3, 22-5 to 22-8, 22-10
spending, 22-1, 22-3, 22-5,

Numbers on this page refer to PROBLEM NUMBERS, not page numbers

22-7, 22-10
Variance, statistical, 32-9, 32-20 to 32-22
Vehicle rental cost, 10-4 to 10-7
Volume discount in advertising, 9-5

Wage-price spiral, 5-36
Wages and wage rates, 7-1, 7-2, 7-5, 7-8 to 7-14, 7-17, 7-20, 7-22 to 7-24, 7-26, 7-28, 7-29
    base rate, 7-2, 7-5, 7-9
    double time, 7-5, 7-10 to 7-12, 7-17, 7-18
    gross wages, 7-28
    net wages, 7-26, 7-27
    overtime, 7-2, 7-5, 7-8, 7-11 to 7-15, 7-18, 7-27, 7-29
    time-and-a-half, 7-2, 7-5, 7-9 to 7-15, 7-17, 7-18, 7-29
Waste allowance, 1-28, 1-29
Water tax, 2-25
Weighted average, 1-39
    inventory methods, 18-7, 18-15
Withholding tax, federal, 2-14, 7-26 to 7-28, 13-3
    partial table, 2-14
    state, 7-26
    table, 7-25 to 7-30
Working capital, 16-4, 16-17, 16-18
    ratio, 15-29
    sources and uses, 16-7

Yearly earnings, 1-46, 7-7

Zero-sum game, 30-13, 30-15